KU-758-534

TEXTBOOK ON
CRIMINAL LAW

40006604

LETTERKENNY RTC

4048 6684

TEXTBOOK ON

CRIMINAL LAW

Second Edition

R.T.C. LIBRARY, LETTERKENNY
344
~ i o

Michael J. Allen, LLB, LLM, Barrister

BLACKSTONE
PRESS LIMITED

First published in Great Britain 1991 by Blackstone Press Limited,
9-15 Aldine Street, London W12 8AW. Telephone 081-740 1173

© Michael J. Allen, 1991

First edition, 1991
Reprinted 1992
Second edition, 1993

ISBN: 1 85431 264 2

British Library Cataloguing in Publication Data
A CIP catalogue record for this book is available from the British Library

Typeset by Style Photosetting Ltd, Mayfield, East Sussex
Printed by BPCC Wheatons Ltd, Exeter

All rights reserved. No part of this book may be reproduced or transmitted in
any form or by any means, electronic or mechanical, including photocopying,
recording, or any information storage or retrieval system without prior
permission from the publisher.

Contents

1 INTRODUCTION   1

2 *ACTUS REUS*   15

3 *MENS REA*   44

4   NEGLIGENCE AND STRICT LIABILITY   81

5   CAPACITY AND INCAPACITATING CONDITIONS   98

6   GENERAL DEFENCES   138

reasonableness of the force used – 6.5.3.2 Excessive force – 6.5.3.3 Mistake **6.5.4** Extent of the justifications **6.5.5** Resisting justifiable conduct

7 PARTIES TO CRIME   165

7.1 Accomplices 7.1.1 Principals and accessories **7.1.2** Aiding, abetting, counselling or procuring – 7.1.2.1 Defining terms – 7.1.2.2 Presence, activity and inactivity **7.1.3** Proving the principal offence – 7.1.3.1 Absence of an *actus reus* – 7.1.3.2 Perpetrator exempt from prosecution – 7.1.3.3 Perpetrator not liable to conviction – 7.1.3.4 Perpetrator and accomplice liable but for different offences **7.1.4** *Mens rea* of an accessory – 7.1.4.1 Intention to assist or encourage the principal – 7.1.4.2 Knowledge of the circumstances constituting the offence – 7.1.4.3 Knowledge of the type of offence – 7.1.4.4 Liability for acts beyond the common design **7.1.5** Withdrawal from the joint enterprise **7.1.6** Victims as accessories **7.1.7** Entrapment and accessorial liability **7.2 Vicarious liability 7.2.1** Vicarious liability by implication **7.2.2** The delegation principle **7.2.3** Limitations on vicarious liability **7.2.4** Statutory defences **7.3 Corporate liability 7.3.1** The principle of identification **7.3.2** Liability of officers

8 INCHOATE OFFENCES   197

8.1 Introduction 8.2 Incitement 8.2.1 *Actus reus* **8.2.2** *Mens rea* **8.2.3** Excluded offences **8.2.4** Impossibility **8.3 Conspiracy 8.3.1** Introduction **8.3.2** Common elements – 8.3.2.1 Agreement – 8.3.2.2 Parties – 8.3.2.3 Acquittal of the other alleged conspirators **8.3.3** Statutory conspiracy – 8.3.3.1 Course of conduct – 8.3.3.2 If the agreement is carried out – 8.3.3.3 In accordance with their intentions – 8.3.3.4 Necessarily amount to or involve the commission of any offence – 8.3.3.5 Impossibility **8.3.4** Jurisdiction **8.3.5** Common law conspiracies – 8.3.5.1 Conspiracy to defraud – 8.3.5.2 Conspiracy to corrupt public morals or to outrage public decency – 8.3.5.3 Impossibility in common law conspiracy **8.4 Attempt 8.4.1** Statutory definition and scope **8.4.2** *Mens rea* **8.4.3** *Actus reus* **8.4.4** Impossibility

9 HOMICIDE   233

9.1 Introduction 9.1.1 *Actus reus* **9.2 Murder 9.3 Manslaughter 9.3.1** Introduction **9.3.2** Voluntary manslaughter – 9.3.2.1 Diminished responsibility – 9.3.2.2 Provocation – 9.3.2.3 Suicide pacts **9.3.3** Involuntary manslaughter – 9.3.3.1 Constructive manslaughter – 9.3.3.2 Reckless manslaughter **9.3.4** Reform **9.3.5** Other unlawful homicides – 9.3.5.1 Causing death by dangerous driving – 9.3.5.2 Infanticide

10 NON-FATAL OFFENCES AGAINST THE PERSON   258

10.1 Non-sexual offences 10.1.1 Assault and battery – 10.1.1.1 Technical assault – 10.1.1.2 Battery – 10.1.1.3 Defences to assault and battery – 10.1.1.4 Aggravated assaults – **10.1.2** Wounding and inflicting grievous bodily harm –

14 CRIMINAL DAMAGE

Preface

Criminal law is a subject of great complexity which students find both fascinating and frustrating. The complexity is in large part caused by the uncertainty created by judges in courts at all levels, who fail to understand or adhere to fundamental principles. As a result the subject is both challenging and potentially frustrating.

Traditionally textbooks on criminal law provide much more detail than students require and may, themselves, add to the confusion. This book will seek to clearly state both the principles fundamental to criminal liability and the current state of the law in the areas covered in most criminal law courses. In addition it will highlight those areas where there are doubts, problems or confusion. It is hoped that this book will help students both to meet the intellectual challenge which criminal law presents them and safely to negotiate those areas where frustration might creep in.

In the two years since the first edition of this book was published there have been numerous developments both statutory and case-law. In particular, a number of changes have been made to the text to take account of the passage of the Criminal Justice Act 1991, the Criminal Procedure (Insanity and Unfitness to Plead) Act 1991, the Road Traffic Act 1991 and the Aggravated Vehicle-Taking Act 1992. New cases have been incorporated into every chapter with the result that some questions posed in the first edition have been answered, while new questions have arisen to which answers now are required.

While the law may change Blackstone Press remain good humoured, helpful and efficient; to them I give my thanks.

The law is stated as it was on 1 February 1993.

Michael J. Allen

Table of Cases

Table of Statutes

ONE

Introduction

1.1 SUBSTANTIVE CRIMINAL LAW

The subject matter of this book is the substantive criminal law; that is, the law which determines what is or is not a crime. This book is not concerned with the reasons why certain conduct is defined as criminal; that is a matter of moral philosophy. Neither is it concerned with the reasons why people commit crimes; that is a matter for criminologists to ponder. Likewise, the procedures by which criminals are arrested, prosecuted, convicted and sentenced are outside the remit of this book. Similarly, the study of punishment and the efficacy of the various sentencing options available to the courts is a matter for penologists to consider.

Having excluded so much it might appear that there is little left to consider. Such a conclusion would be erroneous as the criminal law is a complex and expansive subject. Before studying it, however, it is necessary to place it in context by considering questions such as the following: What is a crime? What purpose or function does the criminal law serve? Why is particular conduct classified as criminal?

1.2 DEFINING A CRIME

A crime may be defined as an act (or omission or a state of affairs) which contravenes the law and which may be followed by prosecution in criminal proceedings with the attendant consequence, following conviction, of punishment. This definition reveals nothing of the characteristics of acts which are defined as criminal. Indeed the same act may give rise to both criminal and civil liability. For example, if D punches P he may be guilty of assault, a crime. The same act also constitutes the tort of assault which is a form of trespass to the person and D, if successfully sued by P, would be liable to pay damages. Likewise, if D sets fire to P's house he may be guilty of the crime of arson. P could also sue him for the tort of trespass to his property.

When Parliament passes legislation making a particular act criminal, the nature of that act does not change but the consequences of performing it do change. For example, until 1930 it was not an offence to take and drive away a motor vehicle without the owner's consent. Section 28 of the Road Traffic Act 1930 made this an offence and in 1968 Parliament extended this offence to cover the taking of any 'conveyance' thus including, for example, boats (see s.12 of the Theft Act 1968). Similarly, until 1978 it was not an offence for a diner in a restaurant to make off without paying for the meal he had consumed. The mischief of customers making off without paying their bills where payment on the spot was expected was dealt with in s. 3 of the Theft Act 1978. In both these cases, the relevant act remains the same and the actor continues to be civilly liable for trespass and debt respectively. Parliament's legislative intervention, however, has meant that both these acts may also result in criminal liability.

By the same token, if Parliament enacts legislation which abolishes a particular crime, the nature of the act which previously constituted a crime remains the same; it is only the consequences of performing that act which differ. For example, s. 1 of the Sexual Offences Act 1967 provided that it would no longer be an offence for a man over the age of twenty-one to commit buggery or gross indecency in private with another man over that age who consented to the act. The nature of these acts did not change after 1967 but the consequence of committing them in particular circumstances changed as the criminal sanction was removed.

The definition of crime is thus of limited usefulness. It only indicates which acts are criminal by reference to consequences which may ensue from their commission; it tells us nothing about the function of the criminal law or why particular conduct is classified as criminal. The definition, therefore, is essentially concerned with the legal consequences of the act.

1.3   THE FUNCTION OF THE CRIMINAL LAW

The function of the criminal law is largely to set the parameters within which the criminal justice system operates. There are two aspects to this. Firstly, the criminal justice system is a tool of social control representing the agglomeration of powers, procedures and sanctions which surround the criminal law. The police are empowered to investigate crime, search for evidence, arrest suspected offenders and question them. The courts are empowered to try persons charged with committing crimes and, if convicted, to sentence them. In setting the parameters within which this coercive State apparatus operates, the criminal law plays a central role; a person may only be arrested where he is suspected of committing a crime; the police may only search for evidence which points towards the commission of a crime; the courts may only try and sentence persons who are charged with, and then convicted of, committing crimes. It is crucial, therefore to define clearly what acts, omissions or states of affairs amount to crimes as all the other powers, procedures and sanctions of the criminal justice system are dependent upon these definitions. The criminal law, accordingly, limits and controls the legitimate exercise by the State of its coercive power to investigate crime and prosecute, convict and punish criminals. Secondly, the criminal law operates as a guide to the citizen indicating the limits of legitimate activity on his part and predicting the consequences of infraction of the criminal law.

If the power of the State is to be effectively limited and if the citizen is to be able confidently to make rational choices regarding his behaviour, the criminal law must be clear, relatively stable and accessible, that is, knowable in advance. Throughout the course of this book judicial decisions on the content and ambit of the substantive criminal law will be subjected to criticism, sometimes trenchant criticism, as there is a tendency for judges to lose sight of the wider role which the criminal law serves in their understandable desire to see persons whom they regard as 'undersirable characters' locked behind bars.

The criminal law is a series of prohibitions backed up with the threat of punishment. An understanding of the function of the criminal law requires further inquiry into the reasons why breaches of the criminal law are met with punishment and why certain behaviour is subjected to prohibition.

1.3.1 Social control and social morality

The criminal law represents the rules of social control within a society. But how are the rules determined? Is there an essential criterion which determines which behaviour merits criminal sanction? The Wolfenden Committee, *Report of the Committee on Homosexual Offences and Prostitution* (1957) Cmnd 247, stated (at paras. 13 and 14) that the function of the criminal law is:

> to preserve public order and decency, to protect the citizen from what is offensive or injurious and to provide sufficient safeguards against exploitation or corruption of others, particularly those who are specially vulnerable because they are young, weak in body or mind or inexperienced or in a state of special physical, official or economic dependence. It is not . . . the function of the law to intervene in the private lives of citizens, or to seek to enforce any particular pattern of behaviour, further than is necessary to carry out the purposes we have outlined.

To this extent the criminal law is a reflection of corporate or societal morality. The wrong-doing which the criminal law seeks to punish is that which threatens the fundamental values upon which a society is founded. While it is harmful to the individual to be robbed or assaulted, it is also harmful to society as such behaviour threatens the security and well-being of that society. The criminal sanction operates then as a form of social control both punishing the offender and re-asserting the mores of that society. This may be seen more clearly when the possible purposes punishment may serve are examined.

1.3.1.1 Retribution
A major purpose which punishment serves is retribution. Punishment is meted out to the offender because this is what he deserves in response to his infraction of the criminal law. This was expressed by Stephen, *A History of the Criminal Law of England* (1883) at pp. 81-82:

the infliction of punishment by law gives definite expression and a solemn ratification and justification to the hatred which is excited by the commission of the offence, and which constitutes the moral or popular as distinguished from the conscientious sanction of that part of morality which is also sanctioned by the criminal law. The criminal law thus proceeds upon the principle that it is morally right to hate criminals, and it confirms and justifies that sentiment by inflicting upon criminals, punishments which express it.

To some extent, therefore, retribution reflects society's desire for vengeance. When people join together in a society governed by law, they relinquish their own right to retaliate to harm done to them in exchange for the protection which the law offers them. H. Gross gives expression to this view in *A Theory of Criminal Justice* (1979) (at pp. 19-20):

But society requires that this right [to repay harm with harm] be surrendered by its members, and in exchange undertakes to protect them by laws that can be effective only if violations are punished. The bargain that is struck, then, places a moral obligation on society to punish crime as it places a moral obligation on its members to refrain from breaking the law.

Vengeance or retaliation is only one aspect of retribution. A further element is that of denunciation. The infliction of punishment signals society's disapproval of the criminal's conduct and reaffirms the values the criminal law is designed to uphold. This reflects the more modern view of the appropriate place for retribution in the criminal justice system. In *Sargeant* (1974) 60 Cr App R 74, a case concerning violent crime, Lawton LJ, after rejecting the idea of 'an eye for an eye', gave expression to this view (at p. 77):

society, through the courts, must show its abhorrence of particular types of crime, and the only way in which the courts can show this is by the sentences they pass. The courts do not have to reflect public opinion. On the other hand they must not disregard it. Perhaps the main duty of the court is to lead public opinion. Anyone who surveys the criminal scene at the present time must be alive to the appalling problem of violence. Society, we are satisfied, expects the courts to deal with violence. . . . Those who indulge in the kind of violence with which we are concerned in this case must expect custodial sentences.

The punishment inflicted, however, must not represent a blind act of vindictive retaliation; it must be both reasoned and reasonable. The idea which has gained ascendancy in recent years is that of 'just deserts' based on the philosophical ideas of Kant. A person who commits a crime has gained an unfair advantage over the other members of society. Punishment cancels out that advantage (particularly where the court orders confiscation, restitution or compensation) while, at the same time, it re-affirms the values of that society by visiting moral disapproval or reprobation on the offender. The punishment the criminal deserves, of course, must bear some relationship to the harm he has caused. Punishment can only be considered reasonable where the courts respect the concept of proportionality.

1.3.1.2 Deterrence A second purpose which punishment may serve is that of deterrence, whether this be *particular* deterrence (i.e. dissuading the individual criminal from re-offending in the future) or *general* deterrence (i.e. dissuading other possible offenders from offending by the example made of each particular offender). It is difficult to assess the effectiveness of individual deterrence. Some offenders may never offend again even if they are not caught or punished; others may only be deterred where the punishment imposed is so severe that it is out of all proportion to the gravity of the wrongdoing. In relation to general deterrence, courts, in the past, sometimes imposed exemplary sentences to deter others where an offence had become prevalent or was particularly grave (see e.g. *Wilson and Tutt* (1981) 3 Cr App R (S) 102; *Poh and To* [1982] Crim LR 132). While judges may have associated severe sentences with deterrence, the connection was not necessarily valid. In *The Sentence of the Court* (5th edn, 1990) published by the Home Office, it is stated (at para. 3.3):

> The simplest way of evaluating the individual deterrent effect of sentencing is to compare the proportions of offenders undergoing different types of sentence who, when free to do so, continue to commit offences. The almost invariable conclusion of the large amount of research which has been undertaken . . . is that it is hard to show any effect that one type of sentence is more likely than any other to reduce the likelihood of reoffending, which is high for all. Similarly, longer periods of custody or particular institutional regimes do not seem to have a significant effect. Studies comparing the reconviction rates of offenders given community service orders with those given custodial sentences have also shown little difference.

Different sentences therefore have little effect in deterring offenders. *The Sentence of the Court* goes on to state, however, (at para. 3.4) that:

> The inference most commonly drawn from research studies is that the probability of arrest and conviction is likely to deter potential offenders whereas the perceived severity of the ensuing penalties has little effect.

Of course, detection and conviction must result in punishment if the rules are not to lose their coercive force. Whether a particular person is susceptible to coercion, however, may depend on other factors. H. Packer, *The Limits of the Criminal Sanction* (1968) observed (at p. 45):

> [T]he deterrent role of the criminal law is effective mainly with those who are subject to the dominant socializing influences of the day . . . Deterrence does not threaten those whose lot in life is already miserable beyond the point of hope. It does not improve the morals of those whose value systems are closed to further modification, either psychologically . . . or culturally. . . .

Thus, the deterrent role of the criminal process is a limited one; those who are set on committing crime may not be deterred by the criminal law. For most members of society, however, the criminal law may serve to educate them on acceptable and unacceptable conduct creating thereby unconscious inhibitions against offending. Gross makes this point (at p. 401):

> The threats are not laid down to deter those tempted to break the rules, but rather to maintain the rules as a set of standards that compel allegiance in spite of violations by those who commit crimes. In short, the rules of conduct laid down in the criminal law are a powerful social force upon which society is dependent for its very existence, and there is punishment for violation of these rules in order to prevent the dissipation of their power that would result if they were violated with impunity.

1.3.1.3 Incapacitation The third purpose which punishment may serve is that of incapacitation. If a term of imprisonment is imposed on an offender, the public are protected from further offences by him for so long as he is in prison.

1.3.1.4 Rehabilitation The pre-1960s penal debate was premised upon the idea of rehabilitation. Probation was introduced as a disposal following conviction to give effect to this rehabilitative ideal. The idea of rehabilitation even found expression in the Prison Rules 1964 which stated that 'the purpose of the training and treatment of convicted prisoners shall be to encourage and assist them to lead a good and useful life'. So far as prison is concerned this ideal has largely been abandoned as the problems of overcrowding and underfunding have taken their toll, making the most immediate concern of prison governors that of containment. The idea of rehabilitation also underpins parole which was introduced by the Criminal Justice Act 1967.

In recent years there has been a movement away from rehabilitation as an objective of punishment. Studies on both sides of the Atlantic reveal that the recidivism rate varies little between offenders who received retributive sentences and those who received rehabilitative sentences (see e.g. Brody, *The Effectiveness of Sentencing* (Home Office Research Study No. 35, 1976)). Similarly, rehabilitation as a basis for sentencing offenders lead to disparity in punishment as the sentencer was looking to the needs of the offender rather than the offence committed as the starting point in determining the appropriate sentence. This is not to say that alternatives to prison are disparaged. On the contrary, there is a growing interest on the part of the Home Office in community sentences as these may be as effective as prison, both in terms of their retributive and deterrent value, and incur a lower financial and social cost as the prisoner can serve his sentence (e.g. community service) in the community.

1.3.1.5 The current approach Until recently the sentencing system in England and Wales lacked a coherent rationale as retribution, deterrence, incapacitation and rehabilitation were all advocated as the aims of sentencing, without there being any explanation of how these aims were to be reconciled or of which was to take priority if they came into conflict (see, for example *Sargeant* (1974) 60 Cr App R 74). In the late 1980s the Government began to consider the sentencing system and the relative merits of the various objectives which may be achieved through punishment. The Government's approach was set out in the White Paper, *Crime, Justice and Protecting the Public* (Cmd 965, 1990). The Government recognised that rehabilitation, while it may be sought, may not always be achieved and cannot be used as a justification for imprisonment (see paras. 2.6–2.7). Deterrence, while it may have immediate appeal, probably operates only with those who are law-abiding in the first place. The White Paper stated (at para. 2.8):

But much crime is committed on impulse, given the opportunity presented by an open window or unlocked door, and it is committed by offenders who live from moment to moment; their crimes are as impulsive as the rest of their feckless, sad or pathetic lives. It is unrealistic to construct sentencing arrangements on the assumption that most offenders will weigh up the possibilities in advance and base their conduct on rational calculation. Often they do not.

The approach the Government opted for, therefore, was one based on the idea of retribution. The White Paper stated (at para. 2.9):

The Government's proposals therefore emphasise the objectives which sentencing is most likely to meet successfully in whole or in part. The first objective for all sentences is denunciation of and retribution for the crime. Depending on the offence and the offender, the sentence may also aim to achieve public protection, reparation and reform of the offender, preferably in the community. This approach points to sentencing policies which are more firmly based on the seriousness of the offence, and just deserts for the offender.

In 1991 the Criminal Justice Act was passed reflecting in its provisions, to a large extent, the views expressed in the White Paper. The emphasis on retribution is apparent in that the concept of proportionality has been made a central principle of sentencing. The Act requires a court in passing a custodial sentence, a community sentence or (in the case of a magistrates' court) a unit fine, to impose a sentence which is 'commensurate with the seriousness of the offence . . .' (see ss. 2(2)(a), 6(2)(b) and 18(2)(a)). Rehabilitation, as an aim of sentencing, has not been abandoned totally although retribution takes priority. The Act seeks to encourage the use of community sentences by making it clear in s. 1(2) that custodial sentences are the sentence of last resort and should be used only where the offence was 'so serious that only such a sentence can be justified for the offence'. In choosing a community sentence rehabilitation may still be an aim as the court is required to choose an order which is both commensurate with the seriousness of the offence (s. 6(2)(b)) and which is 'the most suitable for the offender' (s. 6(2)(a)). The idea of imposing a heavier sentence for deterrent or rehabilitative reasons is eschewed. The Act does permit a court to depart from the principle of proportionality, however, where the offender has been convicted of a sexual or violent offence and the court considers either (a) that only a custodial sentence 'would be adequate to protect the public from serious harm from him' (s. 1(2)(b)) or (b) that a longer custodial sentence 'is necessary to protect the public from serious harm from the offender' (s. 2(2)(b)). In such cases the need to protect the public takes priority over the principle of proportionality.

1.3.2 What conduct should be classified as criminal?

Having looked at the purposes which punishment may serve, it is necessary to consider why particular conduct is prohibited by the criminal law. What is the social morality which the criminal law reflects? Is the fact that certain conduct is regarded as immoral by the majority of citizens a sufficient justification, in itself, for making that conduct punishable by law?

To determine what is immoral is a far from straightforward task. Ideas of what is immoral vary from one society to another and from one generation to another. In any society, however, there is to be found a common core of morality which reflects standards of behaviour to which the majority of citizens in that society conform, deviations from which will provoke censure. Many of these rules of morality will be enforced by the criminal law, such as prohibitions of murder, violence to the person, sexual assaults and theft. As Gross states (at p. 13):

It seems obvious that those crimes of violence, theft and destruction that stand as paradigms of crime and comprise the core of any penal code are also moral wrongs. Everyone has a right to be free of such harm inflicted by others, and when murder, rape, arson, assault or [theft] is committed there is also a moral wrong since a moral duty to refrain from doing harm to others has been breached. The right to be free of such harm does not have its origin in law but in a general consensus on the rights enjoyed by any member of society, or even by any person, no matter how he lives. This consensus is a more fundamental element of society even than the law, and for that reason the violation of such a right is a moral wrong and not simply a legal wrong.

Not all rules of social morality, however, are subject to enforcement by the criminal law. Adultery may be regarded by many as immoral but it is not a crime. Lying may be immoral but it is not necessarily a crime (see Chapter 12 *post*). Similarly, many prohibitions of the criminal law are morally neutral. There is no rule of social morality which dictates that the speed limit for vehicles in built-up areas should be 30 mph, nor does social morality dictate that seat belts should be worn in vehicles or that persons under eighteen should not be served alcohol in licensed premises. These laws may be justified on the basis that they improve safety for, or prevent harm to, citizens. They may be matters on which there is a fair degree of social consensus but this is not due to any common perception of morality.

There has long been disputation amongst legal philosophers as to what the proper sphere of the criminal law should be. The nineteenth century philosopher J.S. Mill in his essay *On Liberty* expressed the view that the only legitimate purpose for which legal coercion could be exercised over any member of a civilised community is to prevent harm to others. The Wolfenden Committee extended this (see 1.3.1 *ante*). By contrast Lord Devlin in *The Enforcement of Morals* (1965) expressed the view that the primary function of the criminal law was to maintain public morality. In his opinion 'intolerance, indignation and disgust' were vital to a society and conduct which aroused such feelings amongst right-thinking members of society deserved suppression by means of the criminal law.

The views expressed by Lord Devlin seemed to receive approval subsequently in the House of Lords. In *Shaw* v *DPP* [1962] AC 220, D was convicted of conspiracy to corrupt public morals arising from his publication of the 'Ladies Directory' advertising the names and addresses of prostitutes, together with photographs and details of the 'services' they were prepared to offer. The House of Lords upheld the conviction, Viscount Simonds stating (at p. 267):

> In the sphere of the criminal law I entertain no doubt that there remains in the courts of law a residual power to enforce the supreme and fundamental purpose of the law, to conserve not only the safety and order but also the moral welfare of the State, and that it is their duty to guard against attacks which may be the more insidious because they are novel and unprepared for.

By contrast, Lord Reid, dissenting, reflected the view of Mill. He was of opinion that there was 'no such general offence known to the law as conspiracy to corrupt public morals.' Lord Reid went on to state (at p. 275):

> Even if there is still a vestigial power [in the courts to extend the law of conspiracy], it ought not, in my view, to be used unless there appears to be general agreement that the offence to which it is applied ought to be criminal if committed by an individual. Notoriously, there are wide differences of opinion today as to how far the law ought to punish immoral acts which are not done in the face of the public. Some think that the law already goes too far, some that it does not go far enough. Parliament is the proper place, and I am firmly of opinion the only proper place, to settle that. When there is sufficient support from public opinion, Parliament does not hesitate to intervene. Where Parliament fears to tread it is not for the courts to rush in.

It is rare for such a stark division to occur in the House of Lords as a result of philosophical differences of opinion regarding the function of the criminal law. While Mill's and Devlin's views are prescriptive it is clear that neither accurately describes the actual province of the criminal law. In reality the justifications for the creation of particular offences may differ. Some offences enforce morality, others are there to protect individuals from harm and others do both. Indeed defining 'harm' is as difficult a task as defining 'morality'. Should harm be limited to physical harm to others or should the law also adopt a paternalistic approach to protect the individual from harming himself? Attempting suicide used to be a crime, possessing prohibited drugs, riding a motor cycle without a helmet or driving a car without wearing a seat-belt are offences. The only person who will suffer from these activities is both perpetrator and victim. Looked at more widely, however, it may be argued that society may also suffer the cost of medical treatment and social security payments to persons maimed or debilitated by, or orphaned or widowed as a result of, these activities. The definition of 'harm' may be widened in another way to include offence to one's sensibilities and psychological harm. Offences under the Obscene Publications Acts 1959 and 1964, or offences such as indecent exposure or brothel-keeping may be regarded as causing harm in this sense apart from offending against morality.

What is clear from this brief examination is that the decision to criminalise or decriminalise particular activities, whether by judicial decision or legislation, is far from straightforward. A range of considerations may be relevant to the ultimate decision, for example, morality, economics, ethics, politics and philosophy. Changes in morality may lead to changes in the law, for example, s. 1 of the Sexual Offences Act 1967 or the Abortion Act 1967. As views change perhaps other offences will be removed from the criminal calendar; many would argue for the legalisation of voluntary euthanasia or of the possession of cannabis.

The decision to use the criminal law to proscribe particular conduct or activities requires a balancing of moral considerations and concepts of harm as well as an assessment of the extent to which the State has a legitimate interest in controlling the acts which an individual does in private which cause harm to no one else. Even if conduct is considered immoral and harmful this will not necessarily justify criminalisation. Other considerations may be relevant such as whether the law would be enforceable and whether a criminal sanction is necessary or appropriate to achieve the end in view. For example, the connection between AIDS and sexual promiscuity may be clearly established and this may lead to a change in attitudes to sexual morality. The majority of people in society may come to regard fornication, adultery and casual sexual relationships with 'intolerance, indignation and disgust'. Greater sexual fidelity may reduce the spread of the disease and the harm to individuals and society. However, to seek to criminalise all sexual relationships outside marriage would be impossible to enforce without gross invasion of privacy; it may also be argued that the State has no legitimate interest in seeking to control private consensual sexual activity. Criminalisation is also not the only possible solution to the problem; greater health education may be sufficient to reduce the spread of the disease. Moral considerations alone are not a sufficient reason for extending the reach of the criminal law. The evidence of the past twenty years also suggests that the view that it is the function of the criminal law to enforce morality is one which is in decline.

It is not possible therefore to present an equation which when applied to particular behaviour will provide the answer whether or not such behaviour should be classified as criminal. Too many factors of varying weight and relevance have to be weighed in the balance. Furthermore the answer may vary over time as public perceptions of the role of the criminal law, the role of the State, the rights of the citizen and social morality change.

1.4 CLASSIFYING OFFENCES

There are now literally thousands of criminal offences, the vast majority being of statutory creation and of a regulatory nature. Our concern, however, is generally with the major offences (e.g. murder, manslaughter, rape, assault, theft, robbery, burglary, criminal damage, deception) and the general principles underlying criminal liability. While most offences are now of statutory creation, the criminal law originally was laid down in the decisions of the judges. Some offences, such as murder and manslaughter, are still common law offences lacking a statutory definition.

At common law, crimes were classifed generally as either felonies or misdemeanours. Subsequently this classification was adopted by Parliament when it came to create offences by legislation. The principal felonies were homicide, rape, theft, burglary, robbery and arson. A misdemeanour was any offence which was not a felony. Felonies were more serious than misdemeanours. The classification had important consequences in terms of the power of arrest and the penalties available on conviction. There was a general power of arrest without warrant in respect of felonies but not in respect of misdemeanours. On conviction of a felony the felon was liable to forfeiture of his land and goods (abolished by the Forfeiture Act 1870) and, if Parliament had declared a crime to be a 'felony without benefit of clergy', the penalty was death. Gradually the distinctions between felonies and misdemeanours were eroded by legislation. Finally, in the Criminal Justice Act 1967, all distinctions between felonies and misdemeanours were abolished. The distinction which this Act created, and which has been perpetuated by the Police and Criminal Evidence Act 1984, is that between arrestable and non-arrestable offences. Arrests without warrants may only be made in respect of arrestable offences. Section 24(1) of the 1984 Act defines 'arrestable offence' generally as any offence 'for which the sentence is fixed by law (i.e. murder, treason and piracy with violence) or for which a person of twenty-one years of age or over (not previously convicted) may be sentenced to imprisonment for a term of five years. . . . '. Section 24(2) specifies further offences which are arrestable although not meeting these criteria. Most arrestable offences are also indictable.

A second mode of classification of offences relates to the mode of trial. The distinction here is between summary and indictable offences. Summary offences are less serious than indictable offences and are tried before a magistrates' court. Indictable offences are more serious and are tried in the Crown Court before a judge and jury. Many offences are triable either way (see s. 17 of and sch. 1 to the Magistrates' Courts Act 1980). The decision whether an offence should be tried summarily or on indictment where it is triable either way is made by the magistrates' court having regard to the representations made by the prosecutor and the accused and all the circumstances of the case (see s. 19 of the 1980 Act). Obvious considerations are the gravity of the offence and the sentence available to the magistrates' court as compared to that available before the Crown Court. Theft, for example, is an offence triable either way. The maximum penalty available on trial on indictment is seven years' imprisonment whereas the maximum sentence which a magistrates' court may impose is generally six months' imprisonment (see s. 31 of the 1980 Act). If the court decides to proceed summarily the consent of the accused is required as he may wish to assert his right to trial by jury (see s. 20 of the 1980 Act) (see further Ingman, *The English Legal Process* (4th edn, 1992) pp. 42-58).

1.5 PROCEDURAL ISSUES

1.5.1 Burden and standard of proof

In criminal cases the burden of proof is on the prosecution; it is for the prosecution to prove the charge against the accused, which may also involve disproving any defence the accused may raise. The prosecution will seek to prove its case by calling evidence such as that of witnesses to the alleged offence, forensic evidence, evidence of incriminating items found in the accused's possession or in his home or car, a confession he may have made to the police, and circumstantial evidence, for example, his presence at the scene of the crime before or shortly after it was committed. If the prosecution fail to establish a prima facie case that the accused committed the alleged offence, the judge will, at the conclusion of the prosecution case, direct the jury to acquit the accused. If a prima facie case is made out, the trial will continue and the accused may call witnesses, present evidence and testify himself if he so desires. At the conclusion of all the evidence the prosecution and defence will make their closing submissions and the judge will sum up to the jury, whose task it then is to reach a verdict. The jury are only entitled to convict the accused if the prosecution has discharged the burden of proof and satisfied them beyond reasonable doubt of the guilt of the accused. If the jury are left with a reasonable doubt as to his guilt they must acquit; they may not be satisfied that he is innocent, but if they are not sure of his guilt the case against him has not been proved.

This rule was expressed clearly in the House of Lords in *Woolmington* v *DPP* [1935] AC 462. D was charged with the murder of his wife who had left him. His defence was that he had gone to his wife taking the gun with him to show her and tell her that he was going to commit suicide, and in showing it to her it had gone off accidentally. The judge directed the jury that once the prosecution proved that the deceased was killed by D, it was for D to show that the killing was not murder. The House of Lords held that this was a misdirection. The accused in a criminal trial is presumed innocent until proved guilty. It was not enough to show that D had done the act, it had also to be proved that he did so with the necessary criminal intent. It was for the prosecution to prove this rather than for the defence to disprove it. Viscount Sankey LC stated (at pp. 481-482):

Throughout the web of the English Criminal Law one golden thread is always to be seen, that it is the duty of the prosecution to prove the prisoner's guilt. . . . If, at the end of and on the whole of the case, there is a reasonable doubt, created by the evidence given by either the prosecution or the prisoner, as to whether the prisoner killed the deceased with a malicious intention, the prosecution has not made out the case and the prisoner is entitled to an acquittal. No matter what the charge or where the trial, the principle that the prosecution must prove the guilt of the prisoner is part of the common law of England and no attempt to whittle it down can be entertained.

While the overall burden of proof is upon the prosecution, the accused may have either an evidential burden or a burden of proof in respect of any defence he may seek to raise. If the accused's defence is anything more than a simple denial that he committed the alleged offence, he will bear an evidential burden to make this a live issue in the trial. The prosecution cannot be expected to anticipate all the possible defences an accused might raise. Accordingly, the burden on them to negate the accused's defence only arises when the accused has raised that defence. In *Woolmington* the accused's defence was accident; it was incumbent upon him to tender some evidence to this effect, either by testifying himself or calling other witnesses or by cross-examination of prosecution witnesses. Once he had raised this issue the prosecution was obliged to disprove it if they were to secure a conviction. Similarly, if the accused wishes to raise other defences such as self-defence, or duress, or automatism, he must discharge this evidential burden.

In some exceptional cases, however, a burden of proof is cast upon the accused in respect of certain defences he may wish to raise. The only such exception at common law is that of insanity. If D wishes to plead that he was insane at the time he committed the offence with which he is charged, he bears the burden of proving insanity. Other exceptions have been created by statute, for example, diminished responsibility (s. 2(2) of the Homicide Act 1957) or 'lawful authority or reasonable excuse' for the possession of an offensive weapon in a public place (s. 1(1) of the Prevention of Crime Act 1953). Where a burden of proof is cast upon the accused he is not required to prove his defence beyond reasonable doubt, but rather to the civil standard of proof, that is, he must prove his defence on a balance of probabilities (see *Carr-Briant* [1943] KB 607 at 610).

1.5.2   The functions of judge and jury

The judge is in overall control of the proceedings. He will decide all legal questions which may arise, for example, whether a particular piece of evidence is admissible, whether a particular witness may be compelled to testify, and whether the prosecution has raised a prima facie case against the accused. At the end of the case he will sum up to the jury. This will usually involve a summary of the evidence which each side has tendered and may involve, in addition, pointing out inconsistencies in the evidence or omissions, or points where both sides are not in dispute thereby highlighting the key issues which will have to be settled by the jury. The judge will also direct the jury on the law. He will instruct them on the necessary requirements of the offence which the prosecution must prove and the requirements of any defence the accused has raised which they must disprove or which he must prove. The jury's task then will be to determine what the facts were and apply the law to these facts to see whether all the requirements of the offence have been proved and the requirements of any defence negated by the prosecution. If the jury are satisfied beyond reasonable doubt that all these requirements have been proved or negated they will convict. If, however, the jury have a doubt as to any requirement of the offence which may not have been proved, or a requirement of the defence which may not have been negated, or, if it is a case where the defence have a burden of proof, they are satisfied that the defence have discharged that burden, they must acquit.

One problem which has arisen in recent years is the tendency of judges to avoid their responsibility to declare and explain the law to the jury. In specifying the requirements of a particular offence, it is the responsibility of the judge to explain to the jury what particular words mean. For example, the offence of burglary is committed, *inter alia*, where the accused enters a building as a trespasser and steals therein (see s. 9(1)(b) of the Theft Act 1968). It is not sufficient for the judge blandly to state to the jury that the prosecution must prove that (i) the accused entered, (ii) that what he entered was a building, (iii) that he was a trespasser and (iv) that he stole therein. The jury may not know what constitutes 'trespass' or what constitutes 'stealing'. Further elucidation of these concepts is therefore required on the part of the judge if the jury are to be equipped to perform their task of applying the law to the facts as they find them. In recent years, however, judges have taken a relaxed view of their own responsibilities. Where a statute uses 'an ordinary word' they have been content to leave it to juries to decide upon the meaning of that word and then apply it to the facts as they find them. Thus judges have resisted defining words like 'intention' or 'dishonesty' being content to leave it to the juries to determine what they mean. At many points in this book this judicial attitude will be subjected to criticism as it presumes a degree of linguistic ability on the part of jurors which may not actually exist. It also leaves to juries the task of determining what the law is before applying it to the case before them. This harbours the obvious danger of inconsistency between juries and, it is suggested, the even greater danger of injustice to the accused. Where the liberty of the citizen is at stake there is a great need for certainty and clarity in the law. These goals can only be attained when the judges accept their responsibility to declare and explain the law.

Further reading
D. A. Thomas, 'Form and Function in Criminal Law', in *Reshaping Criminal Law: Essays in honour of Glanville Williams* (1978, ed. P. R. Glazebrook).
D. J. Galligan, 'The Return of Retribution in Penal Theory', in *Essays in Memory of Rupert Cross* (1981, ed. C. F. H. Tapper).

TWO

Actus Reus

2.1 THE ELEMENTS OF CRIME

2.1.1 General

The criminal law does not seek to punish people for their evil thoughts; an accused must be proved to be responsible for conduct or the existence of a state of affairs prohibited by the criminal law before liability may arise. Whether liability arises will depend further on the accused's state of mind at the time; usually intention or recklessness is required. A Latin maxim encapsulates this principle – *actus non facit reum, nisi mens sit rea* – the act itself does not constitute guilt unless done with a guilty mind. The conduct or state of affairs which a particular offence prohibits is called the *actus reus* and the state of mind which the accused must be proved to have had at the time of the conduct or during the existence of the state of affairs is called the *mens rea*. It is important to note that the terms *actus reus* and *mens rea*, are simply useful labels to be attributed to the constituent parts of any crime being analysed; they do not have any meaning in themselves. They have no greater meaning than, for example, the terms 'obverse' and 'reverse' used when describing coins. Just as the words and designs on coins will vary so too will the *actus reus* and *mens rea* of different crimes.

It is particularly important when analysing the *mens rea* of offences to realise that this term is not prescriptive. In some offences nothing short of intention to bring about the prohibited consequence will suffice (e.g. theft, Chapter 11 *post*) whereas in others the inadvertent taking of an obvious risk will suffice (e.g. some forms of criminal damage, Chapter 14 *post*). While the Latin maxim above is a useful tool it is not a universal truth. There are many offences, largely of a minor and regulatory nature, where *mens rea* is not required. These are called strict liability offences and are of statutory creation (see 4.2 *post*). In such cases proof by the prosecution of *mens rea* is not required in respect of at least one element of the *actus reus*.

The use of the Latin terms *actus reus* and *mens rea* has been criticised. In *Miller* [1983] 2 AC 161, 174 Lord Diplock stated that:

> it would . . . be conducive to clarity of analysis of the ingredients of a crime that is created by statute . . . if we were to avoid bad Latin and instead to think and speak . . . about the conduct of the accused and his state of mind at the time of that conduct, instead of speaking of *actus reus* and *mens rea*.

The Law Commission in its Draft Criminal Code Bill (Law Com No. 177) uses the terms 'external elements' and 'fault element'. However, the terms *actus reus* and *mens rea* are so widely used that they will be retained for the purposes of exposition in this book.

While most crimes may be analysed in terms of *actus reus* and *mens rea*, a few crimes exist where these concepts merge. In some offences the *actus reus* may only be proved by proving *mens rea*. For example, s. 1(1) of the Prevention of Crime Act 1953 makes it an offence for any person, without lawful authority or reasonable excuse, to have with him in any public place any offensive weapon. Section 1(4) defines 'offensive weapon' as 'any article made or adapted for use for causing injury to the person, or intended by the person having it with him for such use'. If, for example, the accused is found carrying a pick-axe handle in a public place, the issue whether this amounts to the *actus reus* of the offence will depend on his intention at the time as this article does not fall into either of the first two categories of articles 'made or adapted for use for causing injury'. If there is no intent to use it to cause injury then there is no offensive weapon and thus no *actus reus*. In some other offences the *actus reus* implies a mental element. For example, if the accused is charged with possession of a controlled drug such as heroin or cannabis contrary to s. 5 of the Misuse of Drugs Act 1971 it is necessary to prove that he knew he possessed the thing which turns out to be the drug even though he does not know its nature (see *DPP v Brooks* [1974] AC 862; *Boyesen* [1982] AC 768); it is not possible to possess something if you do not know of its existence and thus in the absence of this mental element of knowledge there can be no *actus reus*.

2.1.2 Defences
So far the suggestion has been that if the prosecution prove the commission of an *actus reus* by the accused with the necessary *mens rea* criminal liability will have been established. This ignores the fact that the accused may be able to rely upon some justification or excuse to avoid criminal liability. Do justifications or excuses, more commonly referred to as defences, form part of the definition of a crime or are they outside the definition, operating like a trump card in bridge? Glanville Williams in *Criminal Law: The General Part* (2nd edn, 1961) expresses the view that all the constituents of a crime are either *actus reus* or *mens rea* stating (at p. 20):

> *Actus reus* includes . . . not merely the whole objective situation that has to be proved by the prosecution, but also the absence of any ground of justification or excuse, whether such justification or excuse be stated in any

statute creating the crime or implied by the courts in accordance with general principles.

An alternative view expressed by D.J. Lanham, '*Larsonneur* Revisited' [1976] Crim LR 276, is that a crime is 'made up of three ingredients, *actus reus, mens rea* and (a negative element) absence of a valid defence.' Which view is correct is not crucial; it can even be argued that both are partially correct if a distinction is drawn between justifications and excuses. A.T.H. Smith, 'On *Actus Reus* and *Mens Rea*' in *Reshaping the Criminal Law* (ed. Glazebrook, 1978), states (at p. 99):

the distinction is that we excuse the actor because he is not sufficiently culpable or at fault, whereas we justify an act because we regard it as the most appropriate course of action in the circumstances, even though it may result in harm that would, in the absence of justification, amount to a crime.

An example of a justification is self-defence. If, for example, D is charged with unlawfully and maliciously wounding V contrary to s. 20 of the Offences Against the Person Act 1861 he may admit that he did wound V and that he intended to do so, but he would not be convicted if he did so only in response to V's murderous assault upon him. In such circumstances the wounding of V would not be unlawful as it would be justified by the defence of self-defence. As the wounding was not unlawful it can be said that there was no *actus reus*; similarly as D only intended to wound V in circumstances where this was justified, there was no intention to unlawfully wound V (see further 6.5.2.3 *post*). By contrast, if D wounded V because he was told to do so by X who was holding D's wife hostage threatening to kill her if he did not obey, D could plead the defence of duress. In this situation, D intended to wound V and did so unlawfully (as he had no justification for so doing) but the defence of duress would operate to excuse him from the consequences of conviction and punishment. There has been an *actus reus* and *mens rea* but the defence of duress is superimposed much as a trump card might be played in bridge (see further 6.2 *post*).

2.2 DEFINING AN *ACTUS REUS*

Each crime must be looked at individually to determine what must be proved to establish its *actus reus*. In the case of a common law crime (such as murder) the definition of its *actus reus* is to be found in the decisions of the courts; in the case of a statutory crime (such as theft) the definition of the *actus reus* is to be found in the statute as interpreted judicially in decided cases. Generally, however, it is necessary to know which elements of the definition of an offence comprise the *actus reus*. The term *actus reus* has a much wider meaning than the 'act' prohibited by the law which it implies. A useful working definition is that it comprises all the elements of the definition of the offence except those which relate to the mental element (*mens rea*) required on the part of the accused. The definition of an offence may prohibit acts or omissions (conduct);

it may prohibit these only in particular circumstances. In some cases the definition of the offence may require particular consequences to ensue from the conduct. A distinction which flows from this is that between 'conduct crimes' and 'result crimes'. A 'conduct crime' prohibits conduct regardless of consequences whereas a 'result crime' prohibits particular consequences which ensue from conduct on the part of the accused. In a limited number of cases, offences prohibit particular states of affairs without reference to conduct or its consequences. The ambit of the criminal law may be illustrated by the following examples of offences.

An example of a 'conduct crime' is perjury which is committed whenever D makes a statement on oath which he does not believe to be true. The offence is committed whether or not the statement is believed. In other words, the result of D's prohibited conduct is irrelevant; it is the conduct and not the consequence which is prohibited. The relevant circumstance in the *actus reus* of this offence is that the statement is made on oath. Another conduct crime is rape, which is committed where D has sexual intercourse with a woman who does not consent. The relevant circumstance in the *actus reus* of this offence is that the woman is not consenting at the time of the intercourse. An example of a 'result crime' is murder where it must be proved that D's conduct caused the deceased's death. If the intended result of the death of the victim does not occur, the law of attempts, under the Criminal Attempts Act 1981, provides for a charge of attempted murder – a 'conduct crime'. An example of a 'state of affairs' offence, where the definition of the *actus reus* is concerned neither with conduct nor its consequences, is being in charge of a motor vehicle on a road or other public place while unfit to drive through drink or drugs contrary to s. 4(2) of the Road Traffic Act 1988. If D is in charge of the vehicle (a state of affairs) it matters not whether he was driving the vehicle, sitting in it or asleep in it.

2.3 PROVING AN *ACTUS REUS*

It has already been stated that the criminal law does not seek to punish people for their evil thoughts or intentions. If D has the *mens rea* for a particular offence but does not bring about the *actus reus* he is not guilty of committing that offence. This is illustrated by the case of *Deller* (1952) 36 Cr App R 184. P was selling a car to D and accepted D's car in part exchange after D represented to him that it was 'free from all encumbrances'. D believed this representation to be false as he had previously executed a document with a finance company which purported to be a hire purchase agreement in respect of the car. If this agreement was valid the car was not free from encumbrances and D had lied to P. If, however, the agreement was in reality a loan on the security of the car it was void as it had not been registered under the Bills of Sale Act 1878 and thus D's representation would, in fact, be true. D was charged with, and convicted of, obtaining P's car by false pretences contrary to s. 32 of the Larceny Act 1916. As the jury found the agreement was a loan on the security of the car, the Court of Criminal Appeal quashed D's conviction as this agreement was void and thus the car was unencumbered. There were,

R.T.C. LIBRARY, LETTERK...
3 44
.1...

accordingly, no false pretences because 'it may be quite accidentally and, strange as it may sound, dishonestly, the appellant had told the truth' (*per* Hilbery J at 191). D quite clearly intended to make false representations but the representations he made were true; while he had *mens rea* there was no *actus reus*. If such facts were to recur the correct charge would be *attempting* to obtain property by deception.

2.4 CONDUCT MUST BE VOLUNTARY

2.4.1 General

D is driving his car when suddenly, without warning, he suffers a heart attack which renders him incapable of continuing to exercise control over the vehicle. D slumps over the steering wheel and his foot pushes the accelerator pedal to the floor while the car careers through a traffic light which is showing red. The vehicle continues along the road and crashes into the rear of E's car which is stopped at a zebra crossing. E's vehicle is forced on to the crossing where it hits V breaking his leg. If D was charged with failure to stop at a red traffic light, dangerous driving and criminal damage to E's car, and E was charged with failing to accord precedence to a pedestrian on a zebra crossing and causing V grievous bodily harm, could they be convicted, have they committed the *actus reus* of any of these offences?

Where the *actus reus* of an offence requires conduct on the part of the accused, whether an act or omission, liability will only accrue where the conduct is willed; it is not suffficient that the accused by his bodily movements performed the prohibited conduct or brought about the prohibited consequence defined by the *actus reus* of the offence. In *Bratty* v *A-G for Northern Ireland* [1963] AC 386 (at 409), Lord Denning stated that the 'requirement that it should be a voluntary act is essential, not only in a murder case, but also in every criminal case'. In offences requiring *mens rea*, if the conduct is not willed there will also be an absence of *mens rea* on the part of the accused, but even if the offence is one of strict liability, requiring no proof of *mens rea*, it is still necessary to prove that the accused's conduct was voluntary. To convict and impose punishment on an accused who was not responsible for his conduct would be unjust.

In the example above, driving through a red traffic light is a strict liability offence. There is no need to prove that D was aware that the light was red and drove through it intentionally. The only matter which the prosecution need to prove is that D was driving the vehicle when it went through the red traffic light. However, as D had been incapacitated by the heart attack, there was at the time no voluntary act of driving and thus no *actus reus*. The charge of dangerous driving would similarly fail. The charge of criminal damage would also fail as, although D's car caused damage to E's car when it crashed into it, this was not the result of a voluntary or willed act on the part of D. Had D felt warning pains before the heart attack and continued driving he might be liable, particularly if he had previously had such an attack and recognised the pains as warning symptoms. In *Kay* v *Butterworth* (1945) 173 LT 191 (see also *Hill* v *Baxter* [1958] 1 QB 277), D was driving home after night-shift work when, overcome by sleep, he drove into a party of soldiers. He was convicted of driving without due care and attention and dangerous driving as, realising that he was becoming drowsy, he should have stopped and it was immaterial that he was not conscious of his actions when the accident happened. Humphreys J stated:

A person, however, who through no fault of his own, becomes unconscious while driving, for example, by being struck by a stone, or by being taken ill, ought not to be liable at criminal law.

In *Bell* [1984] 3 All ER 842, further examples of involuntary conduct for which no criminal liability may attach were given by Goff LJ who stated (at p. 846):

a motorist . . . [who] has been attacked while driving by, for example, a swarm of bees or a malevolent passenger, or because he has been affected by a sudden blinding pain, or because he has become suddenly unconscious by reason of a black-out, or because his vehicle has suffered some failure, for example, through a blow-out or through the brakes failing.

In the example above E would be acquitted as his failure to accord precedence to a pedestrian was due to the external application of force on his vehicle which was beyond his control (see *Leicester* v *Pearson* [1952] 2 QB 668). Similarly, there was no voluntary act on E's part which caused V's injury.

In the example of D and E a distinction may be drawn between the causes of their involuntary conduct. E's conduct was caused by the external application of physical force. Another example would be where A is carving the Sunday joint when B seizes his hand holding the knife and thrusts it into C killing him. If A was charged with murder he would be acquitted as there was no voluntary act on his part. In our earlier example D's involuntary conduct was due to his loss of consciousness. Where a person does physical acts while in a state of unconsciousness this is referred to as automatism. For example, a person may perform physical acts while concussed or in a state of somnambulism or while suffering a fit or seizure. Automatism will be considered further in Chapter 5.

2.4.2 State of affairs offences

While most offences require voluntary conduct on the part of the accused to establish their *actus reus*, there are some offences which prohibit the existence of a state of affairs. An example given above is s. 4(2) of the Road Traffic Act 1988, being in charge of a motor vehicle on a road or other public place while unfit to drive through drink or drugs. For as long as the accused is in charge of the vehicle while unfit the *actus reus* is committed. This is so even though the accused may not be responsible for his unfitness, as where his soft drink has been laced with alcohol, although this may constitute a special reason for not disqualifying him from driving (see *Shippam* [1971] RTR 209; *Pugsley* v *Hunter* [1973] RTR 284).

While there may be strong public policy reasons for adopting an 'absolute liability' approach to 'situational' road traffic offences because of the obvious dangers involved to members of the public, it is questionable whether this approach should be adopted in other cases of 'state of affairs' offences. The courts, however, have not shown any reluctance to convict people of situational offences where they have not been responsible for bringing about the prohibited state of affairs. In *Larsonneur* (1933) 97 JP 206, L, a French citizen was required to leave the United Kingdom. She went to Eire but was deported and brought back to Holyhead by the Irish police who handed her over to British police officers. On a charge under the Aliens Order 1920 that she 'being an alien to whom leave to land in the United Kingdom has been refused, was found in the United Kingdom' L was convicted. The Court of Criminal Appeal upheld her conviction, Hewart CJ referring to the circumstances of compulsion which brought about her return to the United Kingdom as 'perfectly immaterial'. The Court was totally unconcerned to discover whether L had caused that state of affairs. The suspicion must be that the Court would have upheld her conviction even if a group of kidnappers had removed her from Eire and had brought her to the United Kingdom; a requirement of culpability (i.e. voluntariness) on the part of the accused leading to the creation of the state of affairs would have been desirable and could easily have been implied by the Court of Criminal Appeal in its construction of the statute.

Just when it was thought that *Larsonneur* was an aberrant decision which could be shunted into a siding and forgotten, the Divisional Court revived the controversy with its decision in *Winzar* v *Chief Constable of Kent, The Times,* March 28, 1983. W had been brought to hospital on a stretcher. He was diagnosed as being merely drunk and was asked to leave. When he was later found slumped on a seat in the corridor the police were summoned. They removed him to the road, concluded he was drunk and placed him in their police car. W was charged with being found drunk on the highway contrary to s. 12 of the Licensing Act 1872. The Divisional Court construed the words 'found drunk' to mean 'perceived to be drunk' and upheld his conviction on the basis that, as the purpose of the offence was to deal with the nuisance of public drunkenness, it was sufficient to establish guilt to prove that the person was drunk while in a public place; how he came to be there was considered to be irrelevant. The report does not indicate how W came to be taken to hospital. If he had been found lying in the street originally there might be no cause for complaint. The decision, however, is expressed in broad terms and may be criticised on two bases. First, it is arguable that the officers first perceived W's condition while he was in hospital; by taking him outside to the public highway they had procured the commission of the offence. Secondly, in the absence of express words in the statute dispensing with the need to prove voluntary conduct on the part of the accused bringing into existence the prohibited state of affairs, the requirement of voluntariness should have been implied on the basis that penal statutes should be construed strictly in favour of the accused. (This is a presumption of statutory interpretation honoured more in the breach than in the observance in recent years.)

The decision in *Winzar* may be contrasted with *Martin* v *State* 31 Ala. App. 334, 17 So. 2d 427 (1944) where the Alabama Court of Appeals reversed the trial court's conviction of being drunk on a public highway on the ground that a voluntary appearance on the highway is a prerequisite of a conviction. The appellant had been in his own house drunk when police officers forcibly entered his house, carried him into the street and then arrested him. If this factual situation occurred in England the broad terms of the decisions in *Larsonneur* and *Winzar* would dictate a contrary result. It is to be hoped that courts will apply these two cases narrowly and look for culpability on the part of the accused in bringing about the prohibited state of affairs before convicting. The degree of culpability required need not be very great. An objective requirement that the creation of the state of affairs be reasonably foreseeable at the time the accused embarked on the course of conduct which ultimately led to that state of affairs would suffice. For example, if the accused is drinking in a public house it is reasonably foreseeable that he will end up on the public highway either at closing time or if he leaves or is ejected earlier. If, however, he is drinking at home, it is not reasonably foreseeable that this will happen. Thus if Winzar had been at home unconscious from his drinking when a third party summoned the ambulance to take him to hospital, the reasonable foreseeability test would not be satisfied. If, however, he had been drinking in a public house when he collapsed the test would be satisfied, albeit the roundabout way in which he ended up on the highway could not have been foreseen at the time he commenced his drinking.

2.5 OMISSIONS

2.5.1 General

A, knowing that B cannot swim, pushes him into the deep end of the swimming pool intending that he should drown. C, a swimmer using the pool, ignores B's struggles and his cries for help. D, the life-guard employed by the council to rescue anyone in difficulty, ignores B's cries, believing them to be a prank of which there have been many that day. E, B's father who is swimming in the pool, also ignores B's cries, reckoning that it is time that his wimpish son either sinks to oblivion or learns to swim. B drowns. Will A, C, D and E be liable for unlawful homicide (i.e. either murder or manslaughter depending on their *mens rea*)? A is the only one to have performed a positive act which caused B's death. C, D and E failed to act to save B but they did not do any positive act to cause his death. If liability is to arise it would depend on there being a duty upon them to act to prevent B's death although they are not responsible for the existence of the life-threatening situation.

Generally the common law was concerned to prohibit particular results from occurring and it punished an accused for causing the prohibited result by his positive acts. Gradually the courts came to recognise limited liability for omissions where a duty to act could be implied, the accused failed to act and the prohibited result ensued. Not all offences, however, are capable of commission by omission. It is a question for the courts whether a particular offence is capable of commission by omission. Some offences cannot be committed by omission, for example, burglary and robbery. In some offences the definition of the *actus reus* may make it clear that it may only be committed by an act. In *Ahmad* (1986) 84 Cr App R 64, A, a landlord, was charged with doing acts calculated to interfere with the peace or comfort of a residential occupier with intent to cause him to give up occupation of the premises contrary to s. 1(3) of the Protection from Eviction Act 1977. The relevant acts had been done by A without the necessary intent but he subsequently omitted to rectify the situation with the intention of causing his tenant to give up occupation of the premises. The court strictly construed the statute holding that the requirement of doing acts could not be satisfied by an omission.

Murder or manslaughter may be committed by omission. In the example above D and E could be found liable for unlawful homicide provided *mens rea* could be established as the courts have recognised a duty to arise under contract (see *Pittwood* (1902) 19 TLR 37, 2.5.2.2.1 *post*) and a duty on the part of parents to care for their children and protect them from physical harm (see *Gibbins and Proctor* (1918) 13 Cr App R 134, 2.5.2.2.2 *post*). A problem in relation to D and E, however, is that they did not actually cause B's death in the sense in which causation is generally understood (see 2.6 *post*). The courts do not appear to have grappled with the principles of causation specifically in relation to omissions. The Law Commission in its Draft Criminal Code Bill (Law Com No. 177) specifically addresses this issue in clause 17(1) which states: '. . . a person causes a result . . . when . . . (b) he omits to do an act which might prevent its occurrence and which he is under a duty to do according to the law relating to the offence'.

With regard to C, he would not be liable as there is no general duty to be a 'Good Samaritan'. The position of the common law was summarised in *Lord Macaulay's Works* (ed. Lady Trevelyan), Vol. VII, p. 497:

In general . . . the penal law must content itself with keeping men from doing positive harm, and must leave to public opinion, and to the teachers of morality and religion, the offence of furnishing men with motives for doing positive good. It is evident that to attempt to punish men by law for not rendering to others all the service which it is their [moral] duty to render to others would be preposterous. We must grant impunity to the vast majority of those omissions which a benevolent morality would pronounce reprehensible, and must content ourselves with punishing such omissions only when they are distinguished from the rest by some circumstance which marks them out as peculiarly fit objects of penal legislation.

While C's disregard of B's plight and failure to render assistance may be morally reprehensible it falls outside the ambit of the criminal law.

2.5.2 Classifying omissions

The analysis of offences into *conduct crimes* and *result crimes* is useful when examining liability for omissions. G. P. Fletcher in *Rethinking Criminal Law* (1978) distinguishes two forms of liability for omissions. The first type he designates 'breach of duty to act', where liability may be imposed for breach of a statutory obligation to act. This relates to conduct crimes where there is no requirement for the occurrence of harm to be proved. The second type of liability which relates to result crimes he designates 'commission by omission', where liability is imposed 'for failing to intervene, when necessary, to prevent the occurrence of a serious harm such as death or the destruction of property' (at p. 421). Fletcher's classification will be used to examine the situations in which the criminal law imposes liability for omissions.

2.5.2.1 Breach of duty to act   Various statutes impose duties to act on individuals in specified circumstances. An individual finding himself in the specified circumstances who fails to perform that duty will commit an offence. For example, a motorist who, without reasonable excuse, fails to provide a police officer with a specimen of breath when required to do so under s. 6 of the Road Traffic Act 1988, or who, when at a police station, similarly fails to provide a specimen of breath, blood or urine when required to do so under s. 7 of the 1988 Act, is guilty of an offence. The penalty for these offences of omission is the same as the offences of commission of which the motorist was suspected. Thus a motorist suspected of driving a vehicle while unfit due to drink or drugs is liable to the same penalty whether he provides the specimen which would establish his guilt or whether he refuses to provide it. Another example of an offence of omission created by statute is failure by a motorist to stop and provide his name and address to any person reasonably requiring it where his vehicle has been involved in an accident where there has been *inter alia* injury to another person or damage to another vehicle (s. 170(4) of the Road Traffic Act 1988). A more serious offence relating to the non-disclosure of information is created by s. 18 of the Prevention of Terrorism (Temporary Provisions) Act 1989. If a person has information which he knows or believes might be of material assistance *inter alia* in preventing the commission of an act of terrorism or in securing the apprehension, prosecution or conviction of a person for a terrorist offence, and he fails without reasonable excuse to disclose that information as soon as reasonably practicable to the proper authorities, he is guilty of an offence.

The above examples are all of statutory creation where it is specifically stated that failure to perform the duty imposed by the statute is an offence. In some situations the common law has recognised an offence where a duty imposed by common law or statute has been neglected. In *Dytham* [1979] QB 722, D, a police constable, was on duty in uniform near a club when a man was ejected from the club and kicked to death by a 'bouncer'. D took no steps to intervene and when the incident was over he drove off having told a bystander that he was going off duty. D was charged with the common law offence of misconduct whilst acting as an officer of justice, in that he had wilfully and without reasonable excuse or justification neglected to perform his duty to preserve the Queen's Peace and to protect the person of the deceased or arrest his assailants or otherwise bring them to justice. D contended that there was no such offence known to the law and that misconduct required a positive act or an element of corruption but mere non-feasance was not enough. The Court of Appeal, in upholding his conviction, placed reliance on a passage in Stephen's *Digest of Criminal Law* which stated:

> Every public officer commits a misdemeanour who wilfully neglects to perform any duty which he is bound either by common law or by statute to

perform provided that the discharge of such duty is not attended with greater danger than a man of ordinary firmness and activity may be expected to encounter.

Lord Widgery stipulated the requirements of the offence as being wilful neglect not mere inadvertence, and the neglect must be culpable in the sense that it is without reasonable excuse or justification. He stated (at p. 727):

This . . . element of culpability . . . is not restricted to corruption or dishonesty but . . . must be of such a degree that the misconduct impugned is calculated to injure the public interest so as to call for condemnation and punishment. Whether such a situation is revealed by the evidence is a matter that a jury has to decide.

It is interesting that Dytham was charged with a conduct crime and not the result crime of manslaughter. This is presumably because it was considered that causation could not be established as it would be impossible to prove that the victim would not have died but for Dytham's failure to perform his duty.

Misconduct in a public office would appear to be an offence applicable to all holders of public office. The nature of the offence obviously will vary depending upon the duties, statutory or common law, placed upon the office holder. Another common law offence which may be committed by omission in breach of a duty, in this case a statutory one, is cheating the revenue (see *Mavji* [1987] 1 WLR 1388).

2.5.2.2 Commission by omission The situations examined so far have involved 'conduct crimes'. Is it possible to commit a 'result crime' by omitting to act? Not all omissions will give rise to liability; liability will depend on there being a duty, recognised by the law, to act or intervene in the circumstances. There are several situations in which the law has recognised the existence of such duties; these are outlined below. Most of the cases which have arisen concern murder or manslaughter. There has been some doubt whether less serious offences against the person which require the commission of an assault (i.e. in the broader sense of that term which includes a battery) may be committed by omission. There is no decision which states that an assault requires an act and J.C. Smith argues that such a requirement is unnecessary (see Smith, 'Liability for omissions in criminal law' (1984) 4 *Legal Studies* 88).

2.5.2.2.1 Duty arising out of contract Where the failure to fulfil a contractual obligation is likely to endanger lives, the criminal law will impose a duty to act. The duty will be owed not only to other parties to the contract but also to any other person whose life may be endangered. In *Pittwood* (1902) 19 TLR 37 the accused was convicted of gross negligence manslaughter following the death of a road user who was hit by a train on a level crossing. The accused was employed by the railway company to look after the crossing and ensure that the gate was shut when a train was due to pass. When the collision occurred the accused was away from his post having left the gate open. His actions were regarded as grossly negligent, and his contention that his contractual obligations gave rise to no duty to the public was dismissed as he was paid to keep the gate shut and protect the public.

2.5.2.2.2 Duty arising out of relationship The existence of close relationships can give rise to a duty to act. It is generally accepted at common law (although there is little direct authority) that parents are under a duty to their children to protect them from physical harm and spouses are under a duty to aid each other (see *Smith* [1979] Crim LR 251, *2.5.2.2.3 post*). In *Gibbins and Proctor* (1918) 13 Cr App R 134, a man and woman with whom he was living were convicted of the murder of the man's child, it having starved to death because they withheld food from it. In the case of the man he had breached the duty parents owe their children. The woman, by taking money to buy food, had assumed a duty towards the child (see *2.5.2.2.3 post*).

2.5.2.2.3 Duty arising from the assumption of care for another If a person voluntarily undertakes to care for another person who is unable to care for himself, whether from infancy, mental illness or other infirmity, a duty will be owed to that person (see *Nicholls* (1874) 13 Cox CC 75). The duty may arise from an express undertaking to care for the other, as in *Nicholls* where a grandmother took into her home her grandchild after its mother died, or it may be implied as in *Instan* [1893] 1 QB 450. In the latter case D, who was without independent means, lived with her aunt who became ill and for the last twelve days of her life was unable to care for herself or summon help. D did not give her any food or seek medical assistance but she continued to live with the aunt and eat her food. D was convicted of manslaughter on the basis that by remaining with the aunt a duty was imposed on her to care for the aunt, which duty she had wilfully and deliberately left unperformed.

The principle in *Instan* has been greatly extended by *Stone and Dobinson* [1977] 1 QB 354, so that a duty to care for another may be easily incurred although onerous or difficult to execute. S's sister F came to live with him and his mistress D in 1972. F was suffering from anorexia nervosa and, although initially able to look after herself, her condition deteriorated until she was confined to bed by July 1975. S was 67, partially deaf, nearly blind and of low intelligence. D was 43 but was described as 'ineffectual and inadequate'. S and D tried to find F's doctor but failed. They took F such little food as she required. D and a neighbour once gave her a bedbath. S and D were unable to use a telephone and no one was informed of F's condition. A neighbour was unsuccessful in getting a local doctor to attend. When F died S and D were convicted of manslaughter and on appeal their convictions were upheld, the Court of Appeal being satisfied that the jury were entitled to find that S and D, by the minimal attention they had given F, had assumed a duty to care for her and had been grossly negligent in the performance of this duty as a result of which F had died. It is unclear from the judgment whether it would have been held that S and D had incurred a duty to care for F if, when she became infirm and unable to care for herself, they had simply ignored her.

An issue which is left unresolved is whether a person who is under a duty to care for another, whether due to relationship or because the duty is imposed as a result of care rendered to a helpless or infirm person, may be released from that duty by the person to whom it is owed. For example, if the person wishes to die and does not want medical attention, is the 'carer' under a duty to contravene their requests and obtain medical aid? In *Smith* [1979] Crim LR 251, S was charged with manslaughter following the death of his wife. She had a marked aversion to doctors and medical treatment and would not allow her husband to seek medical attention after she had given birth to a still-born child at home. When she finally gave him permission it was too late and she died before the doctor arrived. Medical evidence was that she could have been saved had medical aid been sought originally. In summing-up to the jury Griffiths J directed them:

> to balance the weight that it is right to give to his wife's wish to avoid calling a doctor against her capacity to make rational decisions. If she does not appear too ill it may be reasonable to abide by her wishes. On the other hand, if she appeared desperately ill then whatever she may say it may be right to override.

The suggestion seems to be that if a person is capable of making rational decisions he may release a carer from his duty of care. In this case the jury could not agree on the charge of manslaughter and were discharged from giving a verdict. This was only a first instance decision and it left unresolved the question whether a person may release another from the duty of care in anticipation of that duty arising. For example, could an aging wife release her husband from his duty of care by telling him that if she falls ill at any time in the future she wants to be left to die at home without medical attention being called?

The answer to this question was given by the House of Lords in the course of its decision in *Airedale NHS Trust v Bland, The Times*, 5 February 1993. An application was made by the Trust for a declaration whether it was lawful for doctors to withdraw life supporting medical treatment, including artificial feeding through a nasogastric tube, from a patient in one of its hospitals who was in a persistent vegetative state with no prospect of recovery or improvement, when it was known that the discontinuance of the treatment would cause his death within a matter of weeks. The House of Lords held that the treatment could be removed and a doctor would not be acting unlawfully in so doing.

Lord Goff of Chieveley, giving the leading judgment, stated several principles which apply in the treatment of patients. Firstly, there was no absolute rule that a patient's life had to be prolonged regardless of the circumstances. While the fundamental principle was the sanctity of human life, this principle was not absolute. His Lordship was recognising that respect for human dignity demands that the quality of the life in question must be considered. Secondly, the principle of self-determination required that respect be given to the expressed wishes of the patient. Thus, if an adult of sound mind refused treatment the doctors responsible for his care had to give effect to his wishes. If the patient was incapable of communicating, an earlier expression of refusal of consent to treatment in certain circumstances would be effective. Where, however, the patient was both incapable of communicating and had given no earlier indication of his wishes there was no absolute obligation upon the doctor to prolong his life regardless of the circumstances. The question was what was in the best interests of the patient. Where a patient is incapable of giving consent, treatment may be provided if it is in his best interests (see *In re F (Mental Patient: Sterilisation)* [1990] 2 AC 1, 10.1.1.3.2 *post*). Likewise it may be discontinued if this is in his best interests. His Lordship considered that the question should be carefully formulated as it was not whether it was in the patient's best interests that treatment should be ended but rather whether it was in his best interests that treatment which had the effect of artificially prolonging his life should be continued. Such treatment would not be appropriate where it had no therapeutic purpose, which would be the case where it was futile because the patient was unconscious and had no prospect of any improvement in his condition.

Thirdly, where the above conditions pertained, the treatment being futile, there was no duty on a doctor to continue life supporting treatment as it was not in the best interests of his patient. Accordingly, although the discontinuance of treatment would amount to an omission, it would not be unlawful as it would not be in breach of duty to the patient. Similar principles applied with regard to the decision whether to put a patient on life supporting treatment in the first place. Finally, Lord Goff emphasised that doctors in deciding whether to initiate or discontinue life support treatment for a patient had to act in accordance with a responsible and competent body of relevant professional opinion on the principles set down in *Bolam* v *Friern Hospital Management Committee* [1957] 1 WLR 582. In *Airedale NHS Trust* v *Bland* guidance was to be found in a 'Discussion Paper on Treatment of Patients in Persistent Vegetative State' issued in September 1992 by the Medical Ethics Committee of the British Medical Association which provided four safeguards which should be observed before discontinuing life support for such patients:

(1) Every effort should be made at rehabilitation for at least six months after injury.
(2) The diagnosis of irreversible PVS should not be considered confirmed until at least 12 months after the injury.
(3) The diagnosis should be agreed by at least two other independent doctors.
(4) Generally, the wishes of the patient's immediate family would be given great weight.

In all cases where it is decided to end life support treatment the opinion of the Family Division of the High Court should be sought. This latter requirement might subsequently be relaxed by the President of the Family Division in light of experience.

2.5.2.2.4 *Duty arising from creation of a dangerous situation*   Where a person inadvertently and without the appropriate *mens rea* does an act which starts a chain of events which, if uninterrupted, will result in harm to another or his property (or any other interest protected by the criminal law), that person, on becoming aware that he was the cause, is under a duty to take such steps as lie within his power to prevent or minimise the risk of harm. If, before the harm occurs, he realises what he has done and with appropriate *mens rea* he fails to take such steps, he will be criminally liable. The authority for this principle is *Miller* [1983] 2 AC 161. D, a vagrant who was squatting in a house, awoke to find that a cigarette he had been smoking had set fire to the mattress on which he was lying. He did not attempt to extinguish the fire but moved to another room. The house caught fire. D was convicted of arson contrary to s. 1(1) and (3) of the Criminal Damage Act 1971. The House of Lords dismissed his appeal against conviction holding that when D became aware of what he had done in setting the mattress on fire he was under a duty to take such steps as were within his power to prevent or minimise the damage to the property at risk. Lord Diplock stated (at p. 181):

> I see no rational ground for excluding from conduct capable of giving rise to criminal liability, conduct which consists of failing to take measures that lie within one's power to counteract a danger that one has oneself created, if at the time of such conduct one's state of mind is such as constitutes a necessary ingredient of the offence.

The steps which an accused is required to take to counteract the danger he has caused are such as are reasonable in the circumstances. Clearly he would not be expected to attempt to put out a raging inferno; all that might be required is a telephone call summoning the fire brigade. In the case of a minor fire he might reasonably be required to extinguish it himself if all that would be required was a bucket of water or that he stamp on it with his shoe.

The incidence of this duty to act arises from the creation by the accused of the dangerous situation. The House of Lords spoke in terms of a physical act on the part of the accused setting the train of events in motion. They did not address the question whether an initial omission which set in motion a train of events which placed a person or property in peril might found liability. For example, D parks his car on a hill and omits to apply the handbrake. He is walking up the path to his house when he remembers this and turns to see his car start to roll down the hill towards children playing in the street. D realises the danger they are in but he hates children and decides to do nothing either to try to stop his car or warn the children of the danger. V, one of the children, is hit by his car sustaining a broken leg. If D is charged with causing grievous bodily harm with intent contrary to s. 18 of the Offences Against the Person Act 1861 would he be liable? There was no physical act on the part of D which caused the injury but rather an omission, i.e. his failure to apply the handbrake. Should the principle of *Miller* be extended?

2.6 CAUSATION

2.6.1 General

Where an accused is charged with a *result crime*, it is necessary for the prosecution to prove that his acts or omissions caused the prohibited consequence. In murder or manslaughter, for example, it is necessary to prove that the accused, by his acts or omissions, caused the death of the victim. Similarly, in criminal damage, it is necessary to prove that the accused's acts or omissions caused damage to, or destruction of, property belonging to another. If the death, damage or destruction occurred because of some other cause then the offence has not been committed even though all the other elements of the *actus reus* are present and the accused had the necessary *mens rea*. The accused, however, may be guilty of some other offence such as attempt (see *White*, 2.6.2 *post*).

The issue of causation is for the jury to decide upon. The cases which have given rise to problems have usually involved homicide. But, even in homicide cases, causation rarely becomes an issue, as how the victim came to die is usually not in dispute. Where there is a dispute it is the duty of the trial judge to direct the jury on the legal principles relating to causation, but it is for the jury, applying those principles, to decide if the causal link between the accused's conduct and the prohibited consequence has been established. Usually it will be sufficient to direct the jury 'simply that in law the accused's act need not be the sole cause, or even the main cause, of the victim's death, it being enough that his act [or omission] contributed significantly to that result' (*Pagett* (1983) 76 Cr App R 279, *per* Robert Goff LJ). Occasionally, when a particular problem relating to causation arises, such as whether the act of a third party has broken the chain of causation, it is (*per* Robert Goff LJ at p. 290):

> for the judge to direct the jury . . . in the most simple terms, in accordance with the legal principles which they have to apply. It would then fall to the jury to decide the relevant factual issues which, identified with reference to those legal principles, will lead to the conclusion whether or not the prosecution have established the guilt of the accused of the crime of which he is charged.

In simplifying causation for the jury, the judge may refer to the two principles of causation namely that an accused can only be convicted if they are satisfied that his conduct was both a *factual cause* and a *legal cause* of the victim's death. The discussion will centre on homicide but the principles are equally applicable to other offences where causation may be in issue.

2.6.2 Factual causation
The accused's conduct must be a *sine qua non* of the prohibited consequence. In other words it must be established that the consequence would not have occurred as and when it did *but for* the accused's conduct. This is sometimes referred to as the 'but for' test. In *White* [1910] 2 KB 124 D put cyanide into his mother's drink with intent to kill her. Later his mother was found dead with the glass containing the posioned drink beside her three parts full. Medical evidence established that she had died of heart failure and not from poisoning. D was acquitted of murder as he had not caused her death and thus there was no *actus reus*. He was, however, convicted of attempted murder.

The fact that factual causation is established, however, does not mean that legal causation can be established. For example, A shows B a job advertisement. B applies for the job and C, the employer, invites her for interview. On her way to the interview B is attacked by D while walking through a park and killed. But for A showing B the advertisement she would not have applied for the job and but for C inviting her for interview she would not have been in the park and been killed as and when she was. No one would argue, however, that A's and C's acts should be regarded as legal causes of B's death. It is D's acts which are the legal cause of B's death.

2.6.3 Legal causation
Not all but-for causes are legal causes of an event. Legal causation is closely connected to ideas of responsibility and culpability. Glanville Williams in *Textbook of Criminal Law* (2nd edn) states (at p. 381):

> When one has settled the question of but-for causation, the further test to be applied to the but-for cause in order to qualify it for legal recognition is not a test of causation but a moral reaction. The question is whether the result can fairly be said to be imputable to the defendant. . . . If the term 'cause' must be used, it can best be distinguished in this meaning as the 'imputable' or 'responsible' or 'blamable' cause, to indicate the value-judgment involved.

The discussion which follows will examine the conditions for the attribution of legal causation.

2.6.3.1 Consequence must be attributable to a culpable act
If the culpable act the accused performed did not contribute to the consequence legal causation will not be established. Thus although D may have been grossly negligent in performing an act he will not be held responsible for a prohibited consequence which would have occurred whether or not he was negligent. This is illustrated by the case of *Dalloway* (1847) 2 Cox 273. D was driving a horse and cart without holding the reins which were lying loose on the horse's back. A child ran in front of the cart and was killed. Erle J directed the jury that if the driver could have saved the child by using the reins they should convict him of mansalaughter, but if they thought he could not have saved the child by pulling the reins they must acquit him. The jury acquitted him presumably satisfied that the child's death could not have been avoided and thus the child's death was not attributable to the accused's negligence. But for the cart being on the road the child would not have died, but driving a cart on the road is not itself a culpable act. The principle in *Dalloway* would similarly apply on a charge of causing death by reckless driving if the death would have occurred regardless of the manner of the accused's driving.

2.6.3.2 The culpable act must be a more than minimal cause of the consequence
In homicide the accused's act may be considered a cause of death if it has accelerated the victim's death. It is no answer to a charge of

murder or manslaughter to say that the victim was dying from a fatal disease or injury and would have died within a short time had the accused not hastened his death (see *Dyson* [1908] 2 KB 454). If, however, the act of the accused produces only a very trivial acceleration of the death of the victim, it may be ignored under the *de minimis* principle (see *Hennigan* [1971] 3 All ER 133 and *Cato* [1976] 1 WLR 110). On occasions judges have stated that the accused's act must be a 'substantial' cause of the victim's death. This would tend to state the principle too favourably for the accused (see *Malcherek and Steel* [1981] 1 WLR 690). In *Pagett*, Robert Goff LJ stated that 'the accused's act need not be the sole cause, or even the main cause, of the victim's death, it being enough that his act contributed significantly to that result'. Whatever the terminology used the idea which is sought to be communicated to the jury is that the accused's contribution to the death of the victim must be more than minimal. The test is far from scientific as what is sought from the jury is not an exact measurement but, to use William's term, a 'moral reaction'; is the death of the victim morally attributable to the accused. This is, perhaps, what Devlin J had in mind when he directed the jury in *Adams* [1957] Crim LR 365. Dr Adams was charged with murder of one of his patients by means of administering pain-relieving drugs. Devlin J directed the jury that it did not matter that the patient's death was inevitable and that her days were numbered:

> If her life were cut short by weeks or months it was just as much murder as if it was cut short by years. The law knows no special defence [by which doctors might be justified in administering drugs which would shorten life in cases of severe pain,] but that did not mean that a doctor who was aiding the sick and dying had to calculate in minutes, or even in hours, and perhaps not in days or weeks, the effect upon a patient's life of the medicines which he administers or else be in peril of a charge of murder. If the first purpose of medicine, the restoration of health, can no longer be achieved there is still much for a doctor to do, and he is entitled to do all that is proper and necessary to relieve pain and suffering, even if the measures he takes may incidentally shorten life. . . . The law is the same for all, and what I have said to you rests simply upon this: no act is murder which does not cause death. 'Cause' means nothing philosophical or technical or scientific. It means what you twelve men and women sitting as a jury in the jury box would regard in a common-sense way as the cause.

In such circumstances a jury would presumably not find causation, as their moral reaction would be that the doctor was seeking to relieve pain and only incidentally accelerated the patient's death. If, however, the pain-relieving drugs were administered not by a doctor but by the sole beneficiary under her will, and were administered to hasten the inheritance, one could assume that a jury would exhibit a different moral reaction and would find causation to be established.

2.6.3.3 The culpable act need not be the sole cause
The act of the accused need be neither the sole nor the main cause of the prohibited

consequence. Other causes contributing to the consequence may be the acts of others or even of the deceased himself.

2.6.3.3.1   The actions of third parties   In *Benge* (1865) 4 F & F 504, the actions of third parties contributed significantly to the deaths. D, the foreman of a track-laying crew, misread the railway time-table so that the track was up at a time when a train was due. D placed a signalman with a flag 540 yards up the line although the company regulations specified 1,000 yards. The driver of the engine was not keeping a good lookout and several deaths resulted from the ensuing accident. D argued that if the signalman had gone the correct distance and the driver had kept a proper lookout there would not have been an accident. D was convicted of manslaughter after Pigott B directed the jury that if D's conduct mainly or substantially caused the accident it mattered not that it might have been avoided if the others had not been negligent.

The facts of cases need not be as unusual as *Benge*. For example, if A and B both attack C, A stabbing him in the lung and B stabbing him in the abdomen, both would be liable for homicide if he dies as a result of the combined effect of the wounds even though neither wound was, of itself, mortal. There are other circumstances, however, where a subsequent act may supercede an antecedent act which otherwise would have caused death. For example, A poisons B with a slow acting poison. Before it takes effect C decapitates B with an axe. In this situation C's act is the sole cause of B's death. A, however, could be charged with attempted murder.

2.6.3.3.2   The actions of the victim   The deceased by his negligence may contribute to his own death. For example, if D is driving in excess of the speed limit when V, who is blind, walks across the road and is hit by D killing him, it matters not that V's negligence contributed to his death if D could have avoided hitting him had he been observing the speed limit (see *Longbottom* (1849) 3 Cox CC 439).

Where the victim brings about his own death this may be legally attributable to the accused where he has caused the victim to reasonably apprehend violence to himself and he has died in seeking to escape. In such a situation D will only be found to have caused V's injuries or death where V's response to D's violence or threat of violence was 'within the range of responses which might be expected from a victim placed in the situation which he was' (*Williams* [1992] 2 All ER 183, 191 *per* Stuart-Smith LJ). V's response must be 'proportionate to the threat, that is to say that it was within the ambit of reasonableness and not so daft as to make it his own voluntary act which amounted to a *novus actus interveniens* and consequently broke the chain of causation' (*ibid*). In deciding whether V's response was reasonably forseeable the jury should bear in mind 'any particular characteristic of the victim and the fact that in the agony of the moment he may act without thought and deliberation' (*ibid*). (See also *Roberts* (1971) 56 Cr App R 95, *Mackie* (1973) 57 Cr App R 453, *DPP v Daley* [1979] 2 WLR 239 and *Hayward*, 2.6.3.4 *post*).

2.6.3.4   The accused must take his victim as he finds him   The accused cannot complain if his victim is particularly susceptible to physical injury as

where, for example, he suffers from brittle bones or haemophilia; if death
ensues from an injury which would not have been fatal in a person of sound
health it will still be attributable to the accused. In *Martin* (1832) 5 C & P 128
Parke J stated (at p. 130):

> It is said that the deceased was in a bad state of health; but that is perfectly
> immaterial, as, if the prisoner was so unfortunate as to accelerate her death,
> he must answer for it.

The accused will be liable, even though he does not physically assault the
victim, if he so frightens the victim that a pre-existing condition is exacerbated
resulting in death. In *Hayward* (1908) 21 Cox CC 692, D, who was in a state
of violent excitement, was heard to express his intention of 'giving his wife
something' when she returned home. When she did so an argument ensued and
D chased her from the house using violent threats. She collapsed in the road
and died. Medical evidence was given that she was suffering from an abnormal
condition such that any combination of fright or strong emotion and physical
exertion might cause death. Ridley J directed the jury that no proof of actual
physical violence was necessary, but that death from fright alone, caused by an
illegal act, such as threats or violence, would be sufficient (cf. *Watson* [1989] 2
All ER 865).

The principle that the accused must take his victim as he finds him is not
limited to consequences flowing from pre-existing medical or physiological
conditions; it has been extended to cover the victim's mental condition or
religious beliefs. In *Blaue* [1975] 1 WLR 1411, D stabbed a girl, the wound
penetrating a lung. At hospital she was told that a blood transfusion and
surgery were necessary to save her life. She died after refusing a blood
transfusion as it was contrary to her beliefs as a Jehovah's Witness. Medical
evidence indicated that she would not have died if she had accepted the
transfusion. On appeal from his conviction for manslaughter, D argued that
the deceased's refusal of a transfusion was unreasonable and broke the chain of
causation. The Court of Appeal rejected this argument in categorical terms.
Lawton LJ stated (at p. 1415):

> It has long been the policy of the law that those who use violence on other
> people must take their victims as they find them. This in our judgment
> means the whole man, not just the physical man. It does not lie in the mouth
> of the assailant to say that the victim's religious beliefs which inhibited him
> from accepting certain kinds of treatment were unreasonable. The question
> for decision is what caused her death. The answer is the stab wound. The
> fact that the victim refused to stop this end coming about did not break the
> causal connection between the act and death.

It has been argued that had the Court of Appeal adopted the 'reasonable
foresight' test used in the 'flight' cases above there would have been no need
for a value judgment to be made on the reasonableness of the victim's religious
beliefs; the only issue would be whether such refusal of treatment was

reasonably forseeable. This is the position in the law of tort. Lawton LJ distinguished between crime and tort stating that 'the criminal law is concerned with the maintenance of law and order and the protection of the public generally'. Glanville Williams, in a casenote (1976) *Cambridge Law Journal* 15, observes that this argument ignores the fact that Blaue was in any event punishable severely for wounding with intent. The need to protect the public could be reflected in the sentence for such an offence just as much as in the sentence for manslaughter. In such a circumstance the label under which punishment is imposed would appear to be purely symbolic. Symbolism, however, may sometimes serve a purpose. Had the victim been unable to obtain medical assistance it would have been unarguable that the wound caused her death. Why should Blaue be allowed to avoid a conviction for manslaughter because of his victim's choice not to accept medical treatment? The victim's omission did nothing to interrupt the chain of causation flowing from Blaue's initiating act.

2.6.3.5 Intervening events and acts Between the initial act or omission of the accused which sets in motion the train of events which result in the prohibited consequence occurring, other events or acts may intervene. The question will arise whether such an event or act amounts to a *novus actus interveniens*, that is a new act which intervenes to break the chain of causation. There are several situations in which it may be argued that the chain of causation has been broken.

2.6.3.5.1 Medical treatment Where the accused inflicts an injury upon his victim which requires medical treatment, is he to be held liable if that treatment is improper or negligent? While it may be foreseeable that a person who is injured will require medical treatment, is it foreseeable that he might receive improper or negligent treatment?

In *Jordan* (1956) 40 Cr App R 152, D stabbed V who was taken to hospital and the wound was stitched. Eight days later V died. D was convicted of murder. On appeal fresh evidence was called which disclosed that at the time of death the wound was healed but D had died as a result of 1) a terramycin injection to prevent infection, administered after V had shown intolerance to a previous injection, and 2) the intravenous introduction of large quantities of liquid which had caused V's lungs to become waterlogged. The treatment was described as 'palpably wrong' and the Court of Appeal quashed the conviction as, if the jury had heard this evidence, they 'would have felt precluded from saying that they were satisfied that death was caused by the stab wound'. The problem with the judgment is that no clear principle was stated for determining when the chain of causation might be broken by medical treatment. Hallett J stated (at p. 157):

> We are disposed to accept it as the law that death resulting from any normal treatment employed to deal with a felonious injury may be regarded as caused by the felonious injury but we do not think it necessary . . . to formulate . . . the correct test which ought to be laid down with regard to

what is necessary to be proved in order to establish causal connection between the death and the felonious injury. It is sufficient to point out here that this was not normal treatment.

Treatment which is 'not normal', however, is not necessarily 'palpably wrong'. In *Smith* [1959] 2 QB 35, D, a soldier, stabbed V twice with a bayonet in a barrack room fight. Another soldier carrying V to the medical reception station twice dropped him. The medical staff were under pressure as others had been injured in the fight. They did not realise that one of V's wounds had pierced a lung and caused a haemorrhage and gave V treatment which, in light of this information, was described at D's trial as 'thoroughly bad and might well have affected his chances of recovery'. V died and D was convicted of murder. On appeal D's counsel sought to argue that the treatment he received was abnormal and that, if the treatment impeded the chance of V recovering, the death did not result from the wound. The appeal was dismissed, Lord Parker CJ stating (at pp. 42-43):

> if at the time of death the original wound is still an operating cause and a substantial cause, then the death can properly be said to be the result of the wound, albeit that some other cause of death is also operating. Only if it can be said that the original wounding is merely the setting in which another cause operates can it be said that the death did not result from the wound. Putting it in another way, only if the second cause is so overwhelming as to make the original wound merely part of the history can it be said that the death does not flow from the wound.

Where the medical treatment is negligent but the wound is still operating, it would seem that both the perpetrator of the wound and the doctor treating it could be said to have caused the death. In such a situation, however, there would be little likelihood of a prosecution for manslaughter being brought against the doctor. Where, however, the wound has healed and negligent treatment independently causes death a prosecution of the doctor may ensue.

It is arguable that had the jury been in full possession of the facts in *Jordan* they legitimately could have found that the wound was simply the setting in which the palpably wrong treatment operated to cause death. An analogous example might be where a doctor administers a drug for V mistaking him for another patient and V dies as a result.

In the latest case, *Cheshire* [1991] 3 All ER 670, the Court of Appeal shifted the point of focus away from the question whether the original wound was still an operating cause at the time of death to whether death was attributable to the *acts* of the accused. D had shot V in the leg and abdomen. Respiratory problems had ensued necessitating a tracheotomy. V suffered further respiratory problems and infections culminating in his death two months after the shooting due to cardio-respiratory arrest. This occurred because V's windpipe had become obstructed due to narrowing where the tracheotomy had been performed, a rare but not unknown complication. The medical staff failed to diagnose and treat this problem. Although the gunshot wounds were healed at the time of death, the Court of Appeal upheld D's conviction of murder on the basis that the respiratory complications were a direct consequence of D's *acts* which, despite medical negligence, remained a significant cause of V's death. This is undoubtedly correct as the failure of diagnosis did not cause V to die but simply hindered measures being taken which might have kept him alive. There are similarities with *Smith* who also suffered the misfortune of misdiagnosis. The Court of Appeal was of opinion that only in the most extraordinary and unusual case would medical treatment break the chain of causation as 'treatment which falls short of the standard expected of the competent medical practitioner is unfortunately only too frequent in human experience for it to be considered abnormal in the sense of extraordinary' (*per* Beldam LJ, at p. 675). By 'extraordinary' it appears his Lordship meant 'unforeseeable'. His Lordship went on to suggest the terms in which a jury should be directed where they have to consider whether negligent medical treatment, rather than the injuries inflicted by D, were the cause of V's death (at p. 677):

[I]t is sufficient for the judge to tell the jury that they must be satisfied that the Crown have proved that the acts of the accused caused the death of the deceased, adding that the accused's acts need not be the sole cause or even the main cause of death, it being sufficient that his acts contributed significantly to that result. Even though negligence in the treatment of the victim was the immediate cause of his death, the jury should not regard it as excluding the responsibility of the accused unless the negligent treatment was so independent of his acts, and in itself so potent in causing death, that they regard the contribution made by his acts as insignificant.

It is submitted that only in rare cases where positive treatment is given, either in terms of surgical operation or medicinal prescription, will medical negligence supervene to become an independent cause of death rendering the accused's acts 'insignificant'. Examples might be where poison is administered in mistake for a drug, or a drug is administered in an excessive quantity resulting in an overdose, or medical staff continue to administer a drug to which V has displayed intolerance and V dies as a result, or an unnecessary operation is performed in the course of which V dies. If, however, due to misdiagnosis treatment which would have been effectual if administered is not given and V dies, the death can still be linked directly to D's original act as in *Smith* and *Cheshire*. The situation is no different from that where D refuses medical treatment (para. 2.6.3.5.2 *post*) or where medical treatment is not available. If there is negligence in the treatment of V, for example, a doctor operating to save his life makes a mistake and V dies during the operation, D's acts will remain a cause of death as such an eventuality is not so extraordinary as to be unforeseeable; the operation was a direct result of D wounding V and thus was not independent of D's acts.

A problem which has arisen in recent years due to advances in medical technology is that of a victim who has suffered serious injuries whose life is sustained by a life support machine. If the machine is switched off by the doctors treating the victim, who is responsible for the death? This issue arose in two appeals heard together by the Court of Appeal: *Malcherek and Steel* [1981] 1 WLR 690. Both appellants had caused serious injuries to their victims whose lives were sustained by life support machines. When the doctors treating the victims concluded, after extensive tests, that they were 'brain dead', they switched off the machines, whereupon the victims ceased breathing, their hearts ceased beating and their blood ceased circulating and 'conventional death' occurred. The Court of Appeal upheld the convictions for murder, Lord Lane CJ stating (at p. 696):

> There is no evidence in the present case here that at the time of conventional death, after the life support machinery was disconnected, the original wound or injury was other than a continuing, operating and indeed substantial cause of the death of the victim.

While it was immaterial whether the doctors' actions were also causes of death, the Court of Appeal did state *obiter* that they regarded such a suggestion by counsel for the appellants as 'bizarre'. This is undoubtedly correct as when the doctors switched off the machines they merely ceased to artificially sustain lives which had been effectively ended by the initial injuries.

Malcherek and Steel dealt with switching off life support machines where the victims are already 'brain dead'. It is assumed that the same principles apply where life supporting treatment is removed from a patient in a persistent vegetative state (see *Airedale NHS Trust* v *Bland, 2.5.2.2.3 ante*). In deciding that case the House of Lords were not addressing the issue of causation, but in the course of his speech Lord Goff stated that in discontinuing life supporting treatment a doctor is 'simply allowing the patient to die in the sense that he [is] desisting from taking a step which might prevent his patient from dying as a result of his pre-existing condition'. If the victim is in a persistent vegetative state as a result of the accused's act, his death after discontinuance of life supporting treatment would also be caused by the accused's act. One remaining problem, however, in respect of liability for homicide is that the death must occur within a year and a day of the accused's act. In many cases life supporting treatment will only be removed after this period has expired; even though it may be possible to establish causation a homicide conviction will be precluded.

2.6.3.5.2 Neglect by the victim If the victim mistreats or neglects to treat injuries perpetrated by the accused, this will not prevent legal attribution of responsibility to the accused where death results. In *Wall* (1802) 28 State Tr 51, the governor of a colony was convicted of murder of a soldier whom he had sentenced to an illegal flogging of 800 lashes, although the soldier aggravated his condition by drinking spirits while in hospital. MacDonald LCB directed the jury that:

> there is no apology for a man if he puts another in so dangerous and hazardous a situation by his treatment of him, that some degree of unskilfulness and mistaken treatment of himself may possibly accelerate the fatal catastrophe. One man is not at liberty to put another into such perilous

circumstances as these, and to make it depend upon his own prudence, knowledge, skill or experience what may hurry on or complete that catastrophe, or on the other hand may render him service.

In *Holland* (1841) 2 Mood & R 351, D cut V severely on the finger. The wound became infected and V ignored medical advice that he should have the finger amputated or his life might be endangered. The wound caused lockjaw and V died. Maule J directed the jury that it made no difference whether the wound was instantly mortal, or whether it became so by reason of the deceased not having adopted the best mode of treatment as 'the real question is, whether in the end the wound inflicted by the prisoner was the cause of death'. The jury convicted D of murder. Medical science has advanced greatly and a refusal of treatment today in such a case might be regarded as unreasonable. The reasonableness of the victim's conduct, however, is not a relevant issue when considering causation (see *Blaue, ante*). It would seem that the accused also has to accept his victim's phobias, irrationality or stupidity. These matters, however, would be pertinent when sentencing an accused convicted of manslaughter where the death could easily have been avoided had the deceased not mistreated or neglected to treat the injury.

2.6.3.5.3 Naturally occurring events   If D renders V unconscious and leaves him lying on a beach with an incoming tide, V's drowning will be attributable to D. In such a situation, while the original injury did not, of itself, cause death, this will not avail D as the event was objectively foreseeable as likely to occur in the normal course of events. By contrast, if D renders V unconscious and leaves him in a building and thereafter the building is blown up by a bomb planted by terrorists, V's death will not be attributable to D as V was not left in a position of obvious danger and such an event would not be expected to occur in the normal course of events.

2.6.3.5.4 Intervention by a third party   The acts of a third party may intervene to break the chain of causation as where, for example, the injured victim dies when the ambulance in which he is being taken to hospital crashes, or, while in hospital he is attacked and killed by an insane patient who has escaped from the psychiatric ward. Where the act of the third party is a reasonable act of self-defence in response to the act of the accused, or a reasonable act done in the execution of a duty to prevent crime or arrest an offender, this will not break the chain of causation (*Pagett* (1983) 76 Cr App R 279). In *Pagett* D fired a shotgun at police officers attempting to arrest him while holding V against her will and using her body as a shield. The officers returned fire and killed V. D was convicted of manslaughter and his conviction upheld by the Court of Appeal. The same principle would apply if the police had returned fire hitting a bystander.

2.7 COINCIDENCE OF *ACTUS REUS* AND *MENS REA*

Where an offence requires *mens rea* the prosecution must prove that the accused had *mens rea* at the time he did the act which caused the *actus reus*

(*Jakeman* (1982) 76 Cr App R 223). In this case D had booked two cases containing cannabis on a flight from Accra to Rome and from there to London. The flight was diverted from Rome to Paris. D had repented of her intention to import the cannabis into England and did not claim her cases in Paris. Officials in Paris, however, sent the cases to London where the cannabis was discovered. D was charged with being knowingly concerned in the importation of cannabis. The court rejected her defence that she had repented of her criminal intent at the time the cannabis entered England. They stated that what mattered was her 'state of mind at the time the relevant acts are done'. In this case the relevant act was booking her luggage to London, at which time she intended it to arrive in London, and it was immaterial that innocent agents at Paris airport subsequently became instrumental in it being sent to London.

Where an *actus reus* may be brought about by a continuing act, it is sufficient that the accused had *mens rea* during its continuance albeit that he did not have *mens rea* at its inception (*Fagan* v *Metropolitan Police Commissioner* [1969] 1 QB 439). In *Fagan* D accidentally drove his car onto a policeman's foot. The officer asked him to move but he delayed doing so. D was convicted of assaulting the constable in the execution of his duty. It was clear that at the time of driving on to the officer's foot D did not have the necessary *mens rea* for the offence. The Divisional Court, however, held that the assault involved a battery (unlawful application of force to another person) and that this battery continued after the car came to rest, and thus there was a continuing act of assault for which D had the necessary *mens rea* at some time during its continuance. The court also stated that if an act is complete, even though results continue to flow from it, the subsequent inception of *mens rea* cannot convert it into an offence. For example, if D accidentally runs over V in his car and V sustains injuries from which he dies some time later, D's desire that V die, formed after the accident, will not convert V's death into murder. The act which caused death was complete prior to the formation of D's desire, even though the results of the act continued to flow up to the point of V's death.

If the facts of *Fagan* were to recur the accused could now be convicted under the 'duty' principle in *Miller*, (*2.5.2.2.4 ante*). The 'continuing act' principle may still be relevant in some circumstances. In *Kaitamaki* [1985] AC 147 (see further *10.2.1.1.1 post*), the Privy Council affirmed the decision of the New Zealand Court of Appeal that, for the purposes of rape, sexual intercourse is a continuing act. Thus, if D penetrates V with consent (or believing he has consent), and then declines to withdraw on consent being revoked (or on realising that V does not consent), he will be guilty of rape as he has formed the *mens rea* for the offence during the continuance of the *actus reus*.

The cases examined so far have involved one act to which *mens rea* may be linked. In several cases the problem has arisen of a consequence ensuing from a combination of several acts but *mens rea* did not exist for the commission of each act. Is it sufficient that the accused had *mens rea* at some stage during the course of events? In *Thabo Meli* [1954] 1 WLR 228, the appellants struck V over the head with intent to kill him. V's body was rolled over a cliff to make his death appear to be an accident. In fact V died from exposure and not from the initial blow to the head. The appellants had *mens rea* when they struck V, but V died from the act of disposal when they did not have *mens rea* as they believed they were disposing of a corpse. The appellants were undoubtedly guilty of attempted murder but the Privy Council upheld the convictions for murder because, as they stated (at p. 230) it was:

> impossible to divide up what was really one series of acts in this way. There is no doubt that the accused set out to do all these acts in order to achieve their plan and as parts of their plan; and it is too refined a ground of judgment to say that, because they were under a misapprehension at one stage and thought that their guilty purpose had been achieved before in fact it was achieved, therefore they are to escape the penalties of the law.

This is essentially a policy decision as there was no *mens rea* when the act causing the *actus reus* was performed. The fact that all the acts were performed in pursuance of an antecedent plan, and death ensued from the execution of that plan, appeared to be crucial to the decision of the Privy Council. In *Church* [1966] 1 QB 59, the Court of Appeal extended the *Thabo Meli* 'series of acts' doctrine to a case of manslaughter where there was no antecedent plan. In the course of a fight with V, D struck and attempted to strangle her. She fell unconscious and D, believing her to be dead, threw her into a river where she drowned. The Court of Criminal Appeal were of opinion that it was sufficient for a conviction if the conduct constituted 'a series of acts which culminated in her death'. The Court stated *obiter* that the jury could have convicted of murder 'if they regarded the appellant's behaviour from the moment he first struck her to the moment when he threw her into the river as a series of acts designed to cause death or grievous bodily harm.' As the act of disposal is for the purpose of disposing of a body, it being the accused's belief that death had occurred already, it is difficult to see how the series of acts could be described as being 'designed to cause death'. The act which caused death was designed to dispose of a corpse! The principle the Court was endeavouring to state has been clarified by the most recent case.

In *Le Brun* [1991] 4 All ER 673, there was neither an antecedent plan nor did D believe that he was dealing with a corpse as he attempted to drag the unconscious body of his wife away from the place where he had assaulted her following an argument in the course of which she had refused to go home. In moving his wife she slipped from his grasp and hit her head on the pavement causing a fractured skull from which she died. D was convicted of manslaughter following a direction to the jury by the trial judge that they could convict of murder or manslaughter, depending on the intention with which the original blow was struck, if D had 'accidentally dropped the victim causing her death whilst either: (a) attempting to move her to her home against her wishes . . ., and/or (b) attempting to dispose of her body or otherwise cover up the previous assault'. The Court of Appeal upheld D's conviction of manslaughter applying *Church*, Lord Lane CJ stated (at pp. 678–9):

> It seems to us that where the unlawful application of force and the eventual act causing death are parts of the same sequence of events, the same

transaction, the fact that there is an appreciable interval of time between the two does not serve to exonerate the defendant from liability. That is certainly so where the appellant's subsequent actions which caused death, after the initial unlawful blow, are designed to conceal his commission of the original unlawful assault . . . In short, in circumstances such as the present, . . . the act which causes death and the necessary mental state to constitute manslaughter need not coincide in point of time.

Accordingly, the 'transaction' principle applies not only where D is disposing of what he believes to be a corpse but also when he is attempting to move V to a place contrary to her will or were D is attempting to cover up his original crime. The Court of Appeal did not expressly declare that the 'transaction' principle is equally applicable to murder, but presumably it is.

In *Thabo Meli*, *Church* and *Le Brun* it was clear that death ensued from the second act. Where it is not possible to determine which of the two acts caused death, the accused may be convicted only if the prosecution prove that he acted with *mens rea* on both occasions (*A-G's Reference (No. 4 of 1980)* [1981] 1 WLR 705). The facts of the *A-G's Reference* were that the D had slapped V on the face causing her to fall down a flight of stairs and bang her head. D dragged her upstairs by a rope tied around her neck, placed her in the bath and drained off her blood before cutting up her body and disposing of the pieces. It was impossible to determine the cause of death. The Court of Appeal held that it is not necessary to prove which act caused death but the jury could only convict of manslaughter if they were satisfied *both* (i) that the fall downstairs was the result of an intentional act by the accused which was unlawful and dangerous (i.e. 'unlawful act' manslaughter), and (ii) that the act of cutting the victim's throat was an act of gross criminal negligence (i.e. gross negligence manslaughter). The same principle would apply on a charge of murder provided the accused had the requisite *mens rea* when he performed each act. For example, D hits V over the head intending to kill him but believing that V is not dead he slits his throat to complete the job before disposing of the body in an incinerator. In this example D has the necessary *mens rea* for murder when he hits V and when he slits his throat. The problem, however, with the principle in *A-G's Reference* is that it is too favourable to the accused as the jury must acquit if they are not satisfied that each act was performed with *mens rea*. It is submitted that if it is proved that the accused had the relevant *mens rea* when he performed the first act, he should be guilty of homicide as either this act caused death and thus *actus reus* and *mens rea* coincided or, if the second act caused death, the 'transaction' principle is applicable.

Further reading

A. C. E. Lynch, 'The mental element in the *actus reus*' (1982) 98 LQR 109.

J. C. Smith, 'Liability for omissions in the criminal law' (1984) 4 LS 88.

H. Gross, 'A note on omissions' (1984) 4 LS 308.

B. Hogan, 'Omissions and the duty myth', in *Criminal Law: Essays in Honour of J. C. Smith* (1986, ed. P. Smith).

G. Williams, 'Criminal omissions – the conventional view' (1991) 107 LQR 86.

A. Norrie, 'A Critique of Criminal Causation' (1991) 54 MLR 685.
J. E. Stannard, 'Medical treatment and the chain of causation' (1993) 57 JCL 88.

THREE

Mens rea

3.1 INTRODUCTION

Where a person has performed acts or brought about consequences which constitute the *actus reus* of an offence he will generally be found guilty of the offence only if he had the necessary *mens rea* at the time he acted. The exceptions to this are offences of strict liability and offences which may be committed negligently, for example, careless driving. *Mens rea* refers to the mental element necessary for a particular crime. This may differ from one crime to another and the definition of each crime must be examined to determine what state of mind is required. Words used in offences to convey a requirement of *mens rea* are, for example, intention, recklessness, maliciousness, wilfulness, knowledge (together with their adjectival and adverbial variants).

Offences which require *mens rea* are generally regarded as being more serious than those which may be committed negligently or for which liability is strict. The term imports a notion of culpability or moral blameworthiness on the part of the offender. For most of this century scholars understood *mens rea* to require an advertent state of mind, whereas those offences which could be committed negligently, or for which liability was strict, imposed liability on the person who may have done the prohibited act or caused the prohibited consequence inadvertently. In recent years, however, the line of demarcation between *mens rea* and negligence has become blurred as judges have struggled to define the meaning of *mens rea* words. After two decades of struggling the outcome is uncertainty and confusion. This is particularly unsatisfactory in the light of the serious consequences for the individual which attend conviction for a criminal offence. It is also unacceptable in a country which purports to adhere to the principles deriving from the idea of the rule of law. J. Raz in 'The rule of law and its virtue' (1977) 93 LQR 195, 198-9 states:

The law must be open and adequately publicised. If it is to guide people they must be able to find out what it is. For the same reason its meaning must be clear. An ambiguous, vague, obscure or imprecise law is likely to mislead or confuse at least some of those who desire to be guided by it.

'Ambiguous', 'vague', 'obscure' and 'imprecise' are all words which could be used to describe judicial pronouncements on the meaning of words which import the requirement of *mens rea* into definitions of offences. It is necessary, however, to seek to make some sense of these judicial pronouncements.

3.2 INTENTION

3.2.1 What might intention mean?

In many offences the *mens rea* required is that of intention to cause the prohibited result. Intention is a word in ordinary use. Its meaning, however, is not clear. When dissenting in *Caldwell* [1982] AC 341, Lord Edmund Davies stated (at p. 357):

The law in action compiles its own dictionary. In time, what was originally the common coinage of speech acquires a different value in the pocket of the lawyer than when in the layman's purse.

It is important, therefore, that technical words, such as 'intention', should be clearly defined. Unfortunately, however, to use Glanville Williams words, 'judges decline to define [intention], and they appear to adjust it from one case to another' (see Williams, 'Oblique intention' [1987] CLJ 417). The *Concise Oxford Dictionary* defines 'intend' as 'have as one's purpose' and 'intention' as 'intending, one's purpose . . . object . . . ultimate aim'. As used in the criminal law, *intention* does not appear to have such a clear or restricted meaning. There are basically four possible states of mind which may be encompassed within the term 'intention'. Let us assume that D has insured V's life. He decides to kill V in order to obtain the insurance moneys. D's *desire* is to kill V and his *motive* is to obtain the money. The following four examples of D killing V illustrate the four states of mind which may constitute intention.

(i) D shoots at V in order to kill him. In this situation V's death is both desired and intended by D. The consequence of V's death may be said to be D's purpose, aim or objective. This variety of intention is referred to as *direct intention*. Even though D may realise that his chances of hitting V may be slim because of the distance or his poor ability with a gun, this does not affect his intention which is to kill V.

(ii) D sees V standing behind a window and shoots at V in order to kill him realising that to do so the bullet must first break the window. In this situation it may be said that D intends also to break the window as this is a necessary precondition to killing V. This may be described as *oblique intention*; breaking the window is D's subsidiary aim or secondary purpose which must be achieved if he is to achieve his ultimate aim or primary purpose. Glanville Williams in 'Oblique intention' *ante*, states (at p. 421):

Direct intention is where the consequence is what you are aiming at. Oblique intention is something you see clearly, but out of the corner of your eye. The consequence is (figuratively speaking) not in the straight line of your purpose, but a side-effect that you accept as an inevitable or 'certain' accompaniment of your direct intent (desire-intent). There are twin consequences of the act, x and y; the doer wants x, and is prepared to accept its unwanted twin y. Oblique intent is, in other words, a kind of knowledge or realisation. . . . Certainty in human affairs means certainty as a matter of common sense – certainty apart from unforeseen events or remote possibilities. Realisation of practical certainty is something higher in the scale than appreciation of high probability.

While there may be a remote possibility that the window may blow open before the bullet passes through it, it is clear at the time D squeezes the trigger that breaking the window is a practical or moral certainty.

(iii) D places a bomb under V's seat timed to kill him in mid-flight as he co-pilots a plane over the Atlantic. In this situation D does not desire to kill the crew or passengers on the plane and their deaths are not a pre-condition to killing V. In the normal course of events, however, their deaths will ensue as the inevitable *by-product* of D's achievement of his primary purpose; they are an inseparable consequence of that end. Again it may be said that at the time of planting the bomb the deaths of the crew and passengers were morally certain if D achieved his primary purpose. Thus, this situation may be regarded as another example of oblique intention.

(iv) D shoots at V, while he is driving a bus, in order to kill him. D foresees that it is highly probable that the passengers on the bus will also be injured or killed. In this situation D does not desire to kill or injure the passengers; their injuries or deaths are not inevitable although highly likely. Does foresight that a consequence is highly probable amount to intention to bring that consequence about or does it only constitute recklessness?

There is much judicial and academic discussion about whether a consequence can be intended if it is not desired. In example (ii) and (iii) above, it may be argued that as D's desire was to kill V the consequences of breaking the window or killing the crew and passengers were undesired. Norrie, 'Oblique intention and legal politics' [1989] Crim LR 793, argues that secondary consequences flowing from D's primary purpose may also be regarded as desired. As D seeks to bring about the primary purpose in a known set of circumstances, secondary consequences which D obliquely intends may be regarded as desired in a broader sense in that they are part and parcel of the package of circumstances within which D chooses to operate.

3.2.2   What should intention mean?
The Law Commission in its Draft Criminal Code (Law Com No. 177) gives the following definition of intention to cause results:

. . . a person acts – . . .

(b) 'intentionally' with respect to – . . .
   (ii) a result when he acts either in order to bring it about or being aware that it will occur in the ordinary course of events . . .

In its commentary on the Code the Law Commission states (at para. 8.14):

> Acting in order to bring about a result is, as it were, the standard case of 'intending' to cause a result. But we are satisfied that a definition of 'intention' for criminal law purposes must refer . . . to 'the means as well as the end and the inseparable consequences of the end as well as the means.' Where a person acts in order to achieve a particular purpose, knowing that this cannot be done without causing another result, he must be held to intend to cause that other result. The other result may be a pre-condition . . . or it may be a necessary concomitant of the first result. . . . The result will occur, and D knows that it will occur, 'in the ordinary course of events . . .. unless something supervenes to prevent it.' It is, and he knows it is, 'a virtual certainty'. We have adopted the phrase, 'in the ordinary course of events' to ensure that 'intention' covers the case of a person who knows that the achievement of his purpose will necessarily cause the result in question, in the absence of some wholly improbable supervening event.

The Law Commission, accordingly, defined *intention* to include the types of situation given in examples (i), (ii) and (iii) above. They went on to reject (iv) as a situation involving intention stating (at para. 8.15):

> A person's awareness of any degree of probability (short of virtual certainty) that a particular result will follow from his acts ought not, we believe, to be classed as an 'intention' to cause that result for criminal law purposes.

The Law Commission's definition of intention has been adopted in the House of Lords, *Report of the Select Committee on Murder and Life Imprisonment* (Session 1988-89, H.L. Paper 78). Professor J.C. Smith, however, is of opinion that the definition could be improved to avoid possible difficulties (see 'A Note on Intention' [1990] Crim LR 85). The most significant difficulty which he considers might arise relates to the type of situation given in example (iii) above. If the bomber knows that bombs of the type he is using have, for example, a 50 per cent failure rate, Smith states (at p. 86):

> It may be argued that the defendant does not . . . intend the death of the crew because he is not virtually certain etc., that they will die – he is not aware that it will happen 'in the ordinary course of events', because there is a 50 per cent chance that it will not happen at all.

Smith suggests the following redraft of the definition:

> A person acts intentionally with respect to – . . .
>   (b) a result when –

(i)   it is his purpose to cause that result; or
(ii) his purpose is to cause some other result and he knows that, if he
      succeeds, his act will, in the ordinary course of events, cause that
      result.

The important point to note about the Law Commission's definition and
Professor Smith's redraft is that both accept that *intention* should have a
meaning wider than in situations like (i) above but that it should not be so wide
as to encompass foresight of probability in situations like (iv) as this is the
domain of recklessness.

3.2.3   How have the courts defined intention?

3.2.3.1   The difficulty of formulating a definition   While it is easy to
state the Law Commission's definition of intention and the states of mind
which this encompasses, it is more difficult to glean from judicial statements a
clear definition of intention. Most of the judgments which refer to intention
suffer from the defect that the judges have been neither clear nor precise in
their use of language, their judgments consequently contain inconsistencies,
contradictions and ambiguities. There are several reasons for this. Some of the
cases in which the meaning of intention has been considered have involved
emotive factual situations which appear to have coloured judicial pronouncements (see e.g. *Steane* [1947] KB 997). The most important cases before the
House of Lords have involved murder where their Lordships had to decide
what the *mens rea* for murder is (see *Hyam* [1975] AC 55, *Moloney* [1985] 1 AC
905, and *Hancock and Shankland* [1986] 1 AC 455). The meaning of intention
was thus subsumed within the discussion of the *mens rea* for murder and
coloured by considerations of the type of conduct which should be caught by
the definition of murder. Their Lordships concluded in *Moloney* that the *mens
rea* for murder was intention to kill or intention to cause grievous bodily harm.
Having given this definition of the *mens rea* of murder their Lordships
considered certain examples of egregious and reprehensible conduct resulting
in death. They concluded that such conduct merited conviction for murder
although, unrecognised by them, it did not fall within any of the three
situations given above which exemplify the meaning of intention. Their
Lordships, in effect, confused policy with principle and as a result have left the
principles of the criminal law in a less than satisfactory condition. One cannot
ignore, however, the pronouncements of the House of Lords and the Court of
Appeal. Accordingly, an attempt must be made to make some sense of the cases.
   A further problem in some of the cases dealing with intention is judicial
confusion of substantive law with the law of evidence. The substantive law lays
down the facts which must be proved if the accused is to be convicted of a
particular offence. For example, if D is charged with murder one of the facts
which must be proved is that he intended to kill or to cause grievous bodily
harm to the deceased. The law of evidence lays down rules relating to the
evidence which may be admitted to prove the existence of this fact. The state
of a person's mind, however, is not an easy fact to prove unless the accused

provides an admissible confession in which he states what his intention or foresight was. In the absence of such a confession the jury (or magistrates in summary proceedings) are left to use their collective common sense to draw inferences from the circumstances and the natural and probable consequences of the accused's conduct in those circumstances. This is provided for specifically by s. 8 of the Criminal Justice Act 1967:

> A court or jury in determining whether a person has committed an offence, –
> (a) shall not be bound in law to infer that he intended or foresaw a result of his actions by reason only of its being a natural and probable consequence of those actions; but
> (b) shall decide whether he did intend or foresee that result by reference to all the evidence, drawing such inferences from the evidence as appear proper in the circumstances.

For example, D is charged with murder having pushed V over a 50 metre high cliff on to rocks below where he died. At his trial, D claims he did not intend to kill or seriously injure V but that he only wished to frighten him to teach him a lesson. If the jury disbelieve D (which they undoubtedly would), they can convict of murder only if they are satisfied beyond reasonable doubt that D intended to kill V or to cause him serious injury. They would be entitled to use their common sense to determine what a person of normal intellect would have foreseen as the outcome of such conduct. One would suggest that the inevitable consequence of such conduct is at least serious injury. They would then be entitled to infer that as D is a person of normal intellect he had such foresight and thus intended to kill or cause serious injury. This is not to say that foresight of a consequence equals intention but rather that, if you foresee a consequence as certain to ensue and persist with your course of conduct, it is reasonable to conclude that you intended that consequence in the absence of any other cogent explanation.

3.2.3.2 Approaching a clear definition The cases are in agreement that intention covers situation (i) above where D does an act with the aim or purpose of causing a particular result. The problem centres on situations (ii) and (iii), that is whether oblique intention will suffice where the definition of the *mens rea* element of an offence requires intention to cause a particular result. In *Mohan* [1976] QB 1 intention was defined as 'a decision to bring about, in so far as it lies within the accused's power, [the prohibited consequence], no matter whether the accused desired that consequence of his act or not.' James LJ also stated (at p. 11):

> . . . evidence of knowledge of likely consequences, or from which knowledge of likely consequences can be inferred, is evidence by which intent may be established but it is not . . . to be equated with intent. If the jury find such knowledge established, they may, and using common sense, they probably will find intent proved, but it is not the case that they must do so.

In this case D was charged with attempting to cause grievous bodily harm with intent having driven a car at a policeman who was blocking his path as he endeavoured to escape. The definition of intention which the Court of Appeal gave clearly included the type of situation given in example (ii) above; D may not have desired to injure the policeman as an end in itself but he was prepared to do so as a pre-condition to escaping which was his ultimate aim or purpose. The court also excluded situation (iv) from the definition of intention. This followed dicta in *Hyam* [1975] AC 55. In that case Lord Hailsham stated (at p. 65):

I do not believe that knowledge or any degree of foresight is enough. Knowledge or foresight is at best material which entitles or compels a jury to draw the necessary inference as to intention.

Lord Hailsham made it clear later in his judgment (at pp. 73-74) that intention was to be distinguished from desire and foresight of probable consequences. He clearly included within his definition of intention, however, both types of situation given in examples (ii) and (iii) stating that intention includes 'the means as well as the end and the inseparable consequences of the end as well as the means.' Thus he went on to state:

. . . a man may desire to blow up an aircraft in flight in order to obtain insurance moneys. But if any passengers are killed he is guilty of murder, as their death will be a moral certainty if he carries out his intention. There is no difference between blowing up the aircraft and intending the death of some or all of the passengers.

After *Mohan* and Lord Hailsham's speech in *Hyam* one would have thought that the meaning of intention was clear. Situations of the type exemplified in (i), (ii) and (iii) above constituted intention and situation (iv) did not. Evidence that a consequence was foreseeable as highly probable was simply circumstantial evidence which might persuade the jury to draw the inference that the accused intended the consequence. But the question always is 'what was the accused's subjective state of mind?' If the jury are not satisfied that the accused actually foresaw the consequence as a moral certainty in situations like (ii) and (iii) the inference of intention would not be appropriate. If the consequence was D's aim or purpose it does not matter that he only foresaw a possibility of achieving it. This view is confirmed by a reading of the case of *Pearman* (1984) 80 Cr App R 259. This distinction between what intention is and how it may be proved is consistent with s. 8 of the Criminal Justice Act 1967 (see 3.2.3.1 *ante*).

Mohan must be contrasted, however, with the cases of *Steane* and *Gillick*. In *Steane* the Court of Criminal Appeal, swayed by the emotive facts of the case, gave a narrow definition to intention confining it to purpose. D was convicted of doing acts likely to assist the enemy with intent to assist the enemy. D gave broadcasts from Germany during the second world war. The Court of Criminal Appeal quashed his conviction as the jury had not been directed to acquit if he may have had 'the innocent intent of a desire to save his wife and children from a concentration camp'. While saving his family may have been his ultimate aim or purpose, assisting the enemy was a necessary pre-condition to achieving that aim. As Glanville Williams points out (see 'Oblique Intention' *ante.*, at p. 428) his intent to save his family did not negative his intent to assist the enemy. Steane, however, did merit having his conviction quashed as the jury had not been directed on duress. The Court of Criminal Appeal, however, wrongly believed that duress might not have succeeded as a defence and thus did violence to the meaning of intention to ensure Steane's acquittal. In *Gillick* v *West Norfolk and Wisbech AHA* [1986] AC 112, the House of Lords balked from recognising a defence of necessity but tampered with the meaning of intention to ensure that a doctor who prescribes contraceptives for a girl under 16 will not be guilty of aiding, abetting, counselling or procuring the offence of unlawful sexual intercourse committed by her with a man, stating that the doctor's 'clinical judgment' is a 'complete negation of the guilty mind which is an essential ingredient of the criminal offence'. But whatever the doctor's motives, if he knows that his act will promote, encourage or facilitate unlawful sexual intercourse, he clearly intends to aid or abet that offence. As *Gillick* did not involve a criminal prosecution what was said was *obiter* and, it is submitted, should be ignored. *Steane*, however, cannot be ignored but it is time that it was overruled as being *per incuriam*. The House of Lords not only neglected to do so in *Moloney* [1985] AC 905, but actually approved of the decision thereby adding more fuel to the fires of confusion as the case is not reconcilable with the speeches of their Lordships!

3.2.3.3 The restoration of confusion The House of Lords have had two further attempts at defining intention, both of which were in the context of appeals from convictions for murder. The problem with *Hyam* was that while Lord Hailsham was clear regarding the meaning of intention, there was uncertainty regarding the actual *mens rea* of murder. The other four law lords appeared to accept that foresight by the accused of a high probability of death or serious bodily harm resulting from his conduct would suffice to constitute the *mens rea* of murder. In *Moloney* the House of Lords declared that the *mens rea* for murder is intention to kill or to cause grievous bodily harm, nothing else will suffice. The issue to be clarified was the meaning of intention.

In *Moloney* the issue was essentially a factual one; there was a dispute between the prosecution and the defence as to whether the appellant knew the gun was pointing at the deceased when he fired it. The appellant's account of the incident was that he had been drinking with his stepfather when the stepfather challenged him to a competition to see who could load, draw and fire a shotgun in the shortest time. In doing so the appellant shot his stepfather killing him. He claimed that he had not aimed the gun and that he had no idea that in firing it he would injure his stepfather. The issue for the jury should have been a simple one as stated by Lord Bridge (at p. 917):

If they were sure that, at the moment of pulling the trigger. . . . the appellant realised that the gun was pointing straight at his stepfather's head, they were bound to convict him of murder. If, on the other hand, they thought it might be true that, in the appellant's drunken condition and in the context of this ridiculous challenge, it never entered the appellant's head when he pulled the trigger that the gun was pointing at his father, he should have been acquitted of murder and convicted of manslaughter.

Either the appellant had the direct intent of killing or seriously injuring his stepfather or he had not. Unfortunately the trial judge confused the issue by directing the jury that 'a man intends the consequence of his voluntary act (a) when he desires it to happen, whether or not he foresees that it probably will happen and (b) when he foresees that it will probably happen, whether he desires it or not.' The equation of intention with foresight of probability rendered an appeal inevitable. Lord Bridge considered the direction on 'foresight of consequences' to be an example of an irrelevant direction which would only confuse a jury. If when the appellant fired the gun he knew that it was pointing at his stepfather's head, the inference was inescapable 'using words in their ordinary, everyday meaning, that he intended to kill his stepfather.'

Lord Bridge went on to consider the correct direction for all crimes where a specific intent is required. (An offence of specific intent is one which requires intention to be proved; recklessness will not suffice as an alternative state of mind.) Lord Bridge considered that 'the golden rule' is to 'avoid any elaboration or paraphrase of what is meant by intent, and leave it to the jury's good sense to decide whether the accused acted with the necessary intent' (at p. 926), although an explanation that intention is something quite different from motive or desire is frequently necessary. Further explanation or elaboration should only be given where necessary to avoid misunderstanding in the light of the facts and the way the case has been presented to the jury in evidence and argument. While Lord Bridge did not express himself particularly clearly at this point, it would appear that he was referring to cases where the evidence suggests that the accused's ultimate aim or purpose was something other than the prohibited consequence which he had caused, that is cases where the accused had an oblique intent. In such cases, Lord Bridge stated, foresight of a high degree of probability is not equivalent to intention but 'as an element bearing on the issue of intention . . . belongs, not to the substantive law, but to the law of evidence.' When elaboration is required, two questions should be put to the jury (at p. 929):

> First, was death or really serious injury in a murder case (or whatever relevant consequence must be proved to have been intended in any other case) a natural consequence of the defendant's voluntary act? Secondly, did the defendant foresee that consequence as being a natural consequence of his act? The jury should then be told that if they answer yes to both questions it is a proper inference for them to draw that he intended that consequence.

Unfortunately this statement is not as clear as it might have been as the term 'natural consequence' is ambiguous. Something may be natural, in the sense of being causally connected to the original act, but it is not necessarily a certain consequence. The example often given is that conception may be a natural consequence of sexual intercourse but it is by no means certain. Lord Bridge appears to have meant to convey, however, the idea that the consequence must have been foreseen as morally certain. Earlier in his speech he stated (at p. 929):

[Natural] conveys the idea that in the ordinary course of events a certain act will lead to a certain consequence unless something unexpected supervenes to prevent it.

Although Lord Bridge regarded as irrational rules of substantive law which sought to define intention in terms of degrees of probability, he did reveal some inconsistency when he stated (at p. 925) that the probability of the consequence taken to have been foreseen must be little short of overwhelming before it will suffice to establish the necessary intent. Such a probability, however, would appear to be indistinguishable from a consequence which is certain unless prevented by some unexpected supervening event. Lord Bridge then illustrated his point by the following example of a person who has an ultimate aim or purpose whose achievement will necessarily involve another consequence (at p. 926):

A man, who, at London airport, boards a plane which he knows to be bound for Manchester, clearly intends to travel to Manchester, even though Manchester is the last place he wants to be and his motive for boarding the plane is simply to escape pursuit. The possibility that the plane may have engine trouble and be diverted to Luton does not affect the matter. By boarding the Manchester plane, the man conclusively demonstrates his intention to go there, because it is a moral certainty that that is where he will arrive.

In this example, Lord Bridge states that boarding the plane 'demonstrates . . . intention'; he does not state that this is evidence from which intention is to be inferred. In other parts of his speech, and particularly when he framed his two-part test, Lord Bridge did speak in terms of drawing inferences. It is his test which has subsequently been taken to have conveyed his intention. Inferring intention from foresight, rather than treating a particular degree of foresight as intention, can create confusion. In a case where the prohibited consequence was not the accused's aim or purpose, nor desired by him as an end in itself or means to an end, the task for the prosecution would be to prove what he foresaw. In the absence of an admission by the accused the jury would be left to infer this from the evidence. If they are satisfied that he foresaw death or serious injury as morally certain at the time he acted it would be correct to say he intended that result in the 'oblique' sense of the word – no further *inferring* should be required. Indeed, as it is not a case where bringing about the prohibited consequence is the accused's aim or purpose, and as intention is something distinct from motive or desire, there would not seem to be any ingredient left which might be inferred to convert foresight into intention.

Doubtless juries will use their common sense and equate foresight of a consequence as morally certain with intention but it would have been much more helpful if Lord Bridge had said so clearly.

A further problem arising from *Moloney* is created by Lord Bridge himself when he provides the example of a terrorist bomber who plants a bomb in a building, giving a warning to enable the building to be evacuated, but realising that it is virtually certain that a bomb disposal squad will attempt to defuse it. If it explodes killing a bomb disposal expert Lord Bridge assumes the terrorist would be guilty of murder. While it may be virtually certain that an attempt will be made to defuse the bomb, it is not, however, certain that anyone will die; bomb disposal experts do not become experts by needlessly throwing their lives away. This example does not illustrate a case of intention to kill but rather recklessness. It may be that Lord Bridge feels that someone like this terrorist should be guilty of murder; that would necessitate a new definition of the *mens rea* of murder.

At the end of his speech in *Moloney* Lord Hailsham stated (at p. 913):

> I conclude with the pious hope that your Lordships will not again have to decide that foresight and foreseeability are not the same thing as intention although either may give rise to an irresistible inference of such. . . .

Lord Hailsham's hopes proved to be in vain as a mere nine months later the House of Lords was considering the meaning of Lord Bridge's judgment in *Hancock and Shankland* [1986] AC 455. The phrase 'natural consequence' had created judicial confusion. This is another example of a case where the only issue was one of fact but the matter was complicated by the trial judge's direction to the jury. The accused were miners on strike. They pushed a block of concrete and a concrete post from a bridge over a three-lane highway on which a miner was being taken to work by taxi. The block hit the taxi killing the driver. The accused were charged with murder the prosecution alleging that they intended to kill or cause serious injury. The accused's case was that their intention was only to block the road and frighten the miner as they believed the block was positioned over the middle lane when the taxi was in the nearside lane. The issue for the jury should have been to determine which version of the facts was to be believed. If the accused were to be believed then a conviction of manslaughter would follow as there clearly was no intention to kill or cause serious injury. If, on the other hand, they disbelieved the accused and the prosecution satisfied them beyond reasonable doubt that the accused knew the block was positioned above the lane along which the taxi was driving, the inference that they intended to kill or cause serious injury would have been inescapable as one could imagine no other reason for dropping the block. The only issue in fact was what was their aim or purpose. If it was to kill or cause serious injury it would not matter whether they only foresaw a slight chance of success. Unfortunately the judge complicated matters by giving the Bridge direction relating to foresight of consequences. He did not explain that 'natural consequence' did not simply mean causally connected and thus the appeal was based on the ambiguity of this phrase. The Court of Appeal quashed the convictions for murder and the House of Lords affirmed this on the basis that the phrase 'natural consequence' required amplification. The amplification which Lord Scarman provided, however, bears little connection to the meaning Lord Bridge attributed to the phrase. Lord Scarman stated (at p. 473):

> [Lord Bridge] omitted any reference in his guidelines to probability. He did so because he included probability in the meaning which he attributed to 'natural' . . . [T]he probability of a consequence is a factor of sufficient importance to be drawn specifically to the attention of the jury and to be explained. In a murder case where it is necessary to direct a jury on the issue of intent by reference to foresight of consequences the probability of death or serious injury resulting from the act done may be critically important. Its importance will depend on the degree of probability: if the likelihood that death or serious injury will result is high, the probability of that result may . . . be seen as overwhelming evidence of the existence of the intent to kill or injure. . . . In my judgment, therefore, the *Moloney* guidelines as they stand are unsafe and misleading. They require a reference to probability. They also require an explanation that the greater the probability of a consequence the more likely it is that the consequence was foreseen and that if that consequence was foreseen the greater the probability is that that consequence was also intended.

A direction in terms of foresight of consequences should only be appropriate where the consequence which occurred was not the accused's direct aim or purpose. Lord Scarman did not state whether such a direction actually was appropriate in the case before him. His judgment serves to dilute the meaning Lord Bridge intended to convey in that a jury, directed in accordance with Lord Scarman's dicta, may infer intention from foresight of high probability whereas Lord Bridge would only permit such an inference where the consequence was foreseen as a moral certainty. On a Scarman direction, different juries may arrive at different verdicts depending on whether they feel the accused's conduct should be condemned as murder. But if foresight of a high probability is not intention, how can a jury infer intention from such foresight unless their decision is effectively a policy one, namely, that they feel that this accused, in these circumstances, deserves to be convicted of murder. Foresight that a consequence is certain to ensue is the other side of the coin of intention, but foresight of probability is a different entity entirely, namely recklessness.

The conflict between *Moloney* and *Hancock and Shankland* led the Court of Appeal to seek to restore some order to the confusion in *Nedrick* [1986] 1 WLR 1025. In that case, the appellant had a grudge against a woman. With the intention of frightening her, he poured paraffin through her letter box and on to the front door of her house and ignited it. A child died in the ensuing fire. The appellant was convicted of murder following a direction to the jury which equated foresight with intention. The Court of Appeal quashed the conviction, substituting a conviction of manslaughter. Lord Lane CJ stated two questions which might be helpful to a jury when determining whether the accused had the necessary intent (at p. 1028). (1) How probable was the consequence which resulted from the defendant's voluntary act? (2) Did he foresee that consequence?

Lord Lane CJ went on to explain that if the accused did not appreciate that death or serious harm was likely to result from his act, he did not intend to bring it about. If he did appreciate the risk but thought that it was only slight, then a jury might easily conclude that he did not intend to bring about the result. Lord Lane CJ continued (at p. 1028):

> On the other hand, if the jury are satisfied that at the material time the defendant recognised that death or serious harm would be virtually certain (barring some unforeseen intervention) to result from his voluntary act, then that is a fact from which they may find it easy to infer that he intended to kill or do serious bodily harm, even though he may not have had any desire to achieve that result. . . . Where a man realises that it is for all practical purposes inevitable that his actions will result in death or serious harm, the inference may be irresistible that he intended that result, however little he may have desired or wished it to happen. The decision is one for the jury to be reached upon a consideration of all the evidence.

Lord Lane CJ appeared to endorse the view that it is only in cases where a consequence is foreseen as virtually certain that intention may be inferred. He expressly stated that on a murder charge if a simple direction would not suffice, the jury should be directed that they are not entitled to infer intention unless satisfied that death or serious bodily harm was virtually certain to result from D's acts and D foresaw this. Lord Lane CJ remained somewhat ambivalent about foresight of degrees of probability in between slight risk and virtual certainty in other offences requiring proof of intention. Lord Lane CJ also caused further confusion, however, in attempting to reconcile Lord Bridge's dicta with those of Lord Scarman when he spoke in terms of the probability of a consequence ensuing from the accused's act.

In the subsequent Court of Appeal pronouncement in *Walker and Hayles* (1990) 90 Cr App R 226, a case involving attempted murder, the court expressed the view that the phrase 'very high degree of probability' meant the same as 'virtual certainty' and a direction using the former phrase could not be faulted. This is a strange assertion as 'certain' conveys a different notion than the word 'probable'. If a consequence is certain it is, to use Lord Lane CJ's words, 'for all practical purposes inevitable' whereas a consequence which is 'very highly probable' is one which has a high likelihood of occurring but it could not be said to be inevitable; it implies a risk, albeit of high degree. It is clear also from his subsequent extra-judicial explanation of his judgment in *Nedrick* that Lord Lane CJ would not equate 'virtual certainty' with the phrase 'very highly probable'. In the debate on the *Report of the Select Committee of the House of Lords on Murder and Life Imprisonment* (H.L. Paper 78-I, 1989), Lord Lane CJ stated that the judgment in *Nedrick* was not as clear as it might have been as he felt bound by the decisions of the House of Lords. Accordingly he had phrased matters in terms of 'inferring' intention when what he had really sought to state was that intention should be defined in the terms used by the Law Commission in the Draft Criminal Code, that is, 'a person acts "intentionally" with respect to . . . a result when he acts in order to bring it about or being aware that it will occur in the ordinary course of events'.

Lord Lane CJ's extra-judicial pronouncement appears to be an acceptance that intention covers situations of the type described in examples (i), (ii) and (iii) above, without the need for confusing references to the drawing of inferences. If only he had stated this in *Nedrick* everything would have been much clearer. Until such a statement is made judicially, courts will be left with the dicta in *Nedrick*, and it is to be hoped that the further gloss added to these by *Walker and Hayles* will be buried.

3.2.4 Basic, specific and ulterior intent

While there may be uncertainty regarding the meaning of the word 'intention' this is compounded by the fact that judges have created further confusion by use of the word 'intent' in differing contexts. When reading judgments the terms 'basic intent', 'specific intent' and 'ulterior intent' will be encountered. It is important that the meaning of these terms is understood.

The term 'basic intent' is used to describe offences for which the mental element required is intention, knowledge or recklessness. The phrase 'basic *mens rea*' would probably be more accurate as one of the ideas which the term seeks to convey is that the offence may be committed recklessly, in that there is no requirement that intention be proved.

The phrase 'basic intent' should be contrasted with both the phrases 'specific intent' and 'ulterior intent'. In *DPP v Morgan* [1976] AC 182, Lord Simon said that crimes of basic intent meant 'those crimes whose definition expresses (or, more often implies) a *mens rea* which does not go beyond the *actus reus*'. Lord Simon was here drawing a distinction between crimes of 'basic intent' and crimes of 'ulterior intent'. A crime of 'ulterior intent' is one where the definition of the *mens rea* requires proof of an intention to bring about a consequence beyond the actual *actus reus* of the offence. This is best explained by examples. Burglary may be committed where a person enters a building as a trespasser with the intention of stealing, causing grievous bodily harm, raping a woman therein or causing criminal damage. The *actus reus* is complete as soon as D enters the building as a trespasser, he need not go on to commit one of these further offences. The *mens rea* required is, firstly, that D knows he is a trespasser or is reckless as to this fact and, secondly, that he intends to commit one of the four further offences. This latter element of the *mens rea* is the 'ulterior intent' as it is a requirement beyond the *actus reus* which is satisfied by proof that D has entered as a trespasser. Other offences of 'ulterior intent' are, for example, wounding with intent to cause grievous bodily harm, wounding with intent to resist or prevent the lawful apprehension of any person and assault with intent to rob.

The term 'specific intent' encompasses both crimes of 'ulterior intent' and other offences in respect of which D may plead that he lacked *mens rea* due to his intoxication at the time he committed the *actus reus*. If an offence is one of 'basic intent' D may not plead intoxication. Offences of 'basic intent' may be committed recklessly whereas offences which the courts have classified as ones of 'specific intent' are either offences of 'ulterior intent' or offences for which proof of intention alone is required in respect of at least one aspect of the *actus reus*, for example, murder.

3.3 KNOWLEDGE

Where an act, omission, state of affairs or event is unlawful where certain circumstances exist, and the offence is one requiring *mens rea*, knowledge of those circumstances on the part of the accused will establish *mens rea*. Many statutory offences impose this *mens rea* requirement by using the word 'knowingly'. But, even where this word is not used, the courts have shown a willingness to imply it into statutory offences (see *Sweet* v *Parsley* [1970] AC 132). In *Roper* v *Taylor's Central Garages* [1951] 2 TLR 284, Devlin J stated that 'knowingly' only says expressly what is normally implied. Of course, the use of the word expressly in a statutory provision avoids all doubt.

In *Roper* Devlin J stated that there were three degrees of knowledge. The first is 'actual knowledge', where the accused knows for a fact that the relevant circumstance exists. Actual knowledge is the equivalent of intention in that if the accused acts knowing the circumstance to exist he may be said to have acted intentionally in respect of it.

The second is 'wilful blindness' which is equivalent to subjective recklessness (discussed 3.4.2.1 *post*). Where knowledge is required a court may be satisfied that wilful blindness suffices (see *Westminster City Council* v *Croyalgrange Ltd* [1986] 2 All ER 353). In this case the defendant company was convicted of knowingly permitting the use of premises as a sex establishment without a licence. Lord Bridge stated (at p. 359):

it is always open to the tribunal of fact, when knowledge on the part of a defendant is required to be proved, to base a finding of knowledge on evidence that the defendant had deliberately shut his eyes to the obvious or refrained from inquiry because he suspected the truth but did not want to have his suspicion confirmed.

In cases of handling stolen goods where the *mens rea* requirement is that the accused did so knowing or believing the goods to be stolen, the courts have held that wilful blindness is not sufficient (see 13.5.2.1 *post*).

The third degree of knowledge is 'constructive knowledge' which is really a species of negligence and rarely suffices to establish criminal liability. Phrases such as 'reasonable cause to believe', 'reason to believe' or 'reason to suspect' in the definitions of offences import this degree of knowledge. Liability is, in effect, incurred where the accused had the means of knowledge had he made the enquiries which a reasonable and prudent person would make.

The amount of knowledge required to establish guilt need extend no further than the circumstance which the definition of the offence prescribes. For example, it is sufficient for a conviction of handling stolen goods that the accused knew the goods to be stolen although he was ignorant or mistaken as to the nature of the goods (*McCullum* (1973) 57 Cr App R 645). Where the offence involved is being knowingly concerned in the fraudulent evasion of a prohibition on the importation of various types of goods contrary to s. 170(2) of the Customs and Excise (Management) Act 1979, different penalties apply depending on the nature of the goods. However, a mistake as to the nature of the goods will not prevent the accused being convicted of a more serious offence than that which he believed he was committing. In *Ellis, Street and Smith* (1986) 84 Cr App R 235, the accused knew they were importing prohibited goods concealed in secret compartments in cars. They believed the goods were pornographic materials when they were, in fact, cannabis, a Class B controlled drug. The maximum penalty for importing Class B controlled drugs is fourteen years imprisonment whereas the maximum for importing pornographic goods is two years. The Court of Appeal held, however, that knowledge that the goods being imported were prohibited was all that was required. This contravenes the principle in *Courtie* [1984] AC 463 that the imposition of separate penalties in a statutory provision creates separate offences. Under the *Courtie* principle, importing pornographic goods is a separate offence to importing controlled drugs. The courts, however, are prepared to accept the *mens rea* of a lesser offence to establish guilt of a greater offence even though the greater offence may have been one which the accused would never have contemplated committing. The potential for injustice is considerable when it is realised that the maximum penalty for importing Class A controlled drugs, such as heroin or cocaine, is life imprisonment.

Where the *mens rea* requirement is knowledge, it must be proved that the accused had the requisite knowledge at the time of committing the offence. If the accused previously knew the prescribed fact but has forgotten it at the time he acted, this will not suffice (see *Russell* (1984) 81 Cr App R 315).

3.4 RECKLESSNESS

3.4.1 What might recklessness mean?

For some offences, such as murder or an attempt, only intention suffices to establish criminal liability. But for most crimes the *mens rea* required is intention or recklessness. Recklessness provides the baseline for liability in most offences and thus it is important to clearly define the parameters of this concept so that it is distinguishable from negligence which generally (subject to a few statutory exceptions and 'gross negligence manslaughter') does not suffice for criminal liability. A person may be reckless as to a consequence or as to a circumstance. The notion that recklessness conveys is that of taking an unjustifiable risk. This is reflected in the Draft Criminal Code where the Law Commission defines the term in Clause 18 as follows:

a person acts – . . .
   (c) 'recklessly' with respect to –
      (i)   a circumstance when he is aware of a risk that it exists or will exist;
     (ii) a result when he is aware of a risk that it will occur;

and it is, in the circumstances known to him, unreasonable to take the risk.

Not all risk-taking is unreasonable; circumstances may exist which justify taking a risk. Whether taking a risk is justifiable depends on a balancing of the social utility or value of the activity involved against the probability and gravity of harm which might be caused. The Law Commission stated in their *Working Paper on the Mental Element in Crime*, Law Com No. 31 (at p. 53):

The operation of public transport, for example, is inevitably accompanied by risks of accident beyond the control of the operator, yet it is socially necessary that these risks be taken. Dangerous surgical operations must be carried out in the interests of the life and health of the patient, yet the taking of these risks is socially justifiable.

The tribunal of fact performs this balancing task using the objective test of whether a reasonable and prudent man would have taken the risk in the circumstances. Thus, if an act has no social utility but involves a slight possiblity of the risk of harm, this would suffice to render the taking of that risk a reckless act.

If the tribunal of fact concludes that the accused has taken an unreasonable risk, is this sufficient to establish criminal liability? Or is awareness of the risk on the part of the accused necessary before criminal liability may be imposed? To put this another way, is it necessary for the accused to have foreseen the risk at the time he acted or is it sufficient that a reasonably prudent person would have foreseen the risk? In most cases the accused is a reasonable person and will have foreseen what other reasonable persons would have foreseen. In some cases, however, the accused, because of mental deficiency, may be incapable of foreseeing what reasonable persons would have foreseen. In such a case is the accused to be found criminally liable for this failure or should criminal liability be limited to those who are, in some way, culpable because they are responsible actors? The views of the courts on this matter have changed over the years. The change was prophesied by Glanville Williams in *Criminal Law: The General Part*, para. 24, who identified the potential for the concept of recklessness to merge with that of carelessness due to three factors: firstly, 'the etymology of the word'; secondly, 'the constant pressure to extend the reach of the criminal law on account of the supposed policy of the individual case'; and thirdly, the need for a formula to be used to instruct juries because of the difficulty of proving recklessness. This third factor can cause a shift of emphasis from asking the jury 'to consider whether the defendant *must* have foreseen the consequence' to asking them 'whether the defendant *ought* as a reasonable man to have foreseen it'.

3.4.2   How have the courts defined recklessness?

3.4.2.1   Subjective recklessness   The courts originally gave recklessness a *subjective* meaning. Thus an accused would be found to be reckless only where he had recognised the possibility of the prohibited consequence occurring (or the particular circumstance existing) and he had carried on regardless. The leading authority on subjective recklessness is *Cunningham* [1957] 2 QB 396; as a result, this concept of recklessness is often referred to as '*Cunningham* recklessness'. In *Cunningham*, D removed a gas meter from an unoccupied house so that he could steal the money it contained. He left behind the fractured pipe from which gas was escaping. The gas seeped into the neighbouring house and P inhaled it. D was convicted of maliciously administering a noxious thing so as to endanger life contrary to s. 23 of the Offences Against the Person Act 1861. D's conviction was quashed as the judge had instructed the jury that 'maliciously' meant 'wickedly'. The Court of Criminal Appeal approved of the definition propounded by Kenny in *Outlines of Criminal Law* (1902) which stated:

> In any statutory definition of a crime, 'malice' must be taken not in the old vague sense of wickedness in general but as requiring either (i) an actual intention to do the particular *kind* of harm that in fact was done or (ii) recklessness as to whether such harm should occur or not (i.e. the accused has foreseen that the particular kind of harm might be done, and yet has gone on to take the risk of it). It is neither limited to, nor does it indeed require, any ill-will towards the person injured.

The issue which had not been clearly left to the jury was whether D had actually foreseen that removal of the gas meter might cause injury to someone but nevertheless had gone on to remove it.

In more recent statutory provisions the word 'maliciously' is not used; Parliament uses the words 'intention' or 'recklessly' expressly. In its Report, *The Mental Element in Crime* (Law Com No. 89), the Law Commission attributed this subjective meaning to recklessness. The Criminal Damage Act 1971 resulted from the work of the Law Commission who in their Report, *Offences of Damage to Property* (Law Com No. 29), approved the Cunningham definition of recklessness. Section 1 of the Act makes it an offence for a person to destroy or damage property belonging to another intentionally or recklessly. Several cases arose in the 1970's concerning the meaning of the word 'reckless' in this section (see *Briggs* [1977] 1 WLR 605; *Parker* [1977] 1 WLR 600; *Stephenson* [1979] 1 QB 695). In all of these cases the Court of Appeal confirmed that the test was subjective – it had to be proved that the accused recognised the risk even though, perhaps because of bad temper, he had suppressed it or driven it out.

In *Stephenson* the accused suffered from schizophrenia. He had crept into a hollow in a large straw stack and lit a fire to keep warm. The stack caught fire. The trial judge directed the jury that they could find the accused guilty if satisfied he had closed his mind to the obvious fact of risk from his act and that schizophrenia might be a reason which made a person close his mind to the obvious fact of risk. In effect he was directing the jury that if a reasonable prudent person would have recognised the risk as obvious they should convict the accused. The Court of Appeal quashed the conviction, Geoffrey Lane LJ stating (at p. 703):

A man is reckless when he carries out the deliberate act appreciating that there is a risk that damage to property may result from his act. It is however not the taking of every risk which could properly be classed as reckless. The risk must be one which it is in all the circumstances unreasonable for him to take. . . . We wish to make it clear that the test remains subjective, that the knowledge or appreciation of risk of some damage must have entered the defendant's mind even though he may have suppressed it or driven it out. . . . The schizophrenia was on the evidence something which might have prevented the idea of danger entering the appellant's mind at all. If that was the truth of the matter, then the appellant was entitled to be acquitted. That was something which was never left clearly to the jury to decide.

3.4.2.2 Caldwell recklessness Unfortunately what seemed clear to the Court of Appeal was far from clear to the House of Lords. Recklessness received radical redefinition in the 1980s in *Caldwell* [1982] AC 341.

3.4.2.2.1 The test of recklessness In *Caldwell* D got drunk and set fire to a hotel in pursuit of a grievance he had against the owner. There were guests in the hotel at the time but the fire was discovered and extinguished before any serious damage was done. D was indicted on two counts of arson. He pleaded guilty to the first count of intentionally or recklessly damaging property belonging to another contrary to s. 1(1) of the Criminal Damage Act 1971 but pleaded not guilty to the second count of damaging property with intent to endanger life or being reckless whether life would be endangered contrary to s. 1(2) of the 1971 Act. He claimed that he was so drunk at the time that the thought that he might be endangering life had never crossed his mind. The trial judge directed the jury that drunkenness was not a defence to this charge and he was convicted. The House of Lords affirmed that where the prosecution indict the accused on the basis that he was reckless whether life was endangered, drunkenness is not a defence as this is an offence of 'basic intent' (see below for a discussion of intoxication, 5.6, *post*). This should have been enough to dispose of the case. Their Lordships, however, took the opportunity to redefine recklessness. Lord Diplock, with whom Lords Keith of Kinkell and Roskill agreed, delivered the judgment of the majority. He stated his test of recklessness as follows (at p. 354):

> In my opinion, a person charged with an offence under s. 1(1) of the 1971 Act is 'reckless as to whether or not property would be destroyed or damaged' if (1) he does an act which in fact creates an obvious risk that property will be destroyed or damaged and (2) when he does the act he either has not given any thought to the possibility of there being any such risk or has recognised that there was some risk involved and has none the less gone on to do it.

The test of recklessness, as framed by Lord Diplock, appears to require that the risk of damage should be obvious before the accused may be found to have been reckless under either limb. This conflicts with Lord Diplock's analysis of recklessness earlier in his judgment where he stated (at pp. 353–354):

[recklessness] includes not only deciding to ignore a risk of harmful consequences resulting from one's acts that one has recognised as existing, but also failing to give any thought to whether or not there is any such risk in circumstances where, if any thought were given to the matter, it would be obvious that there was.

In *Reid* [1992] 3 All ER 673, a case involving causing death by reckless driving, Lord Goff expressed the view that 'the requirement that the risk be obvious . . . cannot be relevant where the defendant is in fact aware that there is some risk of the relevant kind' (at p. 691). It is submitted that this is the correct view and that it should apply generally to all offences where the *Caldwell* recklessness test is used. Thus, if the accused recognises some risk of the harm which ensues occurring but he nevertheless runs that risk, he is reckless in the subjective sense. Alternatively, if the accused fails to give thought to whether the harm which ensues might occur and the risk of such harm would have been obvious to the ordinary prudent person, he is *Caldwell* reckless. The second test of recklessness is an objective one as liability ensues not as a result of what the accused foresaw, but rather on the basis of what he ought to have foreseen.

3.4.2.2.2 Reasons for the redefinition of recklessness Lord Diplock gave several reasons for this extension of the meaning of recklessness. Firstly, he considered that the word 'reckless' in a statute was not a term of art and thus should be given its dictionary meaning of 'careless, regardless, or heedless of the possible harmful consequences of one's acts.' This would seem to merge recklessness with negligence. Secondly, Lord Diplock considered that the two states of mind in his test, of foresight of risk and failure to give thought to the possiblity of there being any such risk, were equally blameworthy. This, to say the least, is highly questionable as the former requires advertence to the risk whereas the latter involves inadvertence. The person who deliberately takes a risk would appear to be much more culpable than the one who does not recognise the risk. It may be that Lord Diplock was concerned to prevent people relying on their own drunkenness as a reason for their failure to recognise a risk. However, such people would not escape liability as the House ruled they could not plead intoxication in respect of an offence for which 'recklessness is enough to constitute the necessary *mens rea*'; there was no need to extend the definition of recklessness to catch what had already been caught by the law relating to self-induced intoxication.

That the inadvertent accused who fails to give thought to an obvious risk is to be regarded as reckless, however, is confirmed by the House of Lords' decision in *Reid (ante)*. Lord Keith of Kinkel and Lord Browne-Wilkinson expressed the view that inadvertence to a risk was as much a subjective state of mind as advertence to a risk as the state of the accused's mind is being examined rather than that of the paradigmatic reasonable person. It is submitted that this misses the point; a person who has failed to give thought to an obvious risk has not subjectively recognised the risk. Whether such a person should be convicted of a criminal offence because he ought to have recognised the risk is a policy question which cannot be answered by an etymological analysis of the word 'reckless'. ✗

The third reason was that the *Cunningham* test of recklessness called for a 'meticulous analysis by the jury of the thoughts that passed through the mind of the accused at or before the time he did the act that caused the damage'. He considered that the distinction between the advertent state of mind and the inadvertent state, for the purposes of a statutory offence of damage to property, 'would not be a practicable distinction for use in a trial by jury' and he could see no reason why Parliament, when it revised the law on offences of damage to property, 'should go out of its way to perpetuate fine and impracticable distinctions'. The whole history of the Criminal Damage Act 1971, from its genesis as a Draft Bill appended to the Law Commission's Report through its debate in Parliament to its enactment, reveals clear acceptance of the subjective meaning of recklessness. It is highly questionable whether the distinction between advertent risk-taking and inadvertent risk-taking is quite as fine as Lord Diplock suggests; it would seem to be fundamental to the distinction between the criminally culpable actor and the negligent actor. As this distinction is fundamental to criminal liability, it is extremely doubtful that Parliament should consider it so fine that it should not be perpetuated. It is also highly questionable whether the distinction is impracticable. Juries are constantly faced with the task of deciding between two versions of events put forward by the prosecution and the defence. If the *mens rea* required for an offence is subjective recklessness, the jury will apply their common sense to this matter. If they would have foreseen the risk of damage or harm in the circumstances in which the accused acted, they may be satisfied that the accused must have foreseen the risk in the absence of some explanation or other evidence raising a reasonable doubt as to whether he foresaw that risk. If the accused is a person of normal intelligence, the inference that he foresaw what other people would have foreseen will, in most cases, be a proper one to draw and does not appear to require the meticulous analysis Lord Diplock envisaged. If for some reason the accused did not foresee the risk, he can always testify to this and seek to raise the doubt in the jury's mind by other evidence or cross-examination of prosecution witnesses. The task appears no more difficult than deciding whether the accused intended a result; in all cases where the accused does not admit to having the prescribed *mens rea* for an offence, the jury's task is one of drawing inferences from all the evidence in light of their own experience. Lord Diplock's approach in this case has a definite flavour of extending 'the reach of the criminal law on account of the supposed policy of the individual case'.

In *Reid* Lord Keith of Kinkel went even further than Lord Diplock in arguing that the subjective test of recklessness is difficult for juries to apply. Lord Keith reasoned that if the alternative test of failure to give thought to an obvious risk did not exist, it would be quite impossible for any juror to be satisfied beyond reasonable doubt that the accused was subjectively reckless and it would be impossible ever to get a conviction. This problem does not appear to have prevented juries convicting defendants on countless occasions of offences requiring subjective recklessness to be proved. Is Lord Keith suggesting that all these convictions are suspect?

3.4.2.2.3 To whom must the risk be obvious? If an accused may be convicted

for failing to give thought to an obvious risk, an important issue to be decided is to whom must the risk be obvious; is it the reasonably prudent person or the accused himself had he bothered to consider the matter? Lord Diplock's views on this matter are contradictory. In *Caldwell* he stated that recklessness 'presupposes that, if thought were given to the matter by the doer of the act before the act was done, it would have been apparent to him that there was a real risk of its having harmful consequences'. This dictum suggests that an accused should only be found reckless if the risk would have been obvious to him had he thought about it. Lord Diplock went on to state that 'the fact that the respondent was unaware of the risk of endangering the lives of residents in the hotel owing to his self-induced intoxication, would be no defence if that risk would have been obvious to him had he been sober'. It appears from this that Caldwell's own responsibility for his state of unawareness is what Lord Diplock considered crucial in dictating that he should not escape criminal liability. Thus, if the schizophrenic *Stephenson* was tried again he should still be acquitted as he was not capable of recognising the risk to which his conduct gave rise. However, Lord Diplock overruled *Stephenson*; this would only be appropriate if Lord Diplock believed that it was sufficient that the reasonably prudent person would recognise the risk as obvious. Dicta in *Lawrence* [1982] AC 510 suggest that this was Lord Diplock's view as he stated (at p. 526):

> Recklessness on the part of the doer of an act does presuppose that there is something in the circumstances that would have drawn the attention of an ordinary prudent individual to the possibility that his act was capable of causing the kind of serious harmful consequences that the section which creates the offence was intended to prevent. . . .

This view was reluctantly accepted by the Divisional Court as the correct one in *Elliott* v *C* [1983] 1 WLR 939. D, who had been out all night without sleep, entered a garden shed where she found white spirit which she poured on to an old carpet and lit to keep warm. The fire spread to the shed which was destroyed. D was fourteen years old and of limited intelligence being in a remedial class at school. The magistrates acquitted her finding that she had given no thought to the risk of the shed being destroyed, but that even if she had given thought to the matter the risk would not have been obvious to her. The Divisional Court directed the magistrates to convict as it was only necessary for the risk to have been obvious to the reasonably prudent man. The Court was not concerned with the reason for the accused's failure to give thought to an obvious risk. The Court felt bound to decide the case in this way because of Lord Diplock's statements in *Lawrence* and *Miller* [1983] AC 161. The case is very disturbing as the doctrine of *mens rea* derives from the idea of responsibility. A person is a responsible actor where he has the capacity to make conscious choices. If a person is incapable of foreseeing the consequences of his actions because of mental deficiency he cannot be considered blameworthy; unless, that is, he is to be blamed for being mentally deficient. It is hardly conceivable that people with inadequacies for which they bear no

R.T.C. LIBRARY, LETTERKENNY

responsibility and over which they have no control, merit the censure of the criminal law. The Divisional Court should have decided the case on its merits without hiding behind a distorted view of the doctrine of precedent; none of the decisions of the House of Lords inevitably led to the conclusion in *Elliott* v *C*, as problems, such as the one contained in this case, were never mooted before their Lordships.

There is a suggestion in the speech by Lord Keith of Kinkel in *Reid* that (at least in respect of reckless driving) an accused should not be regarded as reckless 'where his capacity to appreciate risks was adversely affected by some condition not involving fault on his own part' (at p. 675). It is submitted that this should apply to all offences where *Caldwell* recklessness applies.

In *Stephen (Malcolm R)* (1984) 79 Cr App R 334, it was argued that the reasonably prudent person should at least be of the same age and sex as the accused and bear such of his characteristics as would affect his ability to appreciate the risk involved in his conduct. When the defence of provocation is raised the accused is compared against such a version of the reasonable man (see *9.3.2.2.3 post*). The Court of Appeal rejected this argument and confirmed that the risk need only have been obvious to the reasonably prudent man who is a person of mature years and understanding. Thus the individual is to be judged against a standard which he may be constitutionally incapable of attaining. Once again, when it came to making a choice between doing justice or adhering to precedent, the Court of Appeal preferred to blindly follow the sacred cow of precedent regardless of where that might lead or the gross injustices which might result.

If the reasonable prudent person is not invested with any of the accused's characteristics, might he nevertheless have the benefit of hindsight or expert knowledge? This question arose before the Court of Appeal in *Sangha* [1988] 2 All ER 385. D set fire to furniture in a flat. There was no risk of the lives of any occupants being endangered as they were not present. There was also no danger to occupants of adjacent flats because of the special construction of the building. D was charged with the offence of damaging property being reckless whether the life of another would be thereby endangered, contrary to s. 1(2)(b) of the Criminal Damage Act 1971. It was argued that D could not have been reckless whether life was endangered if there was, in fact, no risk to life. The Court of Appeal held that in deciding whether D had created an obvious risk that the life of another be endangered, the question was whether an ordinary prudent bystander would, at the time when the fire was started, have perceived an obvious risk of damage to property and danger to life. The fact that there may have been special features which prevented the risk from materialising is irrelevant as the ordinary prudent bystander is not to be invested with expert knowledge as to the construction of the property, nor does he have the benefit of hindsight.

There is one situation where the reason for the accused's incapacity to appreciate risks will avail him. If his failure to appreciate an obvious risk was due to intoxication caused by the ingestion of a non-dangerous drug, such as valium, and he was not aware of the drug's intoxicating potential, he will not be criminally liable (see *Hardie* [1985] 1 WLR 64, discussed at *5.6.7 post*). Why a person who is responsible for his incapacity to recognise an obvious risk (Hardie chose to take valium) should receive more favourable treatment than one who is not responsible (such as a schizophrenic, a young person or a mentally retarded person) is far from clear. The decision in *Hardie* makes the decisions in *Elliott* v *C* and *Stephen (Malcolm R)* appear even more incongruous.

3.4.2.2.4 *Thinking about a risk and discounting it* In the previous section we saw how a person who fails to give thought to an obvious risk will be found to be reckless even though he was incapable of recognising the risk. If a person gives thought to the possibility of his conduct involving the risk of damage but wrongly concludes that there is no risk, or that it is negligible in that it is one which a reasonable and prudent person might take in the circumstances, he would not appear to be reckless as he has not failed to give thought to the possibility of risk nor has he recognised a risk and gone on to take it. In *Lawrence* [1982] AC 341, a case involving reckless driving, Lord Diplock stated (at p. 527):

> If satisfied that an obvious and serious risk was created by the manner of the defendant's driving, the jury are entitled to infer that he was in one or other of the states of mind required to constitute the offence and will probably do so; but regard must be had to any explanation he gives as to his state of mind which may displace the inference.

This is the one situation where *Caldwell* recklessness and negligence do not overlap. The concept of negligence includes the person who has given thought to the possibility of the risk existing and unreasonably concluded that it does not exist. This explains the possible continued existence of gross negligence as a basis for manslaughter (see *9.3.3.3.2 post*). If the accused has thought about a risk and concluded that there is no risk and death results, he would not be liable for reckless manslaughter. But if he was grossly negligent in arriving at that conclusion, in that the risk was a grave one which would have been obvious to the reasonable and prudent person, he will be liable.

Another situation which may arise is that of the accused who recognises the risk to which his conduct will give rise and takes precautions to eliminate or minimise the risk but these prove to be inadequate. In *Chief Constable of Avon and Somerset Constabulary* v *Shimmen* (1986) 84 Cr App R 7, D broke a shop window when demonstrating a karate kick to friends. He admitted recognising the risk of breaking the window but said: 'I weighed up the odds and thought I had eliminated as much risk as possible by missing by two inches instead of two millimetres'. His claim, therefore, was that he had minimised the risk. The Divisional Court concluded that he was reckless as he had recognised the risk and had not taken adequate precautions to eliminate it; thus he was a person who had foreseen a risk and gone on to take it. If a person believes he has minimised a risk and there is no social utility in the act to be performed, then there would appear to be no justification for running such a risk. The Divisional Court also suggested that a person would be liable if he believed he had eliminated the risk by his precautions. It is arguable that such a person should not be guilty as he has given thought to the risk and in light of the circumstances (including his proposed precautions) has concluded there is no risk. It is difficult to distinguish such a case from the person who thought about it and concluded there simply was no risk.

3.4.2.2.5   To which crimes does the Caldwell test apply?   This is a crucially important question as it appears that the test of recklessness can vary depending on the offence with which the accused is charged. In this area, as with many others relating to *mens rea*, confusion reigns. In *Seymour*[1983] 2 AC 493, a case of 'motor manslaughter', Lord Roskill, with whose speech the remainder of their Lordships agreed, stated (at p. 506):

> it would be quite wrong to give the adjective 'reckless' or the adverb 'recklessly' a different meaning according to whether the statutory or the common law offence is charged. 'Reckless' should today be given the same meaning in relation to all offences which involve 'recklessness' as one of the elements unless Parliament has otherwise ordained.

After the decision in *Caldwell*, it was believed that the objective test would be applicable wherever the word 'reckless' or its derivatives was used in a statute. The Court of Appeal adopted this approach in *Pigg* [1982] 1 WLR 762 in relation to rape where recklessness as to the consent of the victim is in issue. In *Satnam and Kewal* (1984) 78 Cr App R 149, the Court of Appeal changed its stance and held that the objective test of recklessness did not apply to a charge of rape under s. 1(1) of the Sexual Offences (Amendment) Act 1976. Bristow J explained this decision on the basis that in rape recklessness related to a circumstance, namely the state of mind of the victim, rather than to a consequence. Under the Theft Acts 1968 and 1978, offences of obtaining by deception may be committed by reckless deceptions. In these cases the test is also subjective as the offences require dishonesty to be proved; a person cannot be considered dishonest if he has not recognised the risk that the representation he is making may involve a deception. In *Large v Mainprize* [1989] Crim LR 213, the Divisional Court, on an appeal by the prosecution on a case stated by the justices, applied the subjective test of recklessness to the offence of recklessly furnishing false information as to a fishing catch, contrary to reg. 3(2) of the Sea Fishing (Enforcement of Community Control Measures) Regulations 1985. In dismissing the appeal May LJ blithely stated that he 'was quite certain that [the justices] would have been aware of what "reckless" meant in the circumstances of the instant case.' Ian Kennedy J was so convinced that the meaning of this ordinary word was so self-evident that he doubted whether it 'admits a construction at all.' When it came to expounding its meaning, however, the court did not resort to the numerous criminal cases which have given rise to appellate decisions, nor to the plethora of academic writings thereon, but to two brief statements in two books on the law of tort. *Res ipsa loquitur!* This decision may be a persuasive authority for the many other statutory offences which may be committed by recklessly making false statements. It would appear, therefore, that where the word 'reckless' or its derivatives is used in an offence created by statute, it is impossible to state with certainty whether it is used in its *Caldwell* or *Cunningham* sense in the absence of an appellate decision thereon. In *Reid* Lords Ackner, Goff and Browne-Wilkinson all recognised that the meaning of 'reckless' or 'recklessly' may vary depending on the statutory context in which the word appears.

The offences of common assault, assault occasioning actual bodily harm and indecent assault are statutory offences (see Criminal Justice Act 1988, s. 39 and *DPP* v *Little* [1992] 1 All ER 299, the Offences Against the Person Act 1861, s. 47, and the Sexual Offences Act 1956, ss. 14 and 15, respectively) but assault is defined at common law. Assault may be committed recklessly (see *Venna* [1976] QB 421). In *Kimber* [1983] 1 WLR 1118, a case involving indecent assault, the Court of Appeal adopted the subjective test of recklessness following *Venna*, without referring to *Caldwell*. In *DPP* v *K (a Minor)* [1990] 1 WLR 1067, the Divisional Court held that the *Caldwell* test applied on a charge of assault occasioning actual bodily harm contrary to s. 47 of the Offences Against the Person Act 1861. In *Spratt* [1990] 1 WLR 1073, the Court of Appeal put the issue beyond doubt declaring that *DPP* v *K* was wrongly decided. The Court was of opinion that Lord Roskill's dictum was *obiter* and could not have been intended to cast any doubt on *Cunningham* or *Venna* which had been approved by the House of Lords in both *Majewski* [1977] AC 443 and *Caldwell*. The Court of Appeal stated (at p. 1082):

the history of the interpretation of the Act of 1861 shows that, whether or not the word 'maliciously' appears in the section in question, the courts have consistently held that the *mens rea* of every type of offence against the person covers both intent and recklessness, in the sense of taking the risk of harm ensuing with foresight that it might happen.

Earlier cases such as *W (a Minor)* v *Dolbey* [1983] Crim LR 681, and *Grimshaw* [1984] Crim LR 109, had confirmed that the *Cunningham* test of recklessness applied to all offences under the 1861 Act where the *mens rea* was defined by the term 'maliciously'. In *Savage* and *Parmenter* both reported at [1991] 4 All ER 698, the House of Lords confirmed this, subject to the gloss given to the definition by the Court of Appeal in *Mowatt* [1968] 1 QB 421 (by none other than Diplock LJ) to the effect that in an offence against the person the accused need not foresee the particular harm which occurs but will be held reckless if he foresees that his unlawful act may cause some physical harm to the victim, albeit of a minor character. ✗

3.5 WILFULNESS

The term 'wilfully' is often used in statutes. The cases are inconsistent regarding the question whether or not this imports a requirement of *mens rea*. In *Arrowsmith* v *Jenkins* [1963] 2 QB 561, on a charge of wilful obstruction of the highway contrary to s. 121(1) of the Highways Act 1959, the Divisional Court held that it was sufficient that the accused by an exercise of free will did an act which caused an obstruction. This seemed to import nothing more than a requirement of voluntariness. As such the word 'wilfully' is effectively otiose as the requirement of voluntariness is implied by the general principles of the criminal law. There are, however, a notable number of similar decisions relating to other statutory offences (see e.g. *Maidstone Borough Council* v *Mortimer* [1980] 3 All ER 552; *Hudson* v *MacRae* (1863) 4 B & S 585; *Cotterill* v *Penn* [1936] 1 KB 53).

By contrast, in the earlier case of *Eaton* v *Cobb* [1950] 1 All ER 1016, the Divisional Court held that the word 'wilfully' imported a requirement of *mens rea*. Humphreys J stated (at p. 1017):

> In my view 'wilfully obstruct' in a statute which makes such obstruction a criminal offence means wilfully to obstruct. . . . the test . . . is whether or not the obstruction was intentional.

In this case D had opened his car door in the path of a cyclist after having checked his mirror and seeing the road apparently clear. The Divisional Court took the view that while he wilfully opened the door he did not 'wilfully obstruct' the highway as there was no intention so to do. This decision is similar to those on the offence of wilfully obstructing a police constable in the execution of his duty contrary to s. 51(3) of the Police Act 1964. In *Lewis* v *Cox* [1985] QB 509, Webster J stated (at p. 516):

> the simple facts which the court has to find are whether the defendant's conduct in fact prevented the police from carrying out their duty, or made it more difficult for them to do so, and whether the defendant intended that conduct to prevent the police from carrying out their duty or to make it more difficult to do so.

In this case D had twice opened the rear door of a police van with the object of discovering from his friend who had been arrested where he was being taken. While D's ultimate aim may not have been obstruction, this was, in fact, a necessary pre-condition to the achievement of his ultimate aim. As he knew the van would be prevented from driving away by his opening of the door, he therefore intended the obstruction.

In *Sheppard* [1981] AC 394, the House of Lords imported a *mens rea* requirement into the offence of wilful neglect of a child contrary to s. 1 of the Children and Young Persons Act 1933. Section 1 provides:

> (1) If any person who has attained the age of sixteen years and has the custody, charge, or care of any child or young person under that age, wilfully assaults, ill-treats, neglects, abandons, or exposes him . . . in a manner likely to cause him unnecessary suffering or injury to health . . . that person shall be guilty of a misdemeanour. . . .

The case arose from the failure of parents to procure medical aid for their child who died from malnutrition and hypothermia. In relation to the four positive acts which the section proscribes, Lord Diplock expressed the view that the word 'wilfully' imported *mens rea*. If the word was to be understood as simply requiring a voluntary act, this was not its natural meaning and it would be otiose. Regarding neglect, which in this case involved the failure to provide medical aid, Lord Diplock stated (at pp. 404-405):

> Such a failure . . . could not be properly described as 'wilful' unless the parent *either* (1) had directed his mind to the question whether there was some risk . . . that the child's health might suffer unless he were examined by a doctor and provided with such curative treatment as the examination might reveal as necessary, and had made a conscious decision, for whatever reason, to refrain from arranging for such medical examination, *or* (2) had so refrained because he did not care whether the child might be in need of medical treatment or not.

This is, in effect *Caldwell* recklessness. While the *mens rea* requirement which the word 'wilfully' imports may vary from offence to offence, Lord Diplock's speech clearly suggests that the word does import *mens rea* and should not be understood as simply requiring the act to be voluntary. The earlier cases which attributed such a meaning are, accordingly, of doubtful authority.

3.6 MISTAKE

If the accused makes a mistake will this affect his criminal liability? The answer to this question will depend on the nature of the mistake he makes. His mistake may be such as to negate his *mens rea* in respect of a circumstance which is part of the *actus reus* of the offence. For example, D is charged with the theft of an umbrella which he took from an umbrella-stand in a restaurant. If D believed the umbrella was his own there would be no dishonesty (i.e. *mens rea*) in respect of the appropriation of 'property belonging to another' (i.e. a circumstance in the *actus reus* – see s. 1 of the Theft Act 1968). If, however, *mens rea* is not required in respect of a particular circumstance, a mistake in respect of it may be of no relevance (see *Prince* (1875) LR 2 CCR 154 discussed at 4.2.1 *post*). A mistake may also be made with regard to circumstances which justify or excuse the commission of an offence such as pleas of self-defence or duress.

An issue which has been problematical for many years is whether a mistake must be a reasonable one (i.e. such as a reasonable person might have made in the circumstances) before it will relieve the accused of liability. Needless to say judicial pronouncements on this issue have been contradictory.

Mistakes may be divided into two categories, namely *relevant* mistakes and *irrelevant* mistakes. Figure 1 illustrates the different types of mistake and the relationship between the various sub-categories. Most uncertainty and inconsistency has arisen in respect of relevant mistakes.

Figure 1   MISTAKES

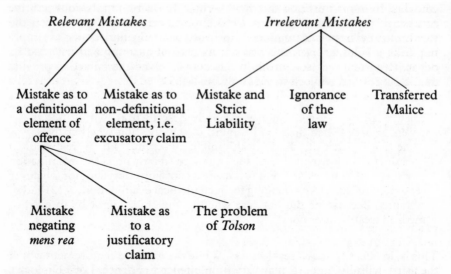

3.6.1 Relevant mistakes

A mistake may be relevant where it relates to either a definitional element of
the offence or an excusatory claim (e.g. duress). The definitional elements of
the offence are the *actus reus* and justificatory claims such as self-defence. The
latter may be viewed as part of the *actus reus* (see 2.1.2 *ante*). At one time only
mistakes which were reasonable could operate to negate liability. In *DPP* v
Morgan [1976] AC 182, the House of Lords removed this requirement in
certain circumstances so that an honest mistake could suffice. Consequently
relevant mistakes have to be divided into those relating to definitional elements
of the offence and those relating to non-definitional elements.

3.6.1.1 Mistake as to a definitional element of the offence There are
three categories of mistake as to a definitional element of an offence.

3.6.1.1.1 Mistake negating mens rea Where an offence is one requiring *mens
rea* the accused must have *mens rea* in relation to every element of the *actus reus*.
If the accused's mistake is to operate to negate his liability it must relate to the
existence of an element of the *actus reus*; it is not sufficient that his mistake is
as to some quality of an element of the *actus reus*. For example, D steals a Jaguar
belonging to V believing it to be green. The car is red but D is colour-blind. His
mistake is one of quality and will not affect his liability. He intended to
appropriate property belonging to another and he did so. In *McCullum* (1973)
57 Cr App R 645, it was held that it was sufficient for a conviction of handling
stolen goods that D knew the goods were stolen albeit that he was ignorant or
mistaken as to the nature of the goods. Similarly, in *Ellis, Street and Smith*
(1986) 84 Cr App R 235 (see 3.3 *ante*), it was sufficient that the accused knew
the goods they were importing were prohibited goods, albeit they thought they

were importing pornography rather than drugs. These examples should be contrasted with the example above of taking the wrong umbrella, where the mistake relates to the existence of an element of the *actus reus*. If D believes that the property he is taking is his own he is not acting dishonestly as he does not believe he is appropriating property belonging to another; his mistake negates his *mens rea* (see further discussion of s. 2 of the Theft Act 1968, *11.2.2.2.1 post*). The result would be the same if D had destroyed the umbrella believing it was his own and had been charged with criminal damage contrary to s. 1(1) of the Criminal Damage Act 1971 (see *Smith (David)* [1974] QB 354).

Formerly a mistake as to the existence of a definitional element would only operate to negate the accused's *mens rea* where the mistake was a reasonable one. The House of Lords considered this issue in *DPP v Morgan* [1976] AC 182. This was a case involving rape where the appellants claimed that they believed the victim was consenting. The trial judge had directed the jury that they should acquit only if they were satisfied that the appellants' mistake as to the victim's consent was reasonable. The House of Lords held this was a misdirection as the only requirement was that the belief in consent be an honest one. Lord Hailsham stated (at p. 214):

Once one has accepted . . . that the prohibited act in rape is non-consensual sexual intercourse, and that the guilty state of mind is an intention to commit it, it seems to me to follow as a matter of inexorable logic that there is no room either for a 'defence' of honest belief or mistake, or of a defence of honest and reasonable belief or mistake. Either the prosecution proves that the accused had the requisite intent, or it does not. In the former case it succeeds, and in the latter it fails.

Thus an honest belief in consent negates *mens rea*; a 'defence' of mistake is, in reality, a denial that the prosecution has proved its case. Of course, the more reasonable the mistake is, the more likely it is that the accused will be believed. Lord Hailsham recognised this when he went on to state (at p. 214):

Since honest belief clearly negatives intent, the reasonableness or otherwise of that belief can only be evidence for or against the view that the belief and therefore the intent was actually held . . ..

The question left unresolved by *Morgan* was whether the decision was confined to the offence of rape or applied generally to all offences requiring *mens rea*. In *Phekoo* [1981] 1 WLR 1117, the Court of Appeal confined the decision to the offence of rape holding that mistakes as to definitional elements in other offences had to be reasonable if they were to negative *mens rea*. In *Kimber* [1983] 1 WLR 1118, the Court of Appeal held that the same inexorable logic which spawned the decision in *Morgan* also dictated that on a charge of indecent assault *mens rea* would be negatived by an honest belief in the victim's consent. This same logic dictates the same result in all offences requiring *mens rea*. Where a particular offence requires only negligence in respect of an element of the *actus reus*, then the mistake must be a reasonable one if it is to negative negligence (see *3.6.1.1.3 post*). If strict liability applies to an element of the *actus reus* a mistake, reasonable or not, will be irrelevant (see 4.2.1 *post*).

3.6.1.1.2 Mistake as to a justificatory claim   D hits V in the belief that V was about to attack him when, in fact, V was simply performing an April Fools' Day prank. Will D's plea of self-defence succeed to negate his liability where it is an honestly held belief or must the belief be a reasonable one. In *Albert* v *Lavin* [1982] AC 546, the Divisional Court held that an accused could rely on his mistaken belief only when pleading self-defence where that belief was based on reasonable grounds. This raises the question whether a justification is something separate from the definitional elements of an offence (see 2.1.2 *ante*). If it is there might be some reason in principle for requiring such mistakes to be reasonable. If, however, the absence of a justificatory claim is part of the definitional elements of the offence the inexorable logic of *Morgan* would seem to apply. In *Kimber*, Lawton LJ disagreed with the reasoning in *Albert* v *Lavin*. When the issue arose directly in *Williams (Gladstone)* (1984) 78 Cr App R 276, the Court of Appeal departed from *Albert* v *Lavin*. D was convicted of assault occasioning actual bodily harm. D had witnessed what he believed to be an assault by M on N. D intervened and punched M. D claimed he honestly believed that N was being unlawfully assaulted by M and that he was trying to rescue N. In fact M was acting lawfully, seeking to arrest N for a robbery he had seen him commit. The jury were directed that D's mistake would be relevant if it was honest and based on reasonable grounds. The Court of Appeal quashed D's conviction. The Court defined 'assault' as 'an act by which the defendant, intentionally or recklessly, applies unlawful force to the complainant.' Thus the force must be unlawful and D must intend to apply unlawful force to the victim. Lord Lane CJ stated that the mental element cannot be substantiated 'by simply showing an intent to apply force and no more.' There are three situations where the use of force is lawful. Firstly, in limited circumstances the victim may consent to the force; secondly, where the defendant is acting in self-defence; and thirdly, where the defendant is using reasonable force in the prevention of crime or to arrest offenders under s. 3 of the Criminal Law Act 1967. If the accused makes a mistake he is to be judged against the facts as he believed them to be. The Court stated (at p.281):

> the jury should be directed first of all that the prosecution have the burden or duty of proving the unlawfulness of the defendant's actions; secondly, if the defendant may have been labouring under a mistake as to the facts, he must be judged according to his mistaken view of the facts; thirdly, that is so whether the mistake was, on an objective view, a reasonable mistake or not.

In *Beckford* [1988] AC 130, the Privy Council approved the decision in *Williams* as correctly stating the law. Lord Griffiths stated (at p. 144):

> If then a genuine beleif, albeit without reasonable grounds, is a defence to rape because it negatives the necessary intention, so also must a genuine

belief in facts which if true would justify self-defence be a defence to a crime of personal violence because the belief negates the intent to act unlawfully.

The element of unlawfulness is thus part of the definitional elements of the offence and requires *mens rea* to be proved in respect of it. If the accused mistakenly believes he is acting in self-defence he does not intend to act unlawfully.

Some statutory offences prohibit conduct where it is done 'without lawful excuse' (see, for example, ss. 1(1), 2 and 3 of the Criminal Damage Act 1971). In these offences the absence of lawful excuse is one of the definitional elements of the offence which the prosecution must prove. Section 5(3) expressly declares that it is sufficient that a belief in one of the circumstances which would constitute a lawful excuse is honest; there is no requirement that the belief be based on reasonable grounds (for a full discussion of s. 5 of the Criminal Damage Act 1971, see 14.2.2.2 post).

3.6.1.1.3 The problem of Tolson The offence of bigamy under s. 57 of the Offences Against the Person Act 1861 is committed where a person 'being married, shall marry any other person during the life of the former husband or wife'. A proviso to the section provides that it shall not extend to second marriages where the first marriage has been dissolved or annulled, or where the husband or wife has been continually absent from the person who is remarrying for seven years, and has not been known by that person to be living within that time. In *Tolson* (1889) 23 QBD 168, a wife remarried five years after last seeing her husband whom she believed to have been lost at sea. She was charged with bigamy when it was discovered that he was still alive. She did not come within the proviso although the jury found that she believed on reasonable grounds and in good faith that he was dead. The Court for Crown Cases Reserved quashed her conviction. In *Gould* [1968] 2 QB 65, it was held that a reasonable belief that the first marriage had been dissolved was a defence. In *Morgan* the decision in *Tolson* was approved along with other bigamy cases which followed it (see *King* [1964] 1 QB 285 and *Gould*). Lord Fraser stated that 'bigamy does not involve any intention except the intention to go through a marriage ceremony'. It is a general principle that *mens rea* is required as to all the elements of the *actus reus* of an offence unless these are excluded expressly or by necessary implication. The approval of *Tolson* can only be explained on the basis that *mens rea* was not required as to the element of 'being married', negligence being sufficient. If this is correct, there is nothing to distinguish the state of mind of the bigamist from that of every other person who marries. As bigamy is a serious offence it is disappointing that the House of Lords did not take the opportunity to disapprove of *Tolson* as the requirement of *mens rea* should not lightly be set aside. *Tolson* should be seen as an aberrant decision and limited to bigamy.

3.6.1.2 Mistake as to a non-definitional element Where an accused seeks to rely on an excusatory defence (see 6.1 *post*) his plea involves an admission that he performed the *actus reus* of the offence with the requisite *mens* *rea*. If the defence is successful the accused is excused the normal consequences of conviction and sentencing which would otherwise ensue. If an accused makes a mistake in respect of an element of an excusatory defence, such as duress, the issue arises whether such a mistake must be a reasonable one. In *Graham* (1982) 74 Cr App R 235, Lord Lane CJ made it clear that an accused may only rely on the defence of duress where his belief that he would be killed or seriously injured if he did not commit the offence was a reasonable one. In *Howe* [1987] AC 417, the House of Lords endorsed this view without further consideration. While the 'absence of duress' is not part of the definitional elements of the offence, there does not appear to be any other reason in principle to treat duress differently to self-defence (see 6.2.3.2 *post*).

This different treatment of mistakes, dependent on whether they relate to matters of justification or of excuse, has the potential for further anomalous consequences. In 'Necessity, duress and self-defence' [1989] Crim LR 611, Professor Elliott gives the example of a motorist, D, who unreasonably believes he is being attacked by V. If D drives away in a dangerous fashion and is charged with dangerous driving, he would not succeed if he raised a plea of duress of circumstances (see 6.3.2 *post*) because of his unreasonable mistake. By contrast, if he drove his car at V, on a charge of dangerous driving he could raise the defence of self-defence.

The Law Commission in its Draft Criminal Code remove this anomaly by clause 41 which provides that 'a person who acts in the belief that a circumstance exists has any defence that he would have if the circumstance existed'; there is no requirement that the belief be reasonable.

3.6.2   Irrelevant Mistakes

3.6.2.1   Mistake and offences of strict liability   An offence is one of strict liability where *mens rea* is not required in respect of an element of the *actus reus*; *mens rea* may be required in respect of other elements of the offence. If the accused makes a mistake in respect of an element for which liability is strict his mistake is irrelevant as his state of mind need not be established in respect of that element in order to determine guilt (see Chapter 4). In *Prince* (1875) LR 2 CCR 154, D was convicted of an offence under s. 55 of the Offences Against the Person Act 1861. Under this provision it is an offence unlawfully to take an unmarried girl under the age of sixteen out of the possession of her father against his will. D was convicted although he had reasonable grounds to believe the girl was over sixteen. The Court of Crown Cases Reserved affirmed his conviction holding that the offence was one of strict liability in respect of the circumstance of the girl's age. As knowledge of the girl's age was not required, a mistake thereto was irrelevant. Lord Bramwell stated, however, that had the accused mistakenly believed the girl's father had consented to her being taken, or if he believed she was not in anyone's possession, care or charge, his conviction would have been quashed as an intention to take the girl out of her father's possession against his will had to be proved.

In *Howells* [1977] QB 614, D was convicted of possession of a revolver without a firearm certificate, contrary to s. 1 of the Firearms Act 1968. D thought the gun was an antique which would have been covered by an exception under s. 58(2); in fact it was a modern reproduction. His appeal against conviction was dismissed by the Court of Appeal on the ground that 'to allow a defence of honest and reasonable belief that the firearm was an antique and therefore excluded would be likely to defeat the clear intention of the Act'.

In Australia and Canada there is a defence of honest and reasonable belief which may be raised to a charge of a strict liability offence. In *Proudman* v *Dayman* (1943) 67 CLR 536 (an Australian case), Dixon J stated (at 540):

> As a general rule an honest and reasonable belief in a state of facts which, if they existed, would make the defendant's act innocent affords an excuse for doing what would otherwise be an offence.

The legislature may expressly exclude this defence in any statutory offence, in which case the offence is one of absolute liability. L.H. Leigh, *Strict and Vicarious Liability* (1982) at pp. 58-61, points out that there are dicta in *Sweet* v *Parsley* [1970] AC 132 and *Morgan* which could be built upon to give recognition to such a defence in England and Wales but so far no court has sought to do so.

3.6.2.2 Ignorance of the law As a general rule, ignorance of, or a mistake as to, the law is irrelevant as the citizen is presumed to know the law of the land. This presumption is applied even if it was impossible for the accused to know the law. In *Bailey* (1800) Russ & Ry 1, D was a sailor who, before the end of a voyage, committed an act which constituted an offence under a statute which had been passed after the voyage had commenced. D was convicted but the judges recommended a pardon. The prosecution have to prove only that an accused brought about the *actus reus* of the offence with which he is charged with the requisite *mens rea*; they do not have to prove that he knew that what he was doing was contrary to the law. For example, if the accused comes from a country where buggery is not an offence and commits an act of buggery with a man under the age of twenty-one in this country in the belief that it is not an offence here, this does not negate his liability as he intentionally did the act which constituted the *actus reus* of the offence (see *Esop* (1836) 7 C & P 456).

There is an exception to the general rule stated above. In some cases the accused's mistake as to the civil law may negate his *mens rea* in respect of an element of the *actus reus* of the offence with which he is charged. In *Smith (David)* [1974] QB 354, D was charged with criminal damage to fixtures in a flat of which he was the tenant. D had installed the fixtures to cover wiring he had installed for his stereo equipment. When he was given notice to quit, D damaged the fixtures in removing the wiring. He claimed he believed he was damaging his own property as he had installed it. D's mistake was as to the civil law; in fact, fixtures become the property of the landlord. D's conviction was quashed as he did not intend to damage 'property belonging to another'. If D had removed the fixtures and taken them with him when he left he would not have been liable for theft as s. 2(1)(a) of the Theft Act 1968 specifically deals with mistakes as to the civil law. It provides that an appropriation of property is not to be regarded as dishonest if the appropriator believed that he had in law the right to deprive the other of it.

In *Secretary of State for Trade and Industry* v *Hart* [1982] 1 WLR 481, D acted as an auditor of two companies although he was disqualifed from doing so by the Companies Acts because he was a director of each company. D was charged with the offence of acting as an auditor of a company knowing that he was disqualifed for appointment to that office. D submitted that he did not know of the statutory provisions which disqualified him. The Divisional Court held it was not sufficient to know the relevant facts rendering him disqualified; it had to be proved that he knew he was disqualified by law from acting as an auditor. D's ignorance of company law meant that he did not have the requisite *mens rea* for the offence. If the accused had admitted that he knew that he was disqualified from acting as an auditor but did not know that this was an offence, he would have been convicted as he would have been in the same position as the accused in *Esop*.

In each case it is crucial to determine the *mens rea* required by the offence. If *mens rea* is not required as to the element of the *actus reus* in respect of which the accused is mistaken, his mistake will be irrelevant. If, however, negligence is required as to that element, the accused's mistake will negate his liability if it was a reasonable one. In the case of bigamy an accused will not be liable if he reasonably, but mistakenly, believed that his first marriage had been dissolved (a mistake of civil law) at the time he entered into the second marriage (see *Gould* [1968] 2 QB 65).

3.6.2.3 Transferred malice   D wishes to kill V. He sees a person whom he believes to be V and shoots at him killing him. In fact he has killed V's twin brother. Can D avoid a conviction for murder because his mistake brought about an unintended result? D will be liable as he intended to unlawfully kill another person and he killed the person at whom he was aiming. His mistake is as to a matter which the law treats as irrelevant, namely the identity of the victim. Likewise if D intends to burn down 10 Downing Street, but in the dark he mistakenly sets fire to No. 11, he will be guilty of arson as he has, without lawful excuse, intentionally damaged property belonging to another.

In the above example would it make any difference if D had shot at V but at the moment D pulled the trigger V had bent over and the bullet had hit and killed a man behind him? In this situation D has not killed the person at whom he was aiming but he has caused the *actus reus* of murder and he did intend to kill. In *Latimer* (1886) 17 QBD 359, D's conviction of unlawfully and maliciously wounding P was upheld, although D had aimed the offending blow with his belt at Q and it had glanced off striking P and causing a severe wound. The Court applied the doctrine of 'transferred malice' Lord Coleridge CJ stating (at p. 361):

> It is common knowledge that a man who has an unlawful and malicious intent against another, and, in attempting to carry it out, injures a third person, is guilty of what the law deems malice against the person injured, because the offender is doing an unlawful act, and has that which the judges call general malice, and that is enough.

If, in *Latimer*, the belt had glanced off Q and the buckle had connected with a valuable vase, breaking it, D would have brought about a different *actus reus* to that intended, namely criminal damage. In such a case if D was charged with criminal damage his intention to injure Q could not be combined with this *actus reus* to support a conviction as the *actus reus* he has caused and *mens rea* he had relate to different offences (see *Pembliton* (1874) LR 2 CCR 119). Of course, if it could be proved that the risk of damage was obvious and D had failed to give thought to this obvious risk (*Caldwell* recklessness) or had foreseen the risk and gone on to take it, D could be convicted of criminal damage on the basis of recklessness. He might also be charged with attempting to wound Q. Professor A. J. Ashworth makes the point that in virtually all cases of transferred malice the accused could have been convicted of attempt and thus there is no need for the doctrine (see 'Transferred malice and punishment for unforeseen consequences' in *Reshaping the Criminal Law* (ed. P. Glazebrook, (1978)). Professor Ashworth argues that charging attempt would be an improvement as then the accused would be prosecuted for the intended harm rather than the accidental result. The Law Commission in its Draft Criminal Code, however, opts to retain the doctrine of transferred fault. In its *Commentary on Draft Criminal Code Bill* (Law Com No. 177) it states its primary reason for this as follows (at para. 8.57):

> Where a person intends to affect one person or thing (X) and actually affects another (Y), he may be charged with an offence of attempt in relation to X; or it may be possible to satisfy a court or jury, without resort to the doctrine, that he was reckless with respect to Y. But an attempt charge may be impossible (where it is not known until trial that the defendant claims to have had X and not Y in contemplation); or inappropriate (as not describing the harm done adequately for labelling or sentencing purposes). Moreover, recklessness with respect to Y may be insufficient to establish the offence or incapable of being proved.

If D shoots at V because he believes that V is about to shoot him but he misses and kills W, D could plead self-defence if charged with W's murder. If he was justified in shooting V (this depends on using only such force as was reasonable in the circumstances), and thus did not intend *unlawfully* to kill another person, he cannot be convicted of murdering W as there is no *mens rea* to transfer.

Further reading
G. Williams, 'Oblique intention' [1987] CLJ 417; 'The *mens rea* for murder: leave it alone' (1989) 105 LQR 387.
S. G. Griffin, 'Inferring the requisite intention to kill' (1989) 139 NLJ 1637.
A. Norrie, 'Oblique intention and legal politics' [1989] Crim LR 793; 'Intention: more loose talk' [1990] Crim LR 642.
R. A. Duff, 'The politics of intention: a response to Norrie' [1990] Crim LR 637.
J. C. Smith, 'A note on 'intention'' [1990] Crim LR 85.
W. Lucy, 'Controversy in the criminal law' (1988) 8 LS 317.

E. Griew, 'States of mind, presumptions and inferences' in *Criminal Law: Essays in Honour of J. C. Smith* (ed P. Smith, 1987).
A. T. H. Smith, 'Error and mistake of law in Anglo-American criminal law' (1985) 14 Anglo-Am. LR 3.
G. Williams, 'Convictions and fair labelling' [1983] CLJ 85.

FOUR
Negligence and strict liability

4.1 NEGLIGENCE

4.1.1 The meaning of negligence

Mens rea, as it has been traditionally understood, requires an advertent state of mind on the part of the accused. Intention and recklessness are states of mind falling within the compass of *mens rea*. Negligence has not been accepted as a *mens rea* term as it does not require advertence on the part of the accused to a particular risk. Negligence is, however, a type of legal fault as it sets an objective standard to which a person's behaviour must conform. The standard set is that of the reasonable (or prudent) man. Thus if a reasonable man would have recognised the risk of a consequence occurring or a circumstance existing in the situation in which the accused acted (or omitted to act), the accused will be liable whether or not he gave any thought to the possibility of there being a risk involved in his conduct.

The *Caldwell* recklessness test overlaps to some degree with negligence as, under *Caldwell*, an accused may be liable where he failed to give thought to an obvious risk. Negligence, however, covers an area which *Caldwell* does not cover. If a person gives thought to a risk but concludes that there is no risk or that it is negligible he will not be liable under *Caldwell*. The concept of negligence, however, includes the person who has given thought to the possibility of the risk existing and unreasonably concluded that it does not exist. Negligence also covers the person who recognises the risk but takes steps which he believes would eliminate it, if the steps he takes fall below the standard of conduct to be expected from the reasonable person.

4.1.2 Criminal liability for negligence

Traditionally the common law did not impose liability for negligence with the exception of manslaughter where 'gross' negligence was a ground of liability (see *9.3.3.3.2 post*). There are few crimes where negligence is the sole basis of liability. The most notable example is s. 3 of the Road Traffic Act 1988 (as substituted by s. 2 of the Road Traffic Act 1991), under which it is an offence to drive a motor vehicle on a road without due care and attention or without reasonable consideration for other persons using the road. This offence is generally referred to as careless driving. In *McCrone* v *Riding* [1938] 1 All ER 157, 158, Lord Hewart CJ stated the standard of driving which is required as follows:

> That standard is an objective standard, impersonal and universal, fixed in relation to the safety of other users of the highway. It is in no way related to the degree of proficiency or degree of experience to be attained by the individual driver.

This standard applies to all drivers, even the inexperienced learner driver. The standard set is that of the reasonably prudent and skilful driver. If the accused drives in a way in which such a reasonable driver would not have driven, he will be liable.

Negligence as to the existence of a circumstance is sometimes sufficient to establish liability. This is sometimes referred to as 'constructive knowledge' (see 3.3 *ante*). For example, under s. 25 of the Firearms Act 1968 it is an offence 'for a person to sell or transfer any firearm or ammunition to . . . another person whom he knows or has reasonable cause for believing to be drunk or of unsound mind.'

Although liability is rarely imposed for negligence there are two other ways in which negligence may become relevant. In certain strict liability offences statute may provide that it is a defence for the accused to prove that he was not negligent. Under the Trade Descriptions Act 1968, which creates a number of offences which require no proof of *mens rea* or negligence by the prosecution, s. 24(1) provides that it is a defence for the person charged to prove:

> (a)   that the commission of the offence was due to a mistake or to reliance on information supplied to him or to the act or default of another person, an accident or some other cause beyond his control; and
> (b)   that he took all reasonable precautions and exercised all due diligence to avoid the commission of such an offence by himself or any person under his control.

The Food and Environment Protection Act 1985 contains a defence in s. 22(1) in similar terms to s. 24(1)(b) above.

The second way in which negligence may be relevant is the converse of the first; negligence in respect of a subsidiary element of the *actus reus* of the offence with which he is charged may deprive the accused of a defence which would otherwise have been available to him. For example, s. 19(1) of the Sexual Offences Act 1956 provides that it is an offence to take an unmarried girl under the age of eighteen out of the possession of her parent or guardian against his will with the intent that she shall have unlawful sexual intercourse with men or with a particular man. It is a defence under s. 19(2) if the accused takes the girl believing her to be of the age of eighteen or over and has reasonable cause for the belief. An honest but unreasonable belief regarding the age of the girl will not avail the accused; proof of negligence in respect of the age of the girl is sufficient to establish liability provided both the intention to take her out of the possession of her parent or guardian, and the ulterior intent relating to sexual intercourse, are proved. Bigamy is another offence where negligence in respect of the subsidiary element of 'being married' is sufficient. Thus if an accused goes through a second ceremony of marriage having made an unreasonable mistake that his former marriage has been annulled or dissolved or that his spouse is dead, he will be guilty of bigamy (see *King* [1964] 1 QB 285).

4.1.3 Does the reasonable man share any of the accused's characteristics?

While the standard against which the accused's conduct is measured is objective, that of the reasonable man, the question arises whether there are situations in which a subjective element may be imported into negligence so that the reasonable man shares any physical or mental limitations from which the accused might suffer. It is clear that if the accused had some special knowledge which the ordinary person would not possess, the standard against which he will be judged is that of the reasonable man possessing that special knowledge (see *Lamb* [1967] 2 QB 981). In one situation a 'no negligence' defence has been held to involve subjective consideration of whether it was unreasonable for the accused to have acted as he did in light of his physical or mental limitations. Under s.7(1) of the Sexual Offences Act 1956 it is an offence for a man to have unlawful sexual intercourse with a woman who is a defective. Under s. 7(2) it is a defence for the accused to prove that he did not know and had no reason to suspect her to be a defective. In *Hudson* [1966] 1 QB 448, the Court of Criminal Appeal held that the proper question for the jury is whether it was reasonable for the accused, having regard to his mental or physical limitations, to have been unaware that the woman was a defective. It is not sufficient that he did not know that she was a defective, but he will succeed in his defence if he can prove that people sharing his limitations would not have realised she was a defective.

The Misuse of Drugs Act 1971 contains a similar provision. Under this Act various offences relating to the production, cultivation, possession and supply of drugs are created. Section 28 provides a defence in relation to some of these offences:

(2) . . . it shall be a defence for the accused to prove that he neither knew of nor suspected nor had reason to suspect the existence of some fact alleged by the prosecution which it is necessary for the prosecution to prove if he is to be convicted of the offence charged.

In *Young* [1984] 1 WLR 654, the accused sought to rely on his intoxication as his reason for not suspecting that he was in possession of a controlled drug. The Courts-Martial Appeal Court held that this would not avail him as a defence based on the ground of 'no reason to suspect' involved the concept of objective rationality. The Court did not refer in its judgment to *Hudson* but referred to other statutory defences based on 'reasonable grounds for belief'. There are many statutory defences based on 'reasonable cause' or 'reasonable grounds' to believe (see e.g. s. 1(5) of the Official Secrets Act 1989) and these have been interpreted as imposing an objective test of whether the reasonable person would have held the requisite belief (see *McArdle* v *Egan* (1933) 150 LT 412).

In light of *Young* and of the decisions in *Elliott* v *C* [1983] 1 WLR 939, and *Stephen (Malcolm R)* (1984) 79 Cr App R 334 (see *3.4.2.2.3 ante*), it is doubtful if *Hudson* continues to be an authority in this area. It would appear that if there was an objective reason to suspect, it will not avail the accused that persons suffering from his mental or physical incapacities would not have been aware of it.

4.2   STRICT LIABILITY

4.2.1   The meaning of strict liability

If *mens rea* or negligence need not be proved in respect of one or more elements of the *actus reus* of an offence, that offence is one of strict liability. This must be contrasted with absolute liability. If an offence is one of absolute liability even the absence of voluntariness on the accused's part will not avail him. Very few offences involve absolute liability (see *Larsonneur* and *Winzar* v *Chief Constable of Kent, 2.4.2 ante*). If an offence is one of strict liability the prosecution must prove the *actus reus* was committed by the accused; this involves establishing that the accused's conduct was voluntary.

While an accused may not be found guilty of a strict liability offence where his conduct was involuntary, just as he could not be convicted of an offence requiring *mens rea* or negligence, he may be convicted even though he caused the prohibited consequence inadvertently and in a totally blameless way. For example, D, a butcher, asked a vet to examine a carcass to check that it was fit for human consumption, and, on receiving the vet's assurance that it was fit, he offered it for sale. D was convicted of the offence of exposing unsound meat for sale because the meat turned out to be unfit for human consumption, the vet having negligently performed his examination (see *Callow* v *Tillstone* (1900) 83 LT 411). D had exercised due care and taken reasonable steps to avoid committing the offence; his conduct was quite blameless. The offence, however, was one of strict liability as neither *mens rea* nor negligence were required in respect of the unsoundness of the meat. Short of not selling meat at all, there was no way for D to avoid liability. Similarly, if the accused is charged with driving a motor vehicle on a road either while unfit through drink contrary to s. 4 of the Road Traffic Act 1988, or with a level of alcohol in his blood, breath or urine above prescribed limits contrary to s. 5, he will be convicted even though he was unaware of his condition and not responsible for it, as where it is due to his soft drink being surreptitiously laced with alcohol. When construing road traffic legislation, the courts have held that these offences are strict liability offences which impose liability on the blamelessly inadvertent driver in the above situation, although the court may treat the 'laced drink' as a special reason for refraining from disqualifying the driver under s. 34(1) of the Road Traffic Offenders Act 1988 (see *Shippam* [1971] RTR 209; *Williams* v *Neale* [1971] RTR 149).

It should be noted that while liability may be strict in respect of one element of the *actus reus*, *mens rea* or negligence may be required in respect of other elements. In *Prince* (1875) LR 2 CCR 154, D was convicted of taking an unmarried girl under the age of sixteen out of the possession of her father against his will, contrary to s. 55 of the Offences Against the Person Act 1861. D believed on reasonable grounds that the girl was eighteen but he knew she was in the custody of her father. D was convicted as knowledge that the girl was under sixteen was not required. By contrast, in *Hibbert* (1869) LR 1 CCR 184, D met a girl of fourteen in the street and took her to another place where they had sexual intercourse. D was acquitted of the s. 55 offence as it was not proved that he knew the girl to be in the custody of her father; *mens rea* was required as to this element.

4.2.2 The origins of strict liability

It is a presumption of the common law that *mens rea* is required to be proved to establish guilt of a criminal offence. There is some doubt as to whether there are any exceptions to this principle at common law. Public nuisance and criminal libel have been cited as common law crimes of strict liability. Public nuisance and libel are also torts and tortious liability is more often pursued than criminal proceedings. The criminal cases on public nuisance are far from clear on whether *mens rea* or negligence are required; but there does not appear to be a clear declaration that they are not required. Those on criminal libel are similarly ambiguous. There must be an intention to publish the words which are alleged to be libellous but it is unclear whether any further *mens rea* is required in respect of the tendency of the words to defame.

A third common law offence which may involve strict liability is that of blasphemous libel. This had fallen into desuetude for over sixty years until it was resurrected for the prosecution of the editor and publishers of *Gay News* (see *Lemon and Gay News Ltd* [1979] AC 617). The majority in the House of Lords held that it was not necessary to prove an intent to blaspheme; all that was necessary was an intention to publish the words which the jury found to be blasphemous. A publication is blasphemous where it uses indecent or offensive language likely to shock or outrage the general community of Christian believers. The dissenting minority considered that the prosecution should prove that the accused intended the words to have this effect or foresaw that they were likely to have this effect. The minority considered that the majority had created an offence of strict liability but the majority denied that blasphemous libel was an offence of strict liability! It is suggested that the minority were right both substantively and in their interpretation of the speeches of the majority.

Strict liability applied to a fourth common law offence, criminal contempt of court involving the publication of material likely to prejudice a fair trial. Contempt of court is now dealt with in the Contempt of Court Act 1981. In s. 1 of this Act, Parliament expressly affirmed the strict liability rule.

Apart from the above examples of possible strict liability at common law, strict liability invariably arises in respect of offences created by statute. The precursors to offences of strict liability are to be found in some eighteenth century regulatory statutes relating to the adulteration of foodstuffs and tobacco, which created defences for merchants and others charged with such offences to prove that the adulteration took place without their knowledge and despite the exercise of due diligence to prevent it (see further L.H. Leigh, *Strict and Vicarious Liability* (1982)). In the nineteenth century there was an increase in regulatory legislation concerned with food and drugs, health, liquor, factories, pollution and other public welfare matters. Faced with this welter of legislation and the difficulties of enforcement, the courts dispensed with the requirement of *mens rea* in many cases where there were no express words in the statute requiring proof of *mens rea*. This development could be justified on several grounds. First, earlier regulatory legislation requiring proof of *mens rea* made convictions difficult to secure. Secondly, later legislation either did not use words, such as 'maliciously', 'intentionally', 'knowingly', 'wilfully' or 'permitting', which would impose a requirement of *mens rea*, or these words were used in some sections of Acts and not in others. Thirdly, most of this regulatory legislation could be regarded as creating offences *mala prohibita* rather than *mala in se*. Offences such as murder, rape, theft are *mala in se* because they are inherently immoral. Regulatory offences generally do not involve inherently immoral activities. Conduct becomes criminal simply because it is prohibited. For example, many strict liability offences relate to driving vehicles and the safety and construction of vehicles. There is nothing inherently immoral in driving at 71 mph as opposed to 69 mph. Driving at 71 mph is an offence, however, because Parliament has decided that, in the interests of safety, a line has to be drawn somewhere between acceptable speed and unacceptable speed. Regulatory offences are created by Parliament for the better running of society and the penalty is imposed to encourage observance of the law. Those who break such laws, however, are not really thought of as criminals.

Strict liability has not been confined to regulatory offences (see *Prince* 4.2.1 *ante*) and, indeed, it was not a necessary consequence of the difficulty of proving such offences. The legislation could have been interpreted to involve a reversal of the burden of proof so that the accused would be convicted unless he proved that he had not been at fault, i.e. a 'no negligence' or 'due diligence' defence could have been implied. While not going this far, courts in recent years have sought to reaffirm the presumption of *mens rea* and are, perhaps, less willing to find that an offence is one of strict liability. How do courts decide when construing a statute whether or not the offence it creates is one of strict liability? This question will be answered in the next section.

4.2.3 Identifying offences of strict liability
If Parliament did its job properly there should never be any room for doubt whether or not an offence is one of strict liability. If *mens rea* is required this could be expressly stated by using one of the long list of words (e.g. intentionally, knowingly, wilfully, permitting, etc.) which impose this require-

ment. Alternatively, if the offence is intended to be one of strict liability, this could be expressly stated as was the case with the Contempt of Court Act 1981. Unfortunately, many statutory provisions remain silent and the courts are left to divination, or, as they prefer to call it, statutory interpretation whereby they seek to discover the intention of Parliament. Certain factors or considerations may assist the courts in this quest.

4.2.3.1 The presumption of *mens rea*

The absence of express words imposing a requirement of proving *mens rea* is not conclusive that the offence is one of strict liability. In the earlier part of this century judges were, perhaps, more easily persuaded that strict liability was intended in such circumstances. In 1969, however, the House of Lords, in its decision in *Sweet* v *Parsley* [1970] AC 132, gave notice of a significant shift in position by reaffirming the presumption of *mens rea*. If it is clearly expressed that an offence is to be one of strict liability, the courts would carry out the will of Parliament. Where, however, the statute is silent, Lord Reid stated the position as follows (at p. 148):

> In such cases there has for centuries been a presumption that Parliament did not intend to make criminals of persons who were in no way blameworthy in what they did. That means that whenever a section is silent as to *mens rea* there is a presumption that, in order to give effect to the will of Parliament, we must read in words appropriate to require *mens rea*. . . . In the absence of a clear indication in the Act that an offence is intended to be an absolute offence, it is necessary to go outside the Act and examine all relevant circumstances in order to establish that this must have been the intention of Parliament. I say 'must have been' because it is a universal principle that if a penal provision is reasonably capable of two interpretations, that interpretation which is most favourable to the accused must be adopted.

Lord Pearce outlined the matters which the court would examine to determine whether Parliament's intention had been to impose strict liability (at p. 156):

> But the nature of the crime, the punishment, the absence of social obloquy, the particular mischief and the field of activity in which it occurs, and the wording of the particular section and its context, may show that Parliament intended that the act should be prevented by punishment regardless of intent or knowledge.

In the case before them the House of Lords concluded that the offence was not one of strict liability. Miss Sweet had been convicted of being concerned in the management of premises which were used for the purpose of smoking cannabis contrary to s. 5(b) of the Dangerous Drugs Act 1965. Miss Sweet had let rooms in a farmhouse to students. She had retained a bedroom for her own use on the occasions when she visited the property, but she resided elsewhere. The House of Lords held that knowledge that the premises were being used for the prohibited purpose was required. Section 8 of the Misuse of Drugs Act 1971, which replaced the 1965 Act, avoids ambiguity by expressly imposing the requirement of knowledge.

The Privy Council in *Gammon (Hong Kong) Ltd* v *A-G of Hong Kong* [1985] AC 1, reaffirmed the presumption of *mens rea*. Lord Scarman indicated in his speech the matters which a court should consider to determine whether that presumption had been rebutted by a particular statutory provision. He stated (at p. 14):

> In their Lordships' opinion, the law . . . may be stated in the following propositions . . . : (1) there is a presumption of law that *mens rea* is required before a person can be held guilty of a criminal offence; (2) the presumption is particularly strong where the offence is 'truly criminal' in character; (3) the presumption applies to statutory offences, and can be displaced only if it is clearly or by necessary implication the effect of the statute; (4) the only situation in which the presumption can be displaced is where the statute is concerned with an issue of social concern; public safety is such an issue; (5) even where a statute is concerned with such an issue, the presumption of *mens rea* stands unless it can also be shown that the creation of strict liability will be effective to promote the objects of the statute by encouraging greater vigilance to prevent the commission of the prohibited act.

In the four sections which follow the factors which courts consider in deciding whether the presumption of *mens rea* has been rebutted will be examined. While a consideration of one factor may point to rebuttal of the presumption, consideration of the others may point to the presumption being upheld. The decision in respect of each particular offence may involve a balancing of competing factors.

4.2.3.2 The statutory context   If words which impose the requirement of *mens rea* are present in the section under consideration, there is no room for confusion as the intention of Parliament will have been clearly expressed. The absence of such words, however, is not conclusive that *mens rea* is not required as it is in this circumstance that the presumption of *mens rea* operates. Assistance may be sought from other sections in the statute. If *mens rea* words are used in other sections but not in the section under consideration, this may suggest that Parliament intended this section to create a strict liability offence. The perceived purpose of the provision may be of importance in arriving at a conclusion. In *Cundy* v *Le Cocq* (1884) 13 QBD 207, D, a publican, was convicted of selling intoxicating liquor to a person who was drunk contrary to s. 13 of the Licensing Act 1872. D did not know the person was drunk nor was there any evidence of negligence. D's conviction was upheld, however, by the Divisional Court which examined other sections of the Act and found that they contained the word 'knowingly' which s. 13 did not contain. Its view that the offence was one which did not require *mens rea* was confirmed by its examination of the purpose of the Act which it concluded was 'for the repression of drunkenness' and it was therefore right to place upon the publican the responsibility of determining whether his customer was sober and thus remove from him the temptation to sell liquor without regard to the sobriety of the customer.

In *Pharmaceutical Society of Great Britain* v *Storkwain Ltd* [1986] 1 WLR 903, the House of Lords adopted the same approach when construing s. 58(2)(a) of the Medicines Act 1968. D had been charged under this provision with supplying 'prescription only' drugs to customers who had presented forged prescriptions. D believed in good faith and on reasonable grounds that the prescriptions were valid. The presence of express requirements of *mens rea* in other sections of the Act and the absence of such a requirement in this section added to the fact that pharmacists were in a position to put illicit drugs on the market, led their Lordships to conclude that Parliament intended to impose strict liability.

The fact that one section of an Act is silent regarding *mens rea* when other sections are not is not, however, conclusive of the question whether that section creates an offence of strict liability. In *Sherras* v *De Rutzen* [1895] 1 QB 918, the Divisional Court had to consider another provision under the Licensing Act 1872. D, a publican, was convicted under s. 16(2) of having unlawfully supplied liquor to a constable on duty. D believed the officer was off duty as he was not wearing his armlet and thus made no enquiry of the officer as to his status. D regularly served officers in uniform if they were off duty and therefore not wearing their armlets. The Court noted that s. 16(1) made it an offence for a licensee to 'knowingly' harbour or suffer to remain on his premises any constable on duty. The Court, however, quashed D's conviction importing a requirement of knowledge into s. 16(2), Wright J stating (at p.923) that:

> if guilty knowledge is not necessary, no care on the part of the publican could save him from conviction . . . since it would be easy for the constable to deny that he was on duty when asked, or to produce a forged permission from his superior officer as to remove his armlet before entering the public house.

Day J concluded that the effect of the absence of the word 'knowingly' from s. 16(2) was to shift the burden of proof on that issue to the accused. This approach, however, has not been generally adopted.

4.2.3.3 The social context Examining the statutory context of an offence may not be sufficient to resolve the question whether the presumption of *mens rea* has been rebutted; in such circumstances the social context of the offence is highly relevant. In *Gammon* (4.2.3.1 *ante*) Lord Scarman stated that the presumption of *mens rea* was particularly strong where an offence was 'truly criminal' but this presumption could be displaced where the offence related to an issue of social concern. This seems to be suggesting that some offences are more 'criminal' than others and that offences relating to issues of social concern are not truly criminal. This raises the problem of how one is to distinguish a 'real crime' from a 'quasi-crime'? The distinction seems to be between offences which involve infractions of the moral code and those offences of a regulatory nature which involve a breach of the law but to which no social stigma attaches, that is those offences 'which are not criminal in any real sense but are acts which in the public interest are prohibited under a penalty' (*per* Wright J, in *Sherras v De Rutzen* [1895] 1 QB 918 at 922). The problem with this dichotomy is that public morality changes from one generation to the next. For example, offences relating to pollution may have been regarded as purely regulatory and not truly criminal when enacted. The present generation, however, is likely to regard those guilty of pollution as being criminals because of increased public awareness of environmental issues. The distinction that should be made is perhaps between regulatory offences and other offences as some regulatory offences may involve moral stigma.

In deciding if an offence is 'quasi-criminal' the courts pay attention to two particular factors. Firstly, they consider whether the offence is one of general application to all members of the public or applies to a specific class of persons who are engaged in a particular activity, trade or profession such as selling food, drugs, liquor or engaging in industrial activities. If the offence is of the latter type the courts will more readily hold it to be one of strict liability. In *Sweet v Parsley* [1970] AC 132, 163, Lord Diplock stated:

> Where penal provisions are of general application to the conduct of ordinary citizens in the course of their everyday life, the presumption is that the standard of care required of them in informing themselves of facts which would make their conduct unlawful is that of the familiar common law duty of care. But where the subject-matter of a statute is the regulation of a particular activity involving potential danger to public health, safety or morals, in which citizens have a choice whether they participate or not, the court may feel driven to infer an intention of Parliament to impose, by penal sanctions, a higher duty of care on those who choose to participate and to place on them an obligation to take whatever measures may be necessary to prevent the prohibited act, without regard to those considerations of cost or business practicability which play a part in the determination of what would be required of them in order to fulfil the ordinary common law duty of care.

This may help to explain the decision in *Pharmaceutical Society of Great Britain v Storkwain Ltd* as the prohibition was specific to pharmacists and the accused had chosen to engage in that profession. It could be argued, however, that Parliament must be presumed to be legislating within the context of what is practicable in the real world. Pharmacists could only avoid dispensing drugs on a forged prescription if they checked every prescription with the doctor who appeared to have written it; such a practice could hardly be considered practicable. The imposition of strict liability thus appears to be harsh and unnecessary; the purpose of the legislation, to encourage pharmacists to take care when dispensing drugs, could have been achieved by the imposition of a requirement that the prosecution must prove negligence.

The second factor which the courts consider is the social danger which the offence is aimed at preventing. The greater the social danger the more likely it is that the presumption of *mens rea* will be found to be rebutted. Consequently many strict liability offences relate to the control of pollution, inflation, drugs and driving, the regulation of industrial activities and hygiene and safety in respect of the production and sale of food. For example, many motoring offences impose strict liability. Motoring is an activity in which citizens generally engage and thus motoring offences might be expected to require proof of *mens rea* or negligence. However, as the potential danger to the public is grave, courts have found the presumption of *mens rea* to have been rebutted. In the field of pollution strict liability is imposed. In *Alphacell Ltd v Woodward* [1972] AC 824, the House of Lords held the accused company guilty of causing polluted matter to enter a river, contrary to s. 2(1)(a) of the Rivers (Prevention of Pollution) Act 1951 although there was no evidence that the company knew of the pollution or that they had been negligent. Lord Salmon stated (at p. 848):

It is of the utmost public importance that rivers should not be polluted. The risk of pollution . . . is very great. The offences created by the Act of 1951 seem to me to be prototypes of offences which 'are not criminal in any real sense, but are acts which in the public interest are prohibited under a penalty.' . . . I can see no valid reason for reading the word 'intentionally', 'knowingly' or 'negligently' into section 2(1)(a). . . . This may be regarded as a not unfair hazard of carrying on a business which may cause pollution on the banks of a river. If . . . it were held . . . that no conviction could be obtained . . . unless the prosecution could discharge the often impossible onus of proving that the pollution was caused intentionally or negligently, a great deal of pollution would go unpunished and undeterred . . .

The House of Lords was influenced by the devastating effects pollution can have, the assumption of responsiblity by voluntarily choosing to conduct a business which may cause pollution and the need to deter others from causing pollution by encouraging greater vigilance. Similar considerations influenced the Privy Council in *Gammon Ltd v A-G of Hong Kong* [1985] AC 1. The appellants, who were respectively the registered contractor, the project manager and the site agent for building works, were charged with deviating in a material way from work shown on an approved plan contrary to the Hong Kong Building Ordinance. Part of a temporary support system on the building site had collapsed. The issue to be decided was whether the appellants had to know that their deviation was *material* or whether liability was strict in relation to this element of the offence. The Privy Council held that the offence was one of strict liablity. They were influenced by the threat to public safety which would arise from material deviations from plans, the need to deter the incompetent from engaging in building work and the need to encourage greater vigilance on the part of those who do engage in such work.

4.2.3.4 The severity of the punishment
The decisions of the courts in this area vary considerably. On the one hand the provision of a low maximum punishment by Parliament may indicate that the offence is one which is not truly criminal, thereby giving support to a finding of strict liability. The assumption is that a high maximum penalty indicates that the offence is truly criminal and that an accused should only be convicted where he is shown to be blameworthy. On the other hand, however, the provision of a severe

punishment, such as prison, may lend support to the contention that the offence deals with a matter of grave social danger for which strict liability is appropriate. In the *Storkwain* decision the House of Lords were not persuaded by the argument that Parliament could not have intended to impose strict liability for an offence which carried a maximum sentence of two years' imprisonment as the other factors which they considered pointed to strict liability. In *Gammon* the Privy Council considered that the maximum penalty of a fine of $250,000 and imprisonment for three years indicated the 'seriousness with which the legislature viewed the offences.' While this was a 'formidable' argument against strict liablity, viewed in light of the ordinance as a whole their Lordships concluded (at p. 17) that:

> there is nothing inconsistent with the purpose of the ordinance in imposing severe penalties for offences of strict liability. The legislature could reasonably have intended severity to be a significant deterrent, bearing in mind the risks to public safety arising from some contraventions of the ordinance.

Similarly, in *Howells* [1977] QB 614, on a charge of possession of a firearm without a firearm certificate contrary to s. 1(1)(a) of the Firearms Act 1968, the Court of Appeal concluded that the fact that the maximum penalty was five years' imprisonment did not preclude the imposition of strict liability. The Court found that other factors such as the wording of the Act and the danger to the community resulting from possession of lethal firearms outweighed this factor.

4.2.3.5 Promoting the enforcement of the law   The fact that a statute deals with an issue of social concern is not sufficient to displace the presumption of *mens rea* unless strict liability will be effective in encouraging vigilance and observance of the law. In *Reynolds* v *G. H. Austin & Sons Ltd* [1951] 2 KB 135, the defendant company was charged with a contravention of the Road Traffic Acts. The company were a private hire coach company who had contracted to take members of a women's guild on an outing. The organiser of the outing advertised to the general public that there were spare tickets available. The company did not have a public service licence and performed the contract unaware that the trip had been advertised to the public. The Divisional Court held that the offence was not one of strict liability. Devlin J stated (at pp. 149-150):

> if a man is punished because of an act done by another, whom he cannot reasonably be expected to influence or control, the law is engaged, not in punishing thoughtlessness or inefficiency, and thereby promoting the welfare of the community, but in pouncing on the most convenient victim. . . . where the punishment of an individual will not promote the observance of the law either by that individual or by others whose conduct he may reasonably be expected to influence then, in the absence of clear and express words, such punishment is not intended.

In *Lim Chin Aik* v *The Queen* [1963] AC 160, the Privy Council quashed the appellant's conviction, under s. 6(2) of the Immigration Ordinance 1952 of the State of Singapore, of remaining in Singapore (after having entered) when he had been prohibited from entering by an order made by the Minister under s. 9. The Privy Council stated that it was not enough to label the statute as one dealing with a grave social evil and infer that strict liability is intended. It was important also to enquire whether strict liability would assist in the enforcement of the regulations. 'There must be something he can do, directly or indirectly, by supervision or inspection, by improvement of his business methods or by exhorting those whom he may be expected to influence or control, which will promote the observance of the regulations.' In the instant case the imposition of strict liability would simply serve to convict a 'luckless victim' as the prohibition had not been published or made known to the appellant. Thus strict liability will not be imposed where the accused either has no means of knowing the law or of taking action to ensure observance of the law.

4.2.4 Justifications for strict liability

The two justifications generally given for the creation of strict liability offences are that they encourage greater safety and improved standards of prevention, thereby offering the public better protection from the risks inherent in particular activities, and that they relieve the prosecution of the difficult task of proving *mens rea*, thereby increasing both administrative efficiency and the deterrent effect of conviction. Is strict liability necessary for the protection of the public and the enforcement of particular laws? A facile answer would be, 'Yes, it must be because Parliament has enacted so many offences which impose strict liability.' The fact that Parliament has created so many strict liability offences, however, does not establish the necessity of their existence. Strict liability offences are only necessary if there is no other means of achieving the ends of protecting the public and enforcing the law.

A distinguished social scientist, Baroness Wootton, argued ardently in favour of the extension of strict liability to cover all crimes. In *Crime and the Criminal Law* (2nd edn, 1981) she stated (at p. 46):

> If, however, the primary function of the courts is conceived as the prevention of forbidden acts, there is little cause to be disturbed by the multiplication of offences of strict liability. If the law says that certain things are not to be done, it is illogical to confine this prohibition to occasions on which they are done from malice aforethought; for at least the material consequences of an action, and the reasons for prohibiting it are the same whether it is the result of sinister malicious plotting, of negligence or of sheer accident.

This begs the very important question of what is a forbidden act? It could be argued that in murder the forbidden act is causing the death of another person. A surgeon who performs an operation on a patient could be found to have committed the forbidden act if his patient dies under anaesthetic even though the chances of success of the operation were low but the risk was taken as, without the operation, the patient would have died in a few weeks or months.

To find such a surgeon guilty of murder would be ludicrous and would involve divorcing the law from the social and moral context in which it operates, not to mention deterring all other surgeons from performing operations involving any risk of death. Such an approach, far from protecting the public, would end up leaving them more at risk. What the law seeks to prevent is forbidden acts in the circumstances where the perpetrator of the act is morally culpable. Baronness Wootton would seek to distinguish the culpable from the blameless by leaving it to the judge to mete out an appropriate sentence. Such an approach, however, does not overcome the stigma attaching to criminal conviction. Nor does it make for efficiency as the courts would be cluttered with prosecutions of blameless individuals who would ultimately be dealt with by means of an absolute discharge. It is not possible to protect people from all harm; the law's role, however, is to seek to protect them from the intentional or reckless infliction of harm and, in some circumstances, from the negligent infliction of harm. If harm could not have been prevented by the exercise of reasonable care, the prosecution of the blamelessly inadvertent will not prevent the occurrence of such harm in the future.

In the area of regulatory offences the social context is important. We need people to engage in industrial processes, to make and sell food, to dispense drugs, to drive motor vehicles. There may be risks involved in all these activities meriting the exercise of care on the part of those engaging in them. The law should encourage such care but not be so harsh as to discourage people from embarking upon these enterprises in the first place. Thus the blamelessly inadvertent pharmacist should not be punished for dispensing drugs on a forged prescription if he was exercising that degree of care to be expected of pharmacists consistent with considerations of economics and practicability. Similarly, the butcher selling meat should take reasonable precautions to avoid selling meat which is unfit. Punishing him where, despite such precautions, he has sold unfit meat serves no purpose unless it is to discourage the sale of meat altogether (see *Callow* v *Tillstone*, 4.2.1 *ante*). Alternatively, if the butcher is forced to employ an analyst to test every carcass this would raise his costs to the extent that meat would become too expensive for many people to afford, which in turn would have detrimental effects on the ordinary consumer, the farmer and all those involved in processing and selling meat. It is also highly questionable whether strict liability leads to a higher standard of care. In *R* v *City of Saulte Ste Marie* (1978) 85 DLR (3d) 161, before the Supreme Court of Canada, Dickson J stated (at p. 171):

> There is no evidence that a higher standard of care results from absolute liability. If a person is already taking every reasonable precautionary measure, is he likely to take additional measures, knowing that however much care he takes, it will not serve as a defence in the event of breach? If he has exercised care and skill, will conviction have a deterrent effect upon him or others?

By contrast, in *Alphacell*, Lord Salmon took the view that strict liability would encourage those who might be potential polluters 'not only to take reasonable steps to prevent pollution but to do everything possible to ensure that they do not cause it.' This may reflect a degree of commercial naivety on the part of Lord Salmon. If expenditure of thousands of pounds for preventive measures will not ultimately prevent the risk of pollution, the factory owner may prefer to save his money, keep his unit costs down, retain his competitiveness, increase his profits and run the risk of being caught and fined several hundred pounds should his operations cause pollution at a time when an inspector is around.

Does strict liability make for efficient law enforcement and effective prevention/deterrence? Clearly the task of the prosecution is facilitated as, in strict liability offences, it is only necessary to prove that the *actus reus* was committed and there is no need to prove the more difficult issue of *mens rea*. In the many regulatory offences that exist this makes for easier enforcement as it is only necessary for a pollution inspector to prove that the accused's factory is discharging effluent into the river, or a health inspector need only prove that meat sold was unfit. No enquiry need be made to discover if the accused knew that he was causing pollution or selling unfit meat. This, however, ignores a problem. How is a sentencer to sentence someone convicted of a strict liability offence if he does not know whether he committed the offence intentionally, recklessly, negligently or inadvertently despite the most stringent precautions? The person who intentionally causes pollution deserves a very much heavier sentence than the one who has exercised reasonable care. As the prosecution only have to establish that pollution was caused by the accused, the facts which would disclose the level of the accused's culpability would not be proved in the trial. This may necessitate a further post conviction hearing to determine the factual basis of the offence (see *Newton* (1982) 4 Cr App R (S) 388). This would seem to cancel out any efficiency benefits deriving from dispensing with the proof of *mens rea* for the purposes of conviction. It also may be difficult to establish the factual basis of the offence as the investigating official may not have inquired into, or obtained evidence relating to, the culpability of the accused as this was not necessary for the purposes of obtaining a conviction. If he does make such inquiries and acquire evidence he is performing the same task as an officer investigating a crime requiring proof of *mens rea* and this will defeat any claim of administrative efficiency. In addition, if there is any doubt as to the factual basis of the offence, this must be resolved in favour of the accused as the normal burden of proof applies (see *Newton* and *Gortat and Pirog* [1973] Crim LR 648). If efficiency is to be obtained and no evidence of culpability sought, all offenders will appear the same and thus will be treated as if they had been blamelessly inadvertent; i.e. culpability is reduced to the level of the lowest common denominator. If this occurs, sentences will not serve to deter the culpable. In addition, if a result arises from blameless inadvertence and could not, by the exercise of reasonable care, have been avoided, the imposition of a penalty will not prevent future infractions unless the offender desists entirely from the activity involved. If penalties which truly reflect the offender's culpability can only be determined by thorough investigation and proof to the same standard required for conviction, there would seem to be little reason for having strict liability offences.

If regulatory offences are seeking to encourage the exercise of reasonable care, strict liability would not appear to be necessary. If a person has exercised reasonable care and the forbidden harm still occurs, punishing him will not make the incidence of that harm any less likely in the future. The punishment appears unjust and serves no purpose. If punishment is not inflicted, as where an absolute discharge is given because the accused is blameless, the whole process of prosecution and trial appears pointless and militates against efficiency in respect of other cases relating to blameworthy offenders. The conclusion thus seems to be that strict liability achieves nothing which could not be achieved by means of a requirement of negligence. It may be that considerations of administrative efficiency might dictate that on proof of the *actus reus* a presumption of negligence is raised, subject to rebuttal by proof on the balance of probabilities by the accused that he was not negligent. This is not unacceptable as if the accused has been exercising reasonable care in respect of a particular activity in which he is engaged he should be able to prove this by evidence of the production system, supervision, checks, safety precautions, etc. involved.

4.2.5 Defences to strict liability

The High Court of Australia in *Proudman* v *Dayman* (1941) 67 CLR 536, and the Supreme Court of Canada in *R* v *City of Sault Ste Marie* developed a general due diligence (or 'no-negligence') defence to offences of strict liability which places the burden of proof on the accused. In the latter case Dickson J stated (at p. 181):

> The correct approach . . . is to relieve the Crown of the burden of proving *mens rea*, having regard to . . . the virtual impossibility in most regulatory cases of proving wrongful intention. In a normal case, the accused alone will have knowledge of what he has done to avoid the breach and it is not improper to expect him to come forward with the evidence of due diligence . . . This involves consideration of what a reasonable man would have done in the circumstances. The defence will be available if the accused reasonably believed in a mistaken set of facts which, if true, would render the act or omission innocent, or if he took all reasonable steps to avoid the particular event.

While the recognition of strict liability offences in England and Wales was a judicial decision, no court has been prepared to import a common law 'due diligence' defence. Parliament, however, has sought to mitigate the worst effects of strict liability by including defences in some statutes. Due diligence defences have been provided in, for example, s. 67 of the Offices, Shops and Railway Premises Act 1963; s. 24(1) of the Trade Descriptions Act 1968; s. 34 of the Weights and Measures Act 1985; and s. 28 of the Misuse of Drugs Act 1971. In some statutes the due diligence defence has been combined with a 'third party' defence requiring the accused to prove both that he exercised due diligence and that the offence was due to the act or default of a third party (see e.g. Food Safety Act 1990, s. 21(2). If successful such a defence leaves the third party liable to conviction on the basis of strict liability. If, for example, a shopkeeper was charged with an offence under s. 8 of the Food Safety Act based on his sale of a bottle of ginger ale to a customer which, when opened, was found to contain the decomposed remains of a snail, the shopkeeper might avoid conviction if he proved that he had exercised all due diligence and that the contravention was due to the act or default of the manufacturer. If the bottle was made of dark glass there would be nothing that the shopkeeper could do to check the contents other than open it and pour them out; this would not be reasonable. But if the bottle was made of clear glass, and the snail was visible, the shopkeeper would fail in his defence as, although not responsible for the contamination, he could have discovered it by a cursory inspection. If the third party responsible for the contravention is not identifiable, the third party defence is not available.

Further reading
L. H. Leigh, *Strict and Vicarious Liability* (1982).
J. C. Smith, 'Responsibility in criminal law' in *Barbara Wootton, Essays in Her Honour* (1986, eds. Bean and Whynes) 141.
M. Smiths and A. Pearson, 'The value of strict liability' [1969] Crim LR 5.
G. Richardson, 'Strict liability for regulatory crime: the empirical research' [1987] Crim LR 295.
F. B. Sayre, 'Public welfare offences' (1933) 33 Col LR 55.
I. Paulus, 'Strict liability: its place in public welfare offences' (1978) 20 Crim LQ 445.
B. Jackson, '*Storkwain*: a case study in strict liability and self-regulation' [1991] Crim LR 892.

FIVE

Capacity and incapacitating conditions

5.1 INTRODUCTION

A person should only be held criminally liable where he has the capacity to understand his actions, in the sense of being able to understand the nature of those actions and the circumstances in which they occur, and to recognise the consequences which may flow from them, and, having understood them, where he has the capacity to control them. Moral culpability should not attach to the person who at the time he acted (or omitted to act) was unable to understand what he was doing and/or unable to control what he was doing, as such a person is not a responsible actor and therefore is not deserving of blame or punishment. The criminal law has recognised this requirement of rational capacity by excepting persons who lack rational capacity from liability in certain circumstances. According to N. L. A. Barlow, 'Drug intoxication and the principle of *Capacitas Rationalis*' (1984) 100 LQR 639 (at p. 647), the principle or presumption of rational capacity operates as 'a pre-condition to punishment; as a standard, a criterion, for determining eligibility for and immunity from punishment.' In this chapter the issues of infancy, insanity, automatism and intoxication will be examined. These conditions are often said to give rise to defences. They will be examined in this chapter, however, rather than Chapter Six, as they specifically relate to the issue of whether the accused had rational capacity at the time of his act. In the case of defences such as duress or self-defence, there is no question of the accused's rational capacity being in doubt; implicit in these defences is the idea that the accused did exercise rational judgment and chose to act as he did but his claim is that his acts were either justified or excusable because of the circumstances in which he found himself.

5.2 INFANCY

Infants are persons under eighteen years of age. For the purposes of criminal procedure, sentencing and criminal liability there are various terms applied to different age groups. A *child* is a person aged ten years or more but under fourteen years of age. A *young person* is aged fourteen years or more but under seventeen years of age. A *young offender* is aged fourteen years or more but under twenty-one years. The procedures before the courts and the sentences available on conviction will vary according to the age of the offender. But before issues of sentencing arise the issue of criminal liability has to be considered. It is an irrebuttable presumption of the criminal law that a child under ten years of age at the time an alleged offence was committed cannot be found guilty of that offence (see s. 50 of the Children and Young Persons Act 1933, as amended). A child under ten is said to be *doli incapax*, that is, incapable of crime. This presumption derives from a recognition of the immaturity of children who will not have a fully developed understanding of what is right and wrong nor the ability to fully appreciate the consequences of their acts. If a child is charged with an offence and it is established that he was under ten years of age at the time the alleged offence was committed, the case against him will be dismissed without any inquiry whether he understood what he was doing. This may mean that precocious children under ten who are given to breaking the law escape liability because the presumption is irrebutable. The solution to this problem is for a local authority or other authorised person to commence proceedings in the family proceedings court in respect of the child under s. 31 of the Children Act 1989 for an order placing the child in the care of a local authority or putting him under the supervision of a local authority or probation officer. In proceedings under the 1989 Act the child's welfare will be the paramount consideration of the court (s. 1(1) of the Children Act 1989) and under s. 31(2) an order may only be made if the court is satisfied –

(a)   that the child concerned is suffering, or is likely to suffer, significant harm; and
(b)   that harm, or the likelihood of harm, is attributable to –
   (i)   the care given to the child, or likely to be given to him if the order were not made, not being what it would be reasonable to expect a parent to give to him; or
   (ii)   the child's being beyond parental control.

These requirements are very stringent and will not be satisfied merely upon proof that the child has committed what would be a criminal offence but for the principle of *doli incapax*.

A consequence of the *doli incapax* principle is that not only is the child not guilty of the crime, but the child has not committed a crime. But, if the offence was instigated by another person, that person, rather than being an aider, abettor, counsellor or procurer, becomes the principal acting through an innocent agent; he commits the crime. The absence of a crime may also negate the criminal liability of others. For example, in *Walters* v *Lunt* [1951] 2 All ER 645, a mother and father were acquitted of the charge of receiving from their son a child's tricycle knowing it to be stolen. As the son was seven years of age he could not steal and thus the tricycle was not stolen. Had the parents instigated the taking of the tricycle by their son they would have stolen it through an innocent agent.

Where a child is ten years of age or over and under the age of fourteen at the time of the alleged offence, there is a common law presumption that he is incapable of committing an offence. This presumption, however, may be rebutted by proof of 'mischievous discretion', an element which must be proved in addition to the *actus reus* and *mens rea* of the offence involved. In *Gorrie* (1918) 83 JP 136, it was held that mischievous discretion required proof that the child knew that what he was doing was seriously wrong. In *JM (a minor)* v *Runeckles* (1984) 79 Cr App R 255, the Divisional Court stated that it was not necessary to prove that the child knew that the act was morally wrong, although such knowledge may help prove that he knew it was seriously wrong, but proof that he knew that what he was doing was merely naughty or mischievous would not suffice. The younger the child is, the stronger the evidence must be to establish mischievous discretion (see *X* v *X* [1958] Crim LR 805).

There are various ways of seeking to prove mischievous discretion. It is not sufficient to prove that normal children of D's age would know that the offence involved was seriously wrong unless the prosecution also prove that D is a child of normal mental capacity (*JBH and JH (Minors)* v *O'Connell* [1981] Crim LR 632; and *Runeckles*). The child's behaviour at the time he committed the offence and thereafter may also provide evidence of mishievous discretion, for example, seeking to cover up the crime, telling lies or running away from the police (see *York* (1748) Fost 70, CCR; and *Runeckles*) but running away on its own is not sufficient to establish mischievous discretion (*A* v *DPP* [1992] Crim LR 34). Evidence may also be given of the child's home background (see *Padwick* [1959] Crim LR 439) or of previous convictions (see *R* v *B, R* v *A* [1979] 3 All ER 460).

Generally proof of mischievous discretion is a separate matter from proof of *mens rea*. Where an offence involves dishonesty, however, proof of dishonesty will involve proof of mischievous discretion. In *T* v *DPP* [1989] Crim LR 498, T, a child aged ten, was charged with theft of a first-aid box from an ambulance. Upon removing the box T threw it over a wall and climbed over after it whereupon he was caught. When questioned by the police he said 'it ain't nothing to do with me, I didn't steal it' and when cautioned, said 'I can speak if I want to'. The Divisional Court held that his acts in climbing over the wall and denying the theft when challenged were sufficient to indicate that he knew that what he was doing was wrong. This mischievous discretion was indistinguishable from the *mens rea* requirement of dishonesty.

Boys under the age of fourteen are irrebuttably presumed to be incapable of sexual intercourse and thus cannot be convicted as perpetrators of rape (*Groombridge* (1836) 7 C & P 582), offences involving sexual intercourse (*Waite* [1892] 2 QB 600) or buggery whether as agent or as patient (*Tatam* (1921) 15 Cr App R 132). Convictions for indecent assault, however, have been upheld where a boy has done acts which, but for his age, would have amounted to one of the above offences. In addition, a boy under fourteen may be convicted of abetting another to commit these offences. It has yet to be decided if a boy under fourteen could be convicted of attempted rape or attempted buggery. Where a boy under fourteen is capable of sexual intercourse it seems illogical to irrebuttably presume him to be incapable (see further 8.3.3.4 *post*). The Criminal Law Revision Committee recommended the abolition of this presumption (*Fifteenth Report: Sexual Offences* (1984) Cmnd 9213, para. 2.48) and the Law Commission follow this recommendation in their Draft Criminal Code (clause 87).

5.3 INSANITY

5.3.1 Introduction

The defence of insanity is concerned with the accused's mental state at the time when the alleged offence was committed. The accused's mental state may be relevant at two other times. Firstly, in a criminal trial it is relevant at the time he is arraigned and called to plead to the charge against him. Under ss. 4 and 4A of the Criminal Procedure (Insanity) Act 1964 (as substituted by s. 2 of the Criminal Procedure (Insanity and Unfitness to Plead) Act 1991) an accused may be found 'unfit to plead' where it is established that because of his mental condition he is unable to understand the charge and the difference between a plea of guilty and a plea of not guilty, to challenge jurors, to instruct counsel and to follow the proceedings.

The issue of the accused's fitness to plead is determined by a jury as soon as it arises (s. 4(3), Criminal Procedure (Insanity) Act 1964). If the judge considers it expedient to do so, having regard to the supposed disability, and where it is in the accused's interests, he may postpone consideration of the issue up to the time of the opening of the case for the defence (s. 4(2)). This is appropriate where the prosecution case appears weak as they may not be able to establish a *prima facie* case to answer, the judge will then direct the jury to acquit. If the issue arises on arraignment a jury should be empanelled to decide the issue (s. 4(5)(a)). If it arises during the course of the trial it should be determined either by the trial jury or a separate jury empanelled for this purpose, as the court may direct (s. 4(5)(b)).

An accused may not be found unfit to plead except on the written or oral evidence of two or more registered medical practitioners, at least one of whom is approved for the purposes of s. 12 of the Mental Health Act 1983 by the Secretary of State as having special experience in the diagnosis or treatment of mental disorder. If the accused is found unfit to plead the trial must not proceed or further proceed. A jury will then determine on the basis of evidence (if any) already adduced or on evidence adduced by the prosecution and/or a person appointed by the court under s. 4A of the 1964 Act to put the case for the defence (i.e. defence counsel), whether the accused did the act or made the omission constituting the *actus reus* of the offence charged against him (s. 4(2)). This jury will be either a new jury where the issue of unfitness to plead arose on the arraignment or, if it arose later, the jury by whom the accused was being tried (s. 4A(5)). If not satisfied that the accused did the act or made the omission, the jury should acquit of the count in question (s. 4A(4)). If the jury are satisfied the accused did the act or made the omission, the judge decides on the correct disposal. He may make an order for admission to a hospital approved by the Secretary of State (with or without an order restricting the accused's discharge), a guardianship order under the Mental Health Act 1983, a supervision and treatment order or an absolute discharge (s. 5(2) of the 1964 Act). If the sentence for the offence is fixed by law (i.e. murder) the court must order detention in hospital with restriction on discharge without limit of time (s. 5(3)).

The second time in a criminal trial when the mental condition of the accused will be relevant is when he has been convicted. His mental condition will be relevant to the question of the appropriate sentence to be imposed (see further M. Wasik, *Emmins on Sentencing* (2nd edn, 1993)).

While much ink is expended in textbooks and academic journals seeking to explain, analyse and rationalise the defence of insanity, it is, in practice, a rarely used defence. Part of the reason for its infrequent use is that many of those accused of murder, who in the past might have raised the defence of insanity, now raise the defence of diminished responsibility under s. 2 of the Homicide Act 1957 (see 5.5 *post*). The most recent study of the operation of the defence by R. D. Mackay, 'Fact and fiction about the insanity defence' [1990] Crim LR 247, reveals that in the fourteen years from 1975 to 1988 there were only forty-nine verdicts of 'not guilty by reason of insanity'. Of these verdicts fourteen were returned in murder cases, twenty-three in cases of non-fatal assaults, and the remainder were returned in a variety of cases involving arson, robbery, burglary, deception and reckless driving.

If an accused is found to have been insane at the time the *actus reus* was committed the verdict the jury return is 'not guilty by reason of insanity' (see s. 1 of the Criminal Procedure (Insanity) Act 1964). This is generally referred to as the 'special verdict'. Previously, on such a verdict being returned the judge had to order the accused to be detained in a hospital to be selected by the Home Secretary (s. 5(1) of and sch. 1 to the Criminal Procedure (Insanity) Act 1964). The fact that the consequence of a special verdict was automatic committal to a mental hospital was one of the deterrents against pleading insanity or, in some cases, from running a line of defence which might have been interpreted by the court as an insanity defence (see *Sullivan* and *Hennessy post*). The prospect of indefinite detention in a mental hospital led some defendants to plead guilty and cast themselves upon the mercy of the judge when sentencing them, rather than rely on a defence which was technically available to them. The Criminal Procedure (Insanity and Unfitness to Plead) Act 1991 gives much greater discretion in disposing of an accused on a special verdict being returned. The court has the same powers of disposal as are available where an accused is found unfit to plead (see above). This may result in the defence being pleaded more frequently.

5.3.2 The rationale for a defence of insanity

There are five different ways in which a person's mental condition may affect his responsibility for his conduct. Firstly, he may perform a prohibited act in a state of impaired consciousness due to some mental condition or internal cause. In such a condition his act is involuntary and he is referred to as an automaton. Secondly, he may be conscious and perform willed bodily movements which consitute the *actus reus* of an offence but due to his mental condition he may not know or understand what he is doing. Thirdly, he may be conscious and able to comprehend what he is doing but due to his mental condition be unaware that it is wrong. Fourthly, he may know what he is doing and that it is wrong but due to his mental condition he may not be able to control what he is doing. Fifthly, he may know what he is doing and that it is wrong but due to a delusional state he may believe that his act is appropriate. In each of these cases it could be said that the accused is not a responsible actor at the time of his act as he is not totally in touch with reality. The capacity for rational judgment has been impaired. As such he may not be an appropriate subject for punishment although, if he continues to be a danger to the community, it may be appropriate for the community to be protected from him.

The five states of impairment listed above vary in their impact on the definitional elements of the offence. In the first state there is no *actus reus* as the act was not voluntary and, necessarily, if it was not voluntary there was no *mens rea* either. In the second state there is an *actus reus* but no *mens rea*. In the third, fourth and fifth states there is an *actus reus* and *mens rea* but serious doubts arise with regard to the rational capacity, and thus responsibility, of the actor.

While it was stated above that the criminal law had recognised the principle of rational capacity by excepting persons from criminal liability who lack it, the recognition of this principle has been almost accidental rather than designed. This becomes evident from a study of the operation of the defence of insanity. The effect of this defence is that in certain circumstances individuals who lacked rational capacity at the time of the commission of the alleged offence are excused from criminal liability; the defence covers the first three conditions outlined above. The defence has developed, however, in the absence of a clearly articulated theoretical foundation and in isolation from modern medical opinion. As a result the defence is deficient in some cases as it does not cover a particular type of individual who clearly lacks rational capacity, namely those who fall within the fourth and fifth situations outlined above. In other circumstances, the defence of insanity itself works injustice as it brings within its ambit individuals who, in any other context, would not be considered insane, for example, the epileptic (*Sullivan*) or the diabetic (*Hennessy*) or the sleepwalker (*Burgess* [1991] 2 QB 92), who technically fall within the first situation outlined above. This problem highlights the difficulty in delineating the dividing line between automatism and insanity, or, as it is often termed non-insane automatism and insane automatism. Not all individuals who are reduced to an automatous condition are insane; some are insane, some are clearly sane and others fall in between because their condition technically fits the criminal law's definition of insanity but does not correspond to any medical definition of insanity. Indeed, psychiatrists do not talk of insanity but prefer to use terms such as mental illness or mental disorder.

While the Criminal Procedure (Insanity and Unfitness to Plead) Act 1991 has addressed the problem of the injustice of the automatic disposal to a mental hospital, it has not addressed the problem of the definition of insanity and the tendency of the defence to cover inappropriate conditions while failing to cover other conditions where rational capacity is absent. There are other problems with the defence in respect of the way in which it conflicts with other general principles of criminal liability which will be dealt with below.

5.3.3 The law
The law relating to the defence of insanity is to be found in the rules set out in *M'Naghten* (1843) 10 Cl & F 200, which delineate the circumstances in which an accused will be held not to have been legally responsible for his conduct. These rules are not concerned with medical definitions of insanity, and, indeed, these may bear little resemblance to the criminal definition. The origin of the *M'Naghten* Rules is interesting. Daniel M'Naghten was found to be insane and acquitted on a charge of murdering Sir Robert Peel's private secretary, it being his intention to kill Peel. He was committed to hospital but there was a public outcry at the perceived leniency of the verdict. The matter was debated in the House of Lords, where it was decided to seek the opinion of the judges on the legal principles relating to insanity. The joint answer given by fourteen judges is not technically binding as a precedent as it is only an opinion rather than a judgment upon a case before a court. The rules, however, have been treated as authoritative ever since.

The principles stated by the judges are as follows:

1.   Everyone is presumed sane and to possess a sufficient degree of reason to be responsible for their crimes until the contrary is proved.

2.   To establish a defence of insanity it must be clearly proved that at the time of committing the act, the accused was labouring under such a defect of reason, from disease of the mind, as (a) not to know the nature and quality of the act he was doing; or (b) if he did know it, not to know he was doing what was wrong.

5.3.3.1 Procedural matters   The first principle refers to the presumption of sanity. If the accused is to raise the defence of insanity the burden of proving it is upon him. Generally it is for the prosecution to prove the guilt of the accused beyond reasonable doubt and to disprove any defence he may raise. In the case of insanity it is not sufficient for the accused to raise the defence, he bears a burden of proving it. He is not required to prove it beyond reasonable doubt but need only do so on a balance of probabilities. This raises a problem: if the accused is claiming that he did not know what he was doing, relying on 2(a) above, he is being asked to prove on the balance of probabilities something the contrary of which the prosecution have not proved. If the prosecution prove beyond reasonable doubt that he knew what he was doing, and thus had *mens rea* that would be an end of the matter. But if they fail to prove this it seems superfluous, and indeed illogical, to require the accused to prove the contrary on a balance of probabilities. The courts, however, have not recognised this problem although Glanville Williams has in *Criminal Law: The General Part,* (2nd edn., 1961, para. 165), where he argues that on ground 2(a) it should only be necessary for the accused to introduce evidence of insanity which raises a reasonable doubt whether he had the necessary *mens rea*. Further support for this argument is gained by the fact that if the accused's defence is one of automatism due to some cause other than a disease of the mind, the burden of proof remains on the prosecution and the accused need only raise a doubt to succeed.

While an accused may not expressly raise the defence of insanity, the nature of his defence may, in effect, amount to an insanity defence as where, for example, he claims he was acting as an automaton or lacked *mens rea* and medical evidence points to this being due to a disease of the mind giving rise to a defect of reason of the appropriate kind outlined in the second principle above. In the past it was obviously in the accused's interests to claim that he was an automaton or lacked *mens rea* without expressly claiming he was insane, as he would hope to be acquitted without suffering committal to a mental hospital which was the automatic consequence of a special verdict being returned. The question whether a defence amounts to one of insanity is one of law to be decided by the judge on the basis of the medical evidence (see *Dickie* [1984] 3 All ER 173). If the judge concludes that the medical evidence supports a defence of insanity he should leave it to the jury to decide if the accused was insane. In several of the cases below the trial judge ruled that the accused's defence of automatism was, in effect, one of insanity as the medical evidence of his mental condition established that it was due to a disease of the mind. In the past in such cases the result was often that the accused changed his plea to guilty to avoid the consequences of a special verdict. It is also open to the prosecution to raise the issue of insanity. In *Bratty* v *Attorney-General for Northern Ireland* [1963] AC 386, Lord Denning stated (at p. 411):

I think that Devlin J was quite right in *Kemp's* case in putting the question of insanity to the jury, even though it had not been raised by the defence. When it is asserted that the accused did an involuntary act in a state of automatism, the defence necessarily puts in issue the state of mind of the accused man: and thereupon it is open to the prosecution to show what his true state of mind was. The old notion that only the defence can raise a defence of insanity is now gone. The prosecution are entitled to raise it and it is their duty to do so rather than allow a dangerous person to be at large.

Where the defence raise a plea of diminished responsibility in response to a charge of murder, it is open to the prosecution to rebut this by adducing or eliciting evidence of insanity (see s. 6 of the Criminal Procedure (Insanity) Act 1964). In such circumstances the burden of proving insanity will be on the prosecution (see *Bastian* [1958] 1 WLR 413).

The ultimate question whether the accused was insane is for the jury to determine; although the medical evidence will be crucial to their decision, it is not for doctors to decide the issue but for the jury to decide it on the basis of their evidence. However, the jury must act on the evidence tendered; if this all points to the accused being insane but the jury convict, such a conviction may be overturned on appeal on the ground that no reasonable jury could have reached such a verdict (*Matheson* (1958) 42 Cr App R 145). But if there is other evidence to the contrary, a jury verdict will not be overturned simply because the medical evidence supported the defence (see *Rivett* (1950) 34 Cr App R 87; *Latham* [1965] Crim LR 434).

5.3.3.2 The constituents of the defence   There are three conditions to be satisfied in any case where a defence of insanity is raised: first that the accused was suffering from a disease of the mind; second, that this gave rise to a defect of reason; and third, that as a result he either did not know the nature and quality of his act or he did not know that what he was doing was wrong. These will be examined in turn.

5.3.3.2.1   Disease of the mind   Disease of the mind is a legal term and not a medical term. The law is concerned with the question whether the accused is to be held legally responsible for his acts. This depends on his mental state and its cause complying with legally defined criteria. The issue for the court is whether the accused had a defect of reason arising from a disease of the mind. The problem, however, is that psychiatrists prefer to use terms such as psychoneurosis and psychosis rather than disease of the mind. The former comprises anxiety states, obsessional states and hysteria; these conditions would not generally meet the criteria for insanity. Most psychoses, on the other hand, satisfy the legal criteria of insanity. Psychoses may be divided into two categories, organic or functional. Organic psychoses are due to a physical cause such as poisoning of the brain by alcohol or drugs, infections such as syphilis, degeneration of the brain due to poor blood supply or tumours, or brain diseases, including senile dementia, atherosclerosis and chorea. Functional psychoses include conditions such as schizophrenia, paranoia, psychopathic personality traits and manic depression. There are other conditions which may cause a malfunctioning of the mind which, while they may have an organic cause, are not neuroses or psychoses, for example, epilepsy or hyperglycaemia arising from diabetes. The problem for the medical witness is whether he should speak the language of the psychiatrist or convert these terms into what he believes they equate to in the legal terminology. This may not be considered a major problem in respect of the questions whether the accused was suffering from a defect of reason due to a disease of the mind as these are for the judge to decide. The danger is there, however, in relation to the medical evidence regarding the effects of such a disease on the accused's mental faculties, as the jury ultimately have to decide if the other criteria of the defence of insanity have been satisfied. If the psychiatrist seeks to translate medical terms into legal terms there is a danger that he will subvert the role of the jury by answering questions which are for their consideration, whereas, if he does not and simply confines himself to the role of the expert witness giving evidence for the jury's evaluation, there is a danger that he will mystify the jury.

This does not answer the question, however, of what constitutes a disease of the mind. In *Kemp* [1957] 1 QB 399, it was argued that 'disease of the mind' meant that there had to be an organic disease of the brain which had caused degeneration of the brain. The accused was charged with causing grievous bodily harm having made a motiveless attack on his wife with a hammer. He suffered from arteriosclerosis which affected the flow of blood in his brain and had caused a temporary loss of consciousness during which the attack was made. He did not suffer from general mental trouble nor had his brain degenerated. Devlin J rejected the arguments of the defence that this was simply a case of automatism and ruled that the defence being raised was one of insanity, stating (at p. 407):

> The law is not concerned with the brain but with the mind, in the sense that 'mind' is ordinarily used, the mental faculties of reason, memory and understanding. If one read for 'disease of the mind' 'disease of the brain', it would follow that in many cases pleas of insanity would not be established because it could not be proved that the brain had been affected in any way, either by degeneration of the cells or in any other way. In my judgment the condition of the brain is irrelevant and so is the question whether the condition of the mind is curable or incurable, transitory or permanent.

Devlin J went on to explain that the words 'disease of the mind' were included in the *M'Naghten* Rules to limit the words 'defect of reason' which were not intended to apply to defects of reason 'caused simply by brutish stupidity without rational power'. This sought to distinguish the untrained mind from the diseased mind.

In *Bratty* Devlin J's dicta in *Kemp* received the approval of Lord Denning in the House of Lords who added a further gloss, stating (at p. 412):

> any mental disorder which has manifested itself in violence and is prone to recur is a disease of the mind. At any rate it is the sort of disease for which a person should be detained in hospital rather than be given an unqualified acquittal.

This represents a particularly ill-considered dictum. Diseases of the mind may manifest themselves in other ways which do not involve violence, for example, pyromania or kleptomania. In addition there are conditions which manifest themselves in violence which do not fall within the definition of disease of the mind as the case of *Quick* [1973] QB 910 discloses. The appellant was a diabetic who committed an assault when suffering from hypoglycaemia. This condition was caused by taking insulin and failing to eat which gave rise to a deficiency of blood sugar causing the appellant to be unaware of what he was doing. The trial judge ruled that his defence of automatism amounted to a plea of insanity, whereupon he pleaded guilty to the charge rather than face the prospect of the jury returning the special verdict. The Court of Appeal quashed his conviction ruling that the cause of his condition was not his diabetes but his use of insulin which was an external factor and his defence of automatism should have been left to the jury. Lawton LJ interpreted the phrase 'disease of the mind' to mean a 'malfunctioning of the mind caused by disease' whereas a 'malfunctioning of the mind of transitory effect caused by some external factor such as violence, drugs including anaesthetics, alcohol and hypnotic influences cannot fairly be said to be due to disease.' The use of the criterion of internal/external causes to distinguish insanity from automatism is fatuous. Hypoglycaemic coma may be caused by overproduction of insulin by the pancreas. As this is an internal cause, it would be classed as a disease and result in a finding of insanity should the sufferer commit an offence while in hypoglycaemic coma due to an overactive pancreas. Is the person suffering from an overactive pancreas more deserving of the label 'criminally insane' than the diabetic who does not control his food and insulin intake? The current state of the law suggests an affirmative answer. To say that the law is an ass is to engage in understatement.

In *Sullivan* [1984] AC 156 the House of Lords had to grapple with the problem of the dividing line between insanity and automatism. The appellant had pleaded guilty to assault occasioning actual bodily harm after the trial judge ruled that his defence of automatism to a charge of inflicting grievous bodily harm was really a defence of insanity. The appellant who had attacked a friend and kicked him about the head and body, claimed that the attack was committed in the course of an epileptic seizure and he was not aware of doing it. Lord Diplock expressed his approval of Devlin J's dictum in *Kemp* and went on to state (at p. 172):

If the effect of a disease is to impair [the faculties of reason, memory and understanding] so severely as to have either of the consequences referred to in the latter part of the rules, it matters not whether the aetiology of the impairment is organic, as in epilepsy, or functional, or whether the impairment itself is permanent or is transient and intermittent, provided that it subsisted at the time of the commission of the act.

Lord Diplock did go on to state that automatism would be available as a defence where temporary impairment resulted from an external physical factor although he did not consider it necessary to examine in detail the possible causes of automatism.

Although Sullivan's attack on his friend appeared to be purposive, although he was unconscious, a result of the decision in the case is that an epileptic who involuntarily connects with someone while his arms and legs are thrashing about in the course of a seizure is insane for the purposes of criminal liability whereas a diabetic in hypoglycaemic coma, caused by a low blood-sugar level, is not. By contrast, however, a diabetic in hyperglycaemic coma, caused by a high blood-sugar level, is insane. This is the conclusion of the Court of Appeal in *Hennessy* [1989] 2 All ER 9. D, a diabetic, was charged with taking a conveyance without authority and driving whilst disqualified. He raised the defence of automatism claiming that due to stress, anxiety and depression he had failed to take his insulin which resulted in a hyperglycaemic coma. The trial judge ruled that this was in reality a defence of insanity as the condition was due to the disease of diabetes. D changed his plea to guilty and appealed. The Court of Appeal took the view that in *Sullivan* Lord Diplock had sought to distinguish between external factors giving rise to a malfunction of the mind and inherent causes giving rise to such a malfunction. The Court upheld the trial judge's ruling that diabetes constituted a disease of the mind as it was an inherent defect. Counsel for D argued further that the stress, anxiety and depression from which he was suffering were external factors. The Court held, however, that while they may be the result of the operation of external factors, (*per* Lord Lane CJ, at p. 14):

> they are not separately or together external factors of the kind capable in law of causing or contributing to a state of automatism. They constitute a state of mind which is prone to recur. They lack the feature of novelty or accident, which is the basis of the distinction drawn by Lord Diplock in *R v Sullivan*.

In *Quick* Lawton LJ had said that 'the law should not give the words "defect of reason from disease of the mind" a meaning which would be regarded with incredulity outside the court.' It is difficult to imagine that the ordinary person would not regard these decisions with incredulity. Is it desirable that epileptics face the prospect of being labelled criminally insane if they are unfortunate enough to suffer a seizure during the course of which they thrash around and involuntarily hit or kick a third party? Society may require protection from epileptics who, in the course of an epileptic seizure, engage in purposive conduct of a violent or dangerous nature (as appeared to be the case in *Bratty*) but no such distinction has been drawn by the courts. Is the distinction between a diabetic in hyperglycaemic coma and one in hypoglycaemic coma so marked in its dangers, consequences and risk of recurrence that the former should be found insane while the latter goes free? In the cases of *Quick* and *Hennessy* the conduct involved appeared to be purposive rather than convulsive but the outcome in each case differed. The fact that the judges in *Quick*, *Sullivan* and *Hennessy* accepted guilty pleas from the defendants tends to indicate dissatisfaction with the operation of the insanity defence.

This judicial dissatisfaction spilled over into open rebellion in Kingston Crown Court on September 10 1990 (see *The Independent*, September 11 1990). In the case of *McFarlane* Judge Bertram Wakely gave a direction to the jury in open and express defiance of the decision of the House of Lords in *Sullivan*. D was charged with inflicting actual bodily harm on a policeman during a search of her home for allegedly stolen property. D had suffered from epilepsy for fourteen years. The defence case was that she struck the officer during an epileptic fit brought on by the strain of a dawn raid by several officers. Rather than directing the jury on the special verdict, Judge Wakely directed them that if they believed that D might have been having an epileptic fit they should return a verdict of not guilty. The jury acquitted D. While Judge Wakely may not have applied the law (as authoritatively declared in *Sullivan*) his judgment was an application of the spirit of Lawton LJ's dictum in *Quick*. One can only hope that one day both law and spirit will be in step!

5.3.3.2.2 *Defect of reason*

If the defence of insanity is to succeed, the disease of the mind must give rise to a defect of reason. This appears to mean that the powers of reasoning must be impaired. If the accused simply fails, because of confusion or absent-mindedness, to use the powers of reasoning which he has, this will not bring him within the *M'Naghten* Rules. In *Clarke* [1972] 1 All ER 219, D was charged with the theft of items from a supermarket. Her defence was that she had no intention of stealing but had absent-mindedly placed the items in her shopping basket. She called medical evidence to establish that her absent-mindedness was due to a combination of depression and diabetes. The trial judge ruled that this was a defence of insanity, whereupon she pleaded guilty and appealed. The Court of Appeal quashed the conviction as D was not someone deprived of her powers of reasoning but simply someone who was momentarily absent-minded or confused who thus lacked the necessary *mens rea* for the offence.

If the accused's defect of reason is to be effective in establishing the defence of insanity, it must affect his legal responsibility for his conduct in one of the two ways specified in the *M'Naghten* Rules. Thus he must prove that either he did not know the nature and quality of his act or, if he did know this, he did not know he was doing what was wrong.

5.3.3.2.3   Nature and quality of the act   In *Codere* (1916) 12 Cr App R 21, it was argued that the word 'nature' referred to the physical character of the act whereas the word 'quality' referred to its moral character. The Court of Criminal Appeal rejected this contention holding that 'nature and quality' referred only to the physical character of the act. Thus it is necessary for the accused to prove that he did not know what he was doing, or did not appreciate the consequences of his act, or did not appreciate the circumstances in which he was acting. In all of these situations the accused would lack *mens rea* but, because his defect of reason is due to a disease of the mind, he is liable to the special verdict rather than simple acquittal. This limb of the defence will cover the automaton who does an act in a state of impaired consciousness (e.g. *Sullivan*, and *Hennessy*). It will also cover the person who acts under a delusion, for example, he believes he is chopping down a tree when, in fact, it is a person. Similarly it covers the person who cuts off a sleeper's head because 'it would be great fun to see him looking for it when he woke up' (see Stephen, *History of the Criminal Law*, vol II, p. 166); such a person does not understand the consequences of his acts. By contrast if D, suffering from a pathological fear of women, kills V because he believes V is a woman, but V is, in fact, a man in drag, his mistake is immaterial and will not avail him as it does not affect his knowledge that he is killing another person.

5.3.3.2.4   Knowledge that the act is wrong   Under this limb of the Rules there is an implicit admission by the accused that he had the *mens rea* for the offence but that he was not a responsible actor as he did not know that he was doing what was wrong. The law in relation to this limb of the defence is not particularly clear. There are two possibilities: (1) that the accused must prove that he did not know that the act was contrary to the law; or (2) that the accused must prove that he did not know that the act was wrong according to the standard adopted by reasonable people. In *M'Naghten* the suggestion was that if the accused knew the act was wrong, in the sense of being one which he knew he ought not to do, this would be fatal to his defence whether or not he knew the actual law prohibiting it as 'the law is administered upon the principle that everyone must be taken conclusively to know it, without proof that he does know it.' This view was reinforced by *Codere* where the Court stated that 'the

standard to be applied is whether according to the ordinary standard adopted by reasonable men the act was right or wrong.' Thus it appeared that the defence of insanity would fail if the accused knew either that his act was prohibited by the law or that it was regarded as wrong by reasonable people.

Doubt has been cast on this proposition by the case of *Windle* [1952] 2 QB 826. D killed his wife by giving her a fatal dose of aspirin. The wife was certifiably insane and had spoken of committing suicide on many occasions. On giving himself up to the police D said, 'I suppose they will hang me for this'. At his trial for murder, medical evidence was given that D suffered from a form of communicated insanity called *folie a deux*, although the experts on both sides agreed he knew that he was doing an act prohibited by the law. Devlin J withdrew the defence of insanity from the jury and D was convicted. The Court of Criminal Appeal upheld the conviction, Lord Goddard CJ stating *obiter* (at pp. 833-834):

> Courts of law can only distinguish between that which is in accordance with law and that which is contrary to law. . . . The law cannot embark on the question, and it would be an unfortunate thing if it were left to juries to consider whether some particular act was morally right or wrong. The test must be whether it is contrary to law. . . . In the opinion of the court there is no doubt that in the *M'Naghten* Rules 'wrong' means contrary to law and not 'wrong' according to the opinion of one man or of a number of people on the question of whether a particular act might or might not be justified.

This judgment appears to widen the defence as an accused who knew his act was morally wrong may still raise the defence if his contention is that because of his defect of reason he did not know it was legally wrong to do what he did.

This limb of the *M'Naghten* Rules has been subjected to criticism. Glanville Williams, *Textbook of Criminal Law* (2nd edn, 1983) at p. 645, argues that 'unless very benevolently interpreted it adds almost nothing to the other questions.' The Butler Committee, *Report of the Committee on Mentally Abnormal Offenders* (Cmnd. 6244, 1975) stated (at p. 218):

> Knowledge of the law is hardly an appropriate test on which to base ascription of responsibility to the mentally disordered. It is a very narrow ground of exemption since even persons who are grossly disturbed generally know that murder and arson are crimes.

This would suggest that this limb of the defence, if applied strictly, will be of little use. This discussion is academic as in practice it appears that almost half of the special verdicts returned in Mackay's study were based on this ground. His study also revealed that trial courts are effectively ignoring the dicta in the appellate cases and special verdicts are being returned in cases where the accused knew his act to be legally wrong but did it because of delusions which caused him to believe it to be morally right! Mackay concluded (at p. 251):

> In many of these cases there seems to have been little attempt made to distinguish between lack of knowledge of legal wrong . . . and unawareness

of moral wrong. Indeed, the general impression gained from reading the documentation in these cases was that the wrongness issue was being treated in a liberal fashion by all concerned, rather than in the strict manner regularly depicted by legal commentators.

One can only state again that it would be desirable for the law, practice and theory to be in harmony.

5.3.3.2.5 Insane delusions and irresistible impulses   Although the jury acquitted M'Naghten, under the test the judges propounded he would have been convicted. He was suffering from paranoia which gave rise to a morbid delusion that he was being persecuted by 'Tories'. This delusion did not prevent him from knowing that he was killing another person and from knowing that it was wrong. It is an arguable point, however, whether he was a responsible actor deserving of punishment.

The judges dealt expressly with the issue of delusions stating:

> if [the accused] labours under [a] partial delusion only, and is not in other respects insane, we think he must be considered in the same situation as to responsibility as if the facts with respect to which the delusion exists were real. For example, if under the influence of his delusion he supposes another man to be in the act of attempting to take away his life, and he kills that man, as he supposes, in self-defence, he would be exempt from punishment. If his delusion was that the deceased had inflicted a serious injury to his character and fortune, and he killed him in revenge for such supposed injury, he would be liable to punishment.

This does not really add anything to the Rules as this situation is already covered by the test relating to the nature and quality of the act. In the example of self-defence the accused did not appreciate the circumstances in which he was acting and thus did not know the nature and quality of his act. In the second example the accused knows that he is killing a person and there is nothing to suggest that he did not know that this was wrong. The problem is that there are delusions which may call into question the responsibility of the accused for his acts but which do not fall within the Rules. For example, there are many cases where the accused kills his victim because he believes that the victim is possessed by the devil, or because he is in a paranoid state believing that the victim is persecuting him or plotting his death. In all these cases the accused would not fall within the Rules if he knows he is killing another person and that killing is wrong. His delusional state, however, would suggest that he is not a responsible actor deserving of punishment even though society deserves to be protected from him. These cases point to a deficiency of the Rules. In practice, however, this deficiency appears to be overlooked as Mackay cites examples of cases where the special verdict has been returned although the Rules do not appear to have been satisfied.

If the accused understands what he is doing and knows that it is wrong, the fact that he could not resist the impulse to do it will be of no avail. The Privy

Council in *Sodeman* [1936] 2 All ER 1138 ruled that the defence could not be founded on uncontrollable impulse (see also *Kopsch* (1925) 19 Cr App R 50). However, medical evidence that in a particular case irresistible impulse was a sympton of the disease from which an accused was suffering, affecting his ability to know the nature and quality of his act or its wrongness, could be left to the jury (see *A-G for South Australia* v *Brown* [1960] AC 432). Thus irresistible impulse on its own will not found a defence, but it may be used to support the claim that the accused either did not know what he was doing or that it was wrong, where there is medical evidence to that effect. Irresistible impulse is relevant, however, to support a defence of diminished responsibility.

5.3.4 Proposals for reform
The *M'Naghten* Rules have been the subject of persistent criticism by lawyers and doctors on several grounds. Firstly, they do not reflect current psychiatric thinking on mental disorder. The language used in the Rules is that of lawyers and has little congruence to the language of psychiatry. Secondly, the Rules lead to absurd distinctions such as those between diabetics suffering from hypoglycaemia and those suffering from hyperglycaemia. The distinctions do not reflect any substantial difference in the responsibility of such persons for their acts and are doubtless regarded with incredulity by ordinary members of the public. Thirdly, the Rules cover persons who normally would not be liable to civil committal to hospital under the Mental Health Act 1983, such as diabetics, epileptics and sleepwalkers, while failing to cover others who are covered by that Act such as the defendant in *Windle,* those suffering from insane delusions which do not prevent them from knowing what they are doing and those subject to uncontrollable impulses.

These criticisms have led to various calls for reform. The most significant report was that of the Butler Committee (Cmnd 6244, 1975). The Butler proposals form the basis for the mental disorder provisions in the Law Commission's Draft Criminal Code. The Draft Code abandons the language of the *M'Naghten* Rules and uses terms such as 'mental disorder', 'severe mental illness' and 'severe mental handicap' which reflect medical terminology. Clause 34 contains definitions which clarify the conditions which amount to a 'mental disorder' and greatly broaden the range of effects which such conditions must have to merit the return of a mental disorder verdict. The effect will be that those who are not responsible but who are not covered by the *M'Naghten* Rules will be covered under these provisions. Clause 34 of the Draft Code provides:

'mental disorder' means –
    (a)   severe mental illness; or
    (b)   a state of arrested or incomplete development of mind; or
    (c)   a state of automatism . . . which is a feature of a disorder, whether organic or functional and whether continuing or recurring, that may cause a similar state on another occasion; . . .
'severe mental illness' means a mental illness which has one or more of the following characteristics –

(a) lasting impairment of intellectual functions shown by failure of memory, orientation, comprehension and learning capacity;

(b) lasting alteration of mood of such degree as to give rise to delusional appraisal of the defendant's situation, his past or his future, or that of others, or lack of any appraisal;

(c) delusional beliefs, persecutory, jealous or grandiose;

(d) abnormal perceptions associated with delusional misinterpretation of events;

(e) thinking so disordered as to prevent reasonable appraisal of the defendant's situation or reasonable communication with others;

'severe mental handicap' means a state of arrested or incomplete development of mind which includes severe impairment of intelligence and social functioning.

The one possible deficiency in these definitions is that 'severe mental illness' does not cover cases where a characteristic of the illness is uncontrollable impulses. If the charge is murder the accused may plead diminished responsibility, but if the charge is attempted murder or causing grievous bodily harm, this defence is not available and conviction would result.

There are two bases upon which a mental disorder verdict should be returned. Firstly, 'if the defendant is proved to have committed an offence but it is proved on the balance of probabilities (whether by the prosecution or the defendant) that he was at the time suffering from severe mental illness or severe mental handicap' (clause 35(1)). This covers cases where the accused may have formed the *mens rea* for the offence but his mind was so disordered that he was not a responsible actor. It is open to the prosecution, however, to prove that 'the offence was not attributable to the severe mental illness or severe mental handicap' (clause 35(1)). Secondly, clause 36 provides:

A mental disorder verdict shall be returned if –

(a) the defendant is acquitted of an offence only because, by reason of evidence of mental disorder or a combination of mental disorder and intoxication, it is found that he acted or may have acted in a state of automatism, or without the fault required for the offence, or believing that an exempting circumstance existed; and

(b) it is proved on the balance of probabilities (whether by the prosecution or by the defendant) that he was suffering from mental disorder at the time of the act.

This provision covers situations where the accused's mental disorder caused him to act as an automaton or it prevented him from knowing what he was doing so that he did not form the *mens rea* required for the offence, or it caused him to believe in a circumstance of defence as, for example, where under a delusional belief that he is under attack he kills in self-defence. In these three circumstances the definitional elements of the offence would not have been proved, or a defence disproved, and the accused would be entitled to an acquittal. The clause provides that, where mental disorder is the reason for the acquittal, a mental disorder verdict should be returned. This recognises that the accused was not a responsible actor but provides protection for the public in the form of the order of disposal which the court may make. Thus diabetics or epileptics will be liable to a mental disorder verdict if their condition reduces them to a state of automatism, but this verdict avoids the stigmatising effect of a finding of insanity and gives the judge discretion in choosing a disposal appropriate to the accused's case.

5.4 AUTOMATISM

5.4.1 Defining automatism

It was stated in para. 2.4.1 *ante* that where the *actus reus* of an offence requires conduct on the part of the accused, whether an act or omission, liability will only accrue where the conduct is willed. Where a person acts while in a state of unconsciousness or impaired consciousness this is referred to as automatism. In such a condition the movements of a person's body or limbs are involuntary (see *Watmore* v *Jenkins* [1962] 2 QB 572). In *Bratty* v *A-G for Northern Ireland* [1963] AC 386, 409, Lord Denning defined an involuntary act or automatism as:

> an act which is done by the muscles without any control by the mind, such as a spasm, a reflex action or a convulsion; or an act done by a person who is not conscious of what he is doing, such as an act done whilst suffering from concussion or whilst sleep-walking.

What is required is that the accused's mind is not controlling his limbs at all; it is not sufficient that the accused's mind is acting imperfectly if he is still reacting to stimuli and controlling his limbs in a purposive way (see *Broome* v *Perkins* [1987] Crim LR 271; *Roberts* v *Ramsbottom* [1980] 1 All ER 7). In *Isitt* (1978) 67 Cr App R 44, D was involved in a road accident and it appeared that he was drunk. He returned to his van and drove off at speed with a police car in pursuit. D evaded the pursuing vehicle, evaded a police road block and finally came to a halt when he drove up a cul-de-sac only to run off through fields. When finally interviewed at home he claimed he could not remember the incident and, at his trial for dangerous driving, he called psychiatric evidence to the effect that the original accident had caused hysterical fugue leading to memory loss. It was claimed that his subconscious mind had taken over so that he did not appreciate what he was doing when he was driving, and although he knew he was trying to get away from the scene of an accident, he was totally unaware of legal restrictions and moral concern. He was convicted and the Court of Appeal dismissed his appeal, Lawton LJ stating (at p. 48):

> It is a matter of human experience that the mind does not always operate in top gear. There may be some difficulty in functioning. If the difficulty does not amount in law to either insanity or automatism, is the accused entitled to say 'I am not guilty because my mind was not working in top gear'? In our judgment he is not. . . .

In our judgment on the psychiatrist's evidence, it is clear that he was accepting that the appellant's mind was working to some extent. The driving was purposeful driving, which was to get away from the scene of the accident. It may well be that, because of panic or stress or alcohol, the appellant's mind was shut to the moral inhibitions which control the lives of most of us. But the fact that his moral inhibitions were not working properly, in our judgment, does not mean that the mind was not working at all.

It is an essential requirement of criminal liability that the accused's acts or omissions which constitute the *actus reus* of the offence were voluntary (see *Bratty*, *per* Lord Denning at p. 409). Thus, if the prosecution cannot prove beyond reasonable doubt that the accused's conduct was voluntary, he will be acquitted. Mental capacity, however, is presumed and the prosecution will only be required to negative an assertion of automatism where the defence have laid a proper evidential foundation for that assertion (*Bratty*). The accused's own evidence will rarely be sufficient and should be supported by medical evidence which points to the cause of the mental incapacity (*Bratty*). Where the cause of the automatism is a disease of the mind within the *M'Naghten* Rules, the acquittal will take the form of the special verdict of not guilty by reason of insanity resulting in committal to a mental hospital. It is therefore crucial to determine which causes of automatism will lead to an outright acquittal and which will lead to a finding of insanity.

5.4.2 The causes of automatism
Where the accused's state of impaired consciousness is due to self-induced intoxication by drink or drugs this will not avail him if the crime with which he is charged is one of 'basic intent', although it may negative *mens rea* for a crime of 'specific intent' (see 5.6.3 *post*). The distinction between automatism due to a disease of the mind and that due to other causes is a very important one. In *Bratty*, D was charged with murder having strangled a girl. He raised three defences: automatism, lack of intent for murder and insanity. The medical evidence pointed to the attack occurring in the course of a psychomotor epileptic seizure. In such a condition the sufferer may perform complicated acts of a purposive, as opposed to convulsive, kind while in an unconscious or somnambulist state. The trial judge ruled that the defence case was one of insanity as the medical evidence pointed to the accused's automatous condition being due to a disease of the mind, and refused to leave the other two defences to the jury. The jury rejected the defence of insanity and convicted. This conviction was upheld by both the Court of Appeal and the House of Lords. Lord Denning accepted that the 'major mental diseases, which doctors call psychoses . . . are clearly diseases of the mind.' To these he added 'any mental disorder which has manifested itself in violence and is prone to recur'. This hardly provided a useful guide for distinguishing automatism from insanity. The distinction which emerges from subsequent cases centres on classifying causes as being either internal or external. In *Quick* [1973] QB 910, Lawton LJ, seeking to define 'disease of the mind' stated (at p. 922):

the fundamental concept is a malfunctioning of the mind caused by disease. A malfunctioning of the mind of transitory effect caused by the application to the body of some external factor such as violence, drugs including anaesthetics, alcohol and hypnotic influences cannot fairly be said to be due to disease.

In *Sullivan* Lord Diplock implicitly accepted the distinction between internal and external causes. A verdict of not guilty would thus be acceptable in 'cases where temporary impairment . . . results from some external physical factor such as a blow on the head causing concussion or the administration of an anaesthetic for therapeutic purposes.' It would appear, therefore, that automatism will not result in a finding of insanity where the cause is external and physical such as concussion resulting from a blow to the head, or impaired consciousness resulting from the administration of drugs (e.g. insulin leading to hypoglycaemia) or anaesthetics. Stress, anxiety or depression which lead to impaired consciousness are not themselves external physical factors (see *Hennessy* [1989] 2 All ER 9), but where they are due to an external physical factor and they lead to impaired consciousness, automatism may be successfully pleaded (see *R* v *T* [1990] Crim LR 256). In the latter case D was charged with robbery and causing actual bodily harm. In her defence she claimed she was acting as an automaton as a result of being raped three days prior to the alleged offences. Medical evidence supported her claim to being raped and a psychiatrist diagnosed that she was suffering from Post Traumatic Stress Disorder which brought about a dissociative state such that the offences had been committed during a psychogenic fugue and she was not acting with a conscious mind or will. Southan J, at Snaresbrook Crown Court, held that the issue of automatism should be allowed to go to the jury as the rape was an external factor and Post Traumatic Stress was not a disease of the mind. In *Rabey* (1977) 37 CCC (2d) 461, where the accused sought to plead automatism based on a dissociative state caused by the psychological blow of rejection by a girl with whom he had become infatuated, the Supreme Court of Canada held that 'the ordinary stresses and disappointments of life which are the common lot of mankind do not constitute an external cause'. The court was of the opinion that the impact of this ordinary event on the accused was primarily due to his psychological or emotional make-up. Rape can hardly be considered one of the 'ordinary stresses or disappointments of life'. Southan J considered that 'such an incident could have an appalling effect on any young woman, however well-balanced normally'. The case is consequently easily distinguishable from *Rabey*.

While the distinction between internal and external causes may appear conceptually simple it has not always been strictly applied. The condition which causes a problem for the courts is that of somnambulism. There are numerous examples of people engaging in purposive conduct while apparently asleep who awake either remembering nothing at all or recalling the events as a dream. If an accused performs an act while asleep the cause for such unconscious conduct would appear to be internal. If, in response to a charge, he pleaded automatism based on somnambulism, the outcome should be a ruling that this was a defence of insanity. However, there are cases where such pleas have been accepted as simple automatism, as in *Lillienfield, The Times,* October 17, 1985. In this case, the Crown Court treated as automatism the actions of the accused who, in a state of somnambulism, had stabbed a friend twenty times. In *Bratty* Lord Denning blithely placed acts done while sleep-walking in the same category as those done while concussed. He cited with approval the dictum of Stephen J in *Tolson* (1889) 23 QBD 168, 187:

> Can anyone doubt that a man who, though he might be perfectly sane, committed what would otherwise be a crime in a state of somnambulism, would be entitled to be acquitted? And why is this. Simply because he would not know what he was doing.'

The fatal flaw in this line of reasoning, however, is the assumption that because, in common parlance, such a person would not be described as insane, the law will treat him similarly. The same questions asked by Stephen J could be asked in respect of the diabetic in hyperglycaemic coma (*Hennessy*) and the epileptic (*Sullivan*); the law, however, regards these people as insane and the case of the sleep-walker is indistinguishable. The Court of Appeal has recently come to this conclusion in *Burgess* [1991] 2 QB 92. D pleaded automatism due to sleep-walking in response to a charge of wounding with intent. The trial judge ruled that this was a case of insane automatism. On appeal against the jury's finding that D was not guilty by reason of insanity, the Court of Appeal upheld the trial judge's ruling; D's automatism was due to an internal cause.

5.4.3 Self-induced automatism.
Automatism is self-induced where it results from something which the accused has done or failed to do. The most frequent example of self-induced automatism is intoxication arising from the voluntary ingestion of alcohol or proscribed drugs. The effect of intoxication on criminal liability is discussed in detail below (see 5.6 *post*). For present purposes it is sufficient to state that self-induced intoxication is not a defence to offences of basic intent, although it may be relevant where the accused is charged with an offence of specific intent, as evidence of intoxication may help the accused to create a doubt as to whether he had formed the intent necessary to be convicted of the offence. Where automatism is due to some cause other than intoxication by alcohol or proscribed drugs, the accused cannot be convicted of an offence of specific intent and it may provide a defence to crimes of basic intent (*Bailey* [1983] 1 WLR 760). In *Bailey*, D raised automatism as his defence to charges under ss. 18 and 20 of the Offences Against the Person Act 1861 of unlawful wounding and wounding with intent. D was a diabetic and claimed he had failed to take sufficient food after taking insulin which caused a hypoglycaemic coma in the course of which he committed the offence. The jury convicted D of the s. 18 offence on the direction from the recorder that self-induced automatism was no defence to offences of specific or basic intent. The Court of Appeal ruled that the recorder's direction was clearly wrong in respect of the s. 18 offence which was one of specific intent. They also held that self-induced

automatism, other than due to intoxication by alcohol or drugs, may provide a defence to crimes of basic intent. Griffiths LJ stated (at p. 765):

> The question in each case will be whether the prosecution have proved the necessary element of recklessness. In cases of assault, if the accused knows that his actions or inaction are likely to make him aggressive, unpredictable or uncontrolled with the result that he may cause some injury to others and he persists in the action or takes no remedial action when he knows it is required, it will be open to the jury to find that he was reckless.

The Court based its ruling on the view that there was an absence of common knowledge amongst diabetics of the possible effects of failure to take food after insulin, whereas it is common knowledge that those who become intoxicated by alcohol or drugs may become aggressive or do dangerous or unpredictable things. If, however, a diabetic did appreciate the risk of becoming aggressive, unpredictable or uncontrollable due to a failure to take food after taking insulin and he deliberately ran that risk, this would amount to recklessness and lead to liability for any offence of basic intent which he committed in that state.

5.5 DIMINISHED RESPONSIBILITY

5.5.1 Operation of the defence

The defence of diminished responsibility is not a general defence; it may only be pleaded in defence to a charge of murder. Its effect, if successfully raised, is in the nature of a partial excuse; the accused is acquitted of murder but is convicted of manslaughter. On a conviction of manslaughter the judge has discretion when sentencing the accused whereas, on conviction for murder, the mandatory sentence is life imprisonment. In sentencing for manslaughter, the judge may reflect in the sentence imposed the degree to which he considers the accused's responsibility for his act was impaired by his mental condition. A defence of diminished responsibility is not required for other offences as, apart from murder, the judge always has discretion as to sentence. The official statistics reveal that between a third and three-fifths of those convicted of manslaughter due to diminished responsibility receive hospital orders under s. 37 of the Mental Health Act 1983, and the majority of these have a restriction order under s. 41 attached. Of the remainder, the sentences range from probation and suspended sentences to various terms of imprisonment. Between the years 1980 and 1990 about 15 per cent of those convicted received life sentences (see *Criminal Statistics: England and Wales* 1990, Cm 1935, 1992). On average, in the period 1980 to 1990 there were about eighty convictions per year of manslaughter due to diminished responsibility. By contrast, over the same period, there were only eight verdicts in total of not guilty by reason of insanity on indictments for murder. The defence has all but replaced the insanity defence on a charge of murder where the accused was suffering from a mental incapacity. The defence covers all cases which would fall within the *M'Naghten* Rules and many other conditions which these do not cover.

The defence was introduced in response to the Royal Commission on Capital Punishment (Cmnd 8932, 1949-1953), which had argued for an expanded insanity defence. The Government accepted that the defence of insanity was limited and that injustices could occur in murder cases but considered that an expanded defence of insanity would cause major difficulties. The defence was created by s. 2 of the Homicide Act 1957. As with insanity, the accused bears the burden of proving the defence (s. 2(2)) on a balance of probabilities (*Dunbar* [1958] 1 QB 1). In practice the accused is rarely put to his proof as a plea of guilty of manslaughter is accepted in about 80 per cent of the cases in which the defence of diminished responsibility is raised (see S. Dell, 'Diminished responsibility reconsidered' [1982] Crim LR 809). In *Vinagre* (1979) 69 Cr App R 104, the Court of Appeal stated that pleas to manslaughter on the grounds of diminished responsibility should only be accepted when there is clear evidence of mental imbalance. The defence will generally be put to their proof where there is disagreement between the psychiatric reports or where these reports do not wholeheartedly support the defence. If the case goes to trial there is about a 60 per cent chance of conviction of murder (see S. Dell, *Murder into Manslaughter* (1984)). Where the accused raises the defence of diminished responsibility, and the prosecution have evidence that he is insane, it may adduce or elicit evidence tending to prove this (see s. 6 of the Criminal Procedure (Insanity) Act 1964), but this power would appear to be rarely used. Section 6 also allows for the converse situation; the prosecution may, where the accused pleads insanity, contend that he was suffering from diminished responsibility. The trial judge has no power to raise the issue of diminished responsibility if the defence do not do so, but if he detects evidence of diminished responsibility he may point this out to defence counsel and leave it so that the defence can decide whether to raise this issue and seek to prove it before the jury (see *Campbell* (1987) 84 Cr App R 255).

5.5.2 Nature of the defence
Section 2 of the Homicide Act 1957 provides:

(1)   Where a person kills or is party to the killing of another, he shall not be convicted of murder if he was suffering from such abnormality of mind (whether arising from a condition of arrested or retarded development of mind or any inherent causes or induced by disease or injury) as substantially impaired his mental responsibility for his acts and omissions in doing or being a party to the killing.

There are three elements to the defence which will be examined in turn.
Medical evidence is crucial to the success of the defence (see *Dix* (1981) 74 Cr App R 306) and a jury may not return a verdict of manslaughter on the ground of diminished responsibility unless there is medical evidence of an abnormality of mind arising from one of the specified causes. While the decision is ultimately for the jury, they must act on the evidence and if the medical evidence supporting a finding of diminished responsibility is unchallenged, and there is nothing in the facts or circumstances to cast doubt on it,

they must accept it (see *Matheson* (1958) 42 Cr App R 145; *Bailey* (1977) 66 Cr App R 31n).

5.5.2.1 Abnormality of mind It must be proved that the accused was suffering from an abnormality of mind at the material time. This is a question for the jury but medical evidence is important. The jury should weigh this up with all the other evidence 'including acts or statements of the accused and his demeanour' (see *Byrne* [1960] 2 QB 396). In *Byrne* Lord Parker CJ defined 'abnormality of mind' (at p. 403) as:

a state of mind so different from that of ordinary human beings that the reasonable man would term it abnormal. It appears to us to be wide enough to cover the mind's activities in all its aspects, not only the perception of physical acts and matters, and the ability to form a rational judgment as to whether an act is right or wrong, but also the ability to exercise will-power to control physical acts in accordance with that rational judgment.

Byrne was a sexual psychopath who strangled a young woman and then mutilated her body. According to the medical evidence he suffered from violent perverted sexual desires which he found difficult, if not impossible, to control, and he had done the killing while under the influence of his perverted sexual desires. The trial judge had directed the jury that without more those facts would not bring the case within s. 2. The Court of Criminal Appeal quashed the conviction for murder and substituted one of manslaughter. Thus an inability or difficulty to control impulses could amount to an abnormality of mind.

In *Byrne*, the medical witnesses had described his condition as amounting to 'partial insanity'. The Court approved this description and an alternative one of 'being on the borderline of insanity'. Such phrases have been used subsequently to direct juries. They inevitably harbour the risk of confusion with the *M'Naghten* Rules definition of insanity. In *Seers* (1984) 79 Cr App R 261, D was convicted of the murder of his wife although there was medical evidence that he was suffering from chronic reactive depression which constituted an abnormality of mind. The defence psychiatrists gave evidence that this was of such a degree as to substantially impair his responsibility whereas the prosecution disputed the severity of his condition. In directing the jury, the judge stated the test as being whether in popular language he was partially insane or on the borderline of insanity. The Court of Appeal quashed his conviction and substituted one of manslaughter holding that the judge should have given a direction in accordance with the substance of the direction in *Byrne* avoiding such concepts as partial insanity. While the use of terms such as partial insanity may be helpful in some cases, there are cases in which the abnormality of mind relied on could not be said to be related to any of the generally recognised types of insanity (see also *Rose* v *The Queen* [1961] AC 496). Thus a depressive illness may found a defence of diminished responsibility although no one would describe the sufferer as being partially insane.

5.5.2.2 Specified causes Unless the abnormality of mind from which the accused is alleged to suffer is shown to arise from one of the causes specified in the parenthesis in s. 2(1), the defence will fail (see *King* [1965] 1 QB 443 at 450). The aetiology of the abnormality of mind is a matter to be determined by medical evidence (*Byrne*). There is little guidance, however, on what is meant by the causes specified in the parenthesis. They were meant to rule out emotions such as hatred, rage or jealousy and external factors such as alcohol or drugs. There are cases, however, where jealousy (see *Miller, The Times,* May 16, 1972; *Asher, The Times,* June 9, 1981) and rage (see *Coles* (1980) 144 JPN 528) have resulted in a s. 2 verdict. Intoxication will not support a verdict but alcoholism may give rise to an abnormality of mind arising from 'disease or injury' if it is proved that the brain had been injured by intoxicants so that there was gross impairment of judgment and emotional responses, or if the drinking was involuntary, arising from a craving for drink which the accused could not resist (see *Tandy* (1988) 87 Cr App R 45; *Inseal* [1992] Crim LR 35). Where the evidence suggests more than one cause for the abnormality of the mind, one of which is intoxication (or some other cause not specified in s. 2), the judge should direct the jury to ignore the effect of the inadmissible causes and consider whether the effect of the admissible cause or causes was an abnormality of the mind such as to substantially impair the accused's mental responsibility (*Fenton* (1975) 61 Cr App R 261; *Gittens* [1984] QB 698). In *Atkinson* [1985] Crim LR 314, the Court of Appeal approved the following direction to juries in such cases:

Have the defence satisfied you on the balance of probabilities – that if the defendant had not taken drink – (i) he would have killed as he in fact did? And (ii) he would have been under diminished responsibility when he did so?

This discretion was approved in *Egan* [1993] Crim LR 131. Juries may as well be asked to predict the future such is the speculative and hypothetical nature of these questions.

The result of the uncertainty as to the meaning of the parenthesis is that psychiatrists vary in their interpretation of the section, with some being more willing than others to use the section in a creative and expansive way. This leads E. Griew, 'The future of diminished responsibility' [1988] Crim LR 75, to conclude (at p. 79) that 'There can be little doubt that the fate of some people charged with murder since 1957 has turned on the qualities of robustness and sophistication shown by those professionally involved in their cases.'

5.5.2.3 Substantially impaired mental responsibility It should be noted that the term 'diminished responsibility' is not used in the s. 2; it appears in the marginal note. Section 2 is hardly a paradigm of legislative clarity as it appears to conflate two ideas, namely, those of impaired capacity and reduced liability. If the accused is to be convicted only of manslaughter rather than murder it is because his impaired capacity diminishes his moral culpability for his act. Griew explains the meaning of s. 2 as follows (at p. 82):

the defendant had an abnormality of mind (of appropriate origin). This had a substantial effect upon one or more relevant functions or capacities (of perception, understanding, judgment, feeling, control). In the context of the case this justifies the view that his culpability is substantially reduced. His liability is on that account to be diminished. More shortly: his abnormality of mind is of such consequence in the context of this offence that his legal liability for it ought to be reduced.

The question ultimately resolves itself into a moral one for the jury: whether they think that the accused deserves to be convicted of murder or manslaughter. This view is supported by Her Majesty's judges who, in evidence to the Butler Committee (see Cmnd 6244, 1975), described the operation of the defence as follows (at para. 19.4):

if the jury think . . . that the defendant has shown recognisably abnormal mental symptoms and that in all the circumstances it would not be right to regard his act as murder in the ordinary sense, it is open to them to bring in a verdict of manslaughter.

The jury's response, however, may vary greatly depending on the extent of their sympathy for the accused and the nature of his offence. Thus manslaughter verdicts may be returned on the basis of very little evidence of abnormality, such as in cases of reactive depression or hysterical dissociation where a person kills in response to extreme anxiety, grief or stress (often in the context of a 'mercy-killing'), whereas horrific killings by someone whom all the pysychiatrists agreed suffered from a severe abnormality of the mind (paranoid schizophrenia) amounting to diminished responsibility, may result in a conviction of murder, as occurred in the case of Peter Sutcliffe (the 'Yorkshire Ripper'). This leads Glanville Williams to conclude, in *Textbook of Criminal Law* (1983) at p. 693, that:

the defence . . . is interpreted in accordance with the morality of the case rather than as an application of psychiatric concepts. Where sympathy is evoked . . . it seems to be dissolving into what is virtually the equivalent of a mitigating circumstance.

After the jury have given their view on the culpability of the accused by returning a s. 2 verdict, the judge can express his in the nature of the sentence he imposes.

The crucial question in a case where diminished responsibility is raised in defence, is whether the abnormality was such as to substantially impair the accused's mental responsibility for his acts. In *Byrne* the Court of Appeal stated that 'mental responsibility for his acts' pointed to 'a consideration of the extent to which the accused's mind is answerable for his physical acts which must include a consideration of the extent of his ability to exercise will-power to control his physical acts.' This was said to be a question of degree and essentially one for the jury. Lord Parker CJ stated (at p. 403):

Medical evidence is, of course, relevant, but the question involves a decision not merely as to whether there was some impairment of the mental responsibility of the accused but whether such impairment can properly be called 'substantial', a matter upon which juries may quite legitimately differ from doctors.

Thus there is no absolute scientific measure; inability to resist impulses is clearly covered but where there is merely difficulty in resisting impulses, the isssue of substantial impairment will depend on the degree of difficulty.

While the question whether the accused's mental responsibility was substantially impaired is one for the jury to decide, it appears that the medical experts are being asked for their opinions on this question. The borderline between murder and manslaughter should be defined by the law. Section 2 of the Homicide Act 1957 fails to do so but leaves it to the jury to determine this matter as a question of moral culpability. Doctors are no more fitted to the task of determining moral issues than juries are, yet courts accept their opinions on these matters and, indeed, solicit them. In *Campbell* the Court of Appeal concluded that there was no *prima facie* case of diminished responsibility as the psychiatrist 'never even addressed himself in his evidence to the final matter which would have to be proved by the defence in order to establish diminished responsibility, namely that the abnormality was such as substantially to impair the mental responsibility of the appellant for his acts. . . . ' The question of substantial impairment is inappropriate for medical witnesses as it is one of degree and whether it exists depends not only on the medical evidence but on all the evidence of the case relating to the facts and circumstances of the killing (see *Walton* [1977] AC 788). Griew points out, however, that it is common practice for psychiatrists in their reports to state whether the accused's mental responsibility was substantially impaired. He states (at p. 84) that one of the reasons why judges have allowed and even encouraged this is 'the convenience of the expert opinion as a device for stretching the scope of the section – for humanely using it to produce a greater range of exemption from liability for murder than its terms really justify.' The existence of this conspiracy between the medical and legal professions to expand the ambit of s. 2 out of motives of humanity was also noted by the Butler Committee (at para. 19.5). This helps to explain both the practice of accepting pleas of diminished responsibility and why mercy-killings or those performed in conditions of reactive depression or dissociation regularly result in s. 2 convictions.

5.5.3 Proposals for reform
Both the Butler Committee and the Criminal Law Revision Committee *Fourteenth Report: Offences Against the Person* (Cmnd. 7844) recommended that the diminished responsibility defence should be revised. They agreed that s. 2 had created problems for doctors, judges and juries. The section confuses issues of legal responsibility or liability and moral culpability. Doctors may be able to testify as to the accused's mental condition and its likely effects but they should not be required to testify as to legal or moral responsibility. Likewise, juries are asked to determine whether there was an abnormality of mind which

is not a medical term, and then to determine if this affected his moral culpability to such an extent as to reduce his legal liability. These are difficult concepts for any jury and it is not surprising that counsel and judges prefer to settle these matters with a guilty plea wherever possible.

The Butler Committee's preferred solution to all these problems was to abolish the mandatory life sentence for murder and leave it to the judge to reflect the offender's culpability in his sentence. The Criminal Law Revision Committee objected to this approach as murder would then cover a very large range of killings. A verdict of guilty of murder would give the judge little guidance as to where on the scale of gravity any particular murder was placed. In addition, juries might be reluctant to convict offenders of murder if they would previously have been convicted of manslaughter on the grounds of diminished responsibility. The Butler Committee recognised that abolition of the mandatory sentence for murder might not prove acceptable and thus suggested a revised version of the s. 2 defence. This was largely accepted by the CLRC with some amendment. The Law Commission in its Draft Criminal Code largely adopts this revised defence. Clause 56 of the Draft Code provides:

(1) A person who, but for this section, would be guilty of murder is not guilty of murder if, at the time of his act, he is suffering from such mental abnormality as is a substantial enough reason to reduce his offence to manslaughter.

(2) In this section 'mental abnormality' means mental illness, arrested or incomplete development of mind, psychopathic disorder, and any other disorder or disability of mind, except intoxication.

(3) Where a person suffering from mental abnormality is also intoxicated, this section applies only where it would apply if he were not intoxicated.

The first point of significance is that under clause 13(1), unless otherwise provided, where evidence is given of a defence, the burden is on the prosecution to disprove that defence rather than upon the accused to prove it. As clause 56 makes no provision to the contrary, the defence is one which the accused is not required to prove, although there must be some evidence to raise the issue. The defence is founded on the concept of 'mental abnormality' which is given a definition which is the same as that of mental disorder in s. 1(2) of the Mental Health Act 1983. This will be of assistance to psychiatrists in that they will be using terms with which they are familiar. The phrase 'any other disorder or disability of mind' has the potential for unlimited scope; it certainly covers reactive depressions, dissociative states and morbid jealousy (see CLRC, Fourteenth Report, para. 92). Accordingly, conditions which were covered by the very liberal interpretation of s. 2 adopted by the courts will also fall within clause 56. There is no requirement, however, for the mental abnormality to arise from 'specified causes'. This is, perhaps, a recognition of the fact that the parenthesis in s. 2 was of little relevance because many psychiatrists were prepared to give, and courts to accept, a very liberal interpretation of the term 'inherent causes'. Clause 56, therefore, simply codifies the practice which has grown up and legitimises it. If enacted it would have the advantage of removing doubt; some psychiatrists are currently unwilling to adopt a cavalier attitude towards s. 2 and strive assiduously to respect it; this may disadvantage their patients as other psychiatrists are quite prepared to declare that the accused was suffering diminished responsibility due to inherent causes because the informal 'rules of the game' permit them to do so (see Griew at p. 80).

On finding the accused to be suffering from a mental abnormality, the jury should return a manslaughter verdict if they consider that the abnormality 'is a substantial enough reason to reduce his offence to manslaughter'. This provision will involve a major change in practice. Psychiatrists have been prepared to testify that the accused's mental responsibility was substantially impaired and courts have engaged in the pretence that this is an expression of expert opinion which justifies their acceptance of a guilty plea to manslaughter. This pretence will not be possible under the proposed test as only a jury can answer the question whether the mental abnormality is a substantial enough reason to reduce the accused's offence to manslaughter. The psychiatrist may not answer this question; it is therefore going to be of crucial importance that his description of the effects of the diagnosed mental abnormality on the accused's behaviour, in terms of his perceptions, comprehension, rationality and will-power, provides the jury with information which will assist them in determining his mental responsibility. But while the psychiatrist may guide them on the likely effects of the accused's mental abnormality on these matters, it does not give them any guidance on how to answer the ultimate question, which is essentially an ethical and legal one, namely, where the boundary between murder and manslaughter is to be drawn. Ethics dictate the kinds of behaviour which should be prohibited and their respective degrees of gravity, while the law seeks to reflect the conclusions of ethics in the definitions of offences; these should clearly define the behaviour prohibited and differentiate it from other offences. The jury will be given no guidance on these matters: it is their decision which will settle both the ethical and legal issues. Manslaughter, in these terms, is unlawful homicide which the jury determine is not murder. Unlawful homicide will not be murder where the moral culpability of the offender is such that he does not deserve to be convicted of murder. Whether an offender deserves to be convicted of murder or manslaughter is for the jury to determine. If a jury was to ask for guidance (to help them from going round in circles for ever), the judge would be reduced to telling them that it is their problem and they must solve it!

Section 2 operates despite the wording of the section because of the practice which has grown up based on the unspoken understanding between psychiatrists, counsel and judges that the former will be allowed to express 'expert opinion' on the ultimate issue. This practice, and the understanding upon which it is founded, would be replaced by a provision which would be unworkable. Section 2 could have been expressed more clearly; clause 56 is not an improvement. Improvement will not occur so long as juries are left with the task of both defining the law and applying their definition.

5.6 INTOXICATION

5.6.1 Intoxication and responsibility

Intoxication may result from the consumption of alcohol or other drugs. As alcohol is the most widely available intoxicant it is not surprising that most cases in which the issue arises relate to alcohol induced intoxication. The principles which apply, however, are the same whether it is alcohol, amphetamines, barbiturates, hallucinogens or other drugs which cause the intoxication. In an intoxicated state a person's mental powers of perception, reasoning, self-control, judgment and ability to foresee consequences may all be impaired as well as his physical reactions and coordination. In some circumstances, intoxication is the essence of a criminal offence as where, for example, D is found drunk in a public place, or is under the influence of drink or drugs when in charge of a motor vehicle in a public place. Other offences may be committed by D when intoxicated, in which case it is important to determine whether his intoxication is relevant to his criminal liability. Is an accused to be acquitted of a criminal offence because he was, due to his voluntary intoxication, deprived of the capacity to control his conduct or to formulate the *mens rea* required for the offence? A person who is insane or an automaton will be acquitted because he bears no responsiblity for his condition and is not, therefore, responsible for, or culpable in respect of, acts he performed in that condition. By contrast, a voluntarily intoxicated person is responsible for his own impaired condition. If the criminal law treats intoxicated offenders differently from those suffering from other incapacitating conditions this may be justifiable on that basis. If the intoxicated offender is convicted of offences he committed whilst in that condition, conviction and punishment may deter him in future from becoming intoxicated, and hopefully, from re-offending.

5.6.2 The effect of voluntary intoxication on criminal liability

Intoxication is not a defence which may be pleaded in answer to a charge; it does not operate to excuse the accused's conduct. It is no excuse for the accused to say that had he been sober he would never have done as he did (see *DPP* v *Majewski* [1977] AC 443), nor may he raise a plea of automatism based on voluntary intoxication (see *Lipman* [1970] 1 QB 152). The only relevance of intoxication is in respect of the question whether the accused had the *mens rea* required for the offence; he may not have formed the *mens rea* because of his intoxication or he may have acted under a drunken mistake which negates his *mens rea*. If he did form the necessary *mens rea*, however, it matters not that he was intoxicated at the time. If the offence is one of negligence or strict liability intoxication will be irrelevant to the accused's liability. Where the offence is one requiring *mens rea*, however, intoxication is only relevant if the offence is one of 'specific intent' as opposed to one of 'basic intent'.

5.6.3 Offences of specific and basic intent

The law relating to intoxication is essentially the result of policy decisions on the part of the courts. On occasions, however, judges engaged in the pretence that their decisions were, in fact, dictated by principle. Upon closer scrutiny the principles proved to be flawed thereby creating doubt and confusion. The flaws were not obvious when the principles were first articulated but became so as the doctrine of *mens rea* developed in a way which meant that it no longer fitted neatly alongside the principles relating to intoxication. In recent years further developments in both areas have resulted in clarification of the principles although they still do not fit neatly side by side.

The early authorities treated drunkenness as an aggravating factor but during the nineteenth century the rigidity of this rule was gradually relaxed in a piecemeal fashion. As the doctrine of *mens rea* became more refined it was realised by judges that this had implications for criminal liability where reliance was placed on the accused's intoxication. These authorities were considered in *DPP* v *Beard* [1920] AC 479, where the term 'specific intent' was first coined by Lord Birkenhead. D raped a girl and, while doing so suffocated her. The House of Lords restored a conviction for murder on the basis of the 'felony murder rule' (which has since been abolished by s. 1 of the Homicide Act 1957). This rule stated that where a person killed in the course of committing a felony the accused would be convicted of murder without any need to prove malice aforethought. As it was not contested that Beard intended to rape his victim and death ensued from this, his drunkenness was irrelevant as it did not affect his formation of the *mens rea* for rape. In the course of his speech Lord Birkenhead, after examining the authorities, stated (at p. 499):

> these decisions establish that where a specific intent is an essential element in the offence, evidence of a state of drunkenness rendering the accused incapable of forming such an intent should be taken into consideration in order to determine whether he had in fact formed the intent necessary to constitute the particular crime.

It is far from clear what Lord Birkenhead meant by the word 'specific'; most probably he meant nothing more than the *mens rea* required by the particular crime in question. This view finds support in statements Lord Birkenhead made later in his speech to the effect that the general principle was that 'a person cannot be convicted of a crime unless the *mens* was *rea*' and thus 'drunkenness rendering a person incapable of the intent, would be an answer'. Subsequent cases, however, have placed the dicta of Lord Birkenhead in a different light. It is now clear that evidence of drunkenness is relevant to consider whether the accused had the necessary intent; it is not necessary that he be rendered incapable of forming the intent by his drunkenness (see *Pordage* [1975] Crim LR 575; *Sheehan* [1975] 1 WLR 739). This is also consistent with the effect of s. 8 of the Criminal Justice Act 1967 (see 3.2.3.1 *ante*). But this principle has been limited in its ambit by judges who seized on the term 'specific intent' and gave it a specialised meaning which Lord Birkenhead probably never intended. They considered that it would be undesirable if those who reduced themselves into an aggressive, dangerous or unpredictable condition escaped all criminal liability; if they did they would be undeterred from reducing themselves into that condition in the future. Thus after *Beard* judges started to speak of offences of 'specific intent' to which intoxication could be pleaded and those of 'basic intent' to which the question of intoxication was irrelevant. Lord Birkenhead had never mentioned the term 'basic intent' and thus had not sought to create any such distinction between offences. He had specifically referred to unlawful homicide stating that if intoxication rendered the accused incapable of forming the intent to kill or to do grievous bodily harm, he would not be guilty of murder but would be guilty of manslaughter. Lord Birkenhead was not sure what the justification for this was; perhaps principle or perhaps the policy that persons who killed when drunk deserved to be punished for their drunkenness. As the principles relating to 'unlawful act manslaughter' were far from clear at this stage his confusion was understandable; he did not say, however, that manslaughter was an offence of basic intent.

The leading case is now that of *DPP* v *Majewski* [1977] AC 443. D was intoxicated as a result of taking barbiturates, amphetamines and alcohol. In this condition he struck a police officer and was charged with assault occasioning actual bodily harm and assaulting a police officer in the execution of his duty. He sought to rely on his intoxication to establish that he was so intoxicated that he did not form the appropriate *mens rea*. The House of Lords held that intoxication was only relevant where the offence charged was one of specific intent, but where, as in the case of assault, the offence was one of basic intent intoxication substituted for *mens rea*. Thus an accused may be convicted of a basic intent offence even though, as a result of his voluntary intoxication, he did not have the *mens rea* normally required to be proved, and even if his intoxication rendered him an automaton. Lord Elwyn Jones LC described this as a substantive rule of the common law unaffected by s. 8 of the Criminal Justice Act 1967. He explained how intoxication operated in an offence of basic intent as follows (at pp. 474-475):

If a man of his own volition takes a substance which causes him to cast off the restraints of reason and conscience, no wrong is done to him by holding him answerable criminally for any injury he may do while in that condition. His course of conduct in reducing himself by drugs and drink to that condition in my view supplies the evidence of *mens rea*, of guilty mind certainly sufficient for crimes of basic intent. It is a reckless course of conduct and recklessness is enough to constitute the necessary *mens rea* in assault cases.

As a statement of principle, this is open to criticism on two grounds. First, a presumption of recklessness conflicts with s. 8 of the Criminal Justice Act 1967, which requires a jury to examine all the evidence before deciding whether the accused did foresee the result which his conduct brought about. Secondly, if becoming intoxicated is reckless, this recklessness arises at a time prior to the commission of the *actus reus* of the offence and thus there is no coincidence of *actus reus* and *mens rea*. In addition, recklessness involves a recognition of the risk which eventuates in the commission of the *actus reus*. At the time the accused becomes intoxicated it is only general or unspecified risks which may exist; there was no suggestion that when Majewski became intoxicated he foresaw the actual risk which eventuated. Thus the recklessness arising from intoxication relates to a time prior to the commission of the *actus reus* and a risk of an unspecified nature unconnected to any specific *actus reus*. If intoxication is to give rise to this irrebuttable presumption of recklessness which will provide the *mens rea* element for offences of basic intent, it can only be supported as a decision based on policy considerations; it is not one which is derived from the principles of the criminal law. Lord Salmon was prepared to admit to this as he stated that the decision was not one which could be supported by logic but was one which accorded with 'justice, ethics and common sense' as it sought to preserve individual liberty, an important aspect of which is the protection of citizens against physical violence.

The problem which remains, however, is how to distinguish crimes of basic intent from those of specific intent. One suggestion was that crimes of specific intent were those of ulterior intent (see 3.2.4 *ante*). Lord Simon recognised a problem with this as murder, an offence universally accepted as being one of specific intent, was not one of ulterior intent. He suggested that the crucial factor is that 'the *mens rea* in a crime of specific intent requires proof of a purposive element'. This suggestion, however, is equally flawed as the *mens rea* of murder does not necessarily involve a purposive element, for example, where the accused intends to cause grievous bodily harm but his victim dies. Rape, which is an offence of basic intent, is one which, by contrast, does involve a purposive element. In Lord Elwyn-Jones' view, the crucial factor in offences of assault, dictating that they were offences of basic intent, was that they could be committed recklessly. Thus, following *Majewski*, there was considerable doubt in relation to the factor which distinguished offences of specific intent from those of basic intent. The only way to be sure was to await a judicial decision in respect of each offence to discover into which category an offence was to be placed.

In *Caldwell* [1982] AC 341, the House of Lords resolved the problem. Lord Diplock stated that *Majewski* is authority for the proposition that 'self-induced intoxication is no defence to a crime in which recklessness is enough to constitute the necessary *mens rea*' (see also *Hardie* [1985] 1 WLR 64). It now appears that the principle is that, if an offence may be committed recklessly, it is one of basic intent whereas, if it is an offence of ulterior intent or an offence where proof of intention alone is required (as in murder), it is an offence of specific intent. Thus offences such as murder, burglary, robbery, wounding or causing grievous bodily harm with intent, and attempt are offences of specific intent whereas offences such as rape, manslaughter, criminal damage, malicious wounding or inflicting grievous bodily harm, and any offence based on assault are offences of basic intent as all these may be committed recklessly.

In cases of offences against the person where the accused successfully pleads intoxication in respect of an offence of specific intent, he will not avoid criminal liability as generally there will be an alternative offence of basic intent of which he may be convicted. For example, if he is charged with murder, he may be convicted of manslaughter; if he is charged with wounding with intent to cause grievous bodily harm contrary to s. 18 of the Offences Against the Person Act 1861, he may be convicted of malicious wounding contrary to s. 20. If, however, he is charged with a property offence of specific intent (e.g. theft), there will generally be no alternative basic intent offence with which he may be charged. In some cases of burglary the accused may have committed criminal damage to gain entry to the premises but many burglaries do not involve any damage.

The effect of the rules relating to voluntary intoxication is that if the accused is charged with an offence of basic intent a plea of intoxication will be fatal as it will relieve the prosecution of the duty of proving *mens rea*. It is still unclear whether the prosecution may seek to prove the accused's intoxication at the outset. There is nothing in the speeches in *Majewski* which would rule this out; as their Lordships treated intoxication as the equivalent of *mens rea* it could be argued that they implicitly accepted the propriety of the prosecution proving it. There is no reason of policy to object to this; if the reason for the intoxication rule is the desire to protect the public, that protection would be effectuated by permitting the prosecution to prove intoxication.

It is worth noting that in cases where '*Caldwell* recklessness' suffices intoxication will only be of relevance where the accused seeks to rely on the lacuna situation; in all other cases he will be reckless in the *Caldwell* sense as he will have failed (because of his intoxication) to give thought to an obvious risk. If he claims that because he was drunk he wrongly concluded there was no risk, he will be liable by an application of the principles in *Majewski*.

5.6.4 Intoxication and defences

If an accused is relying on a defence of duress and claims that he made a mistake because of his intoxicated condition so that, for example, he believed he was under threat when in fact there was no threat, his drunken mistake will not avail him as it will necessarily be unreasonable. Similarly, if the accused seeks to plead provocation in response to a charge of murder he may not rely on his intoxication as a reason for his loss of self-control; he is expected to exercise the self-control of a sober and reasonable person (see *Newell* (1980) 71 Cr App R 331).

Where a defence is one of justification, such as self-defence, a mistaken belief in respect of the circumstances upon which the defence is founded, will not deprive the accused of the right to rely on that defence provided the belief was honestly held; there is no requirement that it also be reasonable (see *Williams (Gladstone)* (1984) 78 Cr App R 276, para. *3.6.1.1.2 ante*). The effect of mistake in such a case is to negate the *mens rea* for the offence as the definition of the offence (whether it be murder, malicious wounding, assault, etc) requires that the act be done *unlawfully*; if the accused believes he is acting in self-defence he does not intend to act *unlawfully*. Thus if D, believing that V is about to kill him, defends himself from the anticipated attack and kills V, he would not be guilty of murder as he did not intend unlawfully to kill or cause grievous bodily harm. If D's mistake was a drunken one, one would expect that he should still be able to rely upon it as the offence of murder is one requiring a specific intent. In *O'Grady* [1987] 3 WLR 321, however, the Court of Appeal took a different view. Lord Lane CJ considered that in such cases there was no difference between offences of basic intent and those of specific intent.

Contradicting his own judgment in *Williams* (although he did not appear to realise this), he stated that the issue of mistake should be considered separately from that of intent. This is, to say the least, a novel idea; it is also fatuous as if a person is mistaken he does not have the requisite intent, mistake and intent being simply two sides of the same coin. In Lord Lane's view, however, where the jury are satisfied that the defendant was mistaken in his belief that any force, or the force which he in fact used, was necessary to defend himself and are further satisfied that the mistake was caused by voluntarily induced intoxication, the defence must fail. The anomalous result of this decision, however, is that if D, when drunk shoots, at what he believes to be a stag, but it turns out to be a person, he may plead intoxication in response to a charge of murder as this will be relevant in considering whether he had the specific intent to kill or seriously injure a person whereas, if D, when drunk, mistakenly believes that V is about to kill him and he shoots and kills V, he will be found guilty of murder. *O'Grady* was followed by the Court of Appeal in *O'Connor* [1991] Crim LR 135, where the Court held that intoxication was irrelevant on the question whether D believed he was acting in self-defence. The conviction for murder was quashed, however, as the trial judge had not directed the jury to take account of D's intoxication when considering whether he had formed the specific intent to cause grievous bodily harm. What better illustration of the illogicality of the *O'Grady* decision could there be? A jury might be forgiven for thinking that a trial judge had taken leave of his senses following a direction that they must ignore the accused's intoxication when considering whether he believed he was acting in self-defence, but that his intoxication must be taken into account in deciding whether he intended to kill or cause grievous bodily harm.

While Lord Lane's judgment in *O'Grady* is unsupportable in terms of principle it was, in fact, a policy decision. Lord Lane considered that where a victim has, through no fault of his own, been injured or killed because of a drunken mistake, '[r]eason recoils from the conclusion that in such circumstances a defendant is entitled to leave the Court without a stain on his character.' In fact, a defendant would not leave the court without a conviction as he could be convicted of an offence of basic intent. In *O'Grady*, the accused was convicted of manslaughter at first instance. In such circumstances a manslaughter verdict could be returned either because manslaughter is an offence of basic intent and thus intoxication supplies the *mens rea* for unlawful act manslaughter, or on the basis that the accused's mistake was grossly negligent or reckless, thereby founding a charge of reckless/gross negligence manslaughter.

To add further to the confusion in the area of intoxication and defences, the courts apply different principles to specific statutory defences which provide that a particular belief provides a defence to the charge. In *Jaggard* v *Dickinson* [1980] 3 All ER 716, D went to a house which she believed belonged to a friend. She believed, correctly, that her friend would not object to her breaking into his house. D was drunk, however, and had gone to the wrong house. D was convicted of criminal damage and appealed, contending that, despite her intoxication, she was entitled to rely on the defence of lawful excuse in s. 5(2) and (3) of the Criminal Damage Act 1971. This provides that a person has a lawful excuse if he believes that the person entitled to consent to the damage would have done so had he known of the circumstances, and that it is immaterial whether a belief is justified or not if it is honestly held. As criminal damage is an offence of basic intent D could not have relied on her intoxication to negative her *mens rea*. The Divisional Court, however, held that she could rely on her intoxication as Parliament had 'specifically required the court to consider the defendant's actual state of belief, not the state of belief which ought to have existed.' The court considered a belief may be honestly held whether it stems from intoxication, stupidity, forgetfulness or inattention. Thus D's intoxication was relevant to the defence of lawful excuse for 'it helped to explain what would otherwise have been inexplicable, and hence lent colour to her evidence about the state of her belief.' The anomalous result of this decision is that if D damages A's property believing, because of a drunken mistake, that it is his own, he will be guilty of criminal damage as this is an offence of basic intent and his drunkenness will substitute for *mens rea*, whereas, if he damages A's property believing, because of a drunken mistake, that it is B's and that B would consent to him doing so, he will have a defence. If intoxication is irrelevant to the issue of intent or recklessness in offences of basic intent, it is difficult to see why it is, nevertheless, relevant to the issue of belief in consent in the context of a statutory defence. The anomaly may be highlighted by recalling that a drunken belief in consent will not avail an accused when he is charged with rape.

5.6.5 The problem of Dutch courage
If D, having decided to commit a particular offence of specific intent, takes drink or drugs to give himself the courage to do so, may he rely on his intoxication at the time he committed the offence to establish that he did not have the *mens rea* required? In *A-G for Northern Ireland* v *Gallagher* [1963] AC 349, D decided to kill his wife and bought a knife and a bottle of whiskey. He drank the whiskey and killed his wife. He sought to argue in the alternative that he either was insane at the time he killed her or he was so drunk that he was incapable of forming the intent to do so. He was convicted of murder. In the House of Lords Lord Denning stated (at p. 382):

> If a man, whilst sane and sober, forms an intention to kill and makes preparation for it, knowing it is a wrong thing to do, and then gets himself drunk so as to give himself Dutch courage to do the killing, and whilst drunk carries out his intention, he cannot rely on this self-induced drunkenness as a defence to a charge of murder, nor even as reducing it to manslaughter. He cannot say that he got himself into such a stupid state that he was incapable of an intent to kill. . . . The wickedness of his mind before he got drunk is enough to condemn him, coupled with the act which he intended to do and did do.

While this may conflict with the requirement of contemporaneity between *actus reus* and *mens rea*, it is an exception justifiable on grounds of policy. As

Smith and Hogan argue, *Criminal Law* at pp. 219-220, if the accused had used an innocent agent to commit the murder he would have been liable and thus the accused in his responsible state should be liable for the acts he intended should be done in his irresponsible state.

5.6.6   Intoxication causing insanity or an abnormality of mind

If the accused's drinking or drug-taking produces a disease of the mind, such as delerium tremens, he may be found insane under the *M'Naghten* Rules. In *Davis* (1881) 14 Cox CC 563, D raised the defence of insanity based on delirium tremens arising from a history of excessive drinking, although he was sober at the time of the offence. In directing the jury Stephen J stated (at 564):

> drunkenness is one thing and diseases to which drunkenness leads are different things; and if a man by drunkenness brings on a state of disease which causes such a degree of madness, even for a time, which would have relieved him from responsibility if it had been caused in any other way, then he would not be criminally responsible.

This direction was approved in *Beard* and *Gallagher*. In *Gallagher* there was evidence that the accused was suffering from psychopathy. The effect of this disease of the mind was to weaken the sufferer's powers of self-control, and this would be aggravated by drink. An impairment of the power of self-control does not fall within the *M'Naghten* Rules although it is relevant to a defence of diminished responsibility (see *Byrne*). The House of Lords made it clear that if the accused's disease of the mind did not bring him within the *M'Naghten* Rules, this defect could not be rectified by taking into account the aggravating effect of alcohol. It is necessary for the alcohol to cause the disease of the mind and for this to result in the accused either not knowing what he is doing or not knowing that it is wrong.

If an accused pleads diminished responsibility based on an abnormality of mind due to some cause other than intoxication, the jury must ignore the effects of the accused's intoxication when seeking to decide whether the abnormality of mind substantially impaired his responsibility. However, a craving for drink or drugs may in itself produce an abnormality of mind where it renders the use of drink or drugs involuntary (*Tandy*). Likewise excessive use of drink or drugs may damage the brain and amount to an injury; this in turn may be such as to substantially impair the accused's responsibility (*Tandy*).

5.6.7   Involuntary intoxication

Involuntary intoxication may arise in three different ways. It may arise where the accused is drugged by others or his drink is laced with alcohol. Second, it may arise from his taking drugs which have been medically prescribed, provided he has taken these drugs in accordance with the instructions. In both these cases he may, in his defence, rely on his intoxication to negative *mens rea* whether the offence be one of specific or basic intent. It is no defence, however, to plead that he would never have committed the offence when sober if he nonetheless formed the requisite *mens rea* in his intoxicated state (see *Davies*

[1983] Crim LR 741). If the accused knows he is drinking alcohol but is mistaken as to its strength, this does not render his intoxication involuntary (see *Allen* [1988] Crim LR 698).

The third situation where intoxication may be treated as involuntary is where the accused takes a non-dangerous drug, provided he was not reckless in taking the drug. In *Hardie* [1985] 1 WLR 64, D was charged with criminal damage with intent to endanger life or being reckless whether life was endangered contrary to s. 1(2) of the Criminal Damage Act 1971. In his defence he claimed he did not have the requisite *mens rea* due to intoxication arising from taking valium. D took the valium tablets, which belonged to another person, to calm his nerves having been told by that person that they would do him no harm. On D's appeal against conviction the Court of Appeal held that *Majewski* did not apply. Unlike alcohol and other dangerous drugs which are liable to cause unpredictability or aggressiveness and thus give rise to the conclusive presumption of recklessness, it was not generally known that taking valium 'would be liable to render a person aggressive or incapable of appreciating risks or have other side effects such that its self-administration would itself have an element of recklessness.' The correct direction to the jury would have been 'that if they came to the conclusion that, as a result of the Valium, the appellant was, at the time, unable to appreciate the risks to property and persons from his actions they should then consider whether the taking of the Valium was itself reckless.' The Court derived support from *Bailey* (see 5.4.3 *ante*). The test of recklessness would thus appear to require subjective awareness, at the time of taking the drug, of the risk of becoming unpredictable, dangerous, aggressive or incapable of appreciating risks to others; there is no need to prove foresight of the particular risk which eventuates. The Court did say, however, that the taking of a soporific or sedative drug would not be an answer to a charge of, for example, reckless driving (and, presumably, dangerous driving contrary to s. 2 of the Road Traffic Act 1988).

While the decision in *Hardie* may be supported on the basis that the accused was not truly responsible for his incapacity due to his being unaware of the effect the Valium might have on him, the decision may be questioned on other grounds. As Hardie was charged with an offence for which *Caldwell* recklessness sufficed, it could be argued that the reason for his failure to give thought to the obvious risk of damage was irrelevant. If the girl in *Elliott* v *C* (see *3.4.2.2.3 ante*) could not rely on her limited intelligence (for which she bore no responsibility) as a reason for failing to give thought to an obvious risk, why should Hardie be allowed to rely on his incapacity which he had caused by his own actions?

5.6.8 Proposals for reform
The Butler Committee (Cmnd 6244, 1975) proposed the creation of a new offence of dangerous intoxication. Where an accused was acquitted of a 'dangerous offence' because he lacked the requisite *mens rea* due to voluntary intoxication, a jury would be able to convict him of dangerous intoxication. This alternative offence would be available where the accused was charged with

any offence involving injury to the person or death or consisting of a sexual attack on another, or involving the destruction of, or causing damage to, property so as to endanger life. The maximum sentence on such a conviction would be one year's imprisonment on a first offence and three years for a subsequent offence. The problem with such a conviction, however, is that it does not distinguish between the types of dangerous offences which the accused may have committed. A minority of the Criminal Law Revision Committee in its Fourteenth Report, *Offences Against the Person*, proposed a modification of the Butler Committee proposal. They proposed that the jury should return a special verdict that the accused had done the act alleged in a state of intoxication, in effect, 'Guilty but intoxicated'. The court would have the same sentencing powers as are available on conviction of the alleged offence but would be able to reflect the culpability of the accused in the sentence it pronounces. This verdict would also reflect the actual harm done by the accused.

The Law Commission in its Draft Criminal Code largely opts for the status quo in clause 22 but avoids use of terms such as 'specific intent' or 'basic intent'. Where the offence charged requires proof of intention, knowledge or belief, evidence of voluntary intoxication may be tendered to show that the accused lacked the state of mind in question. Following the proposal of the majority of the Criminal Law Revision Committee in their Fourteenth Report, the Law Commission proposes to tidy up the law relating to offences of basic intent. Clause 22(1) provides:

> Where an offence requires a fault element of recklessness (however described), a person who was voluntarily intoxicated shall be treated:
> (a)   as having been aware of any risk of which he would have been aware had he been sober;
> (b)   as not having believed in the existence of an exempting circumstance (where the existence of such a belief is in issue) if he would not have so believed had he been sober.

This provision applies to any offence requiring a fault element of recklessness even if it also requires an element of intention or knowledge. Thus the effect of intoxication in respect of a charge of rape would remain unchanged. The effect of clause 221 1(b) would be a partial reversal of *O'Grady*. Where the offence with which the accused is charged cannot be committed recklessly (e.g. murder), and he seeks to rely on an exempting circumstance, such as self-defence, his liability will depend on his beliefs at the time even though he was intoxicated. If, however, he is charged with an offence such as causing grievous bodily harm, which may be committed recklessly, his mistaken belief in circumstances justifying action in self-defence will be immaterial if he would not have held that belief had he been sober.

Further reading
N. L. A. Barlow, 'Drug intoxication and the principle of *Capacitas Rationalis*' (1984) 100 LQR 639.

S. Dell, 'Wanted: an insanity defence that can be used' [1984] Crim LR 431.

R. D. Mackay, 'Fact and fiction about the insanity defence' [1990] Crim LR 247; 'Post-Hinckley insanity in the USA' [1988] Crim LR 88.

C. Wells, 'Whither insanity' [1983] Crim LR 787.

S. White, 'The Criminal Procedure (Insanity and Unfitness to Plead) Act' [1992] Crim LR 4.

SIX

General defences

6.1 INTRODUCTION

When an accused is being tried for an offence and the prosecution have sought to prove that he committed the *actus reus* with the requisite *mens rea*, he may respond by giving an explanation; for example, that he acted under an honest mistake or that he brought about the prohibited consequence accidentally. In common parlance such explanations are referred to as defences. This is, however, inaccurate as such explanations are simply assertions that the prosecution have failed to establish an element of the *actus reus* or the *mens rea* of the offence. By contrast, general defences, such as duress, involve the defendant in conceding that he did commit the *actus reus* and that he intended to bring it about but assert that he should be excused for so doing. Where a defence operates as an excuse the culpability of the accused is negated and he is excused from the normal consequences of conviction and sentencing which would flow from commission of the prohibited act with the requisite *mens rea*. Thus an excuse operates as a shield protecting the accused from conviction and sentence.

Self-defence and prevention of crime are also usually classified as general defences. If raised successfully such a plea provides a justification for the accused's use of force. Where a defence operates as a justification the wrongfulness of the accused's conduct is negated as his conduct is considered to have been an appropriate course of action in the circumstances in which he found himself. Thus a plea of justification operates to cancel the unlawfulness of the accused's conduct; there being no unlawful act, there is thus no crime of which to convict him. Such assertions, accordingly, are not strictly speaking defences but they will be dealt with in this chapter for convenience.

Whether the defence acts as an excuse or a justification is, from the point of view of the accused, irrelevant; in either case he is acquitted. It may, however, be important to others that the nature of the defence be determined as it is possible to be convicted of aiding and abetting an accused who is acquitted by reason of an excuse but not one who is acquitted by reason of a justification. In the latter case there is no offence to aid and abet. It is also thought that conduct which is merely excusable may be resisted by a person threatened by it whereas if the conduct is justifiable it is thought that, in some circumstances, it may not be resisted. This is phrased so tentatively because of the complexities which may arise, as the following example illustrates. PC, a plainclothes police officer, has reasonable grounds for suspecting that an arrestable offence has been committed and he has reasonable grounds for suspecting that D is guilty of it. He seeks to arrest D which he is empowered to do under s. 24(5) of the Police and Criminal Evidence Act 1984. D has not committed any offence and when he sees PC approach him he fears he is about to be assaulted and tries to run off. PC performs a rugby tackle on D seeking to use reasonable force to arrest an offender under s. 3(1) of the Criminal Law Act 1967. D, believing he is being unlawfully attacked, punches PC breaking his nose. If D is charged with unlawfully and maliciously inflicting grievous bodily harm on PC contrary to s. 20 of the Offences Against the Person Act 1861 he could plead self-defence, as he was unaware of PC's identity, but if PC had been in uniform it is thought that he could not resist arrest even though he had not committed any offence.

Classifying defences is important for another reason; it is possible to limit the scope of defences which operate as excuses by limiting their operation to certain offences. In effect the courts are saying that certain types of conduct are excusable in certain circumstances but other types of conduct are not excusable in any circumstances.

When the accused pleads one of these general defences there is a burden on him to lay a proper foundation for the defence, making it a fit and proper issue for the jury to consider. In some cases the facts from which the defence might reasonably be inferred may have emerged in the testimony of prosecution witnesses. If not, the accused must discharge this evidential burden by testifying himself and/or calling witnesses to testify with regard to the defence, thereby making it a live issue in the trial. If this burden is discharged (which is a decision for the judge), the prosecution are given the burden of disproving the defence. If the prosecution fail to discharge this burden by satisfying the jury beyond reasonable doubt that the accused was not acting, for example, under duress, the jury must acquit him.

The defences considered in this chapter have in common the feature that the accused claims he acted as he did because of some compelling circumstance which forced him to choose between so acting or suffering some other form of harm to occur.

6.2 DURESS

6.2.1 General

When an accused pleads duress he is claiming that he committed the *actus reus* of the offence with which he is charged, with the relevant *mens rea* but that he did so because his will had been overborne by the wrongful threats of another to inflict harm on himself and/or his family. Judicial statements to the effect

that duress operates to render the accused's act involuntary are incorrect (see
e.g. Widgery LJ in *Hudson and Taylor* [1971] 2 QB 202, 206). Duress does not
operate in the way that automatism operates (see 5.4 *ante*). The correct
explanation of the way in which duress operates was stated by Lord
Wilberforce in *DPP for Northern Ireland* v *Lynch* [1975] AC 653, at 679-680:

> At the present time, whatever the ultimate analysis in jurisprudence may be,
> the best opinion . . . seems to be that duress . . . is something which is
> superimposed on the other ingredients which by themselves would make up
> an offence, i.e. on the act and intention. *Coactus volui* sums up the
> combination: the victim completes the act and knows that he is doing so; but
> the addition of the element of duress prevents the law from treating what he
> has done as a crime.

The reason for allowing a defence of duress is that it is a concession to human
frailty when faced with the choice of suffering harm or breaking the criminal
law; in such a situation there is no real choice. Professor G. P. Fletcher
describes this as 'moral involuntariness' (*Rethinking Criminal Law* (1978) 803)
undeserving of punishment, a view which echoes Lord Morris in *DPP* v *Lynch*
(at 670):

> it is proper that any rational system of law should take fully into account the
> standards of honest and reasonable men. By those standards it is fair that
> actions and reactions may be tested. If then someone is really threatened with
> death or serious injury unless he does what he is told to do is the law to pay
> no heed to the miserable, agonising plight of such a person? For the law to
> understand not only how the timid but also the stalwart may in a moment of
> crisis behave is not to make the law weak but to make it just. In the calm of
> the court-room measures of fortitude or of heroic behaviour are surely not
> to be demanded when they could not in moments for decision reasonably
> have been expected even of the resolute and the well disposed.

If then it is accepted that there are circumstances in which an accused should
be excused from criminal liability because his act was a response to threats
made to him, what are those circumstances?

6.2.2 The nature of the threat

For a defence of duress to succeed it is not sufficient for the accused to claim
that his will was overborne by threats. The threats must be of a particular kind
if they are to provide the foundation for duress. In *Hudson and Taylor* [1971]
2 QB 202, Lord Widgery CJ stated that the threats must be of death or serious
personal injury (see also *DPP* v *Lynch*). A threat to damage or destroy property
is not sufficient (*M'Growther* (1746) Fost 13) as 'the law must draw a line
somewhere; and, as a result of experience and human valuation, the law draws
it between threats to property and threats to the person' (*per* Lord Simon in
Lynch [1975] AC 653, 687). Threats to expose sexual immorality will also not

suffice (*Singh* [1973] 1 WLR 1600; *Valderrama-Vega* [1985] Crim LR 220). If the accused committed the offence of which he stands charged because of some threat less than death or serious personal injury, while this will not excuse him, it may be considered as a factor mitigating sentence.

While the threats of death or serious injury must be a *sine qua non* of the accused's decision to commit the offence, they need not be the sole reason for so acting (*Valderrama-Vega* [1985] Crim LR 220). In this case the accused claimed that he had imported cocaine because of death threats from a Mafia-type organisation. In addition he said he needed the money which he stood to earn as he was under severe financial pressure due to a large debt he owed his bank. Furthermore he had been threatened with the disclosure of his homosexual propensities. The jury had been directed that duress was available as a defence only if the accused acted *solely* because of the death threats; they should have been left to decide whether the accused would not have acted as he did but for the death threats.

No English case of duress by threats has decided whether threats to kill or injure other persons will suffice to support a plea of duress. In *Ortiz* (1986) 83 Cr App R 173, the Court of Appeal assumed that a threat to injure the accused's wife or family could do so (see also *Valderrama-Vega*). This is confirmed by the 'duress of circumstances' case of *Martin* [1989] 1 All ER 652 (see 6.3.2 *post*). In *Hurley and Murray* [1967] VR 526, the Supreme Court of Victoria held that threats to kill or seriously injure the accused's common law wife could amount to duress. In *Conway* [1988] 3 All ER 1025 (6.3.2 *post*) the defence of duress of circumstances was accorded to the accused where the threat of injury had been made to a passenger in his car. As duress of circumstances is the progeny of duress by threats it is assumed that when such situations arise directly in a case of duress by threats the outcome will be the same. Indeed, it is to be hoped that the defence will be recognised to cover threats to third parties with whom the accused has no special relationship if an ordinary person in the same situation would have responded to the threats as the accused did. For example, would the courts deny D, a passer-by, the defence of duress to a charge of aiding or harbouring an escaped prisoner where D did so solely as a result of the prisoner's threats to kill the prison warders whom he was holding at knife-point, if D would not drive the prison van? Clearly there is no special relationship between D and the warders; but to deny the defence of duress to D on this basis would smack of capriciousness.

6.2.3 The test for duress

Because the defence of duress is founded on the notion that morally involuntary conduct is not blameworthy, some standard is necessary against which to measure the accused's conduct. It is not sufficient that he acted because of a threat; if the ordinary person in that situation would have shown greater fortitude and resisted the threat the accused is morally blameworthy for acceding to the threat. Accordingly, the test for duress involves both subjective and objective elements. These were clearly stated by Lord Lane CJ in *Graham* (1982) 74 Cr App R 235, as two questions to be considered by the jury and have since been affirmed by the House of Lords in *Howe* [1987] 1 AC 417:

(1) Was the defendant, or may he have been, impelled to act as he did because, as a result of what he reasonably believed [the person issuing the threat] had said or done, he had good cause to fear that if he did not so act [that person] would kill him or . . . cause him serious personal injury?

(2) If so, have the prosecution made the jury sure that a sober person of reasonable firmness, sharing the characteristics of the defendant, would not have responded to whatever he reasonably believed [the person making the threat] said or did by taking part in the killing? The fact that a defendant's will to resist has been eroded by the voluntary consumption of drink or drugs or both is not relevant to this test.

There are several points to note about these questions.

6.2.3.1 Burden of proof The questions are framed so as to cast the burden of proof on the prosecution to disprove the defence once it is made a live issue in the trial. Thus, if the jury, while not being convinced that the accused was threatened and committed the offence charged in response to the threat, feel that he may have been threatened and may have acted as he did in response to the threat, they must give him the benefit of the doubt and pass on to consider the next question. Similarly, if they conclude that a reasonable person might have responded to the threat in the same way as the accused, the benefit of the doubt again would have to be given to the accused. It is not for the accused to prove duress but for the prosecution to disprove it.

6.2.3.2 Subjective and objective standards The first question contains both subjective and objective elements. The question focuses on the subjective issue of whether the accused did as he did because of the threats he believed had been made. The accused's belief will only avail him, however, where it is, objectively, a reasonable one. If he makes an honest mistake this will not suffice; there must be reasonable grounds for believing that a threat was being made. This contrasts with Lord Lane's approach in *Williams (Gladstone)* (1984) 78 Cr App R 276 (*3.6.1.1.2 ante*; *6.5.3.3 post*) where, in relation to a plea of self-defence or prevention of crime, he stated that the accused must be judged against the mistaken facts as he believed them to be. There seems to be no obvious rationale to explain the difference of approach unless it is either that defences which are excuses require different treatment from those which are justifications, or that there is a belief on Lord Lane's part that juries are more gullible when considering a plea of duress than they are when considering a plea of self-defence! The divergence in approach between *Graham* and *Williams* is the more remarkable in light of Lord Lane's declaration in the former (at p. 300) that 'consistency of approach in defences to criminal liability is obviously desirable'.

The second element is the objective requirement that the accused's belief must give rise to *good cause* to fear death or serious injury. This suggests that there must be a reasonable likelihood of the threatened harm occurring. If there is no good cause for his fear, albeit the accused does honestly fear the threatened harm occurring, this will not avail him. This leads one to ask whether there is a difference in blameworthiness between the accused whose fear is rational, in that there is a reasonable likelihood of the harm occurring, and the accused whose fear is irrational, though no less compelling? (see 6.2.4 post).

The second question to be considered by the jury sets a purely objective standard. Lord Lane stated (at p. 300):

> As a matter of public policy, it seems to us essential to limit the defence of duress by means of an objective criterion formulated in terms of reasonableness. . . . Provocation and duress are analogous. In provocation the words or actions of one person break the self-control of another. In duress the words or actions of one person break the will of another. The law requires a defendant to have the self-control reasonably to be expected of the ordinary citizen in his situation. It should likewise require him to have the steadfastness reasonably to be expected of the ordinary citizen in his situation.

Thus, if an ordinary person sharing the characteristics of the accused would have resisted the threats, the accused will be convicted as he is blameworthy for failing to show the degree of fortitude which the criminal law demands of all citizens. If the ordinary person would have responded to the threat in the way the accused did, the accused will be acquitted. The characteristics of the accused which are to be attributed to the ordinary person are, by analogy with provocation (9.3.2.2.3 post), presumably age, sex and other non-transitory mental or physical attributes which would affect the gravity of the threat to him.

6.2.3.3 Intoxication and duress

If the accused, because he is intoxicated, mistakenly believes he is being threatened, his mistake will not avail him as such a mistake is necessarily unreasonable. If, rather, he claims that his will to resist was eroded as a result of his intoxication, he will likewise not benefit from this as he is to be judged against the standard of the sober person of reasonable firmness. Lord Lane CJ did not advert to the situation where the accused was involuntarily intoxicated. It is submitted that in such a case the accused's case should be considered in the light of his honest beliefs and his response should be measured against the standard of the ordinary person similarly suffering from involuntary intoxication.

6.2.4 Imminence of the threat and opportunities to escape

If an accused is to be able to plead duress successfully the threat must have been operative at the time he committed the offence. To put this another way, the accused must have committed the offence while under the threat of imminent harm. If he had opportunity to escape from under the threat and failed to do so, his defence of duress will fail (see *M'Growther* (1746) Fost 13). In *Gill* [1963] 1 WLR 841, the accused claimed that he and his wife had been threatened with violence if he did not steal a lorry. The Court of Criminal Appeal, *obiter*, expressed doubts whether duress was open to him as there had been a period of time during which he could have raised the alarm and wrecked the whole enterprise. In *Hurley and Murray* [1967] VR 526, the court held that the defence of duress could be relied on by D even though he was out of range of those issuing the threats, as his common law wife was being held hostage and the threats against her were operating on his mind at the time he committed the offence.

These principles were further elucidated in *Hudson and Taylor* [1971] 2 QB 202. The appellants were teenage girls who were convicted of perjury having been denied the defence of duress by the recorder as the threat of harm to them could not be put immediately into effect in the courtroom when they were testifying. The girls claimed that they had been threatened with violence by a gang if they did not give false evidence at the trial of one of their members. While testifying the girls had seen one of the gang members in the gallery of the court. It was further contended on appeal that the girls should have sought police protection before the trial. On the first point Lord Widgery CJ stated (at p. 207):

> When . . . there is no opportunity for delaying tactics, and the person threatened must make up his mind whether he is to commit the criminal act or not, the existence at that moment of threats sufficient to destroy his will ought to provide him with a defence even though the threatened injury may not follow instantly, but after an interval. . . . [T]he threats . . . were likely to be no less compelling, because their execution could not be effected in the court room, if they could be carried out in the streets of Salford the same night.

On the point of possible police protection Lord Widgery CJ stated (at p. 207):

> The argument does not distinguish cases in which the police would be able to provide effective protection, from those when they would not, and it would, in effect, restrict the defence of duress to cases where the person threatened had been kept in custody by the maker of the threats, or where the time interval between the making of the threats and the commission of the offence had made recourse to the police impossible. We recognise the need to keep the defence of duress within reasonable bounds but cannot accept so severe a restriction on it.

Lord Widgery went on to state what the prosecution had to prove if the defence of duress was to be denied to the accused, namely:

> that the accused failed to avail himself of some opportunity which was reasonably open to him to render the threat ineffective. . . . In deciding whether such an opportunity was reasonably open to the accused the jury should have regard to his age and circumstances, and to any risks to him which may be involved in the course of action relied on.

If the accused is extremely timorous and fears taking an avenue of escape of which the reasonable person would have availed, he will be denied the defence.

6.2.5 Duress arising from voluntary association with criminals

Is the defence of duress available to an accused who has voluntarily associated with criminals who use violence, thereby exposing himself to the risk of compulsion? In *Sharp* [1987] 1 QB 853, D had joined a gang which had carried out a series of armed robberies of sub-post offices culminating in the murder of a sub-postmaster. He claimed he only took part in this last robbery because a gun had been pointed at his head by another gang member who threatened to blow it off if he did not participate. He was convicted of manslaughter when the trial judge rejected duress as a possible defence. The Court of Appeal, relying on codes in other common law jurisdictions, dicta in *Lynch* and the decision of the Northern Ireland Court of Appeal in *Fitzpatrick* [1977] NI 20, dismissed the appeal. Lord Lane CJ stated (at p. 861):

> where a person has voluntarily, and with knowledge of its nature, joined a criminal organisation or gang which he knew might bring pressure on him to commit an offence and was an active member when he was put under such pressure, he cannot avail himself of the defence of duress.

Thus as the defence of duress is a concession to human frailty which will be denied where the accused has failed to avail himself of an opportunity to escape from the duress, so too it is denied to the accused who freely undertakes the risk of being subjected to duress. Where, however, the accused has joined a criminal enterprise not knowing of any propensity to violence on the part of other participants in the enterprise, and thus not anticipating coercion to commit an offence, the defence may be available to him if he was in 'a dilemma in which a reasonable man might have chosen to act as he did' (*per* Mustill LJ in *Shepherd* (1988) 86 Cr App R 47, at 51). In such a case the first question for the jury to decide would be whether the prosecution had satisfied them beyond reasonable doubt that the accused had freely undertaken the risk of being subjected to duress by joining the criminal enterprise. If not the jury would then go on to consider the defence of duress in accordance with the test laid down in *Graham*.

6.2.6 Limits to the defence

Because duress is a defence developed by the common law there has been uncertainty relating to its limits. Should a person be required to sacrifice his own life rather than escape by killing another? This question has been asked and answered differently by the courts over the last twenty years. In *Kray* [1970] 1 QB 125, Widgery LJ stated *obiter* that duress was available to a person charged with being an accessory before the fact to murder. In *DPP for Northern Ireland* v *Lynch* [1975] AC 653, the House of Lords, by a majority of three to two, held that duress was available to a person charged with aiding and abetting murder. Lynch drove a car which contained members of the IRA in Northern Ireland on an expedition in which they shot and killed a police officer. He claimed he was not a member of the IRA and that he believed he would be shot if he did not obey the leader of the group. The trial judge had held that duress was not available to a person charged with aiding and abetting murder. The House of Lords ordered his retrial in which he pleaded duress but he was obviously disbelieved by the jury as he was convicted. In *Abbott* v *The Queen* [1977] AC 755, the Privy Council drew a distinction between principals and secondary parties, holding that duress was not available to a principal charged with murder. While there may be a difference in the mode of participation it is difficult to see that there is necessarily any distinction in the degree of culpability between principal and secondary offenders; is the maker of a bomb necessarily less blameworthy than the one who plants it?

The need to draw this distinction between principal and secondary parties charged with murder has been removed by the decision of the House of Lords in *Howe* [1987] 1 AC 417. Unfortunately their Lordships did so by disallowing duress as a defence to murder whether as a principal or secondary party thereby reversing their decision in *Lynch*. The reasons put forward by their Lordships at times verge on the fatuous. Lord Hailsham, knowing of many acts of heroism by ordinary people, was of opinion that a law which protected the 'coward and the poltroon' could not be regarded as either 'just or humane'; accordingly the ordinary man, rather than kill another, might be expected to sacrifice his own life. However, there is no general duty to heroism in the criminal law and the standard against which the accused is generally measured is that of the reasonable man who might be considered neither heroic (or foolhardy) nor cowardly being a 'sober person of reasonable firmness'. How would Lord Hailsham characterise the ordinary man whose wife and family are held hostage under threat of death by terrorists if he does not plant a bomb intended to cause injury? If he resists the threat at the expense of the lives of his wife and children is he a hero; or if he complies with the threat at the expense of a third party's life is he a poltroon? This scenario, unfortunately, is all too realistic in light of the three car bomb attacks on security forces in Northern Ireland in October 1990, where the IRA held families hostage while the husbands were forced to drive the cars containing bombs to police or army installations.

Lords Hailsham, Griffiths and MacKay expressed the view that to allow duress as a defence to murder would involve overruling *Dudley and Stephens* (1884) 14 QBD 273, which they took to have decided that necessity was not a defence to a charge of murder. Lord Griffiths stated that this decision was based on 'the special sanctity that the law attaches to human life and which denies to a man the right to take an innocent life even at the price of his own or another's life'. This ignores the fact that the taking of one life may lead to a net saving of lives. Their Lordships also ignored the fact that *Dudley and Stephens* is a case whose ratio is far from clear (see 6.3.3 *post*).

Lord Griffiths was of opinion that the defence should not be afforded to a murderer as the 'defence of duress is so easy to raise and may be so difficult for the prosecution to disprove'. If this is so it is an argument for disallowing all defences. It also ignores the fact that in *Graham* the jury convicted where the accused pleaded duress on a charge of murder and, on the retrial of Lynch for murder, the jury in Northern Ireland convicted. Further it contradicts Lord Hailsham who stated that 'juries have been commendably robust' in rejecting the defence where appropriate.

Lords Hailsham and Griffiths expressed the view that the issue of duress in murder would best be dealt with by the executive through the agency of the Parole Board or Royal Pardon. Their views should be contrasted with that of Lord Wilberforce in *Lynch* who stated (at p. 685):

A law which requires innocent victims of terrorist threats to be tried and convicted as murderers, is an unjust law even if the executive, resisting political pressures, may decide, after all, and within the permissible limits of the prerogative to release them. Moreover, if the defence is excluded in law, much of the evidence which would prove the duress would be inadmissible at the trial, not brought out in court, and not tested by cross-examination.

Lord Bridge was of opinion that it was by legislation alone that the scope of the defence of duress could be defined, while Lord MacKay believed the defence was too uncertain for it to be extended to cover an actual killer. As duress is a common law defence one would have expected their Lordships to accept the responsibility placed on judges to develop and clarify the common law. (Their Lordships have not been so loath to extend the ambit of the criminal law when the issue of liability rather than defences has been involved as in *Caldwell* [1982] AC 341.) Once again Lord Wilberforce recognised this in *Lynch* where he stated (at pp. 684-685):

We are here in the domain of the common law: our task is to fit what we can see as principle and authority to the facts before us, and it is no obstacle that these facts are new. The judges have always assumed responsibility for deciding questions of principle relating to criminal liability and guilt, and particularly for setting the standards by which the law expects normal men to act. . . . The House is not inventing a new defence: on the contrary, it would not discharge its judicial duty if it failed to define the law's attitude to this particular defence in particular circumstances.

Following the decision in *Howe* there was uncertainty whether duress would be available as a defence on a charge of attempted murder, although Lord Griffiths stated *obiter* that it was not. The issue arose before the House of Lords in *Gotts*, [1992] 2 WLR 284. D, aged sixteen, was threatened with death by his father unless he killed his mother who had fled to a women's refuge with the other two children to escape the violence, depravity and abuse inflicted upon her and the children by the husband. Subsequently D stabbed his mother but was restrained by bystanders so that, although she sustained serious injuries, she did not die. He was charged with attempted murder and sought to plead duress. The trial judge ruled that duress was not available on a charge of attempted murder whereupon D pleaded guilty and appealed. The Court of Appeal upheld the trial judge's ruling and the House of Lords, by a majority of three to two, dismissed D's further appeal. Lord Jauncey of Tullichettle stated (at p. 293)

It is of course true that withholding the defence in any circumstances will create anomalies but . . . nothing should be done to undermine in any way the highest duty of the law to protect the freedom and lives of those who live under it. I can therefore see no justification in logic, morality or law in affording to an attempted murderer the defence which is withheld from a murderer. The intent required of an attempted murderer is more evil than that required of a murderer and the line which divides the two offences is seldom, if ever, of the deliberate making of the criminal.

The Court of Appeal had been concerned to avoid an anomaly between murder and attempted murder and, in addition, was influenced by the fact that the sentence for attempt was in the discretion of the court. In the instant case the sentence imposed was probation for three years which reflected the mitigating effect duress had in the circumstances. While the Court of Appeal may have been satisfied that no injustice was done to Gotts, they totally ignored the fact that, had his mother died, a matter totally depending on chance and in no way altering D's culpability, there would have been no discretion in sentencing D as the sentence for murder is life imprisonment for an adult and detention at Her Majesty's pleasure for a juvenile. If duress is not to be available as a complete defence on a charge of murder perhaps it should be made a partial defence in the way that provocation operates reducing the offence to manslaughter. On a conviction of manslaughter the sentence is in the discretion of the court, thereby providing the judge with the flexibility required so that he can reflect the mitigating nature of the circumstances in the sentence he imposes.

While *Gotts* dealt with the problem of attempted murder, a further anomaly remains unresolved. It appears that duress may be pleaded as a defence to a charge under s. 18 of the Offences Against the Person Act 1861. Thus an accused may be acquitted of wounding with intent to cause grievous bodily harm following a defence of duress, but if his victim dies within a year and a day he may be convicted of murder. The *mens rea* of murder is intention to kill or intention to cause serious bodily injury. In both cases D's culpability is the same and the gravity of the threats is no different but the outcome hangs on chance – whether the victim lives or dies. Is the logical conclusion therefore that duress should not be available on a charge under s. 18? Or is it conceivable that the House of Lords were right in *Lynch* but wrong in *Howe*? In *Gotts* in the Court of Appeal Lord Lane CJ stated, somewhat dismissively, that there would be anomalies wherever the line was drawn. Lord Jauncey, in the House of Lords, was of the same opinion. It is a sad day when the Lord Chief Justice of England and a Law Lord are not perturbed by anomalies in the criminal law which are the creation of the judges and which are capable of wreaking gross injustices.

The other offence over which there is uncertainty is treason. In *Steane* [1947] KB 997, Lord Goddard CJ took the view that duress was not available on such a charge before doing considerable violence to the definition of intention to permit the quashing of the appellant's conviction (see 3.2.3.2 *ante*). This decision must be considered *per incuriam*; in *Purdy* (1945) 10 JCL 182, Oliver J directed the jury that on a charge of treason based on assisting with German propaganda while a prisoner of war, fear of death would be a defence. In *Lynch* their Lordships cited this case along with *Oldcastle* (1419) 1 Hale PC 50, *M'Growther* (1746) Fost 13, and *Stratton* (1779) 1 Doug KB 239, which all recognised the availabilty of duress on certain charges of treason but it would not be available as a defence to treason involving the death of the Sovereign (see *Axtell* (1660) Kel 13, cited by Lord Simon at 940).

6.3 NECESSITY

6.3.1 General

The question whether there is a general defence of necessity in English law has long taxed criminal lawyers. Duress relates to the situation where a person commits an offence to avoid the greater evil of death or serious injury to himself or another threatened by a third party. Necessity relates to the situation where a person commits an offence to avoid the greater evil to himself or another which would ensue from objective dangers arising from the circumstances in which he or that other are placed. While duress operates as an excuse it was thought that necessity, if it existed as a defence, operated as a justification rendering the accused's conduct lawful. But is there such a defence?

Early writers on English law such as Bracton, Coke and Hale all quoted maxims which conceded that necessity might justify conduct which would otherwise be unlawful. In *Moore* v *Hussey* (1609) Hob 96, Hobart J stated 'All laws admit certain cases of just excuse, when they are offended in the letter, and where the offender is under necessity, either of compulsion or inconvenience.' Examples given by these writers of necessity were pulling down a house to prevent a fire spreading, a prisoner escaping from a burning jail although statute made prison-breach a felony, jettisoning cargo to save a vessel in a storm (see *Mouse's Case* (1620) 12 Co Rep 63).

In several traffic cases there are *obiter dicta* to the effect that there is a defence of necessity. In *Johnson* v *Phillips* [1976] 1 WLR 65, Wien J stated that a constable would be entitled to direct motorists to disobey traffic regulations if this was reasonably necessary for the protection of life or property. In *Woods* v *Richards* [1977] RTR 201, Eveleigh J stated that the defence of necessity depended on the degree of emergency which existed or the alternative danger to be averted.

Despite these authorities and dicta there was still uncertainty in the law as there were other *obiter dicta* which suggested there was no defence of necessity. In *Buckoke* v *GLC* [1971] Ch 655, Lord Denning stated (at p. 668):

A driver of a fire engine with ladders approaches the traffic lights. He sees 200 yards down the road a blazing house with a man at an upstairs window in extreme peril. The road is clear in all directions. At that moment the lights turn red. Is the driver to wait for 60 seconds, or more, for the lights to turn to green? If the driver waits for that time, the man's life will be lost. I suggested to both counsel that the driver might be excused in crossing the lights to save the man. He might have the defence of necessity. Both counsel denied it. They would not allow him any defence in law. The circumstances went to mitigation, they said, and did not take away his guilt. If counsel are correct – and I accept that they are – nevertheless such a man should not be prosecuted. He should be congratulated.

It seems strange that the law should operate in a way such as to discourage appropriate conduct; but this it seems to do and little reliance can be placed on the good sense of prosecuting authorities not to prosecute in such circumstances as the following case illustrates. In *Kitson* (1955) 39 Cr App R 66, D, who had been drinking and had fallen asleep in a car in which he was the passenger, woke to find the driver gone and the car careering down a hill. He took control of the vehicle and steered it to safety. He was prosecuted and convicted of driving under the influence of drink. Obviously he should have preferred to die himself or allow the car to kill others rather than take control of it while under the influence of alcohol! Would Lord Denning have congratulated Mr Kitson if he had shown great fortitude and restraint and, rather than be labelled a criminal, he had permitted the car to continue on its course at the expense of the lives of several pedestrians? Presumably he would as in *London Borough of Southwark* v *Williams* [1971] 2 All ER 175 he stated (at p. 179) 'Necessity would open a door which no man could shut. . . . The plea would be an excuse for all sorts of wrongdoing. So the courts must, for the sake of law and order, take a firm stand'.

A counter argument to this position is that the criminal law should not only be used to discourage inappropriate conduct but should, by means of exceptions to criminal liability, also encourage appropriate conduct.

In several twentieth century cases the defence of necessity has been implicitly recognised. In *Bourne* [1938] 3 All ER 615, an obstetric surgeon was charged with unlawfully using an instrument with intent to procure a miscarriage, contrary to s. 58 of the Offences Against the Person Act 1861, having performed an abortion on a fourteen-year-old girl who was the victim of a violent rape. MacNaghten J dealt with the matter from the point of view of the meaning of 'unlawfully' in s. 58 avoiding express mention of necessity. The jury acquitted after being directed that the accused would not have been acting unlawfully if he acted in good faith to save the girl's life. He stated (at p. 620) that 'the unborn child in the womb must not be destroyed unless the destruction of that child is for the purpose of preserving the yet more precious life of the mother'. If what was done was not unlawful it was justified; the only justification which covers this choice between evils is necessity. A similar approach was adopted in *Gillick* v *West Norfolk and Wisbech A.H.A.* [1986] AC 112, where the House of Lords stated that a doctor who prescribed contraceptives for a girl under sixteen would not be guilty of aiding, abetting, counselling or procuring the offence of unlawful sexual intercourse committed by her with a man, provided he honestly believed his action to be necessary for the physical, mental, and emotional health of the girl. Lord Scarman stated (at p. 190):

The bona fide exercise by a doctor of his clinical judgment must be a complete negation of the guilty mind which is an essential ingredient of the criminal offence of aiding and abetting the commission of unlawful sexual intercourse.

The doctor's motive for prescribing contraceptives is, however, irrelevant if he knows that this will encourage an underage girl to engage in sexual intercourse (see 3.2.3.2 *ante*). Would it not have been more honest for the House of Lords to state openly that necessity would be a defence instead of further confusing intention by declaring that motive may negate guilty mind?

In the most recent House of Lords decision to refer to necessity, *In re F (Mental Patient: Sterilisation)* [1990] 2 AC 1, it was held to be lawful to carry out a sterilisation operation on a mental patient who lacked the capacity to consent as there was a grave risk that she would become pregnant which would have had disastrous psychiatric consequences for her. Lord Brandon of Oakbrook considered that operations on patients incapable of consenting would be lawful provided they were carried out to save life or to ensure improvement or prevent deterioration in the patient's physical or mental health. While Lord Brandon did not expressly mention necessity it is implicit in his speech.

By contrast Lord Goff of Chieveley did mention necessity expressly. He stated that the common law principle of necessity could justify action which would otherwise be unlawful in three groups of cases: first, cases of public necessity where D interferes with another's property in the public interest (e.g. destroying his house to prevent the spread of a fire); secondly, cases of private necessity where D interferes with another's property to save his own person or property from imminent peril (e.g. where he enters upon V's land without his consent in order to prevent the spread of fire on to his own land); and thirdly, 'action taken as a matter of necessity to assist another person without his consent' (e.g. there is no assault where D seizes V and forcibly drags him from the path of an oncoming vehicle thereby saving him from injury or death). Lord Goff stated that there were many emanations of the third principle and that it was 'concerned not only with the preservation of the life or health of the assisted person, but also with the preservation of his property . . . and even with certain conduct on his behalf in the administration of his affairs'. His Lordship considered that the instant case concerned action taken to preserve the life, health or well-being of another who is unable to consent to it. In such a situation two conditions must be satisfied to bring the action within the bounds of necessity:

(a)   there must be a necessity to act when it is not practicable to communicate with the assisted person, and
(b)   the action taken must be such as a reasonable person would in all the circumstances take, acting in the best interests of the assisted person.

Lord Goff's three categories are very narrow and appear to be a long way from providing for a general defence of necessity based on a test of balancing harms (i.e. that D commits an offence to avoid a greater evil to himself or another) (see further 6.3.3 *post*).

6.3.2   Duress of circumstances: necessity by any other name?
Perhaps some judicial reluctance to recognising a defence of necessity was due to the general belief that it operated as a justification. In Canada in *Perka et al*

v *The Queen* (1984) 13 DLR (4th) 1, the Supreme Court of Canada held that necessity should be recognised in Canada as an excuse thereby implying 'no vindication of the deeds of the actor'. Thus the defence was seen as a concession to human frailty and was based on 'society's expectation of appropriate and normal resistance to pressure'. In *Lynch* Lord Simon expressed the view that there was no sustainable distinction in principle between necessity and duress, the latter being 'merely a particular application of the doctrine of necessity'. Might it be possible, therefore to incorporate some forms of necessity within an extended defence of duress without opening 'a door which no man could shut'? This is what appears to have happened almost by sleight of hand in several recent cases before the Court of Appeal. It is a development which was facilitated by Lord Lane's formulation of the test for duress in *Graham*, which did not require that the person from whom the threat emanated should have specified that the accused commit a particular crime; the issue is simply whether the accused may have acted as he did because he feared that if he did not so act he would suffer death or serious injury.

In the first case, *Willer* (1986) 83 Cr App R 225, D was charged with reckless driving. He had been confronted by a gang of youths who threatened to kill him and a passenger in his car. To escape he drove his car over the pavement and into a shopping precinct. When the assistant recorder ruled that the defence of necessity was not available to him he changed his plea to guilty. The Court of Appeal quashed his conviction. While they appeared to accept that the defence of necessity may have been available, they held that the appropriate defence was one of duress. Watkins LJ stated (at p. 227):

> the assistant recorder upon those facts should have directed that he would leave to the jury the question as to whether or not . . . the appellant was wholly driven by force of circumstance into doing what he did and did not drive the car otherwise than under that form of compulsion, i.e. under duress.

In the second case, *Conway* [1988] 3 All ER 1025, D was charged with reckless driving and pleaded necessity on the basis that he drove as he did because his passenger feared an attack from two men who were approaching the car. The two men were, in fact, plainclothes police officers who were approaching the car to arrest the passenger. At the trial the judge did not leave the defence of duress of circumstances or necessity to the jury. The Court of Appeal felt constrained to quash the conviction, regarding the decision in *Willer* as binding on it. It saw the defence of necessity/duress of circumstances as a 'logical consquence of the existence of the defence of duress as that term is ordinarily understood, i.e. "do this or else"; thus it would be subject to the same limitations, namely that the harm sought to be avoided must be death or serious injury. The court found support for this position in the speech of Lord Hailsham LC in *Howe* [1987] AC 417, 429, where he said:

> Duress is only that species of the genus of necessity which is caused by wrongful threats. I cannot see that there is any way in which a person of

ordinary fortitude can be excused from the one type of pressure on his will rather than the other.

In the third case, *Martin* [1989] 1 All ER 652, D drove a car while disqualified from driving after threats from his wife that she would commit suicide if he did not do so. D had pleaded guilty to the charge of driving while disqualified when the trial judge ruled that this was an absolute offence to which necessity was not a defence. The Court of Appeal quashed the conviction and Simon Brown J took the opportunity to summarise the principles governing necessity stating (at p. 653):

> first, English law does, in extreme circumstances, recognise a defence of necessity. Most commonly this defence arises as duress, that is pressure on the accused's will from the wrongful threats or violence of another. Equally however it can arise from objective dangers threatening the accused or others. Arising thus it is conveniently called 'duress of circumstances'.

By formulating the defence of necessity as a form of duress it is clear that English courts regard it as an excuse rather than a justification.

Secondly, Simon Brown J went on to say (at p. 653) 'the defence is available only if, from an objective standpoint, the accused can be said to be acting reasonably and proportionately in order to avoid a threat of death or serious injury'. This acts as a limitation on the circumstances in which necessity may be pleaded. It is not a mere matter of balancing harms so that the defence would be available if the harm committed is less than the harm the accused feared would otherwise occur. The defence is only available if the harm the accused seeks to avoid is that of death or serious injury to himself or another. By comparison in *Perka* the Supreme Court of Canada formulated the defence on the basis of a balancing of harms stating that there had to be proportionality in that the harm caused must be a lesser evil to the harm averted.

Thirdly, Simon Brown J stated (at pp. 653-654):

> assuming the defence to be open to the accused on his account of the facts, the issue should be left to the jury, who should be directed to determine these two questions: first, was the accused, or may he have been, impelled to act as he did because as a result of what he reasonably believed to be the situation he had good cause to fear that otherwise death or serious physical injury would result; second, if so, would a sober person of reasonable firmness, sharing the characteristics of the accused, have responded to that situation by acting as the accused acted? If the answer to both those questions was Yes, then the jury would acquit: the defence of necessity would have been established.

The test for necessity is thus exactly the same as for duress with the exception of the source from which the threat emanates.

As with the defence of duress, D may only rely on the defence of duress of circumstances so long as the threat continues. While initial driving with excess alcohol to escape assailants may have been excusable due to duress of circumstances, it would not be necessary for D to continue to drive a further two and a half miles home (see *DPP* v *Jones* [1990] RTR 34). If D drives off with excess alcohol to escape a threat he will be guilty of the driving offence if the prosecution prove that he continued to drive after the threat had ceased to operate (see *DPP* v *Bell* [1992] Crim LR 176).

6.3.3. The limits of necessity

The defence of necessity recognised as duress of circumstances is subject to the same limitations as the defence of duress. The positive result of this is that it implies that necessity could be pleaded by a thief if he stole food to save himself from starvation thereby refuting the dictum of Lord Denning in *London Borough of Southwark* v *Williams* [1971] 2 All ER 175 at 179, that 'if hunger were once allowed to be an excuse for stealing, it would open a door through which all kinds of lawlessness and disorder would pass'. The negative results, however, are that necessity in this form is an excuse and is not available on a charge of murder or attempted murder. Things have thus come full circle; in *Howe* their Lordships used the case of *Dudley and Stephens* as authority that necessity was not a defence to murder and thus duress should not be a defence to murder. *Howe* was one of the authorities used in *Conway* to develop the defence of duress of circumstances/necessity. The case of *Dudley and Stephens* however is open to several interpretations. In *Lynch* Lord Simon took the ratio to be that there was no defence of necessity known to English law. In *Howe* three of their Lordships interpreted it to mean that necessity was not a defence to murder. The decision could as easily be interpreted as holding there was no necessity to kill in the situation in which the two accused found themselves. They were adrift in an open boat with another man and a boy after being shipwrecked. After several days without food and water they decided to kill the boy who was very weak and they fed on his body. Four days later they were rescued. On their trial for murder the jury returned a special verdict finding that the men would have died before rescue had they not eaten the boy who, because of his weak state, would have died sooner, and that there was no reasonable prospect of relief and no appreciable chance of saving life except by killing; but there was no greater necessity for killing the boy than any of the three men. Lord Coleridge CJ agreed with this last point. Indeed, as the mariners' peril was due to them being adrift, killing any one of them was not going to assure their rescue and thus it could be argued that there was no necessity to kill anyone. The outcome for the two mariners, however, was that they were convicted of murder but the death sentence was commuted to six months inmprisonment.

As *Dudley and Stephens* is such an unsatisfactory authority it would have been possible and more desirable for their Lordships in *Howe* to ignore it and decide the issue *de novo*. There are situations in which killing another may be an appropriate action and even commendable but the criminal law would now discourage such action. Professor J. C. Smith in *Justification and Excuse in the Criminal Law* gives two illustrations. At the inquest into the deaths arising from the *Herald of Free Enterprise* disaster in Zeebrugge harbour an army corporal gave evidence that he led dozens of people to safety up a rope ladder. On the ladder was a petrified passenger who was refusing to move. When persuasion failed the corporal instructed another passenger below this man to push him off the ladder which he did and he was never seen again. If such a situation were to arise again the criminal law now clearly indicates that a person should rather die and allow many others to die than risk killing the person obstructing their avenue of escape. Should not the criminal law promote the net saving of human life? To quote Professor Smith (at p. 77) 'The law has lost touch with reality if it condemns as murder conduct which right-thinking people regard as praiseworthy.'

The second illustration is related by Simpson in *Touching the Void* (1988). One climber slipped off a 19,000-foot cliff in the Andes and was left dangling on a rope attached to his partner. When the partner reached the point of exhaustion and realised that his life was in peril he cut the rope. Miraculously the other survived as he fell on to a snow-covered ice bridge below. Again, if a climber was to seek guidance from the criminal law before going on an expedition, he would discover that it would direct him in such a situation that he should rather die along with his partner than cut the rope to save himself.

The very narrow defence of necessity recognised by Lord Goff in *In re F*, *ante*, as a justification, does not touch on these situations. There would seem to be no need for the exclusion of the defence of necessity in a case of murder. The matter could be adequately dealt with by the jury on a balancing of harms test. It is highly doubtful, in light of the duress of circumstances cases and the dicta in *In re F*, that a general defence of necessity, operating as a justification and founded on a balancing of harms test, will ever be recognised judicially.

6.4 MARITAL COERCION

There is nothing to prevent a spouse pleading duress on the basis of threats from the other spouse. A further defence is available to wives under s. 47 of the Criminal Justice Act 1925 which provides that 'on a charge against a wife for any offence other than treason or murder it shall be a good defence to prove that the offence was committed in the presence of, and under the coercion of, the husband.' This defence is rarely pleaded but several points should be noted. The burden of proving coercion lies on the accused. This is less favourable than the defence of duress but coercion would appear to include threats or intimidation of a lesser degree than required for duress. In *Lynch* [1975] AC 653, 693, Lord Simon stated that 'coercion in its popular sense denotes an external force which cannot be resisted and which impels its subject to act otherwise than he would wish'. While duress suggested threats, he considered that coercion 'extends to any force overbearing the wish' (at 694). At first instance in *Richman* [1982] Crim LR 507, Hutton J directed the jury that coercion could be physical or moral. A wife had to prove that her will was overborne by the wishes of her husband. Coercion, however, differed from trying to persuade someone out of loyalty. It would seem therefore that a wife could not plead coercion on the basis that she committed the offence out of love or a sense of duty; there must be some pressure from the husband.

When duress is pleaded there is no need to show that the person who issued the threats was present at the time the offence was committed; it is sufficient that the threats were imminent. In coercion, however, the husband must be shown to be present when the offence was committed. Duress may be pleaded even though the accused acted under a mistaken belief, provided this mistake was a reasonable one. In coercion a mistaken belief in marriage, albeit a reasonable one, will not avail as the statute is interpreted strictly (see *Ditta, Hussain and Kara* [1988] Crim LR 42).

The need for this defence is highly questionable as it is doubtful whether a woman coerced to commit an offence would give evidence in court which could be used to establish the guilt of her husband as her accomplice. The Law Commission (Law Com No. 83) recommended the abolition of the defence and it is not included in the Draft Criminal Code (Law Com No. 177).

6.5 PRIVATE DEFENCE AND PREVENTION OF CRIME

6.5.1 Generally

An accused charged with an offence may seek to plead that he acted as he did to protect himself, or his property or others from attack or to prevent crime or to effect a lawful arrest. In strict terms such pleas are not 'defences' in the sense in which duress is a defence as, if raised successfully, they provide a justification for the accused's conduct thereby rendering it lawful. For example, it is an offence under s. 20 of the Offences Against the Person Act 1861 to unlawfully and maliciously wound another person. If D is charged with this offence but pleads that he inflicted the wound on V who was attacking him with an axe, his use of reasonable force in the circumstances would be justified and thus lawful. As the use of lawful force is not an offence D would be acquitted of the s. 20 offence as an element of the *actus reus* was missing. Where the accused pleads one of these justifications the onus is on the prosecution to disprove it beyond reasonable doubt. These principles were stated by Lord Griffiths in *Beckford* v *R.* [1988] AC 130, 144, as follows:

> It is because it is an essential element of all crimes of violence that the violence or the threat of violence should be unlawful that self-defence, if raised as an issue in a criminal trial, must be disproved by the prosecution. If the prosecution fail to do so the accused is entitled to be acquitted because the prosecution will have failed to prove an essential element of the crime namely that the violence used by the accused was unlawful.

Self-defence is a justification recognised by the common law. It covers not only defence of oneself but also of others (see *Rose* (1884) 15 Cox CC 540; *Duffy* [1967] 1 QB 63); the term private defence is thus more appropriate and less confusing. Private defence overlaps with s. 3 of the Criminal Law Act 1967 which provides:

(1) A person may use such force as is reasonable in the circumstances in the prevention of crime, or in effecting or assisting in the lawful arrest of offenders or suspected offenders or of persons unlawfully at large.

(2)   Subsection (1) above shall replace the rules of common law on the question when force used for a purpose mentioned in the subsection is justified by that purpose.

Both the common law and s. 3 impose the same requirement that the force used is such as is reasonable in the circumstances (see *Devlin* v *Armstrong* [1971] NI 13; *McInnes* [1971] 1 WLR 1600). If D uses force to defend himself or another from an unlawful attack by P he will usually also be acting to prevent a crime. In most cases it will not matter whether the plea is based in private defence or in prevention of crime. But if s. 3 were interpreted as having superceded the common law on private defence, D would be left defenceless where P, in attacking him, is not committing a crime (as where P is under 10 years of age, insane, in a state of automatism, or under a material mistake of fact) and D knows this. In such a case D could not claim to be acting to prevent a crime; he could, however, claim to be defending himself from an unjustified attack and therefore rely on private defence. It appears that the courts accept that private defence and prevention of crime under s. 3(1) co-exist as justifications (see *Cousins* [1982] QB 526).

6.5.2   The necessity of force
The use of force is not reasonable if it is not necessary. Certain factors will be relevant in considering whether the prosecution have proved beyond reasonable doubt that force was not necessary in the circumstances which existed or which the accused believed to exist. It is not necessary, however, for there to be an actual attack in progress before the accused may use force in private defence. It is sufficient if he apprehends an attack and uses force to prevent it. In *Beckford* Lord Griffiths stated (at p. 144) 'a man about to be attacked does not have to wait for his assailant to strike the first blow or fire the first shot; circumstances may justify a pre-emptive strike'. The danger the accused apprehends, however, must be sufficiently specific or imminent to justify the actions he takes (see *Devlin* v *Armstrong*), and must be of a nature which could not reasonably be met by more pacific means (*Fegan* [1972] NI 80). Where the accused's apprehension may justify his response in using force to defend himself, it does not, however, justify him in inciting others to use force. In such circumstances their use of force would be unlawful unless each individually apprehended the unlawful use of violence on himself and acted in response to this apprehension rather than in response to the accused's incitement (see *Devlin* v *Armstrong*).

6.5.2.1   Preparing for an attack   Where a person apprehends an unlawful attack on himself, may he make preparations to defend himself where those preparations may involve breaches of the criminal law? This issue arose in *Attorney-General's Reference (No 2 of 1983)* [1984] QB 456. D's shop had been attacked and damaged by rioters. Fearing further attacks he made some petrol bombs which he intended to use to protect himself and his property. He was charged with making an explosive substance in such circumstances as to give rise to a reasonable suspicion that he had not made it for a lawful object

contrary to s. 4 of the Explosive Substances Act 1883. He pleaded that his lawful object was self-defence and the jury acquitted. The Attorney-General referred the case to the Court of Appeal. Lord Lane CJ stated (at p. 470):

> The fact that in manufacturing and storing the petrol bombs the respondent committed offences under [the Explosives Act 1875 which prohibits the manufacture and storage of explosives without a licence] did not necessarily involve that when he made them his object in doing so was not lawful. The means by which he sought to fulfil that object were unlawful, but the fact that he could never without committing offences reach the point where he used them in self-defence did not render his object in making them for that purpose unlawful. The object or purpose or end for which the petrol bombs were made was not itself rendered unlawful by the fact that it could not be fulfilled except by unlawful means.

The case is not totally satisfactory as, while it decided in relation to the offence under the 1883 Act that the respondent had made the petrol bombs for a lawful object, it seemed to suggest that he would have been liable for an offence under the 1875 Act. Lord Lane CJ stated (at p. 471):

> a defendant is not left in the paradoxical position of being able to justify acts carried out in self-defence but not acts immediately preparatory to it. There is no warrant for the submission . . . that acts of self-defence will only avail a defendant when they have been done spontaneously. There is no question of a person in danger of attack 'writing his own immunity' for violent future acts of his. . . . He may still arm himself for his own protection, if the exigency arises, although in so doing he may commit other offences. That he may be guilty of other offences will avoid the risk of anarchy contemplated by the reference.

In relation to a charge under s. 1 of the Prevention of Crime Act 1953 of carrying an offensive weapon in a public place, a person could rely on the defence provided in the section of proving that he had lawful authority or reasonable excuse for carrying it. In *Evans* v *Hughes* [1972] 1 WLR 1452, the Divisional Court stated that only 'an imminent particular threat affecting the particular circumstances in which the weapon was carried' could ground a reasonable excuse. Section 139 of the Criminal Justice Act 1988 creates an additional offence of having an article with a blade or point in a public place without 'good reason or lawful authority'. This is aimed at those in the habit of carrying knives and similar articles.

Professor J. C. Smith criticised the *Attorney-General's Reference* decision in *Justification and Excuse in the Criminal Law* (at pp. 122-123) arguing that, if an act is justifiable because done in self-defence or prevention of crime, this ought to be a sufficient answer to a charge of any crime alleged to be involved in the doing of the act. He provided the following illustration:

> If I happen upon a bank robbery and, being shot at by one of the robbers, I pick up the revolver which has been dropped by a wounded policeman and,

quite reasonably, fire it in self-defence, I am surely not guilty of an offence under the Firearms Act 1968, s. 1, of being in possession of a firearm without holding a firearm certificate.

As private defence or prevention of crime may only be pleaded in response to offences involving the use of force the answer to Professor Smith's rhetorical question is that he would be guilty of the offence under s. 1 of the 1968 Act (see Elliott, 'Necessity, duress and self-defence' [1989] Crim LR 611, 618), although a charge under s. 1 of the Prevention of Crime Act 1953 could be met by the specific defence provided by that section as interpreted in *Evans* v *Hughes*. Smith and Hogan, in *Criminal Law* p. 260, argue that the courts should develop the law so that 'where contravention of *any* law is (i) necessary to enable the right of public or private defence to be exercised, and (ii) reasonable in the circumstances, it ought to be excused.' It is submitted that this is what has partially happened by accident through the development of duress of circumstances. In the robbery example above, on a charge under s. 1 of the Firearms Act 1968, duress of circumstances could be pleaded as an excusatory defence. The issue of imminence of the threat necessary for a successful plea of duress/duress of circumstances obviates the use of the defence by a person who arms himself with a gun because he anticipates that one day he may be attacked; the defence would only be available to the person who arms himself immediately prior to what he believes to be an imminent attack. However, duress/duress of circumstances is only available where the accused fears death or serious physical injury whereas private defence may be pleaded in justification where a lesser degree of harm is anticipated. Thus Smith and Hogan's plea for further development of the law still requires further judicial action if all anomalies are to be removed.

6.5.2.2 Duty to retreat?   Formerly it was believed that the common law imposed a requirement that a person could only plead private defence where he had retreated as far as he could before resorting to the use of force. In *Bird* [1985] 1 WLR 816, the Court of Appeal made it clear that there is no such requirement but rather it is a factor to be considered in deciding whether it was necessary to use force, and whether the force used was reasonable. Lord Lane CJ stated (at p. 820) what should have been obvious:

> If the defendant is proved to have been attacking or retaliating or revenging himself, then he was not truly acting in self-defence. Evidence that the defendant tried to retreat or tried to call off the fight may be a cast-iron method of casting doubt on the suggestion that he was the attacker or retaliator or the person trying to revenge himself. But it is not by any means the only method of doing that.

If there were a duty to retreat a person would never be able to use pre-emptive force. Similarly a person is under no duty to refrain from going where he may lawfully go because he knows he is likely to be attacked (see *Field* [1972] Crim LR 435). A distinction must be drawn between the situation where a person acts lawfully but in the realisation that he may be subjected to violence as a result (cf. *Beatty* v *Gillbanks* (1882) 9 QBD 308), and the situation where he deliberately engineers or provokes an attack on himself so that he may respond with force and seek to plead self-defence. In the latter situation the justification of self-defence will not be open to him (cf. *Browne* [1973] NI 96).

6.5.2.3   Unknown circumstances of justification   While the use of force must have been necessary in the circumstances for the accused to be able to rely on one of the justifications under consideration, a problem which has arisen is whether the accused must know or believe that circumstances exist which would justify his use of force even though those circumstances actually do exist. The answer was originally in the affirmative. In *Dadson* (1850) 4 Cox CC 358, D, a constable, was on duty watching a copse from which wood had been stolen. P emerged carrying wood which he had stolen. He ran away when D called to him and D shot him so that he could arrest him. D was convicted of shooting at P with intent to cause him grievous bodily harm. D raised the justification that he was shooting to arrest an escaping felon. Stealing wood was only a felony where the thief had two previous convictions for that offence. In fact P had several such convictions and thus was a felon but D did not know this. D's conviction was upheld as he was not justified in shooting P as the fact that P was committing a felony was not known to him at the time. When the Criminal Law Act 1967 was passed it was argued by some that s. 2 (now replaced by s. 24(4) of the Police and Criminal Evidence Act 1984) and s. 3 had the effect of reversing *Dadson*. Thus it was argued that if a person actually had committed an arrestable offence an arrest of him would be lawful even though the arresting officer did not know nor suspect on reasonable grounds that he had committed that offence. The Law Commission in its reports on *Codification of the Criminal Law* (Law Com Nos.143 and 177) have recommended that an accused should be able to rely on unknown circumstances of justification in any case where the use of force was necessary and reasonable. Professor Brian Hogan has argued strongly against this view in 'The *Dadson* principle' [1989] Crim LR 679. In *Chapman* (1988) 89 Cr App R 190, the Divisional Court effectively reaffirmed *Dadson* (and thus the principle for which it is authority) pointing out that if a person is unaware of circumstances justifying an arrest he cannot perform a lawful arrest as he will not be able to comply with s. 28(3) of the Police and Criminal Evidence Act 1984 which requires that he inform the suspect of the grounds for the arrest. Thus if the arrest is unlawful any force used to effect it is likewise unlawful.

6.5.3   The reasonableness of the force

6.5.3.1   Assessing the reasonableness of the force used   In all the justifications relating to the use of force the ultimate question for the jury is whether the prosecution have proved beyond reasonable doubt that the accused did not use such force as was reasonable in the circumstances. Adapting the test laid down by the Lord Diplock in *Attorney-General for Northern Ireland's Reference (No 1 of 1975)* [1977] AC 105, 137, the jury should be directed to ask themselves:

Are we satisfied that no reasonable man (a) with knowledge of such facts as were known to the accused or . . . believed by him to exist (b) in the circumstances and time available to him for reflection (c) could be of the opinion that the prevention of the risk of harm to which others might be exposed if the suspect were allowed to escape [or the defence of himself or another, or the prevention of crime or the defence of property] justified exposing [the accused's victim] to the risk of harm to him that might result from the kind of force that the accused contemplated using?

While the jury are carrying out this exercise of balancing harms in the 'calm analytical atmosphere of the court-room . . . with the benefit of hindsight' (per Lord Diplock at p. 138) it is important that they seek to place themselves in the position in which the accused found himself, under all the stresses to which he was exposed and with the time which he had available to him in which to make his decision whether to use force. Lord Morris in *Palmer* v *The Queen* [1971] AC 814, 832, stated:

There are no prescribed words which must be employed in or adopted in summing up. All that is needed is a clear exposition, in relation to the particular facts of the case, of the conception of necessary self-defence. . . . If there has been an attack so that defence is reasonably necessary it will be recognised that a person defending himself cannot weigh to a nicety the exact measure of his necessary defensive action.

The accused's own beliefs in the situation are also pertinent to the issue. *Shannon* (1980) 71 Cr App R 192, and *Whyte* [1987] 3 All ER 416, affirmed Lord Morris's view (at p. 832) that:

If a jury thought that in a moment of unexpected anguish a person attacked had only done what he honestly and instinctively thought was necessary that would be most potent evidence that only reasonable defensive action had been taken.

6.5.3.2 Excessive force If, having taken all the above issues into consideration, the jury conclude that while some force may have been necessary in the circumstances, the accused used too much force, his plea of justification will fail. In sentencing the accused the judge may take into account in mitigation the fact that some force would have been justified albeit that the accused used too much. Where, however, the accused is charged with murder there can be no such mitigation as the sentence for murder is a mandatory life sentence. In *MacKay* [1957] VR 560, the Supreme Court of Victoria recognised a qualified defence to murder resulting in a conviction of manslaughter based on the excessive use of force in circumstances where some force would have been justified. The High Court of Australia confirmed this in *Howe* (1958) 100 CLR 448. In *Palmer* Lord Morris stated that self-defence 'either succeeds so as to result in an acquittal or is disproved in which case as a defence it is rejected.' *Palmer* (a Privy Council decision) was followed by the Court of Appeal in

McInnes [1971] 1 WLR 1600. In the *A-G for Northern Ireland's Reference (No 1 of 1975)*, Lord Dilhorne stated that where death resulted from the use of excessive force in prevention of crime or in effecting an arrest, and the accused intended to kill or to do grievous bodily harm, he would be guilty of murder and not manslaughter. The Criminal Law Revision Committee (Fourteenth Report, Cmnd. 7844, para. 288) and the Law Commission (Law Com No. 177) in its Draft Criminal Code recommend the adoption of a defence of excessive force leading to a conviction of manslaughter similar to the Australian qualified defence. In Australia, however, in *Zekevic* (1987) 61 ALJR 375, the High Court of Australia overruled its previous decisions and abolished the qualified defence in order *inter alia* to simplify the task of the jury. One doubts whether the qualified defence is as difficult to understand as the High Court of Australia believed. It is a sad indictment on the Australian judiciary that the accused's right to this qualified defence should be denied because of the inability of the judges to state the law in a form comprehensible to the jury. It is to be hoped that this antipodean retreat will not prevent an English advance.

6.5.3.3 Mistake The reasonableness of the force used by the accused is to be judged in light of the circumstances as he believed them to be; if he makes a mistake he will be judged against the mistaken facts he believed to exist (*Williams* (1984) 78 Cr App R 276; *Beckford* [1988] AC 130) (see *3.6.1.1.2 ante*). In such circumstances, while the accused intended to use force on his victim he did not, because of his mistake, intend to use unlawful force; as Lord Griffiths stated in *Beckford* (at p.144), 'it is an essential element of all crimes of violence that the violence or threat of violence should be unlawful.' Thus, for example, if the accused believes he is about to be attacked when in fact the supposed assailant is a practical joker, or if he believes his actual attacker is armed when he is unarmed, the accused's use of force will be measured against the facts he believed to exist rather than against those which actually did exist. It matters not that his mistake is an unreasonable one; but obviously the more reasonable the mistake the more likely it is that the jury will believe him. If the accused's mistake as to the need to use any force or as to the degree of force necessary to defend himself or prevent crime or the like was caused by his voluntary intoxication, the defence will fail whether or not the offence with which he is charged is one of specific or basic intent (see *O'Grady* [1987] 3 WLR 321; *O'Connor* [1991] Crim LR 135, see *5.6.4 ante*)

6.5.4 Extent of the justifications
While the justifications under consideration are generally raised in response to charges of offences against the person, they are not confined to such offences. In *Renouf* [1986] 1 WLR 522, D was charged with reckless driving. He had driven his car in pursuit of another vehicle, the occupants of which had assaulted him and damaged his car. D forced the vehicle off the road and rammed it. He sought to rely on s. 3(1) of the Criminal Law Act 1967 but was convicted when the trial judge ruled that it was incapable of affording a defence to a charge of reckless driving. The Court of Appeal quashed his conviction as the acts alleged to amount to reckless driving constituted the use of force for

the purpose of assisting in the lawful arrest of offenders and thus it should have been left to the jury to consider whether it was reasonable.

It would appear, however, that these justifications may be pleaded only in relation to offences which are not offences against the person where the circumstances constituting the offence amount to using force. The justifications may not be pleaded in respect of other offences committed incidentally (see 6.5.2.1 *ante*). Had Mr Renouf driven recklessly in pursuit of his assailants and then, drawing alongside their vehicle he had pointed a gun at the driver threatening to shoot if he did not stop, he may have been able to plead that he was using reasonable force to arrest an offender had he been charged with assault. By contrast, if he had been charged with driving recklessly he would have failed in a plea of justification in relation to this charge as his reckless driving did not constitute the force in this situation but rather was incidental to his use of force or, as Lawton LJ put it in *Renouf*, it amounted to a reckless act 'antecedent to the use of force'.

6.5.5 Resisting justifiable conduct

In 6.1 *ante* the example was given of D seeking to resist his arrest by PC. In the first case, where he did not know that PC was a police officer, D thought he was about to be attacked. In the circumstances as he believed them to be he would have been justified in using force; the only question would be whether the force he used was reasonable (see *Williams*; cf. *Kenlin* v *Gardner* (1967) 2 QB 510). In the second case, where he knew PC was a police officer, and the officer was acting lawfully, he would not be justified in resisting arrest even though he had not committed any crime; if D has made a mistake it is not one of fact but rather one of law relating to the circumstances in which a person may be arrested (cf. *Fennell* [1971] 1 QB 428) . If PC, making a lawful arrest, uses more force than is reasonably necessary, D could use force in self-defence as, in this circumstance, the officer would be acting unlawfully in using unjustifiable force. The problematical case would be the situation where PC mistakes D for a dangerous criminal and seeks to use force either to arrest him or to defend himself or others. For example, PC sees D walking along the street and hides in a doorway until D walks past and then tackles him from behind seeking to restrain him. In this circumstance the officer is acting lawfully both in seeking to arrest D and with regard to the use of force, provided he honestly believed that force was necessary either to effect an arrest or to defend himself or others and he used no more force than was reasonably necessary. (The amount of force that may be used to effect an arrest may be less than that which may be necessary in self-defence as it is inconceivable that deadly force would be reasonable to effect an arrest whereas it may be reasonable in self-defence.) Is D, however, obliged to submit to the infliction of this force on him? The case law provides no clear answer, but it is submitted that, if he uses force in return, it is arguable that his force is not being used to resist arrest but to resist what he believes to be an unlawful assault. If Williams could use reasonable force to defend someone whom he believed was being assaulted, who was in fact being lawfully arrested, it would be strange if D, believing he was being assaulted, could not use force to defend himself.

Further reading

G. Williams, 'The theory of excuses' [1982] Crim LR 732.

J. C. Smith, *Justification and Excuse in the Criminal Law* (1989).

D. W. Elliott, 'Necessity, duress and self-defence' [1989] Crim LR 611.

H. P. Milgate, 'Duress and the criminal law: another about turn by the House of Lords' [1988] CLJ 61.

B. Hogan, 'The *Dadson* principle' [1989] Crim LR 679.

E. Colvin, 'Exculpatory defences in criminal law' (1990) 10 OJLS 381.

G. R. Sullivan, 'Bad thoughts and bad acts' [1990] Crim LR 559.

P. A. J. Waddington, '"Overkill" or "minimum force"?' [1990] Crim LR 695.

N. M. Padfield, 'Duress, Necessity and the Law Commission' [1992] Crim LR 778.

SEVEN
Parties to crime

7.1 ACCOMPLICES

7.1.1 Principals and accessories

All the parties to a crime are accomplices. For example, A decides that he wants V killed. He encourages D to perform the murder. B supplies D with a knife to perform the murder, C supplies A with information regarding V's movements, E drives D and F to V's home and acts as lookout, F assists D to kill V by holding him while D stabs him and G, V's discontented butler, shouts encouragement at D and F as they attack V. All seven parties are accomplices to the murder of V but only D is the perpetrator of the offence; the others are accessories.

The person who perpetrates the crime is referred to as the principal. A person is the perpetrator if his act is the most immediate cause of the *actus reus* of the offence; in the example above D's act is clearly the immediate cause of V's death. In some cases D may be liable as principal even though the *actus reus* was brought about by another. D will be liable where he has used another person to procure the commission of the offence and that person is not guilty of the offence due to, for example, infancy, lack of *mens rea* or insanity. Such a person is generally referred to as an 'innocent agent'. For example, D gives E a parcel telling him it is a birthday present and asks him to deliver it to V. The parcel contains a bomb and V is killed when it explodes. D would be guilty of murder as the principal because E, not knowing the nature of the parcel, lacked *mens rea* and was an innocent agent. Similarly, if D employs E, his eight year-old son to climb through windows of houses to steal items, D would be guilty of burglary as principal because E, being an infant, is not criminally liable and is an innocent agent. Problems arise where E is found to be an innocent agent but D is personally incapable of committing the offence as a principal (see 7.1.3 *post*).

Others, not being principals, who participate in the commission of an offence are referred to as accessories and will be liable to conviction if it is proved that they aided, abetted, counselled or procured the commission of the crime by the principal. The law is to be found in s. 8 of the Accessories and Abettors Act 1861, as amended by the Criminal Law Act 1977:

> Whosoever shall aid, abet, counsel or procure the commission of any indictable offence whether the same be an offence at common law or by virtue of any act passed or to be passed, shall be liable to be tried, indicted and punished as a principal offender.

Section 44 of the Magistrates' Courts Act 1980 contains a similar provision for summary offences.

While the consequence of conviction as a principal or an accessory is the same, it is important in some circumstances to be able to distinguish between them. The *mens rea* required of the accessory differs from that of a principal and *mens rea* must always be proved even where the principal's offence is one of strict liability. In some cases an offence may only be committed by persons of a specified class or may not be committed as a principal by persons of a specified class, for example, rape cannot be perpetrated by a boy under fourteen; only a licensee can commit an offence involving a breach of the conditions of the licence (see *Morris* v *Tolman* [1923] 1 KB 166). Where vicarious liability is in issue it is important to identify the principal and the accessory as vicarious liability may only be imposed in respect of the act of a principal (see 7.2 *post*).

Occasionally it is not possible for the prosecution to determine prior to the trial whether more than one person was involved in the offence, and if so, what D's role was. In such circumstances they may allege, in a single count, the alternative allegations that D was principal in the first degree or that he aided and abetted, counselled or procured the offence (see *Gaughan* [1990] Crim LR 880). A problem which may arise, however, was identified by Lamer J in a murder case before the Supreme Court of Canada, *Thatcher* (1987) 39 DLR (4) 275, who stated (at p. 313):

> if the Crown presents evidence which tends to inculpate the accused under one theory and exculpate him under the other, then the trial judge must instruct the jury that if they wish to rely on such evidence, then they must be unanimous as to the theory they adopt.

If the evidence is consistent with both theories then it would not matter, particularly if the jury were split as to the basis for conviction provided they were all satisfied that he had committed the offence either as principal or accessory.

In most cases there will be no problem identifying the principal and the accessory but in some circumstances, while it may be clear an offence has been committed, and that two or more accomplices were involved, it may be unclear who was the principal and who was the accessory. Thus if A and B were involved in the commission of an offence both may be convicted where it is proved that each of them must have been guilty in one capacity or the other (see *Swindall and Osborne* (1846) 2 Car & Kir 230; and *Chan Wing-Siu* v *The Queen* [1985] AC 168)). Both may be principals as where, for example, A and B in pursuance of a joint enterprise attack V, raining blows on him and he dies (see *Macklin and Murphy's Case* (1838) 2 Lew CC 225), or A and B act in concert to rob a bank, A threatening the staff with a gun while B appropriates the money; provided each had the requisite *mens rea* they could be convicted as principals to murder and robbery. The cases tend to talk in terms of there being a joint enterprise, or pre-arranged plan or talk of the accused 'acting in concert'. This is not a prerequisite of liability. If A and B independently embark on an attack on V at the same time and he dies, both may be convicted of murder provided each had the requisite *mens rea* even though there is no pre-arranged plan or agreement between them (see *Mohan* [1967] 2 AC 187). In *Mohan* A and B attacked V with cutlasses killing him. The evidence indicated that only one wound proved fatal but it could not be established who inflicted that wound. A and B appealed against convictions of murder arguing that as there was no pre-arranged plan to attack V the Crown had to show which of them struck the fatal blow. The Privy Council dismissed the appeals on the basis that as A and B were attacking the same man at the same time with similar weapons and with the common intention that he should suffer grievous bodily harm, each of them was present aiding and abetting the other and thus there was no need to prove any pre-arranged plan.

Where the offence is one of strict liability and it is unclear which of the accused was the principal, each may be convicted only where the prosecution prove that each had *mens rea*. In *Smith* v *Mellors and Soar* [1987] RTR 210, both M and S were over the blood-alcohol limit when seen running away from a car which had been driven on the road. Driving with a blood-alcohol level above the prescribed limit is a strict liability offence. As it could not be proved who was driving neither could be convicted unless he had the *mens rea* required for conviction as an accessory. Thus the prosecution had to prove that each accused knew that the other had had too much to drink to be fit to drive.

In some cases it may be clear that an offence has been committed and that either A or B committed it, but it is not clear who did it nor is it clear whether the other was an accessory. In such circumstances if the prosecution cannot bring forward prima facie evidence that each of them is guilty in one capacity or another, the charges against both will be dismissed. In *Lane and Lane* (1986) 82 Cr App R 5, the evidence showed that the child of the accused had been fatally injured between noon and 8.30pm. Each parent had been present for some of the time and absent for some of it but throughout the period the child had always been in the presence of a parent. As it could not be proved who had injured the child nor that each had been involved as principal or accessory, there was no case to answer on the charges of manslaughter against each. If, however, the prosecution can prove that one of the accused committed the offence and the other aided or abetted him in doing so, then both may be convicted. In such circumstances it does not matter that the principal offender cannot be identified as s. 8 of the Accessories and Abettors Act 1861 states that those who aid, abet counsel or procure an offence are 'liable to be indicted, tried and punished as a principal offender' (see *Forman and Ford* [1988] Crim LR 677, 6.1.2.2 *post*).

7.1.2 Aiding, abetting, counselling or procuring

7.1.2.1 Defining terms If an accused is charged as an accessory he will be charged with aiding, abetting, counselling or procuring the particular offence and he is liable to conviction if it is proved that he participated in any one of these four ways (see *Re Smith* (1858) 3 H & N 227; *Ferguson* v *Weaving* [1951] 1 KB 814). There has been much argument regarding the meaning of each individual term and 'aiding and abetting' have generally been paired together as if they were synonymous. In *Attorney-General's Reference (No 1 of 1975)* [1975] QB 773, Lord Widgery CJ took the view that each word probably had a different meaning. 'Aiding' suggests helping or assisting the principal to commit the offence whether before its commission or at the time of its commission. In the scenario given at the beginning of para. 7.1.1 *ante*, B, C and E all assist D prior to the commission of the murder (see *Thambiah* v *R* [1966] AC 37); F is present assisting him at the time of the offence (see *Clarkson* [1971] 1 WLR 1402) and E also assists at that time by keeping watch (see *Betts and Ridley* (1930) 22 Cr App R 148). 'Abetting' suggests the activity of one who incites, instigates or encourages the principal to commit the offence (see *Wilcox* v *Jeffery* [1951] 1 All ER 464). 'Counselling' also suggests advising or encouraging the commission of the offence. In *National Coal Board* v *Gamble* [1959] 1 QB 11, Devlin J expressed the opinion that 'abetting' involved presence at the scene of the crime offering encouragement. At common law 'abetting' denoted encouragement at the time of the offence and 'counselling' encouragement given previously. In the scenario in para. 7.1.1, A would be liable for counselling the commission of the offence and G for abetting it; F, by his presence and assistance, is also offering encouragement and thus is also an abettor.

In *Attorney-General's Reference (ante)*, Lord Widgery CJ considered that in most cases of aiding, abetting or counselling the parties would have met and discussed the offence they had in mind. While this may be generally true, it is not a requirement for liability as an accessory. The principal may have met with the accessories separately or there may have been no discussion at all. For example, in the scenario in para. 7.1.1, G abetted the offence but he never discussed it or planned it with D or any of the other parties. What seems to be necessary is some meeting of minds or consensus, namely that the offence committed is the one encouraged and the principal is aware of that encouragement even if he would have committed it without encouragement (see *Calhaem* [1985] 1 QB 808). In the case of aiding, however, there need not be a meeting of minds. For example, in the scenario in para. 7.1.1, if H, the maid, restrained W, V's wife, and prevented her from phoning the police or from trying to rescue V, H would have assisted D in committing the offence although D was totally unaware of H's intervention.

It is not necessary to prove any causal link between the assistance or encouragement and the commission of the offence (see *A-G's Reference;*

Calhaem). By contrast 'procuring' involves a different concept altogether. In *A-G's Reference (ante)*, Lord Widgery CJ stated that procuring required a causal link to be established between what the procurer did and what the principal did. Procuring, Lord Widgery said, means 'to produce by endeavour'. The facts of the case giving rise to the Reference were that A surreptitiously added alcohol to D's drink knowing that he would shortly be driving his car home. D was convicted of the strict liability offence of driving with an excessive quantity of alcohol in his body contrary to s. 6(1) of the Road Traffic Act 1972. The Court of Appeal held that this amounted to procuring as A had set out to see that a particular state of affairs happened and had taken appropriate steps to produce it. The addition of the alcohol to D's drink was a direct cause of the excess alcohol level in his blood. Thus Lord Widgery stated (at p. 780) the offence had been procured 'because, unknown to the driver and without his collaboration, he has been put in a position in which in fact he has committed an offence which he never would have committed otherwise.'

7.1.2.2 Presence, activity and inactivity Mere presence at the scene of an offence and failure to intervene or prevent it is generally not sufficient to render such a person liable as an accessory, although it may provide prima facie (but not conclusive) evidence of an intention to encourage the perpetrator (see *Coney* (1882) 8 QBD 534). If a person is to be convicted in such circumstances it must be proved that there was encouragement in fact and that there was an intention to encourage (see *Clarkson* [1971] 1 WLR 1402; and *Bland* [1988] Crim LR 41). This may be established by proving that the accused was present as a result of a prior agreement that the offence be committed (see *Smith* v *Reynolds* [1986] Crim LR 559) or that he did some positive act of assistance or encouragement knowing the circumstances which constitute the offence. It is not necessary to establish that commission of the crime was the accessory's purpose in the latter situation (see *National Coal Board* v *Gamble* [1959] 1 QB 11).

Voluntary presence at the scene of a crime, without more, may amount to actual encouragement. In *Wilcox* v *Jeffery* [1951] 1 All ER 464, A's presence as a paying member of the audience at a concert given by D amounted to aiding and abetting D to contravene the Aliens Order 1920. D had been permitted to enter the United Kingdom only on condition that he take no employment. Further evidence of A's intention to encourage D was derived from A's behaviour in that he had met D at the airport and, after the concert, he wrote and published a laudatory review of the concert in the periodical of which he was the proprietor. In this case there would clearly have been no performance if there had been no audience so the presence of each member of the audience was an encouragement to D to perform (see also *Coney, ante*). But presence is not always sufficient to amount to encouragement. In *Allan* [1965] 1 QB 130, A was present at the scene of an affray. He was totally passive doing nothing to offer encouragement to those involved in the fighting, although he harboured a secret intention to join in if help was needed by the side which he favoured. The Court of Criminal Appeal stated (at p. 138):

> In our judgment, before a jury can properly convict an accused person of
> being a principal in the second degree to an affray, they must be convinced

by the evidence that, at the very least, he by some means or other encouraged the participants. To hold otherwise would be, in effect, . . . to convict a man on his thoughts, unaccompanied by any physical act other than the fact of his mere presence.

This case is distinguishable from *Wilcox* v *Jeffery* as, without spectators, the affray would still have occurred so mere presence, without more, did not amount to encouragement.

Where A has the right to control the actions of another and deliberately refrains from doing so, his inactivity may amount to actual encouragement. For example, a publican who takes no steps to make his customers leave his premises after closing time, may be convicted of aiding and abetting their consumption of alcohol outside hours (*Tuck* v *Robson* [1970] 1 WLR 741). Likewise if the owner of a car sits as a passenger in it while it is driven recklessly and does nothing to prevent or discourage this, he may be guilty of aiding and abetting the reckless driving. His failure to exercise his right of control is evidence of encouragement (see *Du Cros* v *Lambourne* [1907] 1 KB 40; *Cassady* v *Reg. Morris* [1975] RTR 470). If the Road Traffic Bill 1990 is enacted the offence of reckless driving will be replaced by that of dangerous driving, but the same principle will apply.

If A is under a duty to act, his omission to do so may give rise to liability as an accessory just as it may as a principal. While A may not have a right to control D, his omission to fulfil his duty may amount to encouragement of D. For example, if one parent ill-treats his child in the presence of the other parent, the latter's failure to fulfil his or her duty to protect the child may amount to encouragement of the former (see *Russell and Russell* (1987) 85 Cr App R 388). The conclusion of encouragement is not automatic as there may not have been time to intervene or the parent may have been in terror of the other. In *Forman and Ford* [1988] Crim LR 677 it was held that, where a suspect was assaulted while in a cell with two officers, it was not established who was the assailant and there was no evidence that they were acting in concert, both could be convicted if the jury are satisfied in respect of each of them that if he himself did not commit the assault he encouraged the other to do so by failing to intervene or report the offence and the other relied on him neither to intervene to prevent nor afterwards to report the offence. In this situation each officer is under a duty to prevent crime and to keep the peace so his inactivity can amount to positive encouragement.

7.1.3 Proving the principal offence

Is it possible to convict A as an accessory without convicting D as the principal? The fact that D has been acquitted in a separate trial does not preclude a court from convicting A as the evidence against D may have been weak. What is necessary is that it be proved beyond reasonable doubt that the principal offence was committed. Several situations may arise.

7.1.3.1 Absence of an *actus reus*

A person cannot be convicted as an accessory unless there was an *actus reus*. In *Thornton* v *Mitchell* [1940] 1 All ER

339, a bus driver reversed his bus relying on the signals of his conductor as he was unable to see behind the bus. Two pedestrians behind the bus were knocked down and injured. The driver was charged with careless driving and the conductor with aiding and abetting that offence. The justices dismissed the charge against the driver as he had done nothing which he should not have done and had not been careless, but they convicted the conductor. The Divisional Court held the conductor could not be convicted as there was no *actus reus* of careless driving. The Court quoted with approval the dictum of Avory J in *Morris* v *Tolman* [1923] 1 KB 166 (at p. 171) 'in order to convict, it would be necessary to show that the respondent was aiding and abetting the principal, but a person cannot aid another in doing something which that other has not done'. As there was no *actus reus* it was not possible to regard the conductor as the principal working through an innocent agent.

7.1.3.2 Perpetrator exempt from prosecution If the perpetrator of the principal offence is, for some special reason, exempt from prosecution, this does not preclude the conviction of another as an accessory for encouraging or assisting the commission of the offence. In *Austin* [1981] 1 All ER 374, the father of a child, assisted by A, snatched the child from the lawful custody of his estranged wife. A was convicted of child stealing contrary to s. 56 of the Offences Against the Person Act 1861 (since repealed). The Court of Appeal held that while the proviso to the section exempted the father from liability to prosecution, he had committed the offence of child stealing. Accordingly, the proviso provided no obstacle to the conviction of A as an accessory to that offence.

7.1.3.3 Perpetrator not liable to conviction Where the principal offence has been committed a person who has encouraged or assisted the principal to commit it will be liable as an accessory even though the offence is one which the accessory could not commit as a principal. Thus a woman or a boy under fourteen may be convicted of rape as an accessory (see *Ram and Ram* (1893) 17 Cox CC 609; *Eldershaw* (1828) 3 C & P 396). What would happen in such a case, however, if the principal was not liable to conviction because he lacked the requisite *mens rea* or had a defence, but the accomplice had the requisite *mens rea* and did encourage or assist in the commission of the *actus reus*? For example, A, a woman, encourages E to have sexual intercourse with V, against V's will, and she restrains V while E has intercourse. If E is under fourteen he would not be guilty of rape because he is presumed incapable of sexual intercourse. A could not be convicted as a principal acting through an innocent agent as she is not capable of committing rape as a principal. The law would appear to be deficient if A was to escape criminal liability for rape because of these technicalities. A possible solution would be to hold that the *actus reus* of rape had been committed in that unlawful sexual intercourse occurred to which V did not consent, and that A had aided and abetted the commission of that *actus reus*.

In *Bourne* (1952) 36 Cr App R 125, A forced his wife to commit buggery with a dog. His conviction of aiding and abetting the commission of the offence was upheld on appeal as, although the wife would not have been guilty as principal because of the defence of duress, the *actus reus* of buggery had been committed. It would also have been true to say that the wife had the *mens rea* for the offence as duress acts merely as an excuse which exempts the accused from conviction where she has committed an offence as a result of the threats of another (see 6.2.1 *ante*). In *Cogan and Leak* [1976] QB 217, Leak compelled his wife to have sexual intercourse with Cogan. Cogan's conviction was quashed following the House of Lords decision in *Morgan* (see *3.6.1.1.1 ante*) as his defence of honest belief in Mrs Cogan's consent had not been left to the jury. Leak's conviction was upheld as he had procured the commission of the offence. Lawton LJ stated (at p. 223):

> the act of sexual intercourse without the wife's consent was the *actus reus*; it had been procured by Leak who had the appropriate *mens rea*, namely his intention that Cogan should have sexual intercourse with her without her consent. . . . . it is irrelevant that the man whom Leak had procured to do the physical act himself did not intend to have sexual intercourse with the wife without her consent. Leak was using him as a means to procure a criminal purpose.

This accords with the decision in *Bourne*. Unfortunately Lawton LJ went on to state that Leak could have been indicted as the principal working through an innocent agent. This creates several difficulties. At that time Leak could not commit rape as a principal as he was cohabiting with his wife (but see *10.2.1.1.2 post*). Further, it is difficult to see how it could be said that 'Leak had sexual intercourse with V without her consent'. While there is no intellectual difficulty in affirming, for example, that D stole, killed, or committed arson through an innocent agent as personal action on the part of the accused is not implicit in the definition of the offence, rape does appear to presume personal action on the part of the perpetrator; Leak most clearly did not have intercourse with his wife at that time. If this basis of the decision is followed it leads to the even more ludicrous conclusion that A, in the scenario at the beginning of this section, could be charged as the principal to the offence of rape even though as a woman she is incapable of performing the *actus reus*; according to s. 1(1) of the Sexual Offences (Amendment) Act 1976 only a man may commit rape! The only conclusion one can arrive at is that this part of the decision in *Cogan and Leak* is wrong and that only the part of the decision which accords with *Bourne* should be followed. Thus A will be liable as an accessory where he has encouraged or assisted the commission of an *actus reus* albeit that the perpetrator is not liable as a principal.

7.1.3.4 Perpetrator and accomplice liable but for different offences
The same facts may supply the *actus reus* of several offences. For example, unlawful homicide includes murder and manslaughter, for which the *actus reus* is the same, conviction of either depending on the *mens rea* of the accused or the availability of the mitigating defences of diminished responsibility or provocation. Accordingly there is nothing wrong in principle with D being convicted of murder as a principal and A being convicted of manslaughter as

an accessory if A lacked the *mens rea* for murder. For example A and D embark on a joint enterprise to burgle a factory agreeing to knock out V the watchman with a cosh. D knows that V has an eggshell skull and that such an assault will cause at least grievous bodily harm to him. A is unaware of this and does not contemplate any injury to V beyond actual bodily harm. If D coshes V and he dies, D would be liable for murder as he intended to cause grievous bodily harm but A would only be liable for manslaughter on the basis of an unlawful and dangerous act. The converse also applies (and is consistent with the principle in *Bourne*) so that A may be convicted of the greater offence whereas D is convicted of the lesser as the *actus reus* has been committed and the accessory's liability depends on his own *mens rea*. In *Howe* [1987] 1 AC 417, Lord Mackay (with whom Lords Bridge, Brandon and Griffiths agreed) considered the following hypothetical situation (at p. 458):

> A hands a gun to D informing him that it is loaded with blank ammunition only and telling him to go and scare X by discharging it. The ammunition is in fact live, as A knows, and X is killed. D is convicted only of manslaughter, as he might be on those facts.

Lord Mackay agreed with the Court of Appeal that it would be absurd if A should thereby escape conviction for murder and that the previous authority of *Richards* [1974] QB 776 was wrongly decided. He stated (at p. 458):

> where a person has been killed and that result is the result intended by another participant, the mere fact that the actual killer may be convicted only of the reduced charge of manslaughter for some reason special to himself does not, in my opinion in any way, result in a compulsory reduction for the other participant.

If the perpetrator, D, intentionally kills in pursuance of a joint enterprise where he and A had agreed only to inflict some minor injury on the victim, the fact that D's act was beyond the common design and uncontemplated by A would absolve A from liability for manslaughter (see *Lovesey and Peterson* [1970] 1 QB 352; *Dunbar* [1988] Crim LR 693 discussed at 7.1.4.4 *post*).

The examples so far have involved a difference in *mens rea* between A and D. Where murder is charged an accused may be convicted of manslaughter if he successfully raises a defence of diminished responsibility or provocation. Section 2(4) of the Homicide Act 1957 specifically provides that the fact that one party to a killing is not liable to be convicted of murder because of diminished responsibility does not affect the question whether the killing amounted to murder in the case of any other party to it. There is no such provision in respect of provocation but it is assumed that the outcome would be the same and Lord Mackay's dictum in *Howe, ante,* appears to confirm this.

7.1.4 *Mens rea* of an accessory
The *mens rea* required of an accessory may be simply stated as an intention to assist or encourage the commission of the principal offence combined with

knowledge of the circumstances which constitute the offence. This statement requires elucidation; this will reveal the problems associated with the *mens rea* of accessories.

7.1.4.1 Intention to assist or encourage the principal Defining the *mens rea* required of accessories has presented major difficulties for the courts. The principal is the one whose act has caused the *actus reus* of the offence and the *mens rea* required of him generally relates to the doing of that act and the bringing about of its causally connected consequences. As the acts of the accessory do not cause the *actus reus* the *mens rea* required cannot equate exactly to that of the principal. For example, D shoots at V intending to kill him and succeeds. D's *mens rea* directly mirrors the *actus reus* he has brought about. A supplied D with the gun knowing that D wished to kill V, although he hoped D would fail. It can be seen that A's act assists D but the *actus reus* of murder does not directly mirror his state of mind. If A is to be liable for murder it will be because he has intended to assist D knowing that D intends to kill rather than on the basis that he, himself, intended to kill V. In *National Coal Board* v *Gamble* [1959] 1 QB 11, the Divisional Court held that intention to assist or encourage had to be proved in addition to knowledge of the circumstances. The commission of the principal offence may not be the accused's desire, motive or purpose. Devlin J stated (at p. 23):

> But an indifference to the result of the crime does not of itself negative abetting. If one man deliberately sells to another a gun to be used for murdering a third, he may be indifferent about whether the third man lives or dies and interested only in the cash profit to be made out of the sale, but he can still be an aider and abettor. To hold otherwise would be to negative the rule that *mens rea* is a matter of intent only and does not depend on desire or motive.

In *NCB* v *Gamble*, A's servant B operated the weighbridge at a colliery. B informed D that his lorry was overladen; driving an overladen lorry on the road was an offence. D said that he was prepared to take the risk whereupon B gave him the weighbridge ticket and the property in (i.e. ownership of) the coal passed to D. Without this ticket D could not have left the colliery. A was charged with aiding, abetting, counselling or procuring D's offence of driving an overladen lorry on the road. For the purposes of the appeal it was assumed that B knew he had the right to prevent the lorry leaving the colliery. A, through its servant B, supplied D with an essential item for the commission of the offence, namely the weighbridge ticket, and did so knowing the circumstances which would render D's act of driving on the road an offence. A's indifference to this consequence was irrelevant to liability as A, through its servant, had voluntarily done an act which assisted D knowing the circumstances which constituted the offence. The intention required, therefore, is the voluntary performance of an act with the realisation that this assists or encourages D in his course of conduct.

There was much discussion in *NCB* v *Gamble* about whether ownership of the coal had passed prior to, or only after, the weighbridge ticket had been handed over. The suggestion was that if A only became aware of D's illegal purpose after ownership in the property had passed, but before delivery, he could not be liable as an accessory when he delivered what was D's property to him. This is unsatisfactory and not required by the law of contract. A contract for an illegal purpose is unenforceable regardless of when the seller learns of that purpose. No distinction should be made between the situation where A sells a gun to D knowing from the outset that D intends to use it to kill someone and the situation where D has paid for the gun (and ownership of it has passed) but before A delivers it to him he tells A that he intends to use it to kill someone (cf. *Garrett* v *Arthur Churchill (Glass) Ltd* [1970] 1 QB 92).

A problem with *NCB* v *Gamble* is that it provides the potential for extensive liability for accessories. For example, A sees D, a motorist, standing beside a vehicle which has a punctured tyre. He offers to change the tyre. When performing this act of charity he notices that one of the other tyres is partially bald, and therefore illegal. If A completes the task will he be liable for aiding and abetting D's offence of driving a vehicle on the road with a defective tyre. Or, similarly, if he had noticed that one of the rear light panels was damaged before he changed the wheel, would he be liable for aiding and abetting D's offence of driving with defective lights? If intention does not require proof of a purpose, motive or desire that the offence be committed, A's voluntary act of assistance with knowledge of the circumstances which constitute the principal offence, would seem to be sufficient for liability as an accessory.

7.1.4.2 Knowledge of the circumstances constituting the offence   In *Johnson* v *Youden* [1950] 1 KB 544, Lord Goddard CJ stated (at p. 546):

> Before a person can be convicted of aiding and abetting the commission of an offence he must at least know the essential matters which constitute that offence. He need not actually know that an offence has been committed, because he may not know that the facts constitute an offence and ignorance of the law is not a defence.

The 'essential matters which constitute that offence' refers to the circumstances of the *actus reus*, its consequences (in the case of a result crime) and, in certain circumstances, the *mens rea* of the principal. A cannot be liable as an accessory if he is unaware of the circumstances which constitute the offence. In *Ferguson* v *Weaving* [1951] 1 KB 814, A, the licensee of a public house, was charged with aiding and abetting customers to commit the offence of consuming intoxicating liquor on licensed premises outside the permitted hours. A did not know that customers were still drinking after closing time. The Divisional Court held she could not be convicted if she did not know that customers were committing the principal offence.

Some matters, however, cannot be known although they may be foreseen, for example, the consequences of the perpetrator's act or his *mens rea*. Thus where A gives assistance prior to the commission of the offence, it is more accurate to refer to his 'contemplation' rather than his knowledge. 'Knowledge' for these purposes includes wilful blindness and subjective recklessness (see *Carter* v *Richardson* [1974] RTR 314 and *Blakely, Sutton* v *DPP* [1991] Crim LR 763).

Where the principal offence is one of strict liability, while the principal may be convicted without proof of *mens rea*, an accessory may be convicted only where *mens rea* is proved. In *Callow* v *Tillstone* (1900) 83 LT 411, A, a veterinary surgeon, was charged with aiding and abetting the exposure for sale by D, a butcher, of unsound meat. A had examined a carcass at D's request and certified it sound. A had performed the examination negligently and the meat was unsound. D was convicted of the strict liability offence of exposing the meat for sale. A's conviction, however, was quashed as he did not know the meat was unsound.

7.1.4.3 Knowledge of the type of offence Where A counsels or procures D to commit a particular crime, A necessarily knows the type of offence involved as the commission of the offence is A's purpose. For example, if A writes to D encouraging him to kill V, A will know that if D does so he will commit murder as he will have done so with the necessary *mens rea*. Where A aids or abets D to commit an offence, commission of that offence may not be A's purpose or object. For example, A may sell D a gun to make a profit indifferent to the fact that D intends to use it to kill V. A may not intend for D to kill V, but he gives assistance intentionally knowing that D has the intention to kill. Several problems may arise, however, in cases of aiding and abetting: (i) A may not know the exact details of the crime D has in mind although he knows D intends to kill; (ii) A may not know the exact crime D intends to commit although he knows D is going to commit one of a range of offences; (iii) A knows that if particular circumstances arise D *will* commit a particular offence; and (iv) A knows that if particular circumstances arise D *may* commit a particular crime. It is crucial, therefore, to determine how precise A's knowledge must be if he is to be convicted as an accessory.

In *Bainbridge* [1960] 1 QB 129, the Court of Criminal Appeal had to consider situation (i) above. A supplied oxygen-cutting equipment to D who used it to break into a branch of the Midland Bank and steal £18,000. A appealed his conviction as an accessory claiming that it had to be proved that he knew the precise details of the intended offence. The Court held it was sufficient that A knew the particular type of offence intended which was later committed. Mere knowledge that the equipment was going to be used for some illegal venture, however, would not be sufficient. In *Bainbridge* the equipment had been used for only one offence. The Court left unresolved the question whether A would have been liable for breaking and entering offences committed on other banks. If A need not know the precise details of the offence the logical answer to this question is that he would be liable for each breaking and entering offence committed by using the equipment he supplied.

In *Maxwell* v *DPP for Northern Ireland* (1979) 68 Cr App R 128, the House of Lords approved of, and extended, the principle in *Bainbridge* to cover situation (ii) above. A drove his car guiding members of the UVF (an illegal organisation) in another car to a public house where he knew a terrorist attack was to be carried out whether by guns or bombs or otherwise. A pipe bomb was thrown into the pub. A was charged with (1) doing an act with intent to cause an explosion likely to endanger life or cause serious injury to property and (2) possession of explosive substances with intent to endanger life or cause serious injury to property. A was convicted and his conviction upheld as, although he did not know the precise type of offence intended to be committed, he knew that one of a limited number of serious crimes was intended and was, in fact, committed. Thus an accessory will be liable where he contemplates the commission of one or more of a range of crimes by the principal and he intentionally lends assistance to the principal who then commits one or more of these offences. Lord Scarman stated (at p. 153) 'An accessory who leaves it to his principal to choose is liable, provided always the choice is made from the range of offences from which the accessory contemplates the choice will be made'. Thus if A gives D a jemmy contemplating only that he will use it to break into houses to steal therein or break open crates to steal their contents, he would be liable for any such offences, but he would not be liable if D used the jemmy to injure a night-watchman who disturbed him. A problem which is unresolved, however, is that burglary is an offence of ulterior intent. The ulterior intent specified under s. 9(2) of the Theft Act 1968 which must be proved for conviction under s. 9(1)(a) is intention to steal, or inflict grievous bodily harm, or rape or cause criminal damage (see 13.2 *post*). If D entered a house as a trespasser with the intention of raping the occupant, V, could A be convicted as an accessory to burglary? The answer depends on whether burglary is a 'type' of crime or the different varieties of burglary are different 'types' of crime. It is arguable that D's *mens rea* is one of 'the essential matters which constitute the offence'. If A only contemplated D stealing, D's intention to rape would appear to render the offence D committed a different type from the offence A contemplated. The contrary argument is that the *actus reus* of burglary is the same regardless of the intent with which it is committed and that A's assistance related to the effecting of the *actus reus*. Perhaps assistance in resolving this conflict may be sought from the cases on deliberate departure by the perpetrator from the joint enterprise. Breaking into a house with intention to rape could be considered a substantial variation from the joint enterprise which envisaged breaking into a house with intent to steal (see 7.1.4.4 *post*). What is not in doubt is that if D does rape the occupant A is not an accessory to the offence of rape.

If A and D decide to rob a bank and agree that D will carry a gun to shoot anyone who offers resistance, A will be liable for wounding or murder if D does shoot a bank clerk or customer who resists. This is situation (iii) above and A will be liable even though he fervently hoped that no one would resist or if he believed that resistance was only a remote possibility on the basis that fifty robberies had been carried out successfully without any resistance being offered. It matters not that A may have foreseen only a small risk of resistance being offered as he has intentionally participated in an enterprise contemplating wounding or killing if necessary; an intention is no less so because it is conditional on the occurrence of other events (see *Betts and Ridley* (1930) 22 Cr App R 148). In some cases the agreement between the parties to use force is not express but implied or, as it is referred to in some cases, 'tacit'. If it is a tacit understanding of the parties before the enterprise is embarked upon that violence will be used if certain circumstances arise, A will be liable. For example, A notices D is carrying a gun, which they had not previously discussed. A asks D what it is for to which D replies 'Just in case!'. If A still goes ahead with the robbery he will be liable to the extent of his contemplation as he is tacitly agreeing to its use for whatever purpose he contemplates D intends. If he contemplated that D would use it to kill or wound he will be liable for murder if D does kill, but he would be liable only for manslaughter if he contemplated that D would use it only to frighten.

In situation (iv) A does not know that D will wound or kill if certain circumstances arise but he contemplates that he might. Is this situation distinguishable from (iii) above? Is liability limited to tacit agreement or is contemplation of the possibility that D might commit the offence sufficient? In *Chan Wing-Siu* [1985] 1 AC 168, the Privy Council gave the leading judgment on joint enterprises. A, D and E, armed with knives, went to a flat intending to steal from V the occupant. V refused to hand over any money whereupon he was stabbed to death. A, D and E were charged with murder. A claimed he was not involved in the killing as he was restraining V's wife in another room when D and E killed V. A argued at the trial and again on appeal that it had to be proved that he foresaw that death or grievous bodily harm would probably result from the joint enterprise if a contingency in which a weapon might be used by one of his companions eventuated. The jury were directed that each was guilty if proved to have contemplated that a knife might be used on the occasion by one of his accomplices with the intention of inflicting serious bodily injury. All three were convicted and appealed. The Privy Council dismissed their appeals. Sir Robin Cooke stated (at p. 175):

> a secondary party is criminally liable for acts by the primary offender of a type which the former foresees but does not necessarily intend. . . . [This principle] turns on contemplation or, putting the same idea in other words, authorisation, which may be express but is more usually implied. It meets the case of a crime foreseen as a possible incident of the common unlawful enterprise. The criminal culpability lies in participating in the venture with that foresight.

This statement is not entirely clear as Sir Robin equates contemplation with authorisation. The latter is more in line with the idea of joint conditional intent whereas the former relates to foresight of possible future *mens rea* which the perpetrator may form. Sir Robin appeared to accept later in his judgment that contemplation of the risk that another party to the offence might inflict harm with an intention adequate for murder would be sufficient. This has been affirmed as the correct basis for liability in subsequent Court of Appeal decisions after a period of some doubt. In *Hyde* [1990] 3 All ER 892, the Court of Appeal reviewed the authorities and concluded that the factor crucial to liability was contemplation rather than tacit agreement. Lord Lane CJ stated (at. p. 896):

If [A] realises (without agreeing to such conduct being used) that [D] may kill or intentionally inflict serious injury, but nevertheless continues to participate with [D] in the venture, that will amount to a sufficient mental element for [A] to be guilty of murder if [D], with the requisite intent, kills in the course of the venture. . . . [A] has in those circumstances lent himself to the enterprise which [A] realises may involve murder.

Hyde was approved by the Privy Council in *Hui Chi-ming* v *R* [1992] 1 AC 34 where Lord Lowry explained Sir Robin Cooke's ambiguous use of the word 'authorisation' (at p. 53):

Their Lordships consider that [he] used this word . . . to emphasise the fact that mere foresight is not enough: the accessory in order to be guilty, must have foreseen the relevant offence which the principal may commit *as a possible incident of the common unlawful enterprise* and must, with such foresight, still have participated in the enterprise. The word 'authorisation' explains what is meant by contemplation but does not add a new ingredient.

It may appear that an accessory is more harshly treated than the principal as the latter can only be convicted of murder where he intended to kill or cause grievous bodily harm, whereas the accessory will be liable if he foresaw this as a possible incident of the joint enterprise. The *mens rea* of the accessory, however, relates not to the *actus reus* of the offence but to his own participation; he is liable because of his intentional participation in the contemplated offence(s). Problems of remoteness may arise where the risk A contemplates is highly improbable. In *Chan Wing-Siu* Sir Robin Cooke confined an accessory's liability to situations where he had foreseen 'a substantial risk, a real risk, a risk that something might well happen.'

7.1.4.4 Liability for acts beyond the common design

Three situations may arise and the liability of an accessory differs between them:

(i) D accidentally commits a different offence in performing the common design or commits the contemplated offence in a different but non-relevant context;

(ii) D commits the contemplated offence in unforeseen circumstances; and

(iii) D deliberately commits an offence outside the scope of the parties common design.

In situation (i) for example, if A encourages D to assault V and D does so but V dies, both A and D will be liable for manslaughter. Death may have been unforeseen but each party to a joint unlawful enterprise is equally liable for the consequences of acts done in pursuance thereof (see *Baldessare* (1930) 22 Cr App R 70). In *Anderson and Morris* [1966] 2 QB 110, Lord Parker stated the principle as follows (at p. 118):

where two persons embark on a joint enterprise, each is liable for the acts done in pursuance of that joint enterprise, [and] . . . that includes liability for unusual consequences if they arise from the execution of the agreed joint enterprise.

Similarly the doctrine of transferred malice applies to the liability of accessories. If D, endeavouring to assault V, had accidentally assaulted W, or assaulted W mistaking him for V, both A and D would be liable for the assault; the context of the offence differs from the common design in a non-relevant way. By contrast, if D had deliberately assaulted W, this would fall within situation (ii) and A would not be liable as the execution varies from the common design in a matter of substance. Hawkins stated the principle as follows (2 PC c29, s. 21):

> But if a man command another to commit a felony on a particular person or thing and he do it on another; as to kill A and he kill B or to burn the house of A and he burn the house of B or to steal an ox and he steal a horse; or to steal such an horse and he steal another; or to commit a felony of one kind and he commit another of a quite different nature; as to rob JS of his plate as he is going to market, and he break open his house in the night and there steal the plate; it is said that the commander is not an accessory because the act done varies in substance from that which was commanded.

What amounts to a variation in substance will not always be easy to define. In the examples Hawkins gives the perpetrator departs from the plan in each case in a significant way. An insignificant variation would be the case of robbing JS; if the principal had robbed him on the way back from market the accessory would remain liable for robbery. A variation from the common design, however, will not relieve an accessory of all liability. He may remain liable for incitement or conspiracy or he may be liable for a necessarily included lesser offence. In the example of stealing JS's plate (which falls within situation (iii) above) the accessory would not be liable for burglary but he would be liable for simple theft as the counselled offence was robbery which involves theft and the offence committed was burglary which in this instance also involved theft. Similarly, if A had encouraged D to indecently assault V and D had raped V, A would not be liable for rape but would still be liable for indecent assault as rape necessarily involves indecent assault.

In *Saunders and Archer* (1573) 2 Plowd 473, S desired to kill his wife and sought the assistance of A who supplied him with poison. S put this poison in an apple and gave it to his wife who ate a little but gave the remainder to their daughter. S watched this without intervening and the daughter died of poisoning. S was held guilty of murder; his failure to intervene amounted to a deliberate variation in substance from the common design and thus A was acquitted. If S had not been present when the wife gave the apple to the daughter the doctrine of transferred malice would have applied. If the facts of *Saunders and Archer* occurred today, A could be convicted of conspiracy to murder or of aiding, abetting, counselling or procuring S's attempt to kill his wife (see *Hapgood and Wyatt* (1870) LR 1 CCR 221).

Where the common design involves a conditional intention, the accessory will only be liable where the condition is fulfilled. For example, A and D suspect that V, their accomplice in crimes of robbery, is cheating them out of their fair share of the loot. A suggests to D that he should kill V if this happens again. After V divides the loot following the next robbery D shoots him although he has not cheated as D wants a bigger share. A would not be liable as an accessory as the condition had not been fulfilled but he could be liable for conspiracy to kill.

In situation (iii), D does not merely commit the agreed offence in circumstances which substantially depart from the common design nor does he merely accidentally commit the *actus reus* of an offence different in type from that intended, but he deliberately goes beyond the common design and commits an offence different in type from that intended or contemplated. The principle was stated by Lord Simmonds LC in *Davies* v *DPP* [1954] AC 378, 401:

> I can see no reason why, if half a dozen boys fight another crowd, and one of them produces a knife and stabs one of the opponents to death, all the rest of his group should be treated as accomplices in the use of a knife and the infliction of mortal injury by that means, unless there is evidence that the rest intended or concerted or at least contemplated an attack with a knife by one of the number, as opposed to a common assault. If all that was designed or envisaged was in fact a common assault, and there was no evidence that [A], a party to that common assault, knew that any of his companions had a knife, then [A] was not an accomplice in the crime consisting in its felonious use.

A problem which arises in relation to homicide in these circumstances is whether A can be convicted of manslaughter if D deliberately kills when the common design was only to injure the victim. Had the victim died as a result of the assault all the parties would be liable for manslaughter as the common design involved the commission of an unlawful and dangerous act. Where, however, D independently kills in the course of the joint enterprise, if A did not contemplate intentional killing or the infliction of grievous bodily harm, this would appear to absolve him of all liability for unlawful homicide (see *Lovesey and Peterson* [1970] 1 QB 352). In this case Lord Widgery stated (at p. 356):

> It is clear that a common design to use unlawful violence, short of the infliction of grievous bodily harm, renders all co-adventurers guilty of manslaughter if the victim's death is an unexpected consequence of the carrying out of that design. Where, however, the victim's death is not a product of the common design but is attributable to one of the co-adventurers going beyond the scope of that design, by using violence which is intended to cause grievous bodily harm, the others are not responsible for that unauthorised act.

In this case the convictions of the two appellants of murder of a jeweller, committed in the course of a robbery, were quashed as one of them had gone beyond the common design to rob by acting with the intent to inflict grievous bodily harm, but the prosecution were unable to prove which. This decision was followed in *Dunbar* [1988] Crim LR 693, where A's conviction of murder was quashed as, although she had contemplated the use of some unlawful violence short of the infliction of grievous bodily harm, the principal had gone beyond the scope of that design and used extreme violence intending to cause grievous bodily harm or death.

Both the above decisions conflict with *Betty* (1963) 48 Cr App R 6, and *Reid* (1975) 62 Cr App R 109. The judgments in these cases, however, are of questionable authority as the issues were never clearly identified and the reasoning is sometimes contradictory. In *Betty* there is a suggestion that the accessory contemplated grievous bodily harm and in *Reid* the Court of Appeal even stated that the appellant knew of his co-accused's murderous intent. These decisions deserve to be ignored and merit overruling.

Three situations remain for consideration. In the first both A and D intend grievous bodily harm to V but D performs the act in a way different to the plan. For example, A tells D to 'kneecap' V and supplies him with a gun for this purpose. D shoots V in the head and he dies. Both had the intention to cause grievous bodily harm but D has performed the act in a way different to that counselled. In such a case A would not have contemplated death as a likely result of kneecapping and D's departure from the agreed plan would appear to amount to a substantial variation absolving A of liability for murder, and it is submitted, manslaughter. In the second situation, A and D agree about the act to be performed but A contemplates a different result to that intended by D. For example, A gives D a cosh to knock out a security guard on premises they intend to burgle. A only contemplates actual bodily harm and does not contemplate that D might intend anything more but D, performing the act, intends grievous bodily harm. The guard dies. In these circumstances D would be guilty of murder and, it is submitted, A would be guilty of manslaughter. The act of coshing the guard was within the common design; it was only the contemplated or intended consequence which differed. In such circumstances each party should be liable to the extent that he had *mens rea*. A intended that the particular unlawful and dangerous act be committed and death ensued. In the third situation A and D intend grievous bodily harm to V but when they come upon V he provokes D who loses his self-control and kills him. If D is convicted of manslaughter by reason of provocation, this rules out liability on the part of A as D, having lost his self-control, was no longer engaged in a joint enterprise with A (see *McKechnie* (1992) 94 Cr App R 51).

7.1.5 Withdrawal from the joint enterprise
If A has encouraged D to commit an offence, or is present assisting D to commit an offence, is it possible for him to escape liability by withdrawing from the enterprise before the offence is committed? Withdrawal will clearly not affect A's liability for incitement or conspiracy or attempt where the principal has reached the stage of performing a 'more than merely preparatory act' (see 8.4.3 *post*) before A withdraws. Actual withdrawal from the enterprise must be effective if A is to escape liability for the completed offence; a mere change of heart without more is not sufficient (see *Becerra* (1975) 62 Cr App R 212). What is required will depend on the assistance or encouragement A has given. If A

has counselled D to commit the offence he may withdraw by expressly countermanding or revoking his encouragement (see *Saunders and Archer* (1573) 2 Plowd 473; *Croft* [1944] 1 KB 295) although he may still be liable for incitement. The communication must, where practicable and reasonable, be timely and 'serve unequivocal notice upon the other party to the common unlawful cause that if he proceeds upon it he does so without the further aid and assistance of those who withdraw' (*per* Sloan J. A. in *Whitehouse* (1941) 1 WWR 112, quoted with approval in *Becerra*).

Where A has supplied the means of committing the crime, a change of heart and quitting of the scene prior to the offence being committed would not be sufficient (*Whitehouse*). In *Becerra*, A, D and E broke into a house intending to steal. A gave D a knife to use if necessary on anyone interrupting them. When V came downstairs to investigate the noise, A said, 'There's a bloke coming. Let's go.' and jumped out of the window. D stabbed V with the knife, killing him. A's conviction of murder was upheld by the Court of Appeal as he had not effectively withdrawn from the joint enterprise. What amounts to effective withdrawal will vary with the circumstances of each case. Sometimes nothing less than physical intervention will suffice. The Court did not state if this would have been necessary in the instant case; it was sufficient for the purposes of disposing of the appeal to state that what A had done was not enough.

In *Grundy* [1977] Crim LR 543, A gave burglars information about premises and the habits of the occupants six weeks before the burglary took place. Four weeks later A tried to dissuade them from committing the offence. His conviction was quashed as this evidence of effective withdrawal had not been left to the jury. In *Whitefield* (1983) 79 Cr App R 36, A gave D similar information and agreed to break into the premises with D. Later he withdrew but D went on alone and A took no steps to stop him. The Court of Appeal held that there was evidence that A had served unequivocal notice on D that if he proceeded with the burglary he would do so without A's aid and assistance, and the judge's ruling that this was not enough and that notification of the police or other steps to prevent the burglary was required, was wrong. Both these cases appear to be unduly liberal towards the accessory. The information supplied remained of use to the burglars and was not negated by the suppliers' subsequent efforts to dissuade the burglars. If the appellants in *Grundy* and *Whitefield* had only counselled the commission of burglary without supplying information which assisted the burglars, verbal communication of withdrawal would suffice. Where something more is 'done, it is submitted that the withdrawal should not be considered effective if the accessory has not notified the police or warned the owners of the premises.

7.1.6 Victims as accessories

The fact that A is a victim of the offence does not, of itself, prevent him being convicted as an aider and abettor. For example, consent is a limited defence to offences against the person operating only where the action can be positively justified by some public interest. If A is a masochist and he permits D, a sadist, to wound him for his sexual gratification, A would be an aider and abettor to D's offence of unlawful wounding as there is no public interest justifying D's action (see further *10.1.1.3.1 post*). Similarly, if A permits D to perform an unlawful abortion on her she can be convicted as an aider and abettor to that offence (see *Sockett* (1908) 1 Cr App R 101). Where a statute is designed to protect a certain class of persons, however, a member of that class who is the victim of the offence cannot be convicted as an accessory. In *Tyrrell* [1894] 1 QB 710, A, a girl between the ages of thirteen and sixteen, was convicted of aiding and abetting D to have unlawful sexual intercourse with her contrary to s. 5 of the Criminal Law Amendment Act 1885. Her conviction was quashed on appeal, Lord Coleridge CJ stating (at p. 712) that 'it is impossible to say that the Act . . . can have intended that the girls for whose protection it was passed should be punishable under it for the offences committed upon themselves.' (see also *Whitehouse* [1977] QB 868). If A, being under sixteen, however, aids, abets, counsels or procures D to have intercourse with V who is under sixteen, A will be liable as, in this instance, she is not the victim of the offence whom Parliament is seeking to protect.

7.1.7 Entrapment and accessorial liability

Many offences are only detected because of proactive policing. For example, undercover drugs officers infiltrating a smuggling operation or drugs dealing enterprise to obtain evidence against the participants, or an undercover officer or informer infiltrating a gang of robbers to obtain information leading to their apprehension *in flagrante delicto*, or undercover officers lingering in public toilets to arrest any person who solicits them for homosexual purposes. Is such an officer ever liable to conviction as an accessory? The situations and persons involved may be divided into four types:

   (i)   those who merely observe the crime but play no part in the instigation of the offence, namely spies;
   (ii)   those decoys who accede to the accused's suggestions and thereby help provide the opportunity for the commission of the offence, namely collaborators;
   (iii) those decoys who expose the accused to temptation and thereby facilitate the commission of the offence by the accused, namely tempters; and
   (iv)   those decoys who actively entice, encourage or persuade the accused to commit an offence, which he would not otherwise commit, for the purpose of entrapping him, namely *agents provocateurs*.

The aim of the spy or decoy in all cases is to obtain evidence of the commission of an offence by the accused which will be sufficient for, or necessary to, a prosecution. The propriety of the behaviour of the spy or decoy in so doing varies from one category to another. The courts appear to approve of the behaviour in the first three categories but consider that the behaviour involved in the fourth situation goes too far and involves the *agent provocateur* in complicity in the offence which the accused ultimately commits. In *Mullins* (1848) 3 Cox CC 526, Maule J stated (at p. 531) that a person acting as a spy does not deserve to be blamed 'if he instigates offences no further than by pretending to concur with the perpetrators.' In *Birtles* (1969) 53 Cr App R 469, Lord Parker CJ stated (at p. 473):

it is vitally important to ensure so far as possible that the informer does not create an offence, that is to say, incite others to commit an offence which those others would not otherwise have committed. It is one thing for the police to make use of information concerning an offence that is already laid on. . . . But it is quite another thing, and something of which this court thoroughly disapproves, to use an informer to encourage another to commit an offence, or indeed an offence of a more serious character, which he would not otherwise commit, still more so if the police themselves take part in carrying it out.

This view has been echoed in subsequent cases such as *McCann* (1971) 56 Cr App R 359, *Mealey and Sheridan* (1975) 60 Cr App R 59 and *McEvilly and Lee* (1973) 60 Cr App R 150.

In the recent case of *Edwards* [1991] Crim LR 45, undercover officers were introduced to E, a suspected drugs dealer. E agreed to supply them with drugs and agreed a discount on future deals. It was clear that this particular conspiracy to supply drugs to the officers would not have taken place but for the officers' enticement of E. E, however, was prosecuted for conspiracy to supply controlled drugs to persons unknown; the officers' evidence was treated as evidence of this wider, established conspiracy which they clearly had not instigated, and thus they had not acted as *agents provocateurs*.

In *Sang* [1979] 2 All ER 1222, Lord Salmon suggested that police officers and informers involved in improper instances of entrapment should be prosecuted. He stated (at p. 1236):

I would now refer to what is, I believe, and hope, the unusual case in which a dishonest policeman, anxious to improve his detection record, tries very hard with the help of an *agent provocateur* to induce a young man with no criminal tendencies to commit a serious crime, and ultimately the young man succumbs to the inducement. . . . The policeman and the informer who acted together in inciting him to commit the crime should . . . both be prosecuted and suitably punished.

Lord Diplock also accepted that a police officer or informer would be liable as accessories (at p. 1226). Lord Salmon includes several superfluous requirements such that the police officer be dishonest, the accused be young and the crime serious. These add nothing to the basic criterion which is that the accused is encouraged to commit an offence which would not otherwise have been committed, that is, to use Lord Parker's words, an offence which was not 'laid on'. The fact that the officer's or informer's motive may have been the detection of crime is irrelevant.

In *Smith* [1960] 2 QB 423, D, a private individual seeking to expose corruption in local government, offered a bribe to the mayor of Castleford. D was convicted of corruption contrary to s. 1(2) of the Public Bodies Corrupt Practices Act 1889, the Court of Appeal holding that the purity of his motives provided him with no defence. Where an offence is 'laid on', however, it may be appropriate in some circumstances for a police officer or informer to participate in the offence. In *Birtles* Lord Parker CJ stated (at p. 473):

In such a case the police are clearly entitled, indeed it is their duty, to mitigate the consequences of the proposed offence, for example, to protect the proposed victim, and to that end it may be perfectly proper for them to encourage the informer to take part in the offence or indeed for a police officer himself to do so.

If an officer or informer does participate his behaviour will be lawful. In *Clarke* (1984) 80 Cr App R 344, Macpherson J enlarged upon Lord Parker's dicta stating (at p. 348):

> In using the expression 'it may be perfectly proper' the Lord Chief Justice was, in our judgment, contemplating that in such exceptional cases where an informer (and/or a policeman) took part in a 'laid on' case there should be no finding that it was unlawful so to do.

For example, D tells A that he is going to commit a burglary. A is unable to dissuade him from so doing but agrees to drive D to the scene of the offence. A then telephones the police and D is caught *in flagrante delicto*. The decision in *Clarke* would suggest that A's assistance was justified. There must be limits to this, however, as offences involving injury to people or irreparable damage to property should not be assisted in any way. This limited defence obviously requires considerable clarification.

Where D commits an offence as a result of improper entrapment, that is the work of an *agent provocateur*, this will be a mitigating factor to be taken into account in sentencing (see *Sang and Mangan* [1979] 2 WLR 439; *Underhill* (1979) 1 Cr App R (S) 270).

7.2 VICARIOUS LIABILITY

In the law of tort an employer is responsible for the torts of his employees acting in the course of their employment. This is known as 'vicarious liability' which is a form of strict liability arising from the master-servant relationship, without reference to any fault of the employer (see further Jones, *Textbook on Torts*, 3rd edn, pp. 252-269). There is no such general rule in criminal law; generally if the master is to be liable it will be on the basis of being an accessory under the principles outlined above. The principle was stated by Raymond CJ in *Huggins* (1730) 2 Strange 883, 885:

> It is a point not to be disputed but that in criminal cases the principal is not answerable for the act of the deputy, as he is in civil cases; they must each answer for their own acts and stand or fall by their own behaviour. All the authors that treat of criminal proceedings, proceed on the foundation of this distinction; that to affect the superior by the act of the deputy, there must be command of the superior which is not found in this case.

Huggins was the warden of Fleet prison who was charged with aiding and abetting B, a turnkey, to murder a prisoner who had died as a result of the turnkey's neglect. As this occurred without Huggins' knowledge he was not guilty.

While this is the general rule, it is subject to exceptions. At common law there were two offences for which an employer could be liable for the acts of his employees even if these had not been authorised and he remained ignorant of them, namely public nuisance (see *Stephens* (1866) LR 1 QB 702) and criminal libel (this was modified by s. 7 of the Libel Act 1843). Occasionally statute expressly imposes vicarious liability. For example, section 59(1) of the Licensing Act 1964 provides:

> Subject to the provisions of this Act, no person shall, except during the permitted hours –
> (a) himself or by his servant or agent sell or supply to any person in licensed premises . . . any intoxicating liquor . . .

More usually, however, vicarious liability is the result of judicial interpretation of statutory offences of a regulatory nature. Various reasons are put forward to support such interpretations. Imposing liability on the employer for contraventions of legislation by his employees may be a more effective way of encouraging compliance with the legislation; the employer, after all, is the one who has overall control of the business and can regulate the conduct of his employees. It may also be considered unjust to punish an employee for the breach of some regulation as he may not have had the means of detecting the breach or of preventing it. A further justification is that vicarious liability is necessary to make certain provisions effective where some *mens rea* offences may only be committed by persons of a particular status, such as licensees. Such legislation would be rendered nugatory if the licensee could claim that the act had been performed without his knowledge by his servant; the response of the courts has been to create the 'delegation principle'. While these justifications have some force, they do represent an attempt by the judges to come to the rescue of the legislature as all these problems could have been met by means of better drafting of the legislation.

7.2.1 Vicarious liability by implication
The approach of the courts to statutory interpretation for the purpose of determining whether a provision imposed vicarious liability was stated by Atkin J in *Mousell Bros v London and North Western Ry* [1917] 2 KB 836, 845:

> [W]hile prima facie a principal is not to be made criminally responsible for the acts of his servants, yet the legislature may prohibit an act or enforce a duty in such words as to make the prohibition or the duty absolute; in which case the principal is in fact liable if the act is in fact done by his servants. To ascertain whether a particular Act of Parliament has that effect or not, regard must be had to the words used, the nature of the duty laid down, the person upon whom it is imposed, the person by whom it would in ordinary circumstances be performed, and the person upon whom the penalty is imposed.

In many statutes it is unclear upon whom the duty is imposed; in such cases the courts generally conclude that it is imposed on the employer as he is the one who has control of the enterprise. Where the performance of the duty requires positive acts the doctrine of vicarious liability is necessary. But where the offence is one of strict liability, consisting of an omission to perform a duty imposed on the employer, he will be personally liable as the perpetrator (without resort to the doctrine of vicarious liability) as, the duty being unfulfilled, the omission is as much his as that of any servant to whom he assigned the task. In *Hodge v Higgins* [1980] 2 Lloyd's Rep 589, a vessel was observed in the River Humber at night without a forward light. The master had retired to bed ill leaving the vessel in the charge of the mate. The master was convicted of neglect of duty contrary to s. 27 of the Merchant Shipping Act 1970, which made it an offence for the master of a ship to omit to do anything required to preserve the ship from loss, destruction or serious damage. The magistrate found, and the Divisional Court upheld his finding, that there was a breach of this duty and the master could not evade his responsibility as the duty was his alone.

Where the offence requires a positive act the courts have to decide if the act of the employee can be attributed to the employer. If it can, without undue strain to the wording of the legislation, and the offence is one of strict liability, the employer will be held to be a joint principal with his employee. Thus words such as 'sell', 'supply' and 'use' have frequently been given this extended meaning. In *Coppen v Moore (No. 2)* [1898] 2 QB 306, D, the owner of several shops, instructed his managers to sell American ham under the description 'breakfast ham'. A shop assistant in one shop, without the knowledge of her manager or D, sold some ham as 'Scotch ham'. It was an offence under s. 2(2) of the Merchandise Marks Act 1887 to sell any goods 'to which any . . . false trade description is applied'. The assistant had done the physical act of selling and committed this offence, but the Divisional Court held that D was also liable as, property in the ham being vested in him, he had in law sold the ham. Had D not been convicted as a principal by means of the implication of vicarious liability, it would not have been possible to convict him as an accessory due to his lack of knowledge.

Other cases establish that an employer is 'in possession' of goods which his servant possesses (*Melias Ltd v Preston* [1957] 2 QB 380), 'uses' a vehicle which his employee uses (*Green v Burnett* [1955] 1 QB 78), and 'presents' a play which his employee presents (*Grade v DPP* [1942] 2 All ER 118). By contrast, however, only the actual driver of a vehicle can be said to be 'driving' (cf. *Thornton v Mitchell* [1940] 1 All ER 339). Likewise, where words which import *mens rea* are used, such as 'knowingly', 'maliciously', 'fraudulently', 'permitting', 'suffering' or 'allowing', the employer can only be liable where he had *mens rea* himself (see *James & Son v Smee* [1955] 1 QB 78); his servant's *mens rea* cannot be imputed to him, unless the case falls within the bounds of the 'delegation principle' (see 7.2.2 *post*).

This approach of extending the meaning of words has been used to impose liability not only in the employer/employee situation but also to impose liability on a principal for the act of his agent or independent contractor (see

Quality Dairies (York) Ltd v *Pedley* [1952] 1 KB 275, and *F. E. Charman Ltd* v *Clow* [1974] 1 WLR 1384), on a partner for the act of his fellow partner (see *Clode* v *Barnes* [1974] 1 All ER 1166), and on a licensee for unlawful sales by the bar staff even though they were not his employees but employees of the owner of the bar (see *Goodfellow* v *Johnson* [1966] 1 QB 83). The issue is whether there is a sufficient nexus between the parties so that it can be said that the accused had some control over the actions of the other. A further consideration is whether the imposition of liability would serve to encourage stricter supervision to ensure compliance with regulatory legislation. Ultimately the matter is one for judicial interpretation. The Law Commission, when considering vicarious liability for the acts of independent contractors, stated (Law Com No. 177) at para. 9.49:

> It is one thing to hold that a person carrying on a business of supplying milk or heavy building materials 'uses' a vehicle if he employs an independent contractor to supply those things in the contractor's vehicle. It would be quite another thing to hold that a householder 'uses' the removal van owned by a firm of removers whom he engages to carry his furniture to a new residence.

7.2.2 The delegation principle

Where the offence is not one of strict liability but requires proof of *mens rea*, the general rule is that a master cannot be convicted on the basis of vicarious liability without it being proved that he knew what was going on. The delegation principle forms an exception to this rule. Under this principle the *mens rea* of the employee may be imputed to the employer where it is established that the latter had delegated his responsibilities to the former. The creation of this principle proved necessary to deal with cases where *mens rea* offences could only be committed by persons of a particular status, such as licensees of licensed premises. If the servant performed the act constituting the *actus reus* of the offence with *mens rea* he could not be convicted as a principal as he was not a person of the requisite status. The licensee, lacking knowledge, could not be a principal and thus the servant could not be convicted as an accessory. The outcome would be that the purpose of the statute in regulating the conditions under which alcohol could be sold would be defeated where the licensee had handed over management responsibilities to his servant.

In *Somerset* v *Hart* (1884) 12 QBD 360, Lord Coleridge CJ suggested that a man could put another in his position so as to represent him for the purpose of knowledge. This was built upon in *Allen* v *Whitehead* [1930] 1 KB 211. Under s. 44 of the Metropolitan Police Act 1839 it was an offence for the owner or keeper of a refreshment house to knowingly permit or suffer prostitutes to meet there. D owned a cafe which was run by a manager. The manager knowingly permitted prostitutes to meet there unknown to D. D was convicted as to hold otherwise would be to render the provision nugatory; the manager's knowledge was imputed to him. In *Linnett* v *Metropolitan Police Commissioner* [1946] KB 290, Lord Goddard CJ indicated the nature of the delegation principle (at p. 294):

The principle underlying these decisions does not depend upon the legal relationship existing between master and servant or between principal and agent; it depends on the fact that the person who is responsible in law, as for example, a licensee under the Licensing Acts, has chosen to delegate his duties, powers and authority to another.

In this case, accordingly, one of two co-licensees, who was absent, was held liable for the acts of the other who had knowingly permitted disorderly conduct in the licensed premises contrary to s. 44 of the Metropolitan Police Act 1839.

What constitutes delegation is not totally clear. In *Vane v Yiannopoullos* [1965] AC 486, D, the licensee of a restaurant was on another floor when a waitress in the restaurant, contrary to instructions, served drinks to two youths who did not order a meal. The magistrate dismissed an information charging him with knowingly selling intoxicating liquor to persons to whom he was not permitted to sell, contrary to s. 22(1)(a) of the Licensing Act 1961. The House of Lords dismissed the prosecutor's appeal. Lord Evershed stated that delegation required the handing over of all effective management of the premises. Lord Hodson stated that it did not cover cases of partial transfer of authority. Lord Reid did not believe there could be delegation where the licensee remained on the premises. In the course of their speeches some of their Lordships expressed disquiet about the doctrine. Lord Donovan stated that 'if a decision that "knowingly" means "knowingly" will make the provision difficult to enforce, the remedy lies with the legislature.' Lord Reid found difficulty justifying the priniciple but considered that it was too long established to overturn it. It appeared, therefore, that what was required was a complete transfer of authority and responsibilities to another person and the absence of the licensee from the premises.

In *Winson* [1969] 1 QB 371, the Court of Appeal confirmed that partial delegation was insufficient to impute knowledge to the licensee (see also *Bradshaw v Ewart-James* [1983] QB 671). In *Howker v Robinson* [1973] 1 QB 178, however, the Divisional Court upheld a conviction of a licensee for selling alcohol to a person under the age of eighteen where this had been done by a barman in the lounge while the licensee was in the public bar. The Divisional Court treated the question of delegation as one of fact and accepted the magistrates finding that there had been delegation. The decision appears unsupportable on two grounds. Firstly, this was not a case of the licensee taking no part in managing the business; if there was any delegation of authority it was only partial. Indeed it is difficult to discover even partial delegation of the licensee's proprietary or managerial functions. Secondly, the justification for the delegation principle is that it is necessary to avoid rendering certain statutory provisions nugatory. In this case, however, a failure to find delegation would not have had this effect as the relevant provision, s. 169(1) of the Licensing Act 1964, specifically prohibited 'the holder of the licence or his servant' from selling alcohol to a person under eighteen. Thus the barman could have been prosecuted for the offence as liability was not limited to persons with the status of licensees. It is submitted, therefore, that *Howker v Robinson* was wrongly decided.

The Law Commission's Draft Criminal Code (Law Com No. 177) excludes the delegation principle from Code offences (see clause 29) proposing instead that if Parliament intends vicarious liability to be imposed on the basis of the fault of another it must do so expressly. Clause 29(2) provides that 'a fault element of an offence may be attributed to a person by reason of the fault of another only if the terms of the enactment creating the offence so provide.'

7.2.3 Limitations on vicarious liability

There are three limitations on vicarious liability. Firstly, vicarious liability can only arise where the person who did the act did so within the scope of his employment or, if not an employee but acting as the accused's agent, within the scope of his authority. For example, if an employee does an authorised activity in an unauthorised way he remains within the scope of his employment (see *Coppen* v *Moore (No. 2)*, 7.2.1 *ante*). By contrast, if the sales assistant had started to sell stolen goods under a false description the employer would not be liable as he would have been performing a wholly unauthorised activity. Similarly, if an employee uses his employer's vehicle to deliver goods, his use of the vehicle is also his employer's use, but, if he uses it as a get-away vehicle for a robbery, his use, being a wholly unauthorised activity, would not be his employer's use. In *Adams* v *Camfoni* [1929] 1 KB 95, D was a licensee charged with selling alcohol outside the permitted hours. The sale had been effected by a messenger boy who had no authority to sell liquor or anything else. Accordingly D was acquitted.

Secondly, where the employee's acts amount to the aiding and abetting of an offence, the employer cannot be held vicariously liable for such aiding and abetting on the basis of imputed knowledge, even though the offence was one which he could have personally aided and abetted (see *Ferguson* v *Weaving*, 7.1.4.2 *ante*).

Thirdly, it was held in *Gardner* v *Akeroyd* [1952] 2 QB 743, that vicarious liability cannot be imposed in respect of an attempt to commit an offence, even though vicarious liability could have been imposed for the completed offence.

7.2.4 Statutory defences

There is no general defence of due diligence which an employer may plead in respect of an offence committed by his employee for which he is vicariously liable. Some statutes do contain express provision for due diligence defences; others combine the due diligence defence with a 'third party' defence (see 4.2.5 *ante*). Where the offence is a strict liability offence which may only be committed by a person of a particular status, the employee cannot be a principal. If he is not a principal there is no 'third party' whom the employer can bring before the court as the actual offender. A third party defence can only operate where the offence is one of strict liability and not limited to persons of a particular status, in which case both employer and employee are joint principals.

7.3 CORPORATE LIABILITY

A corporation is a legal person and therefore may be criminally liable even though it has no physical existence and cannot act or think except through its directors or servants. A corporation is, for example, a limited company, a public corporation like those formed to run nationalised industries (e.g. British Rail), or a local authority. At common law an unincorporated association is not a legal person and therefore not subject to criminal liability. Section 5 of and sch. 1 to the Interpretation Act 1978 provide that in every Act, unless the contrary intention appears, 'person' includes a body of persons corporate or unincorporate. This definition applies prospectively in respect of unincorporated associations so that these bodies may be criminally liable for offences created after 1 January 1979 (the commencement date for the 1978 Act) where the word 'person' is used in the definition of the offence.

A corporation is vicariously liable for strict liability offences to exactly the same extent as a natural person. A corporation will also be criminally liable for the breach of any statutory duty imposed upon it in a particular capacity such as an occupier or keeper (see *Evans & Co Ltd* v *LCC* [1914] 3 KB 315). Its criminal liability extends further than this, however, to cover direct liability for acts performed by natural persons who are identified with it, i.e. the principle of identification (see 7.3.1 *post*). There are two limitations, however, to corporate liability identified in *R* v *ICR Haulage Ltd* [1944] KB 551. Firstly, there are certain offences which, from their very nature, cannot be committed by corporations, for example, bigamy, rape, incest and perjury. In all these cases, if suitable circumstances arose, a corporation could be liable as an accessory. Obiter dicta in some old cases suggested that a corporation could not be convicted of an offence of violence. These were acted on in *Cory Bros & Co* [1927] 1 KB 810 but doubted in *ICR Haulage Ltd*. In *R* v *Coroner for East Kent, ex parte Spooner* (1989) 88 Cr App R 10, where an application for judicial review of the decision of the coroner at the inquest into the deaths resulting from the sinking of the *Herald of Free Enterprise* off Zeebrugge was refused, Bingham LJ, in the Divisional Court, stated *obiter* that a corporation could be convicted of manslaughter on appropriate facts. This was subsequently confirmed by Turner J when P & O European Ferries (Dover) Ltd, two directors and a senior manager were tried for manslaughter in respect of the deaths resulting from the Zeebrugge disaster (see *R* v *P&O European Ferries (Dover) Ltd* (1990) 93 Cr App R 72). Turner J held that a company is 'properly indictable for the crime of manslaughter' through 'the controlling mind of one of its agents' who 'does an act which fulfills the prerequisites of the crime of manslaughter'. The prosecution ended in failure, however, when Turner J withdrew from the jury consideration of the charges as there was no evidence that anyone who constituted 'the controlling mind' of the company had the requisite *mens rea* to support a convition of manslaughter. The only other prosecution of a corporation for manslaughter in the 1960s was also unsuccessful.

Secondly, a corporation will not be convicted of an offence where the only punishment which may be imposed is physical. In *ICR Haulage Ltd,* Stable J stated (at p. 554) that 'the court will not stultify itself by embarking on a trial in which, if a verdict of guilty is returned, no effective order by way of sentence can be made.' Thus a corporation cannot be tried for murder or treason as the only punishments available to the court on conviction are life imprisonment or death. Where a corporation is convicted of an offence it will be punished by the imposition of a fine and/or compensation order.

7.3.1 The principle of identification

In vicarious liability an employer is held liable for the acts of his employee; in corporate liability a corporation is liable for its own acts. As a company has no physical existence and cannot think or act, a fiction has to be applied to convert the acts and thoughts of a human person into those of the corporation thereby attributing personality to it. This fiction is the principle of identification which was explained by Lord Reid in *Tesco Supermarkets Ltd* v *Nattrass* [1972] AC 153 (at 170) as follows:

A living person has a mind which can have knowledge or intention or be negligent and he has hands to carry out his intentions. A corporation has none of these: it must act through living persons, though not always one or the same person. Then the person who acts is not speaking or acting for the company. He is speaking as the company and his mind which directs his acts is the mind of the company. There is no question of the company being vicariously liable. He is not acting as a servant, representative, agent or delegate. He is an embodiment of the company, one could say, he hears and speaks through the persona of the company, within his appropriate sphere, and his mind is the mind of the company. If it is a guilty mind then that guilt is the guilt of the company.

It is a question of law for the judge whether a person is to be regarded as the company or simply its employee or agent. The judge when directing the jury must tell them the facts which they must find if a person is to be regarded as having acted as the company. If those facts are proved and the jury are satisfied that that person did the act (or omitted to act) with the requisite *mens rea*, the company can be convicted of the offence. The corporation will only be liable where the person identified with it was acting within the scope of his office; it will not be liable for acts which he did in his personal capacity (see *DPP* v *Kent and Sussex Contractors Ltd* [1944] KB 146). In determining whether a person acted as the company or simply as its servant or agent, a distinction has to be drawn between those who represent the mind of the company and those who represent its hands. In *H. L. Bolton (Engineering) Co Ltd* v *T. J. Graham & Sons Ltd* [1957] 1 QB 159, Denning LJ stated (at p. 172):

A company may in many ways be likened to a human body. It has a brain and a nerve centre which controls what it does. It also has hands which hold the tools and act in accordance with directions from the centre. Some of the people in the company are mere servants and agents who are nothing more than hands to do the work and cannot be said to represent the mind or will. Others are directors and managers who represent the directing mind and will of the company, and control what it does. The state of mind of these managers is the state of mind of the company and is treated by the law as such.

The fact that a person is involved in 'brain' work rather than manual work is not the test; what is required is that such persons 'represent the directing mind and will of the company and control what it does' (*per* Lord Reid, *Tesco Supermarkets Ltd* v *Nattrass* [1972] AC 153 at 171). This covers directors, the managing director, the company secretary and other superior officers responsible for managing the affairs of the corporation. If one of these persons delegated some part of his management functions, giving the delegate full discretion to act independently, the delegate would also fall within the class of persons whose acts are those of the corporation (see *Lennard's Carrying Co Ltd* v *Asiatic Petroleum Co Ltd* [1915] AC 705 and *Worthy* v *Gordon Plant (Services) Ltd* [1985] CLY 624). Who exactly is covered will vary from case to case but the memorandum and articles of association of the company may provide some guidance.

In the *Tesco* case, the company was charged with an offence under the Trade Descriptions Act 1968. Tesco sought to raise a defence under s. 24(1) of the Act on the grounds that the commission of the offence was due to the act or default of another person, the branch manager of the store, and it had exercised all due diligence to avoid the commission of the offence. The magistrates found that the company had set up a proper system, so it had exercised all due diligence, but they found that the branch manager was not 'another person' as his acts were those of the company. On appeal to the House of Lords the conviction was quashed. The House held that the defence was available as the branch manager was another person being the 'hands' and not the 'brains' of the company; there had been no delegation by the board of directors of any of their managerial functions in respect of the affairs of the company to the branch manager. He had to obey general directions from the company and take orders from his regional and district supervisors. Accordingly, his acts or omissions were not those of the company.

The *Tesco* case indicated that the principle of identification operates not only to establish liability but it can excuse liability for certain regulatory offences where a third party defence is available. As the branch manager did not act as the company, his act was that of a third party. The company, through its superior officers, had established a proper system of supervision and thus had exercised all due diligence.

There are two problems arising from the principle of identification (these have been identified by C. Wells, see Further reading *post*). First, the larger and more diverse a company is, the more likely it is that it will be able to avoid liability. Tesco had over 800 branches; a branch manager would have no control over the company's affairs. In a small company the controlling officers are much closer to the action which may involve the commission of offences. The second problem is that the company will only be liable if the person identified with it is, himself, individually liable in that he had the *mens rea* for the offence. Where there are several superior officers involved, each may not have the requisite degree of knowledge to constitute the *mens rea* of the offence. Can the company be liable where the collective knowledge of these officers is sufficient to constitute the *mens rea*. In *ex parte Spooner* (*ante*) which arose from the Zeebrugge inquest, it was argued that the individual instances of neglect of safety by different company officials should be aggregated for the purposes of determining corporate liability. In the Divisional Court this was dismissed without much consideration; thus the individuals would have to have been individually liable for manslaughter before the company could be liable. If a company is a legal person, however, and the knowledge of its officials is its knowledge, it is at least arguable that the company, being the repository of their collective knowledge, knew the whole facts of which they individually only knew a part. Where an organisation is large and diverse, no one official will know all that there is to know.

7.3.2 Liability of officers

Apart from their liability as perpetrators or accomplices of the offences for which a corporation may be held criminally liable, the officers of a company may be made liable by statutory provision. Many statutes, such as the Betting, Gaming and Lotteries Act 1963 (s. 53) and the Trades Description Act 1968 (s. 20) contain the following provision:

> Where an offence under this Act which has been committed by a body corporate is proved to have been committed with the consent or connivance of, or to be attributable to any neglect on the part of, any director, manager, secretary or other similar officer of the body corporate or any person who was purporting to act in any such capacity, he as well as the body corporate shall be guilty of that offence.

While this largely duplicates the liability imposed by the criminal law on perpetrators or accomplices, it does extend it and it may also make the task of the prosecution easier where proving liability under the normal principles would be difficult. 'Consent' and 'connivance' largely overlap with 'aiding, abetting, counselling or procuring', but they may be easier to prove. In particular 'connivance' may be established by proving wilful blindness to the commission of the offence and acquiescence in it (see *Somerset* v *Hart* (1884) 12 QBD 360). The main extension of liability is effected by the words 'attributable to any neglect on the part of' which imposes liability for negligence where the officer has failed to prevent the commission of an offence by the corporation. Section 18 of the Theft Act 1968 contains a similar provision but it omits any reference to 'attributable to any neglect'.

An offence will not be attributable to the neglect of all directors because it is attributable to the neglect of one or of some other official of the company as there is no general duty upon a director to 'supervise his co-directors or to acquaint himself with all the details of the running of the company' (*per* Lord Parker CJ in *Huckerby* v *Elliott* [1970] 1 All ER 189, 194). Lord Parker went on to state:

> it is perfectly proper for a director to leave matters to another director or to an official of the company, and . . . he is under no obligation to test the accuracy of anything that he is told by such person, or even to make certain that he is complying with the law.

Similarly, where an officer of a company has delegated work to his senior staff it is reasonable for him to expect that work to be completed in accordance with the instructions given, so that he will not be guilty of neglect if he does not check such work (see *Lewin* v *Bland* [1985] RTR 171). However, if a director has reason to distrust another director or official or person to whom work has been delegated, or reason to suspect that that person was not carrying out his duty, and he does nothing, this could amount to neglect. In *R. McMillan Aviation Ltd* [1981] Crim LR 785, the company was charged with selling goods to which a false trade description had been applied contrary to s. 1 of the Trade Descriptions Act 1968, and a director was charged with the same offence on the basis of attributable neglect. Judge Rubin, in directing the jury in Kingston-upon-Thames Crown Court, stated that he would be liable where it was proved 'that he knew the trade description was false, in which case quite clearly he had a duty to prevent the offence, or that he had reasonable cause to suspect that the company was applying a false trade description, in which case he would have a duty to take steps to see if it was false or not and if he failed to do so he was guilty.'

Further reading
I. H. Dennis, 'The mental element for accessories' in *Criminal Law. Essays in Honour of J. C. Smith* (1987, ed. P. Smith).
M. Giles, 'Complicity – the problems of joint enterprise' [1990] Crim LR 383.
D. Lanham, 'Accomplices and transferred malice' (1980) 96 LQR 110; 'Accomplices and withdrawal' (1981) 97 LQR 575.
J. C. Smith, 'Aid, abet, counsel and procure' in *Reshaping the Criminal Law*, (1978, ed. P. Glazebrook).
G. Williams, 'Which of you did it' (1989) 52 MLR 179; 'Complicity, purpose and the Draft Code' [1990] Crim LR 4 and 98; 'Victims and other exempt parties in crime' (1990) 10 LS 245.
M. Allen, 'Entrapment: time for reconsideration' (1984) 13 Anglo-Am LR 57.
P. J. Pace, 'Delegation – a doctrine in search of a definition' [1982] Crim LR 627.
L. H. Leigh, *Strict and Vicarious Liability* (1982).
R. S. Welch, 'The criminal liability of corporations' (1946) 62 LQR 345.
C. Wells, 'The decline and rise of English murder: corporate crime and individual responsibility' [1988] Crim LR 788; 'Manslaughter and corporate crime' (1989) 139 New LJ 931.
D. Bergman, 'Recklessness in the boardroom' (1990) 140 New LJ 1496.

EIGHT
Inchoate offences

8.1 INTRODUCTION

A person does not break the criminal law simply by having evil thoughts (*Higgins* (1801) 2 East 5). To plan and scheme in one's mind to commit an offence is not, in itself, unlawful. Where, however, a person takes steps towards effecting that plan to commit a substantive offence, he may in the process commit one of the inchoate crimes of incitement, conspiracy or attempt. The law would be seriously deficient as a means of protecting persons or property from harm if it could only intervene after a substantive offence had been committed and the harm done. The inchoate offences permit intervention at an earlier stage before any harm has been done but at a time when the accused has moved from mere mental planning to the stage of performing overt acts which manifest his intention that a particular substantive offence be committed. 'Inchoate' means 'just begun or undeveloped'. This accurately reflects the nature of the crimes of incitement, conspiracy and attempt as they are committed when the accused begins to manifest his criminal intention overtly and at a stage prior to the consummation of that intention in the commission of the substantive offence.

For example, (i) A bears a grudge against V and decides to set fire to his house; (ii) A tells B of his decision and encourages B to assist him; (iii) B agrees to help and they formulate a plan to effect their purpose; (iv) A and B go to V's house, having first telephoned to check he is not at home, and douse it with paraffin; (v) they set light to the paraffin at different points around the house. At (i) A commits no offence as he is merely thinking evil thoughts. In (ii) his initial recounting of his decision involves no offence but when he encourages B to participate he commits the offence of incitement. B commits no offence by listening to A's incitement but when he agrees to participate he and A commit the offence of conspiracy (iii). When they set fire to the house (v) they commit the offence of arson. However, at (iv) A and B are guilty of attempted arson.

It is important to note that these inchoate offences are steps on the way to the commission of a substantive offence (but see common law conspiracy, 8.3.5 *post*); they are not crimes existing in the abstract. Thus the indictment would charge A with incitement to commit arson, A and B with conspiracy to commit arson, and attempt to commit arson. An indictment which simply charged the accused with 'incitement' or 'conspiracy' or 'attempt' would be defective.

8.2 INCITEMENT

At common law it was an indictable offence to incite or solicit a person to commit any offence (*Higgins* (1801) 2 East 5). Now incitement to commit a summary offence is triable summarily (s. 45 of the Magistrates' Courts Act 1980) and incitement to commit an offence triable either way is similarly triable either way (s. 17 and sch. 1 para. 35). Where an accused is convicted of incitement to commit a summary offence he will be liable to the same penalty as he would be liable to on conviction of the completed offence (s. 45(3)). Where an accused is convicted summarily of an offence triable either way he will be liable to the same penalty as he would be liable to on summary conviction of the completed offence (s. 32(1)(b)). The penalty for incitement following trial on indictment is imprisonment or a fine or both at the discretion of the court, regardless of the penalty for the completed offence. Parliament has created statutory forms of incitement, for example, incitement to murder contrary to s. 4 of the Offences Against the Person Act 1861 or the Incitement to Mutiny Act 1797 or the Incitement to Disaffection Act 1934. The nature of these offences does not appear to differ from incitement at common law but the penalty is specifically stipulated in the statute.

8.2.1 *Actus reus*
The *actus reus* of incitement requires proof that the accused by means of encouragement, persuasion, threats or pressure sought to influence another to commit an offence (see *Race Relations Board* v *Applin* [1973] QB 815). The solicitation need not be directed to a specific person but may be to all the world. In *Most* (1881) 7 QBD 244, D published in a London newspaper an article urging readers around the world to follow the example of those in Russia and murder their Heads of State. This was held to be incitement to murder contrary to s. 4 of the Offences Against the Person Act 1861 (see also *Invicta Plastics Ltd* v *Clare* [1976] RTR 251). Incitement need not be express but may be implied. In *Invicta Plastics* the company was convicted of inciting readers of a magazine in which they advertised to commit the offence of using unlicensed apparatus for wireless telegraphy contrary to the Wireless Telegraphy Act 1949. The company advertised a device which would give the driver of a vehicle warning of a police radar trap; there was little chance of the licensing authority granting licences for the use of such devices.

Incitement is committed only where the solicitation, express or implied, comes to the notice of the person or persons whom it is intended to incite. A person may be liable for an attempt to incite, however, where the communication containing the solicitation does not reach the intended recipient, for example, where a letter is intercepted (see *Ransford* (1874) 13 Cox CC 9). The offence of incitement is complete, however, upon the communication reaching the intended recipient even though it fails to influence him to commit the offence incited (see *Krause* (1902) 66 JP 121). If the offence incited is committed, the inciter becomes an accessory to that offence and will be dealt with accordingly.

If the act, when done by the person incited, would not amount to a crime, the inciter will not be liable for incitement. In *Whitehouse* [1977] QB 868, D was convicted of inciting his daughter of fifteen to commit incest with him. Had intercourse taken place D would have been guilty of incest but a girl under sixteen commits no offence by permitting it (s. 1(1) of the Sexual Offences Act 1956). D's conviction was quashed. D would now be guilty of an offence as s. 54 of the Criminal Law Act 1977 makes it an offence for a man to incite a girl under sixteen whom he knows to be his grand-daughter, daughter or sister to have sexual intercourse with him. If a person is incapable of being an accessory to an offence because he or she is a victim whom the law seeks to protect (see *Tyrrell* [1894] 1 QB 710, 7.1.6 *ante*), he or she is similarly incapable of inciting the commission of the offence. Where the person incited would not be liable for the complete offence if he committed it because of the defence of duress, the inciter who made the threats to encourage the other to commit the offence, will be liable for incitement as the defence of duress does not cancel the *actus reus* and *mens rea* of the completed offence but simply excuses the accused from the consequences of conviction and punishment (cf. *Bourne* [1976] QB 217).

8.2.2 *Mens rea*
The accused must intend that the offence incited be committed and that any consequence in the *actus reus* result. If D incites E to kneecap V he would be liable for incitement to wound or incitement to cause grievous bodily harm, but he would not be guilty of incitement to murder. If V died from the wounds, however, both D and E would be liable for murder on the basis of their intention to cause grievous bodily harm. In addition to intention, the accused must know (or be wilfully blind as to) all the circumstances of the act incited which make it an offence, but there is no requirement that he know that the act is an offence. One of these circumstances is the *mens rea* of the person incited. If D believes that the person incited will not have *mens rea* for the crime in question, he will not be guilty of incitement. For example, D owns a shop which sells second-hand goods. He asks E to serve in the shop one day when he will be away on business. He tells E that X will be bringing in a video recorder and that E should pay him a previously agreed sum for it. The video recorder is stolen and D knows this. If he believes that E is unaware of its provenance he will not be liable for inciting E to handle stolen goods. If E does receive the video recorder, however, D could be convicted of handling stolen goods as a principal acting through an innocent agent. If, for some reason, the video is not received, D could be charged with an attempt to handle stolen goods by means of an innocent agent as his incitement of E could be construed as being a 'more than merely preparatory act', there being no further act necessary on D's part to procure E to commit the offence (see 8.4.3 *post* and

Law Com No.177, para. 13.10). In *Cogan and Leak* (7.1.3.3 *ante*), for example, if C had been unable to have intercourse with Mrs L due to his inebriation, could L have been convicted of incitement to commit rape? This would depend on whether L believed that C would have the *mens rea* for rape. If he believed that C had believed his story that Mrs L would consent to having intercourse with him, L would not have believed that C would have had the *mens rea* for rape and thus could not be convicted of incitement. In this case, however, it is submitted that he could not be convicted of attempt to rape through an innocent agent (see discussion in 7.1.3.3 *ante*).

The principle stated in the previous paragraph was distorted somewhat by the Court of Appeal in *Curr* [1968] 2 QB 944, which imposed the requirement that the person incited actually had to have the *mens rea* for the offence incited. D lent money to women with families and in return took their family allowance books containing vouchers which they had signed. He used other women agents to cash these vouchers. D was charged with soliciting the commission of a summary offence contrary to s. 9 of the Family Allowances Act 1945. This provision made it an offence for a person to receive money in payment of an allowance which the person knew was not properly payable. The women agents would only be guilty of this summary offence if knowledge was proved. D's conviction of soliciting was quashed as it had not been proved that the women had this knowledge. This decision is clearly wrong. The offence of incitement is committed regardless of whether the person incited committed the offence incited or intended to do so. The state of mind of the person incited is therefore irrelevant; all that is relevant is whether D believed, that if the offence incited was committed, the person incited would have the requisite *mens rea*.

8.2.3 Excluded offences

While a person may be convicted of attempting to incite (see 8.2.1 *ante*), there is doubt whether a conviction of inciting to attempt is possible. Generally an incitement to attempt is an incitement to commit. Schedule 1 to the Magistrates' Courts Act 1980 (paras. 34 and 35) makes no mention of such an offence, which suggests that it does not exist. It is possible to envisage circumstances, however, where such an offence, if it exists, could be committed. For example, D gives E a gun loaded with blanks and encourages E to shoot V. If E shoots at V with the intention to kill he will be guilty of attempted murder (see 8.4.4 *post*). D would be liable for aiding, abetting, counselling or procuring the attempt. If, however, E does not do the act incited, is it not arguable that D should be liable for inciting an attempt to wound or to murder? The Law Commission in their Draft Criminal Code Bill include liability for incitement to attempt (see clause 47(5)(b)).

While a person may be convicted of conspiring to incite, s. 5(7) of the Criminal Law Act 1977 abolished the offence of incitement to conspire, but incitement to incite is an offence known to the law (see *Sirat* (1985) 83 Cr App R 41; *Evans* [1986] Crim LR 470). This creates an anomaly: D may be convicted of incitement to incite where he encourages E to encourage F to commit an offence, but he may not be convicted where he encourages E to encourage and agree with F to commit an offence as this involves an incitement to conspire. The Law Commission recommend that both incitement to incite and incitement to conspire should be offences (see clause 47(5)(b)).

A person may be an accessory to incitement, for example, D may, with knowledge of its contents, post a letter written by E inciting F to commit an offence. However, incitement to aid, abet, counsel or procure an offence appears not to be an offence. This is the substance of a Crown Court decision in *Bodin and Bodin* [1979] Crim LR 176, and it is implicit in the drafting of s. 30(4) of the Criminal Law Act 1977. The rationale for this principle appears to be that aiding, abeting, counselling and procuring is not an offence in itself; liability only arises where the substantive offence is committed. Thus the acts incited may or may not turn out to be criminal. Incitement requires that the acts incited, when done, would be a crime by the person incited.

8.2.4 Impossibility

It has been stated above that there can be no liability for incitement unless the acts incited, when done, would amount to a crime by the person incited. The fact that the incitor believes that the act incited is a crime will not render him guilty of incitement. For example, D, who comes from a country where fornication is a crime, incites E to have intercourse with F. D is guilty of no offence as the act incited is not an offence (see *Taafe* [1984] AC 539). Can an inciter be liable for incitement where it is impossible to commit the offence incited? There are two situations which arise. The first is where the impossibility arises from the inadequacy of the means to be used to commit the crime. Obviously, if D knows that the offence cannot be committed by the means suggested he cannot be guilty of incitement to commit that offence as he lacks *mens rea* (see *Brown* (1899) 63 JP 790). For example, D incites E to shoot X using a gun which D supplies having loaded it with blanks. D will not be liable for incitement to wound or murder but *quaere* incitement to attempt (see 8.2.3 *ante*). But if D believed the bullets were live ammunition he would be liable for incitement to wound or murder as his mistake is simply as to the adequacy of the means to be used to commit the crime. Similarly, D would be liable for incitement to steal where he encouraged D to break into a safe using a jemmy to steal its contents, even though, unknown to D, the jemmy was inadequate to effect this object.

The second type of impossibility arises independently of the means to be employed; commission of the offence incited is impossible regardless of the means to be used. For example, D encourages E to receive a video recorder which they both believe to be stolen. In fact, it is not stolen so E's receipt of it could not amount to handling stolen goods. In *Fitzmaurice* [1983] QB 1083, the Court of Appeal stated *obiter* that the principles in *Haughton* v *Smith* [1975] AC 476, and *DPP* v *Nock* [1978] AC 979, which applied to attempt and conspiracy at common law, should also apply to incitement so that where an offence is factually impossible D will not be liable for incitement to commit it. Thus D would not be liable for incitement to handle stolen goods where the video recorder was not stolen. Similarly, if D incites E to kill V, but V is already dead, D will not be guilty of incitement to murder (see *Sirat* (1985) 83 Cr App R 41, at 43), or if D incites E to steal from V's pocket, which happens to be empty, D will not be guilty of incitement to steal. It is important, however, to examine carefully the course of conduct which the inciter was encouraging. If at the time of the incitement commission of the offence is possible, subsequent intervening impossibility will not protect D from conviction. For example, D encourages E to steal a necklace from V's safe. If the necklace was in the safe at the time of the incitement D will be guilty even though it had been removed by the time E sought to steal it. If D is encouraging E to commit an offence in the future its physical impossibility at the time of the incitement will not preclude conviction of D for incitement if it would be possible at the time D intends E should commit it. In *Shephard* [1919] 2 KB 125, the Court of Criminal Appeal upheld D's conviction of incitement to murder where he had written a letter to a pregnant woman encouraging her to kill the child after it was born. Bray J stated that the essential thing is that 'there should be a person capable of being murdered at the time when the act of murder is to be committed.' What is not clear is whether D would be liable where, although commission of the offence may be possible in the future, circumstances arise so that it is, in fact, impossible; for example, if the child had been born dead. If the actual possibility of committing the offence had to be established rather than its potential possibility, D could not be prosecuted until the necessary future events had occurred. This would clearly be undesirable, particularly if the future event is a long way off. It is submitted that D should be liable for incitement where the future offence is a realistic possibility. D's intention is, essentially, a conditional one; if the conditions are satisfied, he intends the offence to be committed (see also *McDonough* (1962) 42 Cr App R 37).

8.3 CONSPIRACY

8.3.1 Introduction
At common law the offence of conspiracy was committed where two or more persons agreed 'to do an unlawful act, or to do a lawful act by unlawful means' (*Mulcahy* (1868) LR 3 HL 306). This definition did not limit liability to agreements to commit crimes but also included agreements to commit some torts, to defraud, to corrupt public morals or to outrage public decency. In *Kamara* v *DPP* [1974] AC 104, the House of Lords held that an agreement to commit the tort of trespass to land, if accompanied by an intention to inflict more than merely nominal damage, amounted to a criminal conspiracy. The Law Commission (Law Com No. 76, para. 1.113) expressed the view that conspiracy should be confined to agreements to commit criminal offences and it is their aim that legislation should ultimately achieve this result. The other inchoate offences of incitement and attempt may only be charged where the result incited or attempted is itself a crime. The Criminal Law Act 1977, which resulted from the work of the Law Commission and created the offence of statutory conspiracy, has only partially achieved this result. Pending a comprehensive review of offences of fraud and of the law relating to obscenity and indecency, s. 5 of the 1977 Act preserves the offence of conspiracy to defraud and, possibly the offence of conspiracy to corrupt public morals or outrage public decency. Agreements to commit torts, however, are no longer indictable as conspiracy.

8.3.2 Common elements

Certain elements are common to both statutory conspiracies and common law conspiracies.

8.3.2.1 Agreement The essence of conspiracy is an agreement between two or more persons to effect the particular prohibited purpose. The agreement may be express or implied, but whatever form it takes, the offence of conspiracy is complete as soon as the parties agree. There is no requirement that they begin to put the agreement into effect, nor need all the details of the agreement be settled. Thus A and B would be guilty of conspiracy to rob where they had agreed to rob a bank even though they had not settled the time or place where the robbery was to take place. While conspiracy is complete as soon as two parties agree to effect an unlawful purpose, the conspiracy will continue to subsist as long as they agree and will only terminate on its completion by performance or by abandonment or frustration (see *DPP* v *Doot* [1973] AC 807). As conspiracy is a continuing offence, other persons may join an existing conspiracy and become parties to it. For example, if A approaches C and asks him to join him and B in robbing a bank when C agrees he becomes guilty of conspiracy to rob. This illustrates a further point that it is not necessary for all the parties to a conspiracy to be in contact with each other. What is necessary is that all the parties to the conspiracy have a common purpose communicated to at least one other party to the conspiracy (see *Ardalan* [1972] 2 All ER 257; *Scott* (1979) 68 Cr App R 164).

8.3.2.2 Parties While it must be proved that there was an agreement between D and another, that other need not be identified *(Phillips* (1987) 86 Cr App R 18). However, there must be at least two parties to the agreement; agreements with certain persons may not suffice to establish the offence of conspiracy. For example, where the director of a company who is solely responsible for the conduct of the company's business decides to commit an offence in the company's name, he cannot be convicted of conspiring with the company as only one mind was involved albeit that the company has a separate legal personality (see *McDonnell* [1966] 1 QB 233). But where a director conspires in the course of the company's business with other persons or companies, the company may be indicted as a party to that conspiracy (see *R* v *ICR Haulage Ltd* [1944] KB 551).

Where the only parties to an agreement are husband and wife they cannot be guilty of conspiracy, whether statutory (s. 2(2) of the Criminal Law Act 1977) or common law (*Mawji* v *R* [1957] AC 126). However, a husband and wife can be convicted of conspiracy where a third party is also involved (*Whitehouse* (1852) 6 Cox CC 38; *Chrastny* [1991] 1 WLR 1381), or where the agreement was entered into before they married (*R* v *Robinson* (1746) 1 Leach 37).

Where the only other party to an agreement to commit an offence is a child under the age of criminal responsibility, D will not be guilty of conspiracy (s. 2(2)). If the child is between ten and fourteen, D will be liable for conspiracy although that the child will be liable only if he has 'mischievous discretion'. While there is no authority at common law, it is assumed that the principles for statutory conspiracies would also apply.

Where the only other party to an agreement to commit an offence is an intended victim of that offence, D will not be guilty of conspiracy (s. 2(2)). The intended victim of the offence will not be guilty of conspiracy regardless of the number of persons involved in the conspiracy (s. 2(1)). The 1977 Act does not define 'victim'. Smith and Hogan, *Criminal Law*, suggest that the meaning of 'victim' is confined to offences which exist for his protection so that he would not be convicted of that offence as an accessory when it is committed by another with his full knowledge and cooperation (see 7.1.6 *ante*). This may have been the legislature's intention but it is expressed ambiguously. If A, a masochist, agrees to B, a sadist, performing acts upon him which will involve actual bodily harm, it is arguable that neither could be convicted of conspiracy as A is the intended victim. There is no common law authority in respect of victims as parties to conspiracies, but the issue is unlikely to arise as it is difficult to imagine an agreement with the proposed victim of a fraud to defraud him.

We have seen that where a person cannot commit an offence as a principal this does not prevent him being liable as an accessory (see 7.1.3.3 *ante*). His exemption from liability as a principal will likewise not protect him from liability for conspiracy. Thus, for example, a boy under fourteen or a woman may be convicted of conspiracy to rape (see further 8.3.3.4 *post*). Where a person is exempt from liability for an offence, whether as principal or accessory, he will not necessarily be exempt from conviction for conspiracy with another to commit that offence. There is a paucity of authority in this area. The Law Commission recommended that the exemption should extend to liability for conspiracy (see Law Com No. 76, para. 1.56) disapproving of the only authority in favour of liablility, *Whitchurch* (1890) 24 QBD 420, where a woman was convicted of conspiring to procure her own abortion though she was not pregnant and could not commit the substantive offence under s. 58 of the Offences Against the Person Act 1861. Parliament did not adopt this recommendation as it was considered that the provision to implement it would unduly complicate the 1977 Act and, in practice, non-pregnant women would not now be prosecuted. It appears that in practice the court will determine the question of liability by considering the purpose of the statute and whether it would be defeated by holding an exempt person liable for conspiracy or whether its purpose requires the extension of the exemption to cover conspiracy. In *Burns* (1984) 79 Cr App R 173, the question arose directly. The Court of Appeal upheld the conviction of a father of a child of conspiracy with others to steal it from the mother, although he was exempt from prosecution for the substantive offence under s. 56 of the Offences Against the Person Act 1861 (s. 56 has since been repealed by the Child Abduction Act 1984). Watkins LJ stated the considerations which influenced the court in its decision as follows (at p. 179):

> We find [no authority] that leads us to say that it is in any way wrong or unjust for a person who is exempt, in the sense that James Burns was, from prosecution for the substantive offence to be proceeded against for the crime of conspiracy.

> The dangers of permitting a father of children to collect a posse of men and suddenly launch a siege of the home of his erstwhile wife, to break in and

then snatch away sleeping children are surely self-evident. The criminal law does not in our view permit that sort of conduct. When a father who is exempt under s. 56 behaves in that way, it is, in our judgment, not only lawful but right and just that the prosecution should be free to bring a charge of conspiracy against him.

A person who agrees with another who is exempt from prosecution for the substantive offence to commit that offence may be convicted of conspiracy (see *Duguid* (1906) 21 Cox CC 200).

8.3.2.3 Acquittal of the other alleged conspirators There must be at least two parties to a conspiracy. If A is charged with conspiracy with B and B is acquitted, can A be convicted? If other parties, not charged, are alleged to have been involved, the acquittal of B has no consequences for A provided that the prosecution prove that A agreed with at least one other person (see *Anthony* [1965] 2 QB 189). Where A and B are the only alleged conspirators the conviction of one and acquittal of the other need not necessarily involve any inconsistency as the evidence against one may have been much stronger than the evidence against the other; for example, A may have confessed to the conspiracy, such confession being highly probative evidence against A but being of no evidential value against B. If A and B are tried separately the inconsistent verdicts again may be due to the different evidence presented at each trial, or the way in which the case was conducted or simply the different view which different juries take of the witnesses (see *DPP* v *Shannon* [1975] AC 717). There was some doubt, however, at common law whether a jury trying several conspirators together could convict one and acquit the others, there being no other alleged conspirators. To avoid all doubt s. 5(8) and (9) of the Criminal Law Act 1977 provide:

(8) The fact that the person or persons who, so far as appears from the indictment on which any person has been convicted of conspiracy, were the only other parties to the agreement on which his conviction was based have been acquitted of conspiracy by reference to that agreement (whether after being tried with the person convicted or separately) shall not be a ground for quashing his conviction unless under all the circumstances of the case his conviction is inconsistent with the acquittal of the other person or persons in question.

(9) Any rule of law or practice inconsistent with the provisions of subsection (8) above is hereby abolished.

The effect of this provision is that where all the alleged conspirators are tried together and the evidence against each is of roughly equal weight, the judge should direct the jury that they must either convict all or none, and the judge should make it clear that if they are unsure about the guilt of one of the conspirators, they must acquit all (see *Longman and Cribben* (1980) 72 Cr App R 121). But where the judge considers that the weight of the evidence against each conspirator is markedly different, he must direct them to consider each case separately and that they may convict or acquit as is appropriate according to the evidence (see *Roberts* (1983) 78 Cr App R 41).

8.3.3   Statutory conspiracy

The offence of statutory conspiracy is defined by s. 1(1) and (2) of the Criminal Law Act 1977, as amended by s. 5 of the Criminal Attempts Act 1981, as follows:

> (1)   Subject to the following provisions of this Part of this Act, if a person agrees with any other person or persons that a course of conduct shall be pursued which, if the agreement is carried out in accordance with their intentions, either –
>
>   (a)   will necessarily amount to or involve the commission of any offence or offences by one or more parties to the agreement, or
>   (b)   would do so but for the existence of facts which render the commission of the offence or any offences impossible, he is guilty of conspiracy to commit the offence or offences in question.
>
> (2)   Where liability for any offence may be incurred without knowledge on the part of the person committing it of any particular fact or circumstance necessary for the commission of the offence, a person shall nevertheless not be guilty of conspiracy to commit that offence by virtue of subsection (1) above unless he and at least one other party to the agreement intend or know that that fact or circumstance shall or will exist at the time when the conduct constituting the offence is to take place.

As conspiracy is an offence which centres on the agreement between the parties, which involves a meeting of minds, it is difficult to divide the offence into *actus reus* and *mens rea*. It is proposed, therefore, to analyse the separate ingredients contained in s. 1(1) which go to make up the offence.

8.3.3.1   Course of conduct   The essence of conspiracy is that the parties agree upon a course of conduct to be pursued. For the parties to be liable for conspiracy the agreed course of conduct, if pursued in accordance with their intentions, must necessarily amount to or involve the commission of an offence by one or more of the conspirators. Where the agreement is to commit a 'result crime' the phrase 'course of conduct' would be meaningless if confined to their actions divorced from the consequences of those actions. For example, if A and B agree to kill V by placing poison in a bottle of milk in his fridge, this will not necessarily result in murder as V may not drink the milk. If the phrase 'course of conduct' covered only the parties' physical acts, A and B would not be guilty of conspiracy to murder. This phrase must therefore include the intended consequences of those actions which, in this case, are the death of V. Thus the course of conduct agreed includes not only the actions intended to be taken but also the consequences of those actions.

If 'course of conduct' includes intended consequences, it is important to determine what consequences the parties intended as their liability will be limited to these. In *Siracusa* (1990) 90 Cr App R 340, O'Connor LJ stated (at p. 350):

The *mens rea* sufficient to support the commission of a substantive offence will not necessarily be sufficient to support a charge of conspiracy to commit that offence. An intent to cause grievous bodily harm is sufficient to support the charge of murder, but is not sufficient to support a charge of conspiracy to murder or of attempt to murder.

In *Siracusa* the accused were charged, *inter alia*, with conspiracy to import heroin contrary to s. 170(2)(b) of the Customs and Excise Management Act 1979. The jury were directed that if they agreed on a course of conduct to be pursued which, if carried out in accordance with their intentions, would necessarily amount to the offence of being concerned in the fraudulent evasion of the prohibition either on the importation of cannabis or heroin, by one or more of the parties to the agreement, then they were guilty of conspiracy. Case law has established that a person may be convicted of the substantive offence of importing heroin where he believed that cannabis was being imported (see 3.3 *ante*). Where conspiracy is charged, however, this will not suffice. O'Connor LJ stated (at p. 350):

> if the prosecution charge a conspiracy to contravene s. 170(2) of the Customs and Excise Management Act by the importation of heroin, then the prosecution must prove that the agreed course of conduct was the importation of heroin. This is because the essence of the crime of conspiracy is the agreement and in simple terms, you do not prove an agreement to import heroin by proving an agreement to import cannabis.

The course of conduct agreed also includes any circumstances necessary for the commission of the substantive offence. A person cannot be convicted of conspiracy unless he and at least one other party to the agreement intend or know that such circumstances shall or will exist at the time when the conduct constituting the offence is to take place. This is implicit in s. 1(2) which is not particularly clearly expressed. The substance of this provision is that, where recklessness or negligence suffice with respect to a circumstance of the substantive offence or strict liability applies thereto, a person can be convicted of conspiracy to commit such an offence only where he and another party to the agreement intend that the circumstance shall exist or know that it will exist at the time the offence is to take place.

A problem with s. 1(2) however, is that the words 'intend or know' are somewhat restrictive. It is not strictly accurate to state that A intends a circumstance to exist if he has no control over whether or not it exists, nor is it possible for A, at the time of the agreement, to know that a particular circumstance will exist at some future time. For example, if A and B agree to handle particular stolen goods, it may be their intention that the goods be stolen but they have no control over this event. Likewise they cannot know at the time of the agreement that the goods will be stolen when they handle them; they may have been repossessed and thus cease to be stolen. It would be more accurate to say that they 'believe' that the goods will remain stolen at the time they intend to handle them.

If only one of the parties to the agreement has the relevant knowledge or intention there is no conspiracy. For example, if A and B agree to purchase a particular consignment of goods from C, A knowing them to be stolen and B having no such knowledge or belief, neither will be liable for conspiracy to handle stolen goods even though the agreed course of action, if pursued, would necessarily have involved the offence of handling stolen goods by A. Likewise, where the parties differ as to the intended consequences, this will affect their liability for conspiracy. For example, if A and B agree to wound V and A intends that V should die but B only intends that he should sustain grievous bodily harm, there is no conspiracy to kill but there is a conspiracy to cause grievous bodily harm.

8.3.3.2 If the agreement is carried out Sometimes the agreement the parties make is a conditional one, for example, to beat up V on his way home from the pub if he is alone. Have they agreed on a course of conduct which, if it is carried out in accordance with their intentions, will necessarily amount to or involve the commission of an offence? In *Jackson* [1985] Crim LR 444, the appellants' convictions of conspiracy to pervert the course of justice were upheld by the Court of Appeal. The appellants had agreed with W, then on trial for burglary, that if he was convicted they would shoot him in the leg as they considered that the court would then deal with him more leniently. The Court of Appeal held that –

> Planning was taking place for a contingency and if that contingency occurred the conspiracy would necessarily involve the commission of an offence. 'Necessarily' is not to be held to mean that there must inevitably be the carrying out of the offence; it means, if the agreement is carried out in accordance with the plan, there must be the commission of the offence referred to in the conspiracy count.

The object of the agreement was the commission of the offence; if the contingency did not occur no action would be taken. This is to be contrasted with the situation where the object of the agreement is not the commission of that offence but the attainment of some other object, although the parties may contemplate the commission of an offence to attain that object. The following example was given in *Reed* [1982] Crim LR 819, and approved in *Jackson*:

> A and B agree to drive from London to Edinburgh in a time which can be achieved without exceeding the speed limits, but only if the traffic which they encounter is exceptionally light. Their agreement will not necessarily involve the commission of any offence, even if it is carried out in accordance with their intentions, and they do arrive from London to Edinburgh within the agreed time. Accordingly the agreement does not constitute the offence of statutory conspiracy or indeed of any offence.

Driving from London to Edinburgh within a particular time was an object which could be attained without the commission of any offence; if the speed limit was broken, this was incidental to the main object of the agreement. In *Reed* the Court of Appeal contrasted the driving example with that of A and B who agree to rob a bank, if when they arrive at the bank it seems safe to do so. 'Their agreement will necessarily involve the commission of the offence of robbery if it is carried out in accordance with their intentions. Accordingly, they are guilty of the statutory offence of conspiracy.' The object of their agreement was robbery; the commision of the offence was not incidental to any other object.

One situation remains. What if A and B agree to rob the bank and to kill anyone who seeks to prevent their escape. Are they guilty of conspiracy to murder? The driving example might appear to suggest that they are not, as the main object of their agreement is to rob the bank and this can be attained without necessarily killing anyone. But if this agreement to kill is isolated from the agreement to rob, there is little to distinguish it from *Jackson* as it is an agreement to kill subject to a condition precedent. If no one seeks to prevent their escape the course of conduct will not be pursued, but if anyone does seek to prevent their escape, the agreed course of conduct will necessarily invovle the commission of murder. Perhaps the correct approach to this problem is to separate the elements of the agreement from each other. The result is two separate agreements to pursue two courses of conduct: firstly, the agreement to rob the bank, and secondly the agreement, if a particular contingency occurs, to kill. The driving example is not severable in this way; there is one agreement to pursue one course of conduct which may or may not involve the commission of an offence.

8.3.3.3 In accordance with their intentions
At common law the prosecution had to prove not only an agreement to carry out an unlawful purpose but also an intention on the part of any alleged conspirator to carry out the unlawful purpose (see *Thomson* (1965) 50 Cr App R 1). The Law Commission did not recommend any change in the law. In Law Com No. 76, they stated (at para. 7.2):

> A person should be guilty of conspiracy if he agrees with another person that an offence shall be committed. Both must intend that any consequence specified in the definition of the offence will result and both must know of the existence of any state of affairs which it is necessary for them to know in order to be aware that the course of conduct agreed upon will amount to the offence.

The implication of this view was that if A did not intend for the substantive offence to be committed he could not be liable for conspiracy, and if there were only two parties to the alleged agreement, the other party likewise could not be guilty of conspiracy. In *Anderson* [1986] AC 27, the House of Lords was faced with the problem of an alleged conspirator who claimed he did not intend the substantive offence to be committed. D agreed for a fee to supply diamond wire to cut through prison bars to enable a prisoner to escape. He was convicted of conspiracy to effect the escape of a prisoner and appealed claiming that he intended only to supply the wire, receive his fee and then go abroad but that he neither intended nor expected the plan to be carried out. The House of Lords could have upheld D's conviction on the basis that he had aided and abetted the conspiracy as the others involved clearly had the intention that the substantive offence be committed. Their Lordships chose, however, to uphold his conviction as a principal to the conspiracy. Lord Bridge, in a speech with which all the House agreed, stated (at p. 38):

> I am clearly driven by consideration of the diversity of roles which parties may agree to play in criminal conspiracies to reject any construction of the statutory language which would require the prosecution to prove an intention on the part of each conspirator that the criminal offence or offences which will necessarily be committed by one or more of the conspirators if the agreed course of conduct is fully carried out should in fact be committed.

Too great a concern for easing the task of the prosecution has once again led to a distortion of the substantive principles of the criminal law. If it is not necessary to prove an intention on the part of one of the parties to an agreement that the course of conduct be pursued, it would appear to be unnecessary to prove such an intention in relation to any other party. The absurd outcome is that a person may be guilty of conspiracy where no party to the alleged agreement intended the substantive offence to be committed. In such a case there is no agreement to commit a crime, and no statutory conspiracy according to s. 1(1), but yet Lord Bridge would permit the conviction of conspiracy of all the parties to this non-existent agreement!

If a person may be convicted of conspiracy 'irrespective of his intention', what is the *mens rea* of conspiracy? Lord Bridge's answer to this question was distorted by his concern to render immune from liability 'respectable citizens' who enter into agreements for the purpose of 'exposing and frustrating the criminal purpose of the other parties to the agreement.' His concern would have been unnecessary had he adopted the Law Commission's view, as such a person would not intend the offence to be committed. Lord Bridge's abandonment of the requirement of proof of such an intention prima facie rendered such persons involved in entrapping offenders liable for conspiracy. In order to return them to the realms of innocence Lord Bridge invented a new *mens rea* requirement unsupported by the legislation, the Law Commission or any common law authority. He stated (at p. 39):

> the necessary *mens rea* of the crime is, in my opinion, established if, and only if, it is shown that the accused when he entered into the agreement, intended to play some part in the agreed course of conduct in furtherance of the criminal purpose which the agreed course of conduct was intended to achieve. Nothing less will suffice; nothing more is required.

This dictum itself contradicts Lord Bridge's earlier dicta as, if the intention of any alleged conspirator is irrelevant, it is impossible to determine the 'criminal purpose which the agreed course of conduct was intended to achieve.' Ignoring this absurdity, this dictum appears to require proof of an intention on the part of an alleged conspirator to play some part in the agreed course of conduct. Anderson's part was to be supply of the cutting wire and thus their Lordships confirmed his conviction of conspiracy. But it had always been understood that a person could be guilty of conspiracy even though he was to play no active role in the commission of the substantive offence. Lord Bridge's dictum would appear to remove such a person from the realms of liability. For example, A approaches B and asks him to kill C. If B agrees this would have amounted to conspiracy prior to *Anderson*. Now, however, A and B will only be liable for conspiracy to kill where A intended to play some part in the agreed course of conduct, namely the killing of C. Furthermore, far from rendering all persons involved in acceptable entrapment (see 7.1.7 *ante*) immune from criminal liability, Lord Bridge's dictum brings some such persons within the realms of criminal liablity if they intend to play some part in the agreed course of conduct – such action perhaps being necessary either to maintain their credibility as conspirators or to obtain the evidence necessary for a prosecution. Lord Bridge's good intentions only seem to have served to create more problems than he was seeking to resolve.

In *Siracusa* (1990) 90 Cr App R 340, the Court of Appeal sought to effect a damage limitation exercise by 'clarifying' Lord Bridge's dictum that it must be shown that 'the accused, when he entered into the agreement, intended to play some part in the agreed course of conduct. . . . ' O'Connor LJ (a judicial clairvoyant if ever there was one!) stated (at p. 349):

We think it obvious that Lord Bridge cannot have been intending that the organiser of a crime who recruited others to carry it out would not himself be guilty of conspiracy unless it could be proved that he intended to play some active part himself thereafter.

Thus, in the example above where A asks B to kill C, both A and B are, in the opinion of the Court of Appeal, guilty of conspiracy. O'Connor LJ went on to state (at p. 349):

Participation in a conspiracy is infinitely variable: it can be active or passive. If the majority shareholder and director of a company consents to the company being used for drug smuggling carried out in the company's name by a fellow director and minority shareholder, he is guilty of conspiracy. Consent, that is the agreement or adherence to the agreement, can be inferred if it is proved that he knew what was going on and the intention to participate in the furtherance of the criminal purpose is also established by his failure to stop the unlawful activity. Lord Bridge's dictum does not require anything more.

So 'play some part in' means no more than continuing to concur in the activity of another or failure to stop the unlawful activity. It is hard to believe that this is what Lord Bridge meant. A problem with this interpretation, however, is that it presumes activity on the part of other parties in furtherance of the criminal purpose. It had always been accepted that a conspiracy was complete when the parties agree and there was no requirement of activity in furtherance of the agreement. Doubtless, in many cases, it is only possible to prove the existence of the agreement by inference from the overt acts of the parties, but matters of proof should not be confused with substantive principles. In addition, the real problem with Lord Bridge's speech, that of the abandonment of the requirement that a conspirator intend the substantive offence to be committed, remains.

In its Draft Criminal Code the Law Commission reassert the traditional view of conspiracy in clause 48 which specifically requires proof that a person charged with conspiracy, and at least one other party to the agreement, must have intended the offence to be committed.

8.3.3.4 Necessarily amount to or involve the commission of any offence If the course of conduct agreed upon is carried out in accordance with the parties' intentions, will it necessarily amount to or involve the commission of an offence? If A and B agree upon a course of conduct which they believe will amount to an offence but it is not an offence, their belief will not convert their agreement into the offence of conspiracy. For example, believing that it is illegal to import lace into England, A and B agree to smuggle some lace into the country. In fact, there is no restriction on the importation of lace, so the agreement, if executed will not involve the commission of any offence.

The agreement, when executed, must involve one or more of the parties to the agreement in the commission of an offence. Will participation as an aider, abettor, counsellor or procurer of an offence suffice? In *Hollinshead* [1985] 1 All ER 850, the Court of Appeal held that an agreement to aid and abet an offence was not sufficient; a charge of conspiracy would only be sustainable where the agreement envisaged the commission of the offence as a principal by one or more of the parties. On the appeal hearing of that case in the House of Lords [1985] AC 975, their Lordships did not address this question, they upheld the convictions of the accused for common law conspiracy to defraud and considered it unnecessary to decide whether a statutory conspiracy to aid and abet an offence was possible. The wording of s. 1(1) and the fact that their Lordships did not decide that there was a statutory conspiracy seem to imply that a conspiracy to aid and abet is not possible. It should be noted, however, that there are a few statutory offences, whose *actus reus* consists of aiding and abetting or procuring something, for example aiding, abetting, counselling or procuring another's suicide. In these cases the aider and abettor is the principal so that it is possible to conspire to aid and abet a suicide (see *Reed* [1982] Crim LR 819).

One particular problem worthy of mention is an agreement between A, aged thirteen, and B that A will rape V. If the agreement is carried out, A cannot be convicted of rape because there is a presumption of law that a boy under fourteen is physically incapable of committing sexual intercourse (see *10.2.1.1.1 post*). It is important to determine the substance of this rule. If it is an element of the *actus reus* of the offence that the perpetrator be fourteen or over, then performance of the act by a person under fourteen is not an offence. Thus an agreement to rape would be an agreement to do something which is not an offence. If, however, the presumption is one of physical impossibility, that is that, regardless of any evidence to the contrary, a boy under fourteen is presumed incapable of performing the act of sexual intercourse, this would not preclude a conviction of conspiracy (or attempt). In *Waite* [1892] 2 QB 600, Lord Coleridge CJ described the presumption as one of physical incapacity. He was of opinion that it also precluded convictions for attempt. By contrast, in *Williams* [1893] 1 QB 320, Hawkins J considered a conviction of attempt would be possible. As the Criminal Attempts Act 1981 reversed the common law rule on impossibility, a conviction of conspiracy (or attempt where a more than merely preparatory act has been performed) would be possible. The presumption of physical incapacity is equivalent to a case of inadequacy of means (see 8.3.3.5 *post*). An impotent man could be convicted of conspiracy to rape or attempted rape; similarly a boy presumed incapable may be convicted. In the example it would not appear to matter if B was also thirteen or even a woman. Obviously this refined logic would be unnecessary if the presumption of incapacity (which bears no relationship to reality as a pre-pubescent boy is capable of sustaining an erection and thus of penetration) was abolished.

8.3.3.5 Impossibility Section 1(1)(b) (inserted by s. 5 of the Criminal Attempts Act 1981) deals with the problem of impossibility where facts exist which render the commission of the agreed offence impossible. To some extent this provision is unnecessary as the situation is covered by the phrase 'carried out in accordance with their intentions'. For example, A and B agree to kill C by shooting him. Unknown to them he is already dead so commission of the substantive offence of murder is impossible. However, had the agreement been carried out in accordance with their intentions this would necessarily have involved the commission of the offence of murder. The inclusion of s. 1(1)(b), however, is useful as it serves to avoid all doubt. Thus A and B will be liable for conspiracy in the following circumstances:

    (i)   they agree to pick V's pocket which, unknown to them, is empty (the offence of theft is impossible in the circumstances);

    (ii)   they agree to break into a safe to steal the contents using a jemmy which, unknown to them, is incapable of effecting their purpose (the offence of theft is impossible because of the inadequacy of the means chosen to commit it);

    (iii)   they agree to have consensual intercourse with V whom they believe to be fifteen but who has just celebrated her sixteenth birthday (the offence of having sexual intercourse with a girl under sixteen is impossible as V lacks the necessary quality of being under sixteen).

These examples illustrate three types of impossibility: impossibility due to the circumstances (often referred to as physical impossibility), impossibility due to inadequacy of means, and impossibility due to the absence of a quality on the part of a person or subject-matter (e.g. goods being stolen to support a charge of handling stolen goods) necessary for the commission of the offence (this may also be referred to as legal impossibility). At common law, following the decisions in *Haughton* v *Smith* [1975] AC 476 and *DPP* v *Nock* [1978] AC 979, impossibility was a defence except where it arose from inadequacy of means.

8.3.4 Jurisdiction

Section 1(4) of the Criminal Law Act 1977 provides:

> In this Part of this Act 'offence' means an offence triable in England and Wales, except that it includes murder notwithstanding that the murder in question would not be so triable if committed in accordance with the intentions of the parties to the agreement.

If A and B agree in England and Wales to commit an offence in some other country, they will only be guilty of conspiracy if the offence when committed would be triable in England and Wales. Thus if A and B agree to rob a bank in France they will not be guilty of conspiracy as the offence of robbery in France is not triable before an English court. However, if A, being married, agrees with B, who is aware of his married status, to go to France and marry her, they would be guilty of conspiracy to commit bigamy as bigamy is one of the few offences triable in England and Wales although committed abroad by a British citizen. Similarly murder committed abroad by a British citizen is triable in England and Wales. The Act does not deal with agreements abroad to commit an offence abroad, which offence when committed would be triable in England and Wales. For example if two British citizens agree in France to murder V in France, it is conceivable that they could be tried for conspiracy in England as the wording of s. 1(4) does not preclude this.

It should be noted that s. 1(4) also includes an exception to the general rule relating to jurisdiction in that if two foreign nationals agree while in England to kill V in France, they may be tried in England for conspiracy to murder even though, if the agreement is carried out, they could not be tried here for murder.

The Act makes no provision for the case of an agreement abroad to commit an offence in England. In *DPP* v *Doot* [1973] AC 807, the House of Lords held that such a conspiracy could be prosecuted in England if the parties acted in England in concert and in pursuance of the agreement. Lord Wilberforce was prepared to hold that acts by one conspirator in England should be sufficient to establish liability on the part of all the parties to the agreement. In *Somchai Liangsiriprasert* v *United States* [1990] AC 607, the Privy Council held that in Hong Kong, where the law on conspiracy was the same as the common law in England, an agreement abroad to commit an offence within the jursidiction was triable as conspiracy even though no overt acts had been performed within the jurisdiction. Lord Griffiths stated (at p. 620):

> But why should an overt act be necessary to found jurisdiction? In the case of conspiracy in England the crime is complete once the agreement is made and no further overt act need be proved as an ingredient of the crime. The only purpose of looking for an overt act in England in the case of a conspiracy

entered into abroad can be to establish the link between the conspiracy and England or possibly to show the conspiracy is continuing. But if this can be established by other evidence . . . it defeats the preventative purpose of the crime of conspiracy to have to wait until some overt act is performed in pursuance of the conspiracy. . . . Crime is now established on an international scale and the common law must face this new reality. Their Lordships can find nothing in precedent, comity or good sense that should inhibit the common law from regarding as justiciable in England inchoate crimes committed abroad which are intended to result in the commission of criminal offences in England.

In *Sansom* (1991) 92 Cr App R 115, the Court of Appeal held that the principle enunciated in *Somchai* applied to statutory conspiracies.

8.3.5 Common law conspiracies
These are limited to conspiracy to defraud and possibly conspiracy to corrupt public morals or outrage public decency.

8.3.5.1 Conspiracy to defraud Statutory conspiracy involves an agreement to commit an offence. Many frauds are crimes but some are not. Conspiracy to defraud was preserved by s. 5(2) of the Criminal Law Act 1977 to cover those frauds which are not crimes. For some time, however, there was confusion whether a conspiracy to defraud which would involve the commission of an offence could be charged as common law conspiracy. The problem has been resolved by s. 12 of the Criminal Justice Act 1987:

(1) If –
   (a) a person agrees with any other person or persons that a course of conduct shall be pursued; and
   (b) that course of conduct will necessarily amount to or involve the commission of any offence or offences by one or more of the parties to the agreement if the agreement is carried out in accordance with their intentions,
the fact that it will do so shall not preclude a charge of conspiracy to defraud being brought against any of them in respect of the agreement.

The effect of this provision is to recognise the overlap between the two forms of conspiracy – they are not mutually exclusive. This leaves to prosecutors a choice as to how to charge a particular conspiracy, but this choice should be exercised in accordance with guidance issued by the Director of Public Prosecutions under s. 10 of the Prosecution of Offences Act 1985, which indicates the circumstances in which a charge of conspiracy to defraud is appropriate.

8.3.5.1.1 The meaning of 'defraud' A conspiracy to defraud 'is an agreement to practice a fraud on somebody' (*Wai Yu-tsang* v *R* [1991] 4 All ER 664, 671, *per* Lord Goff). There is no need for anyone to be deceived if the course of conduct agreed by the parties is carried out. In *Scott* v *Metropolitan Police Commissioner* [1975] AC 819, D was convicted of conspiracy to defraud the copyright owners of films. D agreed with the employees of cinema owners to remove the films temporarily and to make copies of them without the knowledge or consent of the copyright owners. The copies were then to be distributed on a commercial basis accruing for the conspirators profits which might otherwise have been secured by the copyright owners. Viscount Dilhorne stated (at p. 840):

> an agreement by two or more by dishonesty to deprive a person of something which is his or to which he is or would or might be entitled and an agreement by two or more to injure some proprietary right of his, suffices to constitute the offence of conspiracy to defraud.

In this case the copyright owners suffered a loss in either of two ways: (i) the sales of the unauthorised copies would affect the sales of legitimate copies of their films; and (ii) under *Reading* v *Attorney-General* [1951] AC 507, the accused were bound to account to the copyright owners for any profits they made, which they clearly did not intend to do.

The victim of the conspiracy to defraud, however, may not suffer economic loss if the agreement is carried out. This will not prevent a conviction for conspiracy to defraud where a deception was involved and the victim was dishonestly deceived into taking an economic risk which he would not otherwise have taken as 'interests which are imperilled are less valuable in terms of money than those same interests when they are secure and protected' (*Allsop* (1976) 64 Cr App R 29, 32, *per* Shaw LJ). In this case the appellant, a sub-broker for a hire purchase company, in collusion with others entered false particulars on application forms in order to induce the company to accept applications which they might otherwise have rejected. The Court of Appeal upheld his conviction of conspiracy to defraud the company. If the creditors fulfilled the terms of the hire purchase agreements the company would suffer no loss but would, in fact, make a profit. The creditors, however, fell into higher risk categories than those with whom the company generally contracted.

Where a person is a public official there may be a conspiracy to defraud where he is dishonestly induced by deception to act contrary to his public duty (*Welham* v *DPP* [1961] AC 103).

In *Wai Yu-tsang* v *R*, the Privy Council affirmed the decisions in *Allsop* and *Welham*. A was the chief accountant of a bank in Hong Kong. He was charged with conspiracy with others to defraud the bank and its shareholders, creditors and depositors by dishonestly concealing in the accounts of the bank the dishonouring of cheques the bank had purchased to the sum of US $124m. This sum exceeded the assets of the bank and A concealed this fact to prevent a run on the bank. The agreement to conceal this fact amounted to a conspiracy to defraud as it would or might deceive the victims into acting or failing to act so that they suffered economic loss or their economic interests would be put at risk. Delivering the decision of the Board, Lord Goff of Chieveley quoted with approval from Lord Denning's speech in *Welham* (at p. 133):

The important thing about [the definition of defraud] is that it is not limited to the idea of economic loss, nor to the idea of depriving someone of something of value. It extends generally to the purpose of the fraud and deceit. Put shortly, 'with intent to defraud' means 'with intent to practise a fraud' on someone or other . . . If anyone may be prejudiced in any way by the fraud, that is enough.

Lord Goff considered that this was confirmed by the cases concerned with persons performing public duties, which were not to be regarded as a special category but rather illustrated the principle that conspiracies to defraud are not restricted to cases of intention to cause the victim economic loss. Thus a person may be defrauded when he is 'prejudiced in any way'. This provides the potential for greatly widening the ambit of this offence.

8.3.5.1.2 The mens rea of conspiracy to defraud The *mens rea* of conspiracy to defraud involves an intention to defraud and dishonesty. The problem which arises is determining what is meant by intention. The dicta in the cases are contradictory and confusing; much of the confusion deriving from the fact that there was equal uncertainty as to the meaning of 'defraud' when many of them were decided. The decision in *Wai Yu-tsang (ante)* may provide a means of rationalising the decisions. In *Scott (ante)* Lord Diplock stated that the 'purpose of the conspirators must be to cause the victim economic loss'. In most cases, however, the aim or purpose of the conspirators is to make a profit for themselves; it is rarely their direct purpose to cause a loss to some other person albeit that this might be the inevitable consequence of the performance of the agreed course of conduct. Indeed in *Scott* it would appear that the purpose of the conspirators was to make a profit for themselves, the lost profits to the copyright owners of the films being an inevitable consequence of their enterprise. In truth, therefore, they only had an oblique intent in respect of this loss.

In *Attorney-General's Reference (No 1 of 1982)* [1983] QB 751, the Court of Appeal referred to the 'true object of the agreement' as opposed to side effects or incidental consequences of the conspiracy. In this case loss would have been caused to X Ltd, the makers of whisky, if the defendants' agreement to sell in Lebanon whisky falsely labelled as being made by X Ltd had been put into effect. The Court of Appeal held, however, that this agreement only involved fraud in respect of the Lebanese purchasers who would have been deceived, but would not have involved an agreement to defraud X Ltd as any loss they might have suffered was only incidental to the true object of the agreement. Consequently, the parties could not be charged with conspiracy as it was not the object of the agreement to cause loss to anyone within the jurisdiction. This decision must be contrasted with that of the House of Lords in *Cooke* [1986] AC 909, where this refined and artificial analysis of 'true object' and 'incidental consequences' was not alluded to by their Lordships. The House upheld the convictions of British Rail stewards of conspiracy to defraud British Rail where they had dishonestly sold to passengers their own food, rather than British Rail food, intending to keep the proceeds. Their object was doubtless to make a profit rather than to cause a loss to British Rail, although this was the inevitable consequence of their actions. Their convictions, therefore, could only be upheld on the basis that they had an oblique intent with respect to causing such loss.

In *Allsop (ante)*, the Court of Appeal were of the opinion that it did not matter that the appellant did not desire to cause loss to the company as the deceit he employed deceived the company and imperilled its economic interests. Shaw LJ stated (at p. 32)

> Where a person intends by deceit to induce a course of conduct in another which puts that other's economic interests in jeopardy he is guilty of fraud even though he does not intend or desire that actual loss should ultimately be suffered by that other in this context.

This is in line with the approach of the House of Lords in *Welham (ante)* which established that 'intent to defraud' should not be given a narrow meaning, involving an intention to cause economic loss to another, but rather meant an intention to practise a fraud on another, or an intention to act to the prejudice of another man's right.

In *Wai Yu-tsang* the Privy Council affirmed *Allsop*, doubted Lord Diplock's dictum in *Scott*, approved *Welham* and did not refer to either the *Attorney-General's Reference (No 1 of 1982)* or *Cooke*. It would appear, however, that the continuing authority of the *Attorney-General's Reference (No 1 of 1982)* is questionable in light of the decisions in *Cooke* and the instant case. Lord Goff stated (at pp. 671–672):

> The question whether particular facts reveal a conspiracy to defraud depends upon what the conspirators have dishonestly agreed to do, and in particular whether they have agreed to practise a fraud on somebody. For this purpose it is enough for example that . . . the conspirators have dishonestly agreed to bring about a state of affairs which they realise will or may deceive the victim into so acting, or failing to act, that he will suffer economic loss or his economic interests will be put at risk. It is however important in such a case . . . to distinguish a conspirator's intention (or immediate purpose) dishonestly to bring about such a state of affairs from his motive (or underlying purpose). The latter may be benign to the extent that he does not wish the victim or potential victim to suffer harm; but the mere fact that it is benign will not of itself prevent the agreement from constituting a conspiracy to defraud.

It would appear, therefore, that an intention to bring about a state of affairs which amounts to defrauding another, whether because he will suffer economic loss, or he is deceived into taking an economic risk, or he is deceived into acting contrary to his public duty, or his rights are placed at risk of prejudice, is sufficient. The above dictum of Lord Goff uses the words 'will or may deceive the victim' suggesting that recklessness is sufficient. This was both unnecessary to the decision before the Privy Council and goes beyond what was decided in *Allsop*.

It must also be proved that the accused was dishonest. A person is dishonest if he realises that he is acting contrary to the standards of honesty of ordinary decent people (see *Ghosh* [1982] QB 1053, discussed at *11.2.2.2.2 post*).

8.3.5.1.3 Who is to be the perpetrator of the fraud? Statutory conspiracy is only committed where it is intended that at least one of the parties to the agreement perpetrate the offence. It appears, however, that conspiracy to defraud may be committed even though the fraud is ultimately to be perpetrated by persons who were not parties to the agreement. This is the purport of the decision in *Hollinshead* [1985] AC 975. The House of Lords upheld the convictions of the accused of conspiracy to defraud one or more electricity boards where they had manufactured and sold to a supposed middleman (in fact a police officer seeking to entrap them) devices designed to alter readings of electricity meters. The fraud on the electricty boards would be perpetrated by the ultimate purchasers of the devices when they used them to alter their meter readings. The course of conduct agreed upon by the accused would not have brought them into contact with the perpetrators of the frauds. Completion of their agreed course of conduct, by selling the devices, did not involve fraud on anyone. Nevertheless, the House of Lords held that their purpose was to cause economic loss to the electricity boards. It is clear, however, that their purpose was to make a profit from selling the devices to the middleman; this they would do regardless of what happened to the devices thereafter. Sense may only be made of the decision of their Lordships if 'purpose' is interpreted to mean 'intention'. Conspiracy to defraud, therefore, may be committed where the ultimate fraud is to be perpetrated by a person not a party to the agreement. In *Hollinshead*, however, it would not be correct to state that it was an inevitable consequence that the electricity boards sustain economic loss (the middleman may not have sold the devices or they may have been destroyed in a fire); it would be more accurate to state that this was virtually certain to result. If the parties to the agreement foresaw this, then it would be open to the jury to infer that they intended that result (see 3.2.3.3 *ante*).

8.3.5.2 Conspiracy to corrupt public morals or to outrage public decency Section 5 of the Criminal Law Act 1977 provides:

(1) Subject to the following provisions of this section, the offence of conspiracy at common law is hereby abolished. . . .

(3) Subsection (1) above shall not affect the offence of conspiracy at common law if and in so far as it may be committed by entering into an agreement to engage in conduct which –
    (a) tends to corrupt public morals or outrages public decency; but
    (b) would not amount to involve the commission of an offence if carried out by a single person otherwise than in pursuance of an agreement.

Subsection (3) is expressed in very tentative terms for two reasons. Firstly, it was not clear whether there were substantive offences of corrupting public morals or outraging public decency. Secondly, even if there were such substantive offences, paragraph (b) gives expression to the uncertainty whether corrupting public morals or outraging public decency as the object of a conspiracy perhaps had a wider meaning. If so action which, if done by a person acting alone, would not constitute either substantive offence might, if agreed to be done by two or more persons, constitute common law conspiracy to corrupt public morals or outrage public decency. The outcome of all this is uncertainty. If the meaning of corrupting public morals or outraging public decency is the same whether charged as substantive offences (if such exist) or as a conspiracy, then conspiracy to corrupt public morals or outrage public decency will be statutory conspiracies if these activities constitute substantive offences. It would obviously have been much more desirable if Parliament had taken the intitiative and decided whether corrupting public morals or outraging public decency were substantive offences and, if so, had provided definitions. The Law Commission had recommended the abolition of common law conspiracies to corrupt public morals or outrage public decency, along with substantive common law offences relating to morals and decency (Law Com No. 76, paras. 3.136–3.142), but their recommendations were ignored.

Are there substantive offences of corrupting public morals or outraging public decency and are the definitions of these activities the same whether charged as substantive offences or conspiracy? In *Shaw v DPP* [1962] AC 220, the accused was convicted of conspiracy to corrupt public morals arising from his publication of the 'Ladies Directory' advertising the names and addresses of prostitutes, together with photographs and details of the 'services' they were prepared to offer. The House of Lords upheld his conviction without deciding whether corrupting public morals was a substantive offence although the Court of Criminal Appeal had held that it was. In *Knuller v DPP* [1973] AC 435, the accused were charged with conspiracy to corrupt public morals and to outrage public decency arising from an agreement to publish, in a magazine called *IT*, advertisements soliciting homosexual acts in private between consenting adults. The conviction of conspiracy to corrupt public morals was upheld. Lord Simon expressed the view that 'corrupt' was a strong word meaning more than 'lead morally astray' suggesting 'conduct which a jury might find to be destructive of the very fabric of society.' Lord Reid considered that 'corrupt' was synonymous with 'deprave'. The conviction of conspiracy to outrage public decency was quashed as the direction to the jury was defective, although Lords Reid and Diplock thought that this was not an offence known to the law. Lords Simon, Kilbrandon and Morris held that there was a substantive offence of outraging public decency and thus there could be a conspiracy to do so. The Court of Appeal in *Mayling* [1963] 2 QB 717 had likewise held that it was an offence to outrage public decency. In defining the offence Lord Simon in *Knuller* stated (at pp. 494–495):

> *R v Mayling* shows that the substantive offence (and therefore the conduct the subject of the conspiracy) must be committed in public, in the sense that

the circumstances must be such that the alleged outrageously indecent matter could have been seen by more than one person, even though in fact no more than one did see it. If it is capable of being seen by one person only, no offence is committed. . . .

I do not think that it would necessarily negative the offence that the act or exhibit is superficially hid from view, if the public is expressly or impliedly invited to penetrate the cover. Thus, the public touting for an outrageously indecent exhibition in private would not escape. . . . Another obvious example is an outrageously indecent exhibit with a cover entitled 'Lift in order to see . . . ' This sort of instance could be applied to a book or newspaper. . . . The conduct must at least in some way be so projected as to have an impact in public.

The jury must also consider whether public decency is outraged by the conduct involved. Lord Simon went on to state (at p. 495):

It should be emphasised that 'outrage' . . . is a very strong word. 'Outraging public decency' goes considerably beyond offending the susceptibilities of, or even shocking, reasonable people. Moreover the offence is, in my view, concerned with recognised minimum standards of decency, which are likely to vary from time to time. Finally, notwithstanding that 'public' in the offence is used in a locative sense, public decency must be viewed as a whole; and I think the jury should be invited, where appropriate, to remember that they live in a plural society, with a tradition of tolerance towards minorities, and that this atmosphere of toleration is itself part of public decency.

In a series of recent cases the Court of Appeal confirmed the continued existence of the substantive offence of outraging public decency (see *Gibson* [1990] 2 QB 619; *May* (1989) 91 Cr App R 157; *Lunderbech* [1991] Crim LR 784; *Rowley* [1991] 4 All ER 649). It is difficult to envisage conduct which, when done alone, would not amount to the substantive offence of outraging public decency but which, if done in concert, would amount to conspiracy to outrage public decency. It would seem that there is nothing left for the common law offence of conspiracy to cover so that a conspiracy to outrage public decency should be charged as a statutory conspiracy. It is submitted that the same should apply to conspiracy to corrupt public morals albeit the authorities on the existence of the substantive offence are not so clearcut.

One final point relates to the wording of s. 5(3)(b). If the conduct agreed to be engaged in would 'amount to or involve the commission of an offence', the agreement cannot be charged as common law conspiracy (if this continues to exist). The word 'offence' in paragraph (b) is unqualified; it is not confined to the substantive offences of corrupting public morals or outraging public decency.

8.3.5.3 Impossibility in common law conspiracy The substance of the decision of the House of Lords in *DPP* v *Nock* [1978] AC 979 is that impossibility is generally an answer to a charge of common law conspiracy unless the impossibility arises from the inadequacy of the means to be used to effect the agreed course of conduct. It should be noted, however, that, if, at the time of the agreement, the object of the agreement was capable of being achieved, the fact that it subsequently becomes impossible of achievement due to some supervening event will not provide the accused with a defence as the offence of conspiracy is complete upon conclusion of an agreement without proof of any further steps to effect it being necessary.

8.4 ATTEMPT

8.4.1 Statutory definition and scope

The common law offence of attempt to commit an indictable offence was abolished by the Criminal Attempts Act 1981 which created a new statutory offence of attempt. The Act was largely the result of the work of the Law Commission (see Law Com No. 102). Section 1(1) of the Act provides.

(1) If, with intent to commit an offence to which this section applies, a person does an act which is more than merely preparatory to the commission of the offence, he is guilty of attempting to commit the offence.

By s. 1(4), liability for attempts is confined to offences which, if completed, would be triable in England and Wales as indictable offences. Thus, generally, there is no liability for an attempt to commit a summary offence. Section 1(4) goes on to exclude from liability attempts to commit the following offences, conspiracy, aiding, abetting, counselling, procuring or suborning the commission of an offence, and assisting an offender who has committed an arrestable offence or compounding an arrestable offence contrary to ss. 4(1) and 5(1) of the Criminal Law Act 1967. Where aiding, abetting, counselling or procuring is itself a substantive offence, for example, complicity in another's suicide contrary to s. 2(1) of the Suicide Act 1961, or procuring others to commit homosexual acts contrary to s. 4 of the Sexual Offences Act 1967, a person may be convicted of attempting to commit such an offence.

The definition in s. 1(1) implicitly excludes the possibility of convictions for attempt to commit some other crimes. For example, the requirement of 'an act' means that a person cannot attempt to commit an offence which can only be committed by an omission. Similarly a person cannot be convicted of an attempt to commit a result crime, such as murder, on the basis solely of an omission where he was under a duty to act. Where an offence may not be committed intentionally, as is the case with involuntary manslaughter where the killing is unintentional, there cannot be an attempt to commit that offence. If a person intends to kill he will be liable for attempted murder. It would also appear to be the case that a charge of attempted murder is appropriate even though a verdict of voluntary manslaughter (arising from diminished repsonsiblity, provocation or suicide pact) could have been returned had the intended victim died (see *Bruzas* [1972] Crim LR 367) or if a verdict of infanticide would have been available (but cf. *Smith* [1983] Crim LR 739).

Section 1(4) also adverts to jurisdictional issues. If D is to be liable for attempt to commit an offence, the offence, if completed, must be one for which he could have been indicted in England and Wales. For example, murder by a British citizen is indictable regardless of where it is committed. Thus if D sends a box of chocolates laced with poison to V who is in France, intending to kill him, D will be liable for attempted murder as soon as the chocolates are posted. If D's intention is only that V be made ill by the chocolates he is not liable for an attempt to administer poison contrary to s. 24 of the Offences Against the Person Act 1861 as such an offence committed abroad is not triable in England. If D is in France and gives the chocolates to V intending to kill him, he could, in theory, be prosecuted in England for attempted murder unless the courts take the view that there is no need for such extra-territorial jurisdiction. If so they could give a restrictive meaning to the words 'does an act' construing it to require that the acts which constitute the attempt either be done within the jurisdiction or be intended to have some effect within the jurisdiction. If D is outside the jurisdiction when he does the acts which may constitute an attempt, he will be liable to conviction where the acts are designed to have an effect within the jurisdiction (see *DPP* v *Stonehouse* [1977] 2 All ER 909). Thus if D, in France, sends poisoned chocolates to V, in England, intending to make V ill, he will be guilty of an attempt to administer poison.

8.4.2 *Mens rea*

The essence of the offence of attempt is intention. While it must be proved that the accused did an act which was 'more than merely preparatory to the commission of the offence', the acts which may amount to the *actus reus* derive their significance from the accused's intention. The acts, in themselves, may appear to be innocent but when added to the accused's intention they constitute a crime. For example, if D lights a cigarette lighter beside some curtains in a restaurant this may or may not constitute attempted arson, depending on whether he does so intending to set fire to the curtains or to light a cigarette. Similarly, if D offers V a chocolate this may be a perfectly innocent act of generosity or it may constitute attempted murder if D offers it intending to kill V believing, mistakenly, that the chocolate contains poison. In both cases the act of offering the chocolate is exactly the same but it is D's intention which colours the act and converts the second situation into the *actus reus* of attempted murder.

It is important, therefore, to determine what the meaning of 'intent to commit an offence' is in the context of attempt. The Court of Appeal held in *Pearman* (1984) 80 Cr App R 259, that the word 'intent' in s. 1(1) has the same meaning as at common law. In *Whybrow* (1951) 35 Cr App R 141, the Court of Appeal held that although on a charge of murder proof of an intention to cause grievous bodily harm would suffice to establish *mens rea*, on a charge of attempted murder 'the intent becomes the principal ingredient of the crime'. Accordingly, it had to be proved that the accused intended to kill. Thus where an accused is charged with attempt it must be proved that he had the intention to commit the substantive offence he is alleged to have attempted. Similarly, if recklessness with regard to causing a consequence will suffice for the substantive offence, only intention with regard to that consequence will suffice where attempt is charged (see *O'Toole* [1987] Crim LR 759 where D's conviction of attempted arson was quashed). This is logical as a person cannot be said to be trying to bring about a result where that result is not his aim or object but is merely foreseen as a possible consequence of the achievement of his aim or object.

At common law the word 'intent' was defined by the Court of Appeal in *Mohan* [1976] QB 1, 11, as 'a decision to bring about, in so far as it lies within the accused's power, the commission of the offence which it is alleged the accused attempted to commit, no matter whether the accused desired that consequence of his act or not'. This definition encompassed direct intent and oblique intent (see 3.2.1 *ante*). In *Pearman* the Court of Appeal approved this definition and explained the meaning of the phrase 'no matter whether the accused desired that consequence of his act or not' as follows (at p. 263):

> [These words] are probably designed to deal with a case where the accused has, as a primary purpose, some other object, for example, a man who plants a bomb in an aeroplane, which he knows is going to take off, it being his primary intention that he should claim the insurance on the aeroplane when the freight goes down into the sea. The jury would not be put off from saying that he intended to murder the crew simply by saying that he did not want or desire to kill the crew, but that was something that he inevitably intended to do. Similarly, for example, a man who is cornered by the police when he is in a car may have the primary purpose of simply escaping from that situation. If he drives straight at the police officers at high speed, a jury is likely to conclude that he intended to injure a police officer and maybe cause him serious grievous bodily harm.

Some confusion as to the degree of foresight required where oblique intent is involved has been caused by the Court of Appeal decision in *Walker and Hayles* (1990) 90 Cr App R 226 (see 3.2.3.3 *ante*). In this case W and H threw V from a third floor balcony after banging his head against a wall, threatening him with a knife and declaring that they were going to kill him. V survived and W and H were charged with attempted murder. This was not a case involving oblique intent so the only issue should have been as to their intention in throwing him from the balcony: did they intend to kill him; if they intended some lesser degree of harm this would not suffice for attempted murder. The jury were confused and sought clarification from the judge. Unfortunately the judge directed the jury in terms of inferring intention from the probability of death ensuing: if the accused knew there was a high probability of death the jury were entitled to infer they intended to kill. The Court of Appeal did not disapprove of using 'high probability' as the measure although they expressed a preference for the phrase 'virtual certainty'. This, however, is not the issue. If direct intention is involved, that is the accused has no other aim or purpose in committing the alleged offence than the result involved in that offence, it matters not that achievement of that result is possible, probable or certain. If achievement of that result is his aim or purpose then he intends it whether or not he is likely to achieve it. For example, D aims a gun at V and fires intending to kill V but misses. D is guilty of attempted murder whether he had a 10 per cent chance of succeeding in his purpose or a 99 per cent chance. If there is doubt as to what D's purpose was (was it only to frighten, to wound or to kill) this is a different issue. In this case it may be legitimate to point out that the more probable the result the more likely it is that D intended it, but it must be made clear that this is not conclusive of the matter as all the evidence in the case must be taken into account. It is only where there is evidence that D's aim or purpose was something other than to kill that a direction based on *Nedrick* [1986] 1 WLR 1025 (see 3.2.3.3 *ante*), should be considered; there did not appear to be any such evidence in *Walker and Hayles*. However, if a jury are satisfied that D's direct intent was to cause grievous bodily harm they may (but need not necessarily) convict of attempted murder if satisfied that D knew that death was virtually certain to ensue. For example, if D throws V off a hundred metre high cliff (V miraculously surviving by catching hold of a protruding ledge) and claims 'I only wanted to break his legs', a jury should acquit of attempted murder if they believe D. But if they are satisfied that D realised that death was virtually certain to ensue they could infer the intention to kill from that foresight and convict of attempted murder. The example illustrates the very limited application of the *Nedrick* direction where attempted murder is charged and D claims he only intended to cause grievous bodily harm.

The focus so far has been upon consequences; what *mens rea* is required with regard to the material circumstances of the offence? If D is charged with attempted rape is it sufficient that he intends to have sexual intercourse being reckless whether the woman consents, or must it be proved that he intended to have non-consensual intercourse? Similarly, if D is charged with attempting to have intercourse with a girl under the age of thirteen, is it sufficient to prove that he intended to have intercourse (strict liability applies in respect of the girl's age on a charge of committing the substantive offence), or must it be proved that he intended to have intercourse with a girl under that age? The Law Commission, in their report which preceded the passage of the Act (Law Com No. 102, para. 2.15) took the view that intention as to every element of the offence was required; knowledge as to surrounding circumstances equating with intention as to consequences. The Court of Appeal, however, has decided that if recklessness in respect of a circumstance will suffice for commission of the substantive offence, it will suffice on a charge of attempt to commit that offence. In *Khan* [1990] 2 All ER 783, on a charge of attempted rape, the trial judge directed the jury that the accused were guilty if they were reckless as to whether the victim consented. Dismissing appeals against conviction, Russell LJ stated (at p. 788):

> The only difference between the [offences of rape and attempted rape] is that in rape sexual intercourse takes place whereas in attempted rape it does not, although there has to be some act which is more than preparatory to sexual intercourse. Considered in that way, the intent of the defendant is precisely the same in rape and in attempted rape and the *mens rea* is identical, namely an intention to have intercourse plus a knowledge of or recklessness as to the

woman's absence of consent. . . . Recklessness in rape and attempted rape arises not in relation to the physical act of the accused but only in his state of mind when engaged in the activity of having or attempting to have sexual intercourse. . . . The only 'intent' . . . of the rapist is to have sexual intercourse. He commits the offence because of the circumstances in which he manifests that intent, i.e. when the woman is not consenting and he either knows it or could not care less about the absence of consent.

In cl. 49(2) of the Draft Criminal Code the Law Commission accepts that recklessness as to circumstances is sufficient on a charge of attempt if it would suffice on a charge of the substantive offence. It is anticipated that on a charge of attempting to commit an offence where strict liability as to a circumstance suffices, courts will accept proof of recklessness. It is submitted that they should not accept anything less.

A final problem to be disposed of is that of conditional intention (cf. 8.3.3.2 *ante*). A person has conditional intent where he intends to commit an offence if a particular condition is satisfied; for example, D intends to steal from V's car if he finds any items of value in the car. In such a case there will be an attempted theft where D, with this intent, does an act which is more than merely preparatory to the commission of the offence, for example, opening the door of the car. Provided the prosecution do not charge D with attempt to steal specific items, there is no obstacle to a conviction. If the prosecution specify particular items they would have to prove that D would have stolen these had he discovered them. To avoid such difficulties of proof the prosecution need only charge D with 'attempting to steal from a car'. On such an indictment there is no need to prove that the car contained any items worth stealing, or even any items at all. If the car is completely empty so that theft from it is impossible, this will not prevent a conviction for attempt as the Criminal Attempts Act reversed the decision in *Haughton* v *Smith* [1975] AC 476 relating to impossible attempts (see 8.4.4 *post*).

8.4.3 Actus reus

The *actus reus* of attempt is the doing of 'an act which is more than merely preparatory to the commission of the offence' the accused intends to commit. This is a question of fact for the jury. Section 4(3) provides:

Where, in proceedings against a person for an offence under s. 1 above, there is evidence sufficient in law to support a finding that he did an act falling within subsection (1) of that section, the question whether or not his act fell within that susbsection is a question of fact.

The trial judge must decide whether there is sufficient evidence to support a finding that the accused did such an act. If there is not, he will direct an acquittal and, if there is, the jury will be left with the task of deciding what acts the accused did and whether these were more than merely preparatory to the commission of the offence. At some point D's acts will cross over from being *merely preparatory* to being *more than merely preparatory*. The Criminal

Attempts Act provides no more guidance than the common law for determining the precise point when an attempt is committed.

The test generally settled at common law was known as the 'proximity' test formulated in *Eagleton* (1855) 6 Cox CC 559, 571 by Parke B:

> The mere intention to commit a misdemeanour is not criminal. Some act is required and we do not think that all acts towards committing a misdemeanour are indictable. Acts remotely leading towards the commission of the offence are not to be considered as attempts to commit it, but acts immediately connected with it are.

This test was very vague as there was no indication when acts passed over from being remote to being immediately connected with the intended offence. But, to some extent, this is inevitable as there is an infinite variety of methods of committing offences and an infinite variety of situations will arise. When examining the common law, the Law Commission recognised this (Law Com No. 102) stating (at para. 2.45):

> in our view there is no magic formula which can now be produced to define what precisely constitutes an attempt. . . . Of the various approaches, only the 'proximity' test has produced results which may be thought broadly acceptable. Its disadvantages are that hitherto it has not worked well in some cases, and that it is imprecise. It shares the latter disadvantage with all other approaches but its flexibility does enable difficult cases to be reconsidered and their authority questioned. Further, where cases are so dependent on what are sometimes fine differences of degree, we think it is eminently appropriate for the question whether the conduct in a particular case amounts to an attempt to be left to the jury.

This led the Law Commission to propose a test which did not differ greatly from the proximity test but which was designed to avoid a problem identified in the proximity test. Proximity suggested that an act had to be immediately connected with the commission of the offence. There was a danger that this would be construed very restrictively limiting liability to situations where the accused had performed the last act necessary to commit the offence. Thus the Law Commission changed the terminology to indicate that the parameters of attempt were broader than might be suggested by the proximity test. The difference between the tests is essentially one of perspective. The proximity test looked backwards from the commission of the full offence to see if the acts the accused had performed were close enough to that point. The new test looks forwards from the point of preparatory acts to see whether the acts of the accused have gone beyond the preparatory stage.

From one point of view, all acts, apart from the last one necessary to bring about the commission of the offence, are preparatory acts. The inclusion of the word 'merely', however, suggests a grey area of ill-defined proportions between acts which are purely preparatory and the last act of commission. This grey area covers those acts performed by the accused when he might be described as being 'on the job' as opposed to preparing for it or, as the Court of Appeal put it in *Gullefer* [1987] Crim LR 195, when the accused has 'embarked on the crime proper'. This will obviously vary from case to case. An example may help to illustrate the position. D decides to kill V and with this intention he performs the following acts: (1) he spends several days observing V's movements in order to choose a good place and time for performing the killing; (2) he buys a gun and ammunition; (3) he visits a wood on several occasions for target practice; (4) on the day the offence is to be committed he loads the gun; (5) he drives to the scene of the proposed killing and hides in some bushes awaiting V's arrival; (6) he observes the road watching for V; (7) he sees V and takes aim; (8) he places his finger on the trigger; (9) he squeezes the trigger and fires the gun. Point (9) is the last act to be performed by D in order to bring about commission of the offence of murder. If a police officer had been observing D, however, could he have intervened at some earlier point to prevent the killing while being sure that D would be convicted of attempted murder? To some extent points (1) to (8) were all acts preparatory to the last act but at some stage D moved from performing *merely preparatory* acts to performing *more than merely preparatory* acts. This would appear to be at some stage after point (4) and before point (9) when he might be described as being 'on the job' or as having 'embarked on the crime proper'. Whether a jury would be prepared to convict of attempted murder (assuming the judge leaves the issue to them) if the officer intervened at point (6) or (7) is highly questionable. Some juries might not even convict where D had reached point (8) if they paid undue attention to the fact that D could still relent and withdraw from committing the offence at that stage. What is clear, however, is that the jury's task does not simply involve applying the declared law to the facts as they find them but, in addition, involves them determining what the law is, that is, defining the meaning of 'more than merely prepartory'. This creates a risk of perverse and inconsistent verdicts.

There have been several decisions of the Court of Appeal which have sought to clarify the new test. In *Widdowson* (1985) 82 Cr App R 314, D wishing to obtain a van on hire-purchase terms but realising that he would not be accepted as credit-worthy, filled in a credit enquiries form in the name of another person and was convicted of attempting to obtain services (the hire-purchase of the van) by deception. If the finance company had responded favourably to D's enquiry, it still remained for D to make a formal application for a hire-purchase deal. The Court of Appeal quashed the conviction, referring to common law tests which indicated that this would not be considered an attempt. The Court considered that D had not performed every act necessary to achieve the consequence of obtaining services by deception; his acts were not immediately but only remotely connected with the offence alleged to have been attempted; and, using the words of Lord Diplock in *DPP* v *Stonehouse* [1978] AC 55, 68, he had not 'crossed the Rubicon and burned his boats', that is he had not reached the point of no return but could still have withdrawn from commission of the offence. These tests would greatly reduce the ambit of attempt which the Law Commission had hoped to increase.

In *Boyle and Boyle* (1987) 84 Cr App R 270, the appellants were convicted of attempted burglary having been found by a policeman standing by a door, of which the lock and one hinge were broken. The Court of Appeal upheld their convictions being satisfied that the only thing left for them to do to commit the full offence was for one of them to step over the threshold of the property and enter as a trespasser, there being ample evidence of an intention to steal. The Court also referred to another test which had been approved at common law. This had been propounded in Stephen's *Digest of the Criminal Law* (9th edn) as follows 'An attempt to commit a crime is an act done with intent to commit that crime and forming part of a series of acts which would constitute its actual commission, if it were not interrupted'. This is a very vague test as it would appear to encompass all acts of preparation and those which are more than merely preparatory.

In *Jones* [1990] 1 WLR 1057, the Court of Appeal disapproved of the approach to construction of s. 1(1) of the Act which referred back to previous conflicting case law. Taylor LJ stated that the correct approach was 'to look first at the natural meaning of the statutory words, not to turn back to earlier case law and seek to fit some previous test to the words of the section.' He cited with approval the judgment of Lord Lane CJ in *Gullefer* [1987] Crim LR 195 (reported also at [1990] 1 WLR 1063) where he stated (at p. 1066):

It seems to us that the words of the Act of 1981 seek to steer a midway course. They do not provide, as they might have done, that the . . . *Eagleton* test is to be followed, or that, as Lord Diplock suggested, the defendant must have reached a point from which it was impossible for him to retreat before the *actus reus* of an attempt is proved. On the other hand, the words give perhaps as clear a guidance as is possible in the circumstances on the point of time at which *Stephen's* 'series of acts' begins. It begins when the merely preparatory acts have come to an end and the defendant embarks upon the crime proper. When that is will depend of course upon the facts in any particular case.

Jones had been convicted of attempted murder of his former girlfriend's new boyfriend, F. Jones bought a gun, shortened the barrel, disguised himself, jumped into the rear seat of F's car as he left his daughter at school, pointed the gun at F and said 'You are not going to like this'. F managed to grab the gun and escape with it from the car. It was not established whether Jones had his finger on the trigger of the gun when he pointed it at F. The Court of Appeal dismissed Jones' appeal, Taylor LJ stating (at pp. 1062-3):

Looking at the plain natural meaning of s. 1(1) in the way indicated by the Lord Chief Justice, the question for the judge in the present case was whether there was evidence from which a reasonable jury, properly directed, could conclude that the appellant had done acts which were more than merely preparatory. Clearly his actions in obtaining the gun, in shortening it, in loading it, in putting on his disguise, and in going to the school could only be regarded as preparatory acts. But, in our judgment, once he had got into the car, taken out the loaded gun and pointed it at the victim with the intention of killing him, there was sufficient evidence for the consideration of the jury on the charge of attempted murder. It was a matter for them to decide whether they were sure those acts were more than merely preparatory. In our judgment, therefore, the judge was right to allow the case to go to the jury.

Thus, ultimately, the matter is one for the jury. The accused need not have performed the last act nor reached the point of no return. It is impossible to be any more precise than that (cf. *Campbell* [1991] Crim LR 268).

One final point to note in respect of the *actus reus* of attempt is that the fact that the accused is interrupted or desists prior to doing the last act necessary to commit the substantive offence he intended to commit does not prevent his conviction for attempt if he has performed a more than merely preparatory act. Thus there is no defence of withdrawal if the point has been reached where a more than merely preparatory act has been performed.

8.4.4 Impossibility

If D makes a mistake as to the law, believing that it prohibits what he intends to do, he will not be guilty of attempt if he endeavours to carry out his intention. What he is attempting to do is not a crime and the offence of attempt applies only to attempts to commit indictable offences. For example, D comes from a country where adultery is a crime and he believes it is also a crime in England. He attempts to have consensual intercourse with E, a married woman, but fails. Had he succeeded he would have committed no offence; the fact that he fails does not render him liable for attempt as what he attempted to do is not a crime.

There are three situations, however, where D may fail to commit an offence because it is impossible to commit it in the circumstances (cf. 8.3.3.5 *ante*). For example:

(i)   D attempts to steal from V's pocket which, unknown to him, is empty (physical impossibility);

(ii)   D attempts to break into a safe to steal the contents using a jemmy which, unknown to him, is incapable of effecting his purpose (impossibility arising from inadequacy of means);

(iii)   D attempts to handle stolen goods but, unknown to him, the goods are not stolen (legal impossibility as the goods lack a quality essential for the commission of the offence).

At common law D would have been convicted of attempt only in the second situation (see *Haughton* v *Smith* [1975] AC 476) as it was considered that in this situation the crime was not really impossible as it could have been committed if D had used different or more adequate means. Thus, in *White* [1910] 2 KB 124, the accused was convicted of attempted murder where he tried to kill his mother using an insufficient dose of poison. Had he given her sugar, mistaking it for poison, he would not have been convicted as this would have been a case of physical impossibility. The distinctions which the common law made were considered refined and artificial. The Law Commission recommended that the law should be changed (Law Com No. 102, para. 2.96) placing the emphasis on the intention of the accused provided there was proof of a more than merely preparatory act. This recommendation was put into effect by s. 1(2) and (3) of the Criminal Attempts Act which provide:

(2) A person may be guilty of attempting to commit an offence to which this section applies even though the facts are such that the commission of the offence is impossible.

(3) In any case where –
   (a) apart from this subsection a person's intention would not be regarded as having amounted to an intent to commit an offence: but
   (b) if the facts of the case had been as he believed them to be, his intention would be so regarded,

then, for the purposes of subsection (1) above, he shall be regarded as having had an intent to commit that offence.

The purport of s. 1(2) is to render a person liable to conviction regardless of the category of impossibility which prevented commission of the intended substantive offence. Section 1(3) is, essentially, superfluous but it was included as a precaution to deal with the particular situation of legal impossibility. If D intended to handle a particular video, believing it to be stolen, when, in fact, it was not, he might claim that, as he intended to handle only that particular video, he did not intend to handle stolen goods but intended to handle a 'non-stolen video'. Simply to frame the argument exposes its ludicrous nature as D's subjective state of mind was to handle goods he believed to be stolen, that is, an intention to handle stolen goods. The fact that the objective status of the goods was that they were not stolen does not, in any way, impinge upon D's state of mind, just as the fact that a pocket is empty does not alter D's intention to steal from that pocket; if he were to claim that he intended to take nothing as there was nothing to take, he would be laughed out of court. But, to be doubly sure, Parliament enacted s. 1(3) which simply states that if the facts had been as he believed them to be (if the video had been stolen) he shall be regarded as having an intent to commit that offence (handling stolen goods).

But, be prepared for two surprises. In *Anderton* v *Ryan* [1985] AC 560, the House of Lords held that the Act had not affected cases of legal impossibility so that the appellant's conviction of attempting to handle stolen goods was quashed as the video she sought to handle was not stolen, or, as their Lordships put it, her acts were 'objectively innocent'. The next surprise is that just over a year later the House of Lords in *Shivpuri* [1987] AC 1 overruled this decision, Lord Bridge declaring (at pp. 21-22) that:

the concept of 'objective innocence' is incapable of sensible application in relation to the law of criminal attempts. The reason for this is that any attempt to commit an offence which involves 'an act which is more than merely preparatory to the commission of the offence' but which for any reason fails, so that in the event no offence is committed, must *ex hypothesi*, from the point of view of the criminal law, be 'objectively innocent'. What turns what would otherwise, from the point of view of the criminal law, be

an innocent act into a crime is the intent of the actor to commit an offence.
... A puts his hand into B's pocket. Whether or not there is anything in the
pocket capable of being stolen, if A intends to steal his act is a criminal
attempt; if he does not so intend his act is innocent. ... These considerations
lead me to the conclusion that the distinction sought to be drawn in *Anderton
v Ryan* between innocent and guilty acts considered 'objectively' and
independently of the state of mind of the actor cannot be sensibly
maintained.

As a result, their Lordships dismissed the appellant's appeal from a conviction
of attempting to be knowingly concerned in dealing with prohibited drugs.
Shivpuri was arrested in possession of a suitcase which he believed contained
either heroin or cannabis. He admitted that he intended to receive the drugs
and deal in them. In fact the case contained snuff which was not a prohibited
drug. Shivpuri had the intention to commit the offence and he had done acts
which were more than merely preparatory to the commission of the *intended*
offence.

Further reading
M. Cohen, 'Inciting the impossible' [1979] Crim LR 239.
I. Dennis, 'The rationale of criminal conspiracy' (1977) 93 LQR 39; 'The
elements of attempt' [1980] Crim LR 758.
A. T. H. Smith, 'Conspiracy to defraud: The Law Commission's Working
Paper No. 104' [1988] Crim LR 508.
K. J. M. Smith, 'Proximity in Attempt: Lord Lane's midway course' [1991]
Crim LR 576.
M. Wasik, 'Abandoning criminal intent' [1980] Crim LR 785.
G. Williams, 'The Lords and impossible attempts, or *quis custodiet ipsos
custodes*' (1986) 45 CLJ 33.

NINE
Homicide

9.1 INTRODUCTION

There are several offences of unlawful homicide: murder, manslaughter, infanticide and causing death by reckless driving. There are other offences closely approximating to homicide such as child destruction and abortion. The common element to homicide offences, however, is the *actus reus*.

9.1.1 *Actus reus*
Coke described the *actus reus* of homicide as 'Unlawfully killing a reasonable person who is in being and under the King's Peace, the death following within a year and a day' (Coke, 3 Inst 47). A killing is unlawful where it is not justified (see *Williams* (1984) 78 Cr App R 276, and *Beckford* [1988] AC 130, *3.6.1.1.2 ante*).

To be the victim of homicide a person must be 'in being'. A baby still in the womb cannot be the victim of homicide. It is important therefore to determine when a child being born becomes an independent 'person in being'. It appears that the child must be wholly expelled from the mother (*Poulton* (1832) 5 C & P 329) and be alive having an existence independent of the mother (*Enoch* (1833) 5 C & P 539). It is not necessary for the umbilical cord to have been severed. However, what constitutes an independent existence is problematical. Some cases suggested that the child must have breathed and others added the requirement of having an independent circulation. Medical science now establishes that foetuses have an independent circulation within a couple of months of conception. A further problem is that a child may be born alive but not breathe for several minutes. In *Brain* (1834) 6 C & P 349, Park J stated that breathing was not essential if the child was born alive. The problem of determining the point at which a child acquires an independent existence, however, does not appear to be a major one as the last reported case dealing with the matter was *Handley* (1874) 13 Cox CC 79. Where a child has been poisoned or injured while in the womb, is born alive but dies thereafter from the poison or injury, this may amount to murder or manslaughter depending on the state of mind of the person who administered the poison or inflicted the injury (see *West* (1848) 2 Car & Kir 784; *Senior* (1832) 1 Mood CC 346).

If a person is dead he cannot be the victim of homicide. But what if V's heart has stopped and while a doctor is seeking to resuscitate him D shoots V through the head; can D be convicted of homicide. If the prosecution could not establish that V was alive D could be convicted of attempted murder. In *Malcherek and Steel* [1981] 1 WLR 690, the Court of Appeal adverted to the test of 'brain death', although they did not have to decide whether this was the legal definition of death they accepted that it was the test which the medical profession used. If the courts have to address the issue they will probably accept 'brain death' as the test. If a person is 'brain dead' at the time of D's act, even though being artificially kept alive by mechanical means (perhaps so that vital organs may be used for transplant purposes), it is submitted that he cannot be the victim of homicide.

The phrase 'the King's Peace' is a strange one as it appears that everyone in the world is under the King's or Queen's Peace, except an enemy alien who is killed in the course of war. If an enemy alien is a prisoner of war he is under the Queen's Peace. Murder and manslaughter are exceptional in that an English court may try a British citizen for these offences if committed in any country (see s. 9 of the Offences Against the Person Act 1861 and s. 3 of the British Nationality Act 1948). If the offence takes place on a British ship or aircraft it can be tried here whether the perpetrator is a British subject or an alien, but English courts have no jurisdiction if the offence occurs on a foreign ship outside territorial waters.

The final requirement is that the death occur within a year and a day of the event which is alleged to have caused the victim's death. This rule was originally justified because of the difficulty of proving causation where there was a long interval between the infliction of the injury and death (on causation generally see 2.6 *ante*). Medical science has advanced so that this justification is no longer valid. The rule remains however, presumably because of an alternative justification that a person who has injured another should not remain indefinitely at risk of prosecution for homicide (see Criminal Law Revision Committee, Fourteenth Report: *Offences Against the Person*, Cmnd 7844, paras. 39 and 40). If a person is artificially kept alive by a life support machine for more than a year and a day it would appear that a conviction of homicide is not possible, but indictments for attempted murder or other offences against the person are always available.

In *Dyson* [1908] 2 KB 454, the 'year and a day' rule was applied. D was indicted for the manslaughter of his child who died in March 1908, having inflicted injuries on him in November 1906 and December 1907. The judge directed the jury that they could convict D if they found that death had been caused by the injuries inflicted in November 1906. The Court of Criminal Appeal quashed the conviction. Lord Alverstone CJ stating (at p. 456):

no person can be convicted of manslaughter where the death does not occur within a year and a day after the injury was inflicted, for in that event it must be attributed to some other cause. . . . The proper question to have been submitted to the jury was whether the prisoner accelerated the child's death by the injuries which he inflicted in December 1907.

9.2 MURDER

Murder is unlawful homicide committed with 'malice aforethought'. The penalty for murder is mandatory life imprisonment. 'Malice aforethought' describes the *mens rea* required for a conviction of murder. If malice aforethought is lacking the unlawful homicide will be manslaughter. It should be noted, however, that 'malice aforethought' is a technical term whose meaning implies neither ill-will nor premeditation. Thus a person who kills out of motives of mercy or compassion to alleviate suffering may, nevertheless, be guilty of murder, just as a person who kills in the 'heat of the moment' without prior planning may be guilty of murder.

It is important, therefore, to determine the meaning of 'malice aforethought'. Prior to 1957 it appeared that an accused could be convicted of murder where (1) he intended to kill ('express' malice), or (2) he intended to cause grievous bodily harm ('implied malice'), or (3) he killed in the furtherance of a felony (for example, rape or robbery) or when resisting or preventing a lawful arrest, even though there was no intent to kill or to cause grievous bodily harm ('constructive malice'). The courts had not been consistent in their use of the terms 'express' or 'implied' malice. Precise definition of 'implied malice' was not necessary as this appeared to overlap with 'constructive malice' as causing grievous bodily harm was a felony. In 1957 the Homicide Act abolished 'constructive malice'. Section 1 provides:

(1) Where a person kills another in the course or furtherance of some other offence, the killing shall not amount to murder unless done with the same malice aforethought (express or implied) as is required for a killing to amount to murder when not done in the course or furtherance of another offence.

(2) For the purposes of the foregoing subsection, a killing done in the course or for the purpose of resisting an officer of justice, or of resisting or avoiding or preventing a lawful arrest, or of effecting or assisting an escape or rescue from legal custody, shall be treated as a killing in the course or furtherance of an offence.

The question arose whether, by abolishing 'constructive malice', the Act had abolished liability where an accused intended to cause grievous bodily harm but not to kill. As s. 1(1) reserved liability where an accused had 'express malice' or 'implied malice' it had to be determined whether 'implied malice' meant something other than an intention to cause grievous bodily harm. In *Vickers* [1957] 2 QB 664, the Court of Criminal Appeal held that 'implied malice' meant an intention to cause grievous bodily harm. In *Hyam* [1975] AC

55 the House of Lords failed to arrive at a decision on this issue. In *Cunningham* [1982] AC 566, the House finally decided that an intention to cause grievous bodily harm was 'implied malice' and was something separate from 'constructive malice'. The *mens rea* of murder, therefore, is an intention to kill or an intention to cause grievous bodily harm (as to the meaning of intention see 3.2 *ante*).

'Grievous bodily harm' is a phrase which is to be given its natural meaning (*DPP v Smith* [1961] AC 290). In *Smith* Viscount Kilmuir stated that 'bodily harm' requires no explanation and 'grievous' means 'really serious', although a direction to a jury which omitted the word 'really' would not be a misdirection (*Saunders* [1985] Crim LR 230). Thus a person may be convicted of murder even though he did not intend to kill nor even foresee death as a possibility. For example, D, a member of a terrorist group, performs a 'knee-capping' on V, a member who has broken the rules of he group. D has performed many such 'knee-cappings' in the past and no victim has ever died and he foresees no risk of V dying. V, however, fears hospitals and does not receive medical treatment and dies from septicaemia caused by the wound. As D intended to cause grievous bodily harm he would be convicted of murder. In their Draft Criminal Code (Law Com No. 177), the Law Commission recommend a change in the law. Clause 54 provides:

(1)   A person is guilty of murder if he causes the death of another –
   (a)   intending to cause death; or
   (b)   intending to cause serious personal harm and being aware that he may cause death . . .

The *Report of the Select Committee of the House of Lords on Murder and Life Imprisonment* (HL Paper 78–1, 1989) supports this recommendation stating (at para. 68):

A person is not generally liable to conviction of a serious crime where the prohibited result was not only unintended but also unforeseen. This seems to the Committee to be a good rule of moral responsibility which should certainly apply to the most serious crime of all, murder. While the law continues to have two categories of homicide, unforeseen but unlawful killings are properly left to the law of manslaughter.

9.3   MANSLAUGHTER

9.3.1   Introduction
The offence of manslaughter generally covers all unlawful homicides which are not murder. The punishment for this offence is in the discretion of the court and therefore ranges from absolute discharge to life imprisonment, reflecting the immense range of circumstances which may fall within the compass of this offence.

The offence of manslaughter may be divided into two generic types – voluntary and involuntary. Voluntary manslaughter is committed where the accused has killed with malice aforethought, and thus cou~~~ murder, but there are mitigating circumstances present reduci~~ ity. As the sentence for murder is mandatory life imprisonm~~ sentencing such an accused for murder would not be able to re~~ ~se mitigating circumstances in the sentence. Accordingly, where an accus~ ~ills while suffering from diminished responsibility, or the killing is done under provocation or in pursuance of a suicide pact, he will be convicted of manslaughter. The offence of infanticide serves the same purpose. Involuntary manslaughter is an unlawful killing committed by an accused who did not have malice aforethought but who, nevertheless, had a state of mind which the law treats as culpable.

9.3.2 Voluntary manslaughter

9.3.2.1 Diminished responsibility
A full discussion of the provisions relating to diminished responsibility is to be found in Chapter 5, para. 5.5.

9.3.2.2 Provocation
Provocation is only a defence to a charge of murder. The effect of this defence is to reduce to manslaughter what, in the absence of provocation, would have been murder. If the jury are not satisfied that the accused had the intention to kill or cause grievous bodily harm they must acquit of murder and, necessarily, of voluntary manslaughter (although a conviction of involuntary manslaughter may still be possible). But if the jury are satisfied he had the requisite intention they must convict of manslaughter if the accused may have been provoked. The burden of proof in respect of provocation is upon the prosecution (*Cascoe* [1970] 2 All ER 833); if there is evidence raising the possibility of provocation the burden is upon the prosecution to prove beyond reasonable doubt that the accused was not provoked. If the jury are left feeling that there is a reasonable possibility that the elements of the defence existed, they must convict of manslaughter. It is for the judge to decide if there is evidence raising the possibility of provocation. There may be such evidence even though the defence have not sought to rely on provocation. This often occurs where the defence are seeking to plead that the killing was done in self-defence (see *Lee Chun-Cheun* [1963] AC 220; *Johnson* [1989] 1 WLR 740); the accused may not wish to undermine this defence by giving evidence of provocation. Thus, even if the issue of provocation is inconsistent with the way the defence have chosen to conduct their case, the judge must direct the jury on provocation if there is evidence upon which a jury might find provocation (see Lord Reading in *Hopper* [1915] 2 KB 431, 435; *Newell* [1989] Crim LR 906).

Provocation was a defence at common law, but it has been modified by s. 3 of the Homicide Act 1957, which provides:

Where on a charge of murder there is evidence on which the jury can find that the person charged was provoked (whether by things done or by things said or by both together) to lose his self-control, the question whether the provocation was enough to make a reasonable man do as he did shall be left to be determined by the jury; and in determining that question the jury shall take into account everything both done and said according to the effect which, in their opinion, it would have on a reasonable man.

There are two elements to the defence of provocation: first, the subjective question whether the accused was provoked to lose his self-control; and, second, the objective question whether a reasonable man would have been provoked to lose his self-control and do as he did. Because of the burden of proof being on the prosecution, the defence will succeed if the jury feel the accused may possibly have been provoked to lose his self-control and a reasonable man may possibly have lost his self-control and done as he did. At common law the judge could withdraw the defence from the jury if there was no evidence that a reasonable man would have lost his self-control and done as the accused did (*Mancini* v *DPP* [1942] AC 1). The Act prohibits this; if there is evidence that the accused may have been provoked the second question must be left to the jury to decide.

9.3.2.2.1 What can amount to provocation At common law words alone, except 'in circumstances of a most extreme and exceptional character' could not amount to provocation (*Holmes* v *DPP* [1946] AC 588). With two exceptions, actual violence by the deceased upon the accused was required. The exceptions were discovery by a husband of his wife in the act of committing adultery and discovery by a father of someone committing sodomy on his son. A confession of adultery by the spouse did not constitute provocation (*Holmes*). The Act removed all such restrictions. The provocation need not be illegal or wrongful and may even be something as natural as a baby crying (*Doughty* (1986) 83 Cr App R 319). In *Doughty*, the judge refused to leave the issue of provocation to the jury where D claimed that the persistent crying and restlessness of his seventeen-day old son had caused him to lose his self-control and kill the child. The Court of Appeal quashed the conviction for murder, substituting one of manslaughter, as the Act made it mandatory to leave the issue of provocation to the jury where there was any evidence that the accused was provoked to lose his self-control.

At common law, apart from the two exceptions mentioned above, the provocative acts had to be done by the deceased to the accused (*Duffy* [1949] 1 All ER 932n). The Act removes these limitations so that the provocation may emanate from third parties (*Davies* [1975] QB 691) or be directed at third parties (*Pearson* [1992] Crim LR 193). What is crucial is that there be evidence that D was provoked to lose his self-control. Thus, for example, if X taunts D that D's wife, W, and V are having an affair and D loses his self-control and kills X, or W or V, the defence of provocation would have to be left to the jury. Likewise, if D arrives at his daughter's house to find her being physically and verbally abused by his son-in-law, V, and D loses his self-control and kills him, the defence of provocation would have to be left to the jury. In *Pearson*, two brothers, M and W, killed their violent and abusive father. M had suffered ill-treatment from the father for eight years during which time W had largely lived elsewhere. W had returned home to protect M. M was convicted of manslaughter due to provocation and W of murder. The Court of Appeal quashed W's conviction substituting one of manslaughter as the judge had failed to direct the jury that, in deciding whether W could rely on the defence of provocation, they could have regard to the father's words and conduct not simply against him but against M, especially as his return home had been prompted by a desire to protect M from further violence.

9.3.2.2.2 The subjective question

The first question for the jury to consider is whether there is a reasonable possibility that the accused was provoked to lose his self-control. If the jury are satisfied beyond reasonable doubt that he was not provoked to lose his self-control they will convict without considering whether a reasonable man would have lost his self-control. Thus, for example, if D has a particularly phlegmatic temperament and did not lose his self-control in circumstances in which a reasonable man may have, his defence will fail.

The jury are entitled to look beyond the immediate act which led to the accused's loss of self-control and take into account the relevant background. In *Davies* [1975] QB 691, Widgery CJ stated (at p. 702) that the 'background is material to the provocation as the setting in which the state of mind of the defendant must be judged.' But in all cases the issue hinges on whether the accused lost his self-control (*Davies*; see also *Cocker* [1989] Crim LR 740). In *Ibrams* (1981) 74 Cr App R 154 and *Thornton* [1992] 1 All ER 306, the Court of Appeal approved the dictum of Devlin J in *Duffy* that there must be 'a sudden and temporary loss of self-control, rendering the accused so subject to passion as to make him or her for the moment not master of his mind'. While there may have been a history of provocative acts or words, if at the time of the killing, D was not provoked to lose his self-control, he cannot rely on past provocation. In *Ibrams* the appellants had been terrorised by V over a period up to 7 October. They then agreed a plan and killed V on 14 October, there being no evidence that V had done anything after 7 October to provoke them. The Court of Appeal considered that the interval of time and the formulation of a plan negatived claims of loss of self-control. The Court approved a further passage from *Duffy*:

> Indeed, circumstances which induce a desire for revenge are inconsistent with provocation, since the conscious formulation of a desire for revenge means that a person has had time to think, to reflect, and that would negative a sudden temporary loss of self-control, which is of the essence of provocation.

This does not mean that there cannot be cumulative provocation, that is a series of acts or words over a period of time which culminate in the 'sudden and temporary loss of self-control' by the accused. Thus, provocation is not confined to the last act before the killing occurred; there may have been previous acts or words which, when added together, cause the accused to lose his self-control, although the last act on its own may not be sufficient to constitute provocation (see *Simpson* [1957] Crim LR 815; *Fantle* [1959] Crim LR 584; and M. Wasik, 'Cumulative provocation and domestic killing' [1982]

Crim LR 29). In *Ahluwalia* [1993] Crim LR 63 where D killed her husband after a long history of domestic violence by him, it was argued that in domestic violence 'slow-burn' cases, where the accused only loses self-control after a prolonged period of provocation from the deceased, the *Duffy* test was inappropriate as a delay or 'cooling-off period' between the last act of provocation and the killing might, in fact, cause the accused to react more strongly. The Court of Appeal restated that only Parliament could change the law on provocation but did specifically state with regard to the alleged 'slow-burn' reaction:

> We accept that the subjective element in the defence of provocation would not as a matter of law be negatived simply because of the delayed reaction in such cases, provided that there was at the time of the killing a 'sudden and temporary loss of self-control' caused by the alleged provocation. However, the longer the delay and the stronger the evidence of deliberation on the part of the defendant, the more likely it will be that the prosecution will negative provocation.

The fact that the accused has done something to induce the provocative conduct does not preclude him from seeking to raise the defence of provocation. In *Edwards* [1973] AC 648, D had been blackmailing V. When pressed for payment, V swore at D and began attacking him with a knife. D wrestled the knife from V and killed him in a fit of 'white hot' passion. The judge declined to leave provocation to the jury who convicted D of murder. The Privy Council substituted a conviction of manslaughter stating (at p. 158):

> On principle it seems reasonable to say that (1) a blackmailer cannot rely on the predictable results of his own blackmailing conduct as constituting provocation sufficient to reduce his killing of the victim from murder to manslaughter, and the predictable results may include a considerable degree of hostile reaction by the person sought to be blackmailed, for instance vituperative words and even some hostile action such as blows with a fist; (2) but if the hostile reaction by the person sought to be blackmailed goes to extreme lengths it might constitute sufficient provocation even for the blackmailer; (3) there would in many cases be a question of degree to be decided by the jury.

Section 3, however, requires that where there is any evidence that the accused was provoked the issue must be left to the jury. The Privy Council's decision sought to add a pre-condition in cases of self-induced provocation which the words of the statute do not support. In *Johnson* [1989] 1 WLR 740, the Court of Appeal disapproved of *Edwards*, Watkins LJ stating (at p. 744):

> In view of the express wording of s. 3 . . . we find it impossible to accept that the mere fact that a defendant caused a reaction in others, which in turn led him to lose his self-control, should result in the issue of provocation being

kept outside a jury's consideration. Section 3 clearly provides that the question is whether things done or said or both provoked the defendant to lose his self-control. If there is any evidence that it may have done, the issue must be left to the jury.

Thus the jury must take everything into account regardless of whether it was a predictable result of the accused's own conduct.

9.3.2.2.3   The objective question   The fact that D lost his self-control does not mean that his defence of provocation will succeed; the jury have then to consider the objective question of whether a reasonable man would have been provoked to lose his self-control and do as D did. If the jury feel there is a reasonable possibility that he would, they must return a verdict of manslaughter. It is crucial, therefore, to determine who the reasonable man is. At common law the reasonable man was an adult person with normal physical and mental attributes (*Bedder* v *DPP* [1954] 1 WLR 1119). If the accused was a juvenile he was disadvantaged as he was to be expected to exercise the self-control which an adult would exercise. His age might also affect the gravity of the provocation addressed to him (*Camplin* [1978] AC 705). Furthermore, if the accused had any particular characteristics which singled him out, these were not attributed to the reasonable man. This was consistent with the common law rule that provocation was limited to acts of violence by the deceased upon the accused. Thus, if the accused was disfigured or impotent, taunts about these matters could not constitute provocation so there was no need to attribute these characteristics to the reasonable man.

Section 3 of the Homicide Act changed this by allowing words alone to constitute provocation. In *Camplin* [1978] AC 705, the House of Lords held that the Act reversed the decision in *Bedder*. In *Camplin*, V, a man in his fifties, forcibly buggered D, a boy aged fifteen, and then laughed at him. D lost his self-control and hit V over the head with a chapati pan killing him. At D's trial the judge directed the jury that they should ignore D's age when considering the objective question and decide whether a reasonable adult would have been provoked to do as D did. The Court of Appeal allowed D's appeal and substituted a conviction for manslaughter holding that the reasonable man is a person of the same age as the accused. The House of Lords dismissed the Crown's appeal. The reasonable man was a person of the same age and sex as the accused who is not exceptionally excitable or pugnacious. Lord Diplock stated (at p. 718):

a proper direction to a jury . . . should state . . . that the reasonable man referred to in the question is a person having the power of self-control to be expected of an ordinary person of the sex and age of the accused, but in other respects sharing such of the accused's characteristics as they think would affect the gravity of the provocation to him; and that the question is not merely whether such a person would in like circumstances be provoked to lose his self-control but also whether he would react to the provocation as the accused did.

Ultimately it is for the jury to decide if particular characteristics are relevant to the gravity of the provocation on the accused and what degree of self-control is to be expected of him. But certain matters are not characteristics, namely hot-temperedness or pugnacity or drunkenness. In *Newell* (1980) 71 Cr App R 331, the Court of Appeal developed further the meaning of characteristics following the New Zealand case of *McGregor* [1962] NZLR 1069 where North J stated (at p. 1081):

> The characteristic must be something definite and of sufficient significance to make the offender a different person from the ordinary run of mankind, and have also a sufficient degree of permanence to warrant its being regarded as something constituting part of the individual's character or personality. ... [It covers] not only ... physical qualities but also ... mental qualities and such more indeterminate attributes as colour, race and creed. ... Moreover ... there must be some real connection between the nature of the provocation and the particular characteristic of the offender by which it is sought to modify the ordinary man test. The words or conduct must have been exclusively or particularly provocative to the individual because, and only because, of the characteristic.

Mental qualities could include such things as phobias. For example, if D suffers from arachniphobia and V torments him with a large spider whereupon D loses his self-control and kills V, D's arachniphobia would be a relevant characteristic to be attributed to the reasonable man.

There must be a connection between the characteristic and the provocation. If D is taunted about his race this is a relevant characteristic to attribute to the reasonable man, but if he is taunted about his sexual orientation, his race would be irrelevant. In addition, if something is to be considered a characteristic it must have a sufficient degree of permanence. In *Newell* the Court of Appeal held the trial judge was correct in not inviting the jury to take into account the accused's intoxication, the fact that he had taken an overdose of drugs and written a suicide note a few days previously, and his grief arising from his girlfriend leaving him, when considering whether a reasonable man would have been provoked to lose his self-control by disparaging remarks made by the victim about the former girlfriend. In addition, the Court held that the accused's chronic alcoholism was not relevant to the provocation but it left open whether, in other circumstances, this might be a characteristic.

It is arguable that this is too narrow a view of 'characteristics'. The recent departure of his girl-friend may have affected the gravity of the provocation to the accused. If the girl-friend had left a long time previously the accused would not have been depressed or as susceptible to provocation in this regard. In *Raven* [1982] Crim LR 51, a Crown Court judge relaxed the test to some extent. The accused was aged twenty two but had a mental age of nine. The judge directed the jury to consider this characteristic when applying the reasonable man test. In addition, however, he stated that the reasonable man was someone who had lived the same life as the accused for twenty two years, which included living in squats for the past two to three years.

Having decided who the reasonable man is, the jury then must consider whether he would have lost his self-control and done as the accused did. At common law there was a rule that the 'mode of resentment must bear a reasonable relationship to the provocation' (*Mancini* v *DPP* [1942] AC 1). Thus fists could be answered with fists but not with a deadly weapon (see *Duffy*). This rule, obviously, could not survive s. 3 of the Homicide Act 1957 as, if it did, it would render nugatory the provision that provocation could arise from words alone. In *Camplin* the House of Lords stated that *Mancini* was no longer to be treated as an authority on the law of provocation. On the other hand, however, it is proper for the jury to consider whether a reasonable man would have responded to the provocation in the way the accused did. The relationship between the provocation and the retaliation is simply a factor to be considered by the jury in answering the objective question (see *Brown* [1972] 2 QB 229). There are degrees of provocation such that a reasonable man might respond in one situation with fists but in another with a deadly weapon. This was recognised by the Privy Council in *Phillips* [1969] 2 AC 130, which stated (at p. 137):

the question . . . is not merely whether in their opinion the provocation would have made a reasonable man lose his self-control but also whether, having lost his self-control, he would have retaliated in the same way as the person charged did.

Thus there are degrees of loss of self-control which vary according to the degree of provocation. The Privy Council rejected the suggestion that there was no intermediate stage between icy detachment and going beserk, stating (at pp. 137–138):

This premise, unless the argument is purely semantic, must be based upon human experience and is, in their Lordships view, false. The average man reacts to provocation according to its degree with angry words, with a blow of the hand, possibly, if the provocation is gross and there is a dangerous weapon to hand, with that weapon.

9.3.2.3 Suicide pacts Section 4(1) of the Homicide Act 1957 (as amended by the Suicide Act 1961) provides 'It shall be manslaughter and shall not be murder for a person acting in pursuance of a suicide pact between him and another to kill the other or be party to the other being killed by a third person'. Section 4(3) defines 'suicide pact' as follows:

a common agreement between two or more persons having for its object the death of all of them, whether or not each is to take his own life, but nothing done by a person who enters into a suicide pact shall be treated as done by him in pursuance of the pact unless it is done while he has the settled intention of dying in pursuance of the pact.

If, for example, D enters into an agreement to kill V and then himself, and having killed V he relents or is prevented from killing himself, he may, on a charge of murder, raise the defence of suicide pact. In this case the burden of proof is upon the defence (s. 4(2)) to prove the facts grounding the defence on the balance of probabilities (*Woolmington* v *DPP* [1935] AC 462).

9.3.3 Involuntary manslaughter

Involuntary manslaughter is an offence of ill-defined boundaries covering the middle ground between murder and accidental death. If D did not have the *mens rea* for murder he may be guilty of manslaughter if the killing was 'unlawful'. Seeking to define this element of unlawfulness has taxed judicial minds for most of this century; and even now there remain areas of uncertainty. It appears that involuntary manslaughter takes at least two and possibly three forms.

The first form is constructive manslaughter, the second is reckless manslaughter, and finally there is a possible third form, namely gross negligence manslaughter.

Sometimes the facts of a case may fall within the compass of both constructive and reckless manslaughter so that a verdict of manslaughter may be available on either of those grounds.

9.3.3.1 Constructive manslaughter   Prior to the Homicide Act 1957, the doctrine of constructive malice meant that an accused could be convicted of murder where he killed in the course of committing a felony albeit that he lacked the *mens rea* of murder. A parallel doctrine existed that if an accused killed in the course of doing an unlawful act, which was not a felony, he was guilty of manslaughter. The Homicide Act, by s. 1(1), abolished the doctrine of constructive murder, but constructive manslaughter remains. This is often referred to as 'unlawful act' manslaughter. The fact that death is caused by D's unlawful act, however, is not sufficient to lead to a manslaughter verdict. The term 'unlawful act' is qualified in several ways.

9.3.3.1.1 A crime of commission   In the nineteenth century there was some uncertainty in respect of the nature of the unlawfulness required. In *Fenton* (1830) 1 Lew CC 179, Tindal CJ directed the jury that it was sufficient if the accused did a wrongful act which was a tort. In *Franklin* (1883) 15 Cox CC 163, Field J doubted *Fenton* finding it abhorrent to construct a crime from a civil wrong. The doubts have since been resolved. In *Andrews* v *DPP* [1937] AC 576, Lord Atkin confirmed that something more than negligence (which suffices for civil liability) is required. In this case the accused had been driving dangerously when he killed the deceased. Driving is a lawful act which becomes unlawful when performed negligently. Lord Atkin sought to distinguish between acts which become unlawful when performed negligently and acts which are unlawful for some other reason stating (at p. 585):

> There is an obvious difference in the law of manslaughter between doing an unlawful act and doing a lawful act with a degree of carelessness which the legislature makes criminal. If it were otherwise a man who killed another while driving without due care and attention would *ex necessitate* commit manslaughter.

An act can only be unlawful in these terms, therefore, if it is done with *mens rea* (see *Lamb* [1967] 2 QB 981). In *Lamb*, D, in fun, pointed a revolver at a friend. He knew that there were two bullets in the chambers, but neither was opposite the barrel. He did not appreciate that the cylinder rotated automatically when the trigger was pulled. He pulled the trigger, a bullet was fired and his friend died. D was convicted of manslaughter following a direction from the judge that pointing the revolver and pulling the trigger was an unlawful act even if there was no intent to injure or alarm and that they need not consider whether the pointing of the gun was an assault. (For the definition of assault see 10.1.1 *post*). The Court of Appeal quashed the conviction; if there was no assault there was no unlawful act. Sachs J stated (at p. 988):

> *mens rea*, being now an essential ingredient in manslaughter . . . that could not in the present case be established in relation to the first ground except by proving that element of intent without which there can be no assault.

There was also no *actus reus* of assault in this case as the friend, being a willing participant in the prank, did not apprehend any injury; the *actus reus* of assault is causing the victim to apprehend immediate application of unlawful force to his body.

A problem decision in this area is that of *Cato* [1976] 1 WLR 110, where the Court of Appeal appeared to extend the ambit of unlawful acts. D injected V with heroin which V had supplied to D for this purpose. V died from respiratory failure caused by the heroin. D was convicted of manslaughter and of administering a noxious thing so as to endanger life contrary to s. 23 of the Offences Against the Person Act 1861. In upholding the manslaughter conviction, the Court of Appeal stated that, even if they had not upheld the conviction for the s. 23 offence (which they did), they would still have upheld the manslaughter conviction on the basis that by injecting the deceased with heroin which D had unlawfully taken into his possession, he had done an unlawful act. This appears to be wrong as injecting heroin is not an offence contrary to the Misuse of Drugs Act 1971. Possession of heroin is an offence but V did not die as a result of D's possession of the drug. As this part of the court's decision was *obiter* it cannot, in light of the authorities, be accepted as authority for the proposition that conduct which does not constitute the *actus reus* of an offence may amount to an unlawful act.

Of course, there will be no unlawful act if the accused had a lawful excuse or justification for doing what he did. For example, if D punches V in self-defence, using no more force than is reasonable in the circumstances, but V stumbles and falls on a stone fracturing his skull and dies, D will not be liable for manslaughter as there is no unlawful act. Similarly if a parent uses only moderate and reasonable force to chastise his child and the child unexpectedly dies, the parent will not be guilty of manslaughter as the force used was lawful. In either case if the force used was excessive there would be no justification and the force would be unlawful providing a foundation for a manslaughter verdict.

Where D has committed an unlawful act of basic intent, the fact that he was intoxicated and lacked *mens rea*, will not avail him. In *Lipman* [1970] 1 QB 152, the Court of Appeal upheld D's conviction of manslaughter although the offence had been committed when he was on an hallucinatory trip due to his taking LSD. The unlawful act he performed was a battery which was an offence of basic intent. If the unlawful act alleged is an offence of specific intent, D may rely on his intoxication as evidence that he lacked *mens rea* (*O'Driscoll* (1977) 65 Cr App R 50), but it is difficult to envisage an offence of specific intent which does not necessarily encompass a lesser offence of basic intent.

It should be noted that constructive manslaughter requires the commission of an unlawful 'act'. It appears that an omission will not suffice (but an omission will suffice for reckless/gross negligence manslaughter where there is a duty to act; see 2.5 *ante*). In *Lowe* [1973] QB 702, the Court of Appeal quashed D's conviction of manslaughter founded on the offence of wilful neglect of the child so as to cause unnecessary suffering or injury to its health contrary to s. 1(1) of the Children and Young Persons Act 1933. The trial judge had directed the jury that there was no difference between an omission likely to cause harm and an act likely to cause harm. The Court of Appeal, disapproving of *Senior* [1899] 1 QB 283 where, on similar facts, a conviction of manslaughter had been upheld, distinguished between acts and omissions, Phillimore LJ stating (at p. 707):

> if I strike a child in a manner likely to cause harm it is right that if the child dies I may be charged with manslaughter. If, however, I omit to do something with the result that it suffers injury to its health which results in its death, we think that a charge of manslaughter should not be an inevitable consequence even if the omission is deliberate.

Obviously, if the omission was merely negligent, no liability for manslaughter should arise. But there is a great difference between neglect which is due to a lack of thought and that which is wilful, in the sense that there is a deliberate decision not to give food or liquids or to seek medical attention. Such conduct is just as reprehensible as positive acts which are likely to cause harm. *Lowe* is a decision which clearly requires reconsideration.

Whether the accused has done an unlawful act is a question for the jury to decide; even if all the evidence points to there being an unlawful act, the judge may not decide this issue himself but must leave it to the jury to determine (see *Jennings* [1990] Crim LR 588). If there is no unlawful act, an accused may still be convicted of manslaughter if the judge also directs the jury on reckless manslaughter and the requirements of this offence are satisfied (see *9.3.3.3.1 post*).

9.3.3.1.2 The unlawful act must be dangerous   While it must be established that the accused had the *mens rea* for the offence which constitutes the unlawful act, this is not sufficient to lead to a conviction of manslaughter. An objective condition must also be satisfied, that is that the act was dangerous. This requirement was explained in *Church* [1966] 1 QB 59, where Edmund-Davies J stated (at p. 70):

an unlawful act causing the death of another cannot, simply because it is an unlawful act, render a manslaughter verdict inevitable. For such a verdict inexorably to follow, the unlawful act must be such as all sober and reasonable people would inevitably recognise must subject the other person to, at least, the risk of some harm resulting therefrom, albeit not serious harm.

The degree of harm likely to be caused need not be serious, but it must be physical harm rather than a risk of emotional disturbance (*Dawson* (1985) 81 Cr App R 150). However, shock produced by fright may fall within the definition of harm where it produces some physical injury, such as a heart attack.

It matters not that the accused did not recognise the risk of harm (*DPP* v *Newbury* [1977] AC 500); the issue is whether all sober and reasonable people would recognise the risk of harm. In deciding this issue the sober and reasonable man is credited with the same knowledge as the accused at the time of the offence. In *Dawson* Watkins LJ stated (at p. 157) that the objective test 'can only be undertaken upon the basis of the knowledge gained by the sober and reasonable man as though he were present at the scene of and watched the unlawful act being performed'. It is the responsibility of the judge to inform the jury which facts are relevant for this purpose (*Dawson*). In *Dawson*, D and E robbed V's filling station wearing masks and armed with a pickaxe handle and replica gun. Shortly afterwards V died of a heart attack. It was not known to the accused, nor would it have been apparent, that V suffered from heart disease. The convictions of manslaughter were quashed for several reasons, one being that the trial judge had not made it clear that the jury could not take into account the fact that V suffered from heart disease when deciding if the unlawful act was dangerous. However, the jury may take into account facts of which the accused became aware during the course of committing the unlawful act (*Watson* [1989] 2 All ER 865). In this case D and E threw a brick through the window of V's house and entered it. They confronted V, who was 87, frail and suffering from a serious heart condition. After abusing V verbally they left and V died 90 minutes later from a heart attack. Although quashing the convictions of manslaughter on another ground, the Court of Appeal held that the sober and reasonable person could be credited with knowledge of the facts of which the appellants became aware after entering the house, namely, the victim's age and frailty. While the offence of burglary was complete upon crossing the threshold, the Court held that the unlawful act comprised the whole of the burglarious intrusion.

The sober and reasonable man will also be aware of the background to the unlawful act which includes preparatory acts done by the accused as this sets the act in context for the purpose of determining its objective dangerousness. In *Ball* [1989] Crim LR 730, D loaded a shotgun with two cartridges taken from his pocket which contained live and blank cartridges. He fired the gun at V claiming he only intended to frighten her. The cartridge in the chamber was a live one and V died. On appeal against his conviction of manslaughter it was argued that the objective assessment of the danger of D's act should be based on his mistaken belief that he was firing a blank cartridge and not on the actual fact that he was firing a live cartridge. The Court of Appeal rejected this submission, Lord Lane CJ stating:

> [Once it is] established . . . that the act was both unlawful and that he intended to commit the assaults, the question whether the act is a dangerous one is to be judged not by the appellant's appreciation but by that of the sober and reasonable man, and it is impossible to impute into his appreciation the mistaken belief of the appellant that what he was doing was not dangerous because he thought he had a blank cartridge in the chamber. At that stage the appellant's intention, foresight or knowledge is irrelevant.

9.3.3.1.3 The problem of Dalby   Must the unlawful act performed by D be directed at the victim? This is a problem deriving from the case of *Dalby* [1982] 1 All ER 916. In this case D supplied a drug to V which V took intravenously. He took other intravenous injections of unspecified substances and died subsequently. On appeal against a conviction of manslaughter it was argued that the supply of the drug was not an act 'directed at the victim' and as V administered the drug to himself in too great a quantity this broke the chain of causation between the unlawful act of supply and the death. The Court of Appeal quashed the conviction stating (in a very confused judgment) that supplying the drug was not an act which caused direct harm. All the previous cases involved unlawful acts which 'inevitably would subject the other person to the risk of some harm from the act itself' whereas, in the present case, 'the supply of the drugs would itself have caused no harm unless the deceased had subsequently used the drugs in a form and quantity which was dangerous'. Thus the Court held that the supply of the drug was not an act directed against the victim and the supply did not cause any direct injury to him. Waller LJ concluded (at p. 919) 'In the judgment of this court, where the charge of manslaughter is based on an unlawful and dangerous act, it must be an act directed at the victim and likely to cause immediate injury, however slight'. What the Court appeared to be stating was that the unlawful act was not a cause of death and, incidentally (as this issue did not require decision if causation could not be proved), the act was not dangerous. This was not truly a case of *novus actus interveniens* as the original act was not a substantial cause of death, it did not set in motion a train of events which would result in death; death would only occur where the drug was injected in dangerous amounts. Unfortunately, in some subsequent cases, the concluding comment of Waller LJ was taken out of context and taken to require that an 'unlawful act', if it is to support a conviction of manslaughter, must be directed against the victim, rather than meaning that the harm must flow directly from the act. Waller LJ cited with approval *Newbury* where the appellants dropped a paving stone from a bridge into the path of an oncoming train killing the guard. The unlawful act in this case was probably criminal damage as the conviction was upheld on the basis that there was no need to prove that the appellants foresaw that their act might cause harm to another. Waller LJ could not purport to follow this case if he meant to impose a requirement that the accused must be proved to have directed his unlawful act at the victim. Rather the citation of *Newbury* supported the proposition that the harm ensuing must be causally (or directly) linked to the unlawful act.

In *Goodfellow* (1986) 83 Cr App R 23, D was convicted of manslaughter having set fire to the council house in which he lived as he wished to be rehoused. D rescued two of his children but his wife, another child and another woman died as the fire spread more quickly than he had anticipated. On appeal it was contended that D's unlawful act was not an act directed at the victims. The Court of Appeal dismissed the appeal holding that the decision in *Dalby* only intended to stipulate that 'there must be no fresh intervening cause between the act and the death'. D's act may not have been directed at the victims but it was a direct cause of their deaths and it was, objectively, dangerous. In *Ball* (*ante*) the Court of Appeal referred to the accused's act of firing the shotgun at the deceased as, 'in the phrase of Waller J, in *Dalby*, "an act directed at the victim"'. The Court did not appear to be seeking to revive the misinterpretation of *Dalby*, but it is unclear why it chose to refer to it. If the fact that an act is directed at the victim is material, the Court did not specify in what respect it is material. For the sake of certainty, it is to be hoped that *Goodfellow* will be accepted as having settled the correct interpretation of *Dalby*.

9.3.3.2 Reckless manslaughter The second basis upon which a person may be convicted of involuntary manslaughter is that of recklessness. For many years the courts have used the terms 'recklessness' and 'gross negligence' interchangeably so that it was not clear whether these two concepts were co-extensive. It was also unclear what the exact risk was in respect of which an accused charged with manslaughter of this variety had to be reckless or grossly negligent; was it a risk of death, or serious bodily harm, or would a risk of serious damage to property suffice? A further uncertainty was as to the degree of risk required; was it a high risk, or a slight risk or did the degree of risk vary depending on the type of harm envisaged.

In the classic statement of gross negligence manslaughter in *Bateman* (1925) 19 Cr App R 8, Lord Hewart CJ stated (at p. 11):

in order to establish criminal liability the facts must be such that, in the opinion of the jury, the negligence of the accused went beyond a mere matter of compensation between subjects and showed such disregard for the life and safety of others as to amount to a crime against the state and conduct deserving of punishment.

This test left the issue to the jury to determine whether the negligence of the accused was so gross that it demanded punishment as a crime rather than the mere imposition of civil liability and payment of compensation. The risk involved had to be to the life or safety of the victim. It was for the jury to determine what degree of risk would lead to criminal liability.

The *Bateman* test was approved in *Andrews* v *DPP* [1937] AC 576, Lord Atkin emphasising that (at p. 583):

for the purpose of the criminal law there are degrees of negligence, and a very high degree of negligence is required to be proved before the felony is established. Probably of all the epithets that can be applied 'reckless' most nearly covers the case. . . . . but it is probably not all-embracing, for 'reckless' suggests an indifference to risk, whereas the accused may have appreciated the risk, and intended to avoid it, and yet shown in the means adopted to avoid the risk such a degree of negligence as would justify conviction.

Lord Atkin clearly foresaw the lacuna which the decisions in *Caldwell* and *Lawrence* subsequently left unaddressed (see *3.4.2.2.4 ante*). Thus gross negligence covers a broader range of situations than are covered by recklessness. In *Lamb (9.3.3.1.1 ante)*, the Court of Appeal considered that the facts would have supported a verdict of gross negligence manslaughter. The difference between reckless manslaughter and gross negligence manslaughter appeared to be in respect of the harm risked. In gross negligence manslaughter the risk of harm had to be of death (or possibly grievous bodily harm) whereas a verdict of reckless manslaughter could be returned where the accused subjectively foresaw the risk of death or *some* bodily harm (see *Pike* [1961] Crim LR 114, and *Gray v Barr* [1971] 2 All ER 949). In *Stone* and *Dobinson* [1977] QB 354 (see *2.5.2.2.3 ante*) the Court of Appeal held that subjective recklessness as to an injury to health and welfare would suffice. Recent cases, however, have left in doubt the question whether gross negligence will suffice to support a manslaughter conviction, and have redefined recklessness.

9.3.3.2.1 Reckless manslaughter: recent cases In *Seymour* [1983] 2 AC 493, the House of Lords was faced with an appeal against a conviction for reckless manslaughter arising from the driving of a motor vehicle. At that time the offence of causing death by reckless driving contrary to s. 1(1) of the Road Traffic Act 1972 also existed. This offence had been created because of the reluctance of juries to convict of manslaughter in cases where death was caused by the driving of a motor vehicle (these were referred to as cases of 'motor manslaughter' but there is no difference in principle between manslaughter where death results from driving a vehicle or from any other cause). The maximum penalty for the statutory offence was five years' imprisonment whereas on a conviction of manslaughter the maximum penalty was and is life imprisonment. In *Government of the USA v Jennings* [1983] 1 AC 624, an extradition case, the House of Lords held that the ingredients of manslaughter and causing death by reckless driving were identical, Lord Roskill stating (at p. 644) 'No doubt the prosecuting authorities today would only prosecute for manslaughter in the case of death caused by the reckless driving of a motor vehicle on a road in a very grave case.' Lord Roskill considered that *Seymour* was such a case.

In *Seymour*, D, when driving his lorry, was involved in a slight collision with a car driven by V, a woman with whom he lived and with whom he had recently quarrelled. D drove his lorry again against the car intending to shunt it out of his way and in so doing, V who had got out of her car, was crushed between the car and the lorry, dying subsequently from her injuries. D was convicted of manslaughter. The trial judge gave the '*Lawrence* direction' on recklessness stating:

> You have to be satisfied upon the question of recklessness that he drove in such a manner as to create an obvious and serious risk of causing physical harm to some other person who might happen to be using the road at the time.

This omitted the reference in *Lawrence* [1982] AC 341, which was concerned with reckless driving, to an 'obvious and serious risk of doing substantial damage to property'. Lord Roskill approved this direction stating that the judge had been 'entirely right not to refer to damage to property, a reference which was irrelevant in this case and might well have confused the jury.' This represented an extension of reckless manslaughter as *Lawrence* involved the objective test of recklessness which had not been adverted to in any previous case of reckless manslaughter.

If recklessness, for the purposes of causing death by reckless driving, is the same as for the lesser offence of reckless driving (as defined in *Lawrence*), and causing death by reckless driving has the same ingredients as reckless manslaughter (whatever the cause of death following *Jennings* and *Seymour*), would recklessness as to an obvious and serious risk of doing substantial damage to property suffice for a conviction of manslaughter if death should unexpectedly occur? If so, this would involve an even greater extension of liability for manslaughter. In *Seymour* a reference to damage to property was unnecessary because the risk clearly was of death or injury. Lord Roskill left the issue undecided as his speech contains contradictory dicta. On the one hand he stated that '"reckless" should be given the same meaning in relation to all offences which involve "recklessness" as one of the elements unless Parliament has otherwise ordained.' On the other hand he stated that Parliament must have intended 'motor manslaughter' to be a more grave offence than the statutory offence and thus it would only be appropriate to charge manslaughter where death resulted from the reckless driving of a motor vehicle, where the risk of death from the defendant's driving was very high. What are the ingredients of manslaughter where death results from some other cause? Will recklessness as to an obvious and serious risk of causing physical harm to another person suffice? What of an obvious and serious risk of doing substantial damage to property? Lord Fraser of Tullybelton helpfully stated in his speech that (at p. 500):

> Although the ingredients of the two offences [of manslaughter and causing death by reckless driving] are the same, the degree of recklessness required for the conviction of the statutory offence is less than that required for conviction of the common law crime.

If the degree of recklessness required differs the ingredients of the offences cannot be the same! If the degree of confusion created, rather than clarity, was the yardstick against which the quality of judicial statements were measured, these judgments would be rated as of the highest quality!

In *Kong Cheuk Kwan* v *R* (1985) 82 Cr App R 18, the Privy Council had to consider reckless manslaughter. D was the captain of a hydrofoil which collided at full speed with another hydrofoil in Hong Kong harbour in perfect weather conditions. The captain of the other vessel was acquitted of manslaughter. D was convicted following a direction on recklessness as to the risk of injury or, in the alternative, gross negligence following *Bateman*. The Privy Council quashed D's conviction. Lord Roskill, who read the opinion of the Board, explained that in *Seymour*, the statement he made that 'motor manslaughter' should be charged where the risk of death from a defendant's driving was very high, was not designed 'to alter the pre-existing law as to manslaughter by recklessness but only to point to those cases in which it still might be thought appropriate to charge the common law rather than the statutory offence.' Lord Roskill gave his approval to the judgment of Watkins LJ in the Court of Appeal in *Seymour* (1983) 76 Cr App R 211, where, referring to gross negligence, he stated (at p. 216):

> we are of the view that it is no longer necessary or helpful to make reference to compensation and negligence. The *Lawrence* direction on recklessness is comprehensive and of general application to all offences, including manslaughter involving the driving of motor vehicles recklessly and should be given to juries without in any way being diluted. Whether a driver at the material time was conscious of the risk he was running or gave no thought to its existence, is a matter which affects punishment for which purposes the judge will have to decide, if he can, giving the benefit of doubt to the convicted person, in which state of mind that person had driven at the material time.

Thus, creating an obvious and serious risk of causing physical injury to another person, is sufficient for reckless manslaughter. The unqualified support for Watkins LJ's commendation of the *Lawrence* direction would also suggest that creation of an obvious and serious risk of doing substantial damage to property would also be sufficient. Lord Roskill framed, somewhat ambiguously, the following questions which the trial judge should have left to the jury relating to the alleged recklessness of the captains of the two hydrofoils (at p. 25):

> Did their respective acts of navigation create an obvious and serious risk of causing physical damage to some other ship and thus to other persons who might have been travelling in the area of the collision at the material time. If so did any of the defendants by their respective acts of navigation so navigate either without having given any thought to the possibility of that risk or, while recognising that the risk existed, take that risk.

This appears to suggest that liability for manslaughter, where there was an obvious risk of damage to property, will ensue only if it was also obvious that this would cause physical injury to other persons. If you risk damaging a ship travelling at sea it is obvious that there will be people on board who will also be put at risk. This does not settle the question whether the creation of an obvious risk of substantial damage to property, on its own, would suffice to establish liability for manslaughter if death should unexpectedly occur. In addition, Lord Roskill's suggested direction dilutes the test in *Lawrence* which required 'substantial damage to property'; Lord Roskill only states 'physical damage'

9.3.3.2.2 Gross negligence manslaughter: does it still exist?

Lord Atkin in *Andrews* recognised that gross negligence may cover a state of mind not covered by recklessness, namely where 'the accused may have appreciated the risk, and intended to avoid it, and yet shown in the means adopted to avoid the risk such a degree of negligence as would justify a conviction'. If, as the Privy Council held in *Kong Cheuk Kwan*, references to compensation and negligence are no longer necessary because of the *Lawrence* direction on recklessness, this would seem to abolish gross negligence manslaughter. However, in *Ball* [1989] Crim LR 730, Stuart-Smith LJ appeared to be oblivious to this development stating:

> In the case of a lawful act the question is whether the accused has been guilty of gross or criminal negligence in the sense that the negligence of the accused went beyond a mere matter of compensation between subjects and showed such disregard for the life and safety of others as to amount to a crime against the state and conduct deserving of punishment.

The question remains unresolved, therefore, whether an accused who has given thought to a risk and wrongly concluded that there was no risk, may be convicted of manslaughter on the basis of gross negligence if death ensues from his conduct.

9.3.4 Reform

The Law Commission in its Draft Criminal Code (Law Com No. 177) provides for a radical reform of the law relating to manslaughter. Clause 55 provides:

> A person is guilty of manslaughter if –
> (a) he is not guilty of murder by reason only of the fact that a defence provided by section 56 (diminished responsibility), 58 (provocation) or 59 (use of excessive force) applies; or
> (b) he is not guilty of murder by reason of the fact that, because of voluntary intoxication, he is not aware that death may be caused or believes that an exempting circumstance exists; or
> (c) he causes the death of another –
> (i) intending to cause serious personal harm; or
> (ii) being reckless whether death or serious personal harm will be caused.

In clause 59 the use of excessive force in self-defence would be recognised as a new defence reducing murder to manslaughter. Currently, if D uses excessive force he will be convicted of murder. If a person is intoxicated and lacks the necessary *mens rea* for murder he will be liable to conviction of manslaughter.

Clause 55(b) states this expressly to avoid confusion. In clause 54 the Law Commission reduce the scope of murder. Clause 55 reflects this reduced scope by rendering an accused liable to conviction of manslaughter where he causes death intending to cause serious personal harm (clause 55(c)(i)). Clause 55 also greatly reduces the scope of involuntary manslaughter by removing the category of constructive manslaughter and defining reckless manslaughter in narrow terms requiring subjective recklessness as to the risk of death or serious personal harm.

9.3.5   Other unlawful homicides

9.3.5.1   Causing death by dangerous driving The Road Traffic Act 1991 abolished the offence of causing death by reckless driving contrary to s. 1 of the Road Traffic Act 1988 (see further S. Cooper, *Blackstone's Guide to the Road Traffic Act 1991*). By s. 1 of the Act, a new s. 1 is substituted into the 1988 Act which provides that 'a person who causes the death of another person by driving a mechanically propelled vehicle dangerously on a road or other public place is guilty of an offence'. The offence of reckless driving in s. 2 of the 1988 Act was abolished and replaced by a new s. 2 offence of dangerous driving. 'Dangerous driving' is defined in a new s. 2A to the 1988 Act as follows:

(1)   For the purposes of sections 1 and 2 above a person is to be regarded as driving dangerously if (and, subject to subsection (2) below, only if) –
  (a)   the way he drives falls far below what would be expected of a competent and careful driver, and
  (b)   it would be obvious to a competent and careful driver that driving in that way would be dangerous.
(2)   A person is also to be regarded as driving dangerously for the purposes of sections 1 and 2 above if it would be obvious to a competent and careful driver that driving the vehicle in its current state would be dangerous.
(3)   In subsections (1) and (2) above 'dangerous' refers to a danger either of injury to any person or of serious damage to property; and in determining for the purposes of those subsections what would be expected of, or obvious to, a competent and careful driver in a particular case, regard shall be had not only to the circumstances of which he could be expected to be aware, but also to any circumstances shown to have been within the knowledge of the accused.

The Act resulted from the Report of the North Committee set up by the Home Office and the Department of Transport, *Road Traffic Law Review* (HMSO, 1988). The North Committee identified a number of problems with the offences of reckless driving and causing death by reckless driving. The new offences are of an objective nature and require no advertence on the part of a jury to the accused's state of mind except for 'any circumstances shown to have been within the knowledge of the accused' (s. 2A(3)). He may have recognised that his driving was dangerous or given no thought to the manner of his driving, or have given thought to it and wrongly concluded that it was not dangerous. The focus, rather, is on the quality of the accused's driving. If a jury decide that the accused's driving fell far below the objective standard expected of a competent and careful driver under s. 2A(1)(a), they will convict if satisfied that it would be obvious to the competent and careful driver that driving in that way would be dangerous (s. 2A(1)(b)), in that it created a risk 'either of injury to any person or of serious damage to property' (s. 2A(3)).

Section 2A(2) is designed to deal with the situation where D drives a vehicle which is in a dangerous condition. He may drive very carefully but the vehicle itself is dangerous, that is, driving that vehicle on a road in its current state creates a risk either of injury to a person or of serious damage to property. There are two possible problems with this provision. Firstly, if D is a lorry driver and overloads his vehicle or loads it in such a way that the load is unstable, this may not be obvious to the competent and careful driver although obvious to the competent and careful lorry driver. Section 2A(3) provides for this situation in that the competent and careful driver is expected to be aware of 'any circumstances shown to have been within the knowledge of the accused' which would cover any specialist skill or knowledge which D had. Secondly, the facts about the vehicle's condition may indicate that driving it would be dangerous but s. 2A(2) does not impose any requirement that D have knowledge of those facts. For example, D leaves his vehicle in a garage to be serviced and an inexperienced mechanic drains the brake fluid and forgets to refill the brake fluid reservoir. If a competent and careful driver knew of the vehicle's 'current state' it would be obvious to him that to drive a vehicle which has no working brakes is dangerous. If D drives the vehicle from the garage and kills V on a zebra crossing when the vehicle fails to stop, would he be liable for causing death by dangerous driving? The wording of s. 2A(3) suggests that the competent and careful driver is only taken to be aware of circumstances of which he could be expected to be aware. Thus, on those facts, the competent and careful driver would be someone who did not know that the brakes were not working. If, however, D on trying the brakes found they did not work but dismissed that from his mind as a fluke, believing that the brakes must be working as the car had just come from the garage, and drove on killing V on a zebra crossing, he would be guilty of the s. 1 offence if the jury concluded that, in such circumstances, it would have been obvious to the competent and careful driver, that the vehicle was dangerous.

While the creation of the s. 1 offence of causing death by dangerous driving removes the problem of causing death by reckless driving and motor manslaughter having the same ingredients, it should be noted that some cases of causing death by dangerous driving will also amount to reckless man-slaughter. Where the danger is such that there is an obvious and serious risk of injury to a person or substantial damage to property, and D either recognises the risk and goes on to take it, or fails to give any thought to the possibility of there being a risk, this will constitute both reckless manslaughter and causing death by dangerous driving. Presumably, if a risk of injury is obvious but not serious (whatever serious means in this context, which has not been addressed judicially), this will consitute the s. 1 offence but not manslaughter. Similarly, if D gives thought to the possibility of there being a risk but wrongly concludes that there is none, he will be liable to conviction of the statutory offence but not to conviction of manslaughter.

It should be noted that the Road Traffic Act 1991 creates a new offence in s. 3 of causing death by careless driving when under the influence of drink or drugs to such an extent that the driver is unfit to drive or the proportion of alcohol in his breath, blood or urine at the time exceeds the prescribed limits. Such a person may be driving a vehicle in a way which is not dangerous, although careless. However, he will be liable to conviction of this offence and on conviction will be liable to imprisonment for up to five years, the same as for the s. 1 offence.

9.3.5.2 Infanticide   Section 1(1) of the Infanticide Act 1938 provides:

> Where a woman by any wilful act or omission causes the death of her child being a child under the age of twelve months, but at the time of the act or omission the balance of her mind was disturbed by reason of her not having fully recovered from the effect of giving birth to the child or by reason of the effect of lactation consequent upon the birth of the child, then, notwithstanding that the circumstances were such that but for this Act the offence would have amounted to murder, she shall be guilty of [an offence], to wit of infanticide, and may for such offence be dealt with and punished as if she had been guilty of the offence of manslaughter of the child.

The offence/defence is limited to the mother, and the child must be under twelve months when killed. Where the Crown charge murder, there is an evidential burden on the accused to tender some evidence pointing to the balance of her mind being disturbed; it is then for the Crown to disprove this. If the Crown charge infanticide they bear the burden of proving that the balance of the accused's mind was disturbed, but this is unlikely to be contested. The principal effect of conviction for infanticide rather than murder is to give the judge discretion in sentencing.

There is now considerable doubt whether women who kill their babies in the first year of life do so because of mental imbalance resultant on child birth. The Butler Committee on Mentally Abnormal Offenders (Cmnd 6244) found that in most cases there is only a remote relationship between the effects of childbirth or lactation and the killing of the child. The Committee considered that the defence of diminished responsibility would now cover all cases of mental imbalance. In practice the real reason for child-killing may be stress arising from caring for a child in an unfavourable social environment due to poor housing, poor family support and poverty, or simply the stress of having to care for a difficult and demanding or unwanted infant. These are factors which affect fathers and mothers whether the child is under or over one year of age and manifest themselves in the problem of 'baby-battering'. The Criminal Law Revision Committee in its *Fourteenth Report: Offences Against the Person* (Cmnd 7844) recommended the retention of the defence but its amendment to reflect modern medical knowledge. Their recommendations have been adopted by the Law Commission in its Draft Criminal Code (Law Com No. 177), clause 64(1) of which provides:

A woman who, but for this section, would be guilty of murder or manslaughter of her child is not guilty of murder or manslaughter, but is guilty of infanticide, if her act is done when the child is under the age of twelve months and when the balance of her mind is disturbed by reason of the effect of giving birth or of circumstances consequent upon the birth.

The reference to 'murder or manslaughter' in this provision is due to the earlier recommendations of the Law Commission which reduced the scope of the offence of murder. The new definition is wide enough to encompass difficult circumstances of a social or environmental nature which may ensue from the birth of the child, although only the mother may be convicted of infanticide. If the father (with the *mens rea* for murder) kills his child , or if the mother (with the *mens rea* for murder) kills her child over the age of twelve months, he or she must rely on the defences of provocation or diminished responsibility if the offence is to be reduced from murder to manslaughter.

Further reading
A. Ashworth, 'Reforming the law of murder' [1990] Crim LR 75.
A. Bustill and A. McCall Smith, 'Fright, stress and homicide' 54 JCL 257.
D. Yale, 'A year and a day in homicide' [1989] CLJ 202.
G. Williams, '*Mens rea* for murder: leave it alone' (1989) 105 LQR 387.
W. Wilson, 'A plea for rationality in the law of murder' (1990) 10 LS 307.
R. MacKay, 'Pleading provocation and diminished responsibility together' [1988] Crim LR 411.

TEN

Non-fatal offences against the person

In this chapter the main offences involving violence against the person will be considered. There are a considerable number of different offences, many of which are contained in the Offences Against the Person Act 1861 (this statute will be referred to by the abbreviation OAPA), but space dictates that only the most common of these can be examined. In the first part of this chapter the main non-sexual offences will be covered and in the second part the main sexual offences will be covered.

10.1 NON-SEXUAL OFFENCES

10.1.1 Assault and battery
Common assault and battery were separate common law crimes. Section 39 of the Criminal Justice Act 1988 stipulates that they are summary offences and specifies the maximum penalties which may be imposed. It was believed that they remained common law crimes. However, in *DPP* v *Little* [1992] 1 All ER 299, the Divisional Court held that they are, and have been since 1861, statutory offences. Section 47 of the OAPA prescribed the penalty for these offences. This decision is surprising as the definitions of assault and battery are not found in any statute but in the common law. An indictment charging an indictable offence against the person may include a count of common assault or battery if it is founded on the same facts or evidence as a count charging an indictable offence or is part of a series of offences of the same or similar character as an indictable offence which is also charged (s. 40 of the Criminal Justice Act (CJA) 1988). Thus, if the jury acquit the accused of the more serious indictable offence, they may still convict of the summary offence.

While assault and battery are distinct crimes, judges and statutes often use the term 'assault' or 'common assault' to encompass both these offences (e.g. s. 47 OAPA and s. 40(3)(a) CJA 1988). In this chapter the term 'assault' will be used in its generic sense to cover both offences. When dealing separately with the offences the terms 'technical assault' and 'battery' will be used. It should be noted that assault and battery are also torts.

10.1.1.1 Technical assault A technical assault is committed when the accused intentionally or recklessly causes the victim to apprehend immediate and unlawful personal violence (see *Fagan* v *Metropolitan Police Commissioner* [1969] 1 QB 439).

10.1.1.1.1 Actus reus V must apprehend immediate and unlawful personal violence. The term 'apprehend' is used as it is not necessary for V to be put in fear; it is sufficient that he anticipates immediate and unlawful personal violence being applied to him by D. The term 'unlawful personal violence' may be misleading as it is not necessary for V to apprehend a severe attack; the apprehension of any unwanted touching of him by D is sufficient. Thus all that V need apprehend is a battery, which was defined by Lord Lane CJ in *Faulkner* v *Talbot* [1981] 3 All ER 468, 471, as 'any intentional touching of another person without the consent of that person and without lawful excuse. It need not necessarily be hostile, rude, or aggressive. . . .'

Personal violence is not unlawful if V consents to it (see 10.1.1.3 *post*), or D is justified in using it (e.g., if D is using reasonable force in self-defence, or to prevent a crime or arrest an offender), or D is engaged in lawful correction (see 10.1.1.3 *post*).

Technical assault generally requires some gesture on the part of D causing V to apprehend immediate violence. For example, where D shakes his fist at V or raises a knife as if to stab V or points a gun at V, there would be a technical assault if V apprehended the immediate application of force on him by D. In the example of the gun, however, there would be no assault if V knew, or believed, the gun was not loaded (see *Lamb* [1967] 2 QB 981). If force could not immediately be applied to V there would be no technical assault. For example, if D, standing on one side of a deep, fast-flowing river, shakes his fist at V on the other side, there being no means of crossing, the element of immediacy would be lacking. Likewise, if V, departing from a station in a train, sees D on the platform shaking his fist at him. The courts, however, appear to be adopting a very liberal view of what is immediate. In *Smith* v *Superintendent of Woking Police Station* (1983) 76 Cr App R 234, the Divisional Court held that it was open to the magistrates to infer that V, dressed in her night-clothes at 11 pm, apprehended immediate unlawful personal violence when she was frightened by D looking through her bedroom window, D intending to cause such fear.

While D's actions may amount to a technical assault, the words he speaks at the time may serve to negative this. In *Turberville* v *Savage* (1669) 1 Mod Rep 3, T placed his hand on his sword and said, 'If it were not assize-time, I would not take such language from you.' The court held that this was not an assault as his declaration indicated that as the judges were in town he would not use force on S. By contrast, if D puts a gun to V's head and says, 'Be quiet or I'll blow your brains out', this should constitute a technical assault as D's forebearance is conditional on V doing as he is told. In *Read* v *Coker* (1853) 13

CB 850, V sued successfully for assault where D and his servants surrounded him rolling up their sleeves and threatening to break his neck if he did not leave the premises. The authorities are somewhat confused on the issue whether words alone may constitute an assault. In *Meade and Belt* (1823) 1 Lew CC 184, Holroyd J stated that 'no words or singing are equivalent to an assault.' This creates difficulties. For example, if D approaches V from behind or on a dark night and says 'I have a gun and I'll shoot you if you don't hand over your money', V may well apprehend immediate unlawful personal violence, but Holroyd J's dictum would suggest this could not constitute a technical assault. In *Wilson* [1955] 1 All ER 744, Lord Goddard stated *obiter* (at p. 745) 'He called out "Get the knives", which itself would be an assault, in addition to kicking the gamekeeper'; this *obiter dictum* is supported by the civil case of *Ansell* v *Thomas* [1974] Crim LR 31, where it was held that D's verbal threat to forcibly eject V from a meeting if he did not leave voluntarily constituted an assault. It is submitted that this is the better view.

In *Fagan* it was stated that an omission could not constitute an assault, but the Divisional Court appeared to leave open the possibility of an assault arising from a continuing act. For example, D, a burglar, is in V's kitchen holding a knife when V enters coming face to face with D and the knife. V apprehends immediate unlawful personal violence and D, recognising V's fear, continues to hold the knife in the same position. It is suggested that D has not assaulted V by omission, but rather that by failing to terminate his act of holding the knife in what has become a threatening manner he commits an assault (cf. *Kaitamaki* [1985] AC 147, *10.2.1.1.1 post*).

10.1.1.1.2 Mens rea The *mens rea* of technical assault is an intention to cause the victim to apprehend immediate unlawful personal violence or recklessness as to whether such apprehension is caused (*Venna* [1976] QB 421). In *DPP* v *K* [1990] 1 WLR 1067, the Divisional Court held that the *Caldwell* test of recklessness sufficed. In *Spratt* [1990] 1 WLR 1073, the Court of Appeal held that in every offence against the person recklessness was to be given its *Cunningham* meaning, 'in the sense of taking the risk of harm ensuing with foresight that it might happen' (*per* McCowan LJ at p. 1082). The Court of Appeal went on to state that *DPP* v *K* had been wrongly decided as the Divisional Court were not referred to *Cunningham* or *Venna*. In *Parmenter* (1991) 92 Cr App R 68, the Court of Appeal followed *Spratt*. In the joint hearing of the appeals in *Savage* and *Parmenter* [1991] 4 All ER 698, the House of Lords was not asked to consider this point but there are dicta in their Lordships' speeches which confirm that advertence to the risk of physical contract is required.

10.1.1.2 Battery The *actus reus* of battery consists of the infliction of unlawful personal violence by the accused upon the victim. Often a battery follows from a technical assault, as where V sees D swing his fist at him and then suffers the impact of the blow. It is not necessary, however, for there to be a technical assault for D to be liable for battery. For example, if V is blind or D punches him from behind, D will be guilty of battery even though V has no apprehension of unlawful personal violence. The slightest touching, if unlawful, is sufficient. The courts, however, have recognised that ordinary everyday life involves many incidents of contact with other persons which should not be treated as criminal. Drawing a line between acceptable and unacceptable forms of contact is not easy. In *Collins* v *Wilcock* [1984] 3 All ER 374, Robert Goff LJ stated that there was a general exception 'embracing all physical contact which is generally acceptable in the ordinary conduct of daily life.' Whether conduct falls within this exception will depend upon the facts of each particular case, but Robert Goff LJ provided some examples of acceptable conduct (at p. 378):

> So nobody can complain of the jostling which is inevitable from his presence in, for example, a supermarket, an underground station or a busy street; nor can a person who attends a party complain if his hand is seized in friendship, or even if his back is (within reason) slapped. . . . [Also] among such forms of conduct, long held to be acceptable, is touching a person for the purpose of engaging his attention, though of course using no greater degree of physical contact than is reasonably necessary in the circumstances for that purpose.

Thus a police officer may tap a person on the shoulder to gain his attention but he may not restrain the person (*Collins* v *Wilcock*). In *Wilson* v *Pringle* [1986] 2 All ER 440, a civil case, the Court of Appeal approved *Collins* v *Wilcock,* but Croom-Johnson LJ stated that it was not practicable to define a battery as 'physical contact which is not generally acceptable in the ordinary conduct of daily life.' He stated that the touching had to be proved to be a 'hostile touching'. When a touching is hostile, however, is a question of fact. He considered that the touching in *Collins* v *Wilcock* was hostile as the officer did not merely touch the person but sought to restrain her which was unlawful. Why was it unlawful? It would appear because it went beyond what was generally acceptable in the ordinary conduct of daily life! Such circularity of definition is hardly conducive to clarity in the law.

As with technical assault, an omission to act cannot constitute a battery but, if D inadvertently applies force to V and then refuses to withdraw it this may constitute a battery. In *Fagan* v *Metropolitan Police Commissioner,* D inadvertently parked his car on a police officer's foot. He refused for some time to reverse off when the officer asked him. He was convicted of assaulting a police officer in the execution of his duty. The Divisional Court held that the battery was a continuing act as force continued to be applied to the officer's foot. When D formed the *mens rea* after the inception of the *actus reus*, this was superimposed upon the existing act making it into an assault. What if D's initial act does not apply force to V, but D realises that if he does not terminate it, force will be applied to V? For example, D places a pole across a darkened corridor. He hears V running along the corridor and deliberately leaves the pole there realising that V will fall over it. If D is not to be convicted of battery it will be on the basis of a very fine distinction which it would be difficult to justify. If D had placed the pole there with the intention of tripping V this has always been assumed to constitute a battery (see *Martin* (1881) 8 QBD 54; but see discussion of *Wilson* [1984] AC 242 at 10.1.2.1. *post*).

Martin illustrates another principle namely that the application of force to V need not be direct. Although overruling *DPP* v *K* in respect of *mens rea*, the Court of Appeal did not question it with regard to the *actus reus*. D, a schoolboy, had placed acid, which he had removed without permission from the chemistry laboratory, in a hot air drier to conceal it. The next person to use the drier suffered scarring when the machine squirted acid into his face. D was charged with assault occasioning actual bodily harm contrary to s. 47 OAPA. Parker LJ stated (at p. 1071):

> [I]n my judgment there can be no doubt that if a defendant places acid into a machine with the intent that it shall, when the next user switches the machine on, be ejected onto him and do him harm there is an assault when the harm is done.

In this case, as D was charged with the s. 47 offence, harm had to be proved. There is no need to prove that V suffered harm where the charge is simple battery. Had D simply placed water in the machine, he could have been liable for battery (see *Pursell* v *Horn* (1838) 8 Ad & El 602). Similarly, if D rigs up a 'booby trap' with a bucket of water suspended above a door, he will be liable for battery if the contents spill on to V upon opening the door (see also *Clarence* (1888) 22 QBD 23, at 25; but see discussion of *Wilson* at 10.1.2.1. *post*).

The *mens rea* of battery is intention to apply unlawful force or subjective recklessness as to whether such force might be applied (see *Venna* and *10.1.1.1.2 ante*).

10.1.1.3 Defences to assault and battery The main defences which apply in the case of a charge of assault and battery are private defence (e.g. self-defence), acting in the prevention of crime, consent, and lawful correction. For private defence and prevention of crime, see 8.5 *ante*.

10.1.1.3.1 Consent It is the essence of assault that it is done without the consent of the victim. The burden of proving lack of consent rests upon the prosecution (see *Donovan* [1934] 2 KB 498, and *Kimber* [1983] 1 WLR 1118). If D mistakenly believes that the victim consents this will negative *mens rea* (see *Jones* (1986) 83 Cr App R 375). It is sufficient that D's belief is honest, it need not be reasonable (*Morgan* [1976] AC 182). There are two questions relating to consent which must be considered: to what may V consent and what constitutes valid consent?

(i) To what may V consent?
No one may consent to his own death at another's hands (see *Young* (1838) 8 C & P 644, and *Cuddy* (1843) 1 Car & Kir 210). In *Attorney-General's Reference (No. 6 of 1980)* [1981] 2 All ER 1057, the Court of Appeal stated that 'it was not in the public interest that people should try to cause or should cause each

other actual bodily harm for no good reason.' In *Miller* [1954] 2 QB 282, actual bodily harm was defined as 'any hurt or injury calculated to interfere with the health or comfort of the prosecutor', and this included a hysterical or nervous condition resulting from an assault. In the *A-G's Reference*, however, the Court of Appeal recognised that there were exceptions to this general rule. Lord Lane CJ stated (at 1059):

> Nothing which we have said is intended to cast doubt on the accepted legality of properly conducted games and sports, lawful chastisement or correction, reasonable surgical interference, dangerous exhibitions etc. These apparent exceptions can be justified as involving the exercise of a legal right, in the case of chastisement or correction, or as needed in the public interest in the other cases.

In the instant case, settling an argument by means of a fight would not be within the public interest so both parties could be liable for assault although both consented to the fight. By contrast, however, properly conducted sports are socially approved even though actual bodily harm may incidentally occur, as where, for example, one boxer knocks another unconscious or breaks his nose, or a footballer breaks his leg in a tackle. Foster, *Crown Law* (3rd edn) p. 259, stated that manly diversions (and presumably, nowadays, all sports whether played by men or women) were in the public interest as 'they tend to give strength, skill and activity, and may fit people for defence, public as well as personal, in time of need.' However, something like a prize fight (where the aim is to fight with bare fists until one participant is unable to continue) is not a properly conducted sport needed in the public interest (see *Coney* (1882) 8 QBD 534). Likewise, players of properly conducted sports only consent to such force as can reasonably be expected during the game (*Billinghurst* [1978] Crim LR 553). Thus if one player in a rugby match kicks or punches an opponent in an incident off the ball, this will be a battery. Similarly, if one boxer kicks his opponent or punches his opponent after the contest is over, these would be batteries as they are not reasonably to be expected during the game and thus are not consented to by the opponent.

The list of exceptions which Lord Lane CJ gave in the *A-G's Reference* was not exhaustive as the Court of Appeal recognised another exception in *Jones* (1986) 83 Cr App R 375, where some boys at a youth club tossed two other boys into the air, so that one suffered a ruptured spleen and the other a broken arm. The Court of Appeal held that they ought to have been able to raise the issue of consent as boys have always indulged in rough and undisciplined play among themselves and probably always will (see further *Aitken* [1992] 1 WLR 1006, Cts. Martial AC).

A person may consent to surgery where the operation is for a valid purpose recognised by the law. A person's consent is valid where the operation is for a valid therapeutic purpose. This will cover medically prescribed treatment even though such treatment may involve a risk of harm, provided the possible benefits of the operation outweigh the possible harm from the operation or the failure to perform it. Even a sex-change operation performed for therapeutic reasons would be covered (see *Corbett* v *Corbett* [1971] P 83, at 99). However, if a person was to have his hand surgically removed to avoid military service or so that he could claim a disability allowance, his consent would be invalid and the surgeon would be liable at least for assault occasioning actual bodily harm as the operation would have no therapeutic purpose. The area of cosmetic surgery is problematic as it could be argued that such operations have no therapeutic value. It is likely, however, that such operations will be accepted as involving therapeutic value because of the psychological benefits they offer to the patient. If, however, V sought to have cosmetic surgery performed on him to change his appearance in the hope of avoiding detection for the offences he had committed, this would not be a therapeutic purpose nor would it be in the public interest so the consent would be invalid.

It is always difficult to determine exactly what the public interest permits. The fact that a particular activity is performed in private between consenting persons does not remove it from the reach of the criminal law administered in the public interest (see Lord Lane CJ in *A-G's Reference*). In *Donovan* [1934] 2 KB 498, D was charged with caning a seventeen-year-old girl for the purpose of sexual gratification. He was convicted of indecent assault and common assault. The judge did not direct the jury on the issue of consent. The Court of Criminal Appeal held that consent would be immaterial if the blows were likely or intended to cause bodily harm. The conviction was quashed, however, as the jury had not been directed to decide whether the blows were likely or intended to cause bodily harm. The case establishes that acts of sado-masochism between consenting persons may not be consented to where actual bodily harm is intended or likely; they do not fall within one of the exceptions needed in the public interest. This was confirmed by the Court of Appeal in *Brown* [1992] 2 All ER 552, where convictions of assault occasioning actual bodily harm contrary to s. 47 OAPA and wounding contrary to s. 20 OAPA were confirmed in respect of a group of homosexual sado-masochists who had participated in acts of violence against each other, including genital torture. Lord Lane CJ, following his own judgment in *A-G's Reference (No. 6 of 1980)* stated that 'the satisfying of sado-masochistic libido does not come within the category of good reason nor can the injuries be described as merely transient or trifling'.

An interesting question not resolved by any of the above cases is whether a person who willingly allows injuries to be inflicted upon him by another, is an accessory to the other's offence. Where a statute is designed to protect a certain class of persons, a member of that class who is the victim of the offence cannot be convicted as an accessory (see 7.1.6 *ante*). Sections 20 and 47 OAPA are not designed to protect a particular class of persons but everyone. Accordingly, this principle is inapplicable and it would appear that the 'victim' would be an accessory in these circumstances. If this is so a person would be guilty of aiding and abetting the offence committed by the wounder although, had he simply wounded himself, he would have been guilty of no offence. The illogicality of the paternalist approach of the law in this situation raises the question whether the parternalism of the criminal law is, indeed, necessary. As none of the accused in *Brown* required medical treatment, does the law really need to interfere?

(ii)   What constitutes valid consent?

The fact that V apparently consents to D's act does not mean that the law will treat that apparent consent as valid consent. If V is a child, or mentally retarded, and the prosecution prove that his understanding and knowledge was such that he was not in a position to decide whether or not to consent, his apparent consent will be invalid (see *Howard* [1965] 3 All ER 684). The issue is whether he was unable to comprehend the nature of the act. In *Burrell* v *Harmer* [1967] Crim LR 169, D was convicted of assault occasioning actual bodily harm arising from tattooing two boys aged twelve and thirteen which resulted in their arms becoming inflamed and painful. The court held that there was no consent as the boys did not understand the nature of the act. Presumably they understood what a tattoo was but, it would appear, they did not understand the pain it would involve. In the case of a young child the absence of consent may be inferred from its age as it would not have the intelligence or understanding to give consent (see *R* v *D* [1984] AC 778). In the case of an older child it will be for the jury to decide whether the child was of sufficient understanding and intelligence to give consent, and if so, whether it has been proved that the child did not give its consent (*R* v *D*).

Where V consents only as a result of D's threats or as a result of fear, this will negative consent. It is not entirely clear what kind of threats will suffice; probably threats to dismiss from employment, or to falsely imprison. The issue will have to be determined on the facts of each case, taking into account the nature of the relationship between the parties and then considering whether the threat would be sufficient to overcome the will of a reasonably firm person. In some situations, the threat may be implied from the relationship, for example where D is in a position of authority over V such as a school teacher.

Fraud may vitiate consent where it relates to the nature of the act involved or the identity of the person performing the act, but not if it relates to the surrounding circumstances in which the act is performed. Thus in *Bolduc and Bird* (1967) 63 DLR (2d) 82, it was held that D, a doctor, was not guilty of assault when he performed a vaginal examination on V, a patient, having told her that E, who was present, was a medical student. E was a voyeuristic musician. This did not vitiate V's consent, however, as D did not deceive her as to the nature of the act. This is undoubtedly a very narrow view as clearly V would not have consented had she known the true circumstances in which the act was to be performed. In *Clarence* (1888) 22 QBD 23, D, knowing he had venereal disease, had intercourse with V resulting in her contracting the disease. It was argued that his concealment of his condition constituted a fraud which vitiated V's consent thereby rendering the bodily contact an assault. The court held, however, that there was no deception as to the nature of the act. Again the deceit related to the circumstances in which the act was performed. There is an anomaly here. If V knew that D had venereal disease her consent would not be effective as a person cannot consent to the infliction of actual bodily harm on herself since, presumably, there is no public interest in favour of the spread of venereal disease.

10.1.1.3.2   Necessity   The defence of necessity was examined above (see *6.3.1 ante*). *In re F (Mental Patient: Sterilisation)* [1990] 2 AC 1, Lord Goff of

Chieveley stated that the common law principle of necessity could justify action which would otherwise be unlawful where, inter alia, the 'action [was] taken as a matter of necessity to assist another person without his consent'. Thus there would be no assault where D seizes V and forcibly drags him from the path of an oncoming vehicle thereby saving him from injury or death. A problem which frequently arises is the need to provide care or medical treatment for a person who is incapable of giving consent to it, for example, due to mental incapacity or to being unconscious as a result of illness or accident. Lord Goff concluded that it was the principle of necessity which provided a justification for the care or treatment in these cases. Where there is a situation of emergency, a doctor should do no more than is reasonably required in the best interests of the patient, before he recovers consciousness. Where, however, the inability to consent is permanent or semi-permanent, care or treatment which is in the best interests of the person may be administered if 'it is carried out in order either to save their lives, or to ensure improvement or prevent deterioration in their physical or mental health' (*per* Lord Brandon of Oakbrook). Thus the day to day care of those who are unconscious or who lack mental capacity to consent, is justified by this principle. Lord Brandon made the additional point that it is not only the principle of necessity which justifies treatment where a person is incapable of giving consent; where care has been assumed of a person who cannot consent, there is a common law duty to treat them (see further *2.5.2.2.3 ante*).

One qualification to the above is that 'officious intervention' cannot be justified. Lord Goff stated that intervention would not be justified 'when it is contrary to the known wishes of the assisted person, to the extent that he is capable of rationally forming such a wish'. This raises an interesting problem; suppose P has been diagnosed terminally ill and he takes an overdose of sleeping tablets leaving a note stating that he cannot face the prospect of a slow and painful death and that he does not wish to be resuscitated. Would D, his medically qualified wife, be guilty of assault if she did resuscitate him? Would D's liability depend on whether P was adjudged rational/irrational or on whether D believed him to be irrational?

10.1.1.3.3 Lawful correction   It is lawful for a parent or other person *in loco parentis* to use reasonable force to discipline their children or charges (see *Cleary* v *Booth* [1893] 1 QB 465; *Mackie* (1973) 57 Cr App R 453) provided the child is old enough to understand its purpose (*Griffin* (1869) 11 Cox CC 402). If corporal punishment is administered out of spite or anger or for gratification, or if the degree of force is unreasonable, it is unlawful (see *Hopley* (1860) 2 F & F 202; *Taylor, The Times,* December 28, 1983). At common law teachers are *in loco parentis* and may administer corporal punishment in respect of the conduct of the child at, or on its way to or from school. However, the common law only applies to teachers at independent schools which receive no public funding and in respect of pupils whose fees are not publicly paid or subsidised. In all other cases no member of staff of a school may administer corporal punishment on a pupil 'by virtue of his position' as a member of staff (s. 47(1) of the Education (No. 2) Act 1986). This provision follows the decision of the

European Court of Human Rights which held the United Kingdom in contravention of article 3 of the Convention (see *Campbell and Cozans* v *United Kingdom* (1982) 4 EHRR 293). If, however, a parent has given express permission to teachers at his child's school to administer corporal punishment, a teacher who does so will not have done so 'by virtue of his position' but by virtue of being placed *in loco parentis* by the parent. In these cases the burden is on the prosecution to prove that the corporal punishment was not lawful.

10.1.1.4 Aggravated assaults There are several offences involving assault which are subject to higher penalties because of the presence of aggravating factors. In the case of each of these offences it must be proved that D committed the *actus reus* of technical assault or battery with the requisite *mens rea* and that the aggravating factor was present. In some cases the aggravating factor is the ulterior intent with which the accused committed the assault, for example, assault with intent to rob (s. 8(2) of the Theft Act 1968), assault with intent to commit buggery (s. 16 of the Sexual Offences Act 1956), and assault with intent to resist or prevent the lawful arrest of the accused or another for any offence (s. 38 OAPA; s. 17(1) of and sch. 1 to the Magistrates' Courts Act 1980). In other cases the aggravating factor derives from the circumstances in which the offence is committed, for example, indecent assault (ss.14 and 15 of the Sexual Offences Act 1956), and assault on a constable in the execution of his duty (s. 51(1) of the Police Act 1964). Finally the aggravating factor may be a consequence of the assault such as the occasioning of actual bodily harm (s. 47 OAPA). This latter offence will be examined separately.

10.1.1.4.1 Assault occasioning actual bodily harm An assault occasioning actual bodily harm is an offence triable either summarily or on indictment, the maximum punishment for which is five years' imprisonment. The *actus reus* is satisfied by proof of a technical assault or battery which, in addition, has caused actual bodily harm. 'Actual bodily harm' means any hurt or injury calculated to interfere with the health or comfort of the victim (*Miller* [1954] 2 QB 282 at 292). The hurt or injury need not be serious or permanent but must be more than trifling or transient. Pain or discomfort are sufficient although there is no discernible injury such as a bruise or swelling (see *Reigate Justices, ex parte Counsell* (1984) 148 JP 193). A hysterical or nervous condition resulting from an assault is also sufficient.

There was some doubt about the *mens rea* of this offence. It was clear that the accused had to intend a technical assault or battery or be reckless (in the *Cunningham* sense) whether the victim apprehend or sustain unlawful personal violence (see *Spratt* [1990] 1 WLR 1073). Whether he had to intend in addition to cause actual bodily harm or be reckless thereto was unclear. In *Roberts* (1971) 56 Cr App R 95, D ordered V, a passenger in his car, to remove her clothes and he tried to pull off her coat. She jumped out of the moving car and suffered concussion and grazing as a result. The Court of Appeal treated the issue of actual bodily harm as purely one of causation to be determined objectively: that is, 'was it the natural result of what the alleged assailant said and did, in the sense that it was something that could reasonably have been foreseen as a consequence of what he was saying or doing?' (*per* Stephenson LJ). There was no need to prove that the accused intended to cause actual bodily harm or was reckless thereto. This was confirmed in *Savage* (1990) 91 Cr App R 317. In *Spratt* [1990] 1 WLR 1073, decided by a different panel in the Court of Appeal on the same day as *Savage*, it was held that *mens rea*, amounting to at least subjective recklessness, was required in relation to causing actual bodily harm although this issue was not strictly relevant to the appeal. In neither case was *Roberts* referred to.

In *Parmenter* (1991) 92 Cr App R 68, the Court of Appeal reviewed both cases and expressed a preference for *Spratt*, interpreting it to have decided as *ratio* that foresight of actual bodily harm is necessary for a conviction of the s. 47 offence, when this was strictly *obiter*. In *Savage* and *Parmenter* [1991] 4 All ER 698, the House of Lords overruled *Spratt* on this point, reversed *Parmenter* and held that the statement of principle in *Roberts* was correct.

The one remaining absurdity in this area is the sentence for the s. 47 offence. The maximum penalty is five years' imprisonment which is the same as that available for the more serious offence of maliciously inflicting grievous bodily harm contrary to s. 20 OAPA. So far Parliament has declined to remove this anomaly.

10.1.2 Wounding and inflicting grievous bodily harm
Section 20 OAPA provides:

> Whosoever shall unlawfully and maliciously wound or inflict any grievous bodily harm upon any other person, either with or without any weapon or instrument, shall be guilty of a misdemeanour, and being convicted thereof shall be liable . . . to imprisonment for not more than five years.

10.1.2.1 *Actus reus* The *actus reus* of this offence consists of unlawful wounding or the unlawful infliction of grievous bodily harm. (For the meaning of 'unlawful' see 10.1.1.1 *ante*). To constitute a wound the continuity of the whole skin must be broken (*Moriarty* v *Brookes* (1834) 6 C & P 684). There need be no profusion of blood; one drop would be sufficient. However, a scratch which does not break the inner skin is not a wound (*McLoughlin* (1838) 8 C & P 635), nor is an internal rupture of blood vessels (*C (a Minor)* v *Eisenhower* [1984] QB 331) but a rupture of the inner skin of the cheek or of the urethra resulting in bleeding is a wound (*Waltham* (1849) 3 Cox CC 442).

Grievous bodily harm means 'really serious harm' (*DPP* v *Smith* [1961] AC 290) and is a question of fact for the jury. While many wounds may also constitute really serious harm, it is clear that the most minor wound, for example a pin prick, falls within s. 20. It is difficult to see why it was thought necessary to specify wounding as a separate head as minor wounds could have been covered by the s. 47 offence.

Grievous bodily harm must be 'inflicted'. This contrasts with s. 18 OAPA (see 10.1.3) where the relevant word is 'causing' grievous bodily harm. In a series of cases spread over a century, it has been held that the words 'inflict' and 'wound' require proof of an assault (see *Taylor* (1869) LR 1 CCR 194; *Clarence* (1888) 22 QBD 23; *Snewing* [1972] Crim LR 267; *McCready* [1978] 1 WLR 1383). Thus, in *Clarence*, D could not be convicted of inflicting grievous bodily harm as V consented to intercourse which resulted in her contracting venereal disease from him; as there was consent there was no assault. There were, however, cases in which the requirement for an assault appears to have been ignored (see *Halliday* (1869) 61 LT 701; *Martin* (1881) 8 QBD 54; *Lewis* [1970] Crim LR 647; *Cartledge* v *Allen* [1973] Crim LR 530). The matter was finally resolved by the House of Lords in *Wilson* [1984] AC 242 where the issue was whether on an indictment charging a single count of inflicting grievous bodily harm, a jury could, according to the terms of s. 6(3) of the Criminal Law Act 1967, return a verdict of guilty of assault occasioning actual bodily harm. Such an alternative conviction would only be possible if the allegations in the indictment 'amounted to or included (expressly or by implication)' an allegation of the offence of which he was convicted. Lord Roskill, with whom all their Lordships agreed, stated that the word 'inflict' does not imply an assault. Thus an accused may inflict grievous bodily harm without necessarily committing a technical assault or a battery. However, if on such an indictment a conviction of the s. 47 offence is to be returned, the prosecution must prove an assault and the allegations in the indictment must include, either expressly or by implication, allegations of assault occasioning actual bodily harm.

A problem with the decision in *Wilson* was that the House approved and followed the Australian case of *Salisbury* [1976] VR 452, where the Supreme Court of Victoria stated that although the word 'inflict' had a wider meaning than 'assault' it did not have as wide a meaning as 'cause'. The Supreme Court stated (at p. 461):

In our opinion grievous bodily harm may be inflicted . . . either where the accused has directly and violently 'inflicted' it by assaulting the victim, or where the accused has 'inflicted' it by doing something, intentionally, which, though it is not itself a direct application of force to the body of the victim, does directly result in force being applied violently to the body of the victim, so that he suffers grievous bodily harm. Hence, the lesser misdemeanours of assault occasioning actual bodily harm and common assault . . . are not necessarily included in the misdemeanour of inflicting grievous bodily harm.

This seems to suggest that where D does not directly apply force to the victim but his act results in force being applied, there is no assault. However, it has always been assumed that a battery does not require the direct application of force by D upon the victim as where, for example, D digs a hole and causes V to fall into it or, as in *Martin* he creates panic and causes V to run into a barrier he has previously erected. In such situations, if V only sustained actual bodily harm, could he not now be convicted of the s. 47 offence? Such a conclusion would be absurd but it seems to flow from the distinction sought to be drawn between the definition of 'inflict' and 'assault'. This can hardly have been intended by Lord Roskill, but, as happens so often in criminal cases, he has failed to relate the decision in the immediate case before him to the whole body of the criminal law, thereby creating more problems than he believed he was solving. The reasoning in *Wilson* seems to lead to the conclusion that an assault requires a direct application of force by D upon the victim. Where force upon V results directly from D's act, though not directly applied by D, this is not an assault but an 'infliction' of force. If the resultant harm is grievous D may be convicted of the s. 20 offence. Thus if D digs a hole intending V to fall into it and sustain injury, and V does so breaking his leg, D will be guilty of inflicting grievous bodily harm. If, however, V only sprains his ankle (actual bodily harm), it would appear that he is not guilty of either the s. 47 offence or of common assault. The strange result of the reasoning in *Wilson* is that the more serious the offence charged, the wider the range of activities which fall within the definition of the *actus reus* of that offence; what may amount to 'causing' for the purposes of s. 18 may not amount to 'inflicting' for the purposes of s. 20, and what may amount to 'inflicting' for the purposes of s. 20 may not amount to assault for the purposes of s. 47 or common assault. Thus, in *Clarence*, D did not assault V when he had intercourse with her thereby causing her to contract venereal disease, nor did he inflict venereal disease upon her as force was not directly and violently applied to her. If, by contrast, he had intended her to contract venereal disease he could have been convicted of the s. 18 offence as he 'caused' grievous bodily harm with intent to do so. The ambit of liability for offences against the person, in respect of the activities which fall within the *actus reus* of each offence, appears to take the form of an inverted pyramid!

The limited extent of Lord Roskill's field of vision is illustrated by the fact that had he read s. 23 OAPA he would have discovered the use of the word 'inflict' in the context of the offence of unlawfully and maliciously administering poison to another person so as thereby to inflict grievous bodily harm. Administering poison does not involve an assault nor does it involve the violent application of force to the body of the victim. If s. 23 is not to be rendered nugatory 'inflict' must have some wider meaning. The result is that 'inflict' has a different meaning in s. 20 from s. 23 which neither makes for consistency in the criminal law nor can have been intended by Parliament.

Similar problems arise in relation to a charge of wounding under s. 20. A wound may be very minor and not, in itself, constitute grievous bodily harm. *Wilson* did not address the question whether the word 'wound' implied a requirement to prove an assault; Lord Roskill stated that he would ignore this limb of s. 20. Previous cases, however, did stipulate that an assault had to be proved (see *Taylor* (1869) LR 1 CCR 194, which Lord Roskill thought could only be supported as a decision if 'wound' implied assault; and *Beasley* (1981) 73 Cr App R 44; see also *Springfield* (1969) 53 Cr App R 608, overruled regarding the correct interpretation of s. 6(3) of the Criminal Law Act 1967 but not on this point). In *Savage* (1990) 91 Cr App R 317, Glidewell LJ accepted that wounding required an assault but was of opinion that, other than in quite extraordinary circumstances, the commission of the offence of wounding would involve an assault. Extraordinary circumstances, however, do occur. The result is that a person may be liable for wounding, contrary to s. 20, in even narrower circumstances than for inflicting grievous bodily harm. Thus if D directly applies force to V whereby V sustains a wound he will be liable for the s. 20 offence. If, however, he digs a hole intending V to fall into it and V does so sustaining a minor cut but no other injuries, D will not be guilty of the s. 20 offence nor of the s. 47 offence nor of common assault.

As none of these problems occurred to their Lordships, perhaps *Wilson* should be limited to its own particular facts. It would be much more desirable, however, if their Lordships gave more careful consideration to the wider implications of their decisions.

10.1.2.2   *Mens rea*   D must wound or inflict grievous bodily harm 'maliciously'. 'Maliciously' does not mean spitefully or with ill-will; rather it means intentionally or recklessly and 'recklessly' is given its subjective meaning which requires foresight of the consequence (*Cunningham* [1957] 2 QB 396). What consequence, however, must D be proved to have intended or foreseen? One would have thought that it would be necessary to prove an intention to wound or cause grievous boily harm or foresight of such a consequence possibly occurring. In *Mowatt* [1968] 1 QB 421, Lord Diplock stated (at p. 426):

> the word 'maliciously' does import on the part of the person who unlawfully inflicts the wound or other grievous bodily harm an awareness that his act may have the consequence of causing some physical harm to some other person. . . . It is quite unnecessary that the accused should have foreseen that his unlawful act might cause physical harm of the gravity described in the section, i.e. a wound or serious physical injury. It is enough that he [foresaw] . . . that some physical harm to some person, albeit of a minor character, might result.

Thus D will be liable where his foresight is of a lesser degree of harm than that which resulted and which is prohibited by s. 20. This was affirmed by the House of Lords in *Savage* and *Parmenter* [1991] 4 All ER 698, at 721. This compares with murder where an intention to cause grievous bodily harm is sufficient.

Two final points to note are that an intent to frighten V is not sufficient for the s. 20 offence (*Sullivan* [1981] Crim LR 46), and if D honestly, but mistakenly, believes that he is, for example, acting in self-defence, or that V has consented to his action which has caused the wound or grievous bodily harm (in circumstances where consent would have operated as a defence), he is not intending to *unlawfully* wound or inflict grievous bodily harm.

10.1.3   Wounding or causing grievous bodily harm with intent
Section 18 OAPA provides:

> Whosoever shall unlawfully and maliciously by any means whatsoever wound or cause any grievous bodily harm to any person . . . with intent . . . to do some . . . grievous bodily harm to any person, or with intent to resist

or prevent the lawful apprehension or detainer of any person, shall be guilty of [an offence and shall be liable to imprisonment for life].

10.1.3.1 *Actus reus* 'Wound' and 'grievous bodily harm' have the same meaning as in s. 20. It is not clear whether a wound, for the purposes of s. 18, must result from an assault. The section states 'whosoever shall unlawfully and maliciously by any means whatsoever wound'; this might imply that a wound may form the basis of a s. 18 charge in a wider range of circumstances than for a s. 20 charge, but the issue is, as yet, unresolved. The word 'cause', however, has a wider meaning than 'inflict' used in s. 20. Thus grievous bodily harm may be 'caused' where there was neither a direct application of force by D upon V (a battery) nor the application of violent force to V directly resulting from D's deliberate act. Thus D would commit the *actus reus* where, for example, D deliberately infects V with a serious communicable sexual disease or he causes grievous bodily harm by poisoning V. Grievous bodily harm may also be caused where D deliberately omits to act where he was under a legal duty to act. One subtle difference between s. 18 and s. 20 is that s. 20 requires the wound or grievous bodily harm to be inflicted on some 'other person' whereas s. 18 only requires that the wound or grievous bodily harm be caused to 'any person'. This raises the interesting possibility that if D caused grievous bodily harm to himself with intent to do so, perhaps seeking to gain discharge from military service or to enable him to claim disability benefit, he could be charged with the s. 18 offence.

10.1.3.2 *Mens rea* There are two elements to the *mens rea* of s. 18. Firstly D must 'maliciously' wound or cause grievous bodily harm and, secondly, he must do so with an ulterior intent either to cause grievous bodily harm or to resist or prevent the lawful apprehension or detainer of any person.

What does 'maliciously' mean in the context of s. 18? Where D is charged with 'maliciously causing grievous bodily harm with intent to cause grievous bodily harm', the word 'maliciously' is superfluous as D can be convicted only where he intended to cause grievous bodily harm. If D is charged with 'malicious wounding with intent to cause grievous bodily harm' or with 'malicious wounding (or maliciously causing grievous bodily harm) with intent to resist arrest' the word 'maliciously' requires definition. D may intend to cause grievous bodily harm without foreseeing a wound. For example, he may administer a karate chop to V intending to break his arm without foreseeing the ensuing wound caused when V falls over cutting his head on the corner of a table. Likewise he may push a police officer intending to resist arrest and not foresee the officer's resultant fall against a rock resulting in a fractured skull and cut scalp. If further anomalies are not to be created 'maliciously' should mean the same in s. 18 as it does in s. 20. In *Mowatt* [1968] 1 QB 421, however, the Court of Appeal stated *obiter* that 'in section 18 the word "maliciously" adds nothing'. As the case concerned a charge of inflicting grievous bodily harm under s. 20, little weight should be attached to this dictum. In *Morrison* (1989) 89 Cr App R 17, D was seized by a police officer who stated she was arresting him. He dived through a window pane dragging her with him as far as the glass resulting in her sustaining serious facial lacerations. The trial judge directed the jury that if he intended to resist arrest and was reckless in the *Caldwell* sense as to causing the officer harm, he was guilty of the s. 18 offence. The Court of Appeal quashed the conviction holding that recklessness in the *Cunningham* (subjective) sense was required. The case did not decide what degree of harm D had to foresee to be liable. Under s. 20, foresight of some physical harm is sufficient and this probably suffices for s. 18 but who can foresee what the Court of Appeal or House of Lords might decide if directly confronted with this issue.

In respect of the ulterior intent, intention bears the same meaning as for murder, that is either (i) the consequence (causing grievous bodily harm or resisting arrest etc.) was D's aim or purpose or, (ii) if this consequence was not D's aim or purpose, D knew that it was a virtually certain consequence resulting from achieving his aim or purpose, in which case the jury may use this as evidence from which intention may be inferred.

If D mistakenly believes that he is justified in using force in self-defence or prevention of crime etc, and he uses reasonable force in the circumstances (as he believed them to be), he would not be guilty of wounding with intent or causing grievous bodily harm with intent. If D is using force to resist arrest believing the arrest to be unlawful, and it is unlawful, he likewise would not be guilty of the s. 18 offence (*Walker* (1854) Dears CC 358). But if the arrest is lawful, although D honestly believes it is unlawful, he will be guilty of the s. 18 offence (*Bentley* (1850) 4 Cox CC 406) as ignorance of the law (in this case the officer's powers of arrest) is no excuse. Thus if D, being innocent of any offence, is arrested by an officer who has reasonable grounds to suspect he had committed an arrestable offence, D would be guilty of the s. 18 offence if he pushed the officer to the ground whereupon he cut his knee. If, however, D believed the person arresting him was not a police officer (rather than believing that an officer had no power of arrest in the circumstances) D's mistake being one of fact rather than of law should, under the principle in *Williams* (1984) 78 Cr App R 276 (see *3.6.1.1.2 ante*), avail him.

10.1.4 Administering poison
Section 23 OAPA provides:

> Whosoever shall unlawfully and maliciously administer to or cause to be administered to or taken by any other person any poison or other destructive or noxious thing, so as thereby to endanger the life of such person, or so as thereby to inflict upon such person any grievous bodily harm, shall be guilty of [an offence] . . . and shall be liable . . . [to a maximum penalty of 10 years' imprisonment].

Section 24 OAPA provides:

> Whosoever shall unlawfully and maliciously administer to or cause to be administered to or taken by any other person any poison or other destructive or noxious thing, with intent to injure, aggrieve, or annoy such person, shall

be guilty of an [offence] . . . and shall be liable . . . [to a maximum penalty of 5 years' imprisonment].

10.1.4.1 *Actus reus* Both sections require proof that D administered to, or caused to be administered to or taken by, V some poison or other destructive or noxious thing. Thus, D would commit the offence if he fed V with the poison (administered), if he left the poison in V's food and E subsequently fed him it (caused to be administered), or if he left it in V's food and V subsequently fed himself with it (caused to be taken) (see *Harley* (1830) 4 C & P 369; *Dale* (1852) 6 Cox CC 14). Until V consumes it, however, there is no administration (see *Cadman* (1825) *Carrington's Supplement*) although D's behaviour prior to this could have amounted to an attempt. Recently 'administer' has been given a wider meaning than internal ingestion. In *Gillard* (1988) 87 Cr App R 189, the Court of Appeal held that spraying V with a noxious fluid so that it comes into contact with his body is sufficient.

The courts have experienced problems over the definition of 'poison' or 'other noxious thing'. Ultimately it is for the jury to decide if the substance involved was a poison or noxious thing. In the context of s. 58 OAPA, which relates to the administration of 'poison or other noxious thing' with intent to procure an abortion, the courts have held that the offence may be committed where a 'recognised poison' has been administered although in a quantity too small to be capable of doing any harm (*Cramp* (1880) 5 QBD 307). If the substance is not a 'recognised poison', to constitute a 'noxious thing' it must be administered in such quantity as to be in fact harmful (*Marlow* (1964) 49 Cr App R 49). The problem with this distinction is that many things which are poisons are beneficial in small doses. For example, strychnine in small doses is used as a treatment to stimulate the respiratory system where a person has been poisoned by depressants of the central nervous system, but larger doses of strychnine are fatal. Similarly, warfarin is used in the treatment of people with certain heart conditions as an anti-coagulant to thin the blood. It is also used as rat poison and in larger quantities can kill humans. Are strychnine or warfarin poisons or noxious things? For the purposes of s. 23 it probably does not matter which category they fall into as it appears that the meaning of noxious thing may differ from s. 23 to s. 24. Section 23 requires not only an administration of the poisonous or noxious substance but that the life of V be thereby endangered or that grievous bodily harm be thereby inflicted on V. If the substance is merely 'noxious' the fact that the life of V has been endangered or he has sustained grievous bodily harm from its administration demonstrates that it has been administered in sufficient quantity to be harmful. These definitional problems may be relevant, however, where an attempt to commit the s. 23 offence is charged. In *Cato* [1976] 1 WLR 110, D was convicted of manslaughter and an offence under s. 23, having injected V, with his consent, with heroin which caused his death. Lord Widgery CJ sought to distinguish between substances in common use which may be harmful when taken in an overdose and those which are liable to injure in common use. The former are not 'noxious' simply because of their aptitude, whereas the latter are. He placed heroin in the latter category and thus it was always a 'noxious' thing although it may not harm experienced addicts who have a high tolerance to it.

It appears that the grievous bodily harm or endangerment of life must result from the administration of the substance and would not cover the situtation where, for example, the substance causes drowsiness and V falls down a flight of stairs breaking his neck.

There is no requirement in s. 24 for anything other than proof of administration of the poison or noxious thing. In *Marcus* [1981] 2 All ER 833, D put eight sedative and sleeping pills into her neighbour's bottle of milk. She was convicted of the s. 24 offence and appealed. On appeal it was argued, relying on *Cato*, that as sleeping tablets are harmless in themselves they could not be regarded as 'noxious' simply because D sought to administer an excess quantity of them. The Court of Appeal explained *Cato* taking the view that Lord Widgery was 'not intending to lay down a general proposition that a substance harmless in itself and in small quantities could never be noxious within s. 24 . . . if administered in large quantities.' In the context of s. 24 'noxious thing' had to be interpreted in light of the requisite intent to injure, aggrieve or annoy. This involved taking into account 'not only the quality or nature of the substance but also the quantity administered or sought to be administered.' Thus a substance harmless in small quantities could be 'noxious' in the quantity administered. In the context of s. 24, 'noxious' was not to be limited to substances which might cause bodily harm but would also include substances which were hurtful or unwholesome or objectionable. The Court gave the example of putting a snail in a bottle of ginger beer intending to aggrieve or annoy V. Similarly it would cover putting a large quantity of laxative in V's milk. In *Marcus*, the sedative quality of the drugs could clearly aggrieve or annoy V but the Court also took the view that they might harm V if, for example, in a sedated condition V were to drive a car or cross a busy street. Thus the 'harmful' quality of the substance may arise indirectly.

10.1.4.2 *Mens rea*
In both sections the word 'maliciously' is used which means intentionally or recklessly in its *Cunningham* sense; it is the administration which must be intentional or reckless. In s. 23 no *mens rea* is required with respect to endangering life or inflicting grievous bodily harm; these are matters of causation (see *Cato*).

D cannot be convicted of the s. 24 offence unless the ulterior intent to 'injure, aggrieve or annoy' V is proved. In deciding if D has such an intent, regard is to be had not only to the effect he intends to produce but also to 'his whole object in acting as he has done' (*per* Robert Goff LJ in *Hill* (1985) 81 Cr App R 206). Thus, if D administered a sleeping pill to a woman with intent to rape her when comatose, the tablet would not be intended to produce injury but his 'ulterior motive' would constitute an intent to injure. In *Hill*, D, a homosexual, gave slimming tablets to two boys which D knew could also produce sleeplessness. Keeping someone awake is not necessarily harmful; but it may be depending on whether D's purpose in doing so is benevolent (for example, to keep the pilot of an aircraft awake) or malevolent (for example, to carry out a prolonged interrogation). In the instant case D's intention in giving the tablets was to disinhibit the boys and thereby render them more susceptible to his sexual advances; this constituted an intent to injure. A problem with this approach is that Robert Goff LJ proceeded, *obiter*, to provide an example which somewhat stretched the meaning of injury. He stated that if D drugged V with a view to stealing his property while asleep, his intention to deprive V of his property amounted to an intent to injure him. It is submitted that this should be regarded as an intent to 'aggrieve or annoy', but Robert Goff LJ considered that depriving V of his property involved more than simply causing him distress or annoyance but was actually injurious to him.

Section 25 OAPA provides that a person charged with an offence under s. 23 may be convicted of an offence under s. 24. In such a case, however, the ulterior intent required for s. 24 must be established.

10.1.5 Reform

The Law Commission's Draft Criminal Code (Law Com No. 177) proposes a major overhaul of non-fatal offences against the person. The Draft Criminal Code proposes a hierarchy of offences which forms a coherent whole avoiding the anomalies and inconsistencies of the OAPA. The more serious offences created by clauses 70 and 71, replacing ss. 18 and 20 OAPA, require proof that D caused V serious personal harm which may be committed intentionally or recklessly. There is no requirement that the harm result from an assault and the subtle distinctions between 'inflicting' and 'causing' are removed. The distinction between wounds and grievous bodily harm are also removed; a wound would become the same as any other form of harm to be judged objectively whether it is serious personal harm or not. Clause 72, replacing s. 47 OAPA, makes it an offence to intentionally or recklessly cause personal harm to another. In the case of each of these offences the *mens rea* reflects directly the *actus reus* of the offence. By clause 4(4) and clause 45(c) the common law defence of consent is retained. Clause 75 defines assault:

A person is guilty of assault if he intentionally or recklessly –

(a) applies force to or causes an impact on the body of another; or
(b) causes another to believe that any such force or impact is imminent,

without the consent of the other or, where the act is likely or intended to cause personal harm, with or without his consent.

Causing or intending harm to another for the purposes of sexual gratification, will thus continue to be an offence even though the other consents to it. Clauses 76, 77 and 78 create three offences of aggravated assault; namely assault on a constable acting in the execution of his duty, assault with intent to resist arrest and assault with intent to rob. Clause 73 creates one offence of administering a substance without consent replacing ss. 23 and 24 OAPA. It provides as follows:

(1) A person is guilty of an offence if he administers to, or causes to be taken by, another without his consent any substance which he knows to be capable of interfering substantially with the other's bodily functions.

(2) For the purposes of this section a substance capable of inducing unconsciousness or sleep is capable of interfering substantially with bodily functions.

Again this tidies up this area removing the anomalies created by ss. 23 and 24. No longer will time be wasted trying to decide if a substance is a poison or noxious thing; the only issue will be whether it is capable of interfering substantially with the other's bodily functions. There will be no need to prove actual harm. The ulterior intent of s. 24 is also removed.

10.2 SEXUAL OFFENCES

There are numerous sexual offences but for the purposes of this chapter discussion will be confined to the main offences arising out of indecent assault and heterosexual intercourse.

10.2.1 Rape
It is an offence for a man to rape a woman (s. 1(1) of the Sexual Offences Act 1956, hereafter referred to as SOA 1956) for which the maximum punishment is life imprisonment. Rape is defined in s. 1 of the Sexual Offences (Amendment) Act 1976 (hereafter referred to as SOAA 1976):

1. (1) For the purposes of section 1 of the Sexual Offences Act 1956 . . . a man commits rape if –
    (a) he has unlawful sexual intercourse with a woman who at the time of the intercourse does not consent to it; and
    (b) at that time he knows that she does not consent to the intercourse or he is reckless as to whether she consents to it;
    and references to rape in other enactments . . . shall be construed accordingly.

10.2.1.1 *Actus reus* The *actus reus* of rape is defined in s. 1(1)(a) SOAA 1976. This comprises three elements which will be considered separately.

10.2.1.1.1 Sexual intercourse Section 44 SOA 1956 defines 'sexual intercourse' as follows:

Where, on the trial of any offence under this Act, it is necessary to prove sexual intercourse (whether natural or unnatural), it shall not be necessary to prove the completion of the intercourse by the emission of seed, but the intercourse shall be deemed complete upon proof of penetration only.

By virtue of s. 7(2) SOAA 1976, s. 44, in so far as it relates to natural intercourse, applies to rape. 'Natural intercourse' means vaginal intercourse; there is no offence of rape *per anum* (*Gaston* (1981) 73 Cr App R 164) but there is the separate offence of buggery, i.e. 'unnatural intercourse' (s. 12 SOA 1956). Penetration is established on proof of the slightest entry of the accused's penis into the victim's vagina; the hymen need not be ruptured (*Hughes* (1841) 9 C & P 752). While slight penetration is sufficient to constitute sexual intercourse, sexual intercourse is regarded as continuing until terminated by withdrawal. In *Kaitamaki* [1985] AC 147, D penetrated V with consent or, at least believing she consented. When he became aware she was not consenting or no longer consenting, he did not desist. He was convicted of rape, his conviction being upheld by the New Zealand Court of Appeal and the Privy Council which stated (at p. 151) that the New Zealand equivalent of s. 44 SOA 1956 was there:

> to remove any doubts as to the minimum conduct needed to prove the fact of sexual intercourse. 'Complete' is used in the . . . sense of having come into existence, but not in the sense of being at an end. Sexual intercourse is a continuing act which only ends with withdrawal.

Thus, while the initial act of penetration may not constitute rape if done with consent or if D believed the woman was consenting, the continuation of intercourse after consent has been withdrawn, or upon becoming aware that the woman never had consented, will constitute rape. This is an enlightened decision recognising a woman's autonomy over her own body. The fact that a woman may intitially consent does not mean that she has handed over autonomy over her body to the man. It is to be hoped that this decision will be followed by English courts.

One final problem in this area is the presumption that a boy under fourteen is incapable of sexual intercourse (natural or unnatural) (see *Groombridge* (1836) 7 C & P 582; *Philips* (1839) 8 C & P 736; *Waite* [1892] 2 QB 600). It is not a requirement of the *actus reus* of rape that the perpetrator be fourteen or over, rather the common law developed the presumption of physical incapacity which is irrebuttable. The outcome is that a boy under fourteen may be convicted of attempted rape as physical impossibility is no obstacle to a conviction of attempt or conspiracy (see 8.3.3.4 and 8.4.4 *ante*). Physical incapacity is no different from presumed physical incapacity. It is difficult to justify this arcane presumption. If it is based on an assumption that boys under fourteen have not reached puberty, the presumption is ill-founded in fact. Furthermore, whether or not a boy has reached puberty is irrelevant to his capacity to sustain an erection and therefore to penetrate the victim. Puberty may have been relevant had it been a requirement of rape that a full act of intercourse be proved ending in ejaculation. As this is not required, the presumption is a nonsense made more nonsensical by the fact that a boy who performs the *actus reus* of rape may not be convicted of that offence but may be convicted of attempt. The Criminal Law Revision Committee, *Fifteenth Report, Sexual Offences*, (Cmnd 9213, 1984), recommended the abolition of the presumption (para. 2.48).

10.2.1.1.2 Unlawfulness Is the word 'unlawful' superfluous in the definition of rape it being subsumed within the requirement that the intercourse be without the consent of the woman? At common law, and since the enactment of the SOA 1956, 'unlawful' has always been interpreted to mean 'illicit' in the sense that the intercourse takes place outside the bonds of marriage (see *Chapman* [1959] 1 QB 100; *Jones* [1973] Crim LR 710). Section 1(1) SOAA 1976 retained the word 'unlawful' when defining rape for the purposes of s. 1 SOA 1956 and it has been assumed until recently to have retained the same meaning (see *R* v *R*, [1991] 4 All ER 481 *post*). This is supported by the fact that other sections of the SOA 1956 create offences arising out of 'unlawful sexual intercourse'. For example, s. 6 makes it an offence to have 'unlawful sexual intercourse with a girl under the age of sixteen'. If, by the law of his domicile, a man is lawfully married to a girl under sixteen and they come to reside in England and have sexual intercourse, this would constitute a criminal offence if the word 'unlawful' were to be treated as being meaningless (see also s. 7 SOA 1956).

A problem arising from this conclusion, however, is the assumption underlying the common law for many centuries that a husband may not be convicted of rape if he forces his wife to have intercourse with him without her consent. The fact that intercourse outside of the bonds of marriage constitutes unlawful intercourse for the purposes of rape does not necessarily imply that all intercourse within marriage is lawful. At common law, however, it was believed that a husband could not be convicted of raping his wife. Sir Matthew Hale CJ stated in History of the *Pleas of the Crown* (vol 1 (1736) p. 629):

> But the husband cannot be guilty of a rape committed by himself upon his lawful wife, for by their mutual matrimonial consent and contract the wife hath given up herself in this kind unto her husband, which she cannot retract.

Hale did not conceive of there being any circumstances where this consent could be revoked while the marriage subsisted. This was confirmed in *Miller* [1954] 2 QB 282, although Lynskey J explained that a husband who used force or violence would be liable for any offence against the person he might commit, even common assault.

At common law it was believed that a husband could inflict corporal punishment on his wife and restrict her liberty. Dicta to this effect have since been refuted as the common law adapted to changes in society with regard to the position of women (see *Cochrane* (1840) 8 Dowl 630, and *Jackson* [1891] 1 QB 671). However, the position with regard to implied consent to intercourse had, until the decision in *R* v *R*, been ameliorated rather than refuted. In a series of cases it had been recognised that there are situations in which the marital exemption to liability for rape does not apply. In *Clarke* [1949] 2 All ER 448, the first reported prosecution of a husband for raping his wife, Byrne J held that the wife's deemed consent to intercourse had been revoked by an order made by the justices that she no longer be bound to cohabit with her husband. Byrne J took the view that consent which had been given by process of law, namely by marriage, could be revoked by process of law, namely the justices' order. He stated that the consent was to intercourse 'during such time as the ordinary relations created by the marriage contract subsisted between them'. In *O'Brien* [1974] 3 All ER 663, consent was found to have been revoked by the pronouncement of a decree nisi. In *Steele* (1976) 65 Cr App R 22, Geoffrey Lane LJ listed the situations where consent would be considered to have been revoked (at p. 25):

A separation agreement with a non-cohabitation clause, a decree of divorce, a decree of judicial separation, a separation order in the justices' court containing a non-cohabitation clause and an injunction restraining the husband from molesting the wife or having sexual intercourse with her are all obvious cases in which the wife's consent would be successfully revoked. On the other hand, the mere filing of a petition for divorce would clearly not be enough, the mere issue of proceedings leading up to a magistrates' separation order or the mere issue of proceedings as a preliminary to apply for an *ex parte* injunction to restrain the husband would not be enough but the granting of an injunction to restrain the husband would be enough because the Court is making an order wholly inconsistent with the wife's consent and an order . . . breach of which would or might result in the husband being punished by imprisonment.

In *R* v *R* [1991] 4 All ER 481, the House of Lords, following the approach adopted by the Court of Appeal, swept aside the common law founded on the writings of Hale and declared that there is no matrimonial exception to the law on rape. Lord Keith of Kinkel stated (at pp. 483–484):

The common law is . . . capable of evolving in the light of changing social, economic and cultural developments. Hale's proposition reflected the state of affairs in these respects at the time it was enunciated. Since then the status of women, and particularly of married women, has changed out of all recognition in various ways which are very familiar . . . [O]ne of the most important changes is that marriage is in modern times regarded as a partnership of equals, and no longer one in which the wife must be the subservient chattel of her husband. Hale's proposition involves that by marriage a wife gives her irrevocable consent to sexual intercourse with her husband under all circumstances and irrespective of the state of her health or how she happens to be feeling at the time. In modern times any reasonable person must regard that conception as quite unacceptable.

Their Lordships' willingness to develop the common law in a way which increases the ambit of criminal liability stands in stark contrast to their expressed inability to do so when it came to developing the defence of duress where only Parliament was deemed capable of changing the common law (see 6.2.6 *ante*). Indeed they did not, in fact, develop the common law by recognising a new exception to cover the situation which pertained in *R* v *R*, but rather swept away the need for exceptions. While the policy reasons behind the decision cannot be doubted, the solution their Lordships adopted to the problem of marital rape is more questionable. Section 1(1) SOAA 1976 contained the word 'unlawful' which Parliament had chosen to retain thereby accepting the common law and the recognised exceptions. Parliament had considered an amendment to the Bill rendering a husband liable to conviction for rape but decided to refer this matter to the CLRC for their consideration. Their Lordships ruled, however, that the word 'unlawful' was mere surplusage, Lord Keith stating (at p. 489):

> In order that the exceptions might be preserved, it would be necessary to construe 'unlawfully' as meaning 'outside marriage or within marriage in a situation covered by one of the exceptions to the marital exception' . . . The fact is that it is clearly unlawful to have sexual intercourse with any woman without her consent, and that the use of the word in the subsection adds nothing. In my opinion there are no rational grounds for putting the suggested gloss on the word, and it should be treated as being mere surplusage in this enactment . . .

This appears to be a piece of judicial legislation. Regardless of how desirable the object to be achieved might be, it is not the function of judges to amend legislation, particularly in a way which widens the ambit of the criminal law. Whatever happened to the presumption that if a criminal statute is ambiguous it should be construed in favour of the accused? The Law Commission were considering the problem of marital rape (see Working Paper No. 116, 'Rape within Marriage' (1990)) and they have since reported recommending that the decision in R v R should be confirmed by legislation which would have the advantage of tidying up the whole area and removing other anomalies in the Sexual Offences Act 1956 to which their Lordships did not address their attention (see Law Com. No. 205 'Rape within Marriage' (1992)).

10.2.1.1.3 The absence of consent

Unlawful sexual intercourse becomes rape only where it is engaged in without the woman's consent. It is not necessary to prove that the woman positively dissented, it is sufficient to prove she did not consent (see Lang (1975) 62 Cr App R 50). Thus if D has intercourse with a woman who is asleep (Mayers (1872) 12 Cox CC 311) or unconscious (Camplin (1845) 1 Car & Kir 746) he will be committing rape. The old cases used to talk of consent being vitiated by 'force, fear or fraud'. In Olugboja [1982] QB 320, L raped V and then took her companion into an adjoining room in order to rape her. L's companion, O, told V that he was going to have intercourse with her and asked her to remove her trousers, which she did because she was frightened. O had intercourse with her and she did not resist or struggle. O was convicted of rape and appealed contending that rape required that the submission of the victim be induced by force or threat of force. The Court of Appeal dismissed the appeal holding that in the SOAA 1976 Parliament had accepted the recommendation of the Heilbron Committee, Cmnd 6352 (1975) para. 84, which recommended that legislation should emphasise that it is the lack of consent rather than violence which is the essence of rape. Dunn LJ stated (at p. 331):

> in so far as the actus reus is concerned, the question now is simply: 'At the time of the sexual intercourse did the woman consent to it?' It is not necesary

for the prosecution to prove that what might otherwise appear to have been consent was in reality merely submission induced by force, fear or fraud, although one or more of these factors will no doubt be present in the majority of cases of rape.

It is for the jury to decide if consent was absent. Dunn LJ stated (at p. 332):

> They should be directed that consent, or the absence of it, is to be given its ordinary meaning and if need be, by way of example, that there is a difference between consent and submission; every consent involves a submission, but it by no means follows that a mere submission involves consent.

This dictum is problematic. 'Consent' means 'voluntary agreement or permission' whereas 'submission' implies 'surrender', 'resignation', 'acceptance of authority' or 'ceasing to resist'. It appears incorrect to state that 'every consent involves a submission' as a person who voluntarily agrees to sexual intercourse with her lover could hardly be described as surrendering or accepting his authority when she is agreeing to that which she may passionately desire. Submission rather suggests constraint in that a person does something which, in the absence of some external constraint, she would not choose to do. It is right to suggest that there is a difference between consent and submission but quite wrong to state that every consent involves a submission. The problem, therefore, is to determine when there is not voluntary agreement but rather merely submission resulting from constraint. If there is a threat of force any apparent agreement thereby induced would clearly not be voluntary; similarly, fraud may vitiate consent (see below). But what of threats of action detrimental to V not involving force, or promises of benefits to be conferred on V if she consents, do these vitiate consent? Dunn LJ went on to state (at p. 332):

> the dividing line . . . between real consent on the one hand and mere submission on the other may not be easy to draw. Where it is to be drawn in a given case is for the jury to decide, applying their combined good sense, experience and knowledge of human nature and modern behaviour to all the relevant facts of that case.

It might be helpful in this task if the jury were instructed that promises of benefit should not be considered sufficient to vitiate consent, whether or not the promises were genuine. Thus, for example, the young aspiring film actress who has intercourse with the film director after promises of parts in his films may well be resigning herself to doing something she finds distasteful and would not otherwise do, but she is agreeing to intercourse without any external constraint being imposed upon her. The constraint operating is her own internal ambition; no one is forcing her to be a film actress. By contrast, threats of detriment may vitiate consent. Where there is force or the threat of violence or well grounded fear of violence, as in *Olugboja*, there is no voluntary consent. In other circumstances the jury will have to apply their own good sense to determine whether the constraint rendered V's agreement involuntary. It is submitted that the jury should balance the detriment threatened against the detriment of undesired intercourse. If, taking into account all the circumstances, the detriment threatened was sufficient to render V's agreement involuntary, i.e. she accepted non-consensual intercourse as the lesser of two evils, they may find there was no consent. For example, a threat by a police officer to arrest a young girl for a serious offence if she does not allow him to have intercourse with her, may vitiate consent, whereas a threat by V's fiancé that he will break off their engagement if she does not allow him to have intercourse with her should not be considered sufficiently detrimental to vitiate consent.

An apparent consent should not be considered valid where the woman is not in a position to decide whether or not to consent because her knowledge and understanding are impaired by youth (*Howard* [1965] 3 All ER 684), mental deficiency (*Barratt* (1873) LR 2 CCR 81) or intoxication (*Lang* (1975) 62 Cr App R 50). An apparent consent will also be vitiated where it has been obtained by fraud as to the nature of the act. In *Flattery* (1877) 2 QBD 410, D was convicted of rape having induced V to submit to intercourse by deceiving her into believing that he was performing a surgical operation (see also *Williams* [1923] 1 KB 340). Section 1(2) SOA 1956 provides that 'a man who induces a woman to have sexual intercourse with him by impersonating her husband commits rape.' This re-enacts s. 4 of the Criminal Law Amendment Act 1885 which reversed a line of cases culminating in *Barrow* (1868) 11 Cox CC 191, which held that this was not rape. The implication is that it is not rape if the impersonation is of someone other than V's husband. Thus if V is cohabiting with X and D impersonates X this would not amount to rape. It is difficult to see why this should not amount to rape as the identity of the other party is supremely important. The Criminal Law Revision Committee in its Fifteenth Report (Cmnd 9213) recommends that this should constitute rape (para. 2.25).

10.2.1.2 Mens rea D must intend to have unlawful sexual intercourse. Prior to the decision in *R* v *R* this was understood to mean an intention to have intercourse with someone who was not his wife. If D made a mistake as to V's identity, believing that she was his wife, there was no intent to have unlawful intercourse. If the mistake was a drunken one, however, intoxication provided no defence (*Fotheringham* (1989) 88 Cr App R 206). After the decision in *R* v *R* (see *10.2.1.1.2 ante*), where the House of Lords held that the word 'unlawful' was 'surplusage' in s. 1(1) SOAA 1976, it would appear that the only intention required is to have intercourse. If D mistakes V for his wife this will be irrelevant; everything will hinge on whether he knew the woman did not consent or was reckless thereto.

With regard to the question of consent, recklessness relates to a circumstance, namely V's state of mind. Subjective recklessness is required; D is reckless where he is aware of the possibility that V may not consent but he nevertheless proceeds to have intercourse (see *Satnam and Kewel* (1983) 78 Cr App R 149). If D claims he believed the woman consented, it is sufficient that this is an honest belief, it need not be based on reasonable grounds (*Morgan* [1976] AC 182). However, the jury may take into account the reasonableness of D's belief when deciding whether he could possibly have entertained such a belief. This evidential proposition is now expressly enacted in s. 1(2) SOAA 1976:

It is hereby declared that if at a trial for a rape offence the jury has to consider whether a man believed that a woman was consenting to sexual intercourse, the presence or absence of reasonable grounds for such a belief is a matter to which the jury is to have regard, in conjunction with any other relevant matters in considering whether he so believed.

10.2.2   Other offences involving sexual intercourse

These offences cover situations where 'consent' exists but it may have been improperly obtained or the woman is deemed incapable of giving valid consent. The offences are indictable and punishable with two years' imprisonment, unless otherwise stated.

10.2.2.1   Procuring unlawful sexual intercourse   The SOA 1956 contains several offences (examined individually in the following paragraphs) involving procuring a woman to have unlawful sexual intercourse in any part of the world. 'Unlawful sexual intercourse' has the same meaning as for rape. The procuring may be done by a man or a woman and thus the sexual intercourse may take place with someone other than the procurer. The offences are only committed where intercourse takes place although, if it does not take place, there may be an attempt to procure (*Johnson* [1964] 2 QB 404). The procuring must occur within the jurisdiction although the sexual intercourse may occur outside the jurisdiction. By contrast rape is an offence which is indictable only if the intercourse occurs within the jurisdiction. 'Procuring' means to produce by endeavour (*Christian* (1913) 78 JP 112). Thus the act of intercourse in question must have been one which the woman would not have embarked on spontaneously or of her own volition; if the woman is a willing participant requiring no persuasion there is no procurement (see *Christian*; and *A-G's Reference (No. 1 of 1975)* [1975] QB 773 at 779).

10.2.2.1.1   Procuring by threats or intimidation   Section 2(1) SOA 1956 makes it an offence to procure a woman by threats or intimidation. It is difficult to define the threats which would vitiate consent for the purposes of rape. Any such threats will suffice for this offence, but presumably some threats which would not suffice for rape will suffice under s. 2. Where the line is to be drawn between threats which are sufficient and those which are not is unclear. It is submitted that this is a question for the jury to decide on objective criteria, namely, whether the threat was one which a person of the age of V and sharing other relevant characteristics could not reasonably have been expected to resist in the circumstances. Intimidation appears to cover situations where there is no express threat but one is implied from the circumstances.

10.2.2.1.2   Procuring by false pretences or false representations   Section 3(1) SOA 1956 makes it an offence to procure a woman by false pretences or false representations. This covers frauds which would not suffice for rape (*Williams*

[1923] 1 KB 340). Thus, if impersonation does not constitute rape, it will amount to an offence under s. 3. Under the Larceny Act 1916 'false pretences' was held not to cover statements about future intentions (*Dent* [1955] 2 QB 590). The inclusion of the phrase 'false representations' probably means that such statements are included. The only issue, therefore, should be whether the statement is false and has induced V to give her consent to sexual intercourse which she would not otherwise have given.

10.2.2.1.3 Procuring a defective   Section 9(1) SOA 1956 makes it an offence to procure a woman who is a defective. It is subject to the exception in s. 9(2) that D will not be guilty of an offence 'if he does not know and has no reason to suspect her to be a defective.' It is unclear whether this section applies where D procures V to have intercourse with himself as s. 7 SOA 1956 creates a separate offence, subject to the same exception, of having unlawful sexual intercourse with a woman who is a defective. This may be of importance in one situation, namely where intercourse does not take place and attempt is charged. If s. 9 does not apply where D is seeking to procure V to have sex with himself, acts which are more than merely prepartory to procuring may not be more than merely preparatory to having unlawful sexual intercourse under s. 7. Where D seeks to rely on the exception to either offence he bears the burden of proof (s. 47 SOA 1956) on a balance of probabilities (*Carr-Briant* [1943] KB 607).

Section 45 SOA 1956 defines 'a defective' as 'a person suffering from a state of arrested or incomplete development of mind which includes severe impairment of intelligence and social functioning.' Severe impairment of intelligence and social functioning must be proved in each case. What constitutes severe impairment is to be judged against the standard of normal persons (*Hall* [1987] Crim LR 831).

10.2.2.1.4 Procuring a girl under twenty-one   By s. 23(1) SOA 1956 it is an offence 'to procure a girl under the age of twenty-one to have unlawful sexual intercourse in any part of the world *with a third person.*' It is no offence where D procures the girl to have intercourse with him. It is thought that strict liability applies in respect of the girl's age (see *Prince* (1875) LR 2 CCR 154).

10.2.2.2 Unlawful sexual intercourse with girls under sixteen   By s. 5 SOA 1956 it is an offence punishable with life imprisonment to have unlawful sexual intercourse with a girl under the age of thirteen. By s. 6 SOA it is an offence (triable either way) to have unlawful sexual intercourse with a girl under the age of sixteen. In the case of both offences it is of no consequence that V consented to intercourse. Furthermore, according to *Prince (ante)*, no *mens rea* is required in respect of the girl's age. Thus a belief that the girl is over thirteen, no matter how reasonable it is, will not avail D. Section 6, however, is subject to two exceptions. Firstly, by s. 5(2), if D has married V and the marriage is invalid due to V's age, sexual intercourse will not be an offence if 'he believes her to be his wife and has reasonable cause for the belief.' Secondly, by s. 5(3), D will not be guilty of an offence if he is under twenty-four and he has not previously been charged with a s. 6 offence or an attempt to commit it, and 'he believes V to be of the age of sixteen or over and has reasonable cause for that belief.' This is often referred to as 'the young man's defence' and is available only on the first occasion a person is charged with this offence as he may not be aware of the serious consequences of mistake as to the girl's age; thereafter it is expected he will take much greater care. For the purposes of this section a person is only 'charged' when he appears before a court having jurisdiction to determine the matter (*Rider* [1954] 1 All ER 5). Thus, being charged by the police, or appearing before a magistrates' court in committal proceedings, does not satisfy the requirements of the section. If D relies on either exception he bears the burden of proof (s. 47 SOA 1956) on a balance of probabilities.

10.2.2.3 Administering drugs to obtain or facilitate intercourse
Section 4(1) SOA 1956 provides:

> It is an offence for a person to apply or administer to, or cause to be taken by, a woman any drug, matter or thing with intent to stupefy or overpower her so as thereby to enable any man to have unlawful sexual intercourse with her.

This offence may be committed by any person, male or female, including the man who seeks to have intercourse himself. It is not necessary that intercourse should take place; the offence is complete when the drugs etc. have been applied or administered with the ulterior intent.

10.2.3 Incest
Incest is committed where a man has sexual intercourse with a woman whom he knows to be his granddaughter, daughter, sister or mother (s. 10(1) SOA 1956). If the woman is of the age of sixteen or over, and she permits the man to have intercourse with her with her consent, knowing he is her grandfather, father, brother or son, she is also guilty of incest (s. 11(1)). If she permits sexual intercourse without consenting to it, it will be rape on his part as well as incest. Where the female is a girl under thirteen (and the indictment specifically alleges this), the offence is punishable with life imprisonment and an attempt to commit it is punishable with seven years' imprisonment. In all other cases the maximum sentences are seven years for the full offence and two years for attempt.

For the purposes of incest 'sister' includes 'half-sister' and 'brother' includes 'half-brother' and it also covers illegitimate relationships, but it does not cover relationships by adoption. However, if D believes that E is his sister, when she is in fact adopted, he will be guilty of attempt.

The *mens rea* of incest requires knowledge of the relationship. If D has intercourse with E, believing that she is the daughter of his wife and her first husband when, in fact, she is the issue of his adultery with his wife prior to her divorce and marriage to him, he will not be guilty of incest (see *Carmichael* [1940] 1 KB 630).

At common law it was not an offence for D to incite a girl under sixteen to have incestuous intercourse with him as she was too young to commit incest (see *Whitehouse* [1977] QB 868). Section 1 of the Indecency with Children Act 1960 (see 10.2.4.2 *post*) made it an offence to incite a child under fourteen to commit an act of gross indecency. However, the law left a gap in respect of a child between the ages of fourteen and sixteen. By s. 54 of the Criminal Law Act 1977 it was made an offence for a man to incite to have sexual intercourse with him a girl under sixteen whom he knows to be his granddaughter, daughter or sister (sister includes half-sister and illegitimate relationships are also covered). The offence is punishable on summary conviction with six months' imprisonment or a fine, and on conviction on indictment with two years' imprisonment.

10.2.4 Indecent assault and indecency with children

10.2.4.1 Indecent assault By ss. 14 and 15 SOA 1956 indecent assault on a woman or on a man, respectively, are offences, triable either way. They are punishable on indictment with ten years' imprisonment (s. 4(3) of the Sexual Offences Act 1985). The offences are the same except that s. 14(3) provides that, where a marriage is invalid because the wife was under sixteen and thus incapable of consenting to indecent acts, the husband will not be guilty of the offence if he believes her to be his wife and has reasonable grounds for that belief. There is no such provision where the husband was under sixteen, and thus a wife performing any act which could, in the absence of consent, constitute an indecent assault will be guilty of that offence as the defence of reasonable belief is not available to her. This is clearly an oversight.

If a person consents to the indecent act there cannot be an indecent assault. A person under sixteen, however, is in law incapable of giving consent (ss.14(2) and 15(2)). D's belief that P is sixteen is no defence as the principle in *Prince* (1975) LR 2 CCR 154, of strict liability regarding the age of the victim, applies. D may therefore be convicted of indecent assault even though acquitted of having unlawful intercourse with a girl under sixteen on the basis of the 'young man's' defence in s. 6 SOA 1956 (see para 10.2.2.2 *ante*). A person who is a defective is also incapable of giving consent but if D does not know and has no reason to believe that P is a defective, P's consent will be a defence (ss.14(4) and 15(4)). Consent has the same meaning as in rape so, for example, force or threats or fraud will vitiate consent. In addition, P may not consent to an act the probable consequence of which is the infliction of bodily harm (*Donovan* [1934] 2 KB 498). It was thought that a husband could not be guilty of indecent assault on his wife where the act was proximate to and part of the preparation for intercourse because the wife was deemed to consent to intercourse by the fact of marriage (see *Henry*, 10.2.1.1.2 *ante*). Consent was not deemed to extend to collateral acts (see *Kowalski* (1987) 86 Cr App R 339). Following the House of Lords' decision in *R* v *R* [1991] 4 All ER 481, the fiction of 'deemed consent' no longer exists. Thus a husband may be guilty of indecent assault in any circumstances where the wife does not consent to the act if this would have been an indecent assault if done to anyone else.

While a boy under fourteen is presumed incapable of sexual intercourse and cannot be convicted of rape, he can be convicted of indecent assault; the act of non-consensual intercourse necessarily involves the commission of an indecent assault.

10.2.4.1.1   Actus reus   There must be an assault in the sense of a technical assault or a battery. Thus if D touches V in circumstances of indecency or causes V to apprehend being touched in such circumstances, there will be an indecent assault (see *Rolfe* (1952) 36 Cr App R 4; *Leeson* (1968) 52 Cr App R 185). An invitation by D for V to touch him cannot amount to an assault regardless of the age of the victim unless it is accompanied by force or the threat of force (*Fairclough* v *Whipp* [1951] 2 All ER 834; *Burrows* [1952] 1 All ER 58n). If D is a woman having intercourse with V, a boy under sixteen, she will not be liable for indecent assault if she is a passive participant, but she will be liable if she does anything active which would be an indecent assault in the absence of consent (for example, touching his penis) even though he consents to this act (see *Faulkner* v *Talbot* [1981] 3 All ER 468).

The assault must be 'accompanied by circumstances of indecency'. The test of what is indecent is whether right-minded persons would consider the conduct indecent as being 'offensive to contemporary standards of modesty and privacy' (*Court* [1988] 2 All ER 221). The circumstances include both what D does and what he says; to kiss V may not be an indecent assault but if accompanied by suggestions of sexual intercourse it could be indecent (see *Leeson* (1968) 52 Cr App R 185). If the assault is in the nature of a technical assault, it is necessary for the victim to be aware of the circumstances of indecency or apprehended indecency, but if the assault is a battery there is no need to prove such awareness. Thus D may indecently assault someone who is asleep or unconscious (*Court*).

A problem arises in determining whether something is indecent; D's motive may be indecent but the act or its circumstances may not appear to be indecent. In *Court*, D spanked a twelve-year-old girl twelve times across the seat of her shorts. When asked by the police why he had done so he replied 'I don't know, buttock fetish'. It was contended that this secret motive, which had not been communicated to the girl, could not make the assault an indecent one. The House of Lords, dismissing his appeal against conviction, distinguished between three situations. Firstly, an incident (i.e. the act and its surrounding circumstances) which, viewed objectively, could not be considered indecent by right-minded persons; in such a case it does not matter that D has a secret indecent motive. Thus, in *George* [1956] Crim LR 52, there was no indecent assault where D attempted to remove V's shoe even though this was something he found sexually gratifying, as there were no circumstances of indecency. Secondly, when viewed objectively, an incident may be inherently indecent regardless of D's purpose or motives. The example Lord Ackner gave was of a man stripping a woman of her clothing against her will. Regardless of D's motives in doing so, right-minded people would inevitably regard this as indecent. Another example Lord Ackner gave was that of a doctor who falsely represented that an intimate examination was necessary thereby obtaining the patient's consent. This would not be a true consent because of the doctor's fraud and thus would be an assault. If the examination was one which right-minded persons would consider indecent (for example, any examination of the patient's genitals), the doctor's motives, whether sexual gratification or private research, would be irrelevant. Thirdly, an incident which is capable of being indecent; the crucial factor will be D's motive. Lord Ackner considered that the present case was such an example. He stated (at p. 230):

> The conduct of the appellant in assaulting the girl by spanking her was only *capable* of being an indecent assault. To decide whether or not right-minded persons might think that assault was indecent, the following factors were clearly relevant: the relationship of the defendant to this victim (were they relatives, friends or virtually complete strangers?), how had the defendant come to embark on this conduct and *why* was he behaving in this way?

Thus if D had been her father, or another person *in loco parentis*, administering discipline, this would not have been an indecent assault. However, as D was doing so for sexual gratification, his motive made an incident capable of being considered indecent actually indecent. D's motive is, therefore, a relevant circumstance in cases falling within this category.

10.2.4.1.2   Mens rea   It must first be proved that D had the necessary *mens rea* for assault or battery. Secondly, it must be proved that D intended to commit an indecent assault, i.e. an assault which right-minded persons would think indecent. Thus D must be aware of the circumstances which would amount to indecency, and with that awareness intend to assault V in those circumstances. Evidence of his motives, whether the case falls within the second or third category, will obviously be relevant in establishing this intention. It is not necessary that he have any motive of sexual gratification; it is sufficient that he is aware that right-minded persons would regard his act in the circumstances as indecent. A problem with this statement of the *mens rea* is that, in *Court*, Lord Ackner expressly approved the case of *Pratt* [1984] Crim LR 41, which it is impossible to reconcile with his statement of principle. In *Pratt* D found two thirteen-year-old boys fishing at night. He threatened them with a gun and made them strip naked and shine a torch on each other's genitals. He claimed his sole motive for his actions was to search for cannabis which he believed the boys had stolen from him. The assistant recorder held that he was entitled to put this evidence before the jury to refute the prosecution's contention that he intended to commit an indecent assault. Lord Ackner approved this finding stating that 'if the jury thought that his explanation might be true, they might decide that right-minded persons would not think that what he had done in the circumstances was indecent.' But if a doctor's motives are irrelevant when he fraudulently obtains consent to intimate examinations of his patients, why should D's motives in this case be relevant? It would appear that what he did was inherently indecent as it would offend contemporary standards of modesty and decency. In such circumstances whether his motive is sexual or otherwise is irrelevant. D's evidence might refute a contention that he made the boys perform these acts for his sexual gratification; this is irrelevant, however, to the issue of whether he knew that right-minded persons would regard such an incident as indecent. In referring to the man who stripped a woman of her clothes Lord Ackner stated (at p. 230):

> Those very facts, *devoid of any explanation*, would give rise to the irresistible inference that the defendant intended to assault his victim in a manner which right-minded persons would clearly think was indecent. Whether he did so for his own personal sexual gratification or because, being a misogynist or for some other reason, he wished to embarrass or humiliate his victim seems to me to be irrelevant. He has failed, *ex hypothesi*, to show any lawful justification for his indecent conduct.

In *Pratt*, D similarly had no lawful justification for his conduct; the fact that D suspected that the boys had stolen his property provides no justification in law for him to strip them naked to search them at gunpoint, particularly so where the property involved is something which it is illegal for D to possess. Lord Ackner's approval of *Pratt* accordingly is nonsensical; an example, perhaps, of unconscious judicial oversight.

It was stated above that P may not consent to an act the probable consequence of which is the infliction of bodily harm (*Donovan* [1934] 2 KB 498). What *mens rea* must be proved on the part of D in these circumstances? D would not intend to assault P as he believes P is consenting to his actions. One would assume, therefore, that it would have to be proved that D either intended to cause some injury or at least realised that such injury was likely; either state of mind would suffice to establish a battery in circumstances where the infliction of injury (for which there is no social justification) serves to cancel P's consent. Unfortunately, the Court of Appeal in *Boyea* [1992] Crim LR 574 have arrived at a different conclusion holding that all that need be proved is that bodily harm was objectively likely in the circumstances. The Court purported to rely on *Savage* (see 10.1.4.1 *ante*) where it was held that on a charge of assault occasioning actual bodily harm it was not necessary to prove that D intended to cause bodily harm or was reckless thereto if such harm was objectively likely in the circumstances. However, in *Savage* there was no doubt that D had committed an assault with the requisite *mens rea* which had caused actual bodily harm; the only question was whether subjective foresight of the risk of bodily harm had to be proved. In *Boyea* proof of an assault depended on there being bodily harm caused which would cancel P's consent. If proof of the objective likelihood of bodily harm suffices as the *mens rea* for indecent assault in these circumstances, D will be convicted without any proof as to his subjective state of mind. As assault is an offence which requires proof of intention or *Cunningham* recklessness this conclusion by the Court of Appeal is contrary to principle. If D does not foresee bodily harm his intention is merely to engage in consensual, non-injurious bodily contact; this does not amount to the *mens rea* of battery.

10.2.4.2 Indecency with children As an assault or battery is not committed where D invites V to touch him, the offence of indecent assault failed to provide protection for children invited to perform indecent acts where the invitation was not accompanied by force or the threat of force. In 1960 the Indecency with Children Act was passed. Section 1(1) provides:

> Any person who commits an act of gross indecency with or towards a child under the age of fourteen, or who incites a child under that age to such an act with him or another, shall be liable on conviction on indictment to imprisonment for a term not exceeding two years, or on summary conviction to imprisonment for a term not exceeding six months, to a fine not exceeding the prescribed sum, or to both.

This offence does not protect children over the age of fourteen and thus leaves a gap in the law as children under sixteen cannot give consent to acts of indecency. 'Gross indecency' is probably limited to acts involving genital contact. The offence may be committed both where the act actually takes place, for example D invites V to touch his penis and V does so, and where D merely incites V to perform the act. An act of gross indecency towards a child is one which does not involve any act on the part of the child, for example, if D masturbates in front of a child he would commit an act of gross indecency towards the child. The offence may be committed although D does no positive act if his inactivity is considered by the jury to amount to an invitation to the child to start, or to continue, conduct which is grossly indecent (see *Speck* [1977] 2 All ER 859).

Further reading

G. Williams, 'Force, injury and serious injury' (1990) 140 New LJ 1227.

M. Giles, 'Judicial law-making in the criminal courts: the case of marital rape' [1992] Crim LR 407.

I. Hare, '*R* v *Savage, DPP* v *Parmenter* — A Compelling Case for the Code' (1993) 56 MLR 74.

B. Bell & K. Harrison, '*R* v *Savage, DPP* v *Parmenter* and the Law of Assault' (1993) 56 MLR 83.

ELEVEN

Offences under the Theft Acts 1968 and 1978: theft and related offences

11.1 INTRODUCTION

In 1968 the Theft Act (hereafter referred to as TA 1968) was passed. For seven years the Criminal Law Revision Committee had considered the area of property offences, previously covered by the Larceny Act 1916. Appended to their *Eighth Report: Theft and Related Offences* (Cmnd 2977, 1966) was a draft Bill which, with some amendment, was passed by Parliament as the TA 1968. This Act was a new code which swept away the previous law creating a new range of offences which were framed, so far as possible, in simple language to avoid the technicality and complexity of the old law. The Theft Act 1978 (hereafter referred to as TA 1978) was passed to replace s. 16(2)(a) of the TA 1968 which had proved highly unsatisfactory. The TA 1978 also contains other provisions to fill some gaps left by the TA 1968.

While both Acts aimed to avoid technicality, problems have materialised. The Acts used words, like 'dishonestly', which the courts have sought to leave to juries to define. This creates a problem of inconsistency. A second problem, which also involves inconsistency, is that the courts in applying the law contained in the Acts have often done so in disregard of the civil law. Theft and related offences are concerned with interferences with the rights and interests others have in property. It would seem first to be necessary to determine to whom the property belonged; this cannot be done without reference to the civil law. Unfortunately the criminal courts have often disregarded the civil law in a misplaced desire to keep the criminal law simple. If a criminal statute uses civil law terms such as 'trust', 'trespasser', 'proprietary right or interest' or 'equitable interest', one would have thought that Parliament intended the recognised civil law meaning to apply. The result is that the law relating to offences against property remains confused, inconsistent and, at times, obscure.

11.2   THEFT

Section 1(1) TA 1968 provides that:

A person is guilty of theft if he dishonestly appropriates property belonging to another with the intention of permanently depriving the other of it; and 'thief' and 'steal' shall be construed accordingly.

The maximum penalty on conviction on indictment is ten years' imprisonment (s. 7 TA 1968).

Five facts must be proved to lead to a conviction of theft; three relate to *actus reus* and two to the *mens rea*. The *actus reus* consists in (i) the appropriation (ii) of property (iii) belonging to another. The *mens rea* consists in (i) the dishonest (ii) intention to permanently deprive the other of the property. These five elements of theft will be examined separately for convenience, but it should be noted that they are interconnected and sometimes difficult to separate.

11.2.1   *Actus reus*

11.2.1.1   Property   Conduct which may constitute 'appropriation' must occur in relation to 'property belonging to another'. It is important to determine firstly what constitutes property for the purposes of theft. The property which may be the subject of theft is defined by s. 4 of the TA 1968. Section 4(1) defines property to include 'money and all other property, real or personal, including things in action and other intangible property'. This is a sweeping definition subject to some limitation in the ensuing subsections relating to land, things growing wild on land and wild creatures. Subject to these exceptions, however, the only limitation is whether the property is capable of being appropriated. The provision does, however, merit further analysis.

11.2.1.1.1   Money   Money refers only to current coins and banknotes, including foreign coins and notes. While I may assert that I have £100 in my bank account, if D steals a cheque of £100 I have made payable to X, D has not stolen any money. He has stolen the cheque, which is a piece of paper; he only steals £100 when he cashes the cheque and receives coins or notes to that value (see *Davis* (1988) 88 Cr App R 347). The property in the bank in which I have a proprietary right or interest is not £100 in money but rather a debt of £100 owed me by the bank; a debt is a 'thing in action'.

11.2.1.1.2   Things in action and other intangible property   A thing in action is intangible property but not all items of intangible property are things in action. A 'thing in action' is a personal right of property which can only be claimed or enforced by legal action and not by taking physical possession (see *Torkington* v *Magee* [1902] 2 KB 427). Examples of things in action are debts, a right under a trust, a copyright or a trade mark, a credit balance in a bank account and a contractual right to overdraw the account. If D purports to sell my copyright in this book to X, this is appropriation of a thing in action belonging to me. If D takes a cheque from my chequebook and makes it payable to himself in the sum of £100, when he pays this cheque into his own bank account he will be appropriating a thing in action, namely the debt which the bank owes to me (see *Kohn* (1979) 69 Cr App R 395). On the other hand, if D knows that his own account is not in credit and he has no overdraft facility (or if he has exceeded the limit of his overdraft facility), and he writes a cheque for £50 on his own account made payable to X and backs it with a banker's card so that the bank is obliged to meet the cheque, D does not commit theft. Although the bank's funds will be diminished by this transaction, D has not appropriated a thing in action; he has not taken for himself or another someone else's right to sue as, prior to the cheque being written, there was no specific debt of £50 (or any greater amount of which it formed a part) owed by the bank to anyone (see *Navvabi* [1986] 3 All ER 102; but D may be liable for obtaining a pecuniary advantage by deception, see 12.6 *post*).

By s. 30 of the Patents Act 1977, a patent, or an application for a patent, is declared not to be a thing in action but it is personal property; it is 'other intangible property' and thus is capable of being stolen. An export quota issued by the government confers an expectation that a licence will be granted to export goods to the amount of the quota, but there is no legally enforceable right to such a licence and thus an export quota is not a thing in action. As a person with an export quota may sell it, it has been held that an export quota is 'other intangible property' and therefore capable of being stolen (See *A-G for Hong Kong* v *Nai-keung* (1987) 86 Cr App R 174). Confidential information, such as the questions on an examination paper, is not 'property' (see *Oxford* v *Moss* (1978) 68 Cr App R 183), and by analogy, trade secrets are not property. If D, however, takes the document on which the information is written, he may be guilty of theft of the document. By contrast, s. 7(2)(b) of the Patents Act 1977 treats an invention for which no patent has been granted or applied for as intangible property. As an invention is essentially information it is difficult to see why confidential information cannot constitute property; the information has value and that value will be lost or diminished if its confidentiality is lost. It is arguable that if D takes that information (for example, by making a copy of the document), while he does not deprive P of the information he does deprive him of its secrecy which is an intangible quality giving the information value. It is argued by Griew, *The Theft Acts 1968 & 1978* (6th edn), that confidential information is not capable of being appropriated (paras. 1-139). While Griew's view is worthy of consideration, it is submitted that it is not necessarily correct. To read confidential information is to assume a right of an owner as it is the right of the owner to determine who should have access to it; it is arguable, therefore, that confidential information should be regarded as property which may be appropriated (see further *11.2.2.1.1 post*).

It appears that electricity is not 'other intangible property' as s. 13 TA 1968 creates a specific offence of dishonestly using, wasting or diverting electricity (see *Low* v *Blease* [1975] Crim LR 513). Thus, if D dishonestly reconnects his electricity supply after it has been cut off for non-payment of his electricity bill, he will commit this offence. Using a private telephone without authority also falls within the scope of this offence, as would switching on the appliances in P's home, when he is away, with the intention that he should incur higher electricity bills.

11.2.1.1.3 Limitations on the theft of land

Section 4(2) TA 1968 provides a general limitation that land cannot be stolen subject to three exceptions. Section 4(2) provides that, subject to certain exceptions, a 'person cannot steal land, or things forming part of land and severed from it by him or by his directions'. Thus, as a general rule, land is not stealable. If I dishonestly move my boundary fence to incorporate part of my neighbour's garden within my own garden, this will not constitute theft. Land for the purposes of s. 4(2), however, does not include incorporeal hereditaments. Thus easements, profits and rents are all capable of being stolen by anyone.

There are three exceptions to the general rule where land may be stolen. Firstly, under s. 4(2)(a), a person may steal land:

> when he is a trustee or personal representative, or is authorised by power of attorney, or as liquidator of a company, or otherwise, to sell or dispose of land belonging to another, and he appropriates the land or anything forming part of it by dealing with it in breach of the confidence reposed in him.

For example, if D is authorised as a trustee to sell 100 acres of land and he sells 99 acres and appropriates the remainder for himself, he would be guilty of theft of that acre of land.

Secondly, under s. 4(2)(b), a person may steal land:

> when he is not in possession of the land and appropriates anything forming part of the land by severing it or causing it to be severed, or after it has been severed.

This provision is subject to s. 4(3) below. The difficulty with it is in determining when something forms part of the land. If it is growing on the land or is a permanent structure or integral part of such a structure or a fixture it is part of the land. Thus, if I dig up my neighbour's rose bushes to plant them in my garden, I will be appropriating them by severing them from the land; similarly if I chop down one of his trees for firewood. If my neighbour digs up his rose bushes to move them to another part of the garden and I remove them, I will be appropriating something that has been severed. Likewise I will be appropriating property by severing it from the land where I remove the tiles from his roof or the topsoil from his garden. If, however, I am in possession of the land as a tenant or a licensee and I remove the topsoil or the rose bushes I will not be guilty of theft (but see s. 4(2)(c) *post*).

A further gloss has been added to this second exception by s. 4(3) which provides:

> A person who picks mushrooms growing wild on any land, or who picks flowers, fruit or foliage from a plant growing wild on any land, does not

(although not in possession of the land) steal what he picks, unless he does it for reward or for sale or for other commercial purpose.

For purposes of this subsection 'mushroom' includes any fungus, and 'plant' includes any shrub or tree.

If I uproot a sapling growing wild on my neighbour's land I will not be within this subsection as I am not picking from a plant but rather taking the whole plant; if done dishonestly this is theft. Similarly, if I chop down a tree growing wild for firewood I will not be within this subsection as chopping is not 'picking'; if done dishonestly this is theft. Apart from such examples, if I confine myself to picking from plants growing wild, for example, taking blackberries or mistletoe or flowers, or picking mushrooms, this will not be theft subject to a further exception. If I pick these items for a commercial purpose this will be theft provided dishonesty is also proven. D picks blackberries growing wild along a hedgerow to make blackberry jelly to sell at a 'Blue Peter Bring and Buy Sale'. The picking would thus be 'for sale' and D will be guilty of theft provided dishonesty is proved. A jury would be unlikely to find D dishonest in this case, but if D is a market trader picking wild mushrooms, mistletoe or blackberries for sale on his stall, his enterprise being of a more commercial nature may persuade a jury to find that this is dishonest.

Thirdly, under s. 4(2)(c), a person may steal land:

when, being in possession of the land under a tenancy, he appropriates the whole or part of any fixture or structure let to be used with the land.

If I am the tenant of the property and appropriate a fixture, such as a washbasin or a fireplace or the fitted kitchen cupboards, I will be guilty of theft. Similarly if I appropriate a structure such as a garden shed or a greenhouse. There is no need to prove a severance of the property in this case; it would be sufficient if I contracted with X to sell the fireplace or greenhouse to him. However, I will not be guilty of theft if I remove the topsoil or rose bushes. If a person in possession of the land as a licensee appropriates fixtures he will not be guilty of theft as he is not within the provision, but, if a licensee appropriates a greenhouse, as this is not part of the land, he will be guilty of theft. The distinctions highlighted here are fine and technical and reflect no distinction in culpability. It appears that the differences in liability between licensees and tenants is the result of legislative oversight rather than legislative intent.

Section 4(4) deals with the position of wild creatures. It provides:

Wild creatures, tamed or untamed, shall be regarded as property; but a person cannot steal a wild creature not tamed nor ordinarily kept in captivity, or the carcase of any such creature, unless either it has been reduced into possession by or on behalf of another person and possession of it has not since been lost or abandoned, or another person is in course of reducing it into possession.

The effect of this provision is to limit the circumstances in which theft of wild creatures may occur to the following cases:

(i)   If a creature is tamed or ordinarily kept in captivity it may be stolen. Thus animals kept in a zoo or wildlife safari park may be stolen, even if they escape, as they are ordinarily kept in captivity. If P tames a wild animal it may be stolen.

(ii)   Other wild creatures, including game, while at large are not owned by anyone, not even the landowner or someone with shooting rights on his land. But once an animal, or its carcass, has been reduced into possession by or on behalf of another, or while it is being reduced into possession, it may be stolen. If D takes a rabbit caught in a trap set by P, this will be theft as P was in the course of reducing it into possession. If D takes a pheasant shot by P, for example, before P's dog retrieves it or from the back of P's vehicle, this will be theft. If D, P's gamekeeper, shoots pheasant on P's instructions and keeps one for himself, this will be theft as he has reduced the pheasant into possession on behalf of another. If, after a day's shoot, a grouse is not retrieved and D finds it, this will not be theft as possession has been lost or abandoned.

11.2.1.2   Belonging to another   In order to be the subject of theft, the property D appropriates must, at the time of the appropriation, belong to another. The Theft Act is not concerned to protect only rights of ownership in property but also other interests in property. Accordingly s. 5(1) defines 'belonging' for the purposes of theft:

> Property shall be regarded as belonging to any person having possession or control of it, or having in it any proprietary right or interest (not being an equitable interest arising only from an agreement to transfer or grant an interest).

The different elements of this definition will be examined separately.

11.2.1.2.1   Possession or control

(a)   Possession   In the normal case a person who owns property also has possession of it. For example, P owns a tool hire business storing the tools at his shop. If D enters the shop and dishonestly appropriates a power drill he will be stealing from P the owner who has possession of the power drill at that moment. If P hires a lawnmower to Q, P retains the ownership of the lawnmower but Q has possession of it. If D dishonestly appropriates the lawnmower from Q's garage he will be stealing from both Q who has possession of it and P who has ownership of it. If Q's son R is mowing the lawn when D seizes the lawnmower from him, he will be stealing from R who has control of the lawnmower, if not possession of it, as well as from P and Q. The inclusion of 'possession and control' in the definition of 'belonging' serves two purposes. Firstly, if someone has possession or control of the article it absolves the prosecution from having to prove who the legal owner of the article was at the moment of appropriation. Secondly, a person with a greater interest in property may steal from a person with a lesser interest. If during the period of hire, P had removed the lawnmower from Q's garage he could be convicted of

theft provided he had done so dishonestly. For example, he may have taken the lawnmower as a preliminary to demanding payment from Q for the cost of replacing it or so that he could obtain the hire fee from another customer. In *Turner (No. 2)* (1971) 55 Cr App R 336, the Court of Appeal, in an ill-considered judgment, appears to have extended liability further. D left his car at P's garage for repair. When he completed the repair P parked the car on the road outside the garage. D, using his spare set of keys, removed the car without paying for the repair. P had a lien on the car entitling him to retain possession of it until the repair bill had been paid. The judge directed the jury to ignore the question of liens and D was convicted of theft. If lien was ignored P was a bailee at will. Bailment at will may be terminated at any time by the bailor. The Court of Appeal held, however, that the words 'possession or control' were not to be qualified in any way. The decision creates obvious problems for a bailor who now may be liable for theft of his own goods if he terminates a bailment at will by surreptitiously removing the goods from the bailee's possession, even though the bailee could not have prevented the bailor from doing so had he done it openly (cf. *Meredith* [1973] Crim LR 253).

(b)   Control The problem sometimes arises of determining whether property belongs to anyone. A person may be in control of property without knowing that he possesses it. Generally the owner of land is in 'control' of any property on his land even if he does not know it is there. In *Woodman* [1974] QB 754, English China Clays sold all the scrap metal on its site to another company which removed the bulk of it but left some behind which was too inaccessible to remove economically. ECC, believing that all the metal had been removed, erected a barbed wire fence and notices warning trespassers to keep out. D entered the site and removed the remaining scrap metal. D was convicted of theft. The Court of Appeal upheld that conviction as there was ample evidence that ECC were in control of the site, had sought to exclude trespassers and thus were prima facie in control of property on the site. The Court did go on to say that if a third party had, for example, hidden explosives or drugs on the site and the occupier had no means of knowledge, this would rebut the general presumption that the occupier had control.

(c)   Abandonment If property is lost, for example P's wallet falls out of his jacket pocket, P continues to possess it until someone else assumes control of it. The wallet still belongs to P and may, in certain circumstances, be stolen by a finder (see *11.2.2.2.1 post*). The position is different, however, if P abandons his property, for example, where P buys a new wallet and throws his old wallet into a hedge the old wallet ceases to belong to anyone and thus cannot be the subject of theft. Property will be regarded as abandoned only when the owner is indifferent as to what becomes of it. Abandonment is not readily inferred by the courts. The fact that P has no further use for it is not conclusive. Thus if P had put the wallet in his dustbin rather than throwing it away, he would not be abandoning it as he would be putting it there to be collected by the council refuse collectors rather than presenting an invitation to others to take it (see *Williams* v *Phillips* (1957) 41 Cr App R 5).

11.2.1.2.2 Proprietary right or interest A full examination of the civil law relating to property would be necessary to explain proprietary rights or interests; this is outside the scope of this book. It is proposed to examine briefly some of the situations which may arise.

(a) The owner A person with a proprietary right or interest in property includes the legal owner of the property but this concept is wider than that of ownership. If a co-owner sells property without the other co-owner's consent, or if a partner sells partnership property without his partner's consent, this will be theft as each co-owner or partner has a proprietary right in the property which is defeated by such a sale (see *Bonner* [1970] 2 All ER 97).

(b) Equitable interests While a trustee is the legal owner of property, the beneficiaries under the trust have equitable interests in the property. Thus, if a trustee dishonestly appropriates trust property this will be theft from the beneficiaries as persons with proprietary interests. Similarly, if an executor dishonestly appropriates property under a will, this will be theft from the legatee(s).

Section 5(1) excludes from the meaning of property belonging to another 'an equitable interest arising only from an agreement to transfer or grant an interest'. For example, D contracts to transfer shares to P who pays for them. Before the transfer is effected D transfers the shares to Q. As P, until the transfer is executed, has only an equitable interest in the shares, D is not guilty of theft of the shares. Depending on what D has done, or intends to do, with the money P has paid him, he may be guilty of theft of the money or obtaining property by deception.

A particular problem which has arisen relates to constructive trusts. A constructive trust is one imposed by the principles of equity in order to satisfy the demands of justice and good conscience without reference to any presumed intention of the parties, for example, where a person in a fiduciary position makes a profit a constructive trust is imposed. In *A-G's Reference (No. 1 of 1985)* [1986] QB 491, D, the manager of a tied public house, was obliged by his contract of employment with P Brewery to obtain all liquor from them and pay all takings into their bank account. D secretly bought beer elsewhere and sold this keeping the profits. If he was the constructive trustee of these profits holding them on behalf of P, he could be guilty of theft. The Court of Appeal held there was no constructive trust, but even if there was, a constructive trust would not create a proprietary interest covered by s. 5(1). To exclude constructive trusts from the purview of s. 5(1) would seem to involve adding words to the statutory language which, it is submitted, is not an apropriate task for a court. The authority of this decision, however, is now in doubt. In *Shadrokh-Cigari* [1988] Crim LR 465, the Court of Appeal applied the principle derived from the civil case of *Chase Manhattan Bank N.A.* v *Israel-British Bank (London) Ltd* [1981] Ch 105 that where P transfers property to D under a mistake of fact, P retains an equitable proprietary interest in the property transferred. If D subsequently dishonestly appropriates the property he will be guilty of theft. If P retains an equitable interest in the property it must be because the demands of justice and good conscience impose a constructive trust (see further *11.2.1.3.3 post*).

11.2.1.3   Special cases   Although s. 5(1) of the TA 1968 is quite widely drafted there are certain cases which it has been considered appropriate to label as theft, even though the property in question does not belong to another. In these cases, others either suffer loss or D makes an unconscionable gain, although technically the property with which D is dealing legally belongs to him.

11.2.1.3.1   Trust property   Section 5(2) provides:

> Where property is subject to a trust, the persons to whom it belongs shall be regarded as including any person having a right to enforce the trust, and an intention to defeat the trust shall be regarded accordingly as an intention to deprive of the property any person having that right.

Under s. 5(1) property in a trust is regarded as belonging to both the trustees and the beneficiaries. However, there are some trusts which do not have specific beneficiaries. Charitable trusts do not have specific beneficiaries who could enforce the trust so, if trustees dishonestly appropriated the property of the trust, it would not be property belonging to another. Charitable trusts are enforceable, however, by the Attorney-General and thus this provision deems him to have a beneficial interest in the trust property so that theft by a trustee is theft from him.

11.2.1.3.2   Property received under an obligation   Section 5(3) provides:

> Where a person receives property from or on account of another, and is under an obligation to the other to retain and deal with that property or its proceeds in a particular way, the property or proceeds shall be regarded (as against him) as belonging to the other.

This provision is designed to deal with the situation where D receives property from or on account of P and, in so doing, he obtains not only possession but also legal ownership of the property. It may be that P retains an equitable interest (see *11.2.1.2.2 ante*) but the subsection is designed to avoid the necessity for complex technical analysis. Thus cases which fall within s. 5(3) are probably also covered already by s. 5(1). Section 5(3) would apply where D receives property from P who attaches to it a requirement that he use it in a particular way. For example, P employs D to paint his house and gives him a cheque for £50 to buy paint. D obtains possession and ownership of the cheque but he is under a legal obligation to use the 'proceeds' of that cheque to buy paint. If D cashes the cheque and uses the proceeds to bet on a horse he will be guilty of theft. Alternatively, if he cashes the cheque, buys the paint and uses it to paint his own house, while he has applied the money for the correct purpose of buying paint, he has appropriated the proceeds of the original cheque by using the paint on his own house. By contrast, if P had paid D a deposit of £50 without imposing any obligation on D on how this money was to be used, D would be free to do with it whatever he liked. Even if he never painted P's house he would not be guilty of theft as there was no legal obligation to use that money or its proceeds in a particular way, although if it was his intention at the outset not to paint the house this might be theft or the offence of obtaining property by deception.

In *Hall* [1973] QB 126, D, a travel agent received deposits and payments from clients who had booked air trips to America. D paid the money into the firm's general account but never arranged the trips and was unable to repay the money. His conviction of theft was quashed, however, as it was not proved that he was under an obligation to the clients to retain and deal with the money in a particular way. It would have been different if D had been under an obligation to preserve the money in a separate fund (see *Brewster* (1979) 69 Cr App R 375). A case which contrasts with *Hall* is that of *Hassall* (1861) Le & Ca 56. D was the treasurer of a club into which members paid money each week on the understanding that D would return the money to each member at Christmas. D became the legal owner of the money as it was never expected that he would return the identical coins to each member. However, it is a situation where D is expected to retain the property or its proceeds and deal with it in a particular way. If he dishonestly appropriates it he will be guilty of theft.

Section 5(3) also covers the situation where D receives money on account of P. For example, if D is employed as P's agent to collect the rent from tenants of property owned by P, the tenants will pay the money to D on account of P. If D dishonestly appropriates this money he may be guilty of theft depending upon the nature of the arrangements operating between himself and P. If D is under an obligation to maintain a distinct fund containing the money obtained from the tenants and pay this over to P, D will be guilty of theft. By contrast, if D is merely under a duty to account to P in due course for an equivalent sum (less any commission) there will be no obligation to retain and deal with the property in a particular way; the relationship is merely that of debtor and creditor. Thus, if D was the rent agent for several property owners and paid all rent collected into one account from which he withdrew his commission and then subsequently paid each property owner the amounts they were due, he would not be guilty of theft if he absconded with the money he collected (see *Robertson* [1977] Crim LR 629). In *Lewis* v *Lethbridge* [1987] Crim LR 59, D obtained sponsorship for a particular charity to be paid if X ran the London Marathon. D collected the sponsorship money but did not pay the charity. It was held that there was no obligation upon D to maintain a fund consisting of the money collected or its proceeds; his relationship with the charity was merely that of debtor and creditor. By contrast, if D used a charity's collecting box to collect for it and then appropriated the contents, he would be guilty of theft as he would be obliged to deal with the contents in a particular way. (There would probably be no need to resort to s. 5(3) in the latter case as the box would belong to the charity, D being merely a bailee, and the contents also would belong to it just as the contents of a telephone call box belong to the telephone company (cf. *Martin* v *Marsh* [1955] Crim LR 781)).

While civil law may place D under an obligation to account for property in particular circumstances, this will not necessarily bring D within the reach of s. 5(3). At civil law, an employee who takes a bribe or makes a secret profit by misusing his employer's property or his own position is bound to account to his employer for the profit. This duty to account, however, only creates the relationship of debtor and creditor; D does not receive the bribe 'on account of' the employer (*Powell* v *McRae* [1977] Crim LR 571), nor the profit 'on account of' the employer (*A-G's Reference (No. 1 of 1985)* [1986] QB 491).

It is difficult to formulate any general rules in relation to s. 5(3) as each case will hinge upon its own particular facts. The obligation upon D, however, must be a legal obligation (see *Gilks* (1972) 56 Cr App R 734; *Mainwaring* (1981) 74 Cr App R 99).The judge must initially decide whether the possible facts are capable of being construed to give rise to a legal obligation. It is then for the jury to determine what the actual facts of the case are; if they fall within those that would give rise to a legal obligation, they then have to consider whether the other criteria for theft are established. If they do not, they should acquit D. The legal obligation should exist at the time D dishonestly appropriates the property or its proceeds. This last proposition, however, appears to conflict with the case of *Meech* [1974] QB 549. P gave D a cheque which D agreed to cash and pay the proceeds to P. D then discovered that P had obtained the cheque by fraud. Together with E and F, D planned to stage a fake robbery so that he could tell P that the money had been stolen. D, E and F were convicted of theft of the money being the proceeds of property that D had received from P under an obligation within s. 5(3). It was argued on appeal that P could not have enforced any such obligation having acquired the cheque illegally. The Court of Appeal, turning the law on its head, concluded that the question was to be looked at from D's point of view; he initially assumed an obligation which he believed was legally binding. But the fact that D believes an element of the *actus reus* of an offence exists does not render him guilty of that offence (as opposed to an attempt to commit it) if that element does not exist in fact. It was further argued by D that, as at the time of appropriation (which the Court had held to be when D, E and F divided the proceeds from the cashing of the cheque), D knew the truth, he was not then under any 'obligation'. Again, amazingly, the Court held that the crucial time was 'the time of the creation or acceptance of the obligation'. But, if there was no obligation at the time of the appropriation, there was no property deemed to belong to another. It is essential for the commission of theft that the property belong to another at the time of the dishonest appropriation. Doubtless D, E and F had criminal intentions, and may indeed have been guilty of attempted theft or conspiracy to steal, but this does not justify the Court of Appeal throwing principle out of the window in order to uphold the convictions of those it considers to be undeserving appellants.

11.2.1.3.3 Property 'got' by another's mistake   Section 5(4) provides:

Where a person gets property by another's mistake, and is under an obligation to make restoration (in whole or in part) of the property or its proceeds or of the value thereof, then to the extent of that obligation the property or its proceeds shall be regarded (as against him) as belonging to the person entitled to restoration, and an intention not to make restoration shall be regarded accordingly as an intention to deprive that person of the property or proceeds.

This provision is designed to cover the situation where P transfers property to D under a mistake which does not operate to prevent ownership of the property passing to D. In many cases this provision is not necessary. For example, if P intends to lend E his book but by mistake he lends it to D (E's twin brother), as P only intended to pass possession and not ownership to E, D has only received possession of the book and P retains the proprietary right of ownership under s. 5(1). If D subsequently dishonestly appropriates the book, for example, by selling it, he will have stolen it from P. If P intended to transfer ownership but acts under a mistake known to D, for example he mistakes D for E or he mistakenly hands D the wrong book, such a mistake prevents ownership in the property passing to D, so if D dishonestly appropriates it he commits theft. In some situations, however, P's mistake will not prevent legal ownership in the property passing to D. In such a situation D may commit theft of the property, its proceeds or value thereof, if he dishonestly appropriates it being under a legal obligation to restore it to P.

An example of a situation covered by s. 5(4) would be that disclosed by the facts in *Moynes* v *Cooper* [1956] 1 QB 439. D, having received a partial advance on his week's wages, was paid his full wages by the wages clerk. When D opened his wage packet he discovered the mistake but decided to keep the money he had been overpaid. D was acquitted of larceny. The wages clerk had transferred ownership of the money to D so D could not steal what was his own property. Under s. 5(4), D would be guilty of theft as he would be under a legal obligation to make restitution of the part, or value thereof, overpaid. In *A-G's Reference (No. 1 of 1983)* [1985] QB 182, this provision was held to cover the case where an employee received an overpayment of wages by means of a direct debit transaction between the employer's account and the employee's account. In this case, the thing in action, the debt owed by the bank to D, to the value of the overpayment, had been 'got' by the employer's mistake, and D was under an obligation to make restitution of that amount to her employer. If D had spent all the money in her account on drinking and gambling before realising that she had been overpaid, a subsequent refusal to restore the sum overpaid to the employer could not amount to theft as there would no longer be property (in this case a thing in action in the form of the debt owed by the bank to D) which D could appropriate. If, however, D had bought jewellery this would represent the proceeds of the overpayment in which the employer would have a proprietary interest and which D could steal.

In *Davis* (1988) 88 Cr App R 347, D was in receipt of housing benefit. By computer error he received additional cheques, some before and some after his entitlement to benefit had ceased. While a machine cannot make a mistake a computer error is the manifestation of a human error, namely that of the operator. D could have been charged with theft of the cheques (which would have fallen within s. 5(1)) but the prosecution charged him with theft of the money he received when he cashed the cheques. His conviction of theft was upheld as the cash represented the proceeds of the cheques and he was under an obligation to make restoration of the proceeds of all cheques paid after entitlement to benefit ceased and of the amount by which he was overpaid while entitled to benefit.

D will be guilty of theft only where there is a legal obligation to make restitution; a moral obligation will not suffice. In *Gilks* (1972) 56 Cr App R 734, D had won £10.62 betting on horses. When he claimed his winnings the betting shop manager paid him £117.25 mistakenly believing he had backed one more winner than he had. D realised the mistake but decided to keep the overpayment. He was convicted of theft. The Court of Appeal held that the conviction could not be sustained under s. 5(4) as 'obligation' meant 'legal obligation' and gaming transactions were not legally enforceable. The Court upheld the conviction, however, relying on an old case, *Middleton* (1873) LR 2 CCR 38, stating that, as the property had been transferred under a mistake, ownership did not pass, so the property belonged to the betting shop when D decided to keep it. In *Middleton*, however, the mistake was as to identity of the recipient of the overpayment; there was no such mistake in this case. Nor was there a mistake as to the amount paid; the manager paid D the sum he intended to pay him. There would only have been a mistake as to the property if he had miscounted or mistaken, for example, a £20 note for a £10 note. The ratio of the case is thus wrong. If such a situation were to recur it is submitted that a conviction might be secured under *Shadrokh-Cigari* [1988] Crim LR 465, on the basis that where property is obtained as a result of a mistake on P's part, P retains an equitable interest in the property or its proceeds. Thus, although D may become the legal owner he may steal from P who retains a proprietary interest in the property (see *11.2.1.2.2 ante*). This rule is still in the course of developing and it is submitted that it should be confined to mistakes as to the identity of the recipient or the property transferred (which are already adequately covered) or mistake on P's part that he is under an obligation to transfer the property to D (as was the case in *Shadrokh-Cigari*). It should not be extended to cover other mistakes, for example, where P gives D a painting believing it has little value, although D knows that it is valuable. If D sells the painting he is currently guilty of no offence and should not become so by any further extension of the rule in the absence of legislative intervention.

11.2.1.4   The property must belong to another at the time of appropriation   The fact that property at one time belonged to P does not mean that it necessarily continued to belong to him at the time D did the act alleged to constitute an appropriation of it. In some situations it will be important to determine when ownership in property passes. This will involve the law of contract and sale. The general rule stated in s. 17 of the Sale of Goods Act 1979 is that the property (i.e. ownership) in goods passes to the buyer at the time the parties intend it to pass. In the case of shops, the courts attribute to the parties the intention that ownership shall pass only on payment by the customer. If D dishonestly removes goods from a shop without paying for them he will be appropriating property belonging to another. By contrast, where D fills his tank with petrol at a self-service station and then decides to make off without paying for the petrol, this is not theft as under s. 18, Rule 5 of the 1979 Act, property in the petrol (i.e. ownership of it) passed to him at the time of filling his tank; when he drives off the petrol is his (see *Edwards* v *Ddin* (1976) 63 Cr App R 218; but D would now be guilty of making off without payment under s. 3 TA 1978). In the case of other sales, s. 18, Rule 1 of the 1979 Act provides that ownership may pass under a contract of sale as soon as the contract is made and before the price has been paid. Thus, if this was the intention of the parties and P hands over the property to D and D then absconds with it, this would not be theft as the property D appropriated was his own as it belonged to him from the time the contract was concluded.

In seeking to determine when ownership was intended to pass 'regard shall be had to the terms of the contract, the conduct of the parties and the circumstances of the case' (s. 17(2) of the 1979 Act). In *Dobson* v *General Accident Fire and Life Assurance Corporation* [1990] QB 274, P offered for sale some jewellery which X agreed to buy and pay for by a building society cheque. The cheque had been stolen and thus was invalid. When P sought to claim under his insurance policy with D, D refused to pay arguing that the property had not been stolen but obtained by deception. The Court of Appeal held that there had been a theft. Looking at the facts they found that property was not intended to pass except in exchange for a valid cheque. Thus when X took delivery of the jewellery it was property belonging to another and he appropriated it at that point. The contract had been induced by X's fraud and thus was voidable. Property does pass under a voidable contract. In this case the very act which passed the property to X, delivery, was also X's appropriation of it, and at that time it still belonged to P. The act by which P divested himself of ownership of the property, delivery, also involved X assuming ownership of the property. In support of his view that it is no defence to say that property has passed under the terms of a voidable contract, Parker LJ quoted from the speech of Lord Roskill in *Morris* [1984] AC 320, at p. 334:

> I respectfully suggest that it is on any view wrong to introduce into this branch of the criminal law questions whether particular contracts are void or voidable on the grounds of mistake or fraud or whether any mistake is sufficiently fundamental to vitiate a contract. These difficult questions should so far as possible be confined to those fields of law to which they are immediately relevant and I do not regard them as relevant questions under the Theft Act 1968.

In *Gomez* [1992] 3 WLR 1061, Lord Keith of Kinkel approved of Parker LJ's reasoning, finding further support for this position in the speech of Viscount Dilhorne in *Lawrence* [1972] AC 626, at p. 633, who stated that '"belonging to another" in section 1(1) and in section 15(1) in my view signifies no more than that, at the time of the appropriation or the obtaining, the property belonged to another'. It seems that what is important is the history of the property up to the moment when the rogue appropriates it. If it belonged to someone other than the rogue then that is sufficient to satisfy the requirements of the Act. Whether or not the rogue had acquired a voidable title to the property is treated as irrelevant. It follows from this (and the decision of their Lordships in relation to the issue of consent, see *11.2.1.5.2 post*) that the person who fills his car with petrol at a self-service filling-station intending not to pay for it, appropriates property belonging to another as up to the point when the petrol enters his tank it belongs to another. As a result, it appears that in all contractual situations involving deception by D where property is intended to pass under the contract, D may be convicted of either theft or obtaining property by deception contrary to s. 15 TA 1968.

11.2.1.5 Appropriation The definition of theft requires that D appropriate property belonging to another. The simplest example of appropriation is where D surreptitiously removes P's wallet from his pocket. It is not every appropriation, however, which amounts to theft; the appropriation must be accompanied by dishonesty and an intention to permanently deprive the owner of the property. Thus the pickpocket who intends to spend the money he finds in P's wallet would have the necessary *mens rea*. By contrast, if D is P's son, and is removing the wallet as an April Fools' Day prank, with no intention to permanently deprive his father of it, there would be no theft, not because of a lack of appropriation, but because of the absence of *mens rea*.

When the Criminal Law Revision Committee, in its *Eighth Report, Theft and Related Offences* (Cmnd 2977, 1966), framed the concept of 'dishonest appropriation' it did so in the hope and belief that this concept would be easily understood without the aid of further definition (see para. 34). Unfortunately, it is only after twenty-four years of confusion arising from two apparently conflicting House of Lords decisions and numerous conflicting Court of Appeal and Divisional Court decisions, that the meaning of the word 'appropriation' has finally been resolved in the House of Lords decision in *Gomez* [1992] 3 WLR 1061.

11.2.1.5.1 Assuming the rights of an owner Section 3(1) of the TA 1968 provides:

> Any assumption by a person of the rights of an owner amounts to an appropriation, and this includes, where he has come by the property (innocently or not) without stealing it, any later assumption of a right to it by keeping or dealing with it as owner.

For the moment we are concerned only with the first part of this definition; cases of later assumption of rights to property will be dealt with later (see *11.2.1.5.4 post*). The phrase 'any assumption of the rights of an owner' cannot mean that D actually acquires rights of ownership; rather it suggests that he seeks to assert or exercise these rights, that is that he deals with the property as if he was the owner. The idea which this seeks to convey is that of *usurpation* (in the sense of substitution without necessarily implying any notion of the wrongful ousting of the owner) in that D seeks to occupy the owner's place in relation to the property. The principal rights of the owner are, for example, to possess, use, consume, sell, hire, lend or destroy his property. It should be noted, however, that the offence of theft protects not just ownership but also lesser interests such as possession or control. Thus the act of an owner designed to usurp or defeat the interests of another in the owner's property may amount to theft. For example, if D hires a lawnmower to P he has divested himself of his right to possession of the lawnmower for the period of hire. If D dishonestly removes the lawnmower from P's possession prior to the expiry of the hire period, he will be usurping P's right to possession (see *Turner (No. 2) 11.2.1.2.1 ante*). Similarly, if E removes it from P intending to return it to him after the period of hire has expired, he will be assuming a right of an owner, namely possession.

A problem which s. 3(1) presents is that it states that any assumption by a person of 'the rights of an owner' amounts to an appropriation. In some cases, however, only one such right is assumed, namely, possession. In *Morris* [1984] AC 320, two appeals were heard by the House of Lords relating to dishonest shoppers in supermarkets who had switched the price labels on goods intending to buy the goods at a lower price at the till. In one case D was arrested after paying the lower price while in the other case E was arrested before he paid the lower price. In the first case D would, if charged, have been liable to conviction of obtaining property by deception contrary to s. 15 TA 1968. In the second case he may have reached the point of attempting the s. 15 offence. In both cases, however, the accused were charged with theft. It was clearly one of the owner's rights to fix the price at which his property would be sold. Switching the price labels was an assumption of this right and it did not matter that the dishonest shoppers had not yet assumed all the owner's rights. Lord Roskill stated (at pp. 331-332) that it is sufficient to prove that an accused assumed *any* of the rights of an owner. This is a necessary construction of the provision as there are cases where D has clearly not assumed some of the owner's rights. For example, D may appropriate property without ever being in possession of it, as where D offers to sell, without authority, P's goods to E; at that point D is assuming a right of the owner, namely to sell his property (see *Pitham and Hehl* (1976) 65 Cr App R 45). A problem with this decision, however, is that P knew D was not the owner of the goods, and D knew that P knew this; on its actual facts, therefore, it would appear that D did not truly assume the rights of an owner, but this should not be taken to undermine the general principle. In such a case the theft is committed at the time of the offer to sell; it does not matter that P was never deprived of his property (although it must, of course be proved that D intended to permanently deprive P of his property).

The decision in *Morris* has important implications relating to when and where theft is committed. If D draws an unauthorised cheque on P's bank account, making it payable in favour of himself or in favour of E and presents it to E, D is assuming the rights of an owner as he is doing that which only an owner is entitled to do (see *Kohn* (1979) 69 Cr App R 395; *Governor of Pentonville Prison, ex parte Osman* (1989) 90 Cr App R 281). The property D is appropriating is the debt owed by the bank to P. The offence of theft of this thing in action occurs when D delivers the cheque to E, even if it is never presented (see *Osman*; this case actually involved sending telex instructions to debit P's account) or, if the cheque is made out in his own favour, when D presents it (see *Chan Man-sin* [1988] 1 All ER 1). The offence is committed where D delivers or presents the cheque even though the account may be held in a bank outside the jurisdiction (see *Osman*). If the bank honours such a cheque and debits P's account, such a transaction is a complete nullity; P's rights against the bank remain exactly as before, that is, the debt owed him by the bank is in the same sum as stood in his account prior to the honouring of the unauthorised cheque (see *Chan Man-sin* v *A-G for Hong Kong*). Although P ends up not being deprived of anything by such a transaction, D remains guilty of theft as it is the appropriation which constitutes the *actus reus* of theft; there is no need to prove 'deprivation'. These principles also cover other transactions. In the example above, if D purports to sell P's property to E, the appropriation occurs where the offer to sell is made even though the property may be situate outside the jurisdiction.

11.2.1.5.2 Consent and appropriation The major problem in relation to appropriation has been whether there could be an appropriation where the owner of the property had consented to the 'taking' of it by the alleged thief. In *Gomez* [1992] 3 WLR 1061, as with *Lawrence* [1972] AC 626 and *Dobson* v *General Accident Fire and Life Assurance Corp plc* [1990] QB 274 (see 11.2.1.4 *ante*) the owner consented to the taking of the property but only because of a deception practised upon him by the rogue. While these facts would support a conviction for the offence of obtaining property by deception contrary to s. 15(1) of the Theft Act 1968, would they also enable a conviction to be obtained for the simple offence of theft contained in s. 1(1))? *Lawrence* suggested an affirmative answer while *Morris* had been construed as suggesting the contrary.

In *Gomez* the accused was the assistant manager of an electrical goods shop. X approached him seeking to acquire goods from the shop in exchange for two building society cheques which were stolen. The cheques were undated and bore no payee's name. Gomez approached the manager seeking his authorisation for a sale totalling the amount of £7,950, the amount of one of the cheques. The manager instructed him to confirm with the bank that the cheque was acceptable. Gomez later falsely told the manager that the bank had said the cheque was 'as good as cash'. The sale was authorised and the goods were duly supplied to X. A few days later Gomez presented the manager with the second cheque which was in the amount of £9,250 in support of a further sale and again this transaction was authorised by the manager and the goods supplied to X. Several days later the cheques were returned marked 'Orders not to pay. Stolen cheque'. Gomez was convicted of theft. The Court of Appeal quashed his conviction on the basis that there was no appropriation at the moment when X took possession of the goods because he was entitled to do so under a contract of sale (which although voidable had not been avoided at the time). The Court of Appeal took the view that the manager's consent and authority negated the element of appropriation. In reaching its decision the Court purported to follow *Morris* although the question of property being obtained by trickery had not been considered in that case. Lord Lane CJ, in dealing with the conflict between *Lawrence* and *Morris*, stated 'suffice it to say that if there is a difference between the two decisions, that was not the view taken by their Lordships in *R* v *Morris*, and that is the decision we must follow'.

The House of Lords gave the Crown leave to appeal and the Court of Appeal subsequently certified that a point of law of general public importance was involved in the decision, namely:

When theft is alleged and that which is alleged to be stolen passes to the defendant with the consent of the owner, but that has been obtained by a false representation, has (a) an appropriation within the meaning of section 1(1) of the Theft Act 1968 taken place, or (b) must such a passing of property necessarily involve an element of adverse interference with or usurpation of some right of the owner?

By a majority of four to one (Lord Lowry dissenting) their Lordships allowed the appeal and approved *Lawrence*, answering the certified question (a) in the affirmative and (b) in the negative. The leading speech was delivered by Lord Keith of Kinkel with whom Lords Jauncey of Tullichettle, Slynn of Hadley and Browne-Wilkinson agreed. His Lordship reviewed the earlier decisions of the House in *Lawrence* and *Morris* highlighting the conflict to which the two decisions gave rise.

In *Lawrence* D, a taxi-driver, was convicted of theft where he represented to P, his Italian passenger, that the £1 tendered was insufficient to cover the fare and removed a further £6 from the passenger's wallet, the true fare for the journey being 52p. D argued on appeal that the conviction of theft of this £6 could not stand as P had consented to him taking it. D was seeking to have the words 'without consent of the owner' implied into s. 1(1) TA 1968. The House of Lords rejected this argument stating that there may be an appropriation 'even though the owner has permitted or consented to the property being taken'. At the time D removed the money from the wallet, it was property belonging to P. In removing it D was doing something which only an owner could do. His removal of the money constituted an appropriation. Whether this was theft would hinge on whether D was dishonest. He would not have been dishonest if he believed that P, knowing the circumstances (i.e. that he was being charged a fare far in excess of the legal fare) consented to his appropriation of the money. Viscount Dilhorne stated (at p. 632):

Belief or the absence of belief that the owner had with such knowledge consented to the appropriation is relevant to the issue of dishonesty, not to the question whether or not there has been an appropriation.

The consequence of this is that if A gives to B a book telling B to keep it, in taking it B appropriates it as he assumes the rights of an owner over the book. This is not theft, however, as B is not dishonest. When D took the £6 from the wallet he appropriated it whether or not P consented to him taking it. D was dishonest because he did not believe that P knew the circumstances and, with that knowledge, consented to the £6 being taken.

Viscount Dilhorne's view finds support in another provision of the act. Section 2(1)(b) provides that an appropriation of property is not to be regarded as dishonest if D appropriates the property in the belief that he would have the other's consent if the other knew of the appropriation and the circumstances of it. The section contemplates that an appropriation may be consented to.

In *Morris* the House of Lords did not question the decision in *Lawrence*, Lord Roskill taking the view that the facts of the case clearly disclosed a dishonest appropriation. Section 3(1) of the Theft Act 1968 provides that 'Any assumption by a person of the rights of an owner amounts to an appropriation . . .'. A question which arose in *Morris* was whether or not D had to assume all the rights of an owner in order to appropriate property. Lord Roskill answered this by stating:

[I]t is enough for the prosecution if they have proved . . . the assumption . . . of any of the rights of the owner of the goods in question . . .

In *Gomez*, after approving this dictum, Lord Keith proceeded to label as unnecessary and incorrect certain of the observations which Lord Roskill had made in his speech in *Morris*.

Firstly, Lord Roskill gave the example of the practical joker who switches price labels on items in a supermarket concluding that this act, without more, would not amount to an appropriation. Lord Keith was of opinion that label switching in itself constitutes an appropriation as it involves an assumption of one of the rights of the owner irrespective of whether or not it is accompanied by some other act. It is the absence of dishonesty and an intention to deprive the owner permanently of the property which renders the practical joker not guilty of theft. Lord Roskill's mistake was that he confused appropriation with theft, forgetting that acts which may constitute the *actus reus* of theft only amount to theft when accompanied by *mens rea*. His Lordship was particularly upset by the suggestion that an honest shopper removing goods from a supermarket shelf 'appropriates' them. But this should not have been a cause for concern as the honest shopper could not be guilty of theft. Lord Roskill, however, seemed to think some stigma attached to the word 'appropriation'. He would only consider including within his conception of 'appropriation' acts which, in themselves, evidence a dishonest intention, this is acts which may be considered wrongful in some way or other.

Secondly, and flowing directly from the previous point, Lord Roskill defined 'appropriation' pejoratively, stating that it 'involves not an act expressly or impliedly authorised by the owner but an act by way of adverse interference with or usurpation of those rights'. In response to this Lord Keith stated (at p. 1076):

While it is correct to say that appropriation for purposes of section 3(1) includes the latter sort of act, it does not necessarily follow that no other act can amount to an appropriation and in particular that no act expressly or impliedly authorised by the owner can in any circumstances do so. Indeed, *Lawrence v Commissioner of Metropolitan Police* is a clear decision to the contrary since it laid down unequivocally that an act may be an appropriation notwithstanding that it is done with the consent of the owner. It does not appear to me that any sensible distinction can be made in this context between consent and authorisation.

The distinction between consent and authorisation had been the basis of an attempt by Parker LJ in *Dobson v General Accident Fire and Life Assurance Corporation plc* to reconcile the two conflicting schools of thought following *Lawrence* and *Morris*. *Skipp* [1975] Crim LR 114 and *Fritschy* [1985] Crim LR 745 supported the *Morris* line of reasoning whereas *McPherson* [1973] Crim LR 191, approved in *Anderton v Wish* (1980) 72 Cr App R 23, at p. 25 supported the *Lawrence* line of reasoning. Parker LJ sought to distinguish the cases of *Skipp* and *Fritschy* on the basis that the owners of the goods in these cases had expressly authorised the physical acts of the defendants in that they had instructed them to take possession of the goods alleged to have been stolen and deal with them in a particular manner, rather than simply consenting to the defendants taking the goods. It is no longer necessary to attempt to make such fine distinctions; Lord Keith concluded that the decisions in *Skipp* and *Fritschy* were wrong as they were inconsistent with *Lawrence*. Lord Keith saw no purpose in referring to the Eighth Report of the CLRC concluding that (at p. 1080):

> The decision in *Lawrence* was a clear decision of this House upon the construction of the word 'appropriate' in section 1(1) of the Act, which had stood for twelve years when doubt was thrown upon it by obiter dicta in *Morris*. *Lawrence* must be regarded as authoritative and correct, and there is no question of it now being right to depart from it.

Lord Browne-Wilkinson made some additional observations on the reasoning in *Morris*. His Lordship highlighted the fact that s. 1(1) uses the composite phrase 'dishonest appropriation' observing that it is not every appropriation which could amount to theft but only 'dishonest appropriation'. By contrast he regarded Lord Roskill's definition of appropriation as, in reality, a definition of 'misappropriation', stating (at p. 1110):

> The concept of adverse interference with or usurpation of rights introduces into the word appropriation the mental state of both the owner and the accused. So far as concerns the mental state of the owner (did he consent?), the Act of 1968 expressly refers to such consent when it is a material factor: see sections 2(1)(b), 11(1), 12(1) and 13. So far as concerns the mental state of the accused, the composite phrase in section 1(1) itself indicates that the requirement is dishonesty ... I regard the word 'appropriation' in isolation as being an objective description of the act done irrespective of the mental state of either the owner or the accused.

It is now clear that 'appropriation' is a neutral word which describes the act of a person in relation to property belonging to another. It is not pejorative to say that a person is appropriating property; the stigma derives from the dishonest intention permanently to deprive the owner of his or her property.

It is clear following the decision in *Gomez* that the degree of overlap between theft contrary to s. 1 and obtaining property by deception contrary to s. 15 of the Theft Act 1968 is considerable. It had been suggested in argument before their Lordships that by following *Lawrence* rather than *Morris*, s. 15 would be rendered otiose since a person who, by deception, persuades an owner to consent to parting with his property will necessarily be guilty of theft within s. 1. An example of a situation which would constitute the s. 15 offence but which would not amount to theft, would be where D deceives P into sending him property. At the point when P despatches the property he passes ownership of it to D. At the time when D receives the property it belongs to him so he cannot appropriate it. He has, however, obtained it by deception. In his speech Lord Browne-Wilkinson provided a further example, namely where the property obtained is land which cannot be stolen (subject to the exceptions in s. 4(2) of the Theft Act 1968). For practical purposes, however, most s. 15 offences will also be thefts. This gives the prosecution considerable discretion in deciding which charge to level. Given that consent is irrelevant, it will be easier to prove theft than to prove the s. 15 offence which requires the prosecution to prove that P was deceived by D into parting with his property.

11.2.1.5.3 Appropriating company assets In law a company is a person. As a company may own property it may also be the victim of theft. A company, however, has no mind of its own; the board of directors is the directing mind and will of the company. A director who has authority to deal with the property of the company for the company's purposes can steal from the company where he applies company property for his own purposes 'dishonestly and in fraud of the company' (see *A-G for Hong Kong* v *Nai-keung* (1987) 86 Cr App R 174). A problem arises, however, where a company is wholly owned by one director or several directors. If the sole director, or all the directors together, apply company property for their own purposes, can he or they appropriate property with which he or they, as the mind and will of the company, have authorised him or them to deal? The dictum in *Morris* that 'appropriation involves not an act expressly or impliedly authorised by the owner . . .' spawned a number of conflicting decisions. In *Attorney-General's Reference (No 2 of 1982)* [1984] QB 624, the two defendants who were shareholders and directors of various companies were charged with theft from those companies. It was conceded by counsel that an appropriation had taken place and the case was argued on the sole issue of dishonesty. The Court of Appeal approved the concession that counsel had made and stated *obiter* that where all the directors and shareholders of a company acted illegally or dishonestly in relation to the company, their consent to the illegal or dishonest acts was not to be attributed to the company. In *McHugh and Tringham* (1988) 88 Cr App R 385, the Court of Appeal upheld a conviction of theft by a company director on the basis that the company had not authorised his actions. The Court stated as a proposition that '(4) An act done with the authority of a company cannot in general amount to an appropriation'. On the facts of the case the Court was not required to determine the correctness of this proposition. Mustill LJ, however, stated (at p. 394):

> If we had thought that this was a case of express authority, it would have been necessary to look closely at proposition (4) to work out the extent of the qualification which we have indicated by the words in general: for qualification there must be, since even an express authority which is either obtained by the actor with a view to abuse, or is actually abused, can scarcely render innocuous what would otherwise be a misappropriation.

By 'misappropriation' Mustill LJ presumably meant a 'dishonest appropriation'.

By contrast in the Supreme Court of Victoria in *Roffel* [1985] VR 511, it was held that a sole director and shareholder could not be convicted of theft of the company's assets because the company had consented to Roffel's acts thereby preventing an appropriation from taking place. In *Philippou* (1989) 89 Cr App R 290, the Court of Appeal upheld the convictions of two sole directors of three companies in the United Kingdom who had used assets of one of those companies to purchase property in Spain in the name of another company of which they were also the sole directors and shareholders. The Court of Appeal took the view that the purchase of the property in Spain for their own benefit displayed the directors' dishonest intention permanently to deprive the first company of its property which, in turn, indicated that the original transfer of funds was adverse to the company and thereby was an act without its consent amounting to a dishonest appropriation.

In *Gomez*, Lord Browne-Wilkinson stated that the decision in *Roffel* and the statement of principle in *McHugh and Tringham* (*viz.* proposition (4)) 'are not correct in law and should not be followed'. This was so whether or not the dictum in *Morris* was correct, his Lordship stating (at pp. 1110–1111):

> Where a company is accused of a crime the acts and intentions of those who are the directing minds and will of the company are to be attributed to the company. That is not the law where the charge is that those who are the directing minds and will have themselves committed a crime against the company . . . In any event, your Lordships' decision in this case, re-establishing as it does the decision in *Lawrence*, renders the whole question of consent by the company irrelevant. Whether or not those controlling the company consented or purported to consent to the abstraction of the company's property by the accused, he will have appropriated the property of the company.

His Lordship went on to conclude that in each case the question to be asked is whether or not the taking of the property from the company has been done dishonestly.

The speeches in *Gomez* make it clear that those who are the directing minds and wills of companies who use their position to pillage company assets have always been liable to convictions for theft on the basis of the ruling in *Attorney-General's Reference (No 2 of 1982)* irrespective of the decisions in either *Lawrence* or *Morris*. In deciding whether or not a company director could be convicted of theft it should not have been necessary to refer to either *Lawrence* or *Morris*, but the decision of the majority in *Gomez* puts the issue beyond doubt by making the question of consent irrelevant.

11.2.1.5.4   Appropriation by keeping or dealing   The second part of s. 3(1) TA 1968 deals with the situation where D originally comes by property without stealing it. A later assumption of a right to the property by keeping or dealing with it as owner amounts to an appropriation. For example, if P lends D his book for a week, D obtains possession of it but he is not a thief if he has no intention of depriving P of it. If, however, D subsequently decides to keep the book permanently or if he subsequently sells it (dealing with it), this conduct represents an appropriation as D is assuming the rights of an owner. The same would apply where D receives property as a result of a mistake by P of which D was unaware at the time. For example, P agrees to lend D his books on criminal law. He gives D a pile of books which D later discovers contains a book on contract. If D decides to keep this or otherwise deal with it he would be appropriating it at that time. Similarly if D finds a book and has no means of discovering its owner at the time this would not be theft. If, however, P later tells D that he has lost a book and the facts revealed indicate that the book lost was the one D found, a decision by D at that time to keep it would be an appropriation.

11.2.1.5.5   Excluding the bona fide purchaser from liability   Section 3(2) provides:

> Where property or a right or interest in property is or purports to be transferred for value to a person acting in good faith, no later assumption by him of rights which he believed himself to be acquiring shall, by reason of any defect in the transferor's title amount to theft of the property.

This provision excludes from liability bona fide purchasers who otherwise might be guilty of theft under s. 3(1) (see *11.2.1.5.4 ante*). For example, if D buys a car from E in good faith believing that E has good title to the car, D's subsequent discovery that E had stolen the car from P will not render D liable to conviction for theft if he then keeps the car. The relevant moment when considering D's belief is when he purchased the property (see *Adams* [1993] Crim LR 72). Should D in the above example decide to sell the car, impliedly representing thereby that he has good title to it, he would be liable for obtaining property by deception contrary to s. 15(1) TA 1968 if Q bought the car from him. This exception under s. 3(2) does not apply to anyone who does not acquire the property in good faith and for value. Thus, where E merely gave the car to D as a gift, he would be liable under s. 3(1) if, on discovering that the car was stolen, he decided to keep it. Similarly, if E, a thief, hires stolen property to D, D would be guilty of theft if he discovered that the property was stolen and then sold it or destroyed it, as he would be assuming rights which as a bailee he had not acquired when the initial bailment took place.

11.2.2 Mens rea

The *mens rea* of theft is made up of two elements: an intention of permanently depriving the owner of his property and dishonesty. It is important at the outset to make plain that both these states of mind must be proved. It should also be understood that while most thieves steal property for personal gain, this is not an element of the offence. Section 1(2) TA 1968 provides that 'it is immaterial whether the appropriation is made with a view to gain, or is made for the thief's own benefit'.

Thus D may be guilty of theft where he destroys P's property. In such a situation he will usually be charged with criminal damage contrary to s. 1 of the Criminal Damage Act 1971. If, however, P is simply deprived of the property without it being damaged, for example, D throws P's jewellery into the Thames, there is no criminal damage but there may be theft.

11.2.2.1 With the intention of permanently depriving the other of it

There is no requirement that P be actually deprived of his property permanently; the crucial question is what was D's intent at the time he appropriated the property? As a general rule, an intention to borrow the property cannot amount to an intention to permanently deprive. If, however, D takes P's money, intending to return to P an equivalent amount, D does have the requisite intention as he does not intend to return to P the exact coins or notes he removed. Where P has only a limited interest in the property, for example, where P has hired a lawnmower from Q for the weekend and D takes it knowing of P's limited interest and intending to return it on Monday, this would amount to an intention to permanently deprive P of his interest in the property. In this example, D steals from P because he intends to deprive P of his limited interest in the property; he does not steal from Q because there is no intention permanently to deprive Q of it. If D did not know the facts and, thinking that P owned the lawnmower, he took it intending to keep it for a week, this would not be theft even though P was permanently deprived of his interest in it.

In most cases, D's intention may be inferred from the circumstances. For example, if D takes P's wallet and spends the contents, or if he takes P's video recorder and sells it, or if he takes P's sandwiches and eats them, the evidence of an intention permanently to deprive P of his property is virtually irrefutable. In other cases, however, the correct inference to draw from the facts will not be so obvious. For example, if D removes P's book from his bag and is found reading it in the library, or if D removes P's bicycle from the cycle stands and is found riding it home, it is far from clear whether D was merely borrowing P's property or whether he intended to deprive P of it permanently. Further evidence would be necessary to found a charge of theft.

The issue of intention may usually be left to the jury without too much elaboration. Section 6 TA 1968, however, provides a partial definition of 'intention of permanently depriving'. Section 6 operates to deem a person's intention to amount to an intention to permanently deprive even though he may have intended to return the property or even had returned the property. The section should not be referred to if the issue of D's intention may be resolved without reference to it; it should be referred to in exceptional cases only (see *Lloyd* [1985] QB 829). There are two reasons for this: firstly, the section is only a partial definition designed to deal with a particular form of mischief; secondly, the section is particularly obscurely drafted. Regarding this latter point it should be noted that the section refers to 'property' and 'the thing itself', but appears to mean the same by both terms. In s. 6(1) the word 'meaning' is used as well as 'intention'; it appears that 'meaning' was used in the sense of 'intending'.

11.2.2.1.1   Section 6(1)   Section 6(1) provides:

A person appropriating property belonging to another without meaning the other permanently to lose the thing itself is nevertheless to be regarded as having the intention of permanently depriving the other of it if his intention is to treat the thing as his own to dispose of regardless of the other's rights; and a borrowing or lending of it may amount to so treating it if, but only if, the borrowing or lending is for a period and in circumstances making it equivalent to an outright taking or disposal.

This provision may be divided into two parts which will be examined separately.

(a)   Disposing of the property regardless of the other's rights   'A person . . . is . . . to be regarded as having the intention of permanently depriving the other of it if his intention is to treat the thing as his own to dispose of regardless of the other's rights.' In such cases, D may intend the property to be returned to P so that P is not actually deprived of it. D will be deemed to have the requisite intention, however, on the basis of his treating the property as his own to dispose of regardless of P's rights.

Several situations may fall within this provision. If D takes P's property intending to sell it back to P (the 'buy back principle', D will not intend to deprive P of it permanently, but he will be treating the property as his own to dispose of regardless of P's rights; it is one of the rights of the owner to sell his property (see *Hall* (1849) 1 Den 381). Similarly, if D takes P's property intending to return it only when P pays for it or fulfills some other condition (the 'ransom principle'), he will again be treating the property as his own to dispose of regardless of the other's rights: only an owner may attach conditions to the use or possession of his property (but cf. *Coffey* [1987] Crim LR 498). In *Lloyd* (*ante*), the Court of Appeal affirmed that these situations fell within s. 6(1). The Court, however, considered that s. 6(1) should be given a restricted meaning stating that they would endeavour to interpret the section so that 'nothing is construed as an intention permanently to deprive which would not prior to the 1968 Act have been so construed'. It was a requirement of larceny at common law and under the Larceny Act 1916 that D have an intention of permanently depriving P of his property. Other decisions of the Court of Appeal and of the Privy Council, however, have not taken so restrictive a view of s. 6. In *Downes* (1983) 77 Cr App R 260, D was in lawful possession of vouchers from the Inland Revenue which could be used to obtain certain exemptions from deduction of tax. D sold the vouchers to others who would then use them for this purpose. D was guilty of theft as although the vouchers which belonged to the Inland Revenue would return to them, D was treating them as his own to dispose of regardless of the other's rights by selling them. In *Chan Man-sin* v *A-G for Hong Kong* [1988] 1 All ER 1, D, a company accountant, drew a forged cheque on the company's account. If the fraud was discovered the company's credit balance would have to be restored by the bank as a debit made on a forged cheque is a nullity; but it was, of course, D's hope that the fraud would not be discovered. The Privy Council held that there was 'ample evidence' that D intended to treat the credit balance in the account (a thing in action) as his own to dispose of regardless of the company's rights.

Where P draws a cheque in favour of D, D may still steal it. For example, in anticipation of D performing a contract of service for P (such as painting his house), P writes out a cheque in favour of D for the sum agreed. D finds the cheque on P's desk and takes it without painting the house, goes to the bank and cashes it. As the cheque is a thing in action representing a debt owed by the bank to the payee, it is owned by the payee, in this case D. He cannot steal the thing in action as this belongs to him. When the cheque is paid it will be returned to P's bank and be available to him. The returned cheque will be stamped 'Paid' and thus will no longer be a thing in action. If D is to be liable for theft, it will be on the basis that the cheque will be returned to P only after P has paid for it, that is by the debiting of his account (see Smith, *The Law of Theft* (6th edn) para. 139 where the decision in *Duru* [1973] 3 All ER 715, is criticised). The same principle may be applied to the situation where D removes a ticket from a booking office for a pop concert. The organisers of the concert own the ticket which will be returned to them by D when he hands it to the attendant on the door to gain admission to the concert. The organisers, however, are effectively paying for the return of the ticket by providing D with admission to the concert. Smith states that the same principle would cover someone who takes, for example, milk tokens from a dairy intending to return them in exchange for milk.

In certain circumstances D's borrowing of P's property may fall within this part of s. 6(1). If D borrows P's book to read on a train or plane journey and, having read it, abandons it in the station or airport on his arrival at his destination, his abandonment would tend to show an indifference as to whether P recovers the book, particularly if there is little likelihood of P recovering it. He is dealing with it in a way in which only an owner may do and is treating it as his own to dispose of regardless of the owner's rights. In a case such as this there would not appear to be any need to resort to the second part of s. 6(1).

One final situation worth mentioning is where D purports to sell P's property to Q. By selling it D is appropriating it. He may have no intention that P be deprived of his property; his intention rather being that he deprive Q of his money by means of the deception. His case does, however, fall within s. 6(1) as he is treating the property as his own to dispose of regardless of P's rights and thus 'is . . . to be regarded as having the intention of permanently depriving the other of it'. If there was no risk of P ever being deprived of his property this may be stretching the bounds of theft too far. A more appropriate charge would be obtaining, or attempting to obtain, property by deception contrary to s. 15 TA 1968.

(b) Borrowing or lending   The second part of s. 6(1) simply expands on the first part; a borrowing or lending of P's property by D may amount to an intention to treat the thing as his own to dispose of regardless of P's rights if 'the borrowing or lending [of it] is for a period and in circumstances making it equivalent to an outright taking or disposal.' In *Lloyd (ante)*, Lord Lane CJ stated (at p. 836) that this provision:

> is intended to make clear that a mere borrowing is never enough to constitute the necessary guilty mind unless the intention is to return the thing in such a changed state that it can truly be said that all its goodness or virtue has gone.

This was a statement of the 'essential quality principle'. If D takes P's railway season ticket, intending to return it to him after it has expired, P will receive back a worthless piece of paper. Similarly if D borrows P's battery and uses it only returning it to P when it is exhausted, the thing returned will be deprived of all virtue.

This principle applies equally to the situation where D is the bailee of P's property and he lends it to E, telling E to keep it for as long as he likes. Thus, if P had gone on holiday leaving some of his valuables with D and D lent P's battery operated torch to E, D's lending of the batteries would seem to be for a period and in circumstances making it equivalent to an outright disposal. In the above examples, if D returns the season ticket one day before the expiry date, or returns the battery with a little power remaining in it, the question will be whether this is equivalent to an outright taking. It could be argued that not all 'its goodness or virtue' has gone.

In *11.2.1.1.2 ante* the question arose whether confidential information or trade secrets could constitute property. In *Oxford* v *Moss* (1978) 68 Cr App R 183, it was held that confidential information in a university examination paper was not 'property'. It was submitted that this was questionable and that the secret quality of the information was a form of intangible property; by reading such a document D was assuming the right of an owner and permanently depriving the owner of the secrecy of the information. It is further submitted that a person borrowing a document containing confidential information so that he may copy it, or even simply to read it, could be held to intend to permanently deprive the lender of it; the document, when it is returned, has lost its virtue, namely its confidentiality, the very thing which gave it, or enhanced, its value. Thus it, is submitted, even if confidential information is not to be regarded as a form of intangible property, D may be guilty of the theft of documents containing confidential information where he only borrows such documents.

11.2.2.1.2   Section 6(2)   Section 6(2) provides:

> Without prejudice to the generality of subsection (1) above, where a person, having possession or control (lawfully or not) of property belonging to another, parts with the property under a condition as to its return which he may not be able to perform, this (if done for purposes of his own and without the other's authority) amounts to treating the property as his own to dispose of regardless of the other's rights.

This section covers both the situation where D is the bailee of P's property, or B surreptitiously borrows P's property. In either case if D pledges the property as security for a loan (pawning being the usual situation envisaged), even though he intends to redeem it and return it to P, he will be deemed to intend permanently to deprive P of the property. It is obvious that at the time of pledging the property D cannot be certain that he will be able to redeem it. If D foresees the slightest possibility that he may not be able to perform the condition, he will fall within the section. It is only where D honestly believes that there is no possibility of him being unable to fulfil the condition that he will not be deemed to have had the necessary intent.

11.2.2.1.3   Conditional intent   Will a conditional intent suffice for theft? For example, D takes P's handbag intending to search through it and steal any money he may find; upon finding no money he replaces the handbag where he found it. In such a case D has no intention to deprive P of the handbag, and the property of which he seeks to deprive P does not exist so there is no appropriation of money. He is, however, guilty of attempted theft as a conditional intention suffices for attempt (see 8.4.2 *ante*).

11.2.2.2   Dishonesty   The final element of theft which must be proved is that at the time D appropriated property belonging to another intending permanently to deprive the other of it, he did so dishonestly. Section 2 TA 1968 specifies three situations in which D's appropriation is not to be regarded as dishonest (s. 2(1)) and one situation in which it may be regarded as dishonest (s. 2(2)). If D raises a defence which falls within s. 2(1) he will be entitled to an acquittal unless the prosecution disproves his alleged belief beyond reasonable doubt.

11.2.2.2.1   Section 2   Section 2 provides:

> (1)   A person's appropriation of property belonging to another is not to be regarded as dishonest –
>> (a)   if he appropriates the property in the belief that he has in law the right to deprive the other of it, on behalf of himself or of a third person; or
>> (b)   if he appropriates the property in the belief that he would have the other's consent if the other knew of the appropriation and the circumstances of it; or

(c)   (except where the property came to him as trustee or personal
representative) if he appropriates the property in the belief that the
person to whom the property belongs cannot be discovered by taking
reasonable steps.

(2)   A person's appropriation of property belonging to another may be
dishonest notwithstanding that he is willing to pay for the property.

(a)   Belief in a right to deprive   If D believes he has a legal right to
appropriate P's property he is not dishonest no matter how unreasonable his
belief may be. If D believes the property is his own, there is no intention to
permanently deprive another of the property. Section 2(1)(a), however, relates to
mistakes as to the law. For example, if D sells and delivers goods to P and P fails
to pay for them, D may wrongly believe he has the right in law to take possession
of the goods. In such a case D may rely on s. 2(1)(a). If E, D's employee, is
instructed to seize the goods from P for non-payment and believes that D has a
legal right to them, he similarly may rely on s. 2(1)(a) if charged with theft.

(b)   Belief in the other's consent   D is hungry and has no money. He goes
to P's house and admits himself using a key P has given him for the purposes
of checking on the property while P is on holiday. D takes food from P's
cupboards believing P would have consented to him doing so had he known
the circumstances. If such a belief is honestly held, D is not dishonest.

(c)   Belief that the owner cannot be found   Although s. 2(1)(c) does not refer
to 'finding' property this is the situation which most clearly falls within this
provision. Where D finds property and honestly believes that the owner cannot
be discovered by taking reasonable steps, D's appropriation of the property
will not be dishonest. In considering what steps would be reasonable regard
would be paid to the nature of the property, whether there were any
identification marks or distinguishing features, the nature and value of the
property and the place where it was found; but, it must be stressed, ultimately
the question is what was D's belief. If D honestly believed there were no
reasonable means of discovering the owner he will not be dishonest even if the
reasonable person would have recognised an obvious and simple means of
tracing the owner. It should be noted that if, after finding the property and
concluding that the owner cannot be traced, D discovers who the owner is, or
how he may be traced, any subsequent keeping or dealing with the property as
owner by D would amount to theft (see s. 3(1), *11.2.1.5.4 ante*).

If the beneficiaries under a trust or will cannot be found, in the absence of a
specific clause that the property reverts to the trustee or personal representative, the Crown will be entitled to the property as *bona vacantia*. If a trustee
honestly believes the beneficiaries cannot be found and that he is entitled to the
property he would appear to fall within s. 2(1)(a), but if he knows he is not
entitled to it he is not covered by the exception in s. 2(1)(c).

(d)   Willingness to pay   Section 2(2) states that D's appropriation of
property may be dishonest even though D is willing to pay for it. A wide variety

of situations may arise, hence the provision is framed in permissive rather than mandatory terms. For example, D unexpectedly has visitors but has no coffee. He goes to his flatmate's cupboard and removes a jar of coffee leaving a note and the price of the coffee. A jury would have to decide if this was dishonest in all the circumstances. It may be that D could also rely on s. 2(1)(b). By contrast, P has a valuable painting which D covets but P refuses to sell to him. D removes the painting leaving a sum in excess of the value of the painting. In this case D's willingness to pay would have to be set in the context of P's clear unwillingness to sell and it is submitted that this should be regarded as dishonest.

11.2.2.2.2   Situations not covered by section 2   The fact that D cannot rely on any of the provisions in s. 2(1) does not mean that D is necessarily dishonest. Where D does not raise any of these defences his case will fall to be considered under the general test of dishonesty. Who is to decide, however, what dishonesty means? As the Act only gives a partial definition one might have expected the courts to provide a general definition of this concept and the leave it to the jury in each case to determine whether the facts fall within this definition. The courts, however, have adopted the contrary approach, determining that what is 'dishonest' is not a question of law but a matter for the tribunal of fact. In *Ghosh* [1982] QB 1053, the Court of Appeal laid down a two-part test to be applied by juries. Was what was done dishonest according to the ordinary standards of reasonable honest people? If so, did D realise that what he was doing was by those standards dishonest?

In most cases there will be no dispute regarding dishonesty; if D is shop-lifting, or robbing a bank, or breaking into and stealing from houses, it would be impossible to argue that this was not dishonest according to ordinary standards of reasonable honest people, or that D did not realise it was dishonest. There are, however, some situations which may give rise to difficulty. In *Feely* [1973] QB 530, the manager of a betting shop took £30 from his employer's safe, a practice which the employer had prohibited. When charged with theft he claimed he had only borrowed it and was going to replace an equivalent sum. His conviction was quashed as the trial judge had ruled that this did not amount to a defence. The Court of Appeal held that the question of what was dishonest was for the jury to determine.

Where an employee borrows his employer's money an infinite variety of circumstances may arise: the employer may have expressly prohibited such a practice in all circumstances; the amount taken may be large or small; the period for which it is taken may vary; D's likelihood of paying it back may vary; D may or may not leave an 'IOU'; D may take the money because some unforeseen emergency has arisen or he may take it for some less creditable reason such as betting on a horse race. As the situations vary so may the conclusions of different juries. Even judges have been known to differ greatly. In *Sinclair* v *Neighbour* [1966] 2 QB 279, D removed money from his employer's till to bet on a horse race. The trial judge thought that this was reprehensible conduct but that it was not dishonest. In the Court of Appeal, Sachs LJ considered that the conduct was dishonest while Sellers LJ considered that views as to the honesty of the conduct might differ. If judges, who share the same or similar class, cultural, educational and professional backgrounds cannot agree on what is dishonest, how can we hope for consistency from juries in an increasingly heterogeneous society? At least if judges make errors on questions of law these may be rectified on appeal and a body of precedent is thereby built up to guide future decisions. Jury decisions on questions of fact are not amenable to rectification nor do they provide any guide for the future. In the situation given above it is arguable that if D, when removing the money, did not believe that he would have had his employer's consent (s. 2(1)(b)) he should not be allowed by other means to raise a defence. It is arguable, therefore, that the decision in *Feely* was unnecessary. Unfortunately it has been built upon by *Ghosh* so that it is now the law, whether sensible or not, that the question of what is dishonest is one of fact for the jury to determine.

The second question in *Ghosh* need only be posed where there is some evidence to suggest that D believed that what he did was honest by ordinary people's standards (see *Roberts* (1987) 84 Cr App R 117; *Price* (1989) 90 Cr App R 409; *Squire* [1990] Crim LR 341). It raises a question: why should being out of touch with normal standards of honesty generally held in the community avail D? The Court of Appeal did not address this issue. Indeed the creation of the second question appears to have been based on a misconception. The Court of Appeal asserted that 'dishonestly' was not intended to characterise D's conduct but his state of mind which cannot be established independently of his knowledge and belief. Examining s. 2(1), the Court found that the matters covered related to the accused's belief which could only be established subjectively. It is important therefore to determine what his state of mind was, and for the jury then to determine if this is dishonest. Under s. 2(1), if D claims he believed he had a right to take the property, or that he believed the owner would have consented to his taking it, or that the owner could not reasonably have been found, the jury would find him not dishonest if he may have had that belief. If he claims he was willing to pay, having determined if he might have been willing to pay, the jury would then decide if ordinary people would regard that, in the circumstances, as dishonest. But strangely, if D claims he did not believe that ordinary people would regard what he did as dishonest, a jury, if they find he may have had this belief, must acquit. This is a strange conclusion; if D, charged with murder, claims he did not believe that a jury would regard his state of mind as 'intention' (another ordinary word for the jury to define), this will not avail him if the jury conclude that he did intend to kill regardless of how he might define intention or characterise his own state of mind. In such a case, the jury determine what his state of mind was, and then characterise it either as intention or not. Where dishonesty is involved, why should D's characterisation of his state of mind be relevant? The answer to this conundrum is that the Court of Appeal did not understand their own test. The Court provided the following example (at p. 1063):

a man . . . comes from a country where public transport is free. On his first day here he travels on a bus. He gets off without paying. He never had any intention of paying. His mind is clearly honest; but his conduct, judged objectively by what he has done, is dishonest. It seems to us that in using the word 'dishonestly' in the Theft Act 1968, Parliament cannot have intended to catch dishonest conduct in that sense, that is to say conduct to which no moral obloquy could possibly attach.

If one ignores the fact that there is no offence under the Theft Acts of which such a visitor could be convicted (which indicates the ludicrous nature of the example Lord Lane CJ chose to illustrate the principle), this example is riven with misconceptions. How can D's conduct, judged objectively by what he has done, be dishonest if one of the objective facts is that he did not believe a fare had to be paid. If there was any offence with which D could be charged and the jury had to consider whether he was dishonest, the first question would be whether what he had done was dishonest by the standards of ordinary honest people. The ordinary honest person would have to be placed in the situation as D believed it to be, that is, is it dishonest not to pay a fare if you believe no fare is due? To frame the question thus exposes the ludicrous nature of the example. This was a case of simple mistake of fact, not one of conflicting beliefs as to what is or is not honest. Because the Court of Appeal wrongly adjudged their alien objectively dishonest it then had to create the second question to render him honest. The second question, thus, appears to have been an unnecessary construct. No moral obloquy ever attached to his conduct because he acted in furtherance of a mistake as to facts; his mistake did not relate to his assessment of what ordinary people would regard as dishonest.

Ghosh, however flawed its reasoning, is a decison of the Court of Appeal which has been applied without question in subsequent cases. The outcome, however, is that if D is totally out of touch with ordinary community standards, the *Ghosh* direction would dictate that he be acquitted. For example, if D, a latter-day Robin Hood who is incensed by the plight of the homeless who decides to steal from the rich who can easily afford it and give the money to charities for the homeless, and he honestly believes that no ordinary reasonable person would regard his charitable activities as dishonest, he is entitled to be acquitted. (Strangely Lord Lane CJ thought that the *Ghosh* test would not avail such a person!) In such a case there is no claim by D of a belief that he had a legal right to take the property or that he believed the owners would have consented to him taking their property; on the contrary he is well aware of the fact that he is depriving them of what is rightfully theirs. As Smith, *The Law of Theft* (6th edn), states (at para. 128). 'The law fails in one of its purposes if it does not afford protection to a person against what he quite reasonably regards as a straightforward case of theft'.

This mess would have been avoided if the courts had accepted their responsibility to define what the law is rather than leaving it to juries. Smith (*ante*) suggests (at para. 129) that it would be open to the House of Lords to re-interpret 'dishonestly' to mean 'knowing that the appropriation will or may be detrimental to the interests of the owner in a significant practical way'. This would remove the risk of inconsistency between juries as to how they define dishonesty and would also negate the defence which the latter-day Robin Hood might raise. Regardless of his or the jury's assessment of what may or may not be regarded as dishonest by ordinary people, he would know that taking another's property may be detrimental to the owner's interests; if he does not have his property he cannot possess it, use it, sell it, spend it or do anything else he might wish to do with it. Smith states that the inclusion of the words 'in a significant practical way' is simply to rule out cases where only minimal detriment may be caused to the owner – it is 'no more than an application of the well-known *de minimis* principle to the law of theft.'

11.3   ABSTRACTING ELECTRICITY

Electricity does not fall within the definition of 'property' for the purposes of theft. A separate offence covers the dishonest use of electricity. Section 13 provides:

> A person who dishonestly uses without due authority, or dishonestly causes to be wasted or diverted, any electricity shall on conviction on indictment be liable to imprisonment for a term not exceeding five years.

The partial definition of 'dishonestly' in s. 2 does not apply to this offence. A person who uses electricity, believing, for example, that the supplier or consumer would have consented if he had known of the circumstances of its use, will not be treated as a matter of law as not being dishonest; the issue will be left to be considered by the jury according to the standards of ordinary honest people.

The normal situation in which this offence may be committed will be where D uses some device to by-pass his electricity meter. The offence is wide enough, however, to cover using P's battery-operated torch. The offence need not be committed for D's benefit; it is sufficient that he dishonestly wastes or diverts electricity.

11.4   ROBBERY

Section 8(1) TA 1968 provides:

> A person is guilty of robbery if he steals, and immediately before or at the time of doing so, and in order to do so, he uses force on any person or puts or seeks to put any person in fear of being then and there subjected to force.

Both robbery and assault with intent to rob are punishable with life imprisonment (s. 8(2)).

11.4.1   The need to prove theft
As robbery is an aggravated form of theft it is necessary to prove theft. For the offence of assault with intent to rob it is necessary to prove an intent to steal. If D has not committed a theft, for example, because he believes he has a right

to the property, he cannot be convicted of robbery even though he used force to deprive P of the property and even though he knew he was not entitled to use force (see *Robinson* [1977] Crim LR 173). Similarly, if D uses force to deprive P of his property temporarily, thus lacking the intention to permanently deprive P of his property, there is no theft. In either case, of course, D could be charged with the appropriate offence against the person arising from his threat or use of force.

Robbery is complete when the theft is complete, that is when D has appropriated the property (see 11.2.1.5 *ante*). It can apply where the enterprise may be unsuccessful. In *Corcoran v Anderton* (1980) 71 Cr App R 104, there was found to be a robbery where D tugged a handbag from a woman's grasp, although he then dropped it and made off without it. The Court said that taking hold of the bag could be an appropriation.

11.4.2   The need to prove force or threat of force

11.4.2.1   Force on a person   In *Dawson and James* (1976) 64 Cr App R 170, D and E jostled P so that he lost his balance at which point F was enabled to take his wallet. The Court of Appeal held that 'force' was an ordinary word and that the trial judge was correct in leaving it to the jury to determine whether jostling P constituted force. This approach was confirmed in *Clouden* [1987] Crim LR 56.

Prior to the Theft Act 1968 robbery required that the force be used to overpower P or to make him give up his property; it was not sufficient if the force was applied to the property to wrench it from P's possession. In *Clouden*, however, the Court of Appeal held that the Act had removed all such distinctions. In this case D approached P from behind and wrenched her shopping basket out of her grasp. In using force on the property, force is also applied to the person and the judge was not at fault in leaving the question to the jury whether D had applied force to a person in order to steal.

11.4.2.2   Threat of force   It is sufficient that D 'puts or seeks to put any person in fear of being then and there subjected to force'. A threat of future force will not suffice (but this may constitute blackmail; see 13.4 *post*). While most cases will involve awareness on P's part of D's threat to use force, the provision also covers the situation where D seeks to put P in fear of being subjected to force but P remains oblivious to the threat. Thus D would be guilty of robbery where he waved a knife at P and issued verbal threats in order to steal P's property but P, unknown to D, was deaf and blind.

11.4.2.3   On any person   In most cases, the force, or threat of force, will be used against P, the person in possession or control of the property. D will be liable for robbery, however, where the force, or threat, is used or issued against another in order to steal. For example, D breaks into P's house and is disturbed by the butler, Q. D knocks Q unconscious and proceeds to steal P's silver. Similarly, if D holds a knife to Q's throat threatening to cut it if P does not hand over the contents of his safe, this would fall within s. 8(1).

11.4.2.4 Immediately before or at the time of the stealing In the previous example of the attack on the butler, D used force immediately before he appropriated the silver. The phrase, however, may be interpreted expansively to cover a wider range of situations. It is submitted that it would cover the case where D uses force on Q at the house to acquire the keys to P's shop or factory from which D then steals property.

If Q, the butler, had disturbed D as he was leaving P's dining room with a bag of silver and D had knocked him unconscious, the question would arise whether the force was used at the time of the stealing. Appropriation was complete when D laid hands on the silver. For these purposes, however, appropriation is treated as a continuing act (cf. rape *10.2.1.1.1 ante*). This problem arose in *Hale* (1978) 68 Cr App R 415. D and E entered P's house and, having taken her jewellery box, tied her up. It was submitted that the theft was complete when they laid hands on the jewellery box and thus they did not use force at the time of stealing. Eveleigh LJ stated (at p. 418):

> To say that the conduct is over and done with as soon as he lays hands upon the property, or when he first manifests an intention to deal with it as his, is contrary to common-sense and to the natural meaning of words . . . the act of appropriation does not suddenly cease. It is a continuous act and it is a matter for the jury to decide whether or not the act of appropriation has finished. Moreover, it is quite clear that the intention to deprive the owner permanently . . . was a continuing one at all times. . . . As a matter of common-sense the appellant was in the course of committing theft; he was stealing.

This case rectifies a flaw in the statute so that the whole course of conduct is regarded as stealing rather than the act which satisfies the minimum requirement for appropriation. A line must be drawn somewhere, however, and it would appear that it would be drawn at the point where D ceases to be engaged in removing the property from P. For example, if D had reached the street with the jewellery box before being confronted by P, it is submitted that the stealing would have been completed prior to this point.

11.4.2.5 In order to steal The force or threat of force must be used or issued in order to steal. For example, if D uses force to rape P and then, having committed the rape, makes off with P's handbag which she had dropped, this would not be robbery as the force was used in order to rape rather than to steal. The force, or threat of it, need not be used only to remove the property from P; it is sufficient if it is used to enable D to commit the theft more safely, for example, where he knocks unconscious a nightwatchman before stealing from a factory, in case the watchman might discover him and raise the alarm.

11.5 OFFENCES INVOLVING TEMPORARY DEPRIVATION

Theft requires an intention of permanently depriving the other of the property. The Theft Act 1968 contains two offences to cover particular situations where this intention does not exist. Apart from these offences and those situations which fall within s. 6(1) (see *11.2.2.1.1 ante*), unauthorised borrowing is not an offence under the Act.

11.5.1 Removal of articles from places open to the public

This offence was created to deal with the particular mischief of the removal of property from places, such as art galleries, museums, cathedrals and other buildings open to the public in which valuable property may be housed or displayed, where there may have been no intention of permanently depriving the owner of the property. A work of art, for example, might be taken as a means of making a political statement, or to obtain publicity for a particular cause, or simply as a prank. It is difficult, however, to envisage a more complicated statutory provision. As more things seem to be excluded than are included, and often the only basis for distinction appears to be whim, one is left wondering whether there really was a need for this offence. The maximum punishment for this offence is five years' imprisonment (s. 11(4))

Section 11(1) provides:

Subject to subsections (2) and (3) below, where the public have access to a building in order to view the building or part of it, or a collection or part of a collection housed in it, any person who without lawful authority removes from the building or its grounds the whole or part of any article displayed or kept for display to the public in the building or that part of it or in its grounds shall be guilty of an offence.

For this purpose 'collection' includes a collection got together for a temporary purpose, but references in this section to a collection do not apply to a collection made or exhibited for the purpose of effecting sales or other commercial dealings.

11.5.1.1 *Actus reus* This offence is confined to buildings, or parts of buildings, where the public have access to view the building (or part of it) or a collection (or part of a collection) housed in it. If access is given to the public for some other purpose, for example, a theatre may display paintings in the foyer, removal of such exhibits will not be covered as access to the theatre is for the purpose of viewing performances of plays. If a separate part of the theatre is set aside purely for the display of exhibits, access to this part would be to view the collection. Where, for example, paintings are exhibited in a gallery for the purpose of sale, such exhibits are not protected by this provision. By contrast, where the purpose is to display the paintings to the public and they are incidentally for sale by the individual artists, the exhibitor's purpose is not that of sale and thus they would be protected by the provision.

Strangely, the offence covers only situations where the public have access to a building to view exhibits. If there are also exhibits in the grounds around such a building, these are also protected. By contrast, if the grounds alone are open to the public and, for example, sculptures are displayed there, removal of a sculpture from the grounds would not be covered. The sculptures would also not be covered even though the public had access to the building if that access was not for the purpose of viewing exhibits as where, for example, they are given access to the house to buy teas or souvenirs or to use lavatories. This would seem to be the result of an oversight by the draftsman.

The articles which are protected by this provision are those which are displayed or kept for display. If D removes a painting from the store in the National Gallery, this would be covered as it is kept for display. If D, by contrast, removed a chair from the gallery, this would not fall within the provision as it is not kept for display. A cross placed in a church for purely devotional purposes is not 'displayed' (*Barr* [1978] Crim LR 244).

If an item is displayed in a building or its grounds, D must remove it from the building or the grounds respectively before he will be liable to conviction. It is not enough that he has moved the item to some other place in the building and hidden it there, or likewise in respect of the grounds. It is sufficient, however, that he removes the item from the building and hides it in the grounds (and presumably vice versa).

Where the article taken is part of a collection intended for permanent exhibition (or an article on loan and exhibited with such a collection) the offence may be committed at any time (s. 11(2)). An item in store remains part of a collection intended for permanent exhibition where the items on display from the collection are rotated as it is the collection which is intended for permanent display (see *Durkin* [1973] QB 786). Where the item is not part of a permanent exhibition, the offence will be committed only where it is removed during the times when the building is open to the public. The articles in a privately owned stately home, which is open to the public only at particular times, would not form a collection intended for permanent exhibition (but where the home was owned, for example, by the National Trust, they probably would). This leads to the ludicrous position that if D enters on a day when the home is open to the public and removes a painting he will be guilty of this offence, whereas if he enters on such a day and hides in a cupboard until after midnight and then removes the painting on a day when the home is not open to the public, he will not be guilty of this offence. The distinction between the two situations is one without substance in so far as it relates either to D's moral culpability or the harm, loss or inconvenience caused to the owner of the home.

11.5.1.2 *Mens rea* D must intend to remove the article. He will not be guilty of the offence, however, 'if he believes that he has lawful authority for the removal of the thing in question or that he would have it if the person entitled to give it knew of the removal and the circumstances of it' (s. 11(3)).

11.5.2 Taking a conveyance without authority

Where D takes a vehicle it is often difficult to prove an intention of permanently depriving the owner of it; D may take a car, for example, to joy-ride or to use on a criminal enterprise or to use for his own convenience. Whatever the reason, such behaviour may create a social nuisance, a public danger and personal inconvenience for the person temporarily deprived of his vehicle. Section 12 covers such taking of motor vehicles and also covers the taking of other conveyances such as boats or bicycles.

11.5.2.1   Taking a conveyance other than a pedal cycle   Section 12(1) provides:

> ... a person shall be guilty of an offence if, without having the consent of the owner or other lawful authority, he takes any conveyance for his own or another's use or, knowing that any conveyance has been taken without such authority, drives it or allows himself to be carried in or on it.

This section creates two summary offences punishable with a fine not exceeding level 5 on the standard scale or up to six months' imprisonment or both (s. 12(2) as amended by s. 37(1) of the Criminal Justice Act 1988). On a trial on indictment for theft, a jury may return a verdict of guilty of the s. 12(1) offence if they are not satisfied that the accused is guilty of theft but it is proved that he committed this offence. As the s. 12(1) offence is a summary offence, an attempt to commit it is not an offence, but s. 9 of the Criminal Attempts Act 1981 creates a separate offence of interference with a motor vehicle with the intention that an offence under s. 12(1) shall be committed (interference with something like a yacht, however, would not be covered).

11.5.2.1.1   Conveyance   A 'conveyance' is something 'constructed or adapted for the carriage of a person or persons whether by land, water, or air' excluding a vehicle where the person controlling it is not carried in or on it (see s. 12(7)(a)). Implicit in the definition of the offence in s. 12(1) is the requirement that it be a conveyance which can be driven. Thus the vehicle, vessel or aircraft must be one which carries its 'driver' on it. This is a broad definition and covers cars, lorries, motor-cycles, boats and aircraft. The definition is wide enough to cover a 'soap-box', a wheelchair, a rowing-boat, or a hang-glider but it would not cover roller skates or skis. In *McDonagh* [1974] QB 448, a case concerned with the meaning of 'driving' in the Road Traffic Acts, it was stated that the essence of driving was the use of 'the driver's controls for the purpose of directing the movement of the vehicle'. According to this definition, roller skates or skis would be excluded as there are no 'controls' of even the most rudimentary nature. An animal is not a 'conveyance' (*Neal* v *Gribble* (1978) 68 Cr App R 9).

11.5.2.1.2   Takes for his own or another's use   A person 'takes' a conveyance when he (1) assumes possession or control of it and (2) intentionally causes it to move or be moved (see *Bogacki* [1973] QB 832. There is no need for D to ride on or 'drive' the conveyance; thus the offence was committed where D took a boat, loaded it on a trailer and drove away (*Pearce* [1973] Crim LR 321).

A person in lawful control or possession of a vehicle, such as an employee or a bailee, may, in certain circumstances, 'take' it. In *McKnight* v *Davies* [1974] RTR 4, D, a lorry driver, was under a duty to return the lorry to his employer's depot after completing his deliveries. D drove the lorry to a public house for a drink, drove several friends to their homes, and then drove home and parked the lorry overnight near his home, returning it to the depot in the morning. He was convicted of the s. 12(1) offence, Lord Widgery CJ stating when dismissing his appeal (at p. 8):

Not every brief, unauthorised diversion from his proper route by an employed driver in the course of his working day will necessarily involve a 'taking' of the vehicle for his own use. If, however, . . . he returns to the vehicle after he has parked it for the night and drives it off on an unauthorised errand, he is clearly guilty of an offence. Similarly, if in the course of his working day, or otherwise while his authority to use the vehicle is unexpired, he appropriates it to his own use in a manner which repudiates the rights of the true owner, and shows that he has assumed control of the vehicle for his own purposes, he can be properly regarded as having taken the vehicle within s. 12.

Lord Widgery CJ was satisfied that D took the lorry when he left the first public house as 'at that point he assumed control for his own purposes in a manner which was inconsistent with his duty to his employer to finish his round and drive the vehicle to the depot. Presumably, D's driving to the first public house was regarded as a 'brief, unauthorised diversion'.

An employee only has control of the conveyance; a bailee, who has possession, may also commit the offence if he uses the vehicle for some purpose other than that for which he received permission, or if he uses it after the period of the bailment has ended. In *Phipps and McGill* [1970] RTR 209, D borrowed P's car to take his wife to Victoria Station on the express condition that he would return it by 9.30 pm. D kept the car overnight and drove the following day to Hastings. It was held that at the time D decided not to return the car and drove it for his own purposes, he took it.

The taking of a conveyance must be purposive; that is, D must take it for his own or another's use as a conveyance. Thus the conveyance must either be used as such while it is being taken, as where D, or another, rides in or on it as it moves or is being moved (see *Bow* (1976) 64 Cr App R 54), or D must take it intending it to be used in future as a conveyance (see *Pearce, ante; Marchant and McCallister* (1984) 80 Cr App R 361). Pushing a car down a hill as a prank, or to remove an obstruction it is causing, would not amount to using it as a conveyance.

11.5.2.1.3 Without the consent of the owner or other lawful authority The taking of the vehicle must be without the consent of the owner or other lawful authority. The latter phrase will cover, for example, cases where the police or local authority have a statutory power to remove vehicles. It is no answer to a charge under s. 12(1) that the owner would have given consent had he been asked (*Ambler* [1979] RTR 217; but cf. *11.5.2.1.4 post*). Consent obtained by intimidation or force is not true consent (see *Hogdon* [1962] Crim LR 563).

Where consent has been obtained by fraud it appears that the consent is valid consent for the purposes of this section. In *Whittaker v Campbell* [1984] QB 318, D, who had no driving licence, pretended to be X and presented X's driving licence in order to obtain the hire of a van. The Divisional Court held that even if a mistake induced by fraud rendered a contract void, this would not affect the validity of the consent to the taking of the vehicle. As the parties were dealing face to face, this was not truly a case of mistaken identity as P hired the van to the person before him who asked to hire it. The principle in the case, however, is stated widely enough to cover cases of mistaken identity; thus if P had intended to hire the van to X (but not to Y) and Y, X's twin brother, had taken possession of it, this would have been a fundamental mistake rendering the contract void. It is submitted that Y's taking of the van should be an offence under s. 12 and that the ratio in *Whittaker* v *Campbell* should be limited to the facts of the case which involved a mistake as to D's attributes rather than his identity; such a mistake only serves to render a contract voidable.

A further problem, however, arises in the fraud cases which highlights a conflict between these cases and those above (*11.5.2.1.2 ante*). In *Peart* [1970] 2 QB 672, P obtained the loan of a car by representing to P that he needed to drive from Newcastle upon Tyne to Alnwick, a journey of some 30 miles. D drove in the opposite direction to Burnley, some 100 miles away. D's conviction of the s. 12 offence was quashed as he had not 'taken' the vehicle as P had consented to him using it. This case seems to conflict with *Phipps and McGill*. In that case it was a 'taking' to use the vehicle for an additional purpose after the permitted purpose had been completed. It is difficult to see why the immediate use of the vehicle for some unauthorised purpose should not constitute 'taking' because possession or control of the vehicle has been obtained by a misrepresentation. In *Peart*, had D driven to Alnwick and then gone to Burnley he would have committed an offence; it is difficult to see how driving straight to Burnley alters the substance of what he did. It is submitted that the decision in *Peart* is wrong and that *Phipps and McGill* should be regarded as the correct authority.

11.5.2.1.4   Belief in lawful authority or consent   Section 12(6) provides:

A person does not commit an offence under this section by anything done in the belief that he has lawful authority to do it or that he would have the owner's consent if the owner knew of his doing it and the circumstances of it.

This provision is similar to s. 2(1)(a) and (b) relating to dishonesty for the purposes of theft. D must adduce evidence of his belief but, having done so, the burden is on the prosecution to disprove that belief beyond reasonable doubt.

11.5.2.1.5   Driving or allowing oneself to be carried in or on a conveyance
Where a conveyance has been taken by another without lawful authority (this covers theft or the s. 12 offence; see *Tolley* v *Giddings* [1964] 2 QB 354), and D knows this (wilful blindness will probably suffice), he will be guilty of the second offence created by s. 12(1) if he drives the conveyance or allows himself to be carried in or on it. If D aids, abets, counsels or procures the taking of the vehicle by E he will be liable as an accessory to E's offence of taking. This second offence created by s. 12(1) extends the ambit of secondary liability. If E takes a car and then meets D and offers him a ride, D would commit the s. 12(1) offence if, knowing that E had taken the car without lawful authority, he accepted the offer and was carried as a passenger in the vehicle. He would

not, however, be guilty of aiding and abetting the original taking by E, as this offence was complete prior to D being offered a ride.

To be liable for this second offence, D must either drive the vehicle himself, or he must 'allow himself to be carried' which requires that the vehicle must move while he is in or on it (see *Miller* [1976] Crim LR 147; *Diggin* (1980) 72 Cr App R 204).

11.5.2.2 Aggravated vehicle taking Because of the perceived problem of 'joyriding' Parliament decided that further legislation was necessary in this area. In many cases of joyriding the vehicle involved ends up being damaged or even destroyed. If several individuals were involved it might prove difficult to establish which of them caused the damage. To counter this and other problems the Aggravated Vehicle-Taking Act was passed in 1992. This inserts a new s. 12A into the Theft Act 1968 which provides:

12A (1) Subject to subsection (3) below, a person is guilty of aggravated taking of a vehicle if—

(a)   he commits an offence under section 12(1) above (in this section referred to as the 'basic offence') in relation to a mechanically propelled vehicle; and
(b)   it is proved that, at any time after the vehicle was unlawfully taken (whether by him or another) and before it was recovered, the vehicle was driven, or injury or damage was caused, in one or more of the circumstances set out in paragraphs (a) to (d) of subsection (2) below.

(2) The circumstances referred to in subsection 1(b) above are—
(a)   that the vehicle was driven dangerously on a road or other public place;
(b)   that, owing to the driving of the vehicle, an accident occurred by which injury was caused to any person;
(c)   that, owing to the driving of the vehicle, an accident occured by which damage was caused to any property, other than the vehicle;
(d)   that damage was caused to the vehicle.

(3) A person is not guilty of an offence under this section if he proves that, as regards any such proven driving, injury or damage as is referred to in subsection (1)(b) above, either—
(a)   the driving, accident or damage referred to in subsection (2) above occurred before he committed the basic offence; or
(b)   he was neither in nor on nor in the immediate vicinity of the vehicle when that driving, accident or damage occurred.
. . .

Upon proof of the basic offence in relation to a mechanically propelled vehicle under s. 12(1) of the Theft Act 1968, guilt of the aggravated offence will be established on proof of one of the three circumstances specified in s. 12A(2).

Proof of a certain degree of fault is required in respect of driving dangerously in that it must be proved that 'it would be obvious to a competent and careful driver that driving in that way would be dangerous' (s. 2A(1)(b) Road Traffic Act 1988). No degree of fault, however, need be proved in relation to the other two circumstances. D could be liable for the aggravated offence where the vehicle is hit by another vehicle through no fault of D's. Similarly, D would be liable where, even though he was driving carefully, he had to swerve to avoid another vehicle being driven dangerously and he damaged a parked car. His liability arises from the fact that the vehicle was being driven as s. 12A(2)(b) does not refer to the 'manner' in which it was being driven. It is also worth noting that anyone who allows himself to be carried in a vehicle which he knows has been taken without the owner's consent commits the basic offence and will be guilty of the aggravated offence simply if the eventualities in subsection (2) occur. For example, E a hitch-hiker, obtains a lift from D who is committing the s. 12(1) offence. On learning this E continues to ride in the vehicle. However, when D starts to drive the vehicle in a dangerous manner, thereby committing the aggravated offence under s. 12A(1), E pleads to be let out. It would appear from the wording of the section that E is also guilty of the aggravated offence and there is no possibility of withdrawal. By contrast, E would not be guilty as an accessory to the offence of dangerous driving contrary to s. 2 of the Road Traffic Act 1988 as he would not be aiding or abetting that offence. Similarly, if D did stop to let E out and then either drove off immediately hitting another vehicle or a pedestrian, or set fire to the vehicle, E would again be liable for the aggravated offence as he was in the vicinity when one of the eventualities in s. 12A(2) of the Theft Act 1968 occurred. It is submitted that the net has been cast too widely by the legislators and that some degree of complicity on the part of E should have been required.

11.5.2.3 Taking a pedal cycle Where the conveyance involved is a pedal cycle, s. 12(5) provides that it is an offence where a person either takes it for his own or another's use, without having the consent of the owner or other lawful authority, cr rides it knowing it to have been taken without such authority. This is a summary offence punishable with a fine not exceeding level 2 on the standard scale. The defence of honest belief in s. 12(6) also applies to this offence.

Further reading
R. G. Hammond, 'Theft of information' (1984) 100 LQR 252
A. Coleman, 'Trade secrets and the criminal law: the need for reform' (1985) 5 Comp. L&P 111.
R. Brazier, 'Criminal trustees' (1975) 39 Conv. (NS) 29.
A. T. H. Smith, 'Shoplifting and the Theft Acts' [1981] Crim LR 586.
S. Gardner, 'Is theft a rip-off?' (1990) 10 OJLS 441.
D. W. Elliott, 'Dishonesty in theft: a dispensable concept' [1982] Crim LR 395
E. Griew, 'Dishonesty – the objections to *Feely* and *Ghosh*' [1985] Crim LR 341; 'Theft and obtaining by deception' [1979] Crim LR 292.
J. N. Spencer, 'The Aggravated Vehicle-Taking Act 1992' [1992] Crim LR 699.

TWELVE

Offences involving deception

12.1 INTRODUCTION

The Theft Acts create a range of offences which contain the common element that the proscribed consequence is brought about as a result of the accused's dishonest deception. These offences cover obtaining property, services or a pecuniary advantage by deception and evading liability by deception. Before examining the individual offences, it is necessary to examine the common elements of these offences.

12.2 COMMON ELEMENTS OF DECEPTION OFFENCES

12.2.1 Deception
Section 15(4) TA 1968 provides:

> For the purposes of this section 'deception' means any deception (whether deliberate or reckless) by words or conduct as to fact or as to law, including a deception as to the present intentions of the person using the deception or any other person.

This definition applies to all the offences which will be considered in this chapter (see s. 16(3) TA 1968 and s. 5(1) TA 1978).

12.2.1.1 Deceiver and deceived The deception must arise from D's words or conduct and, in addition, operate to deceive another person. If D makes a representation believing it to be false but it is, in fact, true, there is no offence as P has not been deceived (see *Deller* (1952) 36 Cr App R 184, 2.3 *ante*), but D may be guilty of an attempt. Using a false coin to obtain items from a vending machine does not constitute obtaining property by deception as no person is deceived. If D succeeds in obtaining an item from the machine in these circumstances he may always be prosecuted for theft (see *Wise and Candy, The Independent,* August 21 1990), and if he fails, for attempted theft. Where he obtains a service, for example the use of a washing machine in a launderette, he may be guilty of abstracting electricity contary to s. 13 TA 1968 or making off without payment contrary to s. 3 TA 1978.

12.2.1.2 Deliberate or reckless D will be liable to conviction where he makes a representation knowing it to be false or where he is aware that it may be false (see *Staines* (1974) 60 Cr App R 160). 'Reckless' for these purposes cannot mean '*Caldwell* recklessness' as deception offences require the proof of dishonesty which is a subjective concept.

12.2.1.3 Words or conduct A deception may arise from D's words or conduct. The representation contained in the words or conduct may be express or implied. If D, wrongfully in possession of a charity collecting box, stands on a street corner shaking the box, his conduct would involve an implied representation that he is entitled to collect for the charity concerned and that money so collected will be handed over to the charity. Similarly, if D offers to sell P a painting which he does not own, there is an implied representation in D's conduct that he has a right to do so. A person who orders a meal in a restaurant, registers as a guest in a hotel, or takes a taxi represents that he intends to pay for the service rendered (see *DPP* v *Ray* [1974] AC 370; *Harris* (1975) 62 Cr App R 28; cf. *Waterfall* [1970] 1 QB 148).

The use of cheques, cheque cards and credit cards has presented the courts with particular problems. Where D draws a cheque in favour of P, for example, in payment for property supplied by P, the act of drawing the cheque involves certain implied representations. Firstly, D is representing that he has an account with the bank upon which the cheque is drawn; if D has stolen the cheque his conduct in drawing it in favour of D will involve a deception. In many cases, however, the problem is not that D does not have an account, but rather relates to the state of the account he does have. Where D draws a cheque in favour of P he is representing that the present facts are such that, in the ordinary course of events, the cheque will be honoured by the bank when presented (see *Metropolitan Police Commissioner* v *Charles* [1977] AC 177). This representation will be true provided either (i) D believes that there are currently sufficient funds in the account to meet the cheque; (ii) he intends to pay in sufficient funds; (iii) he believes a third party will pay in sufficient funds (for example, his employer may pay his salary directly into his account); or (iv) in the case of a post-dated cheque, he believes that by the time the date for presentment arrives his account will contain sufficient funds to meet the cheque (see *Gilmartin* [1983] QB 953). If D does not have such a present intention or belief, his drawing of the cheque amounts to a representation of a present fact (his intention or belief) which is untrue.

Where a cheque is supported by a cheque card, the situation is not quite so straightforward. Provided the conditions on a cheque card are observed, the bank is legally bound to honour the cheque even though D's authority to use the card may have been withdrawn or D has neither sufficient funds in his account nor sufficient overdraft facility to cover the cheque. When a person presents a cheque card he makes a contract on behalf of the bank with the payee to the effect that the bank will honour the cheque. In *Charles (ante)*, D obtained gambling chips at a casino in return for twenty-five cheques for £30 each, all supported by a cheque card. D knew his account was overdrawn and that he had no authority to overdraw and thus no authority to draw further cheques. The conditions on the card, however, had been observed so D could not be guilty of a deception in representing that each cheque would be honoured by his bank. In upholding D's conviction of obtaining a pecuniary advantage by deception contrary to s. 16(1), the House of Lords held, however, that D's presentation of the cheque card involved the implied representation that he had the authority of the bank to use the card so as to create a contractual relationship between the bank and the payee. (The question whether the 'obtaining' resulted from this deception will be examined below at 12.2.2 *post*)

The principle in *Charles* was extended to credit cards in *Lambie* [1982] AC 449. Suppliers of goods and services accept credit cards in pursuance of agreements they have entered into with the credit card companies under which the companies agree to honour the vouchers representing credit card transactions provided the supplier complies with certain conditions relating to the validity of the card. In *Lambie* D had a credit card which gave her credit facilities up to a limit of £200. Knowing she had exceeded this limit and that authority to use the card had been withdrawn by the credit card company, D purchased goods from a shop using her credit card. The shop complied with the relevant conditions so that a valid transaction was concluded which the credit card company was bound to honour. The House of Lords held that in presenting the credit card D was representing (falsely) that she had the authority of the credit card company to use the card.

Generally, where contracts for services or for the sale of property are involved, the provider of the service or vendor of the property may charge whatever he likes. An excessive quotation, however, may constitute a deception where a situation of mutual trust exists between D and his customer or, perhaps, where D knows that his customer is naive or inexperienced and is relying on D's expertise and honesty. In *Silverman* [1987] Crim LR 574, D was known to two elderly sisters having done work for them for many years. He charged them grossly excessive prices for work he did on their property. In this situation of mutual trust, the implied representation was that his charge was fair and proper, which D knew to be untrue. The Court of Appeal found that 'his silence on any matter other than the sums to be charged was as eloquent as if he had said that he was going to make no more than a modest profit.'

A deception may arise from D's silence or his omission to disclose the truth. In *DPP v Ray* [1974] AC 370, D ordered a meal in a restaurant intending to pay for it. After eating the meal he decided not to pay and sat at his table until the waiter left the room at which point he departed without paying. The House of Lords held that there was a deception. Lord MacDermott took the view that the initial representation that he would pay, implied from ordering a meal, was a continuing one which remained live and operative and became false upon his change of mind. Lords Morris and Pearson took the view that by remaining at the table after he had changed his mind he continued to make from moment to moment, but now falsely, the representation that he intended to pay. The principle in *Ray* has wide application. For example, P telephones D, in response to D's advertisement that he has a cooker for sale, and D represents that it is in good working order. Subsequently D discovers that the oven is not working. The representation he made was true when he made it. When P inspects the cooker, which is disconnected, and agrees to buy it, D may be guilty of obtaining his money (property) by deception either on the basis that the original representation was a continuing one which remained live and operative until the contract was concluded, or that, while negotiations were being conducted, D continued to make from moment to moment, but now falsely, the representation that the cooker was in good working order.

Where D is under a duty to disclose information and fails to do so, his failure may amount to a deception. In *Firth* (1990) 91 Cr App R 217, D, a consultant obstetrician, referred private patients to an NHS hospital for treatment, omitting to declare that they were private patients. D was convicted of obtaining an exemption from liability to make payment contrary to s. 2(1)(c) TA 1978. The Court of Appeal affirmed the conviction as D was under a duty to give the relevant information to the hospital. By deliberately and dishonestly refraining from so doing, with the result that no charge was levied on himself or his patients, he had obtained the exemption by deception. The deception either arose from his omission to disclose the truth when under a duty to do so, or could be implied as an act of commission deriving from referring patients to the NHS hospital knowing that they would be treated as NHS patients in the absence of any disclosure on his part of their true status.

12.2.1.4 Deception as to fact, law or intention A deception as to law would cover, for example, the situation where D misrepresents to P the legal effect of a document P is executing. Deceptions, however, generally relate to facts whether past or present. The problem arises in relation to statements of opinion. It is the practice of those selling goods or supplying services to make extravagant claims about those goods or services. How many times do secondhand car salesmen seek to induce sales by declaring, 'this car is a good little runner' or 'a genuine bargain'? While this is a statement of opinion, it is also a representation of fact, namely that it is D's opinion honestly held. If D knows that the car in question has several mechanical defects which cause it to regularly stop or breakdown and which would necessitate a considerable expenditure of money to rectify, it would not be his honest opinion that the car is either a 'good little runner' or 'a genuine bargain'. Thus, if D's opinion is not honestly held, his statement, although appearing to be one of opinion, is, in reality, a misrepresentation of fact because he does not hold the opinion expressed.

A statement of present intentions is a statement of fact. For example, if D asks P for money to fund his university course, his intention being to use the money to bet on a horse, he would be guilty of obtaining property by deception. A statement of intention may be implied from D's conduct as in *Ray*. Similarly, if D asks P for a loan he impliedly represents that he will repay it by using the term 'loan' rather than 'gift'. If it is not his present intention to repay he will be guilty of obtaining the money by deception. If, having received the loan, D decides not to repay it he will not be guilty as the obtaining occurred at a time when his present intention was to repay so there was no deception at that time.

12.2.2 The 'obtaining' must be by deception

'Obtaining' is the term used in ss. 15 and 16 TA 1968 and s. 1 TA 1978 to cover the consequence which D must produce by means of his deception; different terms are used in s. 2 TA 1978, but 'obtaining' will be used in this context as a generic term.

D must make a false statement but there will be no offence unless it deceives P and causes him to act in the way appropriate to the relevant offence, for example, to hand over property for the s. 15 offence. If D has already obtained the property before seeking to deceive P, the obtaining cannot be as a result of the deception (see *Collis-Smith* [1971] Crim LR 716; cf. *Wheeler* 12.3.1 *post*). Likewise, if P is not deceived, for example, because he does not believe D, or does not hear or see the words or conduct which constitute the deception, the obtaining is not the result of the deception. In addition, even though D may have been deceived, the actual deception may not have been operative in causing the obtaining, that is D may not have acted in reliance on the false representation but for some other reason. This is a question of fact for the jury to decide applying their common sense (see *King* [1987] 1 All ER 547). It is important that the prosecution identify the representation which they allege caused the obtaining. In *Laverty* [1970] 3 All ER 432, D changed the number plates of a stolen car and sold it to P. He was charged with obtaining the price from P by the deception that it bore its original plates. P stated in evidence that what induced him to buy the car was, rather, the representation that D had title to sell the car. D's conviction was quashed as there was no evidence that P acted in reliance upon the alleged representation, nor could it safely be inferred that he would not have bought the car if he had known the number had been changed. Had the representation alleged been that D had been the owner of the car, then the conviction would have been upheld.

In other cases, however, the courts have been more prepared to permit inferences that P has been deceived and induced to act in reliance upon the false representation even though the representation involved does not appear to have been at the forefront of P's mind. The problem arises in particular where the false representation is implied from D's conduct. In *Metropolitan Police Commissioner* v *Charles* [1977] AC 177, P accepted D's cheques because they were backed by a cheque card which guaranteed that they would be honoured; he was totally unconcerned as to the state of D's account or whether his authority to use the card had been withdrawn. P did state, however, that had he known D had no funds in his account or no authority to overdraw he would not have accepted the cheques. As the false representation construed from the facts was that D had authority to use the card, it would appear that this was a matter of indifference to P who may not have had any belief that the representation was true. The House of Lords, however, upheld D's conviction. This decision is only explicable if deception does not require a positive belief in the truth of the representation which is, in fact, false, it being sufficient that P is ignorant of the truth and acts in reliance upon the representation of authority.

Charles was followed in *Lambie* [1982] AC 449 where the House of Lords held that the only inference to be drawn from the evidence was that P relied upon D's implicit representation that she had authority to use the card and that had P known the truth she would not have concluded the transaction and supplied D with goods. P's evidence, however, was to the effect that the only thing she was concerned about was that the store be paid which would be assured if the conditions on the card were observed. Again, the House seems to have been satisfied that the property is *obtained by* deception if P would not have concluded the transaction had she known the truth; this is somewhat different to saying that P supplied the goods or service etc. because she *believed* that D had authority.

In many situations D's implied representation may have no actual effect on P's mind but the courts will be prepared to leave the matter to the jury to infer that P was deceived and acted in reliance upon the representation. In *Doukas* [1978] 1 WLR 372, D, a waiter at a hotel, was found in possession of bottles of wine which he intended to substitute for his employer's bottles when a customer ordered wine. He would then make out a separate bill and pocket the money paid by the customer. D was convicted of going equipped to cheat contrary to s. 25 TA 1968. For such a conviction there had to be proof that an offence under s. 15 would have been committed. While a customer may not consciously advert to the possible origins of the wine, the Court of Appeal were satisfied that a jury were entitled to conclude that the honest customer would not lend his support to D's fraud on his employer. Thus, such a customer, being ignorant of the true origins of the wine served, would have been deceived as, if he had known the truth, he would not have agreed to pay for the wine supplied. The questions, therefore, for the jury in a case of deception appear to be: (i) did D make a false representation (expressly or impliedly in words or conduct)? and (ii) did P act in response to this representation in a way in which he would not have acted had he known the truth?

One final point to note is that it is sufficient if the property, services, pecuniary advantage etc. which D obtains are obtained from someone other than the person who was deceived and the obtaining results from that deception. In *Charles* and *Lambie* it was the casino employee and shop assistant, respectively, who were deceived but in both cases D obtained a pecuniary advantage from his bank or credit card supplier respectively.

12.2.3 Dishonestly
The obtaining must also be dishonest. No definition of 'dishonestly' for the purposes of deception offences is given in either Theft Act. Dishonesty, however, remains a subjective concept so that the *Ghosh* direction (see 11.2.2.2 *ante*) is also applicable to deception offences (see *Woolven* (1983) 77 Cr App R 231). Doubtless, the fact that D has used a deception will tend to indicate that he was dishonest, but it does not necessarily follow that he is guilty of an offence as, in the case of property, he may believe that he has a right to the property. The Criminal Law Revision Committee stated (*Eighth Report,* para. 88) that in such a case 'though the deception may be dishonest, the obtaining is not.'

12.3   OBTAINING PROPERTY BY DECEPTION

Section 15(1) TA 1968 provides:

(1) A person who by any deception dishonestly obtains property belonging to another, with intention of permanently depriving the other of it, shall on conviction on indictment be liable to imprisonment for a term not exceeding ten years.

It is worth noting that because of the expansive definition of 'appropriation' in theft, many situations which involve deception are thefts. In *Gomez* [1992] 3 WLR 1061 (see 11.2.1.4 and 11.2.1.5.2 *ante*) the theft occurred when D took delivery of the electrical goods which was the same point at which D 'obtained' the property by deception. The only situations where there may be an 'obtaining by deception' and no theft are where either the property involved cannot be stolen but can be obtained by deception (e.g. land) or where D takes possession of property at a time subsequent to P passing ownership in it to him.

12.3.1 *Actus reus*
The definitions of 'property' in s. 4(1) and 'belonging to another' in s. 5(1) (see 11.2.1.1 and 11.2.1.2 *ante*) apply generally to other offences (s. 34(1)). The limitations contained in s. 4(2) relating to the theft of land do not apply so that a person may obtain land by deception in circumstances where he could not steal land. As a person 'obtains' property if he 'obtains ownership, possession or control of it . . . ' (s. 15(2)), D may be guilty of the s. 15 offence even though he never gains possession of the property. For example, in a sale of goods situation where ownership passes on contract, D would be guilty of the s. 15 offence upon inducing P, by deception to conclude the contract and thereby transfer ownership of the goods to him, even though he never subsequently received delivery of the property. If D contracts to buy goods from P and property passes before delivery, D may also commit the s. 15 offence where he uses a deception to induce P to deliver the goods to him, for example by handing over a worthless cheque. In this situation, although D has become the owner of the goods, P has possession of them and a right to retain possession until payment is made by D. D's deception operates to obtain possession. This situation must be compared with that in *Wheeler* (1990) 92 Cr App R 279. D, a market stall holder, agreed to sell a medal to P, a regular customer, for £150. P became owner of the medal upon conclusion of the contract but D was to retain possession until P returned to pay for it. In the interval D discovered that the medal was stolen. When P returned he had heard that some military memorabilia had been stolen and he checked that D was the owner of the medal and entitled to sell it and D affirmed that he was whereupon P paid for it. The Court of Appeal quashed D's conviction of obtaining the purchase price by deception. Section 22 of the Sale of Goods Act 1979 provides that a person who has no title to goods himself can by sale in market overt give a good title to the customer. At the time of D's representation, P was the owner of the medal and thus D did not and could not represent to P that he (D) was entitled to sell it

since it already belonged to P (cf. *Deller*, 2.3 *ante*). Doubtless D was dishonest, but there was no operative deception as he obtained the purchase price from P because of a valid contract for sale under which he had passed to P good title to the medal.

The offence under s. 15 may be committed where D obtains the property for himself or for another or where the deception enables another to obtain or retain the property (s. 15(2)). D would 'enable' another to 'obtain' property where, for example, E offers to sell a painting to P for £10,000 but P rejects E's offer whereupon D dishonestly represents to P that the painting is an 'Old Master' and is worth considerably more. P agrees to buy the painting and pays E £10,000. D's deception enabled E to obtain the purchase price. D would 'enable' another to 'retain' property where, for example, P lends a book to E for a week, and at the end of the week, D dishonestly represents to P that E requires the book for a longer period and P agrees not to seek its return.

12.3.2 Mens rea
The deception must be deliberate or reckless and D must dishonestly obtain the property. In addition he must intend to permanently deprive the other of the property. Section 6 (see 11.2.2.1 *ante*) applies also to s. 15 with the necessary amendment that for 'appropriating' the word 'obtaining' should be substituted (s. 15(3)).

12.4   OBTAINING SERVICES BY DECEPTION

Section 1 TA 1978 provides:

(1)   A person who by any deception dishonestly obtains services from another shall be guilty of an offence.

(2)   It is an obtaining of services where the other is induced to confer a benefit by doing some act, or causing or permitting some act to be done, on the understanding that the benefit has been or will be paid for.

This offence is punishable with up to five years' imprisonment following conviction on indictment and, following summary conviction, with up to six months' imprisonment and/or a fine of up to £2,000.

12.4.1 Actus reus
12.4.1.1 Deception   The services must be obtained by deception. There would be no offence where, for example, D slipped secretly into a theatre to watch a production, or slipped secretly into an hotel and spent the night in an unoccupied room as in neither case has anyone been deceived. 'Deception' has the same meaning as for s. 15 (s. 5(1) TA 1978).

12.4.1.2 The understanding   The services obtained must be rendered 'on the understanding that the benefit has been or will be paid for'. If D dishonestly tells P, his neighbour, that he is afraid of heights and asks him to clear leaves from his gutter and P agrees as an act of neighbourliness, there is no offence.

By contrast, if D had, in addition, offered him £5 to do the job there may be an offence even though D intends to pay, and does pay, for the service. Generally the deception will relate to the question of payment, but the offence is not confined to situations where D induces P to perform a service and then defaults on payment. Thus, if D, aged seventeen, deceives P that he is over eighteen to gain admission to a striptease show, he will be guilty of the offence even though he paid the correct admission charge, provided his conduct is considered dishonest. If there is no understanding regarding payment, there will be no offence. Thus, if D falsely represents to P, a taxi-driver, that he has just been robbed and asks P to drive him home, and P agrees to this free ride, there is no understanding that the service will be paid for. D may be guilty, however, of obtaining exemption from liability to make payment contrary to s. 2(1)(c) TA 1978 (see 12.5 *post*). It is sufficient that the understanding is that someone other than D has made or will make the payment or that the payment has been made or will be made to someone other than P. Payment in kind, or by D performing certain services in return for P's services, should be regarded as sufficient but there is no decision on this point.

12.4.1.3 Services 'Services' for the purposes of this offence involve the conferring of a benefit by doing some act or causing or permitting some act to be done. The benefit may be conferred on D or another. Whether something constitutes a benefit will generally be settled by the fact that there is an understanding that it has been or will be paid for; people do not generally pay for something if it is not beneficial. In cases of doubt it should be sufficient that D was willing to pay for it or expressed such willingness. In some cases, however, the fact that D regards the service as a benefit will not be sufficient if what is to be done is an offence. For example, if D offers to pay P £100 to circumcise her daughter, D intending not to pay, there would be no obtaining of a service by deception. Female circumcision is an offence under s. 1 of the Prohibition of Female Circumcision Act 1985. Even though D, because of her culture, may regard this as a benefit, the law declares that it is an offence. Smith, *The Law of Theft* (6th edn) para. 233, suggests that the doing of an act cannot be a benefit where it involves the commission of an offence 'if the object of the law is to protect D (or the third party on whom the alleged benefit is conferred) against the act in question'. By contrast, if D uses a false driving licence to induce P to hire him a car, while D's driving of the car without a licence is an offence, this law has not been passed to protect D and thus the hire of the car would be a benefit to him.

The benefit will be conferred where either P does some act or causes or permits some act to be done. Thus P may do the act himself, for example, painting D's house or giving D a massage. Alternatively he may cause the act to be done where one of his employees paints D's house. Finally P may permit some act to be done as where he permits D to use his property, for example, by hiring him a car or a lawnmower or permitting him to use a swimming pool or tennis court.

It appears that the obtaining of a mortgage or a loan (on which interest will be paid) is not a 'service' but rather the obtaining of property (*Halai* [1983]

Crim LR 624). While, in many cases, the s. 15 offence will adequately cover the situation where D intends not to repay the loan, it will not cover the case where D obtains the loan by means of a deception as to his credit-worthiness intending all along to repay it. If D had a bad credit-rating such that he would not otherwise have received a loan, it is difficult to see why this should not constitute a service. *Halai* was distinguished in *Widdowson* (1985) 82 Cr App R 314, where it was stated that obtaining property on hire-purchase terms was an obtaining of services. This seems the more sensible decision.

12.4.2   Mens rea
The deception must be deliberate or reckless and the obtaining must be dishonest.

12.5   EVASION OF LIABILITY BY DECEPTION

Evasion of liability was originally dealt with by s. 16(2)(a) TA 1968. This provision proved problematic. Following the Criminal Law Revision Committee's *Thirteenth Report: Section 16 of the Theft Act 1968* (Cmnd 6733), s. 16(2)(a) was repealed and replaced by s. 2 TA 1978 which provides:

(1)   Subject to subsection (2) below, where a person by any deception –
  (a)   dishonestly secures the remission of the whole or part of any existing liability to make a payment, whether his own liability or another's; or
  (b)   with intent to make permanent default in whole or in part on any existing liability to make a payment, or with intent to let another do so, dishonestly induces the creditor or any person claiming payment on behalf of the creditor to wait for payment (whether or not the due date for payment is deferred) or to forgo payment; or
  (c)   dishonestly obtains any exemption from or abatement of liability to make a payment;
he shall be guilty of an offence.

The deception must be deliberate or reckless. The securing, inducing or obtaining must be dishonest.

12.5.1   Liability to make a payment
The liability in s. 2(1)(a) and (b) must be an existing one at the time of the deception albeit that the date when payment is due has not arrived. Section 2(1)(c) refers simply to a 'liability' and thus covers prospective liabilities. In all cases the liability must be a legally enforceable one (s. 2(2)). Thus, for example, if D owes money to his bookmaker, he would not be guilty of this offence if he evaded liability to pay that debt by deception as gaming debts are not legally enforceable. Similarly, if the debt concerned is no longer enforceable because it is statute-barred, D will not commit this offence.

Where D is liable to pay compensation to P for a wrongful act or omission, such as a tort, D will commit the s. 2 offence only where either he has already 'accepted' liability or liability has been 'established', that is P has obtained judgment (s. 2(2)). Thus, for example, if D, having defamed P, tells P falsely that he has no money and is not worth suing, without in any way admitting the libel, so that P drops his action for libel, there is no offence. By contrast, if having admitted the libel, D, intending to evade paying damages, falsely tells P that he has no money so that P accepts his apology and forgoes seeking damages, this would be an offence.

12.5.2 Securing remission of an existing liability
'Remission' of a liability involves the reduction of, or cancellation of, the debtor's debt. This offence may be committed only where the creditor knows that there is a debt and that he is cancelling or reducing the debtor's liability to make payment. If a creditor remits liability in whole or in part, the debtor's liability is, to that extent, extinguished. Where D, by deception, induces P to remit his debt, he commits the offence under s. 2(1)(a). For example, D borrows money from P and subsequently tells him a hard luck story inducing P to cancel the debt. The offence may be committed where D induces P to remit the liability of another. For example, E borrows £100 from P. Subsequently D tells P falsely that E has been away from work with illness thereby inducing P to accept £50 in full settlement of the debt. By contrast, if D tells P falsely, in either case, that the debt has already been paid and P believes this, P is not remitting a liability as P is not extinguishing a liability, rather he believes there is no existing liability. In such a case D could be prosecuted for the offence under s. 2(1)(b).

It is worth noting that a remission secured by fraud is not effective so D's liability to make payment of the full sum due remains. This leads Smith to argue in *The Law of Theft* (6th edn) at paras. 240-243, that in the above examples D has not, in fact, 'secured' remission of an existing liability. If he has committed any offence it is that of dishonestly inducing a creditor to forgo payment under s. 2(1)(b). It is submitted that the courts are unlikely to engage in such refined reasoning and will probably treat the requirements of s. 2(1)(a) as being satisfied by proof of P's agreement to remit the liability. This is borne out by the fact that in *Jackson* [1983] Crim LR 617 it was held that D secured the remission of a liability where he used a stolen credit card to discharge a debt to a trader. If the conditions on the credit card are satisfied the trader will look to the company for the payment of the sum involved rather than to D (cf. *Re Charge Card Services Ltd* [1988] 3 All ER 702).

12.5.3 Inducing a creditor to wait for or forgo payment
Stalling a creditor is not generally an offence but it may be where D dishonestly induces the creditor to wait for or forgo payment by means of a deception with intent to make permanent default in whole or in part of the liability. For example, D owes P rent. When P calls to collect the rent D tells him falsely that his wallet has been stolen and that he will pay double the following week. If D intends to default permanently, for example, by moving without leaving a forwarding address, he will have committed the offence under s. 2(1)(b) as he has dishonestly induced P to wait for payment. Section 2(3) expressly provides that if D pays P by cheque this does not constitute payment as P is being

induced to wait for payment. As a general rule payment by cheque constitutes conditional payment and the creditor's remedies are suspended until the cheque has been met or dishonoured. If s. 2(3) had not been enacted a creditor who accepted a worthless cheque would not have been held to have waited for or forgone payment. In this situation, if D knows that the cheque will not be honoured, he commits the s. 2(1)(b) offence provided he is dishonest and has the necessary intent to make permanent default. In both the above cases, if D had simply not answered the door when P called and had then left the property without providing a forwarding address, there would have been no offence as no deception was employed.

A creditor is induced to 'forgo' payment where, for example, he is deceived into believing that the debt has been paid already, or he is deceived into believing that the debt is irrecoverable and he writes it off.

The offence created in s. 2(1)(b) will typically be committed where D uses a deception to induce a creditor to wait for payment in order to make default on the debt D owes to the creditor. There is, however, another situation which is covered by the phrase 'with intent to let another do so'. This covers the situation where D deceives P into waiting for payment of a debt owed by E so that E may make permanent default. For example, P calls at E's flat to collect the rent. D falsely tells P that E is in hospital and will pay double the following week, intending to assist E to make permanent default as he knows that E is preparing to leave without providing a forwarding address. In this situation, however, it is crucial that the indictment is drafted correctly so that the particulars of the offence allege that D, by a deception, intended to let E make permanent default on E's existing liability to make a payment as a person may only default on his own existing liability; he cannot default on behalf of another as the legal liability to discharge a debt attaches to the debtor (see *Attewell-Hughes* [1991] 4 All ER 810).

12.5.4 Obtaining exemption from or abatement of liabilty

This offence may be committed where D obtains the exemption or abatement for himself or for another or he enables another to obtain it (s. 2(4)). The liability may be a prospective one. The Criminal Law Revision Committee *Thirteenth Report*, envisaged that this provision would cover the ratepayer who obtained a rebate by making a false statement. It would also cover the case where a person obtained services free or at a reduced rate, for example, gaining admission to a theatre or cinema at a reduced rate by falsely representing that he was a student or a pensioner, or gaining free travel on public transport by representing that he was a pensioner. These cases would also be covered by s. 1.

Section 2(1)(c) suffers from the same potential problem as s. 2(1)(a) in that a person who obtains, for example, a reduction in his poll tax by means of false statements on the assessment form that he is a student does not actually obtain an abatement of his liability; his actual liability remains the same. Again it is submitted that the courts will probably be satisfied by proof of an agreement by the relevant authority to abate D's liability or exempt him from liability. If, at the time when the due date for payment arrives, D pays the abated amount, he will be committing the offence under s. 2(1)(b) provided he has the intention to make permanent default on the balance of his true liability.

It appears that s. 2(1)(c) is not confined to the situation where the creditor realises he is granting an abatement or exemption because of D's representations as the following two cases indicate. In *Firth* (1990) Cr App R 217 (see 12.2.1.3 *ante*) the deception related to a prospective liability rather than an existing liability. The hospital simply did not charge as it was unaware that there was any liability; it did not truly grant an exemption. The Court of Appeal, however, were satisfied that this situation fell within s. 2(1)(c).

In *Sibartie* [1983] Crim LR 470, D 'flashed' an invalid season ticket at a ticket inspector to evade paying the fare for a journey on the London underground. He was charged with an attempt to commit the s. 2(1)(c) offence. Had the ticket inspector been deceived, however, he would not have 'exempted' D from a liability to pay, as the deception would have induced a belief that there was no liability as it had already been discharged by purchase of a season ticket. This decision, it is submitted, goes too far in stretching the meaning of 'exempting'. Had D's deception been successful he would have induced the creditor to forgo payment. A charge of attempt to commit the s. 2(1)(b) offence would have been more appropriate. More care is required on the part of prosecutors in their choice of charge.

12.6   OBTAINING A PECUNIARY ADVANTAGE BY DECEPTION

Section 16 TA 1968 provides:

(1)   A person who by any deception dishonestly obtains for himself or another any pecuniary advantage shall on conviction on indictment be liable to imprisonment for a term not exceeding five years.

(2)   The cases in which a pecuniary advantage within the meaning of this section is to be regarded as obtained for a person are cases where –
  (a)   *repealed*
  (b)   he is allowed to borrow by way of overdraft, or to take out any policy of insurance or annuity contract, or obtains an improvement of the terms on which he is allowed to do so; or
  (c)   he is given the opportunity to earn remuneration or greater remuneration in an office or employment, or to win money by betting.

Deception has the same meaning as for s. 15 (s. 16(3)) and must have been made deliberately or recklessly. The obtaining must result from the deception. The pecuniary advantage may be for D or another. D must have acted dishonestly.

12.6.1   Section 16(2)(b)

D commits this offence where he is allowed to borrow by way of overdraft. This may occur where D deceives the bank into granting him an overdraft facility in which case the offence is complete even though D never uses the facility (see *Watkins* [1976] 1 All ER 578). Alternatively, D commits this offence where he writes cheques using a cheque card which the bank is then bound to honour, and either goes into overdraft when he has no authorisation to do so or exceeds his overdraft limit (see *Charles* 12.2.1.3 *ante*). A point not raised in argument in this case, however, is whether D was actually 'allowed' to borrow in the circumstances. The person deceived was the casino manager; he had no authority to authorise an overdraft of D's bank account. The bank had actually forbidden D to write further cheques; it honoured the cheques because of the contract which arose between itself and the casino which accepted the cheque abiding by the conditions on the card. In *Bevan* (1986) 84 Cr App R 143, the Court of Appeal sought to explain the position by stating that the bank could always renege on its obligations – by honouring the cheques it reluctantly, by 'an act of will', agrees to the borrowing. This line of reasoning is both desperate and contrived. It also creates a new problem: at the time the bank 'allows' the borrowing it knows the full facts and thus it is not deceived; it is difficult to see how the pecuniary advantage is 'obtained' as a result of the deception. Whether or not these decisions make sense, however, is irrelevant as, until they are overturned, they represent the law.

If D deceives his bank into granting him a loan, this is not an offence under s. 16 but it may be an obtaining of property or of services.

This offence is also committed where D is allowed to take out an insurance policy or annuity contract, or where he obtains improved terms in relation to either of these. For example, if D takes out an endowment policy falsely representing that he is a non-smoker when he is a smoker, or that he has not had a test for AIDS when he has, and obtains improved terms either in the level of cover or a reduction in the payments, or obtains cover when he would not otherwise have done so, he will be guilty of this offence.

12.6.2   Section 16(2)(c)

If D by deception obtains employment (or a promotion) and then draws his salary he may be convicted of obtaining property by deception if the deception was an operative cause of the obtaining of the property; this is a question of fact for the jury (see *King* [1987] 1 All ER 547). D may be guilty of the s. 16 offence, however, even if he never draws any remuneration. The offence is confined, however, to the earning of remuneration in an 'office or employment' but 'employment' has been construed widely to include contracts for services and is not confined to contracts of service (see *Callender* [1992] 4 All ER 51). A person who by deception obtains the tenancy of a public house from a brewery neither holds an 'office' nor is he in the 'employment' of the brewery (*McNiff* [1986] Crim LR 57).

Where D by deception obtains an opportunity to bet, for example, on a horse race, and wins, the winnings are not obtained by deception but rather because D chose the winning horse (*Clucas* [1949] 2 KB 226). He is not, therefore, guilty of the s. 15 offence but he will fall within the bounds of s. 16(2)(c) whether or not he places a winning bet; it is the 'opportunity' to win money by betting which he obtains by his deception.

Further reading
A. T. H. Smith, 'The idea of criminal deception' [1982] Crim LR 721.
E. Griew, 'Theft and obtaining by deception' [1979] Crim LR 292.

THIRTEEN

Further offences under the Theft Acts

13.1 MAKING OFF WITHOUT PAYMENT

There are certain situations where D obtains property or services, or seeks to evade his liability to pay, which do not fall within the offence of theft or the deception offences examined in Chapter 12. For example, if D obtains ownership and possession of property from P and then decides not to pay, he is not guilty of theft as the property belongs to him (see *Edwards* v *Ddin* (1976) 63 Cr App R 218). If D uses no deception to obtain the property he is not guilty of obtaining it by deception. If D makes off from the place where he obtained the property and where payment was due, for example, by simply driving away from a self-service filling station, he does not evade his liability by deception. Section 3 TA 1978 was enacted to cover situations such as these where a debtor, seeking to avoid paying his debt, removes himself from the scene where his liability was incurred. Such conduct is commonly referred to as 'bilking'. Section 3 does not require proof that the property involved belonged to another, or that there was a deception practised.

Section 3(1) TA 1978 provides:

> Subject to subsection (3) below, a person who, knowing that payment on the spot for any goods supplied or service done is required or expected from him, dishonestly makes off without having paid as required or expected and with intent to avoid payment of the amount due shall be guilty of an offence.

The offence is punishable on conviction on indictment with up to two years' imprisonment (s. 4(2)(b)), and on summary conviction with up to six months' imprisonment and/or a fine not exceeding £2,000 (s. 4(3)).

13.1.1 *Actus reus*

13.1.1.1 Goods supplied or service done The goods must be supplied. This is satisfied either by P delivering the goods to D or D being permitted to take them, for example, by filling his petrol tank at a self-service filling station or by taking goods from a supermarket shelf. If D takes goods from a shop which is not self-service he does not commit this offence although he may commit theft. If he takes goods in a self-service supermarket he may be guilty of both offences.

Where services are involved the service must be 'done'. Mending D's shoes, letting a room in an hotel, supplying a meal in a restaurant, or hiring D a car are all examples of a 'service done'. The latter two examples also, incidentally, involve the supply of goods. The use of a facility which P provides, for example, using a car park, would also be regarded as a 'service done' so that D would commit this offence if he drove out without paying the charge due. By contrast, if D surreptitiously enters P's theatre, watches a performance and leaves without paying, it would be difficult to construe the performance as a 'service done' as P has not permitted D's entry in the way entry is permitted to a car park.

Section 3(3) provides that 'Subsection (1) above shall not apply where the supply of the goods or the doing of the service is contrary to law, or where the service done is such that payment is not legally enforceable'. The supply of goods would be contrary to law, for example, when P sells prohibited drugs to D, or serves alcohol to D who is under eighteen. Likewise the supply of the service may be contrary to law, for example, in a brothel or an unlicensed casino. Finally, payment for the service may not be legally enforceable, for example, gaming debts are not legally enforceable, a prostitute cannot sue her client for payment for her services, and payment for the provision of lawful services to a minor is only legally enforceable where the service provided is a 'necessary'. If a minor has a course of beauty treatment at an expensive salon and makes off without paying she would commit no offence as the treatment is not a 'necessary' and, accordingly, payment is not legally enforceable. By contrast if she goes to the nearest branch of 'Boots' and is supplied with expensive beauty products and leaves without paying, although these are not 'necessaries' and payment would not be legally enforceable, she would be guilty of the s. 3 offence and probably of theft.

13.1.1.2 Making off D must make off from the spot where payment is required (*McDavitt* [1981] Crim LR 843). There may be more than one 'spot' or the 'spot' may cover a very wide area; where a passenger on the underground fails to buy a ticket, the spot where he commits the offence includes the exit barrier to the underground and is not confined to the place where a ticket should be bought before the journey commences (see *Moberly* v *Alsop, The Times*, December 13, 1991, DC). If D is caught climbing through a window to leave an hotel he will not have made off but he may be guilty of attempt. 'Makes off' is a broad term which will cover the situation where D leaves by stealth or where he openly runs off, for example, by jumping out of a taxi and running away when it stops at his destination. It was suggested at one time that there could not be a 'making off' where P consented to D's departure as a result of a deception by D, for example, D tells the hotel manager that he has settled the bill with the receptionist and is then assisted into his taxi by the manager. The

Court of Appeal in *Brooks and Brooks* (1983) 76 Cr App R 66, did not accept that the term was limited in this way taking the view that 'makes off' means 'departs' regardless of how that departure is effected. The Court emphasised that the crucial consideration was whether the 'making off' was 'dishonest.

13.1.1.3 Without having paid as required or expected Payment on the spot for the goods or services must be required or expected. Section 3(2) provides that '"payment on the spot" includes payment at the time of collecting goods on which work has been done or in respect of which service has been provided.' D's departure must be made without paying in the way required or expected. If D gives forged banknotes he does not pay. Where D pays by means of a worthless cheque he may be guilty of the offence under s.2(1)(b) where he intends to make permanent default as s. 2(3) provides specifically for that situation (see 12.5 *ante*). The offence under s. 3 should not be charged. Where the cheque is supported by a cheque card, even though there are no funds in D's account, he will have paid P as the bank will be obliged to honour the cheque. Similarly, where D pays by credit card P will be paid as required or expected even if D uses it without authority (whether because his authority has been revoked or it is stolen) (see *Re Charge Card Services Ltd* [1988] 3 All ER 702).

13.1.2 *Mens rea*
The making off must be dishonest. In addition it must be proved that D knew that payment on the spot was required or expected of him. If D honestly believed that the goods were supplied or the service done on credit and that he would be invoiced later he would not be guilty. Similarly, if D believed that someone else had paid or was going to pay, he would not be guilty.

It was originally believed that the offence was committed where D's intention in making off was merely to avoid payment on the spot at that time, even though he may have intended to pay later. In *Allen* [1985] AC 1029, the House of Lords held that an intention permanently to avoid payment was required.

13.2 BURGLARY

Section 9 TA 1968 provides:

(1) A person is guilty of burglary if –
  (a) he enters any building or part of a building as a trespasser and with intent to commit any such offence as is mentioned in subsection (2) below; or
  (b) having entered any building or part of a building as a trespasser he steals or attempts to steal anything in the building or that part of it or inflicts or attempts to inflict on any person therein any grievous bodily harm.
(2) The offences referred to in subsection (1)(a) above are offences of stealing anything in the building or part of a building in question, of

inflicting on any person therein any grievous bodily harm or raping any woman therein, and of doing unlawful damage to the building or anything therein.

(3)   References in subsections (1) and (2) above to a building shall apply also to an inhabited vehicle or vessel, and shall apply to any such vehicle or vessel at the times when a person having a habitation in it is not there as well as at times when he is.

(4)   A person guilty of burglary shall on conviction on indictment be liable to imprisonment for a term not exceeding fourteen years.

Section 9 creates two separate offences of burglary. The first offence under s. 9(1)(a) requires proof of entry as a trespasser and of the ulterior intent at that time to commit one of the four offences specified in subsection (2). The second offence requires proof of entry as a trespasser and of commission of theft or inflicting grievous bodily harm or an attempt to commit either of these offences. In most cases where the second offence is committed D will also have committed the first offence at an earlier stage. The two offences in subsection (1), however, are separate and on an indictment for one there can be no conviction of the other (*Hollis* [1971] Crim LR 525). The second offence, however, also covers cases where D entered as a trespasser without having the requisite ulterior intent at that time but subsequently did commit theft or inflict grievous bodily harm or attempt to do so.

13.2.1   Entry as a trespasser

13.2.1.1   Entry   In *Collins* [1973] 1 QB 100, D climbed a ladder and observed P lying naked on her bed asleep. He descended, stripped naked (apart from his socks) and ascended again stopping on the window sill. P, thinking this naked person was her boyfriend, beckoned him in and they had sexual intercourse before she discovered her mistake. D was convicted of burglary on the basis that he entered as a trespasser intending to commit rape One of the issues in the case was whether D had entered before P beckoned to him. Edmund-Davies LJ stated that it had to be proved that D had made 'an effective and substantial entry' before consent had been apparently given. This appeared to abandon the old common law rules that entry by a part of the body, however minimal, was sufficient. In *Brown* [1985] Crim LR 611, the Court of Appeal took the view that all that was required was that the entry be 'effective' and that the question was one of fact for the jury. In the instant case the jury were entitled to find that there had been an effective entry where D was found with the top half of his body inside a shop window rummaging for goods. This leaves a problem unresolved namely, what is the purpose for which the entry must be effective? Is the requirement simply that sufficient of D's body be inside the building to effect the purpose he has in mind? A hand inside a building would be sufficient entry to steal if some item was close to the point of entry. By contrast, if D's purpose is rape, on the facts of *Brown* there would not be an effective entry as his lower body remained outside the building. A burglary is complete when D has entered with the ulterior intent whether or not he commits the ulterior offence, it would seem to be going too far to require that his entry by sufficient to effect that purpose. Perhaps a two part test is required, namely either (i) D's entry is sufficient to effect the ulterior offence, or (ii) D's entry is sufficient for the purpose of bringing the remainder of his body into the building. In the latter case, for example, if D has his arms and shoulders inside the building this would be effective for the purpose of pulling the remainder of his body through. Similarly if D has broken a pane of glass and inserted his hand to open the lock on the door this would be effective to facilitate his entry by means of the door. Clearly a further decision is required to clarify the meaning of 'effective'.

A further problem relates to the insertion of instruments into a building either to effect the ulterior offence or to facilitate entry. At common law, if the instrument was inserted to effect the ulterior offence, this constituted an entry whereas, if it was inserted to facilitate access, this did not constitute entry. This probably remains the case. Where the instrument is used to facilitate access there will certainly be an attempt. If it is used to effect the ulterior offence, for example, to grab goods, it can be regarded as an extension of D's body in which case the question will be whether the entry is 'effective'. If entry is not effective there would, again, be liability for attempt.

If D uses an innocent agent to enter the building it is submitted that D commits trespass by that means. There is no reason in principle why burglary should be excluded from the principles relating to the commission of offences by means of innocent agents.

13.2.1.2 As a trespasser

In establishing whether a person enters as a trespaser, three questions arise (1) what is trespass for the purposes of burglary? (2) did the person entering have permission to enter? (3) had he exceeded the limits of that permission?

13.2.1.2.1 What is trespass for the purposes of burglary?

Trespass is a civil concept. Trespass, for the purposes of civil liability, is committed where a person intentionally, recklessly or negligently enters a building in the possession of another without either permission to do so or a legal right to enter. D's entry must be voluntary. There would be no trespass where D tripped and stumbled into a building or where he was dragged unwillingly into a building.

Mere proof of a trespass for the purposes of civil liability is not sufficient, however, for the purposes of criminal liability for burglary. In tort trespass may be committed negligently. For the purposes of burglary *mens rea* must be proved. In *Collins, ante,* Edmund-Davies LJ stated (at p. 105):

> there cannot be a conviction for entering premises 'as a trespasser' . . . unless the person entering does so knowing that he is a trespasser and nevertheless deliberately enters, or, at the very least, is reckless as to whether or not he is entering the premises of another without the other party's consent.

'Reckless' for these purposes has its '*Cunningham*' meaning (see 3.4.2.1 *ante*). It was not clear whether Collins was on the inside window sill when P beckoned to him; if he was he had already entered as a trespasser. On the assumption that he was outside, his conviction had to be quashed as the trial judge had directed the jury that a civil trespass was sufficient for the purposes of burglary and thus the question of D's *mens rea* had not been left to the jury. If D does not enter as a trespasser, he cannot, generally, commit burglary. The exception is where P requests D to leave; if he does not do so within a reasonable time he becomes a trespasser and thus would commit burglary if he then entered another part of the building and, for example, stole P's purse.

13.2.1.2.2 Permission to enter The person who is in possession of a building or a part of it is the person who may give permission to others to enter. Thus it is the tenant of a flat who may give that permission and not the landlord who owns the property. A lodger or a guest in a hotel, however, is not in possession of his room but is a mere licensee so that permission may only be given by the licensor, in this case the landlord or hotelier. The person in possession, however, may authorise others to give permission to enter. For example, a husband who owns the family home expressly or impliedly authorises his wife and children to invite others into the home. Similarly, he may forbid the entry of certain persons, for example, his daughter's boyfriend, D. If the daughter invites D into the house and he enters knowing his entry is forbidden, or being reckless thereto, and then steals, he will be guilty of burglary as he entered as a trespasser. It was suggested in *Collins* that if a person enters having been given permission by one who has no authority to do so, he is not in fact a trespasser for the purposes of burglary. It is submitted that this is wrong. If D enters without the permission of the occupier, this is trespass for civil purposes but only becomes trespass for the purposes of burglary where D knows he does not have the occupier's permission in the circumstances or is reckless thereto. Where the father had changed his mind and, unknown to D, had given his daughter permission to invite him into the house, if D entered believing he was forbidden from entering and then stole, he would be guilty of theft and attempted burglary (cf. 8.4.4 *ante*).

13.2.1.2.3 Exceeding permission A problem which may arise, however, is that of a person exceeding the permission granted. For example, if D had permission to enter but entered intending from the outset to steal, would this nevertheless be burglary on the basis that his permission was impliedly limited to lawful purposes? In *Jones and Smith* (1976) 63 Cr App R 47, S had a general permission to enter his father's house. On the occasion in question he entered with J to steal a television set. The Court of Appeal upheld his conviction of burglary on the basis that the jury were entitled to find that in entering his father's house with the intent to steal, S had knowingly exceeded the permission given to him. Thus a person who is given permission to enter a building for one purpose and enters for another will be a trespasser. For example, if P gives a key to D to enter her house and water her plants while she is on holiday, and D enters to steal her video recorder, he will be trespassing and guilty of burglary (see *Barker* v *R* (1983) 153 CLR 338, High Court of Australia). Similarly, if D has permission to enter one part of a building and enters another he will be trespassing. For example, if D is invited into P's house to mend her television in the living room and enters P's bedroom to search for her purse to steal it, he would commit burglary as he has entered this part of the building as a trespasser.

How far does this principle extend? Will D necessarily become a trespasser when he enters with one of the requisite ulterior intents on the basis that this exceeds the permission granted? *Jones and Smith* would suggest that this is the case, even though the permission granted to Smith by his father had not been expressly limited to a specific purpose. The decision in *Collins* appears to contradict this. It would defy credulity if D had pleaded that he believed P had authority to permit persons to enter to commit rape. But the Court of Appeal quashed Collins' conviction, which might tend to suggest that entry in excess of permission does not negative that permission. It is submitted that, as the effect on permission of an ulterior intent was not directly adverted to in *Collins*, the case cannot be considered an authority on this point; it should be seen as a case relating to the requirement of *mens rea*. Further, as Smith argues, in *The Law of Theft* (6th edn) at para. 436, 'as the girl saw him to be "a naked male with an erect penis" it seems clear that she invited him in for the purpose of sexual intercourse, that he knew he was so invited and that any intention to rape must have lapsed' although his intention to have intercourse obviously persisted. Thus, if a person enters with an ulterior intent, the entry will generally be trespassory unless the occupier has granted permission to enter for that purpose. For example, if P invites D into his house to beat up his lodger, D would not enter as a trespasser. It should be burglary, however, where D enters a shop intending to steal at the outset. The permission the shopkeeper gives to the public is impliedly limited to entry for the purpose of inspecting or purchasing goods. The Court in *Barker* were not prepared to go this far but it would seem to be implicit in the decision in *Jones and Smith*, and it is submitted, rightly so. Thus a person should be regarded as a trespasser where he enters with an intention contrary to the purposes for which permission to enter was granted. If the shopper enters without an intent to steal, but then forms that intent inside the shop, this is not burglary, even if he then proceeds to steal, as the initial entry was not a trespass.

Where D has a legal right to enter a building, for example, a police officer with a warrant to search for stolen goods, or a British Gas official entering to trace a gas leak, his entry for that purpose will not be trespass. If, however, the officer or the official enter intending, for example, to steal this will be a trespass. It will also be trespass where D gains entry into a building by fraud, for example, by deceiving P that he is a British Gas official seeking to read the meter.

13.2.2 Any building or part of a building

13.2.2.1 'Building' For the purposes of burglary the trespassory entry must be made into a building or a part of a building. There is no definition of 'building' but it appears that it must be a fairly permanent structure. Thus a temporary prefabricated structure (such as is used by many schools for temporary classrooms) would be a building but whether transportable containers connected to an electricity supply on a fairly permanent site are buildings is not yet settled (cf. *B and S* v *Leathley* [1979] Crim LR 314 and *Norfolk Constabulary* v *Seekings and Gould* [1986] Crim LR 167). A tent is not a building. It is not clear when a structure in the process of erection becomes a building. If D enters a structure which is complete apart from the roof, doors and windows, with intent to cause criminal damage, has he entered a building? As yet there is no answer to this problem (cf. *Manning* (1871) LR 1 CCR 338).

An inhabited vehicle or vessel is a building (s. 9(3)). Thus both caravans and house-boats are buildings provided they are occupied, although the occupier does not have to be in at the time D enters it as a trespasser. Problems, however, may arise in defining the limits of 'inhabited'. Is a caravan inhabited when left on a site over the winter months when P does not use it? Is a 'dormobile' inhabited when P is using it simply as a vehicle and not as a holiday home? It is likely that neither of these cases would be covered as P is not actively inhabiting the vehicle. The extension to the meaning of 'building' which s. 9(3) provides is a limited one. It would not cover, for example, a mobile library or shop, or a mobile blood transfusion unit or a mobile army recruitment office, all of which are essentially lorries converted for a particular purpose but which are not 'inhabited'. Thus, if D enters a mobile library intending to set fire to the books, he would not be guilty of burglary although if he entered a library building with the same intent he would. The mischief involved would not seem to be any different but Parliament has ordained that the offence of burglary should be restricted. If D is to be liable for burglary where he enters a vehicle or vessel it will have to be proved that he knew that it was inhabited or was reckless thereto.

13.2.2.2 'Part of a building'   For the purposes of burglary it is sufficient that D enters *part* of a building as a trespasser. Thus while D may have permission to be in certain parts of the building there may be other parts to which his permission does not extend. For example, a guest in a hotel has permission to enter his own room and communal rooms, but has no permission to enter another guest's room or parts of the building exclusively for the use of hotel staff. If D, in the hotel bar, goes behind the counter to steal from the till he would be guilty of burglary; the same applies to a customer who goes behind the counter in a shop to steal (see *Walkington* [1979] 2 All ER 716). The intent, however, must be to commit the ulterior offence in that part of the building which he has entered as a trespasser. If D hides between several racks of clothes in a shop waiting for it to close before removing items of clothing, he would not be guilty of burglary as he has simply remained in a part of the shop which he entered with permission. Of course, if at the time of his original entry into the shop he intended to steal, he would have committed burglary at that point.

Certain problems may arise, however, regarding the extent of a building or its constituent parts. If D enters as a trespasser a flat above a shop intending to gain access to the shop and steal therein, has he committed burglary at the point when he entered the flat? Provided the flat and shop are regarded as one building, he has. But what if D is lawfully in flat A and he uses an interconnecting fire door to enter flat B as a trespasser for the purpose of gaining access to the shop below to steal therein – has he entered a building or part of a building as a trespasser with the requisite ulterior intent? If he enters the shop there is no problem, but if he is apprehended in flat B he would not appear to have entered a part of a building with intent to steal therein. A conviction of burglary would only be possible if the remainder of the building, beyond the part which D lawfully entered, was treated as 'part' of the building. This would involve treating the shop and flat B as one part rather than two separate parts (see Smith, *The Law of Theft* (6th edn) paras. 357-360; cf. Griew, *The Theft Acts* (6th edn) para. 4-23). This would seem to be straining the statutory language which should not be justified by a desire to convict D. A charge of attempted burglary would be more appropriate.

13.2.3   The ulterior offence

As we have already seen burglary is committed either (1) where D enters the building or part of it as a trespasser with intent to commit one of the offences in s. 9(2) (s. 9(1)(a)), or (2) having entered the building or part of it as a trespasser he steals or attempts to steal or he inflicts grievous bodily harm on any person therein or attempts to do so (s. 9(1)(b)).

13.2.3.1   Section 9(1)(a)

Under s. 9(1)(a) it is necessary to prove an ulterior intent to commit one of the four offences specified in s. 9(2). A conditional intent is sufficient (*A-G's References (Nos. 1 and 2 of 1979)* [1979] 3 All ER 143). Thus, if D enters as a trespasser intending to steal anything of value he might find, and there is nothing there, or intending to rape P if she is there, and she is not there, he will have a sufficient intent for burglary. In the case of these ulterior offences it must be proved that D *intended* to commit the relevant offence. As attempted rape may now be committed where D is reckless as to consent (*Khan* [1990] 2 All ER 783) and attempt is an offence of specific intent, it is assumed that the same principle will be applied to this form of burglary. Thus if D enters a building intending to have sexual intercourse with P not caring whether or not she consents, this would, following *Khan*, amount to burglary.

The Act speaks of entering a building and stealing anything in it or inflicting grievous bodily harm upon, or raping, a person 'therein' or doing unlawful damage to the building or anything 'therein'. The word 'therein' is ambiguous as it could mean simply performing the act on a person inside the building (this would cover the case of D dragging P into a building with intent to inflict grievous bodily harm on her or to rape her), or it may mean with intent to inflict grievous bodily harm upon, or to rape, a person already in the building. As the purpose of burglary is the protection of persons or property in a building it might be suggested that the latter interpretation is the correct one.

13.2.3.2   Section 9(1)(b)

Under s. 9(1)(b), the theft, infliction of grievous bodily harm or attempt to commit either of these offences must be proved. This requires that both the *actus reus* and *mens rea* of these ulterior offences must be proved. 'Inflicting grievous bodily harm' would appear to cover the offences under ss. 20, 18 or 23 of the Offences Against the Person Act 1861. Recklessly inflicting grievous bodily harm would be sufficient for this form of burglary. Presumably if D murders P he will also be guilty as the commission of grievous bodily harm is a step on the way to causing death and it would be ludicrous to suggest that D intended to kill but did not intend to inflict grievous bodily harm. If D took property intending only to borrow it, there would be no theft and thus no burglary. It is submitted that D in *Dobson* v *General Accident Fire and Assurance Corpn* [1990] QB 274, *11.2.1.3.2 ante* committed burglary as his permission to enter was on the basis that he had come to purchase P's jewellery; his intention was to steal it from the outset. When he appropriated it he committed theft, therefore, having entered the building as a trespasser.

If D has a defence to any of these offences he will not be guilty of burglary. For example, if D enters a building as a trespasser intending to shelter from the rain and P, the occupier, attacks him with an axe seeking to eject him, D would not be guilty of burglary if he inflicted grievous bodily harm on P in reasonable self-defence. Likewise, if D takes property believing he has in law a right to it, he would not commit theft and therefore would not be guilty of burglary.

13.2.3.3 Intoxication Where D is intoxicated this will be of no relevance in relation to the question whether he knew he was trespassing or was reckless thereto. Intoxication may be relevant, however, in respect of the ulterior offence. Where D is charged with burglary with intent to steal, this is an offence of specific intent (see *Durante* [1972] 3 All ER 962). It is submitted that all forms of burglary under s. 9(1)(a) are offences of specific intent. Where D is charged with burglary contrary to s.9(1)(b) on the basis of theft, this is an offence of specific intent as theft is such an offence (see *Ruse* v *Read* [1949] 1 KB 377). Where D is charged with burglary on the basis of inflicting grievous bodily harm, however, it would appear that the offence is one of basic intent as the *mens rea* for inflicting grievous bodily harm is intention or recklessness. If the burglary charge is based upon an attempt to steal or to inflict grievous bodily harm, it is an offence of specific intent as attempt is an offence of specific intent.

13.3 AGGRAVATED BURGLARY

Section 10 TA 1968 provides:

(1)   A person is guilty of aggravated burglary if he commits any burglary and at the time has with him any firearm or imitation firearm, any weapon of offence, or any explosive; and for this purpose –

    (a)   'firearm' includes an airgun or air pistol, and 'imitation firearm' means anything which has the appearance of being a firearm, whether capable of being discharged or not; and

    (b)   'weapon of offence' means any article made or adapted for use for causing injury to or incapacitating a person, or intended by the person having it with him for such use; and

(c) 'explosive' means any article manufactured for the purpose of producing a practical effect by explosion, or intended by the person having it with him for that purpose.

(2) A person guilty of aggravated burglary shall on conviction on indictment be liable to imprisonment for life.

The element of aggravation in this offence is the fact that D *at the time has with him* a firearm or imitation firearm, a weapon of offence of an explosive. Whether something is an imitation firearm will be a question of fact for the jury (cf. *Morris and King* (1984) 79 Cr App R 104). 'Weapon of offence' is a wider term than 'offensive weapon' under s. 1(4) of the Prevention of Crime Act 1953 as it includes items not only made or adapted for use for causing injury or intended for such use but also items made or adapted for use for incapacitating a person or intended for such use. For example, a broken bottle would be an item adapted for use for causing injury, while a hammer could be an item intended for such use. Handcuffs are items made for incapacitation while a rope or a cloth soaked in chloroform could amount to an item intended for use to incapacitate a person, where, for example, D intends to incapacitate the night watchman at a factory. If a question arises whether an article is made or adapted for use for causing injury or incapacitating a person, it will be for the jury to decide (*Williamson* (1977) 67 Cr App R 35). But, with certain items which have no other purpose, for example, a flick-knife or knuckleduster, the jury must take judicial notice that it is so made (*Simpson* [1983] 3 All ER 789). If an article is made or adapted for use for causing injury or incapacitating a person, it is offensive *per se* and it will be sufficient for the prosecution to prove that D had it with him even if he did not intend to use it. If an article is not offensive *per se*, but may be used to cause injury or incapacitate a person, the prosecution must prove that D intended it to be used for such purpose.

D must have the firearm, weapon of offence or explosive with him at the time he commits the burglary. 'Has with him' requires that D knows that he has an article of aggravation with him (cf. *Cugullere* (1961) 45 Cr App R 108), so that if D is unaware of the fact that there is a flick-knife in his tool bag, or if he does not know his accomplice is carrying a weapon, he will not be guilty of aggravated burglary. If D has forgotten that he has, for example, a flick-knife in his bag, he does not know that he has it with him (*Russell* (1984) 81 Cr App R 315). D will have an article with him where he has custody of it or where he knows that an accomplice has custody of it and is carrying it into the building.

The meaning of 'at the time of committing the burglary' depends on whether burglary is committed contrary to s. 9(1)(a) or s. 9(1)(b). Under s.9(1)(a) the relevant time is the time when D entered the building as a trespasser. Under s. 9(1)(b) burglary is committed where D, having entered as a trespasser, commits an ulterior offence; he must have the weapon etc. with him at the time of committing this offence (*Francis* [1982] Crim LR 363). Thus, if D enters as a trespasser, picks up a knife from the kitchen and then commits the ulterior offence, he would be guilty of aggravated burglary (see *O'Leary* (1986) 82 Cr App R 341). If D enters carrying with him, for example, a rope to tie together items he intends to steal and, upon being disturbed by the householder, uses it to tie him up, does he commit aggravated burglary, i.e. does he have with him at the time of committing the burglary an article intended for use to incapacitate a person? The authorities under the Prevention of Crimes Act 1953, on the question whether a person has with him in a public place an offensive weapon, suggested that the person must have formed the intention to use the article for the purpose of causing injury at some time before the occasion for that use occurred (see *Ohlson* v *Hylton* [1975] 2 All ER 490; *Humphreys* [1977] Crim LR 225). These cases can be distinguished, however, as in both cases D was in a public place lawfully going about his business carrying the relevant article without any criminal intent. In the burglary example, D is already engaged on an unlawful purpose and is carrying that article to effect that purpose which he then uses for an additional unlawful purpose. It is difficult to make out a case for extending the reasoning of the above cases to burglary and thus it is suggested that s. 10 should be construed strictly: at the time of committing the ulterior offence did D have the article in his custody intending it for use to cause injury or to incapacitate at that time regardless of any intention in respect of it he may previously have had. The Court of Appeal adopted this position in *Kelly, The Times*, December 2, 1992, holding that the screwdriver D used to break into a house became an offensive weapon when he used it to threaten the occupier who disturbed him, as he intended to use it at that time for causing injury to or incapacitating her.

13.4   BLACKMAIL

Section 21 TA 1968 provides:

(1)   A person is guilty of blackmail if, with a view to gain for himself or another or with intent to cause loss to another, he makes any unwarranted demand with menaces; and for this purpose a demand with menaces is unwarranted unless the person making it does so in the belief –
   (a)   that he has reasonable grounds for making the demand; and
   (b)   that the use of menaces is a proper means of reinforcing the demand.
(2)   The nature of the act or omission is immaterial, and it is also immaterial whether the menaces relate to action to be taken by the person making the demand.
(3)   A person guilty of blackmail shall on conviction on indictment be liable to imprisonment for a term not exceeding fourteen years.

13.4.1   Demand
D must, expressly or impliedly, make a demand of P to do or refrain from doing something. The nature of the act or omission demanded is immaterial (s. 21(2)). In *Collister and Warhurst* (1955) 39 Cr App R 100, two police officers intimated to P that he would be prosecuted for an offence and arranged to meet him the following day intimating that the report of the offence would be held up and was to be filed only if P failed to keep the appointment. At that meeting W asked P if he had brought anything with him, and P handed him £5. C and W were convicted of demanding money with menaces contrary to s. 30 of the

Larceny Act 1916, the judge having directed the jury that they did not need to be satisfied that there had been express threats or demands it being sufficient that:

> the demeanour of the accused and the circumstances of the case were such that an ordinary reasonable man would understand that a demand for money was being made upon him and that that demand was accompanied by menaces . . . so that his ordinary balance of mind was upset. . . .

It is enough that the demand is made regardless of whether P complies with it. A problem may arise, however, in deciding when or where a demand has been made. Is, for example, the posting of a letter, the sending of a fax, the speaking of words, a demand at that point or only when received or heard by P? In *Treacy* v *DPP* [1971] AC 537, D posted a letter in England containing a demand to P in Germany. D argued that the demand was made in Germany when P read the letter and thus she was not triable in England. The House of Lords held, by a majority, that the demand was made when the letter was posted. The same would apply to a telex or fax. Where D makes a verbal demand, it is made when he utters the words even though P is deaf. If D posts a letter abroad addressed to P in England the offence will be committed when delivered to P (see *Treacy* and cf. *Baxter* [1972] 1 QB 1).

13.4.2 Menaces
As with the demand, the menaces may be express or implied from the circumstances (see *Lawrence and Pomroy* (1971) 57 Cr App R 64). Menaces is not defined in the Act but it had developed a wide meaning under the former law. In *Thorne* v *Motor Trade Association* [1937] AC 797, Lord Wright stated (at p. 817):

> I think the word 'menace' is to be liberally construed and not as limited to threats of violence but as including threats of any action detrimental to or unpleasant to the person addressed. It may also include a warning that in certain events such action is intended.

It is immaterial whether the menaces do or do not relate to action to be taken by the person making the demand (s. 21(2)); thus it is sufficient that the act may be carried out by someone else. The threats, however, must cross some threshold of seriousness to constitute 'menaces'. In *Clear* [1968] 1 QB 670 (a pre-1968 Act case; see also *Lawrence and Pomroy*) Sellers LJ stated (at 679) that the threat must be 'of such a nature and extent that the mind of an ordinary person of normal stability and courage might be influenced or made apprehensive so as to accede unwillingly to the demand'. Thus in *Harry* [1974] Crim LR 32, Judge Petre directed the jury to acquit as 'menaces' was a strong word and could not be established on the evidence in the case. The accused was the organiser of a Student Rag Appeal who had written to shopkeepers offering immunity from any 'inconvenience' arising from Rag activities.

As blackmail is committed when the demand with menaces is made, it does not matter that P is not actually intimidated if the threats would have affected the mind of an ordinary person of normal stability (see *Garwood* [1987] 1 All ER 1032, 1034). If, however, P is unusually timorous and would be intimidated by threats where a person of normal stability and courage would be unmoved, this will only constitute 'menaces' if 'the accused . . . was aware of the likely effect of his actions on the victim' (*Garwood*).

13.4.3   Unwarranted demand

If D demands from P that to which he is legally entitled, for example, payment of a debt or the return of bailed property, and threatens to institute legal proceedings to enforce the demand, this would not constitute an 'unwarranted' demand as D is simply seeking to do that which he is legally entitled to do. By contrast, if D demands something to which he is not entitled accompanied by menaces, or demands something to which he is entitled but threatens action which he is not legally entitled to use to enforce the demand, his demand may be found to be 'unwarranted'. Whether or not a demand is unwarranted depends on D's belief. The prosecution must prove beyond doubt either (1) that he did not believe he had reasonable grounds for making the demand, or (2) that he did not believe that the use of menaces was a proper means of reinforcing the demand. The question is 'what was D's subjective belief?' If D does not introduce any evidence that he had both these beliefs, the judge need not direct the jury on this issue (see *Lawrence and Pomroy*). The relevant beliefs will be examined separately.

13.4.3.1   Belief in reasonable grounds for making the demand   The

question is not whether there *were* reasonable grounds for making the demand but rather whether D *believed there were* reasonable grounds for making the demand. Many situations may arise where D could have such a belief. For example, P may owe him money, or P may have committed a tort and D may believe he is entitled to compensation. D may believe that a demand for payment in these circumstances is reasonable. He may have that belief even though it is founded upon a mistake as where, for example, he believes that Q broke his window and he mistakes P, Q's twin brother, for him. The mistake D makes may be an unreasonable one but this will not matter provided D's honest belief is that he has reasonable grounds for making the demand (see *Harvey* (1981) 72 Cr App R 139).

D's belief need not relate to the law. In the above examples he may have believed that he was legally justified in demanding payment but D's belief may be that he is morally justified in demanding something. For example, Q dies without leaving a will and D, a neighbour who is not entitled to inherit anything on the intestacy, demands from P, Q's daughter, some property from the estate believing that she is morally justified in doing so in recognition of all the help she rendered Q. If D honestly believes that the help she rendered provides reasonable grounds for her demand, the requirements of s. 21(1)(a) are satisfied. In all cases, however, D must also have the belief specified in s. 21(1)(b). This is a provision which it is more difficult to satisfy.

13.4.3.2 Belief that menaces are a proper means of reinforcing the demand While D may plausibly say that he believed P owed him money, or that he believed he was entitled to certain property, credulity is much more likely to be strained when he states he believed he was entitled to threaten P with violence or defamatory disclosures to enforce the demand. If the jury consider that D may possibly have believed that the menaces he used were a proper means of reinforcing the demand, they must acquit. To this extent, the standard against which the appropriateness of the menaces is measured is D's understanding of what is morally and socially acceptable in English society. In *Harvey, ante,* D, E and F paid £20,000 to S for what was thought to be a consignment of cannabis but which turned out to be a load of rubbish. They kidnapped S's wife and child and told S they would rape, maim and kill them unless he gave them their money back. The judge directed the jury that threats which were to commit what everybody knew were serious criminal offences could not be proper. D, E and F were convicted of blackmail and appealed. The Court of Appeal applied the proviso and upheld their convictions as, although the trial judge had not left the question of their belief to the jury, they were satisfied that any jury properly directed would inevitably have convicted as there was no suggestion on the part of the accused that they did not know that rape, murder and maiming were crimes. Bingham J stated (at p. 142):

> 'Proper' . . . is, however, plainly a word of wide meaning, certainly wider than (for example) 'lawful'. But the greater includes the less and no act which was not believed to be lawful could be believed to be proper within the meaning of the subsection. Thus no assistance is given to any defendant, even a fanatic or a deranged idealist, who knows or suspects that his threat, or the act threatened, is criminal, but believes it to be justified by his end or his peculiar circumstances.

In the circumstances of this case there was no room for doubt in light of the crimes actually threatened. If what D threatens is not known to him to be a crime, he may still be convicted if he did not believe it to be socially and morally acceptable as a means of enforcing his demand. For example, D demands payment from P of a debt threatening to show to P's neighbours and the editor of a Sunday newspaper explicit photographs of P performing an unnatural sexual act if P does not pay. D may believe that he has reasonable grounds for making the demand. D may not know that showing an obscene photograph to another person may constitute the offence of publishing obscene matter contrary to s. 2 of the Obscene Publications Act 1959. If he believed that showing the photographs was not unlawful, he could only be convicted of blackmail if it was proved that he did not believe that this would generally be regarded as morally and socially acceptable. It is difficult to imagine that D would have a strong chance of success on this point. However, if D, for example, is a person of low intelligence, poor education and from a social background where it is generally accepted that debts may be enforced by threats, he may genuinely believe his threat to be proper, in which case he would have to be acquitted.

13.4.4 With a view to gain or intent to cause loss

In s. 34(2)(a) TA 1968 'gain' and 'loss' are defined as being limited to gain or loss of money or other property, whether temporary or permanent. Many demands may be regarded as improper but they will found a charge of blackmail only if made by D 'with a view to gain for himself or another or with intent to cause loss to another'. Thus, for example, if D threatens to expose P's adultery to her husband unless she has sexual intercourse with him, this is not blackmail as it does not involve any gain in money or property to D or similar loss to P. By contrast if D's demand had been for money or property in return for not revealing P's adultery, this would found a charge of blackmail.

Section 34(2)(a) further provides:

(i) 'gain' includes a gain by keeping what one has, as well as a gain by getting what one has not; and
(ii) 'loss' includes a loss by not getting what one might get, as well as a loss by parting with what one has.

The following examples may serve to illustrate what is covered by s. 34(2)(a), the threat in each case being to expose P's adultery, P being his secretary:

(a) D demands that P allow him to keep the camera she has lent him (see (i));
(b) D demands that P forego her salary for a month (see (ii));
(c) D demands that P repay a loan he made to her (see (i): this is a gain even though D is legally entitled to repayment of the loan; see *Lawrence and Pomroy*);
(d) D demands that P lend him her car for the weekend (both a gain to D and a loss to P);
(e) D demands that P withdraw her writ for damages for injuries sustained due to D's negligence (D has a view to keeping what he has and P will sustain loss by not getting what she might get);
(f) D demands that P destroy photographs of D in a compromising situation which she has (see (ii));
(g) D demands that P feature in a pornographic video he is making and proposing to sell (D has a view to gain, i.e. the proceeds of sale of the video);
(h) D (who has a grudge against Q) demands that P set fire to Q's car (this constitutes a 'loss to another'; there is no requirement that the loss be caused to the person against whom the threats are made).

13.5 HANDLING

Section 22 TA 1968 provides:

(1) A person handles stolen goods if (otherwise than in the course of of the stealing) knowing or believing them to be stolen goods he dishonestly receives the goods, or dishonestly undertakes or assists in their retention,

removal, disposal or realisation by or for the benefit of another person, or if he arranges to do so.

(2) A person guilty of handling stolen goods shall on conviction on indictment be liable to imprisonment for a term not exceeding fourteen years.

A person who handles stolen goods may also, incidentally, commit theft if his act involves an appropriation. The offence of handling, however, is regarded as more serious than theft, as the maximum sentence available indicates, as the existence of professional handlers (commonly referred to as 'fences') helps to generate thefts; many thieves might not be so keen to steal if they did not have a person readily available who was prepared to dispose of their goods.

The offence of handling is quite complex as it may be committed in many different ways. In addition terms like 'stolen' and 'goods' have their own definitions.

13.5.1. *Actus reus*

13.5.1.1 'Stolen' The goods handled must be 'stolen' goods at the time of the handling. If the handler believes the goods to be stolen but they are not, he will not be guilty of handling (see *Haughton* v *Smith* [1975] AC 476) but he may be guilty of attempted handling (see *Shivpuri* [1987] AC 1). For example, goods would not be 'stolen' if the alleged thief believed he had a claim of right to the property. If, however, the alleged thief successfully pleaded the defence of duress on his trial for theft, this would not avail the handler as the defence of duress only operates as an excuse; D admits to committing the offence but is excused from the consequences of conviction and punishment due to the duress operating upon him. If the alleged thief has been tried and acquitted, this is not necessarily inconsistent with a conviction of the handler as, for example, the evidence against the handler may be much stronger than that against the alleged thief. If the thief has been convicted, the alleged handler may, nevertheless, dispute that the goods were stolen, in which case he will have to prove on a balance of probabilities that the thief's conviction was wrong (see s. 74(2) of the Police and Criminal Evidence Act 1984). If the alleged thief has not been tried or, if tried, has not been convicted, the question whether the goods were stolen must be decided on the basis of the evidence produced pointing to that fact in the trial of the alleged handler. The handler's belief that the goods were stolen does not constitute proof that they were (see *A-G's Reference (No. 4 of 1979)* [1981] 1 All ER 1193) but D's admissions in respect of facts within his knowledge (such as the circumstances in which he acquired the goods) may provide a legitimate basis for inferences to be drawn by the jury that the goods were stolen (see *McDonald* (1980) 70 Cr App R 288; *Barnes* [1991] Crim LR 132).

For the purposes of the offence of handling, 'stolen' has an extended meaning to include goods obtained by blackmail or by deception contrary to s. 15(1) (see s. 24(4)). The words 'steal', 'theft' and 'thief' are also to be construed accordingly. Furthermore, the theft etc. need not take place in England or

Wales provided that the activity amounts to theft etc. and is an offence in the country where it was committed (s. 24(1)).

The goods must remain stolen at the time of the handling. Section 24(3) provides:

> But no goods shall be regarded as having continued to be stolen goods after they have been restored to the person from whom they were stolen or to other lawful possession or custody, or after that person and any other person claiming through him have otherwise ceased as regards those goods to have any right to restitution in respect of the theft.

This provision relates to the two situations dealt with below.

13.5.1.1.1 Restoration of goods When do goods cease to be stolen? This problem arises most often when the owner (or his agent) or the police repossess the goods and then return them to the thief to entrap the handler. If the police take possession of the goods this constitutes 'other lawful possession or custody'. In these situations the handler generally will not be guilty of handling as the goods will have ceased to be stolen (see *Haughton* v *Smith, ante; Dolan* (1855) 6 Cox CC 449; *Schmidt* (1866) LR 1 CCR 15; *Villensky* [1892] 2 QB 597). There is one situation where the handler may be convicted, however, namely where it is alleged that he 'arranged' to handle the goods provided that the arrangement was made after the goods were stolen and before they were restored to lawful possession. For the goods to cease to be stolen there must be an act by the owner etc. amounting to the deliberate exercise of control over the goods. Simply to mark goods which have been stolen for the purpose of identifying them later when transferred by the thief to the handler does not constitute the exercise of control over the goods (see *Greater London Metropolitan Police Commissioner* v *Streeter* (1980) 71 Cr App R 113).

In deciding whether goods have been restored to lawful possession, the question whether a person has taken possession of goods for this purpose depends primarily on his intentions when he acted (see *A-G's Reference (No. 1 of 1974)* [1974] QB 744). In this case a police officer correctly suspected that goods in a car were stolen. He immobilised the car by removing the rotor arm and kept watch. When D returned to the car he questioned him and then arrested him. The Court of Appeal (at p. 753) held that:

> if the jury came to the conclusion that the proper explanation of what had happened was that the police officer had not intended at that stage to reduce the goods into his possession or to assume the control of them, and at that stage was merely concerned to ensure that the driver, if he appeared, could not get away without answering questions, then in that case the proper conclusion of the jury would have been to the effect that the goods had not been reduced into the possession of the police. . . .

13.5.1.1.2 The right to restitution has ceased Goods cease to be stolen when the person from whom they were stolen, or any person claiming through him, no longer has any right to restitution of the goods. For example, if E deceives P into agreeing to sell him property, this is a voidable contract of sale. If P discovers the deception but decides to ratify the contract by delivering the property to E, the goods cease to be stolen. Thus, if E sells the property to D who believes that it is stolen, there is no offence of handling as P's right to restitution of the property ceased upon ratification of the voidable contract. Similarly, if E steals property from P and then sells it in market overt to Q, a bona fide purchaser for value, the property ceases to be stolen. Thus if D, knowing the history of the property, receives it from Q he will not be guilty of handling. By contrast, however, if D had received from E the money Q paid him for the property, he could be guilty of handling (see *13.5.1.2.2 post*).

13.5.1.2 Goods and their proceeds Section 34(2)(b) defines 'goods' to include 'money and every other description of property except land, and includes things severed from land by stealing'. The definition of 'goods' is largely co-extensive with that of 'property' for the purposes of theft with the exception that land, if it is to be the subject of handling, must be severed. The requirement of severance acts as a limitation in respect of property obtained as a result of deception or blackmail.

Section 24(2) provides:

> . . . references to stolen goods shall include, in addition to the goods originally stolen and parts of them (whether in their original state or not) –
> (a) any other goods which directly or indirectly represent or have at any time represented the stolen goods in the hands of the thief as being the proceeds of any disposal or realisation of the whole or part of the goods stolen or of goods so representing the stolen goods; and
> (b) any other goods which directly or indirectly represent or have at any time represented the stolen goods in the hands of a handler of the stolen goods or any part of them as being the proceeds of any disposal or realisation of the whole or part of the stolen goods handled by him or of goods so representing them.

The effect of this provision is to extend the range of property which may be regarded as 'stolen' for the purposes of supporting a charge of handling. Thus, if the thief or the intitial handler converts the stolen goods into money or other property (i.e. 'proceeds' of the disposal or realisation of the stolen goods), these proceeds are also regarded as 'stolen' so that anyone who knowingly handles them will be guilty of handling. This can lead to considerable multiplication of the 'goods' which may be regarded as 'stolen' for the purposes of handling. Several examples will serve to illustrate the operation of this provision.

(i) A steals P's car and sells it for £500 to B, who knows it is stolen. Both the car and the money are stolen. The money directly represents the original stolen goods in the hands of the thief being the proceeds of its realisation or disposal (s. 24(2)(a)).

(ii)   A gives the £500 to C in payment of a debt, C knowing of its provenance; C would be guilty of receiving stolen goods.

(iii)   B breaks the car into parts and sells most of the parts to D and E for £300 each. The £600 is now proceeds of stolen goods which were 'in the hands of a handler' resulting from the disposal of part of the stolen goods and the remaining parts represent part of the stolen goods (s. 24(2)(b)). If D and E knew of the provenance of the parts they would be guilty of handling.

(iv)   B buys another car for £300. This car is also 'stolen goods' as it is 'goods so representing' the 'proceeds of any disposal or realisation of the whole or part of the stolen goods handled by him' (s. 24(2)(b)).

(v)   C buys a painting for £500 from Q. The painting is 'stolen goods' being the proceeds of the realisation or disposal of stolen goods (money) in the hands of a handler (s. 24(2)(b)).

(vi)   If B banks the £600 he received from D and E the debt owed him by the bank (a thing in action) indirectly represents the proceeds of the realisation or disposal of part of the stolen goods in the hands of a handler. If B writes a cheque for £500 for G, who knows of its provenance, the cheque (a thing in action) may represent the proceeds (or part of the proceeds) of the stolen goods in the hands of the handler. If the account had only £500 in it, or less than £500 when B lodged the money, then all or part of the cheque is proceeds of the money. If B's account had a balance in excess of £500 before he lodged the money, it cannot be proved that the cheque represents the stolen money rather than the balance which was originally in the account. The *A-G's Reference (No. 4 of 1979)* [1981] 1 All ER 1193, did not resolve whether G would be guilty of handling in such circumstances. Complicated questions relating to equity and the original victim's right to restitution arise which are beyond the scope of this book (see further Smith, *The Law of Theft* (6th edn) para. 405).

13.5.1.3   Handling   'Handling' may be committed in one of four basic ways provided that the conduct involved takes place 'otherwise than in the course of stealing'. There is, however, only one offence (see *Griffiths* v *Freeman* [1970] 1 All ER 1117; *Nicklin* [1977] 2 All ER 444), and 'handling' is simply a generic term to cover the various ways in which the offence may be committed. Accordingly, an indictment which simply alleges 'handling' is not bad for duplicity but the better practice is to particularise the form of handling alleged (see *Griffiths* v *Freeman, ante,* and *Alt* (1972) 56 Cr App R 457). If one particular mode of handling is alleged, such as 'receiving', D cannot be convicted on the basis of a different mode (see *Nicklin, ante*). In any case where there is uncertainty as to the appropriate mode to allege, the indictment should contain separate counts alleging different modes (see *Sloggett* [1972] 1 QB 430).

The four basic modes of committing the offence are:

(i)   *receiving* stolen goods; or
(ii)   *undertaking* the retention, removal, disposal or realisation of the goods for the benefit of another person; or
(iii)   *assisting* in the retention, removal, disposal or realisation of the goods by another person; or

(iv)   *arranging* to do (i), (ii) or (iii).

Two points in particular should be noted. Firstly, in all cases the goods must be stolen at the time the receiving, undertaking, assisting or arranging takes place. If, for example, D arranges with A to receive goods which A is going to steal, D is not guilty of handling as there are no goods then stolen, but he may be guilty of conspiracy to handle stolen goods. Secondly, apart from receiving or arranging to receive, the other forms of handling are subject to a qualification: in (ii) the acts must be done 'for the benefit of another person' and in (iii) the handler must assist another person to do the relevant acts. If D is charged with arranging to undertake or assist the same qualification applies.

13.5.1.3.1   Receiving and arranging to receive   Receiving involves D in taking possession or control of the stolen goods either alone or with others, which may include joint possession with the thief. It is a finite act so that, where D receives on different occasions goods from different thefts, these occasions must be specified as separate counts on the indictment (see *Smythe* (1980) 72 Cr App R 8). If D's servant or agent takes possession of stolen goods with his authority this will constitute receiving by D (see *Miller* (1854) 6 Cox CC 353). There is no requirement that D should receive the goods to keep or otherwise dispose of them nor that he should gain any profit or other benefit from their receipt. It is sufficient that he has possession or control even if he is only receiving them temporarily to hide them (see *Richardson* (1834) 6 C & P 335). There must be evidence, however, that D has possession or control. If D is merely inspecting the goods in the thief's presence during negotiations, he has neither possession nor control of them. Helping a thief to remove stolen goods from a lorry does not amount to receiving (see *Hobson* v *Impett* (1957) 41 Cr App R 138) although it may amount to one of the other forms of handling. If D finds stolen goods and takes possession of them this does not amount to receiving (see *Haider*, unreported, March 22 1985) although this may amount to theft (see *11.2.2.2.1 ante*).

Negotiating with the thief to purchase stolen goods is not itself a complete act of arranging to receive. When agreement is reached, that D will receive the goods, this will constitute the offence of arranging to receive. The arrangement need not be made with the thief; an arrangement made with a person innocently in possession of stolen goods would suffice provided D knew the goods were stolen. Although an agreement may not be concluded, an offer by D to receive stolen goods may constitute an attempt to handle.

13.5.1.3.2   Undertaking or assisting   There are four activities which may constitute handling where either (1) D undertakes those activities for the benefit of another, or (2) D assists another to perform those activities or (3) arranges to undertake or assist in those activities. In *Bloxham* [1982] 1 All ER 582, the House of Lords held that 'the other person' must have the same meaning whether it is alleged that D assisted or undertook the relevant activity. Thus something may only be undertaken for the benefit of another if that other person could have done the act himself. In *Bloxham*, D, believing that a car he had bought was stolen, sold it to E. He was charged with handling stolen goods on the basis that he had undertaken the realisation of the car for the benefit of another person, namely E. The House of Lords was of the view that the person for whose benefit this transaction was undertaken was D and not E. E's purchase of the car may have been of benefit to him, but this was irrelevant as it was D's act of sale (realisation) which was required to have benefitted him. D could only be convicted where the sale was for the benefit of another person as where, for example, he was selling the car as an agent for C (the thief or another handler of it). Furthermore, the act of sale of the car (realisation) was not one which could have been performed *by* E as he did not possess the car.

The four activities involved each have a separate meaning and appear to cover all the various things a person may seek to do with stolen goods.

(a)   Retention   In *Pitchley* (1972) 57 Cr App R 30, the Court of Appeal defined 'retain' to mean 'keep possession of, not lose, continue to have'. A person undertakes the retention of stolen goods where, for example, he stores the goods for the thief or another handler. As retention is a continuing activity, D may commit the offence where, after taking possession of property to retain for another, he discovers that it is stolen. By continuing to keep possession of it he would be undertaking to retain it (but cf. *Pitchley* where the Court of Appeal appears to have treated this as assisting in the retention of stolen goods). D will be guilty of assisting another to retain stolen goods where he does something 'intentionally and dishonestly, for the purpose of enabling the goods to be retained' (*per* Cantley J in *Kanwar* [1982] 2 All ER 528). Examples of such conduct would be where D helps to hide the goods or he puts the thief in touch with someone else who agrees to store them, or where he tells lies to make it more difficult for the police to find or identify the goods (see *Kanwar*). For example, if E is a thief and the police visit E's flat seeking particular goods and D tells the police that items fitting the description of the stolen goods in fact belong to him and he lent them to E, D would be assisting E to retain those goods. By contrast, however, if D is, for example, a lodger in E's flat and knows where the stolen goods are hidden, but simply refuses to answer any police questions (as opposed to giving untruthful answers), this does not constitute assisting (see *Brown* [1970] QB 105). In *Brown*, the Court of Appeal took the view that to hold that a failure to answer questions amounted to 'assisting' would encroach on the principle that a person is not bound to answer police questions. If, however, the stolen goods were hidden in D's room, this would be circumstantial evidence which may point to him having permitted them to be hidden there initially and thus may support a charge of handling on the basis of undertaking to retain the stolen goods.

It appears that D will be convicted only where a purposive intent is proved. In *Kanwar*, D's husband brought home stolen goods which D used to furnish the home being aware of their provenance. Cantley J stated that D would not be guilty of handling where 'she was merely willing for the goods to be kept and used in the house and was thinking it was nice to have them there, although they were stolen goods.' Similarly a person does not assist in the retention of stolen goods merely by using them (see *Sanders* (1982) 75 Cr App R 84).

(b) Removal This involves transporting or carrying stolen goods. If D transports stolen goods for E's benefit he will have undertaken their removal; if he assists E to transport goods, for example, by lending him a van, he will have assisted in their removal.

(c) Disposal This covers destroying, dumping, giving away or transforming stolen goods. An example of transformation would be where D melts down stolen silver items. The fact that D benefits from a disposal of stolen property does not, in itself, amount to assisting in its disposal; assisting requires an act of helping or encouraging (see *Coleman* [1986] Crim LR 56). In *Coleman*, D and his wife purchased a flat in their joint names; the wife, to D's knowledge, used stolen money to pay some of the fees involved. While purchase of the flat benefited D, this did not establish that he had assisted her; there had to be proof that D encouraged her to do so or agreed to her doing so. On a proper direction, however, a jury may have inferred this from the facts.

(d) Realisation Realisation involves the selling of stolen goods or their exchange for anything else of value. If D sells stolen goods as agent for E (the thief or another handler) he undertakes their realisation for the benefit of another. If D introduces a purchaser to E who is seeking to sell stolen goods, he assists in their realisation. If D arranges a meeting between D and E he would be arranging to assist in the realisation of stolen goods.

13.5.1.3.3 Otherwise than in the course of the stealing This limitation in s. 22(1) protects the original thief from liability for handling in respect of the course of conduct which constituted the original theft. This is necessary where two or more persons participate in the original theft. As theft is committed as soon as D appropriates property, subsequent acts to remove the property might otherwise amount to handling but for this limitation (see *Gregory* (1981) 77 Cr App R 41). For example, D and E agree to burgle a house. D enters and passes property through the window to E outside. D and E then carry the goods to a van to transport them to a fence who will pay them for the property. If s. 22(1) did not contain the above limitation, E would be guilty of receiving when D hands him the goods and both D and E would be guilty of assisting each other to remove the goods and to realise them. The phrase 'course of the stealing' extends beyond the time of the appropriation of the property. The difficulty, however, is determining when the course of the stealing ends. For example, if D removes a statue from P's house and hides it in P's shed to return later with E to remove it from the premises, it is submitted that 'the course of the stealing' was over when D first removed the statue so that when E later assisted D to remove it from the garage he was assisting another to remove stolen goods. By contrast, if E had accompanied D and waited in the garage to help D, the whole transaction would have been a continuing one and E would have been an aider and abettor to the burglary or theft rather than a handler. It is, essentially, a question of fact when a course of stealing ends.

A case which has been regarded by some as problematic is *Pitham and Hehl* (1976) 65 Cr App R 45. M offered to sell P's furniture to D and E. D and E inspected the furniture, agreed to buy it, paid M and then removed it from P's house. They were convicted of handling and appealed, contending that their acts did not take place 'otherwise than in the course of the stealing'. The Court of Appeal upheld their convictions on the basis that M's offer to sell the furniture amounted to a completed theft as he was assuming the rights of the owner at that point. Everything D and E did thereafter was after the course of the stealing had transpired. The case has been subjected to criticism but the decision may be supported. Clearly nothing else was necessary to commit theft other than the making of the offer to sell. If the purpose of the limitation in s. 22(1) was to protect accessories from liability for handling arising from their acts which aided and abetted the principal, the decision does not conflict with this purpose as there was no evidence to suggest that D and E had aided, abetted, counselled or procured M's theft. Rather, it appeared that he committed the theft independently of D and E. It may be, however, that in removing the goods D and E themselves committed a theft but this was a separate theft from M's initial theft (cf. *Gregory ante*).

Where D is found in possession of stolen goods several days after the theft it may not be clear whether he is the thief or a handler. If D is charged with handling, must the prosecution prove that he came by the goods 'otherwise than in the course of the stealing'? The Court of Appeal held in *Cash* [1985] QB 801, that unless there was some evidence pointing to D being the thief, the jury were entitled to infer from the evidence of recent possession that he was the handler and, in such a case, the words 'otherwise than in the course of the stealing' should not be mentioned to the jury.

Once the 'course of the stealing' is over a thief may be guilty of handling the goods he has stolen, for example, by helping a receiver of the goods to move them or dispose of them. Similarly, if D is an accessory to the theft and several days later another party to the theft delivers to him his share of the items stolen, D will be guilty of receiving stolen goods.

It is worth noting that a handler generally commits a separate offence of theft by means of his subsequent dealing with the goods as virtually any act of handling (apart from the 'arranging' cases) will amount to an appropriation of property with the intention of permanently depriving the owner of it.

13.5.2 *Mens Rea*

D will be guilty of handling only where he knows or believes that the goods are stolen goods at the time when he does the act which constitutes handling. In the case of receiving or arranging to receive or to do any of the other prohibited acts, this knowledge or belief must exist at the time D receives the goods or makes the arrangement. Where D's acts constitute *undertaking* or *assisting* in the prohibited acts, D will be liable if he learns the truth and continues to undertake or assist in, for example, the disposal of the stolen goods even though his initial participation in this activity was innocent. If D comes by the stolen goods innocently as a bona fide purchaser, his subsequent dealing with the goods, after he learns of their provenance, cannot amount to theft (see s.3(2) TA 1968, *11.2.1.5.4 ante*) but there is no similar provision excluding liability for handling. If, for example, D subsequently assisted E to sell the goods he would appear to have assisted another to realise the goods. By contrast, if D initially received the goods as a gift, his keeping of, or dealing with, them after discovering their provenance would amount to theft (see s. 3(1) TA 1968, *11.2.1.5.3 ante*); any dealing with the goods thereafter may also constitute handling.

13.5.2.1 What constitutes knowledge or belief? Actual knowledge or belief on the part of D must be proved; it is not sufficient that any reasonable person would have realised that the goods were stolen (see *Atwal* v *Massey* (1971) 56 Cr App R 6). It is enough that D knows or believes in the existence of facts which render the goods 'stolen' in law. D need not know the law and, indeed, it would not avail him if he believed the goods had been stolen when, in fact, they had been obtained as a result of blackmail. In addition, D need not know the nature of the goods; if he takes possession of a suitcase having been told that it contains stolen goods, he will be guilty of handling if it does contain stolen goods even though they differ from the goods which D believed the case contained (see *McCullum* (1973) 57 Cr App R 645).

If D has direct evidence as to the provenance of the goods, for example, he witnesses the theft or the thief tells him the goods are stolen, he 'knows' the goods are stolen (*Hall* (1985) 81 Cr App R 260). 'Belief' that goods are stolen, according to Boreham J in *Hall* (at p. 264):

> may be said to be the state of mind of a person who says to himself: 'I cannot say I know for certain that these goods are stolen, but there can be no other reasonable conclusion in the light of all the circumstances, in the light of all that I have heard and seen.

Suspicion, on the other hand, that goods are stolen is not sufficient (see *Hall*; *Grainge* (1974) 59 Cr App R 3; *Pethick* [1980] Crim LR 242), nor does foresight that goods are probably stolen constitute belief (*Reader* (1977) 66 Cr App R 33). Similarly, wilful blindness does not amount to knowledge or belief, although the fact that D suspects that goods are stolen and deliberately shuts his eyes to this is evidence which may point to him having the requisite knowledge or belief, that is it is evidence from which knowledge or belief may be inferred (see *Griffiths* (1974) 60 Cr App R 14). This latter proposition is difficult to follow; if the jury conclude that D suspected the goods were stolen, and suspicion does not constitute knowledge or belief, how can they infer from this knowledge or belief? It would make more sense to hold that wilful blindness constitutes knowledge or belief.

13.5.2.2 Proof of knowledge or belief The prosecution may be assisted in their task of proving knowledge or belief by the common law doctrine of 'recent possession' and by s. 27(3) TA 1968. Where D is found in possession of recently stolen goods and offers no explanation for his possession, or the jury are satisfied beyond reasonable doubt that any explanation offered is untrue, the jury *may* infer guilty knowledge from this fact (see *Abramovitch* (1914) 11 Cr App R 45). The jury are not obliged to draw such an inference and should convict only where satisfied beyond reasonable doubt that D had such knowledge or belief (*Abramovitch*). There is no particular magic in this doctrine; it is, in fact, simply an example of circumstantial evidence.

Section 27(3) is very different. This provision permits the admission of evidence which may have little or no probative value but will have a highly prejudicial effect upon the accused's case. Where D is charged with handling *and* evidence has been given of his having performed an act which could amount to handling, then for the purpose of proving that D knew or believed the goods to be stolen, two classes of evidence may be admitted:

(a)   evidence that he has had in his possession, or has undertaken or assisted in the retention, removal, disposal or realisation of, stolen goods from any theft taking place not earlier than twelve months before the offence charged; and

(b)   (provided that seven days' notice in writing has been given to him of the intention to prove the conviction) evidence that he has within the five years preceding the date of the offence charged been convicted of theft or of handling stolen goods.

This subsection is strictly construed. Under (a) it is only permissible to tender evidence of the actual handling; no evidence as to D's state of mind nor as to the circumstances in which D came into possession of them, is admissible (*Bradley* (1979) 70 Cr App R 200). This has the potential of wreaking injustice as the other incident of handling may not have constituted an offence as D may not have known or believed the goods to be stolen. Thus, if D had innocently bought stolen goods and been acquitted on a charge of handling and then is subsequently found in possession of stolen goods, the other incident may be proved. The only purpose of proving it is to try to persuade a jury to conclude that it is stretching credulity to believe that both incidents are innocent. D may simply have been unfortunate, however, rather than dishonest. The trial judge, of course, has a discretion to refuse to admit evidence under (a) which the prosecution might tender (see *Rasini, The Times,* March 20 1986).

Under paragraph (b) the prosecution may merely prove the fact of D's previous conviction (*Fowler* (1988) 86 Cr App R 219), but again the risk of prejudice is obvious.

13.5.2.3   Dishonesty   The test of dishonesty is the same as for theft (see *11.2.2.2.2 ante*). Obviously, if D receives stolen goods to hand them back to the owner or the police, he would not be dishonest.

Further reading
J. R. Spencer, 'The mishandling of handling' [1981] Crim LR 682; 'Handling, theft and the mala fide purchaser' [1985] Crim LR 92 & 440.

FOURTEEN
Criminal damage

14.1 INTRODUCTION

The Criminal Damage Act 1971 contains the main offences involving damage to property. The Act is largely the result of work by the Law Commission (see in particular Law Com No. 29). The Act largely complements the law of theft.

14.2 DESTROYING OR DAMAGING PROPERTY BELONGING TO ANOTHER

Section 1(1) of the Criminal Damage Act 1971 provides:

A person who without lawful excuse destroys or damages any property belonging to another intending to destroy or damage any such property or being reckless as to whether any such property would be destroyed or damaged shall be guilty of an offence.

The maximum punishment for this offence following trial on indictment is ten years' imprisonment (s. 4(2)). Where, however, the offence is committed by fire it is charged as arson and the maximum punishment is life imprisonment (s. 1(3) and 4(1)). This reflects the extra danger arising from fire-raising.

14.2.1 *Actus reus*

14.2.1.1 Destroy or damage Whether property is damaged is a question of fact and degree (see *Cox* v *Riley* (1986) 83 Cr App R 54). It includes physical harm, whether permanent or temporary, and the permanent or temporary impairment of the value or usefulness of property. Physical harm may result to property in many ways. Trampling down grass, or other vegetation, may constitute damage (see *Gayford* v *Choulder* [1898] 1 QB 316). Dumping rubbish on land may amount to damage where the owner of the land is put to expense in removing it, even though the land underneath is not damaged (*Henderson and Battley*, November 29, 1984, unreported). Drawing or painting on a pavement using water soluble chalks or paints constitutes damage where the local authority is involved in expense in cleaning the pavement (*Hardman v Chief Constable of Avon and Somerset Constabulary* [1986] Crim LR 330). Spitting on a policeman's coat, however, does not constitute damage where the spittle can be removed with a damp cloth (*'A' (a juvenile) v R* [1978] Crim LR 689). The requirement appears to be that if expense on the part of the owner of the property is incurred to restore it to its previous condition a jury or magistrates may conclude that damage has been caused (see *Roe v Kingerlee* [1986] Crim LR 735). Had the policeman's coat required dry cleaning, for example, the result might have been different. The nature of the property involved may also be relevant in addition to the degree of harm caused. In *Morphitis v Salmon* [1990] Crim LR 48, the Divisional Court held that a scratch to a scaffold bar could not constitute damage as it involved no impairment of its value or usefulness since scratching was a normal incident of scaffolding components. By contrast, a scratch to the bonnet of a car could constitute damage as this would involve expense on the part of the owner in remedial work albeit that the secondhand value of the car might not be affected. Of course, if the damage to the paintwork is substantial this might also affect the value of the vehicle. There is no need for the property to be rendered useless if the damage involves diminution in its value. For example, if water is added to beer its value is diminished but it is not useless; this amounts to damage (see *Roper v Knott* [1898] 1 QB 868).

Damage arising from the impairment of the usefulness of property occurs where, for example, a part is removed from a machine (*Tacey* (1821) Russ & Ry 452) or a machine is dismantled or tampered with so that it will not work (*Fisher* (1865) LR 1 CCR 7; *Getty v Antrim County Council* [1950] NI 114). Where a part is removed or a machine dismantled, D should be charged with damaging the machine and not the parts unless these also have been damaged (see *Woolcock* [1977] Crim LR 104 and 161 and *Morphitis v Salmon*). Simply to deny P the use of his property, for example, by placing a wheel clamp on his car, does not amount to damage (*Lloyd* [1992] 1 All ER 982). In *Cox v Riley* (1986) 83 Cr App R 54, erasure of the programmes on a printed circuit card used to control a computerised saw was held to be damage to the card. This was affirmed in *Whiteley, The Times*, February 6 1991, where D had hacked into a computer network and altered data stored on disks. This was held to be damage even though the physical nature of the disks had not been altered or impaired; their usefulness, however, was impaired. The effect of these decisions in so far as they relate to computers has been reversed by s. 3(6) of the Computer Misuse Act 1990 (the offence in *Whiteley* was committed before the Act came into force) which provides:

For the purposes of the Criminal Damage Act 1971 a modification of the contents of a computer shall not be regarded as damaging any computer or computer storage medium unless its effect on that computer or computer storage medium impairs its physical condition.

The accused in *Cox v Riley* and *Whiteley* would now be guilty of the offence of unauthorised modification of computer material contrary to s. 3 of the 1990 Act. The Law Commission, *Computer Misuse* (Law Com No. 186), whose recommendations resulted in the passage of the 1990 Act, did point out, however, (at para 3.78) that:

> This recommendation would not of course prejudice the operation of the 1971 Act in cases where the unauthorised modification [of a computer's memory or computer storage medium] leads to actual physical damage. For example, if a computer-operated saw were reprogrammed so that it ruined a load of timber, then (subject in both cases to the presence of the appropriate *mens rea*) the re-programming would amount to an unauthorised modification and the consequent damage to the timber would come within section 1 of the Criminal Damage Act 1971.

The 1990 Act does not affect the authority of *Cox v Riley* and *Whiteley* in so far as they are appropriate to other situations where information is stored in electro-magnetic form. For example, if D alters or erases P's audio tapes or video tapes, this would constitute damage even though the physical nature of the tapes had not been altered. In *Whitely* it was argued that tampering with the discs altered only intangible information contained on them but caused no tangible or perceptible damage to the disc itself. Lord Lane CJ responded:

> That contention contained a basic fallacy. What the Act required to be proved was that tangible property had been damaged, not necessarily that the damage itself should be tangible. There could be no doubt that the magnetic particles on the metal discs were a part of the discs and if the appellant was proved to have intentionally and without lawful excuse altered the particles in such a way as to cause an impairment of the value or usefulness of the disc to the owner, there would be damage within the meaning of s. 1. The fact that the alteration could only be perceived by operating the computer did not make the alterations any the less real, or the damage . . . any the less within the ambit of the Act.

This statement of principle will continue to apply if the words 'audio or video tape' and 'tape recorder or video recorder' are substituted for 'metal disk' and 'computer' respectively.

Criminal damage is also committed where D destroys property, for example, by demolishing a building, breaking up a machine, killing an animal, laying waste crops (e.g. by mowing a field of wheat, or spraying it with herbicide), by incinerating books etc. It is difficult to envisage a case where damage will not be done to the property in the process of destroying it.

14.2.1.2 Property Section 10(1) provides:

> In this Act 'property' means property of a tangible nature, whether real or personal, including money and -

(a) including wild creatures which have been tamed or are ordinarily kept in captivity, and any other wild creatures or their carcasses if, but only if, they have been reduced into possession which has not been lost or abandoned or are in the course of being reduced into possession; but

(b) not including mushrooms growing wild on any land or flowers, fruit or foliage of a plant growing wild on any land.

For the purposes of this subsection 'mushroom' includes any fungus and 'plant' includes any shrub or tree.

There are some differences between this definition of 'property' and that in s. 4 of the Theft Act 1968, necessitated by the differing mischief to which each Act is directed. Firstly, land may not be stolen but it may be damaged or destroyed; indeed arson is generally committed against land in the form of buildings. Secondly, 'property' is confined to tangible property in the Criminal Damage Act. Thirdly, wild mushrooms, flowers, fruit or foliage cannot be the subject of criminal damage although they may, in certain circumstances, be the subject of theft.

14.2.1.3 Belonging to another   Section 10 provides:

(2) Property shall be treated for the purposes of this Act as belonging to any person -

(a) having the custody or control of it;

(b) having in it any proprietary right or interest (not being an equitable interest arising only from an agreement to transfer or grant an interest); or

(c) having a charge on it.

(3) Where the property is subject to a trust, the persons to whom it belongs shall be so treated as including any person having a right to enforce the trust.

(4) Property of a corporation sole shall be so treated as belonging to the corporation notwithstanding a vacancy in the corporation.

Again these provisions are broadly similar to s. 5 of the Theft Act 1968. In s. 5 TA 1968 theft may be committed where a person has 'possession or control' of property; the equivalent words in s. 10(2) are 'custody or control' suggesting that P must have physical custody of it and were used to provide a clearer concept than the word 'possession' which is a technical term sometimes giving rise to difficulty (see *Warner* v *Metropolitan Police Commissioner* [1969] 2 AC 256). Another difference from the Theft Act is the inclusion of paragraph (c) in subsection (2) relating to charges on property. This provision is superfluous, however, as a charge on property amounts to a proprietary right or interest in property.

Property may be the subject of criminal damage, therefore, where some person has custody or control of it or a proprietary right or interest in it. As with theft, where D may steal property he owns if another also has a proprietary right or interest in it or possession or control of it, a person may cause criminal damage to property he owns if another has such an interest in it. For example, if D hires a car to P and then removes the rotor arm from it rendering it inoperable, he may be guilty of criminal damage. In cases where D is alleged to have damaged property in which he has a proprietary interest proof of *mens rea* or disproof of lawful excuse may be difficult.

If D destroys his own property for a dishonest purpose, for example to make a fraudulent insurance claim, this is not an offence under s. 1(1) despite D's dishonesty as an insurance company has no proprietary interest in property it insures.

14.2.2 *Mens rea*

The destruction or damage to property belonging to another amounts to an offence only if it is done intentionally or recklessly and without lawful excuse.

14.2.2.1 Intention and recklessness As to the meaning of intention see 3.2.3 *ante*. If D is charged with intentionally damaging property belonging to another, it must be proved that he intended to cause damage by his act (or omission) and that he intended to damage property belonging to another. If D mistakenly believes that the property he is damaging or destroying is his own, he will lack the requisite intention. In *Smith (David)* [1974] QB 354, D, not knowing property law, damaged fixtures he had installed in the flat of which he was a tenant when removing wiring for his stereo equipment. He believed that the fixtures belonged to him when, in law, they belonged to the landlord. His conviction of criminal damage was quashed, James LJ stating (at p. 360):

> Applying the ordinary principles of *mens rea*, the intention and recklessness and the absence of lawful excuse required to constitute the offence have reference to property belonging to another. It follows that in our judgment no offence is committed under this section if a person destroys or causes damage to property belonging to another if he does so in the honest though mistaken belief that the property is his own, and provided that belief is honestly held it is irrelevant to consider whether or not it is a justifiable belief.

In this case D's mistake was one of law; it would make no difference if the mistake was one of fact. For example, after his exams D burns a textbook believing it is his when, in fact, it is his flatmate P's textbook which he has picked up by mistake.

Recklessness was defined in *Caldwell* [1982] AC 341 (see discussion at 3.4.2.2 *ante*). As the test of recklessness in *Caldwell* was extended to cover inadvertence to an obvious risk of damage to property, this expanded considerably the ambit of the offence. If the prosecution charge the accused in the alternative, that is intentionally *or* recklessly damaging property belonging to another, he will also be denied the possibility of raising intoxication as a factor relevant to his state of mind as criminal damage where recklessness is charged (both in relation to the s. 1(1) offence and the s. 1(2) offence; see 14.3 *post*) is an offence of basic intent (*Caldwell*; see 5.6.3 *ante*).

14.2.2.2   Lawful excuse   Section 5(2) provides a partial definition of 'lawful excuse' (see s. 5(5)). Thus D may also avail of any other defence, e.g. duress, prevention of crime, arrest of offenders, and self-defence. For example, where D is being attacked by P he may damage property to defend himself where (i) he jumps through a window, breaking it, in seeking to escape from P; or (ii) he pushes P through the window; or (iii) he hits P over the head with a vase belonging to X and breaks it. In (i) D's defence would be duress of circumstances and in (ii) and (iii) it would be self-defence. In each case D will succeed provided the measures he took were objectively reasonable in the circumstances.

Section 5 provides:

(2)   A person charged with an offence to which this section applies shall, whether or not he would be treated for the purposes of this Act as having a lawful excuse apart from this subsection, be treated for those purposes as having a lawful excuse -

(a)   if at the time of the act or acts alleged to constitute the offence he believed that the person or person whom he believed to be entitled to consent to the destruction of or damage to the property in question had so consented, or would have so consented to it if he or they had known of the destruction or damage and its circumstances; or

(b)   if he destroyed or damaged or threatened to destroy or damage the property in question or, in the case of a charge of an offence under s. 3 above, intended to use or cause or permit the use of something to destroy or damage it, in order to protect property belonging to himself or another or a right or interest in property which was or which he believed to be vested in himself or another, and at the time of the act or acts alleged to constitute the offence he believed -

(i)   that the property, right or interest was in immediate need of protection; and

(ii)   that the means of protection adopted or proposed to be adopted were or would be reasonable having regard to all the circumstances.

(3)   For the purposes of this section it is immaterial whether a belief is justified or not if it is not honestly held.

(4)   For the purposes of subsection (2) above a right or interest in property includes any right or privilege in or over land, whether created by grant, licence or otherwise.

Section 5(2)(a) is equivalent to s. 2(1)(b) of TA 1968 (see *11.2.2.2.1 ante*). The only issue is whether D's belief was honestly held regardless of whether or not it was reasonable. It does not even matter that D's mistake was a drunken one (see *Jaggard* v *Dickinson* [1980] 3 All ER 716, *5.6.4 ante*). The burden is on the prosecution to prove beyond reasonable doubt the absence of lawful excuse once the accused has adduced some evidence to raise the issue. D's mistake may relate to one of several matters (or to a combination of these matters): (i) D may mistakenly believe that he has been told to damage or destroy the property; (ii) D may mistakenly believe that the person telling him to damage or destroy the property (or whom he believes is telling him to do so) is the person entitled to consent to its damage or destruction; (iii) D may mistakenly believe that the person entitled to consent to the damage or destruction of the property would do so if he knew of the circumstances in which D has damaged or destroyed it; (iv) D may believe that the person whom he mistakenly believes is entitled to consent to the damage or destruction of the property would do so if he knew of the circumstances in which D has damaged or destroyed it.

If D honestly believes that the owner of property (or some other person entitled to give consent) has consented to his damaging the property, the reason for the damage is irrelevant even if it is for the purpose of perpetrating a fraud. This results from the fact that criminal damage is not an offence of which dishonesty is an element. In *Denton* [1982] 1 All ER 65, D, who was employed at a cotton mill, set fire to the mill and machinery in it because he thought his 'employer' T had asked him to do so in order to make a fraudulent claim against the insurers. Indeed, it appeared that T had asked D to do so. The Court of Appeal quashed his conviction, Lord Lane CJ stating (at p. 68):

one has to decide whether or not an offence is committed at the moment that the acts are alleged to be committed. The fact that somebody may have had a dishonest intent which in the end he was going to carry out, namely a claim from the insurance company, cannot turn what was not originally a crime into a crime. There is no unlawfulness under the 1971 Act in burning a house. It does not become unlawful because there may be an inchoate attempt to commit fraud contained in it; that is to say it does not become a crime under the 1971 Act, whatever may be the situation outside the Act.

If T had asked D to set fire to the mill for the purpose of making a fraudulent insurance claim, both D and T could have been convicted of conspiracy to defraud.

Section 5(2)(b) provides that D has a lawful excuse where he believes his property or that of another (or property which he believes is his property or another's) is in need of immediate protection and he damages or destroys property believing that this is reasonable in the circumstances to protect his property. This is an unusual provision as D is the sole arbiter of what is reasonable in the circumstances. By contrast, for example, self-defence will not avail an accused if he uses more force than was reasonable in the circumstances even though he believed the force used was reasonable (see 6.5.3 *ante*).

If D's purpose is something other than the protection of property this defence will not be available (see *Hunt* (1978) 66 Cr App R 105; *Hill and Hall* [1989] Crim LR 136). Having determined what D's purpose was, it is for the court to rule as a matter of law whether this amounts to a purpose of protecting property; the fact that D believes he is protecting his property is irrelevant. In *Hill and Hall*, the fact that D and E, members of CND, believed that, by cutting the fence surrounding a United States naval base at Brawdy, they would protect their homes was of no avail as the judge ruled that their acts were not for the purpose of protection. D's and E's convoluted reasoning was that if the Russians attacked this nuclear base, their homes would be damaged by the blast or fall-out from a nuclear attack. If enough people breached the perimeter fence the Americans might decide to remove the base and thereby remove the threat of nuclear attack. The trial judge's conclusion was that D's and E's purpose was to encourage the Americans to leave and this was not a purpose of protecting their property. The Court of Appeal affirmed that he had adopted the correct approach which was to decide (i) what was in D's mind (the subjective test) and (ii) whether it could be said, as a matter of law, on the facts as believed by D, that cutting the strand of wire could amount to something done to protect her home or those of others (the objective test). Thus, the question whether property is damaged or destroyed by D 'in order to protect property belonging to himself' is one of law and not a matter of D's belief. The trial judge had also concluded that D and E had not adduced any evidence that they believed that their property was 'in immediate need of protection'. The Court of Appeal held that he was correct in withdrawing this part of the case from the jury.

14.3   DESTROYING OR DAMAGING PROPERTY WITH INTENT TO ENDANGER LIFE

Section 1(2) of the Criminal Damage Act 1971 provides:

> A person who without lawful excuse destroys or damages any property, whether belonging to himself or another -
> (a)   intending to destroy or damage any property or being reckless as to whether any property would be destroyed or damaged; and
> (b)   intending by the destruction or damage to endanger the life of another or being reckless as to whether the life of another would be thereby endangered;
> shall be guilty of an offence.

The maximum punishment for this offence is life imprisonment (s. 4(1)). In many cases where D damages property and endangers life he will do so with the specific intent to kill and would be liable to conviction of attempted murder. This offence, however, is wider in some respects than attempted murder, as it is sufficient that D is reckless whether life will be endangered (but attempted murder does not require proof of damage to property). This offence, if appropriate on the facts, also avoids the difficulties of proving that D has done a 'more than merely preparatory act'.

14.3.1   *Actus reus*
The meaning of 'damage', 'destroy' and 'property' is the same as for s. 1(1). There is a major difference, however, in that the property destroyed or damaged need not belong to another; D may commit this offence where he destroys or damages his own property if he does so with intent to endanger life or being reckless thereto. For example, if D, a landlord wishing to evict a

squatter who is refusing to leave, throws a petrol bomb into the house thereby damaging the property, he is liable to conviction of the s. 1(2) offence if he had the requisite *mens rea* specified in s. 1(2)(b).

14.3.2   *Mens rea*

D must intend to damage or destroy property or be reckless thereto. In addition, D must intend *by* that damage to endanger life or be reckless thereto. In *Steer* [1987] 2 All ER 833, D fired a shot through a window pane behind which P and Q were standing. It was accepted that he did not intend to endanger their lives. The question remained, however, whether he damaged property being reckless whether the life of another would be endangered. D was convicted and appealed submitting that it had to be proved that the endangering arose from the damage to the window and not the act which caused the damage to the window (i.e. the firing of the bullet which smashed it). The House of Lords affirmed the decision of the Court of Appeal allowing his appeal as it was the shooting which endangered the lives and not the breaking of the window.

The fact that lives are not endangered is irrelevant if it was D's intention by the damage to endanger life (see *Dudley* [1989] Crim LR 57) or he was reckless thereto (*Sangha* [1988] 2 All ER 385). In *Dudley*, D had set fire to P's house in pursuit of a grievance. D threw a fire bomb at the house but P and his family quickly extinguished the fire and only trivial damage was caused. D's conviction of arson being reckless whether life would be endangered was affirmed by the Court of Appeal. The relevant time was when D did the act which caused the damage; if at that time there was an obvious risk of danger to life or if he intended to endanger life, he had the requisite *mens rea*. In *Sangha*, D claimed that he had not created a risk to life as the flat which he set on fire was empty and the construction of the building was such that there was no danger of the fire spreading to adjoining properties. The Court of Appeal dismissed his appeal, Tucker J stating (at p. 390):

> In our judgment, when consideration is given to whether an act of setting fire to something creates an obvious . . . risk of damaging property and thereby endangering the life of another, the test to be applied is this: is it proved that an ordinary prudent bystander would have perceived an obvious risk that property would be damaged and that life would thereby be endangered? The ordinary prudent bystander is not deemed to be invested with expert knowledge relating to the construction of the property, nor to have the benefit of hindsight. The time at which the perception is material is the time when the fire is started.

As objective recklessness suffices in respect of both the damage to property and endangering life, this provision has the potential to create even greater injustices than those arising under s. 1(1). The accused may have failed to give thought to an obvious risk of damage and failed to give thought to an obvious risk of danger to life but yet be liable to conviction of an offence with a possible life sentence; it does not matter that the risk would not have been obvious to D even if he had thought about it (see *Elliott* v *C* and *Stephen (Malcolm R.)*, *3.4.2.2.3 ante*). An example may help illustrate the potential for injustice which the courts appear quite prepared to countenance in relation to the s. 1(1) offence; there is no reason to believe that they would respond differently to a charge under s. 1(2). D, a fourteen year old girl is baby-sitting for P. P tells D to light the fire if it gets cold. D has never lit a fire before because she is used to central heating. D attempts to light the coal fire but fails. She finds some white spirit and, without recognising any risk that might be involved, throws a considerable amount over the coal. On lighting the fire a conflagration ensues as the white spirit has spread from the open hearth to the carpet. The children asleep upstairs are rescued by the fire brigade suffering from smoke inhalation. If there was an obvious risk of damage arising from lighting a fire in these circumstances (it is submitted that there was such a risk which a prudent adult would have recognised), D recklessly damaged the property. If that damage created an obvious risk of endangering life (it is submitted that a prudent adult would have recognised such a risk having recognised the original risk of damage), D was likewise reckless as to endangering life. D will not be able to rely on the defence of lawful excuse (see 14.3.3 *post*). It is hard to believe that the statute was enacted to make criminals of persons such as D, but then, prior to *Elliott* v *C*, few of us believed it was enacted to make criminals of people like C. The problem, of course, would not arise if recklessness had been confined to its subjective meaning which was the Law Commission's understanding of the term when they drew up their proposals for the Criminal Damage Act.

14.3.3 Without lawful excuse

'Without lawful excuse' in s. 1(2) does not have the same meaning as for s. 1(1). The definition in s. 5 does not apply to offences under s. 1(2). Thus, even though D may have P's consent to damage his property, if he does so intending to endanger the life of another or being reckless thereto, he will be guilty of the s. 1(2) offence. The limited circumstances in which D would have a lawful excuse appear to be confined to situations where he damages property to prevent crime or defend himself or apprehend an offender and the reasonable force he uses endangers life. For example, if E is attacking D with a hatchet and D smashes P's vase over E's head to defend himself intending to kill E, D will have damaged property belonging to another intending to endanger the life of another. If the force used, however, was reasonable in the circumstances, D will have been acting with lawful excuse in damaging the property and thereby endangering life.

14.4 THREATS TO DESTROY OR DAMAGE PROPERTY

Section 2 of the Criminal Damage Act 1971 provides:

A person who without lawful excuse makes to another a threat, intending that that other would fear it would be carried out -
    (a)   to destroy or damage any property belonging to that other or a third person; or

(b)   to destroy or damage his own property in a way which he knows is
      likely to endanger the life of that other or a third person; shall be
      guilty of an offence.

On conviction on indictment the maximum punishment for this offence is ten
years' imprisonment (s. 4(2)).

The threat may be made by any means. The Law Commission stated that
'the only limitation that needs to be imposed is that the threats should be
intended to create fear that what is threatened will be carried out' (Law Com
No. 29, para. 55). There is no requirement that D intend to carry out the
threats; the essence of the offence is the intention to create fear. If P is not, in
fact, put in fear as he does not believe D would carry out the threat, this will
not avail D provided it is proved D intended to cause fear in P.

The conduct threatened must be an offence under s. 1 of the Act. If D
threatens an offence under s. 1(1), the definition of 'without lawful excuse' in s. 5
applies, but if he threatens an offence under s. 1(2) this definition is inapplicable.

14.5   POSSESSING ANYTHING WITH INTENT TO DESTROY OR
DAMAGE PROPERTY

Section 3 of the Criminal Damage Act 1971 provides:

A person who has anything in his custody or under his control intending
without lawful excuse to use it or cause or permit another to use it -
(a)   to destroy or damage any property belonging to some other person; or
(b)   to destroy or damage his own property in a way which he knows is
      likely to endanger the life of some other person;
      shall be guilty of an offence.

On conviction on indictment the maximum punishment for this offence is ten
years' imprisonment (s. 4(2)).

It is necessary to prove a purposive intention, that is that D possessed the
item for the purpose of committing an offence under s. 1 himself or for another
to use it to commit such an offence. A conditional intention, to use the item to
cause damage should it prove necessary, will suffice (*Buckingham* (1976) 63 Cr
App R 159). 'Without lawful excuse' applies in the same way as for the s. 2
offence (see 14.3 *ante*). D must have actual custody or control of the item at the
time he formulates the intention. If, for example, D gives E a brick and
subsequently suggests to him that he should use it to damage P's property, D
has the necessary intention but he does not have custody or control of the brick
(he would, however, be liable to conviction for incitement). By contrast, if D
picks up a brick intending to give it to E so that he can damage P's property,
D will have custody and control of the brick with the intention to permit E to
use it to cause criminal damage.

There is no definition of 'anything'; the essence of the offence is D's intent.
If D has the requisite intent it does not matter what the thing is which he has
in his custody or control.

Index